Managerial Economics

Managerial Economics

Firms, Markets, and Business Decisions

Ian M. Dobbs

Reader in Business Economics and Finance,
University of Newcastle-upon-Tyne

OXFORD

UNIVERSITY PRESS

OXFORD

UNIVERSITY PRESS

Great Clarendon Street, Oxford OX2 6DP

Oxford University Press is a department of the University of Oxford.
It furthers the University's objective of excellence in research, scholarship,
and education by publishing worldwide in

Oxford New York

Athens Auckland Bangkok Bogotá Buenos Aires Calcutta
Cape Town Chennai Dar es Salaam Delhi Florence Hong Kong Istanbul
Karachi Kuala Lumpur Madrid Melbourne Mexico City Mumbai
Nairobi Paris São Paulo Singapore Taipei Tokyo Toronto Warsaw

and associated companies in Berlin Ibadan

Oxford is a registered trade mark of Oxford University Press
in the UK and certain other countries

Published in the United States
by Oxford University Press Inc., New York

British Library Cataloguing in Publication Data

Data available

Library of Congress Cataloging in Publication Data
Dobbs, Ian M.
Managerial economics / Ian M. Dobbs.
p. cm.
Includes bibliographical references and index.
1. Managerial economics. I. Title.
HD30.22.D627   1999   338.5′024′658–dc21   99–24058

ISBN 0–19–877570–9

1 3 5 7 9 10 8 6 4 2

Typeset in Minion
by J&L Composition Ltd, Filey, North Yorkshire
Printed in Great Britain
on acid-free paper by
The Bath Press, Bath

Preface

This text aims to provide materials and coverage for both an intermediate-level course in microeconomic analysis, with or without a business orientation, and for intermediate- and advanced-level courses in managerial economics, including those where structuring the internal organization of the firm is emphasized. It should also be appropriate for use in graduate courses in managerial economics in most accounting, business, and economics programmes and also for MBA programmes where managerial economics is one of the major subject options. The proliferation of relatively short modular courses often causes some difficulty for students in that the number of core texts also tends to multiply, along with the attendant purchase costs. It is hoped that this book may help in this regard by proving useful as a core text for a variety of such courses. (It could be used, as a core text for a single-module course in project appraisal and capital budgeting, in decision analysis, in price theory, or in the economics of organizational architecture, for example, as well as for managerial, business, and microeconomic principles courses).

Most managerial economics texts currently available on the market assume little background knowledge and offer the same syllabus at a remarkably uniform level of treatment. This is often appropriate, for example, for those MBA or business students who have little prior knowledge of economics, and little technical ability. However, not all students fall into this category. In many undergraduate degree programmes, managerial economics is taught at the intermediate or final-year level. Equally, in the better-quality MBA programmes, students majoring in managerial economics may be required to have a relevant degree. In such cases, students have some degree of numeracy and some appreciation of the economic approach to understanding reality. For such students and such courses, it would thus appear that there is a significant need for a text which recognizes and makes greater use of their talents. My aim, in writing this book, is to go some way towards this end.

Most current texts in managerial economics also pay little attention to the economics of market structure or the internal organization of the firm. Here, both are treated in some depth (four chapters on each). The text also provides a reasonably detailed exposition of all the key topics found in microeconomics principles courses (for example, game theory, choice under uncertainty, managerial discretion, oligopoly, agency theory, etc.). The rationale for this is the observation that many intermediate and final-year business-oriented economics courses also attempt to further develop student understanding of microeconomic foundations.

Pedagogical Features

Most texts of this genre follow the 'American model': slick presentation, extensive case studies, vignettes on prominent business leaders, economists, or management gurus, along with companion study guides and workbooks. In the author's experience, much of this material does not get used, particularly in the better UK, Continental, and North American institutions. Any self-respecting academic delivering a programme will typically follow his or her own ideas, and will selectively use case-study material from various sources to underpin these ideas. By and large, the textbook functions to support such courses—not vice versa. In the light of this, although there are several extended case studies examined within this text, I have chosen to give primarily short and focused cases in support of the material delivered. The space saved has allowed the coverage of topics, and the level of detail within each topic, to be extended.

Many of the chapters can be regarded as stand-alone units (chapter prerequisites spell out the cases where some previous elements of the text are required reading). It is not expected that students will simply start at the first page and plough on through; one would expect instructors to specify particular chapter reading for particular courses. Many authors favour a chatty, informal, story-telling style of exposition. Indeed it is probably the dominant paradigm. I have taken something of a stand against this; in my view, students may appreciate some level of chat, but are also goal-directed and time-constrained; they appreciate a text that tells them clearly and succinctly all they need to know. I have tried, in the exposition, to make the key assumptions, definitions, theorems, facts, etc. stand out typographically. This not only helps the student get clear the fundamental structure of the models, ideas, etc. under discussion, but also facilitates review and, in particular, revision when it comes to preparation for those inevitable end-of-semester examinations.

Contents and Structure

The text starts in Part I with a review of methodology, of how to evaluate and compare theories and models, and follows this with a review of normative evaluation, in which criteria are set out by which policies practised by agents (individuals or firms) can be judged as being in the public interest or not. This is of relevance in business and managerial economics because such evaluations can motivate state or government intervention in the market economy. Part II then turns to tools and techniques used both in the construction of economic models and for the direct solution of business problems (optimization techniques, decision-making under uncertainty, game theory, investment appraisal). Part III then considers demand and cost analysis. The traditional neo-classical theory is reviewed in each case, but the focus here is also on the practice of demand and cost analysis, and two chapters are devoted to statistical aspects of demand and cost estimation. Part IV then examines the various forms of market structure which can be observed (competition, monopoly, monopolistic competition, oligopoly) along with some further consideration of the nature and boundaries of the firm. Part V examines extensions to the basic pricing model, to include topics such as price discrimination, multi-product pricing, pricing over time, advertizing, etc. Part VI deals with the impact of state regulation on the firm: the rationale for it and the different ways in which it can be practised. Finally, Part VII deals with the economics of organizational architecture (the internal organization of the firm; whether it should be centralized or decentralized; how jobs should be designed, monitored and rewarded etc.).

At various places I have discussed the use of spreadsheet modelling as an analytical aid, and given worked-out examples and also set problems. For example, I discuss its use in constrained numerical optimization in Chapter 3, for sensitivity and risk analysis in Chapter 7, and for econometric analysis in Chapters 9 and 11. In my opinion, a facility for spreadsheet modelling is one of the most useful transferable skills a student can take into the world of real work, and hence is one well worth working at.

Acknowledgements

I would like to thank the anonymous referees for helpful and constructive advice (in particular, for encouraging me to include the material on organizational architecture). I would like to thank the editors, Tracy Mawson and Brendan Lambon for their early encouragement (and for commissioning the text), Ruth Marshall for the efficient managing of a sometimes painful production process, and Tim Bartel for the copy editing (and for some thought provoking comments which helped improve the exposition in various places).

The text is an outgrowth of lecture material I have developed and delivered to a variety of classes, at undergraduate, master's, and MBA levels. The outgrowth does, however, feature more material than has been explicitly class-tested; as a consequence I am sure many improvements can be made, both to content and quality of exposition. Constructive feedback, suggestions, and corrections on such matters are very welcome (either through e-mail or at my university address below).

Ian M. Dobbs

Newcastle School of Management
University of Newcastle upon Tyne NE1 7RU
E-mail: I.M.Dobbs@ncl.ac.uk

Contents

Detailed Contents

Part I

Introduction

Part I provides background and overview materials useful at various points throughout the text. Chapter 1 gives an outline of the scope of the text and then proceeds to examine the distinction between positive and normative economics, and the role of models and theories and on what grounds they can be evaluated. Chapter 2 then explains the concept of economic welfare as widely used in normative economic analysis. This is of relevance when considering many of the issues that arise in managerial and business economics, since there is often a public interest dimension associated with a firm's decisions—regarding whether government should intervene and either take over or regulate private sector firm behaviour. It might be thought that the subject matter of a text on managerial and business economics could eschew such normative issues, but a moment's reflection should indicate that this is not the case; firms operating in the private sector have to work within the framework imposed by government, and also need to take into account the possibility that certain types of behaviour may trigger further state intervention. If taken to court, such firms also need to be aware of the economic ideas that may legitimize their behaviour. In the UK for example, such firms are increasingly turning to economists to defend their business practices against further state 'interference'. Any defence of a business practice (such as price discrimination, predatory pricing, access pricing, product tying, etc.) necessarily has to address equity and welfare considerations.

1 Introduction

Objectives This Chapter defines the subject matter to be addressed, sets out the scope of the text, discusses the distinction between positive and normative economics, the nature and use of models and theories, and the criteria for assessing the relative performance of models and theories. Following this, there is a short introduction to the objectives of the firm.

Prerequisites none specific.

Keywords conduct, deterministic, industrial economics, industrial organization, macroeconomics, microeconomics, model, neo-classical economics, performance, positive economics, present value, regulatory economics, stochastic, structure, theory, value judgement, value maximization, welfare economics.

1.1 **Introduction**

Figure 1.1 illustrates the family tree of economics. **Macroeconomics** is the study, broadly speaking, of economic aggregates at the national or possibly international level; the relationships between unemployment, money supply, inflation, and GNP; etc. **Microeconomics** is concerned with the study of the way economic agents operate within such economies; it examines the structure of the markets within which they find themselves and the decision processes by which they make choices within these environments.[1] Microeconomics in its turn subdivides into a variety of sub-disciplines. The subject matter of this text is microeconomic analysis, with a particular focus on what is termed managerial economics, but this material is also at the interface of several overlapping sub-disciplines. The four of primary interest can be briefly characterized as follows:

Definition 1.1 Managerial economics is the application of microeconomic tools and techniques to the key decisions firms need to make; e.g. pricing, output, investment, and advertizing.

Definition 1.2 Welfare economics is concerned with analysing alternative definitions of what constitutes social

welfare and of developing operational measures of such definitions of it.

Definition 1.3 Industrial economics (or **industrial organization**) is concerned with the characteristics and structure of industries and the behaviour of firms within such industries.

Definition 1.4 Regulatory economics is concerned with the reasons for state intervention in the market economy and in particular, the consequences for efficiency and social welfare arising from the state using different types of regulatory control to restrict the behaviour of private sector firms.

Managerial economics is primarily concerned with the theory of the firm, although any study of decisions at the firm level requires an understanding of the structure of the industry within which the firm is located (the number of firms in competition, the nature of that competition, etc.). Firms, in taking decisions, must also be aware of the institutional framework within which they operate. Inevitably we will need to stray across the rather fuzzy boundaries which supposedly demarcate the sub-disciplines of managerial, welfare, industrial, and regulatory economics, as well as those of management accounting (particularly in considering cost analysis and estimation) and corporate finance (when considering investment appraisal and capital budgeting).

The general approach adopted in the text is that of **neo-classical economics**. This approach emphasizes analysis beginning at the level of the individual, with individuals being viewed as having objectives in their economic life which can be identified to some

---

[1] This is a typical pedagogical (i.e. teaching) distinction. However, from a methodological perspective, it can be argued that macroeconomics should be built on micro-foundations. See e.g. Begg (1982) on this.

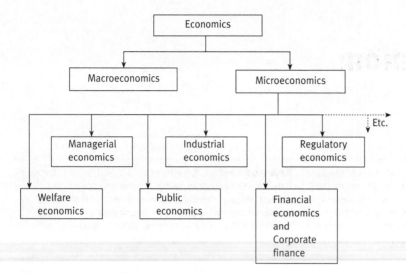

Fig. 1.1 Sub-disciplines within economics

degree of approximation (think of entrepreneurs trying to maximize profits, or consumers trying to choose consumption bundles which yield the maximum utility for particular prices and expenditure). Such agents are assumed to make choices which, given the constraints they face, maximize the value of their objective functions. This optimizing view of individual and firm decision-making is generally very flexible; for example, uncertainty and risk, altruism and inter-temporal time horizons can all be introduced into the neo-classical approach.

Critics of the neo-classical approach often caricature it by focusing on textbook expositions. They note that textbooks depict it as usually a static and certain world with costless information, the rational agents having infinite computing power. However, this is a caricature of the approach; although static single-period, single-product models will feature significantly throughout this text, the extensions to include multiple products, multiple time periods, uncertainty, bounded calculating ability, and so on can be found throughout the academic literature and are addressed at various points here. Neo-classical economics has a chameleon-like nature and is constantly being extended in ways which accommodate (admittedly to varying degrees) the views associated with other schools of thought.[2]

Figure 1.2 illustrates the structure of the text. The idea is that the core material is the theory of the firm (decisions on pricing, investment, advertizing, etc.). However, these decisions are necessarily conditional on having information on how much it costs to produce output (cost analysis), on how pricing and advertizing affect the volume of sales (demand analysis), and on market structure, the nature of competition. Other inputs to such decision-making are the principles for dealing with inter-temporal cash flows and with uncertainty and risk (investment appraisal and capital budgeting).

A central idea in discussing the theory of the firm is that the firm is embedded in a particular market structure and this market structure has implications for the firm's conduct and performance. Figure 1.3 illustrates what is referred to as the **structure–conduct–performance** (SCP) paradigm. Early work (pre-circa 1970) suggested that the direction of causation was principally in the direction S → C → P. However, the modern view is that the directions of causation are complex (see e.g. Tirole 1993), although the fundamental importance of the nature of the production technology is recognized. However, this does not alter the fact that the inter-relationships do exist and that the SCP view of the

---

[2] Behaviourist models of limited calculating ability, satisficing behaviour, and rules of thumb can all be studied within the neo-classical framework. Likewise Marxist views about the evolution of the economy as a whole, and for example on the internal

working of the firm (of management versus workers or unions etc.) has been extensively analysed using economic dynamics and game theory (Chap. 5). Even the Austrian view of the economy as a process continually in flux can arguably also be addressed using the analytic approach.

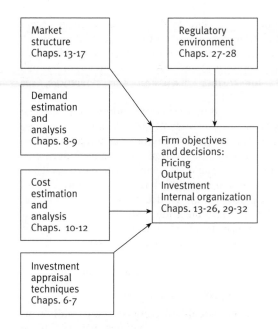

Fig. 1.2 Structure of the text

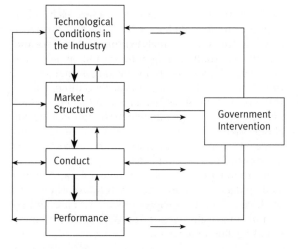

Fig. 1.3 The SCP paradigm

structure. Thus predatory pricing or a firm's merger policy are forms of conduct which will affect the numbers of firms in the industry and hence the extent of competition in that industry.

An additional box has been added in Figure 1.3 for the impact of government policy (G). The idea is that state intervention may influence S, C, and P. In the UK, the government, through privatization and regulatory policy, has substantially changed the structure of many industries (S) along with the way they are able to conduct their affairs (C) and their economic performance (P): industries such as water, gas, electricity, railways, and buses, for example. Again there are feedback effects; behaviour by firms can provoke state intervention. For example, what were deemed to be excess profits in the water and electricity industries, P, led the regulators to lower the price caps in those industries. Thus the arrows again point in both directions; government intervention influences S, C, and P, but equally, S, C, and P may influence policy, G.

1.2 Positive and Normative Economics

Positive economics is about 'what is' whilst **normative economics** is about 'what ought to be'. This is sometimes referred to as the is/ought distinction. Positive economics is concerned with explaining what actually happens in the real world (the so-called *facts*) without making any judgement as to whether what happens is desirable or not. Normative economics, by contrast, is concerned with making judgements about whether one state of affairs is preferable to or better than another.[3] Much of the focus of this text is on the way people actually behave, and is concerned with the analysis of what they need to do in order better to achieve their goals. However, at various points, we shall also be concerned with whether the modes of economic behaviour under discussion are acceptable, a good thing or not. This arises for example in considering price discrimination, predatory pricing, and the regulation of natural monopolies, for example.

world is a useful way of organizing preliminary thinking about the problems facing an individual firm. In Figure 1.3, the arrows indicate directions of influence, and are double-headed; this indicates that there are influences in one direction but also feedback influences. Thus market structure S affects the possible conduct and performance of firms; however, it is equally true that conduct C and performance P can feed back and affect market

[3] The philosopher David Hume (1711–1776) has the reputation of first emphasizing the idea of the is/ought distinction (Hume 1739/1967, 1751/1962). Friedman (1953) emphasizes the distinction in the context of economic analysis.

Economists very commonly use a simple and operational measure (basically, the sum of consumer and producer surplus) for judging whether policies or actions by agents in the economy are a good thing or not. This measure is discussed in further detail in Chapter 2. However, in view of the importance of the is/ought distinction, it is worth considering it here in rather more detail. Consider the following statements:

(i) If I am a twin, then I must have had, at some stage, a brother or a sister.

(ii) That spinster has been recently widowed.

(iii) The planet Neptune is made of Stilton cheese.

(iv) Nurses ought to be paid more than teachers.

(v) Increase the pay of all nurses!

These are clearly different types of statement. The first is logically true, whilst the second is logically false. That is, we can determine whether they are true or false by an analysis of the meaning of the terms contained within them in conjunction with the application of the usual rules of logic. The third statement I shall call an empirical statement. It could in principle be true or false that is, it is not logically true or false. Its truth or falsehood can in principle be determined through a study of the empirical evidence. Statement (iv) is clearly rather different. It is termed a value judgement; it is, or implies, a commendation or recommendation. It is possible to agree or disagree with such a statement but one cannot determine its truth by examination of some empirical evidence. Statement (v) is an imperative, or order. It does not seem to be either an empirical statement or a value judgement (although this point can be debated—see Hare 1952). The individual who issues such an order may, or may not, hold to a value judgement such as (iv).

Definition 1.5 Any statement which implies a recommendation is termed a **value judgement**.

The above examples suggest that one can usefully categorize statements as either (1) logically true, (2) logically false, or (3) neither, and that one can also classify statements as (1) empirical statements, (2) value judgements, or (3) neither. The fundamental distinction of interest here is between empirical statements and value judgements. The idea is that they are basically different types of statement. This is sometimes referred to as Hume's law: 'no value judgement can be deduced from wholly empirical premises' (see Hare 1963). Most economists accept Hume's law as a logical truth (including the author). However, it is worth noting that some philosophers (and economists) have disputed the truth of Hume's law; for further discussion and references, see Sugden (1981).

In commending or recommending, an individual will usually have reasons for so doing. Now these reasons may not be systematic or coherent but economists usually like to argue that value judgements should be capable of being systematized. If an individual holds views that are self-contradictory then clearly no rational debate is possible with that person. Indeed, one could argue that it is a fundamental tenet of individual rationality that the value judgements held by such a person should be mutually or internally consistent. To make this point clear, consider the following value judgements:

(vi) Killing people is always wrong.

(vii) For individuals suffering from a painful terminal illness, it is sometimes permissible to administer a lethal injection.

These value judgements contradict each other. Suppose an individual agreed with each of the above value judgements, and suppose someone pointed out the contradiction; a rational individual could be expected to respond by making some revision to his professed views. (For further discussion of this point, see Ng 1979). The point I am making here is that it is possible to have rational debate about value judgements. The value judgements made in Chapter 2 will have the property that they are not mutually contradictory.

In deciding on whether a statement is or is not a value judgement, a useful check is to ask whether its truth value is (in principle) testable by an examination of empirical evidence. If it is, then the statement is not a value judgement.

EXAMPLE 1.1 Consider the following statements and see whether you agree with the categorization which follows each of them (V denotes a value judgement, P denotes a positive statement):

(viii) Nurses should have a pay rise above the rate of inflation next year.   (V)

(ix) Nurses received a pay increase above the rate of inflation last year.   (P)

(x) You ought to maximize profits if you want to stay in business.   (P)

In each case, if you are uncertain, ask yourself the

question, 'Does it make sense to speak of approving or disapproving it?' Thus (viii) is clearly a value judgement, whilst (ix) is an empirical statement. (Although there might be some debate about definitions of the inflation rate etc., once these are specified, the statement is either true or false.) Statement (x) is a little tricky because it uses the word 'ought' and thus sounds as though it is implying a recommendation. However, this is a *conditional* use of the word 'ought'. The statement has the structure 'if *A* then *B*', where *A* = 'You want to stay in business' and *B* = 'You should maximize profits'. Thus it is really an empirical statement; does maximizing profits mean that you are more likely to stay in business? It is value-neutral because it says nothing about whether staying in business, or maximizing profits, is a good thing.

In part, this text is concerned with studying how individuals and firms actually behave. However, at various points, the analysis can be described as prescriptive. For example, everyone familiar with a first-level economics course will recognize the following statement:

EXAMPLE 1.2 If you wish to maximize profits, then you should choose the output level such that the marginal revenue from the last unit of output equals the marginal cost of producing it.

This comes in the same category as statement (x) above. It is important to recognize that this prescriptive statement is a conditional and empirical statement; that is, it is not a recommendation and hence not a value judgement. Of course such positive statements may be found in conjunction with value judgements, as in the following example.

EXAMPLE 1.3 It is in the public interest to have unfettered capitalism in which entrepreneurs maximize profits by setting marginal revenue equal to marginal cost.

The first part of this sentence, 'It is in the public interest to have unfettered capitalism', is a value judgement; the second part by contrast is an empirical statement. This should be clear since it is meaningful to ask whether entrepreneurs do in fact maximize profits by setting marginal revenue equal to marginal cost (and whether this is an essential element of 'unfettered capitalism').

This completes the discussion of the distinction between positive or empirical statements and value judgements. Apart from its use in this text, a good

understanding of this distinction is one well worth carrying with you through the rest of your life. Much muddled thinking in business, politics, and everyday life can be traced to a lack of appreciation of the distinction.[4]

1.3 Models, Theories, and their Purposes

Most courses on managerial economics will require, amongst other things, that the student can critically assess theories and models. This section provides some ideas for how to go about this process.

1.3.1 Distinguishing Models and Theories

Many writers (including virtually all economists) treat the terms 'model' and 'theory' as synonymous. If there is a useful distinction to draw, it is that outlined in what follows.

Definition 1.6 A **model** is a simplified representation of some part of reality; its function is to exhibit relationships and interdependencies. The model necessarily abstracts from what is assumed to be unimportant detail in order to clarify what are considered to be the key variables and relationships. Models can be physical (made from wood or clay, etc.) but can also be verbal, geometric, or algebraic (so-called symbolic models).

Thus models are focused; that is, they are only intended to deal with one particular area or aspect of reality; they do not explain the world, the universe, and everything. Models are usually mathematical, graphical, or verbal descriptions of the way variables interrelate. It is important to realize that it is not possible to provide a complete and full description of reality. Any description, whether verbal or mathematical (and mathematics is simply another language), or diagrammatic, must of necessity abstract from what the describer considers to be unimportant detail. It is worth noting that we would normally expect any symbolic model to be internally

---

[4] Whilst we are careful to distinguish between empirical statements and value judgements in this text, some writers would argue that the very selection of material in a text represents in itself a value judgement on the part of the author. For example, on this view, the focus on profit maximization in this (and so many other) texts would be viewed as an implicit approval of a type of society which operates in this way. To pursue this debate, however, is beyond the scope of the present Chapter.

logically consistent (i.e. it should not contain any logical inconsistencies).

Given the above definition of the term 'model', what constitutes a theory? I shall adopt the following definition:

Definition 1.7 A **theory** can be regarded as a model along with a specification of the empirical variables and facts whose changes it is supposed to explain/predict.[5]

Thus the variables in the model require operational definitions. (Consider unemployment or inflation, for example: there are no unique measures of these economic phenomena; one has to choose one definition or another.) As noted above, in practice, writers often slur over the above distinction between model and theory, using the terms largely interchangeably. The distinction can be useful, however, as the following discussion of the alternative purposes of a model helps to make clear.

1.3.2 The Uses of Models and Theories

(a) Pedagogic (Teaching) Purposes

You will find in this text models which are much more basic, simple, and straightforward than would ever get published in an academic journal. These are not intended to provide especially good theories, i.e. predictions about the way the world really works, although they may do so in some circumstances. Such models are designed to communicate some of the more basic interrelationships between economic variables. Thus the model of a single-product, single-period profit-maximizing monopolist with linear demand and constant marginal cost is a common pedagogic device. Reality may deviate significantly from such assumptions; for example, if there are multiple products, longer time horizons, uncertainty over costs, demands, and non-linearities everywhere (and such complications can be addressed; see Part V below). However, the simplest models do facilitate communication of basic and important ideas (such as the relationship between price, output, marginal cost, and demand elasticity—see Chapter 14). Such models may also perform satisfactorily, but, clearly, are only likely to do so in situations where their underlying assumptions are satisfied to some reasonable degree of approximation.

(b) Prediction

Theories, particularly in economics, often entail predictions which are **stochastic** rather than **deterministic**. Whilst the observation of a single black swan would refute the theory or hypothesis that all swans are white, it is harder to refute (or confirm) the proposition that, in a coin-tossing experiment, the probability of the coin landing heads is 0.5 (getting 10 heads in 10 tosses of the coin might lead you to suspect that the probability might not be one-half,[6] but it is an admissible outcome even if the probability really is 0.5). Thus theories typically offer only conditional and often probabilistic prediction. It follows that any individual outcome may be consistent with the theory's prediction. However, repeatedly large divergences between the theory's predictions and actual outcomes would constitute poor predictive performance. In judging such predictive performance, it is normal to compare the relative performance of different theories.

(c) Explanation

Here the concern is with causality. It is based ultimately on a view of the nature of reality—that there are causes and effects. The notion of causality is a complex issue, particularly when we admit the possibility of statistical or non-deterministic causality. Friedman (1953) argued (from an instrumentalist perspective) that there is no need for assumptions to be valid or testable—all that matters is prediction. Many theories, however, may work adequately for prediction without having any real causal underpinnings. For example, I may be able to predict the dawn by the time of arrival of the milk bottles or the daily newspaper. X may be observed to be a leading indicator for Y (that is, when X starts to increase, it is expected that, in some specified time period, Y can also be expected to increase). Neither of these models provide causal explanations. Observed regularities can be useful, but they are not generally regarded as explanations.

A key idea in explanation is that a theory should make predictions of a wide range of phenomena, all of which are validated. Thus, suppose model A predicts outcomes of type Y quite well, but not outcomes of type Z, whilst model B predicts Z but not Y. Then we may be able to use the two theories to give us reasonable predictive power (horses for courses; use A to predict Y but B to predict Z),

---

[5] See e.g. Friedman (1953).

[6] And to suspect a double-headed coin.

but this does not constitute explanation. Explanation requires a theory which, from common assumptions, satisfactorily predicts both Y and Z.

A theory which is successful in predicting events of a particular type, but is a failure in predicting other types of phenomena, is clearly not an explanation. It follows that one is unlikely to have great faith in such a theory for predicting other or new phenomena.[7] A theory which is a good explanation should also lead us to look for new kinds of phenomena which the theory will also correctly predict.

In a sense, any prediction failure suggests that a theory is inadequate for explanation. Of course, it is important to acknowledge that failure is often the stimulus to an examination of the assumptions that may be incorrect, to theory modification and development. An upbeat view of the development of economics is thus that the theories currently in use are in continuous development in search of this (impossible) ideal, of perfect explanation.[8]

---

[7] Or for use for policy purposes. A classic example was the Phillips curve (Phillips 1958), which noted an empirical regularity (a negative relationship) between inflation (wage, price) and unemployment. The attempt to utilize this relationship for policy purposes rapidly led to the disappearance of the empirical regularity.

[8] Karl Popper has written at length on the nature of explanation and on falsification (see e.g. Popper 1963). As a matter of logic, if a theory predicts a certain outcome, and that outcome fails to materialize, then the theory must be false; it cannot be an explanation of the phenomena in question. To be precise, at least one of the assumptions or axioms of the theory cannot hold. An issue of some importance here is whether reality is inherently deterministic or stochastic (probabilistic). Albert Einstein famously pronounced that 'God does not play dice with the universe', meaning that ultimate explanations should be deterministic rather than stochastic. However, a major alternative view of reality is that of quantum mechanics. In this view, sub-atomic relationships are inherently stochastic (although implied behaviour at the macro-level can be viewed as 'effectively' deterministic). The problem of assessing predictive performance when causality is viewed as inherently stochastic is much less straightforward. For example, a theory might predict with probability 0.95 (95%) that inflation next quarter will lie in the range 2.3–2.4%. If it transpires that inflation is 2.7% in this period, this clearly does not falsify the statement. If an experiment is replicable (repeatable), it is possible to develop a statistical test of whether one theory's predictions are superior to another's (see any text on econometrics, e.g. Thomas 1989). Economic problems are rarely in the form of replicable experiments; this makes the judgement of whether one theory is superior to another more difficult to establish, and the assessment must always be provisional. Thus on one body of data, theory A may outperform theory B (based on some statistical test/definition of predictive performance). However, it is always possible to imagine more data coming in (say as time elapses) such that B outperforms A on the new data. Any judgement that one theory is predictively superior to another might, at least in principle, be overturned by further replications.

1.4 Evaluating Theories and Models

First, let us deal with models: so long as they are internally logically consistent and seem to capture at least some important aspects of reality, even if they do not predict very well, it can be argued that we should not judge them too harshly, for they can serve useful pedagogical purposes. Theories, by contrast, are more difficult, for this is where models are expected to confront the empirical evidence. The useful idea to keep in mind here is that:

Fact 1.1 Performance is relative.

The idea is that theories are only thrown away when new and better ones can be established. Prediction failure in an absolute sense is clearly a motivation toward looking for new and better theories (and to 'tweaking' the existing theories to improve performance) but in practice, the issue always becomes one of appraising competing theories. Thus, any new theory needs to outperform the old theories before it can replace them. Hence there are different types of performance criteria: simple ones are as follows:

1. Predictive performance
   If one theory always predicts future events more accurately than another model, then the latter can be said to be predictively dominated.

2. Explanation
   (*a*) Does one theory explain a larger set of observed phenomena?
   One theory might explain the relationship between, say, inflation and unemployment—and nothing else. Another might do this and also explain how these variables are related to money supply, interest rates, etc. A theory which seeks to establish causal links between more facets of the real world is, *ceteris paribus* (i.e. other things being equal), a superior theory.
   (*b*) Is one theory more parsimonious/coherent in its assumptions/axioms?
   Does one theory achieve more from less (fewer or simpler assumptions/axioms)? This is the criterion of elegance.
   Does it draw on a common set of assumptions used in related models/theories, or are the assumptions to a greater extent *ad hoc*? This is the criterion of coherence.

Thus in evaluating competing theories, the above criteria provide a useful way of categorizing and assessing their relative performance. Naturally, one theory may come out on top based on one criterion, whilst another criterion may rank the theories differently. The expectation is that, since economic models and theories necessarily omit many elements of reality, they cannot provide a perfect explanation of reality (whatever that might be). In a sense, all models/theories can be viewed as stepping stones along the way toward more complete systems.[9]

1.5 The Firm's Objectives

The standard textbook assumption is that the firm aims to maximize profits. Why is this—and what does it mean? It is important to realize that the term 'profit maximization' itself is rather ambiguous. In a one-period model of the firm, it may make sense, but in the real world, firms are concerned not only with profits today but also those in the future. The inter-temporal equivalent of the single-period profit maximization under certainty is to maximize the **present value** of the firm. This objective of **value maximization** is explained in some detail in Chapter 6 (notably section 6.7). In a nutshell, the story goes as follows. Suppose there is a single owner of the firm, and there is a multi-period time horizon. Why should such an owner attempt to maximize the present value of the firm? Why don't the owner's preferences for consumption today vis-à-vis consumption tomorrow play a part? The answer is that the existence of a capital market in which a rate of interest can be obtained introduces a separation between the consumption decisions of the individual owner of the firm and optimal investment decisions. This **separation theorem** is explained in

section 6.7. Things also become more complex when it is recognized that there is uncertainty; the owner may be risk-averse—should he/she still aim to maximize value? The answer is, with certain qualifications, yes—this issue is discussed in Chapter 7. Of course in practice, firms are more often joint stock companies; that is, there are many owners (shareholders) and these may well have different preferences for consumption over time. The separation theorem establishes that such shareholders will all agree on a single investment plan for the firm despite the heterogeneity of their consumption preferences. That is, they will agree that the firm's objective should be to maximize value. As shown in Chapter 6, the implication is that, for project appraisal, all projects with positive net present value should be undertaken (qualifications to this principle are discussed in Chapter 7).

In practice there is considerable evidence that firms do not always, or even often, attempt to maximize value. Managerial discretion models (Chapter 16) focus on the idea that shareholders exert only weak control over managers and also have less information than managers regarding the potential performance of the firm. This gives management discretion to pursue their own objectives (salary, power, prestige, the quiet life . . .). The consequences for the theory of the firm are discussed in Chapter 16, whilst the issue of how to improve goal congruence (shareholders and top management wanting the same things for the firm) through the design of executive remuneration packages etc. is addressed in Chapters 29–31. However, the profit maximization hypothesis is a powerful and simple one. Empirically, it has reasonable predictive power, and remains the cornerstone of the theory of the firm. Accordingly it will remain centre stage through much of this text.

---

[9] The usual preference in neo-classical economic analysis is to develop relatively simple models using fairly standardized assumptions (which are common to many models) in order to make fairly sharp predictions which can then be confronted with the empirical evidence. More assumptions and model complexity tend to lead to less sharp predictions. For example, the neo-classical theory of consumer choice appears at first glance not to rule out any kind of behaviour at all (if a commodity price goes up, the theory predicts that the consumer may buy more, the same, or less of the good!). This model is examined in some detail in Chap. 8.

2 An Evaluative Framework

Objectives The object of this Chapter is to set out a simple criterion (consumers' plus producers' surplus) which will be used at various points in the text to evaluate whether policies are in the public interest or not. The pros and cons of the various assumptions and value judgements that underpin the criterion are then briefly discussed.

Prerequisites Chapter 1 discusses value judgements and the distinction between positive and normative economics. A basic understanding of demand theory is assumed.

Keywords compensating variation, consumer surplus, deadweight welfare loss, economic welfare, equivalent variation (in footnote), Pareto-efficient, Pareto improvement, Pareto-optimal, potential Pareto improvement, producer surplus, value judgement.

2.1 Introduction

Much of this text is concerned with positive economic analysis; that is, the models discussed are intended to give insight into the way the world works. However, it is often the case that the consequences of particular policies or forms of behaviour need to be evaluated from a public interest or social welfare perspective. Is price discrimination against the public interest? is it better to have state-run or private monopolies? should such monopolies be regulated? etc. This Chapter sets out and discusses the pros and cons of a simple measure (consumer plus producer surplus) which will be used throughout this text as an index of economic welfare.

Recall that any statement which implies a recommendation is termed a value judgement (see section 1.3). Section 2.2 sets out the basic value judgements and assumptions which suffice to establish a simple and operational criterion for judging whether any observed policy (or change in policy) is in the public interest. The essential problem with defining any such index lies with the fact that, in the final analysis, it rests upon some set of value judgements. Unfortunately, an index that 'works' in the sense of giving a complete ranking of alternative states of the world tends to require rather strong value judgements, so that more people are likely to find it difficult to accept the value judgements which underpin the criterion.

In what follows, the term 'state' or 'social state' is shorthand for a 'full description' of the economy. Thus in posing questions such as 'Is social state *A* preferable to social state *B*?', the state *B* might be the current status quo, and the move to state *A* might involve changing *B* by building a new reservoir, or by introducing a new income tax regime, or a new price cap scheme for the regulation of private sector monopoly, or whatever.

The discussion in section 2.2 is concerned with assessing the value judgements and assumptions which underpin the following definition of economic welfare:

Definition 2.1 Economic welfare is deemed to have increased (decreased) as a consequence of some action or decision if the aggregate sum of changes in consumer surplus, firm profits, and tax revenues is positive (negative).

2.2 Value Judgements Underpinning the Welfare Measure

These are first listed, and then discussed in some detail.

2.2.1 The Key Paretian[1] Value Judgements

(a) Society is viewed simply as the collection of all the individuals contained within it.

(b) The welfare of each and every individual in the society should count in deciding whether one state of affairs is preferable to another.

(c) The individual is the best judge of his or her own welfare.

(d) The **Paretian value judgement**: a state of affairs A is socially preferred to a state B if A is preferred to B by at least one individual, and no one prefers B (i.e. anyone who does not prefer A to B is simply indifferent between the two). This is referred to as a **Pareto welfare improvement** or simply a **Pareto improvement**.

(a) Society is Viewed Simply as the Collection of all the Individuals Contained Within it

This is clearly a controversial judgement, as there are informed differences of opinion about what constitutes the relevant community of individuals whose welfare is to be taken into account (and some argue that animals other than *homo sapiens* should be included in the definition of community[2]). This is not merely a 'philosophical' or 'academic' issue; it can have practical significance. A cost–benefit analysis of many policies might draw different conclusions if the welfare of only a subset of individuals is taken into account (e.g. on atmospheric sulphur emissions, if the consequences for those outside the UK are ignored[3]).

(b) The Welfare of Each and Every Individual in the Society Should Count

This is clearly a value judgement: one can either approve or disapprove of it. Individuals in Western cultures with democratic and liberal tendencies are more likely to be comfortable with this kind of value judgement. There might be less agreement in other cultures (say China or the Islamic republics?). Clearly disagreement over this value judgement is less likely to the extent that individuals in the community have relatively homogeneous views and an individualistic outlook.

(c) The Individual is the Best Judge of His or Her Own Welfare

This judgement is less easy to classify, and it can be argued that it is not a value judgement at all; Ng (1974) for example refers to it as a 'subjective judgement of fact'.[4] A necessary condition for a statement to be a value judgement is that its truth value is not, even in principle, testable. The above statement does seem amenable to a form of testing. That is, it seems meaningful to pose the question 'Do I always know what is in my best interests better than anyone else?' A five-year-old child, on being posed the question, 'Do you ever want to go to school again?', may well reject schooling. But, at a later date, such a child might also agree that she did not know her own best interest.[5] As a matter of common sense, most individuals would accept that they do not always know what is in their own best interests (because they lack information relative to others, or because they lack the skills required to process or evaluate such information). However, whatever its philosophical status, at a pragmatic level it is probably better to assume that the individual knows her own preferences better than anyone else. After all, regarding what is in my interests, who is likely to know better, if not me? Thus it seems that most individuals in Western societies seem to have little quarrel with this assumption. Of course other cultures (and those who believe that society breeds false consciousness) might well disagree.

(d) The Paretian Value Judgement

This is the key value judgement. For those comfortable with Western cultural individualism, it commands a ready assent:

Definition 2.2 A situation is said to be **Pareto-optimal** (or **Pareto-efficient**[6]) if it is such that there are no feasible

---

[1] So called after Vilfredo Pareto (see e.g. Pareto 1939), an Italian economist who has a good claim to be one of the founding fathers of welfare economics.

[2] The definition is thus anthropocentric (in ignoring the welfare of other species).

[3] Or on eating any form of meat, if the relevant species is part of the community.

[4] See Ng (1979) for a more extended discussion of 'subjective judgements of fact'.

[5] One problem concerns the continuity of the self (an older self might express regret—but would it be the same person?). See e.g. Parfit (1984) for a careful analysis of the issues.

[6] Thus a Pareto improvement is equivalently a gain in Pareto efficiency, or, as some economists would describe it, simply a gain in efficiency. Anyone with an engineering or scientific background would find this a puzzling use of the term given that the definition involves individual preferences, and I tend to agree. Indeed, for pedagogic reasons, I prefer to avoid using the term 'efficiency' altogether in this context.

changes which would make someone better off without simultaneously making someone worse off.

A Pareto-optimal situation is thus a situation in which there is no further room for Pareto improvements. It can be shown that a property of a (perfectly) competitive market system is that (given a careful specification of the nature of perfect competition[7]).

Theorem 2.1 Every perfectly competitive equilibrium is a Pareto optimum.

The idea is that if no agents have market power (they are all price-takers), and if there are no external effects (no missing markets, or goods/bads which are unpriced, such as pollution and congestion), then the competitive market, in equilibrium, has the desirable welfare property of being Pareto-optimal. Thus, in a competitive equilibrium, it is not possible to make anyone better off without making someone worse off. The intuition for this is straightforward. In such an economy, individuals enter voluntarily into trade with each other (selling their labour, produce, etc.); rational individuals will only agree to be party to any given deal so long as it is advantageous to them in some way (which need not be simply or purely in financial terms). Such individuals can always walk away from deals that are disadvantageous. Equilibrium is a state of rest in which there are no further mutually advantageous deals available to agents in the economy. Theorem 2.1 is a limited result because the conditions under which it holds are very restrictive and are very poorly approximated in the real world (which clearly features monopoly power and many forms of market failure). It is also worth emphasizing that there may be many Pareto-optimal situations which at least some and possibly many individuals would regard as not socially very desirable. Thus Pareto-optimality does not rule out possibly substantial inequalities in the wealth/asset/commodity holdings of individuals in the competitive equilibrium. For example, in a simple barter economy involving two individuals, voluntary trade will make both individuals better off. However, if one starts out with a greater endowment of goods, he or she will typically end up with more after the trading has taken place. Trading makes both individuals better off, but it does not necessarily reduce the level of inequality. If there is no way of making the poor better off without making someone

worse off (say, someone who is richer), then the situation is still a Pareto optimum.

Another important point to be aware of with the Pareto-improvement criterion is that it refers to an individual's welfare, not their financial position. Suppose I am a rich man and currently giving no money to charities. I may well feel better off if I give some of my money away to needy causes. Giving money away might well increase my welfare. This is despite the fact that it makes me financially worse off. If a money transfer raises the welfare of others, then I too may feel better off. In such a case, the transfer is clearly a Pareto improvement. Of course, more generally, financial transfers which are involuntary (such as taxes) are likely to make some individuals feel worse off!

The problem with the concept of the Pareto improvement as a criterion for judging social welfare is that it yields only a partial ordering of states of the world. As such, it is a conservative criterion which favours the status quo, the existing position. This is so because most changes involve actually making some people worse off as well as some (possibly many) people better off. Whenever a change involves some being made better and some being made worse off, the criterion says nothing about whether one state is preferable to the other or not (hence many states are not Pareto-comparable; the Pareto criterion does not tell us which state is to be preferred).

Given the desire to provide an operational index of social welfare, the traditional route out of the above impasse (i.e. not being able to compare some, possibly many, states) is to follow a line suggested by John Hicks (1939) and Nicholas Kaldor (1940), who proposed the following criterion, called the potential Pareto improvement (PPI) criterion. Consider a project which changes state X to state Y (X might be the status quo, and Y might then be the state after, such as changing the rate of income tax or VAT, or building a reservoir):

Definition 2.3 A state Y is said to be socially preferable to a state X if, in state Y, it is hypothetically possible for those who feel better off to compensate those who feel worse off such that, after the compensation, the gainers still feel better off, but the losers no longer feel worse off. This situation is referred to as a **potential Pareto improvement**.

This is the Kaldor version of the criterion and is the one I shall confine myself to discussing, although there are other criteria of relevance.[8]

---

[7] The seminal reference (but not easy reading) is Debreu (1959).

[8] The Hicks criterion is as follows: Consider a change of state $X \to Y$. Then Y is preferred to X if, in state X, it is not possible for

Four key points are worth emphasizing about this criterion:

(i) If the compensation was effected, then we would have an **actual Pareto improvement**.

(ii) Compensation might be financial, but need not be (it could be in goods and services).

(iii) The compensation is hypothetical; compensation need not actually be paid.

(iv) It follows that on the basis of this criterion, some individuals will gain—and more importantly, some individuals will lose.

In view of (iv), which most individuals are likely to regard as a serious criticism of the criterion, we now consider some possible defences for such a criterion.

2.2.2 Problems with using the Potential Pareto Improvement Criterion

(a) Separation of Allocative and Redistributive Decisions (Musgrave 1959)

According to this argument, the branch of government responsible for allocative decisions (such as building roads and reservoirs) is viewed as separate from the branch responsible for redistributing income and wealth amongst citizens. The idea is that, in considering public decisions regarding projects which involve allocative changes (building reservoirs, regulating specified firms' rates of return or prices, etc.), the test should simply be one of deciding whether there is a potential Pareto improvement. The idea is that it is then up to another branch of government to deal with the distributional consequences of undertaking such

those who would be losers (if the change were implemented) to compensate the would-be gainers for not implementing the change. That is, the change is OK if in advance of the change, the losers are unable to compensate the gainers in order not to have the change.

The Kaldor and Hicks compensation tests do not necessarily give the same answer (essentially because of income effects). Consider an old-age pensioner with little wealth or income whose house lies in the path of a proposed motorway. On the Kaldor version of the test, we have to ask, 'What sum of money would compensate you for being relocated?' The answer may be that no finite sum of money could compensate her. However, on the Hicks criterion, things are very different. Here, we ask, 'How much are you prepared to pay for us not to drive the motorway through your home?' The latter is likely to be a relatively small sum of money, simply because the maximum she could pay is limited by her wealth.

projects. The projects themselves create the potential—it is up to another branch of the state to convert it into an actual Pareto improvement.

Unfortunately, in reality, there is no branch of the state which is responsible for seeing to it that the losers of any such project are in fact compensated. Redistribution occurs, but in general at a macroscopic or broad-brush level. It occurs between broad classes of individuals through instruments such as income taxes, expenditure taxes (such as VAT), and wealth and inheritance taxes. Redistribution is rarely fine-tuned to the individual level. Yet projects can often affect individuals in very different ways (consider a new motorway, which necessarily destroys individual properties). Thus, projects involve losers who do in practice lose. It may be true that one can effect some degree of compensation (as in the case of compulsory purchase), but these forms of payment do not necessarily represent full compensation in the utility dimension—individuals may continue to feel worse off after the change, even in the presence of some financial compensation.

(b) The Multi-project Statistical Defence

This is a means-to-an-end argument. Essentially, it does not regard the criterion *per se* as desirable, merely the overall effect of applying such a criterion. It is in my view probably the only credible defence of the PPI criterion. The focus is on the fact that the state is continually implementing a multiplicity of different types of project (from physical projects such as building new towns, roads, and bridges to wider-scale changes such as alterations to the tax system, to macroeconomic policy, and to industrial policy).

The statistical argument is as follows: if the benefits and costs which individuals incur due to particular public sector projects or policies are sufficiently randomly distributed, then, over a large number of such projects, if each project passes the potential Pareto improvement test, then the overall effect is that each individual will in fact be made better off. The idea here is one of swings and roundabouts: some projects will impose costs on an individual whilst others will benefit him/her. Given the large number of projects which impinge on each individual in some way or other, it is argued that the aggregate benefits to any individual will actually outweigh the costs to that individual. This statistical argument can be made more precise, although I shall not pursue a theoretical derivation here (see Polinsky 1974).

The principal counter to this argument is the observation that benefits and costs may not be sufficiently randomly distributed across the population. That is, it might be argued that there are some individuals who systematically seem to do well out of state projects, whilst other individuals systematically do badly. The issue then becomes an empirical one: if the potential Pareto criterion is adopted, does it in practice lead to individuals being made better off?

(c) Technical Objections

Apart from the ethical difficulties associated with the PPI, there are also some that might be termed 'technical' difficulties. It turns out that it is possible for two social states X and Y to be such that the change $X \rightarrow Y$ is a PPI, as is the change $Y \rightarrow X$. Thus there are possibilities of intransitivity and hence an inconsistent ranking of social states.[9] It can be argued that, whilst these difficulties may be of concern in particular applications, they are not of serious practical concern. Thus, it is conventional to sweep them under the carpet with the argument that the criterion will do a reasonable job in most practical applications.

Having set out the criterion for judging whether a change is socially desirable, we still face the problem of rendering the concept operational. How do we in fact judge whether a change passes the test of being a PPI? The starting point for such a measure is the concept of a compensating variation. Again, we consider a project which changes the state of the world from a state labelled X to one labelled Y:

Definition 2.4 The **compensating variation**, CV_i, for individual i, is the sum of money we should need to give to, or take from, the individual in state Y such that it leaves the individual feeling no better or worse off than before the change from X to Y.[10]

Thus for gainers the compensating variation is a positive sum, the amount they are willing to pay for getting the change, whilst for losers it is a negative sum, the amount they feel would compensate them for being subjected to the change. (It may be that no

finite sum will suffice for compensation, but for most projects, some finite sum of money will do the trick.)

The compensating variation (CV) provides a monetary measure of the extent to which the project makes an individual better or worse off. It follows that a test for a potential Pareto improvement (Kaldor version) can be assessed by summing CVs over the society of individuals concerned. Indeed, although there are certain theoretical difficulties associated with the use of the compensating variation (on which see Boadway and Bruce 1985), we shall assume the following:

Definition 2.5 If, for a change $X \rightarrow Y$, the sum of compensating variations (positive for gainers, negative for losers) is positive, then the gainers are (usually[11]) able to compensate the losers, so a potential Pareto improvement exists.

As before, it is worth emphasizing that this is hypothetical compensation, not actual; the caveats on the use of the criterion, as discussed above, remain.

(d) Truth Revelation Problems

In addition to the drawbacks already discussed, it is not yet clear how even this criterion can be made operational. Whilst the compensating variation (CV) is a conceptually well-defined measure of welfare change for an individual, we have yet to find a method of discovering what this CV might be in any given practical situation. Certainly, simply asking individuals to assess their CVs is unsatisfactory since there is an incentive for individuals to misreport the true values. If an individual suspects that revelation of a CV will lead to actual compensation, then there will be under-reporting of willingness to pay, and over-reporting of compensation required by losers. Alternatively, if individuals feel that their reported CVs will affect the assessment of the project, but will not lead to them having to pay any actual compensations, then gainers will over-report gains, whilst losers will continue to exaggerate the compensation they need. Furthermore, any questionnaire approach suffers from being hypothetical; individuals are not required to back their judgements with money outlays. For these reasons, economists prefer to try to deduce individuals' CVs from

[9] For further details of these possibilities, the reader is referred to Ng (1979) and Boadway and Bruce (1985).

[10] The parallel concept associated with the Hicks version of the PPI (see n. 6) is the **equivalent variation**. This is the sum of money needed to be given/taken away from an individual in state X (i.e. before the change) such that the individual then feels no worse off than he or she would have done after the change from $Y \rightarrow X$.

[11] There can be exceptions, but these are not regarded as of great practical importance. For details of the potential complications see e.g. Boadway and Bruce (1988).

observing individual behaviour in the market place (where trades and consumption are backed by money).

For goods traded on competitive markets, the compensating variation for giving someone, or depriving someone, of a traded item is simply its market price. Likewise, if a policy has a consequence of reducing the net profit of a firm by £100, this simply deprives asset-holders of the firm of that amount; thus the *CV* for them is −£100. However, things are more complex when there are price changes. I shall examine this issue in more detail in Chapter 8. The principal result of that analysis is that, to a reasonable approximation, the compensating variation is measured by the change in consumer surplus. Furthermore, this is so both for an individual and at the aggregate level; the only difference is that the change in consumer surplus is measured as the area between the two prices (before and after the price change) to the left of the individual's ordinary demand curve, whilst the aggregate of all individual consumer surpluses is given as the same area, but this time to the left of the market demand curve. This point is illustrated in Figure 2.1 (where the demand curve can be interpreted as either an individual's or the market as a whole). In this text, therefore, we shall generally aggregate benefits to all the individuals affected by any policy or decision. The individuals will typically be consumers, workers, shareholders, or taxpayers.

Definition 2.6 The change in **economic welfare** arising from a decision or policy change is measured as the sum of changes in **consumer surplus**, profits, and, where relevant, tax revenues.

The idea is that if this sum is positive, then there is a reasonable expectation that aggregate *CV* is positive; this in turn means that the gainers can usually (if only hypothetically) compensate the losers. Thus the above criterion provides a reasonable and operational measure for judging whether a potential Pareto improvement exists.

Before moving on to the application of this welfare measure, it is worth emphasizing the distributional consequences of the welfare measure that has finally been settled on. For example, a lump-sum financial transfer of, say, £100 from a rich man to a poor man makes no difference to the level of economic welfare. (Since we measure the aggregate benefit over the whole of society, this redistribution has no effect on the aggregate measure—the gain simply balances the loss.) It can be argued that this is

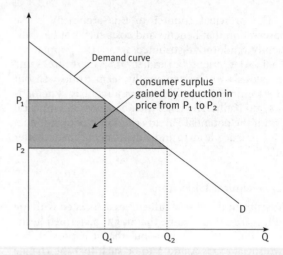

Fig. 2.1 Consumer surplus

acceptable so long as the distribution of income is viewed as acceptable (and so long as lump-sum redistribution is possible to get to it). There are clearly problems with the measure in so far as redistribution is generally effected by distortionary taxation—in which case it can be argued that compensating variations ought to be weighted according to some measure of income or wealth (see for example Harberger 1978, Le Grand 1984). However, there is little consensus on what the weights ought to be, and it has been conventional in most economic analysis of policy issues to stick with Definition 2.8.

2.3 Examples: Monopoly and Taxes as Deadweight Loss

2.3.1 Monopoly Welfare Loss

Figure 2.2 illustrates a simple linear model of a monopoly firm producing a product at constant marginal cost (denoted *MC*) with zero fixed costs. By assumption there is a downward-sloping demand curve. The associated marginal revenue (*MR*) curve has the same intercept and twice the gradient. The monopolist maximizes profits in this model by expanding output until the marginal revenue gained from the last unit of output just equals the marginal cost of producing it. The profit-maximizing output and price are denoted q_m and p_m respectively. Social benefit (area *A* + *B*) is measured as consumer surplus (area *A*) plus profits (area *B*; profit equals

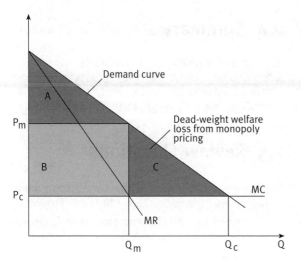

Fig. 2.2 Monopoly welfare loss

revenue minus cost, and the area below the price line and to the left of Q_m is revenue while the area below the marginal cost line is cost).[12]

One alternative pricing policy is that of marginal-cost pricing. Under this policy, welfare is equal to areas $A + B + C$. To see this, note that price is $P_c = MC$, output is Q_c, and consumer surplus is given by area $A + B + C$, whilst profit is zero (since price equals marginal cost for each unit sold). If we compare these two pricing policies, we shall see that there is a welfare gain, equal to area C, when moving from the monopoly price to marginal-cost pricing. This is usually referred to as **dead-weight welfare loss**. Since areas A and C are equal, and each is also equal to half of area B, the welfare loss, area C, comprises 25% of total attainable welfare under marginal-cost pricing. The key point is that the move to marginal-cost pricing represents a Pareto improvement (given our assumptions). To see this, consider groups who gain and those who lose in changing the price from P_m to P_c. Consumers gain by the amount $B + C$ whilst shareholders lose by amount B. Consumers gain by more than shareholders lose. There is a potential Pareto improvement because, after the change, it is possible for the

gainers to compensate the losers and still to have some gains left over.

The existence of a welfare loss under profit-maximizing monopoly pricing provides the fundamental insight that monopoly can be against the public interest. In Chapter 29, the theory of monopoly is revisited in greater detail. It turns out that marginal-cost pricing also has its drawbacks and that there are many other issues which arise in deciding whether any given private sector monopoly needs to be taken into the public sector, or whether it should be regulated (and how), or simply left alone.

2.3.2 Welfare Loss from Taxation

Figure 2.3 illustrates a competitive industry in which MC indicates the supply curve of the industry (it also indicates the marginal cost associated with producing an extra unit of output, for any given output level). The market price is P and the associated consumer surplus is CS. The area PS represents **producer surplus**, which is just another term for profits going to firms.[13] If this market is subject to a per unit sales tax of amount τ per unit, this shifts the supply curve upward by the amount of the tax. The consequence is depicted in Figure 2.4; output shrinks, as does consumer surplus and producer surplus. The government now takes tax revenue equal to the area between the original supply schedule and the after-tax supply schedule. Total welfare is now $CS + PS + TAX$ but the total welfare is now smaller than in the absence of a tax by the triangle indicated; again, this is referred to as deadweight welfare loss. Its magnitude clearly depends on the slopes of the demand and supply schedules.[14]

---

[12] Most readers will have met the concepts of marginal cost and marginal revenue in an introductory course in economics. For readers unfamiliar with these concepts, it is recommended that they skip this section, returning to it only after having read Chs. 8 (for MR), 10 (for MC), and 14 (for an extended discussion of the monopoly pricing problem).

[13] There are some conceptual issues that ought to be clarified here—for example, if the industry is perfectly competitive, with no barriers to entry, then all firms produce the output which minimizes average total cost and earn zero profits. In this case the supply curve is flat and there is no producer surplus.

[14] This analysis indicates the impact of a single tax; the calculation of the welfare loss associated with a change in a single tax, given that there are many taxes on other goods and services (and other distortions—see especially Chap. 29), is much more complex. This is because any change has impacts on the markets for related goods (both close substitutes and complements) and hence on the tax revenues raised on those goods (see e.g. Harberger 1971).

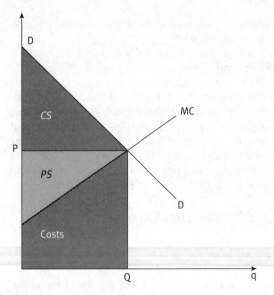

Fig. 2.3 Demand and supply

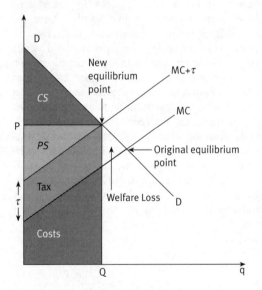

Fig. 2.4 Welfare loss from per unit tax

2.4 Summary

This Chapter provides some justification for a welfare criterion (consumer plus producer surplus) which is used at various points in the text to evaluate whether or not policies are in the public interest.

2.5 Review Questions

1. 'No one could object to the key Paretian value judgements (section 2.2), could they?' Discuss.

2. 'The problem with the potential Pareto improvement criterion is the word *Potential*.' Discuss.

3. Suppose the marginal cost curve in Figure 2.3 is flat. How then does the magnitude of the welfare loss vary with the slope of the demand curve? (Hint: sketch alternative demand curves.) Does this have any policy implications? Discuss.

4. Is monopoly welfare loss necessarily 25%? (Consider redrawing Figure 2.2 with non-linear demand functions, and explore what the welfare loss seems to depend on.)

2.6 Further Reading

The definition of welfare, and the difficulties associated with providing an operational measure, are discussed in some detail but in a fairly technically demanding way in Boadway (1988). Ng (1979) is more accessible, and discusses the nature of value judgements in some detail; note also that Chapter 8 of this book provides some extra detail on the concepts of compensating variation, equivalent variation, and consumer surplus.

Part II

Decision Analysis: Tools and Techniques

Part II gathers together some of the tools and techniques which find practical use in business decision-making and/or in models and theories developed throughout the rest of the text. Chapter 3 deals with optimization, a foundation stone for neo-classical economic analysis; all economic agents, whether they be consumers, firms, managers, workers, etc. are all assumed to be optimizers who aim to maximize something (often profit, or individual utility) subject to the constraints under which they find themselves. Apart from their use in neo-classical economic theorizing, optimization techniques can also find direct use in a firm's decision-making (for example, in the optimization of its production, inventory, or distribution processes). Chapter 4 deals with decision-making under risk and uncertainty, and gives an account and assessment of the expected utility model, which continues to be widely used as a building block of many models in economics and finance which deal with risk and uncertainty (in this text, for example—in Chapter 5 on game theory, in Chapter 22 on pricing under uncertainty, and in Chapter 29, where agency theory is discussed). Chapter 5 deals with game theory; this concerns the interactions between optimizing (typically expected utility maximizing) agents; again, this is a key building block for neo-classical economic analysis. For example, in oligopoly, an industry in which a small number of firms compete, choice of price, output, advertizing, etc. by one firm has a significant impact on the other firms in the industry—so their possible reactions need to be taken into account. Game theory is the study of how such agents should play the game and of likely outcomes (through a range of equilibrium concepts). The last two Chapters in Part II deal with the valuation of risky cash flows which lie in the future, since so many of the decisions the firm faces have a time dimension.

3 Optimization

Objectives This Chapter provides a practical and non-rigorous approach to the analysis of unconstrained optimization problems along with those which feature constraints (either equality or inequality constraints). It includes consideration of the Lagrangian method for equality-constrained optimization, the Kuhn–Tucker conditions for inequality-constrained optimization, and the special case of linear programming.

Prerequisites Some understanding of basic concepts in linear algebra (primarily, how to solve systems of linear equations) and calculus (in particular, the concept of a partial derivative).

Keywords concave function, continuous function, convex function, domain, first-order necessary condition, global maximum, Kuhn–Tucker conditions, Lagrange multiplier, Lagrangian, linear programming, local maximum, necessary condition, quasi-concave function, smooth function, strictly concave function, sufficient condition.

3.1 Introduction

This Chapter provides a practical and non-rigorous approach to the analysis of unconstrained optimization problems along with those which feature either equality or inequality constraints. It presumes some familiarity with concepts such as that of a function (in particular linear and non-linear functions), the concept of a derivative and a partial derivative and the ability to solve systems of linear equations. In any economic application which involves analytic functions, these are restricted exclusively to linear or quadratic type. The following example provides a quick means of checking your understanding of these concepts and their application.

EXAMPLE 3.1

(i) Example of a linear function: $f(\mathbf{x}) = 3x_1 + 2x_2 + x_3$ (each variable, x_1, x_2, and x_3, enters raised to the power of unity).[1]

(ii) Example of a quadratic function: $g(\mathbf{x}) = 3 + x_1 + x_1^2 + 2x_1x_2 + x_3 + x_2x_3$ (where there are product terms, the sum of the power indices on the variables is ≤ 2).

(iii) Partial derivatives: from the function in (ii) above, $\partial g(\mathbf{x})/\partial x_1 = 1 + 2x_1 + 2x_2$, $\partial g(\mathbf{x})/\partial x_2 = 2x_1$, $\partial g(\mathbf{x})/\partial x_3 = 1$, etc.

(iv) Solving systems of linear equations: Consider the equations

$$3x_1 + 2x_2 = 3$$

and

$$2x_1 - 3x_2 = 1.$$

What values of x_1 and x_2 simultaneously solve these equations? The procedure is first to make x_1 the subject of (say) the second equation; $2x_1 - 3x_2 = 1 \Rightarrow x_1 = (1 + 3x_2)/2$. This is then used to replace x_1 in the first equation, to give: $3x_1 + 2x_2 = 3 \Rightarrow 3((1 + 3x_2)/2) + 2x_2 = 3$. This equation is solved to give $x_2 = 3/13$; hence substituting back to obtain the value for x_1 gives $x_1 = (1 + 3x_2)/2 = (1 + 3[3/13])/2 = 11/13$.

This Chapter can be visited as required; that is, the techniques presented here are utilized at various points in the text, and the reader may prefer to review elements of this Chapter on encountering problems in understanding the applications which occur later. Of primary interest from this perspective are sections 3.2 and 3.3. The more general analysis presented in section 3.4, on inequality-constrained optimization, is only occasionally illustrated in applications in footnotes or appendices (although

---

[1] Different letters denote different functions: $f(\mathbf{x})$, $g(\mathbf{x})$, $h(\mathbf{x})$, $\alpha(\mathbf{x})$, $\beta(\mathbf{x})$, etc. all denote functions. Often the letters chosen have mnemonic properties, for example, $C(q)$ denotes total cost associated with producing output q.

many of the problems I analyse could be viewed in a more general context as problems of inequality-constrained optimization).

An understanding of optimization techniques is useful for the understanding of the models and theories—but it is also of use in real-world business applications. This is especially true of linear programming techniques, which find wide use in industry and commerce, but it is also true for the non-linear techniques described below. However, whilst economic analysis emphasizes the intuition obtained from the study of what are called necessary conditions, non-linear constrained optimization in business practice typically involves powerful software packages. All that is required for the solution of most optimization problems in practice is a fairly careful specification of the problem to be solved: the computer software does the rest (simple non-linear optimization problems can be solved using the SOLVER function in EXCEL, for example; see section 3.8 for examples). Thus, the organization of efficient production, of transportation and distribution, of stock and inventory control, of efficient portfolios, of yield management (the fine-tuning of complex pricing policies, such as can be seen with most airlines) are all business problems which can be addressed through the mathematical modelling and optimization approach.

The optimization problem addressed in sections 3.2 to 3.4 below allows objective functions and constraints to be non-linear; however, the special case where both objectives and constraints are linear is important because many practical problems can be assumed to be (at least approximately) linear in character—and because there are special and powerful algorithms available for the solution of such problems; this is the linear programming problem addressed in section 3.5.

Economics is the study of the allocation of scarce resources, and scarcity implies constraints. Most economic agents are assumed to behave as if they are maximizing some type of objective function (typically a non-linear function) subject to constraints (which may be linear or non-linear). Thus the consumer is characterized as maximizing utility, subject to a (linear) budget constraint, firms may aim to maximize profits (or sales revenues) subject to the constraint of a production function (the relationship between inputs and maximum attainable output) and so on. At this stage, however, the examples are selected as mathematical rather than economic applications. This means we can focus primarily on an understanding of the mathematical process involved, which will facilitate a good understanding when we come to the many applications of optimization in economic and business problems which will be encountered throughout this text.

3.2 Unconstrained Optimization

The general problem under consideration here is the following:

$$\text{Maximize } f(\mathbf{x}), \qquad (3.1)$$

where $\mathbf{x}$ is a vector of choice variables; $\mathbf{x} = (x_1, x_2 \ldots, x_n)$. A minimization problem can be converted to a maximization problem simply by attaching a minus sign to the objective function; that is, the problem of minimizing $f(\mathbf{x})$ has the same solution as that of maximizing $-f(\mathbf{x})$.

EXAMPLE 3.2 The problem

$$\text{Minimize } g(\mathbf{x}) = x_1^2 + x_2^2$$

has the same solution as that for the following problem:

$$\text{Maximize } f(\mathbf{x}) = -x_1^2 - x_2^2.$$

In both cases, the maximum is achieved at the point $x_1 = 0$, $x_2 = 0$ (see Example 3.3 for how this optimum can be found).

I shall generally assume that functions are smooth and defined on a given **domain**. The domain of a function is simply the set of points for each of which the function is defined and takes a unique value.[2] For example, the function $C(q)$, representing the total cost of producing an output q, might be defined only for non-negative values of q. A **smooth function** has no kinks, corners, or discontinuities. (Figure 3.1 illustrates both a smooth and a non-smooth function; the latter is discontinuous at x^a and its derivative is undefined[3] at x^b, where the function has a corner). In general, it is assumed

---

[2] The domain is thus the range of x values under consideration; here it is any point between 0 and 4.

[3] For those familiar with the concepts, the left- and right-hand derivatives exist but are clearly not equal at x^b; the left-hand derivative measures the gradient of the curve as one approaches x^b from the left, whilst the right-hand derivative measures the gradient of the curve as one approaches x^b from the right. For formal definitions of 'continuity' and 'derivative', see any text on mathematical analysis, e.g. Apostol (1974) or Beavis and Dobbs (1991).

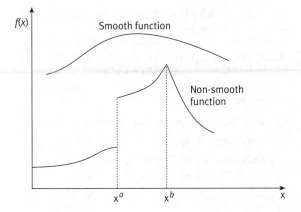

Fig. 3.1 Smooth and non-smooth functions

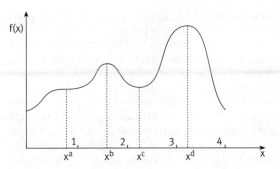

Fig. 3.2 Turning points

that, in the problems addressed in this text, there are no such corners.

The point of imposing this restriction on the types of functions dealt with is that it simplifies the identification of optimal solutions. In particular, for such functions, we can say that a maximum value for the function, if one exists, will occur either at

(i) an interior point in the domain, when it must be the case that the gradient in all directions is zero, or

(ii) a point on the boundary of the domain (in which case, the gradients need not be zero).

Both these points are highly intuitive and can be understood in the context of Figure 3.2 below, which gives the graph of a univariate (one-variable) function. The domain is the region of x-space on which the function is defined. It is sketched on the interval $0 \leq x \leq 4$. If this is the domain of the function, then clearly a global maximum[4] occurs at the point x^d. However, if the domain was $0 \leq x \leq 3$ then clearly the maximum would occur at $x = 3$, a point at which the gradient is positive.

The relevant solutions to problems in this text will generally occur at interior points rather than at boundaries of the domain. Focusing on interior points means the only points of interest are those at which the function has zero gradient, since all points which do not have zero gradient are clearly not candidates for giving a maximum value for the function. This observation indicates a way to locate the point (or points) at which a function attains a

maximum value. The idea is simply to compute the partial derivatives (loosely, the gradients along each dimension of the vector x) associated with the function, and attempt to solve the set of equations generated by setting these derivatives equal to zero. The ith derivative of $f(\mathbf{x})$ is denoted $\partial f(\mathbf{x})/\partial x_i$; it measures the rate of change of f as is x_i is increased (holding the other elements of $\mathbf{x}$ fixed). If the function involves n variables, then there will be n partial derivatives, and hence n equations to solve:

$$\partial f(\mathbf{x})/\partial x_i = 0, \ i = 1, \ldots, n. \quad (3.2)$$

Applying this principle to the objective function in Example 3.2:

EXAMPLE 3.3 Given the problem is:

$$\text{Maximize } f(\mathbf{x}) = -x_1^2 - x_2^2,$$

the partial derivatives are

$$\partial f(\mathbf{x})/\partial x_1 = -2x_1$$

and

$$\partial f(\mathbf{x})/\partial x_2 = -2x_2.$$

Thus the solution is given by setting

$$\partial f(\mathbf{x})/\partial x_1 = -2x_1 = 0$$

and

$$\partial f(\mathbf{x})/\partial x_2 = -2x_2 = 0$$

and the solution is, $x_1 = 0$, $x_2 = 0$ as originally suggested in Example 3.2.

The above example seems to suggest that our algorithm is pretty efficient at identifying a solution. The problem with this algorithm (finding the derivatives, and setting them equal to zero) is that it does not always work, even for the types of functions to which I have restricted attention. This should be immediately clear from a perusal of Figure 3.2, which illustrates a univariate function having four points in the domain at which the derivative is zero.

---

[4] The highest point on a smooth, dome-shaped hill corresponds to the point at which the gradient in every direction is 0.

Point x^a is a point of inflection, at point x^c there is a local minimum, whilst at points x^b, x^d there are local maxima. A local maximum occurs at a point where the value of the function at that point is at least as large as the value of the function at all the surrounding points, for some neighbourhood of the point in question. The neighbourhood can be arbitrarily small. A strict local maximum occurs if the value of the function is strictly greater at that point than at all surrounding points in the neighbourhood.[5] The concept of a local maximum should be clearly distinguished from that of a global maximum. A global maximum occurs at a point in the domain where the function attains its largest value (there could be several global maxima, of course, but at each one the function would have to take on the same value).[6] In Figure 3.2, point x^b looks like a strict local maximum, but is clearly not a global maximum. Point x^d is a strict local maximum and also a strict global maximum for the domain $\{x: 0 \leq x \leq 4\}$.

Thus Figure 3.2 illustrates the fact that identifying points at which the gradient is zero does not necessarily identify a global maximum; such points may also be minima or inflection points. Thus, identifying points which have zero gradient is not a sufficient condition for identifying a global maximum, but it is a necessary condition; that is, any point in the interior of the domain at which a smooth function attains a global maximum must be a point at which the partial derivatives are equal to zero. This is worth stating as a theorem:

Theorem 3.1 For a smooth function $f(\mathbf{x})$, where $\mathbf{x} = (x_1, \dots, x_n)$, a necessary condition for a local or global maximum to occur at a particular point, denoted x^*, is that $\partial f(\mathbf{x}^*)/\partial x_i = 0$, $i = 1, \dots, n$.

This condition is often referred to as a **first-order necessary condition** (since it concerns first-order partial derivatives). Most of the problems encountered in this text are well behaved in the sense that solving equations of type (3.2) will identify the solution required (namely, a global maximum for

objective functions such as profits, or a global minimum for costs, etc.).

However, the above discussion should make it clear that in more general applications, some care has to be taken to ensure that the point identified is indeed one associated with a global maximum value for the function.[7]

EXAMPLE 3.4 Consider the two variable problem

$$\text{Maximize } f(\mathbf{x}) = x_1 - x_1^2 + x_2 - x_2^2 + x_1 x_2. \quad \text{(i)}$$

The necessary conditions are that

$$\partial f(\mathbf{x})/\partial x_1 = 1 - 2x_1 + x_2 = 0 \quad \text{(ii)}$$

and

$$\partial f(\mathbf{x})/\partial x_2 = 1 - 2x_2 + x_1 = 0. \quad \text{(iii)}$$

Solving these two equations yields $x_1^* = x_2^* = 1$. The value of the objective function is then given by substituting these values back into (i); thus

$$f(\mathbf{x}^*) = 1 - 1^2 + 1 - 1^2 + 1 \times 1 = 1.$$

In general the solution could be a minimum, maximum, or inflection point. In fact in this case, the solution is a unique global maximum.

In practice, it is extremely helpful to know whether, having found a solution which satisfies the first-order necessary conditions, it is one at which the function attains a global maximum and indeed whether this is unique. This is addressed in section 3.3 below.

3.3 Concave Functions and their Role in Optimization

If the objective function is concave or quasi-concave, then any point which satisfies the first-order necessary conditions in fact identifies a global maximum for the function. This is particularly useful in

---

[5] All these concepts, including that of a neighbourhood, can be more precisely defined. However, I choose to emphasize intuition rather than formal rigour.

[6] Think of mountains. If the domain is England, and the function involved reports height above sea level at each grid reference point, then the global maximum occurs at the summit of Scafell Pike; if the domain is increased to include Scotland and Wales, then the global maximum occurs at the top of Ben Nevis. Thus a specification of the domain on which the function is defined can be of importance. However, such complications will not arise in this text.

[7] It is possible to look for so-called second-order necessary conditions; in problems involving a single-variable, it is a necessary condition for a maximum that the second derivative is non-positive (whilst for a minimum, it should be non-negative). The intuition for this is straightforward in the single variable case; if, for example, the second derivative at a turning point was strictly positive, then the first derivative would be turning from negative to positive as we increase x and pass through the point; it certainly cannot then be a maximum point. The equivalent conditions for the multi-variable problem are that at a local maximum, the Hessian matrix must be negative semi-definite, whilst at a local minimum, it must be positive semi-definite. However, I shall not go into this level of detail here; for further details see e.g. Beavis and Dobbs (1991) or Takayama (1990).

economic analysis, since many of the functions encountered in economic analysis can often reasonably be assumed concave or quasi-concave: profit functions, cost functions, revenue functions, etc. Concavity is a special case of quasi-concavity and the latter is in fact the more fundamental and important concept.[8] However, concavity is more straightforward to explain and it also plays an important role in the analysis of choice under uncertainty in Chapter 4, so for simplicity the focus here is on this.[9]

Definition 3.1 A function $f(\mathbf{x})$ is said to be **concave** if, for any two distinct points $\mathbf{x}$, $\mathbf{y}$, and any point $\mathbf{z} = \alpha\mathbf{x} + (1 - \alpha)\mathbf{y}$, where α is a scalar such that $0 \le \alpha \le 1$ (i.e. such that $\mathbf{z}$ lies on the line segment between $\mathbf{x}$ and $\mathbf{y}$), $f(\mathbf{z}) \ge \alpha f(\mathbf{x}) + (1 - \alpha)f(\mathbf{y})$. If the inequality is strict (whenever $\mathbf{z}$ is not equal to $\mathbf{x}$ or $\mathbf{y}$), then the function is **strictly concave**.

Figure 3.3 illustrates the definition of concavity, for the case of a univariate function. The key point to understand in this Figure is that $\mathbf{z}$ is a linear combination of $\mathbf{x}$ and $\mathbf{y}$, and so lies on a straight line between them, whilst $\alpha f(\mathbf{x}) + (1 - \alpha)f(\mathbf{y})$ is the point on the line segment immediately above $\mathbf{z}$. A function is concave if, for any $\mathbf{x}$, $\mathbf{y}$, for every value of $\mathbf{z}$ between $\mathbf{x}$ and $\mathbf{y}$, the value of $\alpha f(\mathbf{x}) + (1 - \alpha)f(\mathbf{y})$ is less than or equal to the value of the function at that point (i.e. the line segment at no point goes above the graph of the function).

A related concept is that of convexity:

Definition 3.2 A function $f(\mathbf{x})$ is said to be **convex** if $-f(\mathbf{x})$ is concave, and **strictly convex** if $-f(\mathbf{x})$ is strictly concave.

For the univariate case, a function is said to be convex if, taking any two points, the line segment never goes below the graph of the function. The idea of mentally drawing a line segment between arbitrary points on the function and checking that the line segment is below or above is straightforward; try it yourself to verify the properties of the functions depicted in Figure 3.4 below.

It is easy to verify from the definition (and Figure 3.4) that any linear function of one or more variables is a concave, but not a strictly concave, function. Equally, linear functions are also convex but not strictly convex: That is, they are simultaneously

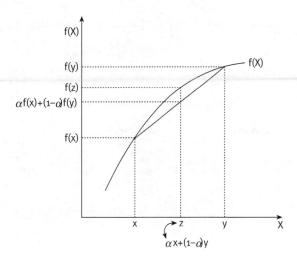

Fig. 3.3 Concave function

concave and convex. If we note the shape of the function in Figure 3.4, panel (*a*), it is fairly clear that a univariate function whose second derivative is negative everywhere[10] will be strictly concave (concomitantly, if the second derivative is positive, the function is convex, as in Figure 3.4, panel (*b*)).

The importance of concavity for optimization is captured in the following theorem (stated without proof; see e.g. Beavis and Dobbs 1990):

Theorem 3.2 If a function $f(\mathbf{x})$ is concave, where $\mathbf{x} = (x_1, x_2, \ldots, x_n)$, then if there exists a point $\mathbf{x}^*$ such that $\partial f(\mathbf{x}^*)/\partial x_i = 0$, $i = 1, \ldots, n$, then $\mathbf{x}^*$ yields a global maximum value for the function. If the function is strictly concave, then $\mathbf{x}^*$ is unique (all other points yield strictly lower values for the function).

If we refer to Definition 3.2, it should be no surprise to learn that the above theorem also holds if the word 'concave' is replaced by 'convex' and 'maximum' is replaced with 'minimum'.

The power of Theorem 3.2 is that, if the function is concave, then a solution which satisfies the first-order necessary conditions yields a global maximum (and if it is convex, the solution yields a global minimum). If the function is strictly concave (or strictly convex), then there is a unique solution to the first-order conditions. Equally, if the objective function is neither concave nor convex, then it is possible for solutions to satisfy the first-order conditions without being global maxima or minima

---

[8] For example, the utility function in consumer theory can be reasonably assumed to be quasi-concave, but not concave.

[9] For details on interrelationships, and on 'quasi-concave programming', see e.g. Beavis and Dobbs (1990) or Takayama (1985).

[10] This means the gradient of the function is continually decreasing as x increases.

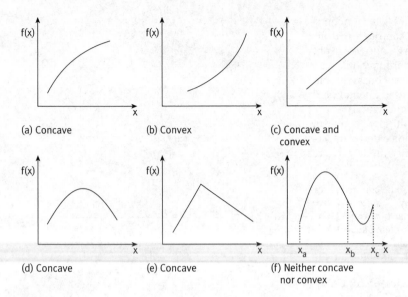

Fig. 3.4 Concave and convex functions

(see Figure 3.2; they may only identify local maxima, minima, or turning points). Often the objective function can be simply assumed to be strictly concave (or strictly convex); this is often reasonable for the firm's profit, revenue, or cost functions.

3.4 Optimization Subject to Equality Constraints

The general problem under consideration is now modified by introducing equality constraints as follows:

$$\text{Maximize } f(\mathbf{x}) \qquad (3.3)$$

$$\text{subject to } g^i(\mathbf{x}) = 0, \, i = 1, \ldots, m, \, m < n, \qquad (3.4)$$

where $\mathbf{x}$ is a vector of choice variables $\mathbf{x} = (x_1, x_2, \ldots, x_n)$, $f(\mathbf{x})$ denotes the objective function, and $g^i(\mathbf{x}) = 0$ denotes the ith constraint function. Note that the number of constraints is assumed to be less than the number of choice variables.[11]

The most natural way to solve the above problem involves substituting in the constraints to eliminate m variables, so reducing the problem to one of

[11] If there are the same number of independent equality constraints as there are choice variables, there will be at most one value for x which satisfies the constraints—there is no scope for optimization.

unconstrained optimization, discussed in section 3.3. Example 3.5 illustrates this approach.

EXAMPLE 3.5 Consider the problem

$$\text{Maximize } f(\mathbf{x}) = x_1 - x_1^2 + x_2 - x_2^2 + x_1 x_2 \qquad (i)$$

$$\text{subject to } 2x_1 + 4x_2 = 5. \qquad (ii)$$

Constraint (ii) implies

$$x_2 = \frac{(5 - 2x_1)}{4} \qquad (iii)$$

This can be substituted directly into the objective function, yielding

$$f(\mathbf{x}) = x_1 - x_1^2 + x_2 - x_2^2 + x_1 x_2$$

$$= x_1 - x_1^2 + \frac{(5 - 2x_1)}{4} - \left(\frac{(5 - 2x_1)}{4}\right)^2$$

$$+ x_1 \frac{(5 - 2x_1)}{4}$$

$$= (-28x_1^2 + 48x_1 - 5)/16 = -(7/4)x_1^2$$

$$+ 3x_1 - (5/16).$$

The first-order condition is that

$$\partial f/\partial x_1 = -(7/2)x_1 + 3 = 0 \Rightarrow x_1^* = 6/7.$$

The solution for x_2 is then given, using the constraint (iii):

$$x_2^* = (5 - 2x_1)/4 = 0.8214.$$

Substituting these values for x_1 and x_2 then gives the value of the objective function as $f(\mathbf{x}^*) = 0.9732$.

However, it is not always convenient to approach the problem in this way. This is for two reasons:

(i) the mathematical manipulations may become rather complex;

(ii) in economic analysis, it is often the case that the functions are not analytic. For example, the constraint that the output q produced by a given vector $\mathbf{x}$ of inputs may be characterized as $q = f(\mathbf{x})$, where the function $f(\mathbf{x})$ may be assumed to be smooth (along with possibly some other properties such as being concave or quasi-concave). In many applications, it is unnecessary to specify an explicit analytical form for the function.[12]

An alternative approach, using an artificially constructed **Lagrangian** function, is better suited to the analysis of these types of problem. This function is defined as follows:

$$L(\mathbf{x},\lambda) = f(\mathbf{x}) + \sum_{i=1}^{m}\lambda_i g^i(\mathbf{x}). \qquad (3.5)$$

The first-order necessary conditions associated with a maximum (or a minimum, by the way) can now be expressed in the form of the following theorem:

Theorem 3.3 If $f(\mathbf{x})$ and the constraint functions $g^i(\mathbf{x})$ are smooth and if the constraint functions are suitably well behaved, then if a particular point, denoted $\mathbf{x}^*$, gives a local maximum (or minimum) for the function (subject to the constraints), then there exists a unique vector of **Lagrange multipliers**, λ^*, such that the following first-order necessary conditions hold:

$$\frac{\partial L(\mathbf{x}^*,\lambda^*)}{\partial x_i} = \frac{\partial f(\mathbf{x}^*)}{\partial x_i} + \sum_{i=1}^{m}\lambda_j^*\frac{\partial g^j(\mathbf{x}^*)}{\partial x_i} = 0, \ i = 1, \ldots, n. \qquad (3.6)$$

In all the problems faced in this text, the constraints are suitably well behaved.[13] Given that equation (3.6) provides n equations, and the m constraint equations must also hold, it follows that there are $m + n$ equations and $m + n$ unknowns (namely $x_1, \ldots, x_n$ and $\lambda_1, \ldots, \lambda_m$); the procedure thus involves manipulating these equations in order to determine solution values for these variables. Most of the problems encountered will involve just one constraint, so this is not a major exercise; however, to illustrate the technique in action in a slightly more complex case, consider the following analytic problem.

EXAMPLE 3.6 Maximize $f(\mathbf{x}) = 1 - x_1^2 - x_2^2 - x_3^2$ subject to

$$g^1(\mathbf{x}) = x_1 + x_2 - 1 = 0 \qquad (i)$$

and

$$g^2(\mathbf{x}) = x_2 + x_3 - 1 = 0. \qquad (ii)$$

The Lagrangian for this problem is

$$L(\mathbf{x},\lambda) = f(\mathbf{x}) + \lambda_1 g^1(\mathbf{x}) + \lambda_2 g^2(\mathbf{x})$$
$$= 1 - x_1^2 - x_2^2 - x_3^2 + \lambda_1(x_1 + x_2 - 1)$$
$$+ \lambda_2(x_2 + x_3 - 1). \qquad (iii)$$

The necessary conditions for a maximum (or minimum, of course) are that (i) and (ii) hold and, from equation (3.6), that

$$\partial L(\mathbf{x},\lambda)/\partial x_1 = \lambda_1 - 2x_1 = 0, \qquad (iv)$$
$$\partial L(\mathbf{x},\lambda)/\partial x_2 = \lambda_1 + \lambda_2 - 2x_2 = 0, \qquad (v)$$

and

$$\partial L(\mathbf{x},\lambda)/\partial x_3 = \lambda_2 - 2x_3 = 0. \qquad (vi)$$

The five equations (i), (ii), (iv)–(vi) can be solved to yield the unique solution as follows. First note that (iv) implies that $\lambda_1 = 2x_1$ and (vi) that $\lambda_2 = 2x_3$. Substituting these into (v) gives

$$2x_1 + 2x_3 - 2x_2 = 0. \qquad (vii)$$

Now, (i) implies $x_1 = 1 - x_2$ and (ii) implies $x_3 = 1 - x_2$. Substituting these into (vii) yields $2(1 - x_2) + 2(1 - x_2) - 2x_2 = 0$, which implies $x_2 = 2/3$. Hence $x_1 = x_3 = 1 - x_2 = 1 - (2/3) = 1/3$, so the solution is $\mathbf{x}^* = (1/3, 2/3, 1/3)$ and $\lambda^* = (2/3, 2/3)$. The value at the maximum is

$$f(\mathbf{x}^*) = 1 - (1/3)^2 - (2/3)^2 - (1/3)^2 = 1/3.$$

The solution in Example 3.6 does in fact identify a global maximum, although the analysis of first-order conditions guarantees only that it is either a local maximum, a local minimum, or a turning point. A final point of some interest is the interpretation of the Lagrange multipliers, λ^*. For a well-behaved problem of the type discussed above, the value of the multipliers at the optimum can be shown to measure the rate at which the maximum attainable value changes as the constraints are relaxed. Thus, in Example 3.4, slackening either constraint by a small amount δ leads to an increase in the objective

---

[12] Analytic here means functions such as $x^2 + 2xy + y^2$ etc. In economic analysis, there is a general preference for avoiding the use of analytic functions. For example, a demand function might be assumed to be continuous and smooth, and have downward slope, but it may not be necessary to make any stronger assumptions (such as that the demand function is linear).

[13] 'Suitably well behaved' here includes the requirement, when solving the system of linear equations, that the equations be linearly independent. For more details, see Lambert (1985) or Beavis and Dobbs (1990).

function of amount $(2/3)\delta$. However this holds in general only for small changes.

As mentioned earlier, it is possible to test the solution further, or to examine so-called 'sufficient conditions' for a solution to the first-order conditions to constitute a unique global maximum. These issues, whilst of some importance, are beyond the scope of the present text (for more details see e.g. Lambert 1985, Beavis and Dobbs 1990, or Takayama 1985). In all the problems analysed in this text, the first-order conditions will identify the optimal solution. However, it is worth emphasizing that the approach adopted in most intermediate texts, which focuses simply on identifying the solutions which satisfy the first-order conditions, as in Example 3.6, is far from rigorous.

3.5 Optimization Subject to Inequality Constraints

As explained in section 3.1, most economic problems can be viewed as optimization subject to inequality constraints. In many cases, the solution will obviously involve certain binding constraints; for this reason, many texts simplify the analysis by treating such constraints as equality constraints. A good example of this is that of the consumer's utility-maximization problem, in which it is conventional simply to assume that the budget constraint will bind. However, in more complex problems, things may not be so obvious, and a less informal approach to the identification of the optimum solution is required.

The general problem under consideration is here modified by introducing inequality constraints as follows:

$$\text{Maximize } f(\mathbf{x}) \qquad (3.7)$$

$$\text{subject to } g^i(\mathbf{x}) \geq 0, \, i = 1, \ldots, m, \qquad (3.8)$$

where $\mathbf{x}$ is a vector of choice variables $\mathbf{x} = (x_1, x_2, \ldots, x_n$. As in section 3.2, a minimization problem can be converted to a maximization problem simply by attaching a minus to the objective function; that is, the problem involving minimizing $f(\mathbf{x})$ has the same solution as that of maximizing $-f(\mathbf{x})$. Equally, a constraint $\alpha(\mathbf{x}) \leq 0$ can be written as $-\alpha(\mathbf{x}) \geq 0$. Equality constraints such as $\alpha(\mathbf{x}) = 0$ can be accommodated by writing two constraints, namely $\alpha(\mathbf{x}) \geq 0$ and $-\alpha(\mathbf{x}) \geq 0$ (although equality constraints can often also be directly substituted out of the problem, as in Example 3.5).

The above problem is much more complex than the equality-constrained problem, since it is not known whether each constraint will be active (i.e. $g^i(\mathbf{x}) = 0$) or inactive (i.e. $g^i(\mathbf{x}) > 0$) in the optimal solution. Accordingly, a step-by-step or 'recipe' approach is adopted. This approach is not usually computationally efficient, but, for well-posed and well-behaved problems, it will get the solution in the end; for example, it can be guaranteed to work if the objective and constraint functions are concave. The approach again involves the Lagrange function, which will be familiar from the analysis of equality-constrained optimization. The Lagrange function associated with the above problem is defined as:

$$L(\mathbf{x},\boldsymbol{\lambda}) = f(\mathbf{x}) + \sum_{j=1}^{m} \lambda_j g^j(\mathbf{x}). \qquad (3.9)$$

The equality-constrained optimization problem reduced to finding particular values for the choice variables x_i, $i = 1, \ldots, n$, and the Lagrange multipliers λ_i, $i = 1, \ldots, m$, which simultaneously satisfied a set of equations (the first-order conditions). The particular vector of x-variables which did this was denoted $\mathbf{x}^*$ and the associated vector of multipliers was denoted $\boldsymbol{\lambda}^*$. The inequality-constrained optimization here likewise involves finding particular values $\mathbf{x}^*$ and $\boldsymbol{\lambda}^*$ which satisfy a set of necessary conditions; in this case, they are referred to as the Kuhn–Tucker conditions.

The Kuhn–Tucker conditions are as follows:

$$\partial L(\mathbf{x}^*,\boldsymbol{\lambda}^*)/\partial x_i = 0, \quad i = 1, \ldots, n, \qquad (3.10)$$

$$g^i(\mathbf{x}^*) \geq 0, \quad i = 1, \ldots, m, \qquad (3.11)$$

$$\lambda_i^* g^i(\mathbf{x}^*) = 0, \quad i = 1, \ldots, m, \qquad (3.12)$$

and

$$\lambda_i^* \geq 0, \quad i = 1, \ldots, m. \qquad (3.13)$$

The equations in line (3.12) are often termed the **complementary slackness** conditions. This is because they require either $\lambda_i = 0$ or $g^i(\mathbf{x}) = 0$ (or both). Thus if a constraint is slack ($g^i(\mathbf{x}) > 0$), then implies that $\lambda_i = 0$. Or, if $\lambda_i > 0$ then it must be that $g^i(\mathbf{x}) = 0$.

The basic results are as follows:[14]

---

[14] Note that it is assumed the functions are defined on an unbounded domain; there are no boundary problems in the analysis.

Theorem 3.4 (**necessary conditions**): If a 'constraint qualification'[15] holds and the objective and constraint functions are smooth functions, then if a particular point yields a local maximum (subject to satisfying the constraints), then the Kuhn–Tucker conditions are necessary conditions: they must hold at this point.

Theorem 3.5 (**sufficient conditions**): If the objective and constraint functions are smooth concave functions, and a particular point satisfies the Kuhn–Tucker conditions, then at that point the objective function attains a global maximum (subject to satisfying the constraints). If the objective function is strictly concave, then the solution is unique.

The bottom line is that in many cases, it can simply be assumed that the functions involved are in fact concave (remember that all linear functions are concave); then, if a point can be found which satisfies the Kuhn–Tucker conditions (KTC), this is the global optimal solution. A simple algorithm to determine the solution in such a case is as follows:

Algorithm The following process terminates as soon as a solution which satisfies the KTC is found.

Check the KTC for
(i) interior solutions (no binding constraints).
If none exist that satisfy the KTC, then consider
(ii) solutions involving one binding constraint (take each constraint in turn as a separate possibility).
If none exist that satisfy the KTC, then consider
(iii) solutions involving two binding constraints (take each combination of two constraints in turn).
If none exist that satisfy the KTC, then consider
(iv) solutions with three binding constraints, and so on, until the final case is reached, where the solution involves all binding constraints.

Given the assumptions about the nature of the functions involved, a unique optimal solution exists; it follows that the above analysis will eventually find a solution which does satisfy the Kuhn–Tucker conditions. The approach is best illustrated with a simple algebraic example.

Example 3.7 Consider the problem

$$\text{Maximize } f(\mathbf{x}) = x_1 - x_1^2 + x_2 - x_2^2 + x_1 x_2 \qquad \text{(i)}$$

---

[15] Constraint qualifications are beyond the scope of this book (see e.g. Takayama (1985) or Beavis and Dobbs (1990)) but are usually satisfied in most economic problems (and rarely even considered).

subject to

$$2x_1 + 4x_2 \leq 5 \qquad \text{(ii)}$$

and

$$x_2 \geq 1. \qquad \text{(iii)}$$

First rearrange both constraints so they are in the form $g^i(\mathbf{x}) \geq 0$: (ii) becomes

$$g^1(\mathbf{x}) = 5 - 2x_1 - 4x_2 \geq 0 \qquad \text{(iv)}$$

and (iii) becomes

$$g^2(\mathbf{x}) = x_2 - 1 \geq 0. \qquad \text{(v)}$$

In fact the objective function is concave and the constraints are linear, hence also concave. Thus Theorem 3.5 applies; if a solution is found to the Kuhn–Tucker conditions, it constitutes an optimal solution. The Lagrangian is

$$L = x_1 - x_1^2 + x_2 - x_2^2 + x_1 x_2 + \lambda_1(5 - 2x_1 - 4x_2) + \lambda_2(x_2 - 1) \qquad \text{(vi)}$$

and the Kuhn–Tucker conditions are

$$\partial L/\partial x_1 = 1 - 2x_1 + x_2 - 2\lambda_1 = 0 \qquad \text{(vii)}$$

$$\partial L/\partial x_2 = 1 - 2x_2 + x_1 - 4\lambda_1 + \lambda_2 = 0 \qquad \text{(viii)}$$

$$\lambda_1(5 - 2x_1 - 4x_2) = 0 \qquad \text{(ix)}$$

$$\lambda_2(x_2 - 1) = 0. \qquad \text{(x)}$$

Now consider possible solutions:

1. Suppose no constraints bind. If so, then $5 - 2x_1 - 4x_2 > 0$ and $x_2 - 1 > 0$. These imply, from (ix), that $\lambda_1 = 0$ and from (x), that $\lambda_2 = 0$. Using these values reduces (vii) and (viii) to two equations involving x_1, x_2. Solving gives $x_1 = x_2 = 1$ (as the reader can verify). Now substituting these values into the left-hand side of (iv) gives $5 - 2 - 4 = -1$, when it should be non-negative. Thus this candidate solution does not satisfy the KTC.

2a. Suppose constraint (iv) alone binds so that

$$2x_1 = 5 - 4x_2, \qquad (2a1)$$

but (v) is a strict inequality. Then from (x), since $x_2 - 1 > 0$, it follows that $\lambda_2 = 0$. Substituting these values into (viii) gives

$$1 - 2x_2 + x_1 - 4\lambda_1 = 0 \Rightarrow \lambda_1$$
$$= (1 - 2x_2 + x_1)/4. \qquad (2a2)$$

Using this to eliminate λ_1 from (vii) gives

$$1 - 2x_2 + x_1 - 2(1 - 2x_2 + x_1)/4 = 0. \qquad (2a3)$$

Simplifying, this gives

$$1 - 5x_1 + 4x_2 = 0. \qquad (2a4)$$

Solving $(2a1)$ and $(2a4)$ gives $x_1 = 6/7$ and

$x_2 = 23/28$. Unfortunately this contradicts the constraint that $x_2 \geq 1$. Thus this candidate solution also violates the KTC.

2b. Suppose (v) alone binds, but (iv) is a strict inequality. Then $x_2 = 1$ and since $5 - 2x_1 - 4x_2 > 0$, from (ix), $\lambda_1 = 0$. Substituting these values into (vii) gives $x_1 = 1$. However, this in conjunction with $x_2 = 1$ contradicts (iv), that $5 - 2x_1 - 4x_2 > 0$. So this is not the solution.

3. Suppose both constraints bind. (This is the last possibility, so it must be the solution!) Then $x_2 = 1$ and $2x_1 = 5 - 4x_2$, so $x_1 = 1/2$. Substituting these values into (vii) and (viii) and solving gives $\lambda_1 = 1/2 > 0$ and $\lambda_2 = 5/2 > 0$. Thus all the constraints and all the Kuhn–Tucker conditions are satisfied. This is the optimal solution: $x_1^* = 1/2$ and $x_2^* = 1$, and $f(\mathbf{x}^*) = 0.75$.

It turned out that the solution cropped up in the last case to be considered; if it had turned up in the first, there would have been no need to continue the analysis. Often, it is worth pondering a little on the structure of the problem; if you have an idea of where the solution may be (i.e. which constraints are likely to be binding in the solution), it may be worth analysing such cases first. However, the general procedure is as above; clearly, it becomes rather tedious when there are several constraints, but for the case where there are only one, two , or three constraints, the analysis is readily manageable. This solution identified by the Kuhn–Tucker conditions gives the unique global optimum because the objective function and constraints are concave functions; the constraints are clearly concave, since they are linear, whilst the objective function is strictly concave.[16] Theorems 3.4 and 3.5 both apply.

Whilst the Kuhn–Tucker conditions are of great importance in the analysis of economic models, and in particular where only the qualitative properties of functions are known (such as that demand curves have negative slope or that costs increase with output), in business applications, constrained optimization will more generally concern explicit analytic functions. In such cases, it is also possible (so long as the problem is reasonably well behaved) to find the optimum using gradient search methods. A variety of software packages exists to facilitate this approach. In particular, most spreadsheet packages incorporate a SOLVER routine which will deal with constrained optimizations of the type discussed in Example 3.7 (see the Appendix to this chapter).

3.6 Linear Programming

Many business problems can be characterized as problems involving the maximization of an objective function subject to constraints, where all the functions involved are linear or approximately linear. This type of problem, a special case of problem (3.1), is referred to as the **linear programming** problem. Because of its special structure, the linear programming problem is rather more straightforward to solve, and solution methodology lends itself to routine and computerized algorithms. Solving linear programming problems by hand (or hand calculator) is a straightforward but singularly tedious business. In this section I shall confine my attention to two-variable problems; these give an insight into the nature of the problem and can be solved straightforwardly by graphical means. This approach is used to solve mixed-strategy game theory problems in Chapter 5, and in capital budgeting in Chapter 7. The algorithms available for solving more complex linear programming problems and the issue of sensitivity analysis[17] are beyond the scope of the present text; these are major topics which form the centrepiece of any course in operations research. For further details of these, including the use of the so-called dual problem, see any text on operations research (e.g. Taha 1989). However, for small- to medium-scale problems, it is possible to tackle the linear programming optimization problem using EXCEL's SOLVER function (and most spreadsheets have a similar facility). This is straightforward to use, and the approach is the same as described for more general non-linear constrained optimization problems; for a brief exposition, see the appendix below.

The general format of the linear programming problem is

$$\text{Maximize } z = \mathbf{c}'\mathbf{x} \qquad (3.14)$$
$$\text{subject to } \mathbf{A}\mathbf{x} \leq \mathbf{b}, \qquad (3.15)$$

---

[16] Although showing this goes beyond my remit; see e.g. Lambert (1985) or Beavis and Dobbs (1990) for appropriate tests for concavity etc.

[17] Sensitivity analysis here concerns the extent to which the value of the objective function and optimal values for the choice variables $\mathbf{x}^*$ are affected by changes in the parameters of the $\mathbf{A}$ matrix or the right-hand constants $\mathbf{b}$ in equation (3.15).

where $\mathbf{c}' = (c_1, c_2, \ldots, c_n)$, $\mathbf{x}' = (x_1, x_2, \ldots, x_n)$, $\mathbf{b}' = (b_1, b_2, \ldots, b_m)$, and $\mathbf{A}$ is an $m \times n$ matrix. Written out more fully, this becomes:

$$\text{Maximize } z = c_1 x_1 + c_2 x_2 + \ldots c_n x_n \quad (3.16)$$

subject to

$$a_{11} x_1 + a_{12} x_2 + \ldots a_{1n} x_n \leq b_1$$
$$a_{21} x_1 + a_{22} x_2 + \ldots a_{2n} x_n \leq b_2$$
$$\ldots$$
$$a_{m1} x_1 + a_{m2} x_2 + \ldots a_{mn} x_n \leq b_m. \quad (3.17)$$

Notice that we could have written the constraints in precisely the same form as in (3.8). It follows that the Kuhn–Tucker approach could be adopted here to obtain a solution. However, the linear structure facilitates alternative and computationally more efficient solution procedures; one reason for this is that in a linear problem, the solution will necessarily occur on the boundary of the feasible set, and not inside it. The solution procedure essentially needs only to consider the value of the objective function at such corner points on this boundary. The linear program (equations (3.14) plus (3.15)) can also be written to include 'equality' and 'greater than' constraints (and linear-programming software packages are always set up so that they can address problems which include these alternative forms of linear constraint).

In what follows, a simple graphical approach is used to study the problem. This is useful in that it gives a good insight into the nature of the optimization problem (and is sufficient for all the applications discussed later in the text, but is restrictive in that it only works for problems involving two choice variables). Any more complex problem would be solved using either the spreadsheet SOLVER or, for more complex, larger-scale problems, standard commercially available software.

EXAMPLE 3.8 Consider the problem

$$\text{Maximize } z = x_1 + 3x_2 \quad (i)$$

subject to

$$x_1 + x_2 \leq 1 \quad (c1)$$
$$x_1 + 2x_2 \leq 1 \quad (c2)$$
$$2x_1 + x_2 \leq 1 \quad (c3)$$
$$x_1 \geq 0 \quad (c4)$$
$$x_2 \geq 0. \quad (c5)$$

Constraints $(c4)$ and $(c5)$ are non-negativity constraints. The constraints are drawn in Figure 3.5 and the feasible set is shaded. I refer to a constraint as binding if it holds with equality.

Figure 3.5 involves constructing the graphs for each of the constraints, assuming it is binding. This involves making x_1 the subject of each equation; for example, when it binds, constraint $(c1)$ can be written as $x_1 = 1 - x_2$, $(c3)$ as $x_1 = \frac{1}{2} - \frac{1}{2} x_2$, etc. The shaded region in Figure 3.5 is termed the feasible set. Only points within this set satisfy all the constraints simultaneously. Rearranging the objective function, again to make x_1 the subject of the equation, gives $x_1 = z - 3x_2$. For a given value of z this function can be graphed. For example, if we set $z = 0$, then the graph of the objective function is that labelled z_1 in the figure. For all points on the dotted line, $z = 0$; the dotted line is thus a level curve for z. All points on the level curve labelled z_2 have z-value of 0.5, and the further to the north and east the level curve is, the higher the value of the objective function value z. Clearly the optimal solution occurs at the boundary of the feasible set at the point where $x_1 = 0$, $x_2 = 1/2$, at which point the objective function takes the value $z = 1 \times 0 + 3 \times (1/2) = 3/2$.

The two-variable graphical problem can be solved by first sketching out the feasible set and determining the slope of the indifference or level curves associated with the objective function, as illustrated in Figure 3.5. The solution, if it exists, will involve one of the corners in the feasible set, so it should be clear which constraints are binding at that point.

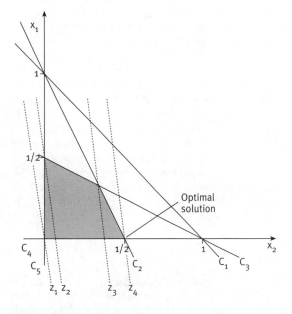

Fig. 3.5 LP graphical solution

The graphical analysis does not have to be conducted to any great level of accuracy; so long as it can be determined from a sketch of the problem which constraints are binding at the optimum, then these constraints hold with equality, and can be analytically solved to obtain the exact co-ordinates of the optimal solution. In the above case, even a rough sketch of the problem will determine that it is constraints ($c2$) and ($c4$) which bind. These hold with equality, so the optimum is given as the solution to the equations

$$x_1 + 2x_2 = 1$$

and

$$x_1 = 0.$$

Thus $x_1 = 0$, hence $2x_2 = 1$, and so $x_2 = 1/2$. The point of this analysis is that only a rough sketch of the feasible set is usually necessary before it becomes clear which are the binding constraints; once these have been determined, the solution can be obtained algebraically (and hence more accurately) by solving these constraints as equations. Note that the feasible set is convex[18] and bounded. The feasible set is clearly always convex, but it does not need to be bounded for there to be an optimal solution. For example, taking away the constraint ($c5$) in Example 3.8 leaves the optimal solution unaffected; the feasible set in this case is illustrated in Figure 3.6. However, take away constraint ($c4$) instead and a solution no longer exists. Thus if the feasible set is bounded, an optimal solution must exist, but boundedness is by no means a necessary condition for the existence of a finite optimal solution.

If we look at Figure 3.5, it is fairly clear that, since level-curves are always parallel straight lines, the optimal solution, if it exists, must lie at one of the extreme points of the feasible set. Indeed, one simple algorithm for obtaining the solution to a linear program involves evaluating the objective function at each extreme point, and then simply choosing the point with the largest z-value. When there are many variables and many constraints, however, more efficient algorithms are available, along with methods for studying the sensitivity of the solution to variations in parameter values (see e.g. Taha 1989). A

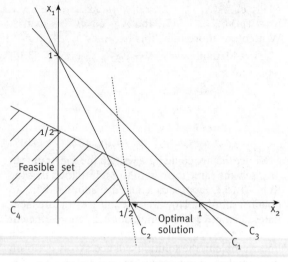

Fig. 3.6 Example where an optimal solution exists although the feasible set is unbounded

whole text could be devoted to these techniques, so the details are beyond the scope of this book. The graphical approach discussed above finds application at various places, however.

3.7 Summary

This chapter covered all the mathematical optimization techniques used in the theoretical analysis, applications, and examples in this text, namely unconstrained optimization, equality-constrained optimization, inequality-constrained optimization, and linear programming. It also discussed (in the appendix) the use of EXCEL software for use in optimization in cases where numerical solutions are possible. The examples discussed here were deliberately purely mathematical/analytical and non-economic in nature in order to enable the reader to gain a good grasp of the solution techniques involved. The relevance of these techniques for business practice will become clear as we meet such applications through the rest of the text.

---

[18] A convex set is a set of points such that, if you take any pair of points in the set and draw a straight line between them, every point on the line between the two points is also in the set. Confirm this in relation to the feasible set in Fig. 3.5.

3.8 Review Questions

1. Unconstrained optimization:

(a) Find the values for x_1, x_2, x_3 which maximize the function

$$f(\mathbf{x}) = 1 + x_1 - 2x_1^2 - x_2^2 - 3x_3^2.$$

(b) If a monopolistic firm has a linear inverse demand function of the form

$$p = 100 - q,$$

where p is price (in £) and q is the number of units of output sold, and the firm has a constant marginal cost of £10 per unit, what is the revenue-maximizing output and price? What is the profit-maximizing output and price?

2. Equality-constrained optimization: Find the values for x_1, x_2, and x_3 which maximize the function

$$f(\mathbf{x}) = 1 - x_1^2 - x_2^2 - x_3^2$$

subject to the constraint that

$$g(\mathbf{x}) = x_1 + x_2 - 1 = 0.$$

3. Inequality-constrained optimization:

(a) Find the values for x_1, x_2 which minimize the function

$$f(\mathbf{x}) = x_1 - x_2^2$$

subject to the constraints

$$x_1 \geq 0, x_2 \geq 0, x_1 + x_2 \geq 1.$$

(Hint: recall that to minimize $f(\mathbf{x})$, it suffices to maximize $-f(\mathbf{x})$).

(b) In the consumer's utility maximization problem, treated in some detail in section 8.3, it is assumed that the budget constraint will bind. A more general formulation (using the same notation) would be as follows:

Maximize $U(\mathbf{x})$

subject to $\sum_{i=1}^{n} p_i x_i \leq Y$.

Show that the optimal solution requires that the budget constraint must bind. (Hint: set up the Lagrangian and explore the necessary conditions; show that the multiplier on the constraint must be positive, and hence, using the complementary slackness condition, that the constraint must bind.)

4. Linear programming: With the information provided in Table 3.1 below, determine the output combination that will maximize daily total profits.

Table 3.1 Profits and Processing Requirements for Products 1 and 2

	Hours of processing needed per ton		Daily capacity (hours)
	Product 1	Product 2	
Cutting	1	2	10
Mixing	2.5	0	10
Packing	0	1.25	10
Painting	0	2.5	10
Profits per ton (£)	30	30	

5. Use the EXCEL SOLVER function to verify the numerical solutions to the problems posed in Examples 3.3 to 3.8.

3.9 Further Reading

Given that the reader has taken a foundation course in calculus and linear algebra, Lambert (1985) provides a good, more detailed, but still fairly intuitive introduction to the mathematics involved in sections 3.2 to 3.5 on non-linear optimization. Beavis and Dobbs (1990) and Takayama (1985) give a rather more rigorous and detailed analysis of concepts and theorems associated with static, and dynamic, optimization along with economic applications. For an excellent text on linear programming which details many algorithms and applications, see Taha (1992).

Appendix: Numerical Solutions to Analytic Problems

This appendix gives an illustration of how the EXCEL SOLVER function may be used to solve analytic constrained optimization problems. The problem to be solved is that given in Example 3.7, repeated here for convenience:

Maximize $f(\mathbf{x}) = x_1 - x_1^2 + x_2 - x_2^2 + x_1 x_2$

subject to

$$g^1(\mathbf{x}) = 5 - 2x_1 - 4x_2 \geq 0 \qquad \text{(i)}$$

and

$$g^2(\mathbf{x}) = x_2 - 1 \geq 0. \qquad \text{(ii)}$$

This problem can easily be solved using the spreadsheet approach as follows (Table 3.2).

Table 3.2 Optimization using EXCEL

	F	G
13	x_1	0
14	x_2	0
15	$f(x)$	0
16	$g^1(x)$	5
17	$g^2(x)$	−1

Columns are labelled in the spreadsheet by the letters F, G, etc. and rows by numbers. Thus F13, F14, F15, etc. identify a particular cell. Cells F13 to F17 are just descriptions of associated cells G13 to G17. Cells G13 and G14 contain simple numbers (random guesses for the solution values for x_1, x_2). Cell G15 contains '= G13 − G13^2 + G14 − G14^2 + G13*G14', that is, it gives the value of the objective function for given values of x_1, x_2 in cells G13, G14. Cell G16 contains '= 5 − 2 *G13 − 4*G14', which is the value of the left-hand side of the first constraint, whilst cell G17 contains '= G14 − 1', the left-hand side of the second. The solution is then obtained by clicking on the SOLVER button (from the TOOLS menu); the 'wizard' then takes you step by step through the final setting-up of the problem. The SOLVER then produces various standard reports which describe the solution; EXCEL answer and sensitivity reports are illustrated in Tables 3.3 and 3.4.

The answer report indicates that the solution obtained is precisely that obtained in Example 3.7. The sensitivity report gives the values of the Lagrange multipliers. (The Lagrangian is set up for 'less than or equal to' constraints in EXCEL, and the Kuhn–Tucker conditions discussed in this section deal with 'greater than or equal to' constraints; it can be shown that this leads to the multipliers being of equal magnitude but opposite sign.) However, they again indicate the sensitivity of the solution to (small) changes in the tightness of the constraints. For example, if the constraint $g^2(x) \geq 0$ was replaced with, say, $g^2(x) \geq 0.1$, then this tightening of the constraint would reduce the value of the objective function at the optimum by the amount $0.1 \times 2.5 = 0.25$. However, it is important to note that the value of the Lagrange multipliers in general only gives an estimate of sensitivity for small changes in the tightness of constraints.

Whilst the spreadsheet approach is both simple to apply in practice and can be used to solve quite complex constrained-optimization problems, two points are worth noting. First, the problem needs to be well specified and reasonably well behaved as the optimization process works through a gradient search process. It is possible that such processes may end up at local maxima and not global maxima (and that there may be no solution, if the problem is ill

Table 3.3 EXCEL answer report

Target Cell (Max)

Cell	Name	Original Value	Final Value
G15	$f(x)$	0	0.75

Adjustable Cells

Cell	Name	Original Value	Final Value
G13	x1	0	0.5
G14	x2	0	1

Constraints

Cell	Name	Cell Value	Formula	Status	Slack
G16	g1(x)	−7.37188E−14	G16>=0	Binding	0
G17	g2(x)	0	G17>=0	Binding	0

Table 3.4 EXCEL sensitivity report

Changing Cells

Cell	Name	Final Value	Reduced Gradient
G13	x1	0.5	0
G14	x2	1	0

Constraints

Cell	Name	Final Value	Lagrange Multiplier
G16	g1(x)	−7.37188E−14	−0.499999754
G17	g2(x)	0	−2.50000006

posed). Secondly, whilst the approach can be applied to numerical or analytic problems, it is of little use in the study and analysis of economic models where only qualitative information regarding the properties of functions is known; in such cases the aim is usually to describe the characteristics of solutions in a more general way. The Lagrangian approach is of particular importance in such cases, as we shall see in applications throughout this text.

4 Decision-making Under Uncertainty

Objectives To distinguish risk and uncertainty and to outline and assess the expected utility model as a positive and normative theory for decision-making under risk and uncertainty.

Prerequisites None required, although some familiarity with the idea of a utility function, from the theory of consumer choice (covered in Chapter 8), may be helpful.

Keywords actuarially fair, Allais' Paradox, ambiguity, certainty, certainty-equivalent wealth, classical probability, Comparability Axiom, Compound Probabilities Axiom, Ellsberg's Urn, event, expected utility, expected value, gamble, Greater Probability of Success Axiom, Independence Axiom, lottery, prospect, relative frequency, risk, risk-averse, risk-neutral, risk preference, St Petersburg Paradox, subjective probability, transivity axiom, uncertainty, utility function, von Neumann–Morgenstern (VNM) function.

4.1 Introduction

This Chapter is concerned with decision-making under risk and uncertainty; how people actually choose, and how they ought to choose if they wish their choices to be in some sense rational. It can be viewed as a stand-alone unit, which may be omitted if not part of the syllabus. However, some familiarity with the concepts of subjective probability and expected utility are helpful for a more complete understanding at various points in the text, notably for game theory (Chapter 5), risk analysis (Chapter 7), and bargaining (Chapter 27).

Most choices involve some form of uncertainty. This is obviously true in games of chance (such as betting on the toss of a coin), but is also true for most business decisions. The consortium which chose to build the Channel Tunnel between England and France would have had estimates of the overall construction cost, but the final cost was always going to be highly uncertain, as indeed were the projected future profits from running the business. Any enterprise, after setting a product price, will face fluctuations in the level of sales. As a consumer, if you buy a second-hand car or a piece of antique furniture, you may get a 'lemon'.[1] Thus uncertainty is endemic to most decisions. Two questions then naturally arise:

1. *What constitutes a satisfactory positive model of choice under uncertainty?* Is it possible to construct a model which seems to describe how individuals actually behave? Note that such a descriptive model would be particularly useful if it was capable of being embedded into more complex models.

2. *What constitutes a satisfactory normative model of choice under uncertainty?* Is it possible to construct a theory about how a decision-maker who desires to be rational should make decisions?

It can be argued that the expected utility model outlined in section 4.3 provides an account of how people actually behave and of how, if they wish to be rational, they ought to behave. It has to be said that the model's performance in describing how people actually behave has come in for considerable criticism in recent years. There is now mounting evidence that individuals seem to behave, at least in some situations, in ways which systematically contradict the model's predictions. This is worrying since the model forms a building block for many other models used in economic analysis; for exam-

---

[1] 'Lemon' is the American term for a used car of low quality (having been clocked, or whatever). The antique furniture may not be what the dealer claimed; it may even be repro.

ple, in game theory (Chapter 5) and the theory of finance (see Chapter 7). By contrast, as a normative model, expected utility would appear to be on firmer ground. The axiomatic[2] foundations are really quite appealing to anyone who wishes to take rational and consistent decisions (although even here, there are several difficulties—see section 4.7).

Choice under uncertainty has been a major growth area for research in economics, particularly experimental economics, in recent years. Some of the problems associated with expected utility and a brief review of new (and older) directions is presented in section 4.8.

4.2 Risk and Uncertainty

The introduction suggested that risk or uncertainty related in some way to the possibility that one of several outcomes could occur once the choice or decision was made. The following classification scheme is often used:

Definition 4.1
 (i) A choice under **certainty** leads to a unique outcome.
 (ii) A choice under **risk** is a choice which may lead to one of several, possibly infinitely many, outcomes, where the probability of each potential outcome is known.
 (iii) A choice under **uncertainty** (or **ambiguity**) may lead to several (possibly infinitely many) outcomes, where the probability of any particular outcome is unknown.

This nomenclature is due to Knight (1933). Most economists have tended to use the term 'uncertainty' as a general term for either risk or uncertainty in the above sense. Recent work in this area has used the word 'ambiguity' to represent uncertainty of the type described in (iii) above, perhaps as a reflection of the lack of agreement over the use of the term 'uncertainty'.

In the light of Definition 4.1, it is clear that most business decisions are in practice decisions made under uncertainty rather than risk. That is, probabilities associated with outcomes are generally unknown. A common approach here, taking the normative perspective, is that it is possible to convert decision problems under uncertainty into problems under risk, essentially through the use of the concept of **subjective probability**.

Whilst this works well from a normative perspective from a positive perspective, the question is slightly different; namely, do individuals behave 'as if' they calculate subjective probabilities? This question is addressed in more detail in section 4.8.

Before proceeding, it may be useful to review the basic axioms and mathematical properties of probability, along with alternative interpretations. It is conventional to start with the idea of a sample space and the concept of events. For simplicity, the following exposition is restricted to cases where outcomes are discrete. Consider an experiment in which a six-sided die is rolled once. There are thus six possible outcomes. Letting '1' stand for the event of the number one showing uppermost (and so on), the set of possible outcomes is denoted $\Omega = \{1,2,3,4,5,6\}$. Ω denotes the sample space. An **event** is then defined as a subset of Ω—for example, the event E of the die showing either 1 or 2. This is denoted $E = \{1,2\}$. The event of an odd number showing is the event $E = \{1,3,5\}$. Both events are subsets of Ω. Basically, a **probability function**, denoted $p(E)$, assigns a number to any event E in the sample space. These probability numbers must have certain properties, as follows:

Definition 4.2 The Axioms of Probability
1. Probabilities are non-negative numbers that sum to unity.
2. If an event E is certain, its probability is unity; i.e. $p(E) = 1$.
3. If two events E_1, E_2 are mutually exclusive, then
$$p(E_1 \text{ or } E_2) = p(E_1) + p(E_2).$$

EXAMPLE 4.1 For a single roll of the die, if $p(\{1\} = 1/6$ and $p(\{2\}) = 1/6$, then $p(\{1,2\}) = 1/3$. Likewise, $p(\{\phi\} = 0$ and $p(\{1,2,3,4,5,6\}) = 1$.[3]

4.2.1 Interpretations of Probability

What meaning can we give to probability numbers? Consider the following possible interpretations:

Definition 4.3 *Classical* or *a priori* Probability: If there are n possible events which are equally likely (because of symmetric characteristics in the structure of the process, such as the symmetry of a fair dice, then the probability of each outcome is $1/n$.

Definition 4.4 The **Relative Frequency** Interpretation: If an experiment is repeated n times and a particular outcome occurs q times out of the possible n, then the

---

[2] In economic analysis, an axiom is essentially a very simple assumption which can be stated in a simple mathematical form, and whose truth is supposedly self-evident.

[3] '$\{\phi\}$' denotes the null, or empty, set.

probability associated with that outcome is $\text{Lim}_{n \to \infty}(q/n)$, the limit of the ratio as the number of experiments goes to infinity.

The *a priori* interpretation merely redefines probability in terms of events being equally likely. Certainly, in practice, this is not especially helpful, except in stylized gambling situations (such as roulette) where apparent symmetry suggests the outcomes do appear to be equally likely (though note that even here, appearance may be deceptive—the wheel may be loaded). The relative frequency definition is also non-operational in practice (since an infinite number of experiments are required), but it does suggest for repeatable experiments that it is possible to estimate probabilities by conducting a (finite) number of experiments. The relative frequency estimate of probability for an event is then simply the number of times the event of interest occurs divided by the total number of experiments (probabilities can only be estimated, but the law of large numbers implies that we know the confidence interval shrinks as *n* is increased, so an arbitrary degree of precision is possible). Unfortunately, there are many 'experiments' which are not easily repeatable (e.g. building the Channel Tunnel). Indeed, it can be argued that most business decisions are not identically repeatable experiments. In such circumstances, there is uncertainty, but no empirical basis for estimating probabilities. If the definition of probability is to play a useful role in such circumstances, the definition needs extending somehow. This is where the concept of subjective probability comes into its own:

Definition 4.5 Subjective Probability: The assignment of probability numbers to events such that the numbers satisfy the axioms of probability (Definition 4.2), and such that the numbers reflect the individual decision-maker's assessment of the chances of the event occurring.

The idea is that the assignment reflects the knowledge the individual has about the 'experiment'. For example, consider a horse race; given the information you have on the past form of a particular horse, you may consider that the odds being offered are either fair or unfair in a particular direction. That is, you have some idea of what you consider to be fair odds. Subjective probability assessments are unique to an individual, although economists like to assume that, if individuals are in some sense rational and have the same information, they will make the same subjective probability assessments. This, of course, is

an hypothesis susceptible in principle to empirical test.[4]

EXAMPLE 4.2 Here are some uncertain outcomes over which an individual may form subjective probability assessments; what subjective probabilities would you assign to the following events?

   (i) After 25 consecutive blacks (Monte Carlo, 18 August 1913), the next spin of the roulette wheel will show a red.

  (ii) The baby a couple are expecting will be another girl, given that their other three are all girls.

 (iii) The Labour Party will win the next general election in the UK.

 (iv) Inflation will be in excess of 3% throughout the next government's term of office.

  (v) John F. Kennedy was killed in 1966.

Different individuals will bring to the above questions different levels of background information, and may also process differently the information presented in each case. In (i), for example, some might stick to the idea that the wheel is fair, so the probability of a red is 18/37 (there are 36 numbers, half being red, plus a zero). Others may consider that such a run (25 blacks) suggests the wheel may be biased—and so might adjust their prior probabilities (of, say, 18/37) to some lower number. Some might argue that the probability of another black was zero on the next turn of the wheel on that night—since the run obviously stopped after 25 blacks (they would have been wrong, as the actual run was of 26 blacks!). Notice that in this case, there is no uncertainty about the event itself (the next turn of the wheel must have turned up a black or something else). The uncertainty is in my (or your) belief about what is true. The same point applies in (v); if you know that JFK was killed in 1963, your subjective probability of the assassination being in 1966 would naturally be zero. However, if you don't know, or are unsure, then it is only possible to assign a subjective probability that it occurred in 1966. Essentially this is what happens in a quiz. Asked the question 'when was JFK killed?', you would naturally select the date with your highest subjective probability. Furthermore, if you had to bet on the date, the odds you would be willing to offer or take would be influenced by your assessment of this

---

[4] Kreps (1990) gives an introductory discussion and further reading on this so-called 'common prior assumption'.

probability. Of course, in many cases, it is possible to invest in obtaining further information on which to base the subjective probabilities; for example, it would not take long to look up the year of JFK's assassination. The point to draw from the above discussion is that subjective probability is a useful way of thinking about uncertain events (particularly in the normative version of the expected utility model, as we shall see).

In general, the rewards or pay-offs associated with outcomes under risk or uncertainty need not be money sums. However, in this text, attention is restricted to the case where pay-offs are purely financial. The following standard notation is used:

Definition 4.6 A **gamble**, **prospect**, or **lottery** is denoted

$$G(x_1,p_1; x_2,p_2; \ldots; x_n,p_n),$$

where x_1, x_2, ..., x_n denote monetary pay-offs and p_1, p_2, ..., p_n denote the associated probabilities of these outcomes ($\sum_{i=1}^{n} p_i = 1$ with $0 \leq p_i \leq 1$ for $i = 1, \ldots, n$).

Thus the characteristics of a gamble are simply and solely the pay-offs and their associated probabilities.

Definition 4.7 The **expected value** of a gamble G is denoted

$$E(G) = \sum_{i=1}^{n} p_i x_i \; (= p_1 x_1 + p_2 p_x + \ldots + p_n x_n).$$

Definition 4.8 A gamble with zero expected value, that is, one for which $E(G) = \sum_{i=1}^{n} p_i x_i = 0$, is termed **actuarially fair**.

Definition 4.9 An individual is said to be **risk-averse** if he/she always rejects actuarially fair gambles. The individual is said to be **risk-neutral** if indifferent to such gambles, and to have **risk preference** if he/she always accepts such gambles.

Consider the gamble where you win or lose £1000 on the toss of a coin. This is an example of an actuarially fair gamble (the expected net gain is zero). If you would not wish to accept such a gamble, you are risk-averse. If you reject all types of actuarially fair gambles, then you are said to be globally risk-averse. Things might not be so straightforward, of course; you might, for example, reject the above gamble, but be quite happy to take a gamble on winning or losing £10 on the toss of a coin. That is, your risk attitude may vary with the kind of pay-offs involved. For example, people often exhibit risk aversion in many situations (insuring a house, possessions, a car, etc.) whilst enjoying gambling on small-stake, large pay-off gambles (the pools, Premium Bonds, etc.). Both the insurance and the gambles are actuarially unfair, of course.[5]

[5] See Friedman and Savage (1976) and Dobbs (1991) for some discussion of how these observations can be rationalized.

4.3 The Expected Utility Model

The most influential and still the most widely accepted theory of individual decision-making under uncertainty is the so-called expected utility model. As previously mentioned, this model can be viewed two ways:

(i)   as a positive economic model—as a description of how people actually behave.

(ii) as a prescriptive model—as a model which prescribes how people ought to evaluate alternatives if they wish their decisions to satisfy certain basic principles of rationality.[6]

Before discussing these alternative interpretations, I present some motivation for the model and then outline its essential characteristics.

4.3.1 The St Petersburg Paradox

There are several varieties of the famous St Petersburg game (see Samuelson 1965 for an extended discussion, including an historical account of it, dating back to Daniel Bernoulli (1738).

EXAMPLE 4.3 The St Petersburg Paradox: The simplest version of the game involves tossing a coin repeatedly; if the coin lands tails (T), the game continues to another toss, until the coin lands heads (H), at which point the game terminates and the player is awarded the pay-off of £2^n if the head turned up on the nth throw of the coin. Thus the sequence TTH pays off £8, whilst TTTH pays £16, and so on. The expected value of the game is

$$EU(G) = \sum_{n=1}^{\infty} p(\text{H on trial } n) \times 2^n$$
$$= (1/2) \times 2 + (1/4) \times 4 + (1/8) \times 8 + \ldots$$
$$= 1 + 1 + 1 + \ldots = \infty.$$

However, few individuals, if offered such a gamble, would be willing to pay a great deal to play such a game. (Think about how much you would be willing to pay). An expected value maximizer would be willing to risk bankruptcy to buy an opportunity to play the game. It thus follows

[6] Note that there is no value judgement involved in statement (ii), since it merely states an operational rule: 'if you want to achieve X, then you need to use Y'. It does not suggest that achieving X is a good thing, or something people ought to do. Of course, suggesting people ought to be rational in this sense would be a value judgement—see Chap. 1.

that most individuals are clearly not expected value maximizers.

As an explanation of the St Petersburg phenomenon, Bernoulli suggested that individuals valued money at a diminishing rate, such that the utility of money was a concave function as illustrated in Figure 4.1.

The idea was that individuals made choices based not on the average or expected pay-off, but on the average or **expected utility** they got from the gamble. The expected utility (denoted EU) of a gamble $G(x_1, p_1; x_2, p_2; \ldots; x_n, p_n)$ is defined as

$$EU(G) = \sum_{i=1}^{n} p_i u(x_i) \ (= p_1 u(x_1) + p_2 u(x_2) + \ldots + p_n u(x_n)), \tag{4.1}$$

where p_i denotes the probability of the ith outcome occurring, x_i is the pay-off, and $U(x_i)$ the utility associated with that pay-off. In the context of the St Petersburg game, the log-function was suggested; that is, $U(x) = \ln(x)$, so that $EU(G) = \sum_{i=1}^{\infty} p_i \ln(x)$. In this case, the expected utility of the St Petersburg gamble becomes

$$EU = (1/2)\ln(2) + (1/4)\ln(4) + \ldots = 0.888 \text{ (approx.)} \tag{4.2}$$

For example, a money sum offered with certainty having the same utility, 0.888, is[7]

$$U = \ln x = 0.888 \Rightarrow x = £2.43 \text{ (approx.)} \tag{4.3}$$

This is a closer valuation to that which most individuals seem to place on the gamble.

However, the idea of utility as a psychological measure of value is only one way of motivating the idea of the expected utility valuation function. John von Neumann and Oscar Morgenstern (1955) provided axiomatic foundations for the expected utility approach to choice under risk. The approach is in fact very similar in spirit to that adopted in neo-classical consumer theory, discussed in section 8.2. There, an individual's preferences over consumption bundles are assumed to satisfy certain axioms (such as transitivity, non-satiation, etc.) and it turns out that this implies the individual's preferences can be represented by a mathematical function such that, whenever the consumer prefers consumption bundle A to another bundle, B, the mathematical function assigns a larger number to A than to B. The function is merely a way of representing preferences, but is traditionally called a utility function, although

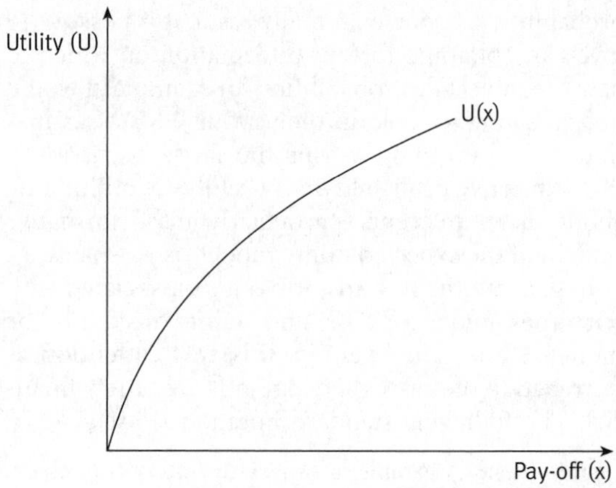

Fig. 4.1 A utility function

in this interpretation, it does not need to be identified with some psychological attribute (such as 'happiness').[8]

If we assume that an individual is able to rank gambles (from most preferred to least preferred, for any given set of gambles), and that gambles have only two types of characteristic, namely pay-offs and their probabilities, then the ordering of such gambles can be represented by a utility function of the form

$$U = U(x_1, p_1; x_2, p_2; \ldots; x_n, p_n). \tag{4.4}$$

Thus, utility depends solely on the pay-offs and their probabilities. The utility function assigns a number to each possible gamble G, such that for any pair of gambles, G_1, G_2, if the individual prefers G_1 then the utility function assigns a bigger number to G_1 than to G_2. The utility function will in general be different for different individuals (since individuals have different attitudes to risk, etc.).

The assumption that the individual can rank gambles means a utility function exists—but what are its characteristics? Clearly we would expect the utility or value of a gamble for an individual to vary with variations in the probabilities and also the pay-offs. In particular, we would expect $\partial U/\partial x_i > 0$ for any pay-off which has a positive probability. But is it likely that the ranking function (4.4) has the simple expected utility form of equation (4.1)? That is, can it simply be written as

---

[7] Note that $\ln(e^x) = x$ for all x and $e^{\ln x} = x$ for all $x > 0$. Here, $\ln x = 0.888$ so $x = e^{\ln x} = e^{0.888} = 2.43$.

[8] Indeed, both here and in consumer theory (Chap. 8), it seems a pity that economists chose to call this preference function a 'utility' function, given the psychological baggage the latter term continues to carry with it.

$$U(x_1,p_1;\ x_2,p_2,\ \ldots,\ x_n,p_n) = \sum_{i=1}^{n} p_i u(x_i), \quad (4.5)$$

where $u(x_i)$ denotes the value associated with the pay-off x_i? It turns out that there is a variety of axiom sets under which the utility function simplifies in this way. Below, I describe a typical axiom set for the case of choice under risk (probabilities are known). It is also possible to construct axiom sets for the case of choice under uncertainty, such that an individual's choices conform to expected utility in the sense that the individual behaves as if he or she attaches subjective probability weights to outcomes, and utility numbers to pay-offs, and ranks gambles according to expected utility (the simple sum of utility numbers times their subjective probabilities). This case, of subjective expected utility, originally developed by Savage (1971), is more important, but also more complex. It is discussed further in section 4.7 below.

4.3.2 The (VNM) Axioms: Von Neumann–Morgenstern

Gambles are denoted by upper case italics, A, B, C, etc. and the notation $A > B$ means 'the individual prefers gamble A to gamble B'. whilst $A \sim B$ means 'the individual is indifferent as between gamble A and gamble B' (they are both equally attractive or unattractive). Also, to save clutter, when there are just two outcomes to a gamble G, I write (p, A, B); in this notation, p is the probability of getting outcome A (note that both A and B could also be gambles); implicitly, the probability of getting outcome B is simply $1 - p$. It is best just to scan the axioms and then review them in the light of the ensuing discussion.

A1 **Comparability**
Either $A > B$, $A \sim B$, or $B > A$.

A2 **Transitivity**
If $A > B$ and $B > C$, then $A > C$ (likewise, if $A \sim B$ and $B \sim C$, then $A \sim C$, etc.).

A3 **Independence**
If $A \sim B$ and if C is some other prospect, then $(p, A, C) \sim (p, B, C)$ for all p such that $0 \le p \le 1$ and for all C.

A4 **Continuity**
If $A > B > C$, then there exists a p, $0 < p < 1$, such that $B \sim (p, A, C)$.

A5 **Desire for a greater probability of success**
If $A > B$ then $(p_1, A, B) \sim (p_2, A, B)$ if $p_1 > p_2$.

A6 **Compound Probabilities**
Compound gambles can be reduced to simple gambles using the standard rules of probability (simply multiplying out the probabilities as appropriate). Specifically, $(p_1, A, B) \sim [p_2, (p_3, A, B), (p_4, A, B)]$ if $p_1 = p_2 p_3 + (1 - p_2)p_4$.

Axioms are supposed to be extremely natural or appealing assumptions. In the ensuing discussion, you should ask yourself in each case to what extent the axioms seem plausible, reasonable, unobjectionable or self-evident.

The first two axioms parallel those for neo-classical consumer theory, and are essential for the existence of a preference ordering. The first is merely the assumption that, for any pair of gambles, the individual is able to decide which she prefers. The second, transitivity, is a consistency property. If an individual prefers gamble A to B, and also B to C, then that individual should also state that she prefers A to C (etc.). Axioms A1 and A2 are essential for the existence of a preference ordering (and for many, this is an essential element in any definition of what it is to be rational, although this can be disputed[9]). Axiom A3, the independence axiom, proposes that an individual's preferences are such that they are unaffected by common consequences. This is illustrated in Figure 4.2.

In axiom A3, the gambles give outcomes A and B with the same probability, and the same alternative consequence C (often referred to as the common consequence). Since $A \sim B$, and C is the same for both gambles, it is argued that whatever the value of p, it should be the case that the gambles (p, A, C) and (p, B, C) are equally attractive. This seems a plausible (and rational) assumption, although in section 4.8, we shall see that it is an assumption that is systematically violated by observed individual behaviour.

---

[9] For example, Loomes and Sugden (1982), in their presentation of regret theory, which dispenses with the transitivity axiom, claim that intransitivity does not preclude rationality. However, the so-called 'money pump' is a major argument against intransitivity being rational. Intransitivity means that it is possible to find a chain of preference of the type $G_1 > G_2 > G_3 \ldots G_m > G_1$ (where G_i denotes a gamble). The point is then that an individual would be willing to give up money to exchange G_1 for G_2 and so on down to giving money to swap G_m for G_1. Thus the individual would end up with the same thing, G_1, but less money. There are problems with this argument, of course (taking money on the first exchange might perturb the rest of the ranking), but it is a nice argument in favour of transitivity; intransitive individuals can be exploited.

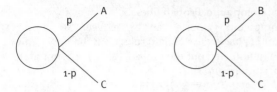

Fig. 4.2 Axiom of independence

A4 proposes that preferences are continuously defined. If three gambles A, B, C are such that $A > B > C$, then the gamble (p, A, C), as p varies from 0 to 1, offers something worse than B through to something definitely better than B. The argument is simply that there must be some intermediate value for p, $0 < p < 1$, such that $(p, A, C) \sim B$ (a fairly uncontroversial assumption). A5 is likewise uncontroversial; if $A > B$ then the individual views the gamble (p, A, B) as getting better and better the higher the probability p (of getting A) is.

The compound probabilities axiom A6 is illustrated in Figure 4.3. Outcome A is realized by moving <up, up> across the right hand tree, with probability $p_2 p_3$, or by moving <down, up>, with probability $(1 - p_2)p_4$. Hence the overall probability of getting A in the two-stage gamble is $p_2 p_3 + (1 - p_2)p_4$. The gambles in the left and right panels in Figure 4.3 are then identical if the individual behaves as if he/she calculates probabilities according to the laws of probability *and* if $p_1 = p_2 p_3 + (1 - p_2)p_4$ (that is, the probabilities of getting A, B are the same in both gambles).

If the individual's preferences satisfy the above axioms, then it is possible to prove the following theorem (see e.g. Gravelle and Rees 1993 or Luce and Raiffa 1965; note that the expected utility of a gamble G, denoted $EU(G)$, is defined by Equation (4.1):

Theorem 4.1 The Expected Utility Theorem: If an individual's preferences over prospects obeys axioms A1–A6,

then there exists a **utility function** $u(x)$ such that, for any 2 prospects A,B, if $A > B$ then $EU(A) > EU(B)$; that is, the expected utility for A is greater than that for B.

The theorem implies that we can find a mathematical function which represents the individual's preferences by correctly ranking gambles according to their expected utility. Whenever the individual prefers one gamble to another, the utility function is such that the expected utility from the former exceeds the latter. I examine in section 4.4 how it is possible to estimate such a utility function for an individual (assuming the individual obeys the above axioms), and then illustrate the uses to which it can be put in sections 4.5 and 4.6. For the moment, I continue to explore the properties of this function.

Fact 4.1 Non-uniqueness of the Utility Function: The VNM utility function is unique up to a positive linear transformation.

The idea is that, if $u(x)$ is a utility function, then so is $z(x)$ defined as

$$z(x) = \alpha + \beta u(x), \qquad (4.6)$$

where α can take any value, and β any positive value.

The function $u(.)$ is a utility function for an individual if, for any pair of gambles A, B, where the individual prefers A to B, then $EU(A) > EU(B)$. That is, if $u(.)$ is a utility function, then expected utility will correctly rank the gambles. Now, Fact 4.1 claims that the function $z(.)$ in equation (4.6) will also do the job. To see this, first note, for any gamble $G(x_1, p_1; x_2 p_2; \ldots; x_n, p_n)$, that implies

$$EZ(G) = \sum_{i=1}^{n} p_i z(x_i) = \sum_{i=1}^{n} p_i[\alpha + \beta u(x_i)]$$
$$= \alpha \sum_{i=1}^{n} p_i + \beta \sum_{i=1}^{n} p_i u(x_i) = \alpha + \beta EU(G)$$
$$(4.7)$$

(since $\sum_{i=1}^{n} p_i = p_1 + p_2 + \ldots + p_n = 1$).[10] Thus consider any pair of gambles, A, B, which an individual ranks as $A > B$; then if $u(.)$ is a utility function, $EU(A) > EU(B)$. However, notice that

$$EU(A) > EU(B) \Rightarrow \alpha + \beta EU(A) > \alpha + \beta EU(B)$$
$$\Rightarrow EZ(A) > EZ(B).$$
$$(4.8)$$

Thus, using $z(.)$ to compute expected utility necessarily gives the same ranking of the gambles as $u(.)$ (and this is true for any pair of gambles). Hence if $u(.)$ is a utility function, so is $z(.)$; both correctly represent the individual's preferences. To

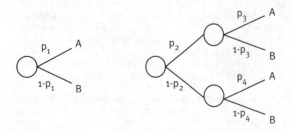

Fig. 4.3 Axiom of compound probabilities

[10] Note that the constants can be moved out of summations here.

emphasize all this, note that Fact 4.1 can be restated as:

Fact 4.2 Any positive linear transformation of a utility function is also a utility function.

This should make it clear that, although the VNM utility function is often referred to as a cardinal utility, it only acts as a ranking mechanism. In particular, suppose, for two gambles, A, B, that it is calculated that $EU(A) = 40$ and $EU(B) = 20$; this does not tell us that the gamble A is twice as good as gamble B—merely that it is preferred.[11]

EXAMPLE 4.4 Suppose, for a given utility function $u(x)$, that for two gambles A, B, $EU(A) = 40$ and $EU(B) = 20$. The difference looks significant. However, it is a mistake to infer anything more than that $A > B$. To see this, note that we can define an alternative utility function such as $z(x) = 10,000 + 0.0001u(x)$ such that the difference looks remarkably small. In this case, $EZ(A) = 10,000.004$ and $EZ(B) = 10,000.002$. The correct interpretation, in both cases, is only that $A > B$; the utility values do not indicate by how much.

4.4 Estimating an Individual's Utility Function

It is possible to estimate an individual's utility function (so long as that individual's preferences over gambles satisfies to some degree of approximation the axioms outlined above). The estimation procedure involves estimating a utility function based on establishing the individual's preferences over very simple types of gamble. Once this is done, the expected utility model allows this information to be used in the evaluation of much more complex gambles. In essence, the approach allows the individual to be confident that all his/her choices will be consistent with the underlying axioms, no matter how complex the problem or calculation involved.

As established in Fact 4.2, the utility function is unique up to a linear transformation. This means that we can choose two points arbitrarily and define

the utility of these points (in the same way as for temperature; the Celsius and Fahrenheit scales assign two arbitrary numbers for the freezing and boiling points of water); the definition of two such points, in conjunction with the individual's revealed preferences over simple gambles, suffices to estimate that individual's utility function.

Often the two points selected are the worst outcome and best outcome imaginable. However, since only financial outcomes are considered here, payoffs are measured as changes relative to the individual's current wealth position. Thus let $u(x)$ denote the individual's VNM utility function, where x denotes gain/loss relative to initial wealth (in £). The function u is assumed continuous and increasing in x (the individual prefers more money to less). Let $u(£0) = 0$ and $u(£1000) = 1000$ (the two points marked in Figure 4.4 with larger circles. Note that this assignment is arbitrary, (subject only to the requirement that the utility function is strictly increasing; $u(£1000)$ must be assigned a larger number than $u(£0)$. We could equally have chosen, say, $u(£55) = -1000$, and $u(£1000) = 3$; that is, the money pay-offs and utility numbers could have been chosen differently so that the utility function would be different, but it would still give the same ranking of gambles.

The individual is then invited to compare a series of simple gambles. There are various ways of setting up the gambles over which the individual is asked to choose. My personal preference is to focus on 50–50 gambles, as these are particularly straightforward to understand; everyone understands gambles based on the flip of a coin. Accordingly, consider the following (and also refer to Figure 4.4):

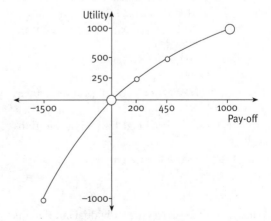

Fig. 4.4 Estimating the utility function

---

[11] Utility is a cardinal index in much the same way as temperature is. For example, compare Celsius and Fahrenheit; it is not meaningful to say that 40°C is twice as hot as 20°C. (To appreciate this point, note that 40°C = 104°F whilst 20°C = 68°F; 104 is not twice 68.)

1. The individual is asked to compare gambles

A: £w for certain

and

B: $(p, £1000, £0)$ with $p = 0.5$
(a 50–50 chance of winning £1000 or nothing).

The individual is asked to judge what value of £w would make him/her indifferent between the two gambles.

Suppose the answer is £450—the individual suggests that receiving £450 for certain is just as attractive as the prospect of £0 or £1000 on the toss of a coin. Then we can apply the expected utility theorem as follows:

$$A \sim B \Rightarrow EU(A) = EU(B) \qquad \text{(i)}$$

$$EU(B) = (1/2)U(1000) + (1/2)U(0)$$
$$= (1/2)1000 + (1/2)0$$
$$= 500 \qquad \text{(ii)}$$

$$EU(A) = U(450), \qquad \text{(iii)}$$

so, substituting (ii) and (iii) into (i), we get

$$U(450) = 500. \qquad \text{(iv)}$$

This establishes a new point on the graph of the utility function (see Figure 4.4).

2. Further points on the graph may be established by using pairs of points already defined, and asking the individual questions similar to those in 1 above. For example, we might ask the individual to compare

A: £w for certain

and

B: $(p, £450, £0)$ with $p = 0.5$.

What value of £w makes the individual indifferent between the two gambles? If the individual replies '£200', then

$$EU(A) = EU(B) \Rightarrow u(£200) = (1/2)u(£450)$$
$$+ (1/2)u(£0)$$
$$= (1/2)500 + (1/2)0$$
$$= 250.$$

The utility of £200 for certain is thus 250, as marked in Figure 4.4.

3. The range can be extended by asking questions such as

A: £1000 for certain

or

B: $(p, £w, £0)$ with $p = 0.5$.

What value of £w makes the individual indifferent? For example, suppose the response is £3000; then

$$EU(A) = EU(B) \Rightarrow u(£1000) = (1/2)u(£0)$$
$$+ (1/2)u(3000)$$
$$\Rightarrow 1000 = (1/2)0$$
$$+ (1/2)u(3000)$$
$$\Rightarrow u(3000) = 2000.$$

The range of negative pay-offs can equally be explored; consider

A: £0 for certain

or

B: $(p, £w, £1000)$ with $p = 0.5$

If the answer is $w = -£1500$, then

$$EU(A) = EU(B) \Rightarrow u(o) = (1/2)u(1000)$$
$$+ (1/2)u(-£1500)$$
$$\Rightarrow 0 = (1/2)1000$$
$$+ (1/2)u(-£1500)$$
$$\Rightarrow U(-£1500) = -1000.$$

Once sufficient points have been established, it should be possible to sketch a smooth approximation to the individual's utility function through these points, as in Figure 4.4. (It is also possible to estimate a mathematical functional form which fits the curve to an acceptable degree of approximation; this can be useful in computer modelling of decision problems or in conducting more complex analysis; see section 4.6.)

The key idea is that the utility function can be constructed from the individual's responses to questions involving their preferences over very simple types of gamble. Once this has been established, the utility function can be used to evaluate choices involving much more complex gambles. Choices made in such a way will then be consistent with the VNM axioms and correctly reflect the estimated structure of the utility function.

4.5 Risk Attitudes and the Shape of the Utility Function

An individual who obeys the VNM axioms is said to feature risk aversion/neutrality/preference over some interval of wealth if that person's VNM utility function is concave/linear/convex over that interval of wealth (concavity and convexity are discussed in Chapter 3). This is illustrated in Figure 4.5 for the case of concavity.

Recall Definition 4.9, that risk aversion means that the individual always rejects an actuarially fair gamble. In Figure 4.5, the individual starts with

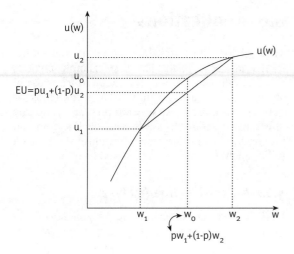

Fig. 4.5 Concavity and risk aversion

wealth w_0. In this figure, an actuarially fair gamble is offered which will move him to wealth level w_1 with probability p and wealth level w_2 with probability $1 - p$ (where w_1 and w_2 are arbitrary wealth levels). By assumption, the gamble is actuarially fair (in expected value terms, accepting the gamble involves neither a gain nor a loss); that is,

$$w_0 = pw_1 + (1 - p)w_2. \qquad (4.9)$$

The utility levels associated with w_0, w_1, w_2 are denoted u_0, u_1, u_2. The initial utility level is u_0 and the expected utility of the gamble is $EU = pu_1 + (1 - p)u_2$. It should be clear that if $w_0 = pw_1 + (1 - p)w_2$, then expected utility $EU = pu_1 + (1 - p)u_2$ can be read off the line segment, as in Figure 4.5. If the utility function is concave, as in the diagram, then clearly $EU < u_0$. This means the individual will reject the gamble. Equally clearly, had the utility function been linear, then EU would have been equal to u_0, whilst if the function had been convex, then EU would have been greater than u_0 (and the individual would have accepted the actuarially fair gamble).

It is sometimes useful to ask what financial sum (for certain) has the same value to the individual as a risky prospect. This concept is defined as follows:

Definition 4.10 Certainty-Equivalent Wealth (*CEW*). The **certainty-equivalent wealth** associated with a gamble is the level of wealth for certain which yields the same level of utility as the expected utility from the gamble.

That is, for a gamble G,

$$u(CEW) = EU(G) \qquad (4.10)$$

EXAMPLE 4.5 Consider the gamble $(0.5; 100, -90)$. Suppose initial wealth is $w_0 = £100$ and the individual's preferences can be represented by the utility function $u(w) = w^{1/2}$. Then the expected utility of the gamble is

$$EU(G) = 0.5(100 + 100)^{1/2} + 0.5(100 - 90)^{1/2}$$
$$= 8.6522.$$

Thus $u(CEW) = 8.6522 \Rightarrow CEW^{1/2} = 8.6522 \Rightarrow CEW = £74.86$.

Thus, even though the gamble has expected value, $EV = 0.5 \times 100 + 0.5 \times (-90) = +5$, the individual will not gamble. If forced to take the gamble, this is equivalent to a reduction in her wealth for certain from £100 to £74.86.

Having defined the effect on the individual's wealth level, we have

Definition 4.11 Certainty Equivalent of a gamble (*CE*): the certainty equivalent of a gamble is the sum of money which gives the same utility to the individual as the gamble. Thus,

$$CE = CEW - w_0. \qquad (4.11)$$

The certainty equivalent is the value for certain that is equivalent to the risky prospect. The concept sometimes finds application in project appraisal where future cash flows are risky. The idea is that it is possible to compute the certainty equivalents for these, and then value them by then discounting at a riskless rate of interest; see Chapter 7 for further discussion of such matters.

EXAMPLE 4.6 Consider an individual with utility function and initial wealth as in Example 4.5, and faced with the same gamble; then the certainty equivalent of the gamble, $CE = £(74.86 - 100) = -£25.14$. Thus, given the individual's initial wealth position, taking the gamble is equivalent to making her £25.14 worse off with certainty.

It is important to note that the certainty equivalent in general depends upon the individual's initial wealth level. Thus if, in Examples 4.5 and 4.6, the individual started with £1000 of wealth, then the *CE* of the gamble rises to $+£2.75$ (as the reader can verify). The *CE* rises towards the expected value as the individual gets wealthier, essentially because the utility function, $u = w^{1/2}$, has less curvature as wealth increases and so displays less risk aversion. The difference between expected value and certainty equivalent is termed the cost of risk bearing:

Definition 4.12 The **Cost of Risk Bearing** (*CRB*): The cost of risk bearing is the difference between the expected value of a gamble and its certainty equivalent: $CRB = EV - CE$.

EXAMPLE 4.7 In Example 4.5, it was shown that the expected value of the gamble (*EV*) is 5. Hence its $CRB = EV - CE = 5 - (-25.14) = 30.14$.

Essentially, the cost of risk bearing is a monetary measure of how much the individual's attitude to risk alters the individual's valuation of the gamble. In the above example, a risk-neutral individual would value the gamble at £5; due to risk aversion, the individual regards it as equivalent to being made worse off by £25.14; thus risk aversion reduces the valuation by £30.14. Of course, increasing wealth means the *CE* rises toward expected value and hence that the *CRB* falls toward zero (with initial wealth at £1000, the *CRB* = £2.25). The cost of risk bearing is positive for a risk-averse individual, is zero for risk neutrality, and is negative for someone who manifests risk preference.

4.6 Applications

This section illustrates how the expected utility model can be applied. The first example involves the use of decision trees (a technique which is useful and straightforwardly acquired). The second looks at optimal insurance. These examples are primarily illustrative (section 4.7 deals with qualifications on the usefulness of direct applications of expected utility analysis for one-off projects).

4.6.1 A Decision Tree Analysis

Decision trees are often a useful way of organizing material, particularly when outcomes can be categorized into a number of discrete possible categories. The following example is a very simple illustration of the technique, showing its usefulness for depicting decision points (indicated in Figure 4.6 by the square box), and points at which there are random outcomes (circles) (either because 'nature' takes a

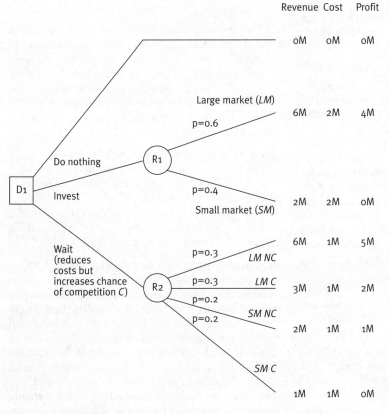

Fig. 4.6 Decision tree

turn, or there is uncertainty regarding the actions of other players). Figures 4.2 and 4.3 are also illustrations of the depiction of random outcomes; for others, see Chapter 5.

EXAMPLE 4.8 Waiting to Invest: A firm has the opportunity to set up a plant in a new country. The stylized choices are not to invest at all, to invest immediately, or to defer investment whilst improvements in plant design are finalized. Set-up costs are £2m (m = million) immediately, or £1m if the firm waits and adopts the new plant design. The market will turn out to be either large (with probability 0.6) or small (with probability 0.4); however, a delay introduces the possibility of competition: with a delay, there is a 50–50 chance of local competition (C); thus, denoting the absence of competition as NC, there are four possible outcomes (namely LM,NC; LM,C; SM,NC; SM,C), as depicted in Figure 4.6. Given the net profits associated with the various outcomes, it is a straightforward matter to compute expected profit, or expected utility.

The expected values are:

EV (doing nothing) = 0;

EV (investing) = $0.6 \times 4m + 0.4 \times 0m$ = £2.4m;

EV (waiting) = $0.3 \times 5m + 0.3 \times 2m + 0.2 \times 1m$
$\qquad + 0.2 \times 0m$ = £2.2m.

So, using expected value, the optimal decision would be to invest immediately.

Expected utility, if the utility function is u(x) = $x^{1/2}$, where x is the net profit, is:

EU (doing nothing) = $0^{1/2}$ = 0;

EU (investing) = $0.6 \times 4^{1/2} + 0.4 \times 0^{1/2}$ = 1.2;

EU (waiting) = $0.3 \times 5^{1/2} + 0.3 \times 2^{1/2} + 0.2 \times 1^{1/2}$
$\qquad + 0.2 \times 0^{1/2}$ = 1.295.

Hence, taking account of the decision-maker's risk aversion, the preferred option is to wait and then invest.

The decision tree approach can also be used to represent problems which involve intermediate decision points; for examples, see Chapter 5.

4.6.2 Optimal Insurance

In practice, most individuals are risk-averse; they reject actuarially fair and even better than actuarially fair gambles. However, if individuals are expected utility maximizers and are able to obtain actuarially

fair insurance, then such individuals will make choices as if they were expected value maximizers. In practice, insurance is usually actuarially unfair in that the expected value of the pay-offs is less than the premium that has to be paid.[12] In such circumstances, the individual may still find that taking out insurance is desirable; however, the individual may now choose to be less than fully insured. With less than fair insurance, individual behaviour in the presence of risk will still manifest some overt degree of risk aversion. These points are illustrated in the example below.

EXAMPLE 4.9 Expected utility maximization: how much insurance? Consider a farmer who has current net worth w_0 (all wealth numbers represent thousands of pounds) and whose preferences are characterized by a VNM utility function $u(w) = \ln w$, where w denotes the individual's wealth level. The farmer's income this period depends on the weather, which in this stylized problem is either good (pay-off 100) or poor (pay-off 0) with equal probability. An insurance premium of £x pays off £0 in good weather, but αx if the weather is poor. Clearly if $\alpha = 2$, the insurance is fair (since £1 premium pays out £2 in bad weather, with probability 0.5), whilst if $\alpha < 2$, it is less than fair. Clearly, $\alpha > 1$ or you do not get your money back in any state of the world! Given this information, what is the optimal level of insurance?

The objective is simply to maximize expected utility. In good weather, the farmer ends up with wealth of $w_0 + 100 - x$ (having paid the premium x), whilst if there is bad weather, the wealth level is $w_0 + \alpha x - x$ (having paid the premium x but receiving the pay-off αx). Expected utility is thus as follows:

$$EU = 0.5\ln(w_0 + 100 - x) + 0.5\ln(w_0 + \alpha x - x).$$
$$\text{(i)}$$

A necessary condition for a maximum at some finite x is that $\partial EU/\partial x = 0$:[13]

---

[12] Administrative costs guarantee that it will usually be less than actuarially fair (imperfect competition in the supply of insurance would only make matters worse). However, some individuals undoubtedly do rather well out of insurance; the issues that arise in the supply of insurance, in particular moral hazard and adverse selection, are discussed in Chap. 29.

[13] Differentiate (i) term by term. Note that $d(\ln z)/dz = 1/z$. If z is a function of x, then by the chain rule,

$\qquad \partial \ln z(x)/\partial x = (\partial \ln z/\partial z) \times \partial z(x)/\partial x = (1/z)\partial z/\partial x.$

Here, for the first term on the right-hand side of (i), $z = w_0 + 100 - x$ so $\partial z/\partial x = -1$. For the second term, $\partial z/\partial x = \alpha - 1$.

$$\frac{\partial EU}{\partial x} = 0.5 \frac{-1}{w_0 + 100 - x} + 0.5 \frac{\alpha - 1}{w_0 + (\alpha - 1)x} = 0.$$
(ii)

Solving for x gives

$$x = 0.5\left[(w_0 + 100) - \frac{w_0}{\alpha - 1}\right].$$
(iii)

Now consider how x varies with α (the index of how fair the insurance is) and w_0, the farmer's level of wealth. Differentiating (iii) gives

$$\frac{\partial x}{\partial \alpha} = \frac{0.5w_0}{(1 - \alpha)^2} > 0$$
(iv)

and

$$\frac{\partial x}{\partial w_0} = 0.5\left(1 - \frac{1}{\alpha - 1}\right) = 0.5\left(\frac{\alpha - 2}{\alpha - 1}\right).$$
(v)

Now, $\partial x/\partial \alpha > 0$ merely indicates that the fairer the insurance, the more the individual insures. If $\alpha = 2$ (actuarially fair insurance), the individual pays a premium of 50 (we get this by plugging $\alpha = 2$ into (iii) above). This is full insurance; the wealth levels are equalized across all states of the world, so the individual is completely indifferent as to what the weather is. Thus in good weather he is better off by 100 minus the premium of 50, which leaves 50, whilst the insurance pays off in bad weather, leaving him better off by 0 + the pay-off (100) minus the premium (50), which also equals 50.

As mentioned above, α has to be greater than 1 for the farmer to take any insurance. Now, if insurance is unfair ($\alpha < 2$), then from (v), $\partial x/\partial w_0$ is negative; that is, the higher his wealth, the less he insures (this is intuitive; the utility function flattens out as wealth increases, making the individual less risk-averse).

4.7 Limitations of the Expected Utility Model in Decision-Making

As indicated in section 4.5, it is straightforward to apply the expected utility model in decision analysis. The decision-maker's utility function can be estimated and then used to rank projects. However, although the expected utility approach is advocated in many managerial economics texts, it is rarely used in practice. Why is this? The following are possible explanations—in increasing order of significance.

1. *Ignorance.* One argument is that the techniques have simply not yet permeated through to business. This is a poor argument; the proliferation of MBA and related business qualifications amongst management, at least in the larger companies, means that at least some of these decision-makers are aware of the technique.

2. *Complexity.* The approach is somewhat intricate. However, for large-scale projects it would seem that the benefits of attaining consistency and coherence in decision-making would outweigh the costs of implementation (but see 6 and 7 below).

3. *Transparency.* Perhaps there is an aversion to making the basis of a decision too transparent; in an organizational context, an individual manager may be more risk-averse (and exhibit more short-termism) than his or her superiors might wish. If so, such a manager would not wish to broadcast such attitudes. This problem, of 'goal incongruence', is discussed further in Chapter 29.

4. *Problems associated with group or team decision-making.* Conflict may arise due to individuals in a team having different attitudes to risk. At least conceptually, this is no real problem; the questions (in section 4.4) required to establish the function are merely posed to the group as a whole. The group would have to come to a unique decision in each case (by whatever process it normally uses for decision-making). This would suffice to establish a team utility function.

5. *Intertemporal Cash flows.* An apparent problem with the formulation in section 4.3 of the expected utility model is that it does not indicate how cash flows at different points in time should be treated, particularly if they have differential risk (as is often the case). One possible approach is to calculate present values for outcomes and use these as gains/losses in wealth in the utility function (although this is not conceptually very satisfactory; there are alternative and better ways of taking time into account).[14]

6. *Portfolio Theory.* Portfolio and asset pricing theory provide a substantial critique of the direct use of expected utility. The problem with the approach used in the examples in section 4.6 is that it is a partial equilibrium approach to decision-making. That is, it focuses on each new project and asks whether the project increases expected util-

---

[14] See sect. 7.3, where it is argued that a present value is simply a value—and hence it is unclear what a 'risky' present value might be.

ity. This piecemeal approach to decision-making can easily lead to sub-optimal decision-making. The following example illustrates this point.

EXAMPLE 4.10 Consider the individual in Example 4.5, having initial wealth w_0 of £100 and utility function $u(w) = \ln(w)$. Suppose the individual has two investment opportunities A, B, both of which require no outlay and generate returns as shown in Table 4.1 below:

Table 4.1 A partial equilibrium approach to decision making

	State of the world	
	S1	S2
Probability of state occurring	0.5	0.5
Pay-offs to A	40	−30
Pay-offs to B	−30	+40

Undertaking no project, the utility level is $\ln(100) = 4.605$.

Undertaking A, or B, gives expected utility of

$$EU(A) = EU(B) = 0.5\ln(140) + 0.5\ln(70) = 4.595.$$

Thus the individual would reject A (or B) if it was evaluated on its own. However, undertaking A and B is preferred to the status quo:

$$EU(A + B) = 0.5\ln(110) + 0.5\ln(110) = 4.7.$$

When there are multiple project opportunities, the correct way to use expected utility analysis appears to be to analyse the global portfolio/project implementation choice problem of the decision-maker (that is, to consider all combinations of projects). That is, it appears that it is no longer satisfactory to undertake piecemeal project evaluation, where each project is evaluated in isolation. However, to evaluate all projects and combinations of projects simultaneously would appear to be both a difficult and cumbersome procedure (and one that does not facilitate decentralized decision-making); it is clearly highly desirable to be able to evaluate projects separately and in a piecemeal fashion. Fortunately this is conceptually possible (see 7 below).

7. *Portfolio effects and Asset pricing theory.* The argument in 6 above suggested that portfolio effects need to be considered. Fortunately, if this observation is pursued sufficiently far, it turns out that it is in theory possible to evaluate individual projects separately. However, the procedure does not involve the direct use of the expected utility model. For a firm undertaking many projects, the risk of an individual project can in part be diversified away (as illustrated in Example 4.10). If the decision-maker aims to act in the interests of the firm's shareholders, at least part of the project's total risk is irrelevant (see Chapter 7). For example, in most versions of what is now called the capital asset pricing model (CAPM), the only risk which has an effect on the value of a project is the covariance between the project returns and the returns on the market of assets as a whole. In the asset pricing approach, expected utility is no longer explicitly used to evaluate projects. However, it should be noted that the notion that individuals maximize expected utility is a cornerstone of many of these asset pricing models (see e.g. Jarrow 1988). These models merely recognize that the theory of individual decision-making has to be embedded into models which take account of the equilibrium processes in financial markets. Indeed, the importance of the capital market to individual decisions is enshrined in the separation theorem (see section 6.7).[15]

Thus using the expected utility model in piecemeal project appraisal (of the type often discussed in managerial textbooks on this topic) is theoretically dubious. From a pragmatic viewpoint, one can understand why it does get used (particularly where the project is large relative to the size of the company, so the portfolio diversification argument works less well). However, for run-of-the-mill project appraisal, it would seem preferable to adopt the sort of approach outlined in section 7.4 (based on the CAPM).

4.8 Expected Utility and Actual Behaviour

Does actual individual behaviour under risk and uncertainty conform to the expected utility model? This question is of importance since most models in economics and finance continue to make use of the idea that individuals behave at least approximately as expected utility maximizers. However, the last two decades or so have seen considerable work on testing

[15] It should be noted that the general approach to discounting risky cash flows is either to estimate their certainty-equivalent values (sect. 4.5), and discount these at a riskless rate, or to discount expected values at a 'risky' discount rate (see Chap. 7).

the expected utility hypothesis, and systematic deviations in individual behaviour are now established as stylized facts. I shall confine attention to two of the more celebrated examples of violations, namely Allais' Paradox and Ellsberg's Urn.

4.8.1 The Allais' Paradox

Individuals are asked to choose between the following two gambles:

$$A1: -£45$$
$$A2: (-£100, 0.5; £0, 0.5).$$

That is, under $A1$, there is a certainty of losing £45 whilst under $A2$, there is a 50–50 chance of losing £100. The modal choice is $A2$ (i.e. most people choose $A2$). The same individuals are then asked to choose between the following two gambles:

$$B1: (-£45, 0.1; £0, 0.9)$$
$$B2: (-£100, 0.05; £0, 0.95).$$

In this case the modal choice was $B1$; that is, most people preferred a 10% chance of losing £45 to a 5% chance of losing £100.

Now, suppose an individual who chose $A2$ and then $B1$ is an expected utility maximizer. Denote such an individual's utility function as $u(x)$. Then from the expected utility theorem we have

$$A2 > A1 \Rightarrow EU(A2) > EU(A1)$$
$$\Rightarrow 0.5u(-100) + 0.5u(0) > u(-45)$$

(i)

and

$$B2 > B1 \Rightarrow EU(B2) > EU(B1)$$
$$\Rightarrow 0.0u(-100) + 0.95u(0) < 0.1u(-45)$$
$$+ 0.9u(0).$$

(ii)

Subtracting $0.9u(0)$ from both sides of (ii) and then multiplying through the inequality by 10 gives

$$0.5u(-100) + 0.5u(0) < u(-45).$$ (iii)

This contradicts (i) (which has the inequality the other way round), hence such an individual cannot be an expected utility maximizer.

Allais' Paradox amounts to a violation of the independence axiom (section 4.3.2), which states that

if $A2 > A1$ then $(p, A2, C) > (p, A1, C)$ for all $p, 0 < p < 1$

(where C is some other prospect). In this particular case C denotes the prospect of getting £0 for sure (see Figure 4.2).

Table 4.2 The Ellsberg's Paradox gambles

Gambles	Colour drawn		
	Red	White	Blue
$A1$	£500	£0	£0
$A2$	£0	£500	£0
$B1$	£500	£0	£500
$B2$	£0	£500	£500

4.8.2 Ellsberg's Paradox

This is an experiment in which an individual is told there are 90 balls in an urn; 30 are known to be red, the other 60 being white or blue in unknown proportion (so along with the 30 reds, there might be 0, or 1, or 2, . . . , or 60 whites, the rest of the 60 being blues). A single ball is to be drawn out of the urn at random. Consider the gambles in Table 4.2, which involve guessing what colour will be drawn.

According to this table, gamble $A1$ offers £500 if a red is drawn, and nothing if the ball is another colour; gamble $A2$ offers £500 if a white is drawn, nothing otherwise; and so on. Individuals are first asked to choose between gambles $A1$ and $A2$. The modal preference is to choose $A1$ (most individuals choose $A1$, although some choose $A2$ and some express indifference between the gambles). The individuals are then invited to choose between $B1$ and $B2$. In this case the modal preference is for $B2$.[16]

Individuals who choose $A1$ in the first case and $B2$ in the second violate the subjective expected utility theorem. To see this, suppose the individual is an expected utility maximizer; then he or she possesses a utility function which defines a utility index for any given pay-off x. In the Ellsberg experiment, no probabilities are given. However, in the subjective expected utility model[17] it is assumed that the individual is able to assign subjective probabilities to all outcomes; accordingly, denote the individual's subjective probabilities of drawing a red, white, or blue

---

[16] There are a variety of experimental issues which need to be controlled; for example, whether the sequencing of questions matters. (See Ellsberg 1962 for details and discussion of the original experiments; Dobbs 1991 discusses these experiments in the light of developments in the theory of choice under uncertainty.)

[17] I have discussed expected utility under the assumption that the individual is able to assign subjective probabilities to outcomes; see Savage (1972) for a formal analysis of the case where objective probabilities are not available.

as p_r, p_w, and p_b respectively. Then, from the expected utility theorem, we have

$$A1 > A2 \Rightarrow EU(A1) > EU(A2)$$
$$\Rightarrow p_r u(500) + p_w u(0) + p_b u(0) > p_r u(0)$$
$$+ p_w u(500) + p_b u(0). \qquad \text{(i)}$$

Collecting terms in $u(0)$ and $u(500)$ gives

$$(p_r - p_w)u(500) > (p_r + p_b - p_w - p_b)u(0) \qquad \text{(ii)}$$

or

$$(p_r - p_w)[u(500) - u(0)] > 0.$$

Since the utility function is strictly increasing, $u(500) - u(0)] > 0$; hence we can infer that $p_r > p_w$. The same idea is now applied to the second pair of choices; more briefly, this gives

$$B1 > B2 \Rightarrow EU(B2) > EU(B1)$$
$$\Rightarrow p_r u(0) + p_w u(500) + p_b u(500)$$
$$> p_r u(500) + p_w u(0) + p_b u(500). \qquad \text{(iii)}$$

Collecting terms, this gives

$$(p_r - p_w)[u(500) - u(0)] < 0. \qquad \text{(iv)}$$

By the same reasoning as before, it follows that $p_r < p_w$. However, we originally showed that if the individual was an expected utility maximizer, then $p_r > p_w$. Hence there is a contradiction, and hence such an individual cannot be an expected utility maximizer. This is a violation of the independence axiom; the difference between $A1$, $A2$ and $B1$, $B2$ is merely a common consequence (+£500 if a blue is drawn) is added to the original bets $A1$, $A2$. More on all this and the issues raised can be found in Dobbs (1991).

4.8.3 New Directions

The violations discussed in the two previous paradoxes are the tip of an iceberg; there is now a considerable body of empirical evidence that individuals make choices which do not conform to the expected utility axioms outlined in section 4.3. Interestingly, many of these violations are systematic. Whether this is because individuals simply make mistakes (Hey 1991) or use some different but equally rational methodology for assessing alternatives remains an open question on which there is much ongoing research. The interested reader is referred to Schoemaker (1982) for an early but very readable exposition and general survey of the subjective expected utility model; three influential non-expected utility models in recent years are, Kahneman and Tversky (1979), Machina (1979), and Loomes and Sugden (1982, 1985). New lines

of enquiry are continually opening up—for example, the evolutionary perspective (e.g. Hirshleifer 1977, Hansson and Stuart 1990), which suggests that preferences may be viewed as being subject to an evolutionary 'survival of the fittest'. However, having set out several criticisms of the model it may be worth finishing by redressing the balance slightly; although individuals do not exactly behave as 'good' expected utility maximizers, it can be argued that they do do so to some degree of approximation. So far, although there are many alternative theories, none has really managed to usurp the central role that expected utility continues to play.

4.9 Summary

This Chapter first reviewed the concepts of risk, uncertainty, and subjective probability. Following this, it gave an exposition of the expected utility model, which remains a principal building block for much economic theory. I examined how the model might be used to aid rational decision-making; although some texts have advocated it as a practical decision-making tool, it was noted that it has to be used with care, and that there are important caveats to its use, notably because of what are termed portfolio effects in decision-making.[18] Following this, I considered the extent to which people actually behave in a manner consistent with the underlying assumptions of the model, noting certain apparently systematic forms of violation (the Allais and Ellsberg paradoxes). The expected utility model finds application at various points in the text, including the next Chapter, where the problem of decision-making in strategic situations is considered.

4.10 Review Questions

1. What is an actuarially fair gamble?
2. Consider the VNM utility function depicted in Figure 4.7; what does this imply about the individual's attitude to risk? (Consider gambling on the lottery, insuring the house, small-stake, small pay-off, gambles etc.)

---

[18] These issues are returned to in Chap. 7 when the problem of taking account of risk is again addressed, in a rather more practical fashion.

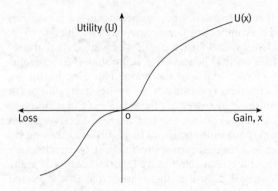

Fig. 4.7 Utility functions manifesting both risk aversion and risk preference

3. What is the point of including an analysis of the expected utility model in a text on managerial economics, given that it is rarely used by businessmen for decision analysis?

4. Swan-Turkey are considering building a new shipyard (set-up cost £0.9m). This is a risky business; suppose orders will either be high (with net operating profit £3m) or low (with net operating profit of only £1m), with equal probability (treat these as one-off returns). Alternatively, they can commission market research (at a cost of £100,000) which will study the market further. Clearly, the consultants will predict either high or low demand for the product. If they are always right in their predictions, is it worth commissioning the study? Assume that the decision-maker wishes to use a utility function $u(w) = w^{1/2}$ with initial wealth $w = £4m$. Note that this problem is straightforward, but involves intermediate decisions (if you hire the consultant, you have a subsequent decision as to whether to invest or not). Work out optimal decisions at these later points first.

4.11 Further Reading

Baumol (1972a), Gravelle and Rees (1992), and Kreps (1990) give an outline of the theory of expected utility at increasing levels of sophistication, whilst Savage (1970) is the seminal (if rather difficult) work on subjective expected utility. Schoemaker (1982) is a readable introduction to alternative versions of the model and to problems associated with it. Hey (1991) gives a clear and useful summary of some of the major extensions and variants of the expected utility model, and also surveys the tests designed to compare their relative performance in describing the ways in which people make risky decisions. John von Neumann's work is legendary in economics (and mathematics) but the seminal text (von Neumann and Morgenstern 1944) which first developed the axiomatic foundations for expected utility is no easy read.

5 Game Theory

Objectives This Chapter examines situations where the pay-offs to economic agents (consumers, firms, governments, etc.) depend significantly upon the actions of other agents, as occurs in so many economic situations where there are small numbers of interacting agents. Game theory is concerned with developing models of such interactive behaviour and with predicting likely outcomes.

Prerequisites None specific, although some understanding of decision-making under uncertainty (and in particular, the concept of von Neumann–Morgenstern utility) is helpful; this is covered in Chapter 4.

Keywords backward induction, cheap talk, common knowledge, complete information, constant-sum, dominance, equilibrium, extensive form, information set, iterated dominance, mixed strategy, move, Nash equilibrium, normal form, prisoner's dilemma, pure strategy, reaction function, solution, strategic form, strategy, strict dominance, subgame, subgame-perfect equilibrium, weak dominance, zero-sum.

5.1 Introduction

Game theory is the study of multi-player decision-making in situations where the choices of each player may affect the pay-offs received by other players. Game theory is central to economic analysis because, in so many economic situations, the pay-offs to one agent depend not only on his/her choice, but also on the choices of others; consider for example an oligopolistic industry where the output or price decision of each firm has an impact on the other firms in the industry, a trade union negotiating with management over a wage settlement, production and sales divisions negotiating over the setting of a transfer price, etc. In this Chapter, basic ideas of rational game-play and the concepts of equilibrium or solution to games are discussed along with some important economic examples (in particular, the so-called prisoners' dilemma, which is at the root of so many instances of market failure). Although there are some economic applications in this Chapter, it concentrates on the basic ideas in game theory; applications can be found at various points in the text (in the Chapters on oligopoly, advertizing, and agency theory, for example).

Game theory is the theory of rational game-play when there is interdependence; that is, the choices of each player have consequences (which may be adverse or beneficial) for the other players. The general approach in game theory is usually to make assumptions about the individual players (regarding their calculating ability and what they know about pay-offs etc.) in order to make predictions regarding the likely outcome of the game.[1]

5.1.1 Assumptions

The following assumptions, which are fairly standard, are assumed throughout this Chapter:

(i) there is a well-defined set of possible outcomes or pay-offs for each player;

(ii) individual players have well-defined preferences (they are von Neumann–Morgenstern expected utility maximizers);

(iii) players have unlimited reasoning and calculational ability (the perfect player assumption).

Clearly these are stylized assumptions: assumption (i) is reasonably innocuous, but there is mounting evidence that assumption (ii) does not hold;

---

[1] It used to be lamented that game theory had not lived up to its promise, essentially because there had been little progress beyond relatively simple and highly stylized games. Nowadays, it is clear that game theory has significantly advanced our understanding of many types of economic situation. If there is sometimes a lack of robustness (a sensitivity of predictions to the detailed assumptions made in modelling the economic game), such lack of robustness, whilst in a sense disappointing, is in itself probably no more than another insight into reality.

individuals in practice do not behave as expected utility maximizers. A traditional defence here has been that (ii) is a reasonable approximation in most applications (see Chapter 4 for a discussion of this point). Risk neutrality is of course a special case of expected utility maximization, and is often assumed in economic applications (for example, oligopolistic firms might be assumed to maximize expected profits). Finally, (iii), the assumption of perfect players, simplifies the analysis although clearly real players suffer from what is often termed 'bounded rationality' (consider the game of chess, where in trying to examine longer and longer sequences of moves and possible counter-moves, the burgeoning volume of information to be stored limits how far ahead you can see).

5.1.2 Types of Game

Games may be categorized as:

Sequential-move games
Key idea: a player observes the opponent's move prior to making a decision (e.g. chess, or wage negotiations, where each party sequentially makes an offer that can be accepted or rejected).

Simultaneous-move games
Key idea: at the time of making a move, the other players' moves cannot be observed and can only be guessed at (e.g. cross-channel ferry operators setting prices, or promotional campaigns).

Games can also be categorized as:

Co-operative games
Collusion and cartel formation in oligopolistic industries are multi-player games where the agents choose to co-operate rather than compete.

Non-co-operative games
These kinds of games occur where agents or firms find communication difficult or where outcomes are mutually antagonistic. Many economic games feature one agent gaining at the expense of others, although there is usually some need to co-operate as well as to compete (e.g. in wage negotiations, where there is a mutual interest in not driving the firm into liquidation).

In this Chapter, attention is restricted to non-co-operative games (with simultaneous or sequential moves). This is in line with the current trend in game theory, which seeks to explain co-operative behaviour as the outcome of games in which indi-

vidual agents act as purely self-interested ('solipsistic') individuals.

Games can also be classified as:

Constant-sum
A constant-sum game is one in which the sum of pay-offs to the players is a constant. One player gets a higher return only at the expense of the others, who lose an equal amount.

Zero-sum
A zero-sum game is simply a constant-sum game in which the sum is equal to zero. Any constant-sum game can be transformed into an equivalent zero-sum game (see section 5.5).

Non-constant-sum
Non-constant-sum games are those in which the total pay-off as well as the share of this to the various players can vary depending on the individual choices.

Most economic situations modelled as games are non-constant-sum, although there are a significant number of situations that can be reasonably characterized as zero-sum (speculation, say in futures markets is essentially zero sum; two parties enter into a contract and thereafter, what one gains, the other loses).

5.1.3 Some Further Definitions

Definition 5.1 A **move** is what the player can choose to do, given the current position (cf. chess).

Definition 5.2 A **pure strategy** prescribes the move to be played for every state that the individual could find himself in (in chess, a strategy prescribes the individual's next move for every conceivable position that could occur on the chessboard).

It follows that if the game is characterized as one in which the individuals select pure strategies, then once each player has selected a strategy, the outcome of the game is determined (however, in section 5.4, the possibility that individuals can randomize their choice of strategy is considered).

Definition 5.3 The **extensive** form of a game is where the moves are played sequentially.

Definition 5.4 The **strategic** (or **Normal**[2]) **form** of a game

---

[2] Von Neumann and Morgenstern (1944), in their seminal work on game theory, gave preference to the strategic form, and referred to it as the 'normal' form of a game; this view no longer holds sway.

is where the players simply choose a strategy (or, in section 5.4, a probability mixture of strategies).

Definition 5.5 An **equilibrium** or **solution** to a game is a predicted outcome for the game (it will turn out that there are several solution concepts).

One might think that the extensive form is more appropriate for dynamic games in which moves are taken in turn by the players, whilst static, simultaneous-move games are better characterized in strategic form, and often this is the case. However, any game, whether it involves sequential and/or simultaneous moves, can be characterized in either the extensive or the strategic form (section 5.6 discusses the pros and cons of strategic and extensive forms).

Definition 5.6 A game is said to be one of **complete information** if, for any given set of the strategy choices by the players, all the pay-offs to all the players are known by all the players.

A game of **incomplete information**, by contrast, is one in which, for at least some strategy choices, at least one player is uncertain about the pay-off to one or more of the players. Whilst this is an important class of games, it is beyond the scope of the present Chapter (see e.g. Kreps 1990 or Fudenberg and Tirole 1991); we deal only with games of full information. In sections 5.2 to 5.5, the reader can assume that the games discussed are simple 'single-shot' simultaneous-move games. Section 5.6 then deals with sequential-move games, the extensive form, and how simultaneous- and sequential-move games can be modelled in either strategic or extensive form.

5.2 Solutions to Games via the Dominance Approach

Definition 5.7 Given a player has a set of strategies from which to choose, a strategy within that set is said to be **strictly dominated** if the player can choose another strategy and guarantee to be better off whatever the other players choose as their strategies. A strategy is said to be **weakly dominated** if the player can choose another strategy and guarantee to be no worse off, and sometimes definitely better off, whatever the other players choose as their strategies.

The idea here is that no rational player would choose to play a strictly dominated strategy. As a consequence, strictly dominated strategies can be eliminated from the game. Each player's own strictly dominated strategies can be eliminated, but equally importantly, since the player assumes the other players are also rational, he/she can also eliminate theirs. Thus all players can delete these strategies, and simplify the game; this is illustrated in section 5.2.2 below. Sometimes, this approach will eliminate all but one of each player's strategies; in this case, the game is solved (as in the prisoners' dilemma example below), and is referred to as a strict dominance solution to the game. Having deleted any strictly dominated strategies, if the game is not solved one can also look to delete weakly dominated strategies; this is discussed below. It is important to note that this approach, of deleting dominated strategies, will often not take us very far toward solving games (that is, it only works in some cases).[3]

5.2.1 The Prisoners' Dilemma

The so-called prisoners' dilemma is an extremely important non-constant-sum game which can bear many economic interpretations. In addition, it illustrates the dominance approach to solving a game.

Consider the matrix in Figure 5.1. The original scenario is as follows. Two criminals are currently held in separate cells by the police; they have committed a serious crime and the police know this, but lack convincing evidence on which to secure a conviction. Being in separate cells, the prisoners are unable to communicate with each other. The police interrogate them separately and offer each of them two choices; either to confess (C) or not to confess (N). Both prisoners are informed what the consequences of their actions will be, and these are depicted in Figure 5.1; in each cell, the left number represents the number of years in gaol that prisoner A gets, the right number represents the number of years that B gets (the numbers are negative, representing years of life lost), and clearly the objective of each player will be to maximize the 'pay-off' (minimize the number of years in gaol) they eventually receive (each naturally prefers a shorter prison sentence to a longer one). If both play N, the police are unable to convict them of the major crime but promise to 'frame' them; they will be found guilty of some petty larceny or for being found in possession of illegal substances and will both get 1 year in prison. If both confess to the crime, they are both

---

[3] There are further issues associated with the deletion of weakly dominated strategies; see for example Kreps (1990).

		B's strategies	
		N	C
A's strategies	N	−1, −1	−12, 0
	C	0, −12	−9, −9

Fig. 5.1 The prisoners' dilemma: strict dominance solution

convicted and get 9 years (the fact that they confessed is taken into account and they are given a reduced sentence; without confession, if they are convicted they will be gaoled for 12 years). If *A* confesses (*C*) but *B* does not (*N*), the police will use the evidence provided by *A* to send *B* to prison for the full 12 years. *A*, in 'grassing' on *B*, gets away with no sentence at all. Likewise, in the top right cell, the diametrically opposite result occurs; *B* gets off free if he confesses (plays *C*) and grasses on *A*, who gets 12 years for not confessing (playing *N*).

The prisoners' dilemma is a simultaneous-move game. This is true even if the prisoners are interviewed at different points in time; the key point is that each prisoner, in making his decision, does not know the decision made by the other prisoner.

Clearly, for each player, *C* strictly dominates *N*. That is, whichever strategy *B* chooses, *A* is better off choosing *C* to *N*. Thus, if *B* chooses *N*, *A* gets 1 year with *N*, and 0 years with *C*, so *C* is preferred, whilst if *B* chooses *C*, *A* gets 12 years by choosing *N* and 9 years with *C*, so again *C* is preferred by player *A*. This is also true for *B*; whichever strategy *A* chooses, *B* gets a better pay-off by choosing *C* rather than *N*. The strict dominance solution to the game is thus (*C,C*) and they both end up with 9 years in gaol.

The co-operative outcome (*N,N*), where both choose not to confess, would make both prisoners better off (they would only receive 1 year rather than 9 years). Unfortunately each of them has an incentive to cheat on any pre-arranged agreement not to confess, so the predicted outcome remains (*C,C*).

Many situations can be interpreted as prisoners'-dilemma-type games. For example,

EXAMPLE 5.1 The nuclear arms race: During the Cold War, both the USSR and the USA had the option of instigating heavy or light expenditure on nuclear development. If both had chosen light (*N* in the matrix), they would have retained the nuclear balance at low cost. If they both had chosen heavy (*C* in the matrix), again there is

nuclear balance, but at much greater cost. If the US chooses heavy expenditure and the USSR light, although the US incurs greater costs it achieves nuclear superiority (and vice versa if the US chooses light and the USSR heavy). According to the dominance solution to the game, the outcome will be that both choose heavy expenditure on the arms race—despite the fact that both would prefer the outcome where both choose low expenditure.

EXAMPLE 5.2 North Sea Fish Stocks (or whaling): Identify *N* as the case where fishermen all stick to their quotas (or use nets with the appropriate mesh gauge to allow young fish to escape), and *C* as the case where they go out and simply try to catch as many fish as they can. The dominance solution is again that everyone fishes until the stocks are depleted, despite the fact that everyone would be better off if the fish catch per fisherman is controlled. Again, every fisherman has an incentive to cheat on any agreement to restrict their fish catch (including EU or international agreements!). The consequence can be disastrous; fish stocks may be depleted so there are simply no fish left to catch at all.

EXAMPLE 5.3 Cartels (e.g. OPEC): Here, interpret *N* as sticking to the cartel's agreed price, and *C* as the act of 'chiselling', i.e. reducing price in order to attract customers away from other members of the cartel. Again the strategy of chiselling, of choosing *C*, dominates choosing *N* (sticking to the agreed price). The ideal for an individual is for all the others to hold the price high and for he/she to grab market share by chiselling. Since everybody chooses *N*, the outcome is one of low price and hence relatively lower profits for all the members of the cartel (see Chapter 16).

Obviously in practice prisoners' dilemma games are often repeated plays (oligopolists setting prices, for example). It is easy to see that if there is a finite number of plays, then cheating may still be predicted. The argument is simply one of **backward induction**. Thus, consider the last period. This is effectively a one-period prisoners' dilemma game for which the dominance solution is to confess. Moving back one period, the players know that in the last period they will both confess (or cheat), so, given the last-period outcome has been decided, the next to last period becomes effectively the new last period. Hence the players will again cheat, . . . This process of reasoning can be repeated all the way back

	B's strategies	
	N	C
A's strategies — N	0, 0	−12, 0
A's strategies — C	0, −12	−9, −9

Fig. 5.2 The prisoners' dilemma: Weak dominance solution

to the first period. This backwards induction argument works because there is a finite number of periods. In infinite games, where there is no known final period, the backwards induction argument breaks down. In this case it becomes possible for the players to try alternative strategies in order to improve on the disastrous outcome of both players confessing (or cheating). In this case, it becomes possible to build trust through signalling behaviour (see Dixit and Nalebuff 1991).

Suppose, in Figure 5.2, the pay-offs for non-confession are replaced with zeros; that is, as we change the story slightly, so that if neither confesses, they both get off without any sentence at all. Then strict dominance does not apply, but weak dominance can be used to rule out N, non-confession, as a strategy; it is weakly dominated by C, confessing. To see this, note that, for player A, if player B plays N, A is indifferent now between N and C, but if B plays C, A definitely prefers to play C. Thus for A, C weakly dominates N. By similar reasoning, C also weakly dominates N for player B. Thus the weak dominance solution is (C,C). The prediction is unchanged, although the solution concept is now weak rather than strong dominance.[4]

Note that in the original prisoners' dilemma (Figure 5.1), the predicted game outcome changes if the pay-offs are changed. For example, in Figure 5.1, it is assumed that if a player 'grasses', he gets away with no prison sentence and no other adverse consequences. In practice, friends of the man left inside may track him down, with adverse consequences. Suppose the adverse consequence is equivalent to, say, 2 years in prison; if the zeros in Figure 5.1 are replaced with 2 years, then there is no dominance solution, either weak or strict (in this new game, both (C,C) and (N,N) turn out to be Nash equilibria—see section 5.3 below; that is, non-confession

as well as confession becomes a possible solution to the game).

5.2.2 Iterated Dominance

Consider the game in Figure 5.3. There is no unique strategy for each of A and B such that a dominance solution is immediately obtained (as occurred in the prisoners' dilemma in Figure 5.1). For A, neither A1 nor A2 is strictly dominated. However, it may still be that a dominance solution exists. The idea of iterated dominance is that the game is simplified by eliminating dominated strategies (either strictly dominated or weakly dominated). In Figures 5.3–5.5, strict dominance can be applied in a series of iterations as follows. For B in Figure 5.3, B3 is strictly dominated by B2 (that is, whatever strategy A chooses, B does better with B2 than with B3). Each player has full knowledge of the pay-offs to both players and knows that the other player is also rational, so each knows neither player will play a dominated strategy (this is referred to as the **common knowledge assumption**). It follows that both players can eliminate B3 from the game (B can do so directly, and A can do so because he/she knows that B is rational.

This leaves the game looking like Figure 5.4. Clearly here, A1 dominates A2, so now both players

	B's strategies		
	B1	B2	B3
A's strategies — A1	2, 0	2, 4	0, 2
A's strategies — A2	0, 6	0, 2	4, 0

Fig. 5.3 An example of iterated dominance (1)

	B's strategies	
	B1	B2
A's strategies — A1	2, 0	2, 4
A's strategies — A2	0, 6	0, 2

Fig. 5.4 An example of iterated dominance (2)

	B's strategies	
	B1	B2
A's strategies — A1	2, 0	2, 4

Fig. 5.5 An example of iterated dominance (3)

[4] In looking for obvious ways to play the game, strong dominance is more convincing than weak dominance (see e.g. Kreps (1990)).

		B's strategies		
		B1	B2	B3
A's strategies	A1	0, 2	3, 1	1, 0
	A2	2, 1	1, 2	3, 2
	A3	2, 3	2, 4	5, 6

Fig. 5.6 Possible non-existence of iterated dominance solutions in pure-strategy games

can delete A2 from the game, leaving the game as in Figure 5.5; here B2 dominates B1. Deleting B1 leaves the solution as (A1, B2) with pay-offs of 2 to A and 4 to B. This is referred to as an **iterated (strict) dominance solution**. Notice that, in Figure 5.3, if the cell pay-offs for strategy choices A2, B3 are changed from (4,0) to (4,2), then B2 does not strictly dominate B3, but it does weakly dominate B3. Thus B3 can be deleted by weak dominance. Following through as before, the solution A1, B2 is again obtained, this time as a weak dominance solution.

Although a weaker solution concept than dominance, it is still (very) possible that a game has *no* iterated dominance solution. To see this, consider the game in Figure 5.6. In this game, no strategies can be eliminated at all (using either strict or weak dominance, as the reader may care to verify). Thus it would appear that the dominance (or iterated dominance) approach solves some games, but not others. In such a case, the dominance approach leaves no unique prediction for the likely outcome of the game. However, as might be expected, with stronger assumptions regarding how the individuals play the game, a prediction for the outcome of the game again becomes possible (see the next section).

5.3 The Nash Equilibrium Concept

For the moment, the case where players are restricted to choosing a single strategy is considered. Section 5.4 then deals with the possibility of players randomizing their strategies (good practice in games such as poker).

Definition 5.8 When each player is required to select a single strategy from his/her strategy set, the game is termed a **pure-strategy game,**

whilst

Definition 5.9 Games in which players choose probability mixes of strategies are referred to as **mixed-strategy games**.

For a pure-strategy game, the Nash equilibrium is defined as follows:

Definition 5.10 An outcome of a game is a **Nash**[5] **equilibrium** if each player's chosen strategy is a best response to the other players' chosen strategies.

To represent this mathematically, suppose there are m players, denoted $i = 1, \ldots, m$, and each player i has a set of strategies, denoted S^i, from which i must select a particular strategy s^i (in the prisoners' dilemma game of Figure 5.1, $S^1 = S^2 = (N,C)$ and player 1 would select either $s^1 = N$ or $s^1 = C$, etc.). The pay-off to individual i, denoted U^i (where U^i represents von Neumann–Morgenstern utility) depends on the strategy choices of all the players, $(s^1, \ldots, s^m)$; this is indicated by writing U^i as a function of $(s^1, \ldots, s^m)$; that is, as $U^i(s^1, \ldots, s^m)$. Then the strategy labelled $(s^{1*}, \ldots, s^{m*})$ constitutes a Nash equilibrium if

$$U^i(s^{1*}, \ldots, s^{i*}, \ldots s^{m*}) \geq U^i(s^{1*}, \ldots, s^i, \ldots s^{m*})$$
$$\text{for } i = 1, \ldots, m. \tag{5.1}$$

That is, given each other player j, $j \neq i$, chooses strategy s^{j*}, the choice of s^{i*} gives i at least as good a pay-off as any other choice $s^i \in S^i$ the player i could make. For example, (C,C) is a Nash equilibrium for the prisoners' dilemma game in Figure 5.1.[6]

The Nash equilibrium is often referred to as 'strategically stable' or 'self-enforcing', for the obvious reason that no player has any incentive to deviate from it. Thus, given the other players' choices, a player cannot do any better by changing strategy. A corollary, which in part motivates the concept of Nash equilibrium as a predicted outcome to a game, is that if an outcome of a game is not a Nash equilibrium, then at least one player has an incentive to deviate. For example, if the players engaged in **cheap talk**,[7] the argument is that the

---

[5] Named after John Nash; see for example Nash (1950).
[6] Thus $U^1(C,C) = -9 > U^1(N,C) = -12$ and $U^2(C,C) = -9 > U^2(C,N) = -12$.
[7] Cheap talk occurs if players are allowed to discuss how they intend to play the game prior to playing it. Cheap talk may help players to co-ordinate on a equilibrium, but cheap talk does not involve any commitment or legally binding contract. For example, in the prisoners' dilemma game, the prisoners, if they have the opportunity to discuss matters before their separate interviews with the police, might agree on both playing N, non-confession. This would be cheap talk because nothing stops the individuals from playing C once they are interviewed.

only outcomes they could all agree to co-ordinate on would have to be Nash equilibria.

The technique for identifying Nash equilibria in pure-strategy games is first to identify A's best responses to B's strategies, and then B's best responses to A's strategies. After this, we look for strategy pairs (an A-strategy and a B-strategy) that are both best responses to each other. Consider Figure 5.7. A's best responses to each of B's possible strategies are indicated in Figure 5.7 by underlining the pay-off that player A gets from the best response with a '~'; likewise, player B's best responses to A's strategies are indicated by underlining the pay-off B gets from the best response with a '_'. Thus if B chooses $B1$, A's potential pay-offs, given in the first column, are 0,2,2 depending on whether A plays strategy $A1,A2$ or $A3$. Thus A's best responses to B's playing $B1$ is to play either $A2$ or $A3$ (they are equally good). A's best response to B's playing $B2$ is to play $A1$ and A's best response to B's playing $B3$ is to play $A3$. Turning to B, B's best responses to A's playing $A1$ is to play $B1$ (note that B's pay-offs are the right-hand numbers in the cells; if A plays $A1$, B gets 2,1,0 by playing $B1$, $B2$, and $B3$ respectively; hence $B1$ is the best response). If A plays $A2$, B's best response is to play either $B2$ or $B3$, and if A plays $A3$, B's best response is to play $B3$. Once we have identified each player's best response(s) to strategy choices by the other player, then from Definition 5.8, it follows that if the best responses of both players match up (i.e. occur in the same cell) then this is a Nash equilibrium. Thus, in Figure 5.7, the only cell with both a '_' and '_' is that identified with strategies $(A3,B3)$; $A3$ is a best response to $B3$ and vice versa. If A chooses $A3$ and B chooses $B3$, neither would have an incentive to deviate from this choice (since they are best responses to each other). This solution $(A3,B3)$ is a Nash equilibrium in pure strategies.

The Nash equilibrium is unique in the game described in Figure 5.7. However, there may be no pure-strategy Nash equilibrium or there may be

		B's strategies	
		B1	B2
A's strategies	A1	2, 1	−1, −1
	A2	0, 0	1, 2

Fig. 5.8 Possible existence of multiple Nash equilibra

multiple equilibria. An illustration of multiple equilibria is given in Figure 5.8, where both $(A1,B1)$ and $(A2,B2)$ are Nash equilibria; again the best responses are marked using the same method and notation as in Figure 5.7.[8] In this case, there is no prediction as to which outcome would be the more likely outcome of the game (unless additional criteria are invoked to select one Nash equilibrium in preference to the other; see section 5.6 for further discussion of this).

As noted above, the Prisoners' Dilemma game (Figure 5.1) has a dominance solution (C,C) which is also a Nash equilibrium. As it happens,

Fact 5.1 A dominance solution is always a Nash equilibrium.

but

Fact 5.2 A Nash equilibrium may not be a dominance solution.

These facts are not formally demonstrated here, although Fact 5.2 is established immediately by noting that the game in Figures 5.6 and 5.7 establishes a counter-example that refutes the proposition that all Nash equilibria are dominance solutions.

As with dominance it is possible that a pure strategy Nash equilibrium does not exist. Figure 5.9 provides an illustration of this fact. The best responses of the two players are indicated in the standard way and there is no match-up. Whatever the two players choose as a strategy, at least one of them has an incentive to deviate. That is, for any given strategy pair, at least one of the players' strategy choices is not a best response to the opponent's strategy. To see this, suppose $(A1,B1)$ were chosen. Then B would rather switch to $B2$. If

		B's strategies		
		B1	B2	B3
A's strategies	A1	0, 2	3, 1	1, 0
	A2	2, 1	1, 2	3, 2
	A3	2, 3	2, 4	5, 6

Fig. 5.7 Nash equilibrium in a pure-strategy game

[8] An early interpretation of this type of matrix was that of the 'battle of the sexes', with A and B as husband and wife, strategies 1,2 being to go to the opera or a boxing match (both occur on the same night). Thus $(A1,B1)$ means that they both go to the opera, $(A1,B2)$ that the husband goes to the opera and the wife goes to the boxing match, etc. They prefer to go out together rather than separately, but A has a preference for the boxing (he gets utility 2, she gets utility 1 if they go to the fight) and B for the opera (she gets utility 2 and he gets utility 1).

		B's strategies	
		B1	B2
A's strategies	A1	70, 30	30, 70
	A2	50, 50	100, 0

Fig. 5.9 Possible non-existence of Nash equilibrium in a pure-strategy game

(A1,B2) were chosen, then A would prefer to choose A2. If (A2,B2) were chosen, then B would rather choose B1 and if (A2,B1) were chosen, A would rather switch to A1. There is always an incentive for one or the other to change their strategy. Thus, when players are restricted to selecting pure strategies, there is no obvious way to play the game and each player has an incentive to try to outguess the other player. This suggests the players are likely to be uncertain as to what strategy the other player will choose; this observation motivates the next section, where the set of choices is extended to include the possibility of players being able to randomize their strategies.

5.4 Mixed-Strategy Solutions

In the game in Figure 5.9, there is no pure-strategy Nash equilibrium. To motivate initially the concept of a mixed strategy, consider Figure 5.9 as a repeated game; suppose that in each play, A always chose the same strategy. Clearly, player B would be able to exploit the observed pattern in A's play. For example, if A always chose A1, B could exploit this by choosing B2, while if A always chose A2, B's best choice would be B1. Many games are like this, poker being the classic example. For example, if you only bid aggressively when you have a good hand, the other players will soon learn to fold their cards quickly (so you never make a killing from holding a good hand). It pays to bluff at least some of the time so you can carry some of the opponents with you when you do have a winning hand. According to this argument, randomizing your strategy should improve your average pay-off in a repeated-play game like poker (of course there is more to playing a successful game of poker than simply randomizing strategies, but it is an important component!). Now, let us return to the non-repeated or single-shot game, as in Figure 5.9. Even in this case, the concept of a mixed strategy

can still be meaningful. For example, the probabilities can be taken as indicating each player's uncertainty over what the other player will do (Harsanyi 1973 suggests this interpretation). On this interpretation, each player, given the uncertainty over which strategy the opponent will play, treats this as if the opponent plays a probability mix of his/her strategies.[9]

The mixed-strategy approach to analysing games that do not have pure-strategy Nash equilibria associates a probability distribution with each player's set of strategy choices.

Definition 5.11 In a normal-form game, if the ith player has n^i strategies to choose from, a mixed strategy for that player is a probability distribution $p^i = (p_1^i, \ldots, p_{n^i}^i)$ such that $0 \leq p_j^i \leq 1$ for $j = 1, \ldots, n^i$ is the probability that the ith player plays his/her jth strategy. The probabilities sum to unity: $\sum_{j=1}^{n^i} p_j^i = 1$.

The problem for the ith player then becomes one of choosing the probabilities $p^i = (p_1^i, \ldots, p_{n^i}^i)$ in order to maximize his or her expected utility (if the pay-offs are VNM utilities), or expected return (if the player is risk-neutral), from the game.

Notice that if a player chooses a probability of 1 for a particular strategy, this implies the other probabilities are zero (since the probabilities sum to unity); such a choice is a pure-strategy choice; thus pure-strategy choices can arise out of mixed-strategy analysis as a special case.

5.4.1 Dominance Solutions with Mixed Strategies

Consider B's strategies and pay-offs (the right-hand numbers in the cells) in the game in Figure 5.10. B's strategies B1, B2, B3 are not dominated as pure strategies, but probability mixes of B1 and B3 exist which dominate B2. For example, if (q_1,q_2,q_3) denotes the probabilities with which B plays these three strategies, the mixed strategy in which $(q_1,q_2,q_3) = (\frac{1}{2},0,\frac{1}{2})$ gives $1\frac{1}{2}$ to B whether A chooses A1 or A2, and this clearly strictly dominates strategy B2 (which yields 1 to B whether A chooses A1 or A2). Hence B2 can be eliminated from the game, leaving the game as in Figure 5.11, which now has a pure-strategy iterated dominance solution (A1,B3). To see this, note that A1 now dominates

[9] For other interpretations (for example, in terms of Bayesian games) and a critical assessment, see e.g. Kreps (1990) or Fudenberg and Tirole (1991).

		B's strategies	
	B1	B2	B3
A's strategies A1	1, 0	0, 1	2, 3
A2	0, 3	1, 1	1, 0

Fig. 5.10 Dominance solutions with mixed strategies (1)

		B's strategies
	B1	B3
A's strategies A1	1, 0	2, 3
A2	0, 3	1, 0

Fig. 5.11 Dominance solutions with mixed strategies (2)

A2 in Figure 5.11, so A2 can be deleted, and then B3 is a dominant strategy.

5.4.2 The Nash Equilibrium in Mixed Strategies

However, as in the case of pure strategies, the dominance approach does not necessarily solve the game. By contrast, a Nash equilibrium, for finite-player, finite-strategy games, always exists. I first present a general definition of the concept of a mixed-strategy Nash equilibrium and then discuss the solution concept in the context of a simple two-player game in which the players each have two pure strategies over which they can randomize.

Definition 5.12 The mixed-strategy choices of all the players constitute a Nash equilibrium if the mixed-strategy choice of each player is a best response to the mixed-strategy choices of all the other players.

In the general case where there are m players and each player i has n^i strategies, the expected utility pay-off to player i, denoted U^i, depends on the choices of probability vector $p^i = (p_1^i, \ldots, p_{n^i}^i)$ by each player i, $i = 1, \ldots, m$; thus we can write $U^i(p^1, \ldots p^m)$. A set of mixed strategies constitutes a Nash equilibrium if

$$U^i(p^{1\star}, p^{2\star}, \ldots, p^{i\star}, \ldots p^{m\star})$$
$$\geq U^i(p^{1\star}, p^{2\star}, \ldots, p^i, \ldots p^{m\star})$$

for all p_i, $0 \leq p_i \leq 1$ and all players $i = 1, \ldots m$.
(5.2)

That is, for each player i, the choice of probability vector $p^{i\star} = (p_1^{i\star}, \ldots, p_{n^i}^{i\star})$ is the best mixed-strategy choice for that player, given that the

mixed-strategy choices of the other players are also best responses.

Consider the game in Figure 5.9 (which had no pure-strategy solution). Let p denote the probability that player A plays strategy A1, and hence $1 - p$ the probability that A plays A2 (since the probabilities sum to unity). Likewise let q denote the probability that B plays B1, and $1 - q$ the probability that B plays B2. Consider the expected utility pay-off to A from the game as a function of the probabilities p, q. Denote this as $U^A(p, q)$. Player A can choose the probability p, but A's best choice for p depends on B's choice of q, as follows. Referring to the pay-offs in Figure 5.9, A's problem is to

Maximize $U^A(p, q) = 70pq + 30p(1 - q) + 50(1 - p)q$
$$+ 100(1 - p)(1 - q)$$
$$= 100 - 50q - 70p + 90pq$$
$$= 100 - 50q + p(90q - 70). \quad (5.3)$$

The expected pay-off in (5.3) is obtained by calculating probability times pay-off for each pay-off and then summing these. Thus A gets 70 if A plays A1 (probability p) and B plays B1 (probability q). The contribution of this to expected value is thus $70pq$. Likewise A gets 30 if A plays A1 (probability p) and B plays B2 (probability $1-q$). The contribution of this to expected value is thus $30p(1 - q)$, etc. The problem for A in (5.3) is to choose p to get the maximum expected return. Note that p is under A's control but not q (A can only conjecture as to the value of q).

Now, from (5.3), $U^A(p, q) = (100 - 50q) + (90q - 70)p$, which increases with p if $90q - 70 > 0$, in which case A's optimal choice is $p = 1$ (recall $0 \leq p \leq 1$), and decreases with p if $90q - 70 < 0$, in which case A's optimal choice is $p = 0$. To summarize,

if $90q - 70 > 0$ then set $p = 1$; (5.4)
if $90q - 70 < 0$ then set $p = 0$;
if $90q - 70 = 0$ then any p will do, $0 \leq p \leq 1$.

The critical value of q is clearly $q = 7/9$. A's optimal choice of p thus depends on his/her conjecture as to the value of q. The relationship between A's choice of p and the value of q is depicted in Figure 5.12.

The same analysis may be conducted for B; using the pay-offs to B in Figure 5.9, player B's optimization problem is to maximize

$$U^B(p, q) = (100 - 50q) + (90q - 70)p. \quad (5.5)$$

Here B can choose q, but not p (B can only conjecture as to the value of p chosen by A). The same reasoning as that for A establishes that the optimal choice of q depends on p and is given as:

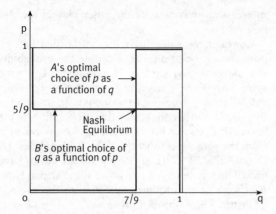

Fig. 5.12 Nash equlibrium in mixed strategies

if $90p - 50 > 0$ then set $q = 1$; (5.6)
if $90p - 50 < 0$ then set $q = 0$;
if $90p - 50 = 0$ then any q will do, $0 \leq q \leq 1$.

Thus $p = 5/9$ is a critical value determining B's choice of q. The relationship of B's optimal choice q (as a function of p) is also illustrated in Figure 5.12.

If we apply definition 5.12 and, in particular, Equation (5.2) to the case of the two-person, two-strategy game in Figure 5.9, then for a particular choice of probabilities by A,B, denoted $(p^\star,q^\star)$, to be a Nash equilibrium, it must be that

$$U^A(p^\star,q^\star) \geq U^A(p,q^\star) \qquad (5.7)$$

for any $p \neq p^\star$ and

$$U^B(p^\star,q^\star) \geq U^B(p^\star, q) \qquad (5.8)$$

for any $q \neq q^\star$.

The two arms of the swastika are termed **reaction functions** and indicate each player's best responses as functions of the other player's choice of probability. The probabilities associated with the intersection point identify the Nash equilibrium (at this point, each player's mixed strategy is a best response to the other player's mixed strategy). Thus the Nash equilibrium in Figure 5.12 is $(p^\star,q^\star) = (5/9,7/9)$.

Solution algorithms exist for the case in which the players have more than two pure strategies over which they can randomize; a linear programming algorithm is discussed in the next section.

5.5 Constant-Sum and Zero-Sum Games

When a two-person game is non-constant-sum, the interests of the players need not be directly opposed. By contrast, in a two-person constant-sum game, they are. Figure 5.9 gave an example of a game in which the pay-offs to the individuals add up in each cell of the matrix to a constant total of 100.[10] There are difficulties of interpretation underlying the idea that it is somehow legitimate to sum pay-offs to the players. For example, if players are risk-averse and the pay-offs are interpreted as utility numbers, then this involves interpersonal comparisons of utility. The issues raised by this are beyond the scope of the present Chapter (see Binmore 1992 for a reasonably accessible and careful discussion). However, in cases such as poker, played between individuals who are risk-neutral, it is true that what one player gains, another loses. Such a game is termed a zero-sum game. A constant-sum game such as that in Figure 5.9 (where pay-offs sum to 100) can always be transformed into a zero-sum game by subtracting an appropriate constant from the pay-offs to each player (namely 50 from each). This generates a new matrix of pay-offs, as in Figure 5.13, where the game in Figure 5.9 is repeated for convenience.

The solution of the zero-sum game is of course identical to that of the original constant-sum game (although the interpretations of the pay-offs are relative to a new benchmark; a pay-off of zero is in fact a case where the two players share the market equally; +20 in Figure 5.13 is a pay-off of 20% above this benchmark; and so on). In what follows, constant-sum games are not transformed into zero-sum games, since the solution methods are in fact identical.

Figure 5.14 illustrates a two-person game in the now standard format; player A has n possible strategies $A_1, A_2, \ldots, A_n$, and B, has m strategies $B_1, \ldots, B_m$. A and B choose mixed strategies $\mathbf{p} = (p_1, \ldots p_n)$ and $\mathbf{q} = (q_1, \ldots q_m)$ respectively, where p_i ($i = 1, \ldots, n$) denotes the probability of A playing strategy A_i and q_i ($i = 1, \ldots, n$) the probability of B playing strategy B_i, etc. If A plays strategy

[10] This could be interpreted as market shares in a duopoly game, for example; however, note that firms are typically concerned about the total size of the market as well as their market share.

Constant-sum

		B's strategies	
		B1	B2
A's strategies	A1	70, 30	30, 70
	A2	50, 50	100, 0

Zero-sum

		B's strategies	
		B1	B2
A's strategies	A1	20, −20	−20, 20
	A2	0, 0	50, −50

Fig. 5.13 Constant-sum and zero-sum games

		B's strategies			
		B1	B2	. . .	B_m
A's strategies	A1	a_{11}, b_{11}	a_{12}, b_{12}	. . .	a_{1m}, b_{1m}
	A2	a_{21}, b_{21}	a_{22}, b_{22}	. . .	a_{2m}, b_{2m}
	A3	. . .			. . .
	A_n	a_{n1}, b_{n1}	a_{n2}, b_{n2}	. . .	a_{nm}, b_{nm}

Fig. 5.14 Game pay off matrix

A_i and B plays B_j, they get a pay-off of a_{ij} and b_{ij} respectively.

The problem of determining Nash equilibria was discussed in section 5.4 for the case of non-constant-sum games, where it was shown how to obtain a solution for the two-person two-strategy case. Naturally, this approach can be applied here. However, when two-person games are constant-sum, a simple linear programming approach can be used to determine the players' optimal mixed strategies (even when there are many possible strategies).

Consider the expected return to A if B plays pure strategy B_j. Then A would get an expected return $p_1a_{1j} + p_2a_{2j} + \ldots + p_na_{nj}$. For a given set of probabilities $\mathbf{p} = (p_1, \ldots p_n)$, the expected return to A will vary depending on B's choice of pure strategy, B_j, $j = 1, \ldots, m$. If A pursues a 'maximin' strategy, in which the aim is to choose the probabilities $\mathbf{p}$ so as to maximize the minimum of these possible expected returns, the solution will in fact identify player A's optimal mixed strategy. This problem can be set up as a linear program as follows:

Maximize L_A

subject to

$$p_1a_{11} + p_2a_{21} + p_3a_{31} + \ldots + p_na_{n1} \geq L_A, \quad (5.9)$$

$$p_1a_{12} + p_2a_{22} + p_3a_{32} + \ldots$$
$$+ p_na_{n2} \geq L_A, \quad (5.10)$$

.
.
.

$$p_1a_{1m} + p_2a_{2m} + p_3a_{3m} + \ldots$$
$$+ p_na_{nm} \geq L_A, \quad (5.11)$$

$$p_1, p_2, \ldots, p_n \geq 0, \quad (5.12)$$

and

$$\sum_{i=1}^{n} p_i = 1. \quad (5.13)$$

The choice variables are $L_A, p_1, \ldots, p_n$. The left sides of the first m inequalities in this linear programming problem are the expected returns that A gets from each of B's strategies. L_A represents a 'floor value' below the minimum of these expected returns; $L_A, p_1, \ldots, p_n$ are chosen so as to raise this floor value as far as possible; in this way the minimum expected return to A is maximized. This program may be solved using standard linear programming techniques. Furthermore, if A has no more than two strategies, it is possible to solve the linear program for A's problem graphically (however many strategies B has).[11] To illustrate this approach, consider the game of Figure 5.15.

The linear program above for A's problem in this case becomes:

Maximize L_A

subject to

$$70p_1 + 50p_2 \geq L_A, \quad (5.14)$$

$$30p_1 + 100p_2 \geq L_A, \quad (5.15)$$

$$40p_1 + 90p_2 \geq L_A, \quad (5.16)$$

$$p_1, p_2 \geq 0, \quad (5.17)$$

and

$$p_1 + p_2 = 0. \quad (5.18)$$

The last equality constraint implies that $p_2 = 1 - p_1$, so this may be used to eliminate p_2 in (5.14)–(5.17) leaving these inequality constraints as

$$70p_1 + 50(1 - p_1) = 50 + 20p_1 \geq L_A, \quad (5.19)$$

$$30p_1 + 100(1 - p_1) = 100 - 70p_1 \geq L_A, \quad (5.20)$$

and

$$40p_1 + 90(1 - p_1) = 90 - 50p_1 \geq L_A, \quad (5.21)$$

---

[11] If A has more than two strategies, the program can be solved using one of the standard linear programming algorithms (such as the simplex method).

		B's strategies		
		B1	B2	B3
A's strategies	A1	70, 30	30, 70	40, 60
	A2	50, 50	100, 0	90, 10

Fig. 5.15 Game payoff matrix

which now features just the two variables L_A and p_1. These constraints are depicted in Figure 5.16.

Since $0 \leq p_1 \leq 1$, the feasible set is the shaded area in Figure 5.16. Since the aim is to choose the point in this feasible set which corresponds to the point where L_A is at its maximum, this is clearly point a, where the two constraints (5.19) and (5.20) both hold with equality. The solution value for p_1 is given by solving these two inequalities as equations, to give

$$100 - 70p_1 = 50 + 20p_1, \qquad (5.22)$$

so

$$90p_1 = 50, \text{ or } p_1 = 5/9. \qquad (5.23)$$

Hence

$$p_2 = 1 - p_1 = 4/9$$

and

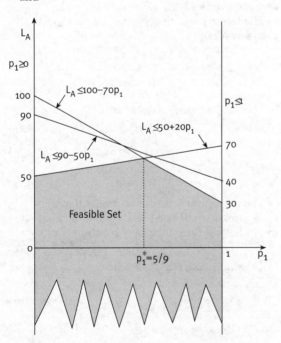

Fig. 5.16 Linear programming solution for player A

$$L_A = 100 - 70p_1 = 100 - 70(5/9) = 61.111.$$

B's problem involves three strategies. The linear program may be written as

Maximize L_B

subject to

$$30q_1 + 70q_2 + 60q_3 \geq L_B, \qquad (5.24)$$
$$50q_1 + 0q_2 + 10q_3 \geq L_B, \qquad (5.25)$$
$$q_1 + q_2 + q_3 = 1, \qquad (5.26)$$

and

$$q_1, q_2, q_3 \geq 0. \qquad (5.27)$$

Although the equality constraint (5.26) can be used to eliminate one probability (say q_3) from the problem, this still leaves three variables (q_1, q_2, L_B), so a graphical solution does not appear possible.[12] However, it can be proved (from linear programming duality theory; see e.g. Taha 1992) that any constraint in A's problem which is redundant is associated with a B-strategy which is not played (i.e. played with probability zero). In Figure 5.16, notice that constraint (5.21) plays no role in A's optimal solution. This constraint is associated with strategy $B3$. Hence we can set the probability associated with this constraint, q_3, to 0. Then (5.26) implies that $q_2 = 1 - q_1$, and using this in the constraints (5.24) and (5.25), they become

$$30q_1 + 70(1 - q_1) = 70 - 40q_1 \geq L_B \qquad (5.28)$$

and

$$50q_1 \geq L_B. \qquad (5.29)$$

If the feasible set is sketched, it is clear that the solution is the point at which these two constraints hold with equality; that is, such that

$$50q_1 = 70 - 40q_1. \qquad (5.30)$$

Hence B's optimal mixed strategy is that

$$q_1 = 7/9, q_2 = 2/9, q_3 = 0, L_B = 38.888.$$

Notice that the solution is precisely the same as that obtained earlier in Figure 5.12, and also that $L_A + L_B = 100$. That is, the expected pay-offs to the two players sum to 100 (as they must). This is because this particular game is also a constant-sum game in which the total pay-off to the two players is always 100.

The above discussion suggests that $n \times 2$ and $2 \times n$ (where $n > 2$) games can easily be solved graphically. By contrast, $n \times m$ games (with player A

---

[12] It can of course be solved using an appropriate linear programming algorithm; see Chap. 3.

having n strategies and player B, m strategies), where $n,m>2$, require more general linear programming techniques. However, solutions are readily obtained if the appropriate linear programming software is available.

5.6 Games in Extensive Form

Previous sections analysed the strategic game form in which players choose strategies (or mixed strategies) 'simultaneously'. The term 'simultaneously' is understood in the sense that each player has to choose a strategy in ignorance of the choices of the other players (moves need not be synchronous). Of course there are many games which feature sequences of moves and in which individual players learn at least something about the play that has gone before (for example, wage negotiations, where there are proposals followed by counter-proposals). Although the extensive game form is descriptively rather clumsy, it is better able fully to describe games which feature at least some sequential moves.[13]

While the strategic form specifies

1. the players,

2. the strategies, and

3. the pay-offs to the players,

the extensive form further specifies

4. decision points or nodes at which each player has the move and

5. what the player knows when it is his/her turn to move.

Consider the game in Figure 5.17. Nodes are identified by the labels I, II, III, etc. and at each node, the player who is to move is indicated. Moves are indicated by the lines, play proceeds in a downward direction in all the Figures in this text, and the final pay-offs are indicated at the foot of the tree. The pay-offs are given at the foot of the tree. Thus, for example, if A confesses (C) and B does not (N), the outcome is (0,12), where A gets 0 years and B gets 12 years in prison, etc.

Definition 5.13 A **pure strategy** for a player is a complete

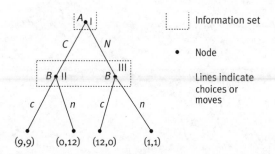

Fig. 5.17 The prisoners' dilemma game in extensive form

plan of action; it specifies the player's choice for every node at which the player has the move.

Definition 5.14 A **mixed strategy** for a player specifies the probabilities for each possible move by a player at each and every node at which the player has the move.

The following definition of an information set is crucial to an understanding of the extensive-form game structure.

Definition 5.15: An information set for a given player i defines a collection of nodes for which
  (i) player i has the move at all nodes in the information set;
 (ii) when play reaches a node in an information set, the player to move does not know which node has been reached; so
(iii) the action taken by a player must be the same at all nodes in an information set.

Figure 5.17 is in fact the prisoners' dilemma game represented in extensive form (cf. Figure 5.1). Although the prisoner's dilemma game involves simultaneous moves, it can still be represented in extensive form. Node I represents player A's choice (to confess, C, or not to confess, N), whilst nodes II and III represent decision points for player B; whatever A does, B also has to choose either to confess (C) or not confess (N). However, since the game is one of 'simultaneous' moves, player B, in making a choice, does not know what choice A makes at node I. This is represented in Figure 5.17, where nodes II and III are indicated as belonging to the same information set by enclosing them in a box. It is worth emphasizing that whatever B chooses at node II, the same choice must be made at node III. Even though B does not know which node (II or III) applies, B has a dominant strategy, namely to play C (as does A to play C). The dominance solution is thus exactly the same as that obtained when the game was represented in strategic form (Figure 5.1); namely, both players confess and end up with 9 years each.

---

[13] As remarked in sect. 5.1, both sequential- and simultaneous-move games can be represented in either the extensive or the strategic form; however, with sequential moves, it is probably safer to represent the game in extensive form, for the reasons discussed in this section.

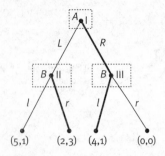

Fig. 5.18 Backward induction for games in extensive form (1)

Fig. 5.19 Backward induction for games in extensive form (2)

An equally valid representation of the Prisoners' Dilemma game would be the same diagram, but with the positions of A (at node I) and B (at nodes II and III) interchanged; extensive-form representations of games which involve some 'simultaneous' moves are not unique, although this does not affect any conclusions regarding equilibria in such games.

Consider the game in Figure 5.18, where, as usual, the payoffs at the foot of the tree, such as (5,1), indicate payoffs of 5 to A and 1 to B.[14] In this game, all information sets are singletons (each set contains just one node). When play reaches a node which is in such an information set, the player to move 'knows the history of the game', since knowing which node one is at implies knowing the route through the tree up to that point, all the way from node I. Indeed, we can extend this observation by remarking that

Definition 5.16 A game is of **perfect information** if all information sets are singletons.

A game of imperfect information, by contrast, is one which features at least one information set which is not a singleton. (For simplicity, subsequent

figures omit boxing of nodes which are in singleton information sets; 'unboxed' nodes are understood as singleton information sets.)

The game in Figure 5.18 is easily solved by applying strict dominance and backward induction. The backward induction principle starts at the bottom of the tree and determines play there, and then moves up the tree using this knowledge. Thus at node II, the optimal choice for B is r (r gives B a pay-off of 3, whilst l gives only 1). The move r at node II is thickened to indicate that this is B's optimal play if the play in the game arrives at node II. Likewise, at node III, the strictly dominant strategy is to choose l (l gives 1 and r gives 0). Again the optimal move is indicated by the thickened line. Now, A knows that B plays rationally, so A knows that if he chooses L, B will choose r, giving (2,3), whilst if he chooses R, B will choose l, giving (4,1). Thus A is able to replace the game in Figure 5.18 with the reduced game in Figure 5.19, which has the dominant solution that A chooses R (this move has also been thickened in Figure 5.18 to indicate that it is the optimal play for A). To sum up, when strict dominance works (so that there is an obvious optimal play for a player at a node), you can rub out the sub-trees below that node and replace them with the dominant strategy payoffs. Having done this, you can move up a level in the tree and apply the same procedure. The backwards induction procedure in this form breaks down, of course, if a player does not have a strictly dominant strategy. For example, at node II in Figure 5.18, if the payoffs were altered to (5,1) for l and (2,1) for r, then player B does not have a strictly dominant strategy, so A cannot predict (using dominance) which strategy B will play at node II.

5.6.1 Inadequacy of the Nash Equilibrium Concept in Games Featuring Sequential Moves

As mentioned in section 5.1, an extensive game form can be turned into a strategic game form. Consider the game in Figure 5.18; clearly A has two strategy choices at node I, namely L or R. A full description of player B's strategies must describe choices at every node at which B has the move; that is, nodes II and III. The strategies are thus (ll, lr, rl, rr) where 'rl' means 'choose r at node II and l at node III', etc. Figure 5.20 indicates the strategic form of the game.

Adopting the procedure discussed in section 5.4 for identifying the security levels, we note that there

---

[14] Only the prisoners' dilemma will feature costs (years in prison) as a payoff; in what follows, the payoffs are all benefits (in either the financial or utility dimension; this was discussed in sect. 5.4).

	B's strategies			
	ll	*lr*	*rl*	*rr*
A's strategies *L*	5̲, 1	5̲, 1	2, 3̲	2, 3̲
R	4, 1̲	0, 0	4̲, 1̲	0, 0

Fig. 5.20 Game payoff matrix

are two Nash equilibria, (L,rr) and (R,rl). Now whilst (R,rl) is the backwards induction solution to the game, the other Nash equilibrium involves a strategy which is not individually rational for player B. That is, the strategy rr implies B would play r if A initially played R; however, this would only net B a payoff of 0 whilst playing l here would give B the payoff 1. The point is that, if A makes an irrational first move (by choosing R), this can be exploited by B since, given the sequential nature of the game, B can observe A's play before making the move. Thus B would never select the strategy rr. The strategic form of the game omits this important piece of information; in the strategic form, there is no reason to predict (R,rl) rather than (L,rr) as the outcome of the game, whilst in the extensive form, we can see that player B would never wish to play rr. Indeed, when viewed in the extensive form, backward induction generates a unique and sensible prediction for the outcome of the game. For this reason, any game involving some sequential moves is probably best tackled by setting the game out in the extensive form rather than the strategic form.

5.6.2 Subgame-Perfect Nash Equilibrium

Backwards induction only yields a unique solution if dominance can be applied all the way up the tree. In many games, this need not be the case. How then do we predict solutions in such cases? Subgame-perfect Nash equilibrium is perhaps one of the most important solution concepts for such games.

Definition 5.17: A **subgame** in an extensive-form game
  (i) begins at a node in a singleton information set and includes all decisions (moves) and subsequent nodes that can be reached therefrom;
  (ii) for any node in the subgame, the associated information set must not involve any nodes outside of those nodes involved in the subgame.

The concept of a subgame is illustrated in Figure 5.21.

Thus the trees down from nodes I, IV, V, and VI are subgames, but those from nodes II, III, VII, VIII,

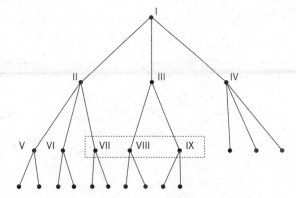

Fig. 5.21 Illustrating the concept of a subgame

and IX are not: those from VII, VIII, and IX because the nodes are not in a singleton information set (they are all in the same information set) and nodes II and III because they involve cutting an information set (treating the tree below II in isolation would ignore the fact that the information set extends across to include node IX).

Definition 5.18 A Nash equilibrium is **subgame-perfect** if the players' (mixed- or pure-) strategy choices are a Nash equilibrium for *every* subgame.

The strategy of solving for a subgame-perfect Nash equilibrium in a game in extensive form thus becomes that of solving for Nash equilibria in the lowest forms of subgame, replacing these subgames with the Nash equilibrium solution values for A, B and then operating on subgames at the next level, and so on until the top of the tree (node I) is reached. Note that in the game in Figure 5.17, the strict dominance solutions at nodes II and III are, of course, Nash equilibria (recall Fact 5.1 in section 5.2: a dominance solution is a Nash equilibrium), so the backward induction argument generates a subgame-perfect Nash equilibrium (where strict dominance can be applied). The following example illustrates a subgame-perfect Nash equilibrium when part of the solution involves mixed strategies.

EXAMPLE 5.4 Consider the game in Figure 5.22. Here the players' choices are to move left (L) or right (R) and their choices are labelled by the nodes from which they emanate (L_I, R_I, L_{II}, R_{II}, etc.). There are subgames at nodes I, II, and III, but not at IV or V (because of the information set linking them). In fact the subgame at node III can be interpreted as the game of 'matching pennies', in which two players choose simultaneously to show

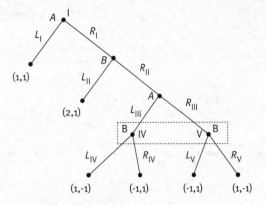

Fig. 5.22 Subgame perfection (1)

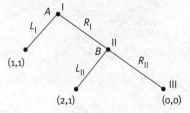

Fig. 5.24 Subgame perfection (2)

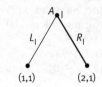

Fig. 5.25 Subgame perfection (3)

L: show heads R: show tails		B's strategies	
		L	R
A's strategies	L	1, −1	−1, 1
	R	−1, 1	1, −1

Fig. 5.23 The matching pennies subgame

a penny (say L_{IV} is when B shows heads, R_{IV} when B shows tails, etc.; A wins £1 and B loses £1 if the pennies match, whilst B wins £1 and A loses £1 if they don't match). If, in this subgame, B could observe A's move, then B would always win (the dominant strategy being L_{IV},R_V). Unfortunately nodes IV and V, are in the same information set; B does not know which of these nodes he/she is at. Thus B must choose L at both nodes (i.e. L_{IV} and L_V) or R at both nodes (i.e. R_{IV} and R_V). Indeed, we can collapse the extensive-form subgame to strategic form with no loss of information; this is depicted in Figure 5.23.

There is clearly no pure-strategy solution to the subgame in Figure 5.23 (as the reader may care to check). However, this subgame can be solved by the technique discussed in section 5.4, or, since it is zero-sum, as a linear programming problem (as in section 5.5); given the symmetry of the problem, the mixed-strategy solution will obviously involve the contestants playing each of their strategies with probability 0.5, the consequence being that each will get an expected return of zero. Thus, the tree in Figure 5.22 can be replaced with a new tree, Figure 5.24, in which the mixed-strategy Nash equilibrium yields expected payoffs of (0,0) to the players at node III.

In Figure 5.24, the Nash equilibrium for the subgame at node II (which only involves player B) is for B to play L_{II}, getting a payoff of 1 (in preference to playing R_{II} and getting 0). Thus this subgame can be replaced with the values (2,1) at node II, as in Figure 5.25; this subgame at node I now finally has the Nash equilibrium solution that A chooses R_I getting the payoff of 2. To sum up, the subgame-perfect Nash equilibrium is for A to play R_I and a mixed strategy of L_{III}, R_{III} with equal probability, whilst B plays L_{II} and a mixed strategy at nodes IV and V of L or R with equal probability. The subgame-perfect outcome is that first A plays R_I and then B plays L_{II}, with payoff (2,1) (and the matching pennies game never gets played).

The idea of requiring a Nash equilibrium for every subgame is clearly a refinement of the Nash equilibrium concept, and one which, in games with some elements of sequential play, eliminates several implausible solutions (that is, the set of solutions which are subgame-perfect is a subset of the set which are simply Nash equilibria).

The above analysis only skims the surface of the subject of game theory. One can criticize solution concepts such as backward induction and also subgame perfection; however, these solution concepts are fairly compelling if we restrict attention to simple two-stage games between just two players. The solution concepts are less watertight in terms of the predictions for the outcomes of games when there are many (> 2) players or multiple (>2) stages (see e.g. Kreps 1991 or Fudenberg and Tirole 1991 for further discussion).

5.7 Empirical Evidence on Game Theory

Most texts on game theory omit any discussion of whether game theory provides useful predictions regarding the way people actually behave in practice. However, experimental economics is now a major research programme, and economists' understanding of the way people behave in real games and economic situations is continually improving. Davis and Holt (1993) provides a useful review of recent experimental work in this area (and in decision-making under uncertainty). In experimental situations, it appears that naive players may be able to eliminate dominated strategies, but they often have difficulty in finding Nash equilibria in pure strategies. However, once subjects become experienced in the playing of such games (against different opponents), where there is a unique Nash equilibrium in pure strategies, this does have significant predictive power regarding the likely outcome of the game. Furthermore, again where the Nash equilibrium is unique, this holds to some extent for more complex (multi-stage and repeated) games. However, other game-theoretic predictions are less well supported by the experimental evidence. Shubik (1984), for example, notes the fact that most individuals in practice are unable to come up with the optimal mixed strategies, but argues that the justification for using Nash equilibrium mixed strategies is normative; that is, such a mixed strategy is worth recommending because it protects the player against the play of any opponent (whether rational or not). Likewise, the idea of applying backwards induction in sequential-move games does not usually occur to naive subjects in experimental situations (or, if it does, only after much game-playing). Thus, the evidence on game theory as a positive description of how economic agents actually play economic or experimental games is somewhat mixed. However, there is no doubt that game theory provides a powerful modelling framework for better understanding the structure of the problem economic agents face—that is, developments in game theory have forced economists to give much greater attention to systematizing the institutional and structural detail within which decisions are made.[15]

5.8 Summary

This Chapter has covered most of the basic and key ideas in game theory, including various equilibrium concepts, such as dominance, the Nash equilibrium, and the subgame-perfect equilibrium. Game theory is concerned with how agents should behave in strategic situations, where an agent's payoff depends not only on his or her own action, but also on that of other players. This kind of interdependence between agents is typical in many economic situations, and for this reason, the game-theoretic approach has come to be dominant in large areas of economic analysis. Applications of game theory occur at various points in the text. For example, Chapter 14 considers how monopolists can attempt to deter entry, whilst Chapter 16 on oligopoly examines how a small number of firms compete against each other within an industry.

5.9 Review Questions

1. What is meant by a Nash equilibrium?

2. In the original prisoners' dilemma game, with payoffs as in Figure 5.1, when one prisoner confesses and 'grasses' on his accomplice, the 'grass' gets off with no jail sentence at all. Consider the case where both partners in crime make it clear to each other that if they grass and go free, they will subsequently be visited and punished by a friend of the jailed felon. Suppose the punishment counts as equivalent to a 2-year stretch in jail. Find the Nash equilibria for this new game.

3. Identify pure-strategy Nash equilibria, if any, in the following games (using the standard notation):

Table 5.1 Identifying pure-strategy Nash equilibria (i)

	B_1	B_2	B_3
A_1	10, 10	20, 0	14, 6
A_2	6, 14	0, 20	30, −10
A_3	16, 4	24, −4	20, 0

[15] If you review the Chapter, you will see just how much specification is required to structure a game; specification involves the payoffs, who moves and when, and what each player knows when they are about to make a move. This detail needs to be specified in modelling any economic situation as a game.

Table 5.2 Identifying pure-strategy Nash equilibria (ii)

	B1	B2	B3	B4
A1	10, 10	0, 20	−10, 30	50, −30
A2	20, 0	10, 10	−20, 40	60, −40
A3	40, −20	20, 0	−40, 60	0, 20

Table 5.3 Identifying pure-strategy Nash equilibria (iii)

	B1	B2	B3
A1	20, 0	30, −10	10, 10
A2	30, −10	50, −30	20, 0
A3	60, −40	0, 20	20, 0
A4	40, −20	40, −20	40, −20

4. Find the optimal mixed strategies and expected payoffs for players A and B in the following game (which uses standard notation).

Table 5.4 Identifying the optimal mixed strategy

	B1	B2
A1	80; 120	40; 160
A2	40; 160	50; 150
A3	100; 100	20; 180

5.10 Further Reading

Gibbons (1992) gives a fairly thorough coverage of basic concepts in a very readable style. Binmore (1992) is also highly recommended (and entertaining). However, for practical and business applications, showing just how insightful game theory can be as an aid to thinking about real-life problems, Dixit and Nalebuff (1991) is hard to beat.

6 Investment Appraisal

Objectives Many decisions taken by the firm lead to a flow of benefits and costs over time (projects such as investment, pricing and advertizing decisions, etc.). This Chapter examines the valuation of cash flows which occur at different points in time and the decision criteria used for assessing such projects.

Prerequisites None.

Keyword annual percentage rate (APR), annuity, benefit–cost ratio, borrowing rate, discount factor, discounted cash flow analysis (DCF), extended yield, incremental IRR, inflation, internal rate of return (IRR), modified internal rate of return (MIRR), money cash flow, net benefit–cost ratio (NBCR), net present value (NPV), normal form, payback period (PBP), real cash flow, real discount rate, real interest rate, return on capital employed (ROC), saving rate, separation theorem, terminal net worth (TNW), yield.

6.1 Introduction: Reasons for Time Preference

Virtually all the decisions faced by a firm have a time dimension; investment projects (such as building a new power station) naturally generate a profile of costs and benefits over time, but even a simple change in price or a short advertizing campaign will typically give rise to a change in the profile of sales over time, and not a simple single-period effect. In this Chapter, such changes are all referred to as 'projects', and the problem of how to assess such projects is analysed. Whilst in many cases, the decision is one of either accepting or rejecting a project, sometimes the decision also involves some degree of optimization. For example, capacity investment may require a choice of the level of capacity to install (and capacity may be available in discrete sizes, or may be continuously variable). Examples involving optimization of this type can be found in Chapter 7 (budget constraints and optimal deferment of projects, optimal project life) and Chapter 23 (capacity planning).

The basic building block for this project appraisal can be found in the concept of net present value, introduced in section 6.2. This chapter introduces the basic ideas, compares various appraisal criteria, and examines how to adjust for the impact of inflation. Chapter 7 then follows on by discussing risk analysis, project finance, and capital budgeting under financial constraints and discusses how spreadsheet modelling can be used to facilitate sensitivity analysis in project appraisal.

There are three central reasons for time preference: reasons why an individual, if offered (for example) the choice of a gift of £1 today or £1 next year, will typically prefer the gift today:

1. risk,

2. inflation,

3. interest.

Risk often (but not always) increases with futurity; cash flows further into the future tend to be riskier than those in the near future. Since, as established in Chapter 4, individuals by and large dislike risk, this provides a reason for time preference. In most economies, prices tend to rise over time rather than fall,[1] and this inflation erodes the purchasing power of money; £1 today will buy more goods and services now than £1 next year will buy then. Finally, money today is worth more than money tomorrow because it is bankable and can earn a positive rate of interest; for example, with an interest rate of 10%, the £1 today can be transformed into £1.10 next year.

---

[1] Although there have been periods in the UK economy when prices have fallen (e.g. around 1920), and more recently the Japanese economy has occasionally seen some (very mild) deflation. However, it is usually and reasonably assumed that, for most economies, prices increase over time.

In sections 6.1–6.5, it is assumed that there is no inflation and no risk; inflation is then dealt with in section 6.6 whilst risk is analysed in Chapter 7. Also, there is no discussion of cash flow estimation in this chapter (demand estimation is discussed in Chapter 9 and cost estimation in Chapter 11); by assumption, cash flows have already been estimated. As a general point, however, it is important to identify all the cash flow consequences; these might include

1. tax consequences,
2. tax allowances,
3. cash grants etc.

which arise from implementing the project.

Finally, in this chapter, it is assumed there is a single rate of interest for borrowing or lending (except where explicitly stated to the contrary). In practice, firms and individuals face different borrowing and saving rates and firms have a variety of ways of raising finance. The effective rate of interest that a firm has to pay on the money it raises for financing investment projects is termed the firm's cost of capital (the estimation of which is discussed briefly in Chapter 7).

6.2 The Concept of Present Value

This concept is most simply introduced under the following set of simplifying assumptions (which are later relaxed).

6.2.1 Assumptions

1. no uncertainty or risk,
2. no inflation,
3. a constant rate of interest (r) per annum can be obtained for both borrowing and lending,
4. no borrowing (or lending) constraints.

These assumptions hold at best approximately; in practice, cash flows are typically risky, there is some inflation, the borrowing rate does not equal the saving rate, and no one can borrow unlimited funds. The consequence of recognizing such facts is examined in subsequent sections (and also in Chapter 7). For the present, assumptions 1–4 hold as we deal with the simplest case, in which the only problem with borrowing is that debt grows at the rate of interest.

Consider investing £1 today. This yields £$(1 + r)$ in 1 years' time, £$(1 + r)(1 + r) = $ £$(1 + r)^2$ in 2 years' time, and £$(1 + r)^t$ in t years' time. Equivalently, dividing through by $(1 + r)$, an investment of £$1/(1 + r)$ will yield £$(1 + r)/(1 + r) = $ £1 next year. Similarly, £$1/(1 + r)^2$ will yield £$(1 + r)^2/(1 + r)^2 = $ £1 after 2 years and £$1/(1 + r)^t$ yields £1 after t years.

Definition 6.1 The **present value** of £1 received in t years' time is £$1 / (1 + r)^t$ now if the rate of interest r is constant over the time interval.

The interpretation of present value is straightforward; if you are offered a cash flow of £1 in year t (for certain), then this is equivalent to being given the money sum £$1/(1 + r)^t$ today. For example, suppose the interest rate is 10% per annum and you are offered £1 in 2 years' time. The present value to you of this promised payment is simply £$1/1.1^2 = $ £0.826. The promise of £1 in 2 years is equivalent to an increase in your wealth today of amount £0.826. To emphasize this point, note that, even if you have no money today, on being promised £1 for certain in 2 years' time, you can borrow £0.826 from the bank (and spend it on consumer goods now if you so wish). The debt incurred with the bank increases over 2 years to exactly £1, but you receive the promised £1 then, and this can be used to pay off the debt.

It is worth mentioning that **borrowing rates** are normally in excess of **saving** or **lending rates** of interest; it follows that, in calculating present values, the relevant discount rate depends on whether the individual has savings (when the discount rate should be the savings rate) or is in overdraft (when the discount rate should be the borrowing rate). Note that an individual should not (rationally) simultaneously borrow and save when the rates differ.[2] Also, in theory, both rates would be needed if the cash flows in and out of the bank caused the balance there to swing from positive to negative or vice versa (this is not considered further here).

The idea in these calculations is that the rate of accumulation in the bank is used as a benchmark for comparison. Money is worth less when received in the future because £1 received today can be invested

---

[2] Of course, one might rationally choose to lock money into longer-term savings plans (for example, in order to achieve higher interest rates), and, as a consequence, occasionally have recourse to credit or borrowing. However, the general principle is that such borrowing should not occur on a persistent basis if you have savings. It is generally cheaper to borrow from yourself (i.e. from your savings) than from any bank or loan institution.

Table 6.1 Compounding/discounting with time varying interest rates

	Time				
	0	1	2	3	etc.
Compounding	£1	$(1 + r_1)$	$(1 + r_1)(1 + r_2)$	$(1 + r_1)(1 + r_2)(1 + r_3)$	etc.
Discounting	£1	$1/(1 + r_1)$	$1/[(1 + r_1)(1 + r_2)]$	$1/[(1 + r_1)(1 + r_2)(1 + r_3)]$	etc.

in the bank and will generate a larger sum at that future date.

Definition 6.2 The **discount factor** for period t is $1/(1 + r)^t$ and the rate of interest r is often referred to as the **discount rate**.

The product of cash flow with the appropriate discount factor gives the cash flow's present value. Thus £1 received in year t has value $£1/(1 + r)^t$, and so $£X$ received in year t has value $£X/(1 + r)^t$. Multiplying by the factor $1/(1 + r)^t$ thus gives the present value of the future sum.

6.2.2 The Period of Discount and the Annual Equivalent Rate (AER)

Although in this section and elsewhere in this text, it is assumed that discounting is on an annual basis, this is normally only an approximation. It may be that interest earned on an account is compounded at more regular intervals; every six months is quite common, but compounding may be monthly, weekly, or even daily. Discounting on an annual basis assumes that cash flows through the year can be lumped as if they occurred at the end of the year. This is a good enough approximation for many purposes. However, in certain applications it may be that a more finely tuned analysis is required. For example, if the monthly rate of interest is r, then £1 received in 6 months' time is worth $£1/(1 + r)^6$, and so on. The principles remain the same. Note that it is important to distinguish here between the monthly rate r and the **annual equivalent rate**, AER, sometimes termed the **annual percentage rate** (APR). These are related by the formula

$$(1 + \text{AER}) = (1 + r)^{12}. \qquad (6.1)$$

Notice that the annual rate is not simply 12 times the monthly rate (because the interest is compounded; for example a 1% per month rate gives an annual rate of 12.68%[3]). Banks and other institu-

tions involved in borrowing/lending money often quote the AER (indeed they are required by law to display it), even when they compound money at a different interval. This annual equivalent rate AER gives the rate per annum at which money grows once invested.

6.2.3 Time-varying Interest Rates

Suppose that interest rates are expected to change systematically over time. Then it is sensible to adapt the discounting procedure to take this into account. Let r_t denote the interest rate expected to hold for time period t (these one-period rates are generally referred to as forward rates of interest). Then money invested in the bank compounds and discounts over time in an obvious way, as shown in Table 6.1

In practice, project appraisal is usually conducted under the assumption that the interest/discount rate is a constant over time; this usually serves as a reasonable approximation, and one which facilitates sensitivity analysis (through variations of a single interest rate). However, it is possible to 'fine tune' the NPV calculation by estimating forward rates over time, and using this information in computing present values.[4]

6.3 Appraisal Criteria

Consider then the problem of deciding whether to accept or reject a project which generates known and certain cash flows over a known and fixed lifetime. This section deals briefly with some widely used non-discounting criteria and then sets out definitions of various discounting criteria. In each case, the pros and cons are briefly assessed.

---

[3] $1 + R = 1.1^{12} = 1.1268.$

[4] Forward rates can be estimated, for example, by examining the market prices of government securities (termed 'gilts') of bonds of different maturities and coupon rates of interest (see e.g. Brealey and Myers 1991). The graph of forward rates against time is known as 'the term structure of interest rates'.

Let π_t denote operating profit (or loss) in year t, $t = 1, 2, \ldots, T$, where T is the (assumed known) project life. It is useful to distinguish the capital outlay if this occurs at time 0, as is assumed in what follows; this is denoted K (more complex projects may involve capital outlays over several periods, of course—see below). The simple numerical example in Table 6.2 will be used to illustrate the calculations involved.

Table 6.2 Project cash flows example (1)

	Time		
	0	1	2
Cash flow	−100	50	70
	(−K)	(π_1)	(π_2)

6.3.1 Non-Discounting Appraisal Criteria

(a) Payback Period (*PBP*)

This is simply the time required to recover or payback the initial investment, the idea being that a project with a faster payback is a better project. The *PBP* is calculated by simply summing the money cash flows until the sum turns positive.

Thus after 1 year the cumulative cash flow is $-100 + 50 = -50$ and after 2 years, it is $-100 + 50 + 70 = 20$. So the payback period is 2 years. A common refinement is to interpolate by assuming the cash flow is uniform over time. Thus at $t = 1$, the sum is -50 whilst at $t = 2$, the sum is 20. Interpolating gives the *PBP* estimate as $PBP = 1 + (50/70) = 1.71$ years.

Pros The *PBP* is a useful rule of thumb since it is very easy to calculate and understand. This facilitates communication, particularly to managers who are not familiar with the discounted cash flow (*DCF*) approach.

Cons Although it focuses attention on projects which give better returns earlier (and so is a crude way of taking account of risk, in so far as risk increases with the futurity of the cash flow), it does not take account of the time value of money in a systematic way and furthermore, it ignores cash flows after the payback period.

Consider for example the projects in Table 6.3.

All three projects have the same payback period, yet clearly *B* or *C* would be preferred to *A* given positive time preference. The comparison of *A* with *B* illustrates the point that the timing of cash flows

Table 6.3 Project cash flow examples (2)

	Time				
	0	1	2	3	4
Project A	−200	50	100	100	0
Project B	−200	100	50	100	0
Project C	−200	50	100	100	1000

before the *PBP* is ignored (cash flows at times 1 and 2 are interchanged, but this does not affect *PBP*[5]), whilst the comparison of *A* with *C* illustrates the fact that the *PBP* ignores cash flows after the *PBP* (here, the £1000 in year 3). It follows that whilst the criterion may be satisfactory for projects which all have the same life and a constant profit per period, it is seriously deficient if used to assess projects when project life varies and cash flows differ significantly from period to period.[6]

(b) Average Return on Capital Employed (*ROC*)

There are several variants of this; a simple version is as follows. First, the average operating profit (denoted $\bar{\pi}$) over the project life is calculated. The *ROC* is then defined as the ratio of this to the initial capital outlay; $ROC = \bar{\pi}/K$. The average profit for the example in Table 6.2 is $(50 + 70)/2 = 60$, so $ROC = 60/100 = 0.6$.

Pros Again, it is simple to calculate and easy to understand. It also takes into account all the cash flows (unlike the payback approach).

Cons Again, it ignores the time value of money. Projects *A* and *B* in Table 6.3 both have the same *ROC* but *B* is preferable because it gets higher returns earlier.

6.3.2 Discounted Cash Flow Appraisal Criteria

This sub-section presents a variety of criteria which can be used for appraising projects, all of which are based on the concept of discounting outlined in section 6.1. This sub-section deals purely with def-

[5] The so called 'discounted payback' criterion does take into account the timing of cash flows, but again ignores the cash flows after the (discounted) payback period. This rule is discussed in sect. 7.2, as a measure worth calculating in any project sensitivity analysis.

[6] For a more detailed discussion of *PBP* and related measures, see Levi and Sarnat (1991) and Dobbs (1996). The latter paper provides a commentary on the uses and abuses of *PBP*, with particular reference to its use in devolved budgeting.

initions and interpretations of the concepts. Section 6.4 deals with the relative advantages of each.

(a) Net Present Value (NPV)

The net present value of the cash flow $\{-K, \pi_1, \pi_2, \ldots, \pi_T\}$ is given as

$$NPV = -K + \sum_{i=1}^{T} \frac{\pi_t}{(1 + r)^t} \qquad (6.2)$$

or, written out,

$$NPV = -K + \frac{\pi_1}{1 + r} + \frac{\pi_2}{(1 + r)^2} + \frac{\pi_3}{(1 + r)^3}$$

$$+ \frac{\pi_T}{(1 + r)^T}. \qquad (6.3)$$

By assumption, the capital outlay K occurs at time 0, and hence has present value $-K$ (since it is an outlay). The cash flow at time 1 of π_1 has present value $\pi_1/(1 + r)$, and so on. The overall present value is simply the sum of the present values of each of the cash flows which arise from the project.

Decision rule
accept the project if $NPV > 0$,
reject if $NPV < 0$,
indifference of $NPV = 0$.

Interpretation The net present value of a project is the immediate cash value of it. Accepting and undertaking the project increases your current wealth by the money sum NPV today.

For the project in Table 6.1, assuming an annual rate of interest of 10%, $r = 0.1$, so[7]

$$NPV = -100 + \frac{50}{1 + r} + \frac{70}{(1 + r)^2}$$

$$= -100 + \frac{50}{1.1} + \frac{70}{1.1} = 3.3. \qquad (6.4)$$

Thus at this rate of interest, the project is worth accepting; it adds value of £3.30 to the individual who undertakes it. Notice that it is not relevant that the NPV is only just positive. The assumption is that there is no risk attached to the cash flows, so any project with positive NPV is worth taking. A project with an NPV of £1 which requires an outlay of £1 million is just as good as a project with NPV of £1 which requires outlay of only £10. Both increase your wealth by £1 and both are feasible (because

by assumption you have unlimited borrowing capacity; you can actually borrow the £1 million). Naturally, when the analysis is extended to introduce risk and, in particular, borrowing or budget constraints, this will no longer hold true.

(b) Net Benefit–Cost Ratio (NBCR)

The $NBCR$ is defined as net present value divided by the present value of the capital outlays. It is assumed here that the capital outlay occurs in a lump at time 0, so

$$NBCR = NPV/K. \qquad (6.5)$$

That is, net present value is expressed relative to the capital outlay which generated it.

Decision rule
accept if $NBCR > 0$,
reject if $NBCR < 0$,
indifference if $NBCR = 0$.

Interpretation $NBCR$ is a measure of the NPV generated per pound of initial capital outlay.

Naturally, since $K > 0$, this gives precisely the same answers as the NPV rule to the decision of whether to accept or reject a project ($NPV > 0 \Leftrightarrow NBCR > 0$).[8] For this purpose, the two criteria are equivalent.[9]

Why might the $NBCR$ be useful over and above the NPV rule? Essentially, if there are no constraints on investment funds for projects, the problem for each project is simply whether to accept it or not, and as already noted, the two criteria give the same answers here. However, suppose that there is a budget constraint on the decision-maker. In this case, more NPV will be generated in total if projects are selected in order of their $NBCR$ until the budget is exhausted. There are several qualifications regarding the validity of this procedure; the conditions under which the rule is appropriate or inappropriate are discussed in some detail in section 7.5.

(c) Benefit–Cost Ratio (BCR)

A concept closely related to the $NBCR$ is the benefit–cost ratio (BCR). This is defined as the present value of the operating cash flows (excluding capital outlays), denoted 'PV' divided by the present value of the capital outlays. Thus PV is defined as

---

[7] All spreadsheets provide a function for the evaluation of net present value. For example, in EXCEL, the net present value of a cash flow starting in period 1 and lasting to period T is given by the function NPV(interest rate, $X_1, X_2, \ldots, X_T$), where $X_1, \ldots, X_T$ are the cash flows at time $1, \ldots, T$.

[8] The notation $A \Leftrightarrow B$ signifies equivalence; that is, A implies B ($A \Rightarrow B$) and B implies A ($B \Rightarrow A$). To spell this out fully, $NPV > 0 \Rightarrow NPV/K = NBCR > 0$ and $NBCR > 0 \Rightarrow NPV/K > 0$, and since $K > 0$ it follows that $NPV > 0$.

[9] If capital outlays occur over several periods, K can be calculated as the present value of these money sums.

$$PV = \sum_{i=1}^{T} \frac{\pi_t}{(1 + r)^t} \qquad (6.6)$$

(present value of all cash flows except the initial capital outlay), and so

$$BCR = PV/K. \qquad (6.7)$$

Decision rule
  accept if $BCR > 1$,
  reject if $BCR < 0$,
  indifference if $BCR = 0$.

This decision rule follows immediately from that for *NPV*. To see this, note that

$$NPV > 0 \Leftrightarrow PV - K > 0 \Leftrightarrow PV/K > 1$$
$$\Leftrightarrow BCR > 1 \qquad (6.8)$$

(and similarly, $NPV < 0 \Leftrightarrow BCR < 1$). Also note that

$$NBCR = NPV/K = (PV - K)/K = BCR - 1 \quad (6.9)$$

The *BCR* is a perfect substitute for the *NBCR*; they have identical information content, and give the same accept–reject decision for any given project. For the project in Table 6.2, $BCR = 1.033$ (>1, and so is acceptable).

(d) Terminal Net Worth (*TNW*)

The net present value criterion values cash flows at a common point in time, namely time zero. However, it is possible to value a cash flow which occurs at time t at any other time τ (so long as the appropriate discount factor is known, as is assumed here). The terminal net worth (*TNW*) criterion values the cash flows at the end of the project's life. Essentially, it tracks the effect of the project on the cash flows into and out of the bank. The terminal net worth of a project measures the extent to which the project has increased one's bank balance by the end of its life. The formula is given as

$$TNW = -K(1 + r)^T + \sum_{t=1}^{T} \pi_t(1 + r)^{T-t}, \quad (6.10)$$

or, written out fully, as

$$TNW = -K(1 + r)^T + \pi_1(1 + r)^{T-1}$$
$$+ \pi_2(1 + r)^{T-2} + \ldots + \pi_{T-1}(1 + r)$$
$$+ \pi_T. \qquad (6.11)$$

Thus each cash flow is compounded forward to the end of the project's life.

Decision rule
  accept if $TNW > 0$,
  reject if $TNW < 0$,
  indifference if $TNW = 0$.

Interpretation *TNW* measures the additional cash which will be in the bank at the end of the project life if the project is implemented.

For the project in Table 6.2,

$$TNW = -100(1 + r)^2 + 50(1 + r) + 70$$
$$= -100(1.1)^2 + 50(1.1) + 70 = 4.0$$

(>0, hence acceptable).
Note that, from equations (6.2) and (6.10),

$$NPV = \frac{TNW}{(1 + r)^T}. \qquad (6.12)$$

Thus

$$TNW > 0 \Leftrightarrow NPV > 0. \qquad (6.13)$$

That is, *TNW* is positive (negative) whenever *NPV* is positive (negative) and vice versa. For any given project, the criteria thus give identical accept–reject decisions.

To sum up the results obtained so far: *NPV*, *NBCR*, *BCR*, and *TNW* all give the same (correct) answer for a decision to accept or reject a project.

Whilst *TNW* is satisfactory for accept/reject decisions, it is less good for the comparison of projects, since different projects can have different expected lifespans.[10] Thus, whilst *NPV*s are all values at time 0 (and so are directly comparable with each other), the *TNW* by contrast is a value at the end of a project's life. The *TNW* of a 4-year project is a value at year 4, whilst the *TNW* of a 6-year project is at year 6; to compare these *TNW*s would require the 4-year value to be compounded forward 2 years, or the 6-year value to be discounted by 2 years. In view of this, there is a general preference for using *NPV* rather than *TNW*. (Although there is no conceivable added value in using *TNW* rather than *NPV*, the criterion was until recently used in some large UK organizations.)

(e) The Internal Rate of Return (*IRR*)

Suppose $\{-K, \pi_1, \ldots, \pi_T\}$ denotes the set of cash flows associated with a given project. Before discussing the concept of the internal rate of return (*IRR*), it is useful to introduce a special case of the cash flow, termed a normal-form cash flow:

Definition 6.3 A cash flow $\{X_1, X_2, \ldots, X_T\}$, where X_t denotes the cash flow in period t, is said to be a **normal-form cash flow** if $X_0 < 0$, $X_t > 0$ for $t = 1, \ldots, T$, and $\sum_{t=0}^{t=T} X_t > 0$. That is, the signs of the cash flows are of the form $\{-,+,+,+ \ldots +\}$ and the cash flow more than pays back in nominal terms.

The net present value of the cash flow $\{-K, \pi_1, \ldots, \pi_T\}$ (normal form or not) at an arbitrary rate of interest i is

---

[10] Capital rationing and the need to rank or choose between projects is discussed in more detail in sect. 6.5.2 and 7.5.

$$NPV_i = -K + \sum_{t=1}^{T}\frac{\pi_t}{(1+i)^t}. \qquad (6.14)$$

Now, suppose the cash flow is of normal form. Thus, when $i = 0$, $NPV_i > 0$. That is, the project at least breaks even in money terms, and, given that $\pi_t > 0$ for $t = 1, \ldots, T$, the present value of each cash flow π_t decreases with increases in the interest rate i. Thus, as i increases, each term in the summation in (6.14) decreases, so NPV_i clearly starts positive (when $i = 0$) and then decreases ($\partial NPV_i / \partial i < 0$), until it finally turns negative (as $i \to \infty$, $NPV_i \to -K$). It follows that there must be a unique positive value for i for which $NPV_i = 0$. This value, denoted i^*, is termed the **internal rate of return** (**IRR**), or discounted cash flow (*DCF*) return, for the cash flow. It is thus defined as

$$NPV_{i^*} = -K + \sum_{t=1}^{T}\frac{\pi_t}{(1+i^*)^t} = 0. \qquad (6.15)$$

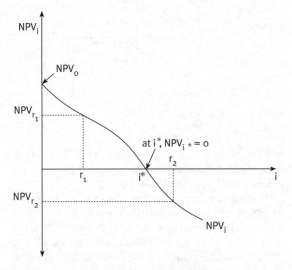

Fig. 6.1 NPV profile for the case of a normal cash flow

Figure 6.1 illustrates the *NPV* profile for this case; clearly, if the bank or market rate of interest is less than i^*, this implies that the *NPV* at the interest rate r is positive (e.g. NPV_{r_1} at interest rate r_1). If the bank interest rate is greater than the internal rate of return, *NPV* is negative (as with NPV_{r_2} at r_2). This suggests the following investment appraisal criterion:

Decision rule If the cash flow is in normal form,
accept the project if $i^* > r$,
reject if $i^* < r$,
indifference if $i^* = r$.

Interpretation The *IRR*, i^*, is the interest rate at which the project is just marginal ($NPV_{i^*} = 0$). It can thus be thought of as the average rate of return earned over the project life by this project.

Qualification If the cash flow is not in normal form, a modified form of the *IRR* is required (see below).

The simple form of internal rate of return outlined above will not in general be a good guide for accept/reject decisions if the cash flow is not in normal form. Furthermore, it cannot be used directly to choose between projects. In fact, the complications that need to be taken into account often lead many writers to recommend dispensing with the *IRR* criterion, since the *NPV* rule is superior on all these counts. However, in practice, many companies continue to use the *IRR* criterion, so it is important to be aware of the qualifications and adjustments required if it is to give correct investment advice. These issues are discussed at length in section 6.5 below. As a general observation, in any project appraisal in which discounted cash flow analysis is conducted, it is usually worth computing the *IRR* as well because it gives some idea of the robustness of the project to variations in the market rate of interest. Thus an *IRR* of 20% indicates that market interest rates can rise to 20% before the project becomes marginal (see section 7.3).

Investment appraisal software (including all the standard spreadsheet packages) incorporate an *IRR* function which facilitates its calculation.[11] In the absence of such software, given that i^* is a solution to a T-order polynomial equation, the standard approach is one of trial and error. In what follows, the case of a normal cash flow is examined; in this case there is a unique positive solution for the *IRR*. Section 6.5 discusses the problems and pitfalls associated with the *IRR* method when the cash flow is not in normal form — in this latter case there may none, one, or several real and positive roots to the polynomial equation.

In the absence of the appropriate computer software, it is possible to compute the *IRR* using a hand calculator as follows. With a cash flow in normal form there is a unique and positive *IRR*. Furthermore, increasing the interest rate i decreases NPV_i. Thus intelligent trial and error should rapidly converge on the value i^* for which $NPV_{i^*} = 0$. The trial and error approach involves making a preliminary

[11] EXCEL has the function IRR (cash flow values, guess), which returns an *IRR* for a set of cash flows (guess is a preliminary estimate of the *IRR*).

guess for i^* and an evaluation of NPV using this guess. If NPV is positive, the value for i is increased and the NPV recomputed (if NPV is negative, decrease the value for i and recompute NPV). Continue until the NPV changes sign. Suppose these computations lead to a value i_1 at which $NPV_{i_1} > 0$ and a value i_2 at which $NPV_{i_2} < 0$. Then the IRR lies between i_1 and i_2. Further guesses and evaluations within this interval narrow it until an acceptable level of accuracy is achieved. Thus if i_3 is a guess for the IRR, selected as a point somewhere in the interval, (i_1,i_2) then on computing the NPV at this value, if $NPV_{i_3} > 0$ the IRR lies in the interval (i_3,i_2), whilst if $NPV_{i_3} < 0$ the IRR lies in the interval (i_1,i_3). This procedure can be repeated until a satisfactory level of accuracy is obtained. To illustrate this technique, consider the project in Table 6.1. NPV_i is calculated as follows:

$$NPV_i = -100 + \frac{50}{1+i} + \frac{70}{(1+i)^2}. \quad (6.16)$$

This is in fact a quadratic in i so it may be solved analytically; however, if $T > 2$, trial and error methods (or the computer!) are usually adopted. The enumeration of (6.16) for different values of i is given in Table 6.4.

Table 6.4 Finding the IRR

i	NPV_i
0.0	20.0
0.1	3.3
0.13	−0.932

Clearly i^* lies between 10% and 13%. We could try further guesses (casual inspection suggests a guess of about 12%) or, perhaps, given the interval is fairly small already, we might use linear interpolation (by graph or algebra). Figure 6.2 illustrates the use of interpolation and makes the point that the polynomial function NPV_i for $T > 1$ is non-linear. Linear interpolation will thus give only an approximation to the answer. However, if at least one of the NPV values computed lies reasonably close to the

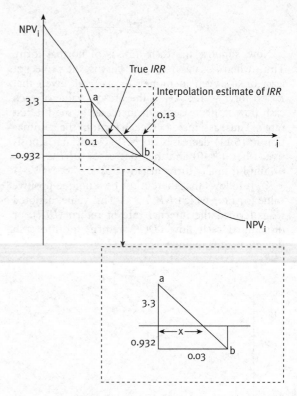

Fig. 6.2 Estimating the IRR

horizontal axis and the gradient at this point is reasonably steep, the error in making a linear interpolation will be relatively small.

The linear interpolation involves similar triangles; in Figure 6.2, $x/3.3 = 0.03/(3.3 + 0.932)$. Thus $x = 0.0234$. The estimate of the IRR, denoted $\hat{i}^*$, is 0.1 $+ x = 0.1234$ or 12.34% (the exact answer, solving the quadratic equation, is 12.32%, to two decimal places). Note that whilst analytic solutions can be obtained for $T \leq 2$, this is not generally possible. By contrast, the iterative approach described above always works, given the cash flow is in normal form. If the cash flow is not in normal form, the strategy is first to convert it to normal form, and then to apply this type of approach (see section 6.5 for further details).

6.4 Annuity Formulae

The present value of £B per annum for T years, commencing in year 1, is given by the annuity formula:[12]

$$PV = (B/r)[(1 - (1 + r)^{-T}].\qquad(6.17)$$

For example, £5 per annum for 20 years, commencing in one years' time, with $r = 0.06$ (6%), has a PV equal to £57.40.

Most spreadsheets provide functions for estimating one of the variables in (6.17) given the others (for example, given B, T, and PV, it is possible to solve for the rate of interest, or given r, B, PV, to solve for T, etc.).[13]

The present value of £B per annum for ever,

---

[12] This is straightforward to prove. Written out in full,

$$PV = \frac{B}{1+r} + \frac{B}{(1+r)^2} + \frac{B}{(1+r)^3} + \ldots + \frac{B}{(1+r)^T}.$$
(i)

Multiplying by $1+r$ and then subtracting B from both sides gives

$$PV(1 + r) - B = \frac{B}{(1+r)} + \frac{B}{(1+r)^2} + \ldots + \frac{B}{(1+r)^{T-1}}$$

$$= PV - \frac{B}{(1+r)^T}$$

(using (i)). Collecting terms in PV then gives

$$PV = (B/r)[1 - (1 + r)^{-T}],$$

as in (6.17).

[13] EXCEL for example has a variety of annuity-type functions as follows:

(i) Net present value:

PV(rate, number of periods, payment-per-period, fv, type)

Type = 0 if end of period payment due, = 1 if beginning of payment period due.

(ii) Payment to give specified fv (future value) starting with specified initial pv

PMT(interest rate, number of periods, pv, fv, type)

This function solves for x for the following profiles:

0	1	2		$T-1$	T	
$PV-x$	$-x$	$-x$	$-x$	$-x$	FV	Type=1
or PV	$-x$	$-x$	$-x$	$-x$	FV$-x$	Type=0.

Related functions:

(iii) RATE(number of periods, payment, pv, fv, type, guess): finds the interest rate (IRR) such that the payment generates fv from pv in the given number of periods.

(iv) NPER(interestrate, payment, pv, fv, type): returns the number of periods required to get fv from pv, given the payment per period.

(v) FV(interestrate, number of periods, payment, pv, type): gives the Future Value of an annuity.

---

commencing in one year's time, is given by the perpetual annuity formula:

$$PV = B/r.\qquad(6.18)$$

This follows from (6.17) since $(1 + r)^{-T} \to 0$ as $T \to \infty$.

Thus the present value of a perpetual annuity is given simply by dividing the annual cash flow by the interest rate. These formulae prove useful in that they simplify the calculations whenever the cash flow is constant per period, as the following example illustrates.

EXAMPLE 6.1 Consider the IRR of a 10% coupon bond which has a maturity of 10 years. Suppose this bond has a face value of £100 and is currently selling in the market at £80. This bond pays 10% on its face value, i.e. £10 per annum. The bond holder receives £100 at the end of the 10 years. Thus the cash flow is:

Year	0	1	2	...	9	10
Cash flow	-80	10	10	...	10	110

The easiest way to calculate the IRR uses the annuity formula to evaluate NPV. Thus

$$NPV_i = -80 + \frac{10}{i}[1 - (1 + i)^{-10}] + \frac{100}{(1 + i)^{10}}.$$

The approach then simply involves iteratively evaluating this at different rates i until the value of i is found for which $NPV_i \approx 0$. (The solution is 13.8%, as the reader may care to verify.) In bond analysis, such an IRR is termed the yield to maturity, or simply the **yield**, on the bond.

EXAMPLE 6.2 Calculation of AER (annual equivalent rate): Suppose £1000 is borrowed over 1 year and the lender asks this to be paid back at £100 per month for 12 months (an apparent interest rate of 20%, but this ignores the timing of the repayments). First compute the implied monthly interest rate r_m: this is given as the solution to the equation

$$NPV_{r_m} = -1000 + \left(\frac{100}{r_m}\right)(1 - (1 + r_m)^{-12}) = 0.$$

The solution is $r_m = 0.02923$. The AER is then calculated as

$$1 + AER = (1 + r_m)^{12} = (1.02923)^{12} = 1.413.$$

Thus AER = 0.413, or 41.3%.

Example 6.2 illustrates how misleading the naive view of the effective interest rate can be; the point here is that viewing the interest rate as 20% forgets that you repay the money every month (the AER would be 20% of course if you repaid the £120 as a lump sum at the end of the year).

6.5 The Comparative Advantages and Disadvantages of *IRR* Versus *NPV*

The *IRR* is quite widely used in finance and investment. Accordingly, it is useful to be aware that it has certain undesirable character traits (and to be aware of how these can be treated). It has already been demonstrated in section 6.3 that the *IRR* gives the correct accept/reject decision when the cash flow is in normal form and, indeed, the same answer as the *NPV*, *BCR*, *NBCR*, and *TNW* criteria. Unfortunately, when the cash flow is not of this form, the simple *IRR* rule breaks down. With non-normal cash flows, there may be several positive *IRRs* which satisfy the $NPV_i = 0$ equation (or indeed, none) and it is no longer clear what the criterion should be. Section 6.5.1 deals with this case. It is worth noting that non-normal cash flows are fairly common in practice. Consider, for example, mining or nuclear power, where there are substantial decommissioning costs at the end of the project's life. Even more significantly, any after-tax analysis will tend to result in at least two changes in the sign of the cash flow; this is because taxes are paid in arrears, so even if a project returns positive profits in all periods, there will be a negative cash flow (the tax outflow) in the year after the project is wound up.

A further problem arises if the issue is not one of simple project acceptance or rejection, but one in which projects are mutually exclusive and need to be compared or ranked. A naive use of *IRRs* to rank projects can lead to the wrong projects being selected. This problem is addressed in section 6.5.2, whilst section 6.5.3 summarizes the pros and cons of the *IRR* vis-à-vis the *NPV* criterion.

6.5.1 Multiple or Non-Existent Positive Real Roots

The following rule of thumb suggests that there may be multiple roots if the cash flow changes sign more than once.

Rule of thumb[14] The maximum possible number of positive real roots is equal to the number of changes in sign of the cash flow.

Unfortunately, this rule of thumb does not provide a count of the actual number of *IRRs*, only a count of the maximum possible number. The following examples illustrate this fact and the fact that the *IRR* is problematic when the cash flow is not of normal form.

EXAMPLE 6.3

t	0	1
π_t	100	-120

A plot of *NPV* against the interest rate is given in Figure 6.3. Here the *IRR* is 20% but the project should be accepted if the market rate of interest is greater than the internal rate of return. Here, with a single change in the sign of the cash flow, there is a single positive root, but the traditional rule (accept a project if its *IRR* > *r*, the market rate) gives an incorrect decision—using the traditional *IRR* rule would lead to incorrectly accepting such a project (if the market rate *r* was less than 20%) or incorrectly rejecting it (if *r* > 20%).

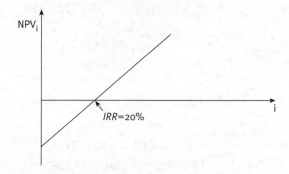

Fig. 6.3 Problems with interpreting *IRR* (1)

EXAMPLE 6.4

t	0	1	2
π_t	-100	500	-600

A plot of *NPV* against the interest rate is given in Figure 6.4. The *IRRs* are 100% and 200%. Suppose the interest rate were 10%; $NPV = -141.3$ at this rate and the project should be rejected despite the apparently extremely attractive high rates of internal rate of return generated by the project.

---

[14] Sometimes referred to as 'Descartes' rule of signs'.

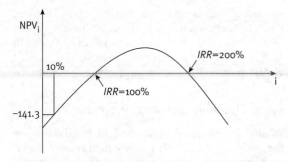

Fig. 6.4 Problems with interpreting *IRR* (2): multiple roots

EXAMPLE 6.5

t	0	1	2
π_t	100	−300	300

A plot of *NPV* against the interest rate is given in Figure 6.5. The *NPV* of this project is positive at all positive rates of interest, yet there is no real and positive *IRR*—the roots of the quadratic equation $NPV_i = 0$ are both complex numbers; $i^* = 0.5 \pm 0.866i$, where i denotes that 0.866 is the imaginary part of the complex number.

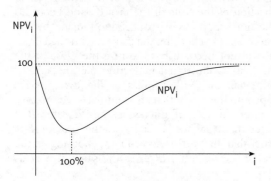

Fig. 6.5 Problems with interpreting IRR (3): non-existence

The above examples illustrate the fact that simply observing that $i^* > r$ does not inform us whether to accept or reject a project when it is not in normal form. Fortunately (or perhaps unfortunately) there are several ways of modifying the *IRR* criterion to overcome the problem of multiple roots. The so called *extended yield method* uses simple discounting to reformulate the cash flow in normal form; clearly this provides a method of resurrecting the *IRR* criterion and making it consistent with the *NPV* criterion.

The principle involved is very simple; whenever there are multiple changes in the sign of the cash

flow, negative cash flows are discounted leftward until the cash flow exhibits normal form. The principle is best illustrated by an example.

EXAMPLE 6.6 Assume a market rate of interest of 10% ($r = 0.1$):

Table 6.5 Modified cash flow (i)

t	0	1	2	3	4	5
π_t	−100	200	−60	300	40	−100
π_t'	−100	145.5	0	253.7	0	0

The modified cash flow π_t' has cash flow 145.5 in year 1, obtained by discounting −60 by one period (i.e. 145.5 = 200−60/1.1). The year 3 cash flow of 253.7 is given by discounting the −100 by one period, giving −50.9 in period 4 (i.e. 40−100/1.1) and further discounting this another period so that 300 − 50.9/1.1 = 253.7.

The cash flow π_t' in Example 6.6 is in normal form. If an *IRR* is computed for this modified cash flow and used in the standard way (if $i^* > r$ then accept the project) it will give the same (and correct) accept–reject decisions as the *NPV* rule.[15]

Most investment appraisal software packages automatically handle the problem of negative cash flows using a type of method similar to that described above. For example, the EXCEL spreadsheet offers a modified *IRR* (*MIRR*), defined as follows:

$$(1 + MIRR)^T = -TNW_{r_s}\left(\begin{array}{c}\text{positive}\\\text{cash flows}\end{array}\right)$$

$$/\ NPV_{r_b}\left(\begin{array}{c}\text{negative}\\\text{cash flows}\end{array}\right), \qquad (6.19)$$

where r_s is the saving rate of interest and r_b is the borrowing rate. It provides the option of using a different rate of interest for borrowing and saving (so you need to consider whether this is appropriate; for example, a project may have some negative cash flows, but if this is simply a reduction in your savings at the bank, then both rates entered into

---

[15] In cases such as Ex. 6.3, one approach (ignoring the more appealing alternative of simply abandoning the *IRR*) is to establish a modified cash flow of the form {+,−,−,−, . . .} and then reverse the decision criterion; that is, to accept such a project if $i^* < r$. However, given all the complexities involved in getting the analysis correct, one can see why most finance academics argue strongly for the *NPV* criterion in comparison with the *IRR*.

this formula should be the savings rate). Notice that this calculation takes all the negative cash flows and revalues them at time 0, whilst taking all the positive cash flows and compounding them to the end of the project life. Thus we get a modified cash flow of the form

Table 6.6 Modified cash flow (ii)

	Time			
	0	1	2 . . . $T-1$	T
Modified cash flow	NPV_{rb} (negative cash flows)	0	0 . . . 0	TNW_{rs} (positive cash flows)

The modified cash flow is in normal form, so the *MIRR* is clearly unique. As can be seen from equation (6.19), the *MIRR* is a measure of the average rate of return earned by the project. Rearranging gives the explicit solution of the *MIRR* as

$$MIRR = \left[\left(-TNW_{r_s} \left(\begin{array}{c} \text{positive} \\ \text{cash flows} \end{array} \right) \right. \right.$$
$$\left. \left. / NPV_{r_b} \left(\begin{array}{c} \text{negative} \\ \text{cash flows} \end{array} \right) \right)^{1/T} - 1. \right. \quad (6.20)$$

In most applications it will be appropriate to use the *same* rate for r_b and r_s (*either* the saving rate *or* the borrowing rate). Even so, these different procedures (*MIRR* and *EYM*) will generally give different values for the internal rate of return. However, each has the important property that whenever the calculated *IRR* (either *MIRR* or extended yield) beats the market rate of interest, the *NPV* at the market rate of interest will be positive and the project should be accepted. That is, they both give consistent investment advice (and advice which is consistent with that given by the other *DCF* criteria: *NPV*, *BCR*, *NBCR*, and *TNW*).

One of the arguments in favour of the *IRR* (and against *NPV*) is that, having estimated the cash flows associated with a project, if the cash flows are in normal form, it can be calculated without reference to the hurdle rate of interest used to judge project acceptability. This provides a separation of analysis from the final decision. Project appraisers merely calculate and submit *IRR*s to decision-makers. Thus top management need not get involved in the detailed project analysis but can make decisions on whether to accept projects depending on their judgement of what the cost of capital (the rate of interest r) will be over the lifetime of the project. Unfortunately, such a separation no longer applies when projects feature non-normal cash flows; in such a case it is necessary to calculate an extended yield, which requires knowledge of the discount rate.

6.5.2 Choosing Between Projects

Whilst the extended yield method largely resolves the problem of multiple roots, a further, and major, problem arises when it is necessary to choose between mutually exclusive projects. Mutually exclusive projects can arise because of their technical nature (e.g. in choosing the sites for drilling for oil within a given field) or simply because of budget constraints (so not all the projects available can be funded).

Suppose there are two projects A and B. Using the *NPV* method, the choice is simple; choose the project with the largest *NPV* (so long as this is positive; otherwise do neither). If the *IRR* is to be used, things are more complicated. First, it is unsatisfactory simply to choose the project with the largest *IRR*. The problem is that the *IRR* gives no indication of the scale of the project, and hence no indication of the *NPV* contribution made by the project. Simply choosing the project with the largest *IRR* will not necessarily maximize the value of the firm. This is illustrated in Figures 6.6 and 6.7. In Figure 6.6, the *NPV* profiles of the two projects happen to be such that B dominates A; that is, whatever the rate of interest r, the *NPV* for B is greater than that for A. Likewise, the *IRR* for B is greater than that for A. Accordingly, choosing on the basis of the highest *IRR* gives the same answer as

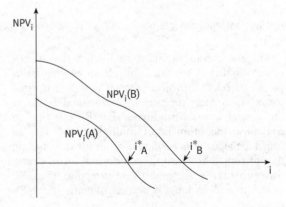

Fig. 6.6 Problems with interpreting *IRR*: choosing between mutually exclusive projects (1)

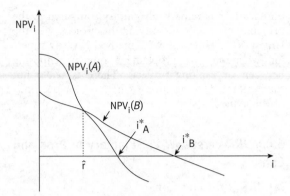

Fig. 6.7 Problems with interpreting *IRR*: choosing between mutually exclusive projects (2)

that of choosing the project with the highest *NPV*. Figure 6.7 by contrast illustrates the possibility that the *NPV* profiles might intersect. In this example, for simplicity, the case where there is just one intersection is considered;[16] the *IRR* for *B* continues to be greater than that for *A*, but *NPV* for *B* is greater than or less than that for *A*, depending on whether the market rate of interest *r* is greater than or less than, the rate associated with the intersection point of the two *NPV* profiles. Thus, choosing on the basis of the largest *IRR* gives an incorrect answer to the project choice decision when the rate *r* is less than $\hat{r}$. For this reason a simple application of the principle of choosing the project with the largest *IRR* cannot be relied on to give correct answers.

It is possible to extend the *IRR* method to accommodate the problem of choosing between projects. This method is often referred to as the **incremental IRR**. However, whilst the method is discussed below, it is worth stressing that it is rather clumsy, particularly when a choice between more than two projects is required. The so-called incremental method operates by utilizing the fact that in its extended-yield form, the *IRR* gives the correct answer to the accept/reject decision. That is, for any project *X*, letting i^*_X denote the *IRR* for *X*, then $i^*_X > r \Leftrightarrow NPV_r(X) > 0$. The incremental method is as follows. For two projects *A* and *B*, calculate i^*_A and i^*_B, the incre-

mental cash flow *B* − *A*, and the internal rate of return on the incremental cash flow i^*_{B-A} (this is referred to as the incremental *IRR*). The incremental *IRR* approach is illustrated in Example 6.7 and explained in Figure 6.8. The approach works because the *IRR* is used only to decide whether to accept or reject projects, a task for which, in extended-yield form, it gives correct answers. Thus if $i^*_A > r$ then $NPV_r(A) > 0$ (this comes from the consistency of *IRR* and *NPV* for accept/reject decisions). If $i^*_{B-A} > r$ this implies $NPV_r(B - A) > 0$. Since $NPV_r(B - A) = NPV_r(B) - NPV_r(A)$ (*NPVs* are additive), it follows that $NPV_r(B) > NPV_r(A)$. The incremental *IRR* method thus tests whether the extra investment required by *B* over that required for *A* generates sufficient extra future cash flows (i.e. whether the additional investment in *B* over and above that required for *A* generates a positive *NPV*).

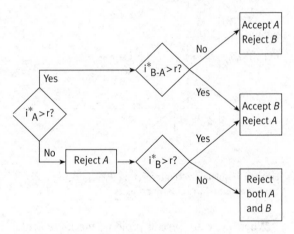

Fig. 6.8 Choosing between projects using the incremental *IRR*

EXAMPLE 6.7 Consider the following two projects *A* and *B* (assume a market rate of interest of 10%):

Table 6.7 Problems with calculating the internal rate of return: Choosing between mutually exclusive projects: a solution

t	0	1	2	3
A	−100	50	70	50
B	−200	100	50	150
B−A	−100	50	−20	100
A normal form for B−A	−100	31.8	0	100

---

[16] There could be multiple intersections, of course; if so, the possibility that the *IRR* gives an incorrect ranking of the projects remains. (You can check this by sketching two *NPV* profiles which do feature multiple intersections and then examining how the *NPV* ranking varies with the rate of interest—the *IRR* ranking remains invariant to the level of the market rate of interest, of course.)

Calculating the *IRRs*, we get $i_A^* > 31.8\%$, $i_B^* = 21.4\%$, and $i_{B-A}^* = 11.8\%$. ($B - A$ denotes the incremental cash flow; note that it is necessary to use the extended yield method to deal with the negative cash flow -20 in period 2; this involves discounting the -20 one period left, leaving a cash flow of $50 - (20/1.1) = 31.8$ at year 2.) On an accept–reject basis, either A or B is clearly viable (both $i_A^*, i_B^* > r = 0.1$). However, project B is preferred because the extra investment ($B - A$) generates a satisfactory return ($i_{B-A}^* = 11.8\% > r = 10\%$). Note that $NPV(A) = 40.9$ and $NPV(B) = 44.9$, so B is preferred using the *NPV* approach; thus the recommendations using the incremental *IRR* and *NPV* are consistent. The profiles are illustrated in Figure 6.9.

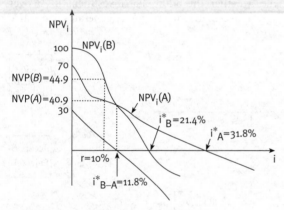

Fig. 6.9 Problems with interpreting *IRR*: choosing between mutually exclusive projects (3)

When there are several projects, the incremental *IRR* method can still be used (although it becomes extremely cumbersome). The procedure is as follows:

1. Rank projects by size of capital outlay from smallest to largest. Let $j = 1, \dots, n$ denote these projects ranked by size.

2. Use the above incremental method to choose between projects 1 and 2.

3. The winner is then compared with the next largest, again using the above incremental *IRR* method, and whichever is preferred, the other is discarded.

4. Repeat 3 until the final (largest) project has been tested.

This process eventually generates an overall winner

but clearly it is remarkably clumsy compared to the principle of simply identifying the project with the largest *NPV*. Thus, the *NPV* method is vastly superior whenever the problem is one of choosing between or ranking projects. There is really not much point in using the *IRR* method for decisions of this type.

6.5.3 *IRR* versus *NPV*: Summary of Pros and Cons

(a) *IRR*: Pros and Cons

· The *IRR* is more complex to calculate. This is not really a substantive criticism, however—software packages take the strain of calculation, which in any case is not particularly time-consuming.

· It is sometimes argued that businesspersons understand rate of return concepts better than *NPV*. Yet there is also a clear danger of confusing the *IRR* with the non-discounting return on capital, *ROC*. (Recall the original cash flow calculations from Table 6.1. The *IRR* = 0.1234 whilst the *ROC* = 0.6; the concepts are different, they give rise to different numbers, and these numbers need to be interpreted differently!)

· Probably the most important and useful feature of the *IRR* is that it indicates the robustness of *NPV* to interest rate uncertainty; if interest rates fluctuate, the *IRR* gives an idea of how high they can go before the project becomes marginal.

· For simple problems, the *IRR* can have the advantage of separating the analysis from the decision. This has already been discussed; whilst the point is correct for cash flows in normal form, whenever there are several changes in the sign of the cash flow, the extended yield method is required. This requires use of the firm's or individual decision-maker's discount rate, so the separation is no longer achieved.

· A disadvantage of the *IRR* is that it cannot easily be used to rank or choose between projects.

(b) *NPV*: Pros and Cons

· *NPVs* are additive.
· Varying interest rates can be used. This is a definite advantage. The *IRR* criterion works on project accept–reject decisions so long as it is compared with a market rate of interest which by assumption is constant over the project life. If the market rate of interest varies over time, it is no longer clear

what the appropriate decision rule for the *IRR* should be. Requiring that the *IRR* beat the highest level of interest rate that may occur over the life of the project is clearly too demanding a criterion. The *NPV* method handles time-varying interest rates (see also section 6.2) as follows.

Let $r_1, r_2, \ldots r_n$ denote the one-period forward rates of interest. The *NPV* is calculated thus:

$$NPV = -K + \frac{\pi_1}{(1 + r_1)} + \frac{\pi_2}{(1 + r_1)(1 + r_2)}$$
$$+ \frac{\pi_1}{(1 + r_1)(1 + r_2)(1 + r_3)} + \ldots$$
$$+ \frac{\pi_n}{(1 + r_1)(1 + r_2) \ldots (1 + r_n)}. \quad (6.21)$$

· *NPV*s are easy to calculate.
· *NPV*s are easier to use for problems where the choice is between several projects (see section 6.5.2).
· On the other hand, *NPV*s give no indication of interest rate sensitivity (but sensitivity analysis eliminates this drawback; see section 7.3).

The general recommendation is that, if a *DCF* analysis of the project accept–reject decision is to be conducted, then both *NPV* and *IRR* (suitably modified) will give correct advice. Furthermore, both are worth calculating since they provide different information concerning the quality of the project; *NPV* indicates its immediate cash value, whilst the *IRR* gives some indication of project robustness to variations in the market rate of interest. However, in choosing between projects, the *IRR* approach is defective and the *NPV* approach should be adopted.

6.6 Taking Account of Inflation

So far, the analysis has assumed zero inflation and no risk. This section is concerned with taking account of expected future inflation rates. For simplicity, the following assumptions are made:

(i) the inflation rate is a constant per-period rate f;
(ii) the money or nominal bank interest rate is a constant per-period rate r_m.

Given these assumptions, it follows that the real rate of interest, denoted r, will also be constant. The following discussion clarifies what is meant by the term 'real rate of interest', and then examines its role in discounted cash flow analysis.

A year 0 pound ($£_0$) in year 0 has a certain purchasing power over goods and services. A year 1 pound ($£_1$) in year 1 buys the same quantity of goods and services as would $£_0 1/(1 + f)$ at that time. If $f > 0$, prices are rising through time, and next year's money buys fewer goods and services. For example, if inflation runs at 5%, then $£_1 1$ buys the same quantity of goods and services as only $£_0 1/1.05 = £_0 0.952$ would have done (note that it buys the goods and services in year 1, not year 0; 'discounting' by the inflation rate does *not* give a present value). 'Discounting' by the factor $1 + f$ simply revalues a future cash flow in terms of today's purchasing power. Thus, a cash flow of amount $£_t X$ in money terms in year t can be translated into a **real cash flow** of $£_0 X/(1 + f)^t$ in that same year, t.

Now, consider investing $£_0 1$ in the bank at time 0. This generates in period 1 the nominal or money return $£_1(1 + r_m)$. In terms of its purchasing power, this only buys the same quantity of goods and services as $£_0(1 + r_m)/(1 + f)$. Thus, in terms of its command over goods and services, the rate growth in real purchasing power is $(1 + r_m)/(1 + f)$. This is termed the real rate of interest. Thus, the **real rate of interest** is defined as

$$1 + r = (1 + r_m)/(1 + f), \quad (6.22)$$

or, approximately,[17]

$$r = r_m - f. \quad (6.23)$$

EXAMPLE 6.8 Suppose $r_m = 0.15$ (15%), and $f = 0.08$ (8%). Then the real rate is, from (6.22), $1 + r = 1.15/1.08 = 1.0648$, so $r = 6.48\%$. According to the approximate formula (6.23), it is $r = 15 - 8 = 7\%$. Thus the error in using the approximate formula is around 0.5% in this case.

Clearly, if the inflation rate is equal to the bank rate of interest (the nominal or money rate of interest), the real rate of interest is zero. In this case, nominal wealth may grow in the bank, but as time passes, it will not buy any more goods and services than it did at time 0. Clearly, whilst the money rate of interest is generally positive, the real rate need

---

[17] Cross-multiplying gives $(1 + r)(1+f) = 1 + r_m$. Expanding, $1 + r + f + rf = 1 + r_m$, so $r = r_m - f - rf$. The term rf is often sufficiently small to be ignored to a reasonable degree of approximation, so $r \approx r_m - f$. However, there is no reason why one should not use the correct formula (6.22) rather than the approximation (6.23).

not be so (for example, the real rate was negative in the late 1970s in the UK, during a period of high inflation).

The correct approach to appraisal in the presence of inflation requires consistency; the alternative methods are:

1. Given cash flows in money terms, use the money discount rate r_m.

2. Given cash flows in real terms, use the real discount rate r.

EXAMPLE 6.9 Suppose $r_m = 0.15$ and $f = 0.08$, so $r = 0.0648$ (as in Example 6.8).

Table 6.8 Cash flow in Money Terms

	t		
	0	1	2
π_t (money terms, £$_t$)	−100	60	80
π_t (real terms, £$_0$)	−100	55.55	68.58

(the real cash flows are calculated as 60/1.08=£55.55 and 80/1.08^2=£68.58). Thus NPV can be calculated either directly, applying the money rate to the money cash flows, as

$$\text{money terms} \quad NPV = -100 + \frac{60}{1.15} + \frac{80}{1.15^2}$$
$$= 12.67,$$

or indirectly, using the real cash flows and applying the real discount rate, as

$$\text{real terms} \quad NPV = -100 + \frac{55.55}{1.0648} + \frac{68.58}{1.0648}$$
$$= 12.67.$$

Thus if one starts with cash flows in money terms, these can first be converted into real terms and then discounted at the real rate of interest, or—more directly—they can be simply discounted at the money rate of interest. However, either method, consistently applied, gives the correct answer.

The above example makes it clear that there is little point in converting cash flows in money terms to real cash flows first; the NPV can be calculated directly using the money discount rate. That is, if you start with cash flows in money terms, simply use the money rate of discount.

Why then is there any need for calculating the real discount rate? Well, suppose the cash flows are initially given in real terms (i.e. cash flows which lie in the future, but are valued in terms of today's money). Then NPV is best calculated by discounting these cash flows directly at the real rate of discount (rather than first computing money cash flows and then applying the money discount rate). Thus in Example 6.9, suppose only the second line of cash flows (the real cash flows) are given. Whilst it is possible to calculate the money cash flows (this time by multiplying by the factor $(1 + f)^t$ for the t-period cash flow) and then discounting these at the money rate, it is clearly quicker simply to use the real rate in the first place to discount the real cash flows.

In fact, there are many situations where the cash flows estimated for a project are naturally interpreted as real cash flows (that is, the estimates are not money cash flows). It is thus important to think carefully as to whether cash flows are in real or money terms. Once this is decided, the appropriate rate of discount is straightforward to assess.

EXAMPLE 6.10 Suppose again that $r_m = 0.15$ and $f = 0.08$, so $r = 0.0648$, as in Example 6.8. Pimax University is reassessing the viability of its MBA programme. As part of the calculation, it needs to put a value on the fee income this programme generates. The MBA is a one-year full-time programme and the target intake is 100 students (a target which is always achieved). Current fees are £7000 per student so revenue per annum is £700,000. What is the present value of this?

Assume that fee income continues year on year for ever. The present value of an annuity of £B per annum for ever is, from (6.18), £B/r, where r is the discount rate. Clearly, the £700,000 per annum is not a money cash flow; with inflation one would predict that the university will raise prices through time. It may be possible to raise prices by more than inflation—or it may be the case that increasing competition implies that prices rise by less than inflation. Ideally, one would want to assess which is likely to be the case. However, suppose we assume that prices rise in line with inflation. Then the fees are constant in real terms. It follows that we should use the real discount rate to value this cash flow. Thus the present value is £700,000/0.0648 = £10.8 million.

A very common error in this type of calculation is to mix up the discount rates; in particular, to use a money rate of discount to discount a real cash flow. This will in general tend to reduce the value of future cash flows and so tend to make projects appear less viable than they really are. In Example 6.10, the *PV* of the fee income is £10.8 million. If the money discount rate had (erroneously) been used, the *PV* would have been calculated as £700,000/0.15 = £4.67 million (less than half the correct figure). Don't make this mistake.

Figure 6.10 is a self-explanatory diagram which may prove helpful in noting the factors by which one can move between money cash flows, real cash flows, and present values.

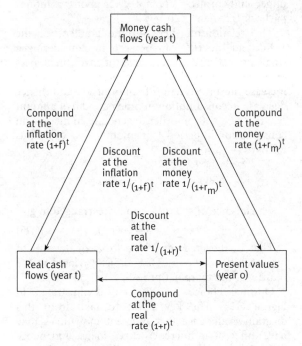

Fig. 6.10 Compounding and discounting factors for moving between money cash flows, real cash flows, and present values

6.7 Value Maximization and the Separation Theorem

The analysis in this Chapter suggests that, when an individual can borrow/save at a fixed rate of interest, the *NPV* criterion indicates whether projects should be undertaken. In this section, the argument is considered in more detail. In particular, it is shown that the existence of a capital market on which individuals and firms can borrow/lend at a fixed rate of interest leads the owners (shareholders) of a company to ask its management to maximize the value (i.e. net present value) of the company, by choosing only those projects which generate positive *NPV* (or have an *IRR* at least equal to the rate of interest). They agree on this even though they may have very different preferences for consumption over time. By contrast, in the absence of a capital market (and hence of a rate of interest at which one can borrow and lend), shareholders may well rationally disagree over which projects the firm should undertake. Thus the ability to borrow and lend at a fixed rate of interest resolves disagreements over the firm's choice of projects and its overall volume of investment (so long as the shareholders have homogeneous beliefs regarding the cash flows expected to be generated by the various projects available to the firm, of course).

The simplest framework within which to discuss these ideas involves just two periods. To begin with, suppose there is just one owner and both the owner and the firm exist for just these two periods (and all projects involve just two periods). Furthermore, suppose there is no capital market in which it is possible to borrow/lend.

Figure 6.11 illustrates the set of consumption opportunities available to the individual who has neither the possibility to undertake projects in which an investment today gives returns tomorrow nor access to a bank or other institution which offers a positive rate of interest for borrowing or saving. In this situation, the individual can only choose

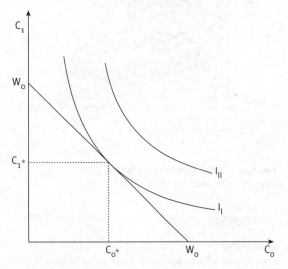

Fig. 6.11 Consumption opportunities in the absence of projects or banks

consumption levels in periods 1, 2 of amounts C_0, C_1 such that these satisfy $C_0 + C_1 \leq W_0$. Thus the individual could spend the whole of W_0 in period 0 and leave nothing for period 1, or could spend nothing today and spend up to the amount W_0 in period 1, or any combination of (C_0, C_1) subject only to $C_0 + C_1 \leq W_0$. The individual can defer consumption until period 1, simply by keeping the money 'under the mattress'.

By assumption the individual's preferences can be represented by a set of indifference curves in (C_0, C_1) space, with the optimal choice being depicted as a point on the outer boundary of the feasible set. It follows that in the above situation, the optimal choice of consumption in the two periods will be represented by a point of tangency between an indifference curve and the outer bound of the feasible set, as depicted in Figure 6.11.

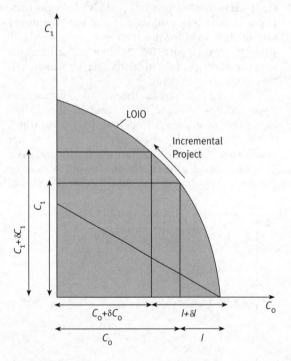

Fig. 6.12 Consumption opportunities: effect of implementing projects

In contrast to Figure 6.11, Figure 6.12 illustrates the case when the individual does have a set of investment projects which involve cash outlays at time 0 but which generate returns in period 1 (but there is still no access to a capital market in which there is borrowing/saving at a positive interest rate).

The locus of investment opportunities ($LOIO$) represents a rank ordering of such investment opportunities, with the gradient of the locus being $-(1 + i^\star)$, where $i^\star$ is the internal rate of return of the marginal project. The gradient is steepest near W_0. These are the best projects; a small sacrifice of consumption today, invested in the project, generates a significant increase in consumption next period. The locus is drawn such that close to W_0, the projects significantly more than pay back their initial investment (the gradient < -1) whilst at the upper end, projects are not even giving a money payback (gradient < 0 but > -1).

The relationship between the gradient of the $LOIO$ and the IRR can be seen by considering a small project at a current level of investment I, as depicted in Figure 6.12. The project requires an increase in investment of amount δI and hence decrease in consumption in time period 0 of amount δC_0 (i.e. $\delta C_0 < 0$) in order to generate an increase in consumption in period 1 of amount $\delta C_1 > 0$. Thus we have

$$NPV_{i^\star} = -\delta I + \left(\frac{\delta C_1}{1 + i^\star}\right) = 0$$

which, since $\delta I = -\delta C_0$, can be rearranged to give

$$\delta C_1 / \delta C_0 = -(1 + i^\star) \qquad (6.25)$$

That is, the gradient of the locus of investment opportunities, $-(1 + i^\star)$, is directly related to the return on the marginal project, $i^\star$.

Optimal choice in this case is illustrated in Figure 6.13. The key point to take from this diagram is the idea that different individuals may have different indifference curve maps, and hence different points of tangency, different choices of consumption in the two time periods, and different levels of investment; that is, the individual's consumption preferences matter in deciding how many projects to undertake.

6.7.1 Choice in the Presence of a Capital Market

Now consider introducing a bank or institution which pays a rate r on savings, and charges the same rate on borrowings by an individual. Figure 6.14 illustrates how this affects the opportunity set in the absence of investment projects; if the sum W_0 is invested, it becomes $W_0(1 + r)$ in period 1. Any point on the line ab is feasible (as is any point in the interior of the shaded region, simply by 'throwing

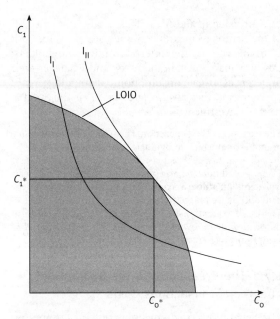

Fig. 6.13 Consumption choices

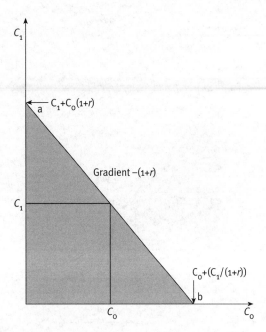

Fig. 6.15 Effect of interest rate

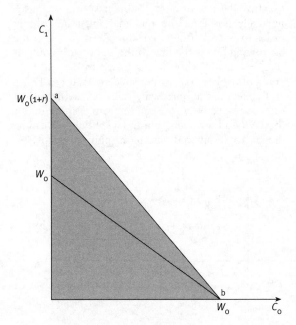

Fig. 6.14 Effect of interest rate

intercept on the horizontal axis represents the present value of the cash flows (C_0, C_1), whilst the vertical intercept represents the terminal net worth (at period 1). Clearly if (C_0, C_1) is a feasible consumption bundle, so are all points on the line segment ab (such points can be reached by either borrowing or saving in period 0 at the rate of interest r).

Now reconsider the *LOIO* in the presence of borrowing/saving at the rate r (Figure 6.16). Through every point on the *LOIO* we can draw a line with gradient $-(1 + r)$, and every point on this line is a feasible consumption point. Clearly, the feasible set of consumption choices is maximized by constructing a borrowing/saving line drawn tangential to the *LOIO* (note that borrowing/saving lines through all other points on the *LOIO* lie inside the outer bound ab in Figure 6.16). The individual will always choose a point on the outer bound of the opportunity set[18] and this is maximized by drawing this line with gradient $-(1 + r)$ tangentially to the *LOIO*. The

away' wealth). The gradient of this line is $-(1 + r)$; the higher the rate of interest r, the steeper the line is.

A key idea is that through any point in (C_0, C_1) space, there is a borrowing/saving line with gradient $-(1 + r)$. This is illustrated in Figure 6.15. The

[18] To labour a rather obvious point, this follows because the individual is assumed to prefer more consumption to less. Any point to the left and below the line ab in Fig. 6.16 has feasible points lying to its north-east; that is, for any point inside the feasible set, there is a point on the line ab which has strictly more consumption in both periods. It follows that the individual will never choose an interior point, but will always choose a point on the line ab (see Chap. 8 for further discussion of this point).

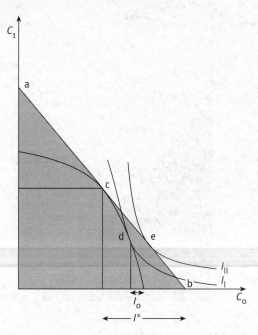

Fig. 6.16 Optimal choice with borrowing and saving at a

individual therefore chooses a level of investment I^* and then attains the highest indifference curve possible by choosing a point of tangency between the indifference curve labelled I_{II} and the line segment ab. In Figure 6.16, the original choice in the absence of a capital market is the point d. This tangency point varies with the individual's preferences (the structure of the indifference map). However, the tangency point c is independent of the individual's preferences; whatever the structure of the individual's indifference map, the same level of investment I^* will be chosen. In Figure 6.16, the case is illustrated where, having undertaken investment I^*, the individual chooses to borrow on the strength of the future returns which the projects will generate in order to move to point e. An alternative case would occur if the tangency point e is to the left of point c on the line segment ab. In that case, the individual chooses the same level of investment I^*, but then also saves some money at the rate r in order to have greater consumption in period 1 (at the expense of consumption in period 0, of course).

The value (present value) of the firm is depicted as the point b on the horizontal axis in Figure 6.16. It should be clear that choosing I^* maximizes the present value of the firm. Any other level of investment will tend to shrink the consumption opportunity set (the shaded area) and hence reduce the

present value of the firm. This is why the objective of the firm is to maximize value (present value) if it is to be run in the interests of its shareholders; however many owners there are, and whatever their preferences over consumption (their indifference curve maps), they always agree that I^* is the optimal level of investment.

Theorem 6.1 (The **Separation Theorem**). If there is a rate of interest r at which individuals can borrow/save, then the owners of a firm will agree that all projects which satisfy $NPV_r > 0$ should be accepted. Thus all such individuals will agree on value maximization as the objective of the firm and hence on the investment programme of the firm. There is a separation between the investment decision of the firm and the owners' individual inter-temporal consumption preferences.

6.7.2 The Breakdown in the Separation Theorem: Transactions Costs

The Separation Theorem holds only as an approximation, since it assumes transactions costs away. In practice, the rate of interest obtainable on savings is normally less than the rate that must be paid in order to borrow funds. For any given (C_0, C_1), the borrowing line is the line to the right, with gradient $-(1 + r_b)$, whilst the saving line is to the left, with gradient $-(1 + r_b)$, as depicted in Figure 6.17 (r_b and r_s denote the borrowing rate and saving rate of interest respectively). As before, from every point on the *LOIO*, a borrowing line and a lending line can be drawn (to the left and right of the point respectively).

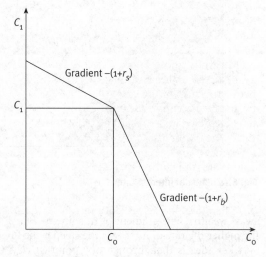

Fig. 6.17 Divergence in borrowing and saving rates of interest

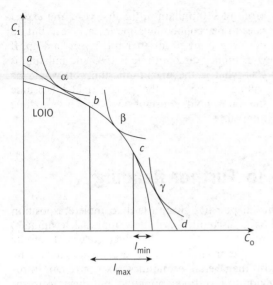

Fig. 6.18 Breakdown of the separation theorem

The only lines of interest are those which expand the opportunity set. Moving around the *LOIO*, there are two tangency points, *b* and *c*, which are of interest since they correspond to levels of investment beyond which no individual would choose for the firm. The feasible set is thus expanded as depicted by the shaded region in Figure 6.18. An individual might realize an optimal solution (tangency between the opportunity set *abcd* and the highest attainable indifference curve) at a point such as α, β, or γ. Individuals with solutions such as γ desire a level of investment I_{min} (and would propose a discount rate for *NPV* calculations of r_b), those with solutions such as α desire investment I_{max} and a discount rate r_s, whilst those in between, with solutions such as β, desire a level of investment somewhere in between. Thus, in the case where the firm is owned by many shareholders, in so far as they have different preferences regarding consumption over time, they will disagree over the desired level of investment for the firm and the appropriate discount rate (in Figure 6.18, if the borrowing rate were equal to the saving rate, they would all agree on the level of investment and the discount rate, since $r_b = r_s$). Therefore, in the presence of transactions costs, there is no separation of the investment decision from preferences over consumption; the Separation Theorem breaks down.

However, it is important to note that the difference between I_{min} and I_{max} is purely a function of the

extent to which the borrowing and saving rates of interest diverge. The closer they are, the nearer the kinked borrowing/saving line of Figure 6.17 approximates a straight line, and the more the minimum and maximum levels of investment converge in Figure 6.18. Thus, to the extent that borrowing and lending rates are fairly close together, the separation theorem holds approximately. On this argument, it is a useful working hypothesis that the objective of the firm is one of value maximization.

6.8 Summary

This Chapter gives a fairly detailed exposition of how to value projects which generate cash flows at different points in time. It covers most of the discounted cash flow appraisal techniques the reader is likely to come across in practice (net present value, benefit–cost ratio, terminal net worth, internal rate of return) and provides a comparison of these with each other and with more traditional non-discounting criteria. The exposition also considers how to take account of inflation in project appraisal, noting a particular type of mistake which is commonplace in practice. The following Chapter extends the above analysis to consider a variety of further issues in capital budgeting; in particular it deals with the valuation of risky cash flows and also the case where project choice is subject to financial or other resource constraints.

6.9 Review Questions

1. Academics often castigate the Payback Period but it continues to be widely used in practice. Why is this?

2. It is possible to correct the defects in the internal rate of return as a decision-making tool. Hence why is it so often argued that net present value is a superior criterion? Is it? Discuss.

3. Calculate the payback period, net present value, benefit–cost ratio, and internal rate of return for the following cash flow profile (use a discount rate of 10% where necessary).

	Time				
	0	1	2	3	4
Cash flow	100	60	20	60	20

4. You have won a prize in a lottery—but there is a choice. You can choose to take the hamper of foodstuffs delivered this Christmas, and every following Christmas for 10 years (11 in all) or you can simply take a cheque for £600 right now. The hamper has a current market value of £100. From a financial point of view, which option is to be preferred? (Assume the hamper, if not required, can always be sold at its market value, that your personal borrowing/saving rate is 15% and that inflation is 5% per annum, that these rates are constant over the period in question, and also that it is close to Christmas right now). How much difference does it make to the value of the hamper option if you have to wait a whole year to receive the first hamper?

5. The patent holder of a new invention, the Robovac (a robot vacuum cleaner), has offered to sell you the patent. The patent lasts 5 years, and you expect that tooling up for production will cost £20 million but that this will earn you a profit of £10 million in the first year. You expect sales to be roughly the same in each year, but do not expect any profit after the 5 years are up. If your money discount rate is 15% and inflation is 4%, what is the maximum sum you would be willing to pay for the patent rights? (Assume the rates hold constant over the 5-year time interval.)

6.10 Further Reading

This chapter has given a fairly complete exposition of basic discounted cash flow appraisal techniques. Lumby (1994) gives a lengthier treatment of the subject, at around the same level as presented here. Most managerial economics texts give an introduction to investment appraisal, but their treatment is often cursory and rarely covers more than the basic ideas.

7 Issues in Capital Budgeting

Objectives This chapter addresses various topics associated with project appraisal in corporate enterprise, including the raising of finance and constraints on financing, methods of handling risk, optimal economic life, and abandonment issues.

Prerequisites Chapter 4 introduces important concepts for risk analysis, and Chapter 6 the problem of valuing cash flows which occur at different points in time (in the absence of risk).

Keywords beta, capital asset pricing model (CAPM), debt, hard capital rationing, market risk premium, option value, retained earnings, return on equity, risk-adjusted discount rate, risk profiles, security market line, sensitivity analysis, simulation, soft capital rationing, systematic risk, tax shield, unsystematic risk, weighted average cost of capital (*WACC*).

7.1 Introduction

This Chapter examines various issues of practical significance in capital budgeting, namely risk, financial or budget constraints, and project economic life. These issues are clearly of practical concern; risk and budget constraints are a fact of life for most project managers, and for most projects there is a question of when to implement and how long to run the project.

Section 7.2 raises the question of what is the appropriate rate of discount when a firm has a range of alternative sources of finance; it discusses the concept of the weighted average cost of capital, and the pros and cons of its use in project appraisal. Sections 7.3 and 7.4 examine in more detail the problem of project appraisal when the cash flows are risky. Three alternative methods of taking account of risk are examined, namely, sensitivity analysis, simulation (and risk profile analysis), and finally the use of risk-adjusted discounted rates. Section 7.5 then deals with the impact of budget constraints on project appraisal and implementation. The net present value rule discussed in Chapter 6 presumes that unlimited capital can be raised at a fixed rate of interest. In practice, this is rarely a reasonable assumption; managers are typically constrained in the amount of finance they have at their disposal. This has important consequences for ranking and implementation. Section 7.6 then

reviews the final topic, that of project deferral and economic life (often it is possible to delay the start of projects, and to truncate them if they are not performing satisfactorily).

7.2 The Firm's Cost of Capital

In Chapter 6, the discount rate was a straightforward concept because it was assumed that a single financial institution offered a constant rate of interest at which the individual could borrow or lend. In practice, firms raise finance for investment from a variety of sources. Each source is costly, but it often appears that the costs associated with different sources are not the same. It is usually argued that a firm wishes to minimize costs, and so it would seem rational for it to choose the cheapest source of finance. If the cost were to vary depending on the volume of finance raised, it would pay to raise finance from each source such that the last unit of finance raised had exactly the same cost.[1] This principle suggests that there might be an optimal mix of finance. Thus there are two natural questions to pose:

1. Does the mix of finance used by the firm matter? (Would an alternative mix be cheaper, add value to the firm?)

---

[1] This principle, of equalizing marginal costs, is discussed in detail in sect. 10.5.

2. What is the firm's discount rate (for a given financial mix)?

Before addressing these questions, consider first the alternative sources of finance available to the firm:

1. issuing ordinary shares (equity);
2. using retained earnings;
3. issuing corporate bonds (loan stocks, debentures);
4. bank borrowing;
5. issuing preference shares, convertible debt, etc.

The first option is to sell new shares. These have a cost, of course. Shares only have value if the investor expects to get a return in the future from their investment. This arises in part in the form of dividend payments, and in part in the form of capital gains. The overall return on a share is called the **return on equity**.[2] This is the effective rate of interest the firm has to pay when it issues ordinary shares. **Retained earnings** are a major source of investment funds, but again there is a cost. Retained earnings are earnings not issued as dividends to shareholders, so an increase in retained earnings is at their expense. Shareholders will only be happy with this if the money earns a satisfactory return (i.e. at least equal to the return on equity), since this will generate increases in dividends at some point in the future. Hence it is usually argued that the effective rate of interest the firm has to pay on retained earnings is the equity rate of return (although it is often regarded as slightly cheaper because it avoids share issue costs etc.[3]). Bonds and bank borrowing are referred to as **debt**. In essence, the firm enters into a commitment, in both cases, to pay interest on the debt, and a return of principle at a given future point in time. Again, it is possible to calculate the effective

rate of interest the firm has to pay for each source of debt finance.[4]

The choice of financial structure lies outside the scope of this text (for an introductory treatment, see e.g. Ross *et al.* 1996). However, given the choice of financial mix, it is possible to estimate the average cost of capital across the different funding sources. For example, if a company is funded entirely by equity and retained earnings, then the discount rate is simply R^e, the return on its equity stock. The cost of debt capital is, for bank loans, simply the rate of interest required on it, whilst for a corporate bond, the rate can be measured as the *IRR* associated with the bond.

Definition 7.1 The **weighted average cost of capital** (*WACC*). If a company has various types of finance, it is possible to calculate a *WACC* as follows. If there are n types of finance,

$$WACC = \frac{V_1 R_1 + V_2 R_2 + \ldots + V_n R_n}{\sum_{i=1}^{n} V_i R_i},$$

where V_i denotes the market value of the ith type of finance and R_i the associated cost (in %).

The market value of different forms of finance is straightforwardly calculated:

Definition 7.2 Market Values:

· Equity stock: market price times number of shares outstanding.
· Retained earnings: simply the amount retained.
· Debt: market price of each bond times the number of bonds.
· Bank loans: simply the amount borrowed.

EXAMPLE 7.1 Suppose there are

(i) 1m (m = million) equity shares, current market price £1 $\Rightarrow V_1 = $ £1m, and the average return on equity (R_1) has been, say, 15%.

(ii) 5,000 debentures with market price £90 $\Rightarrow V_2 = $ £0.45m, with *IRR* of, say, 8% $\Rightarrow R_2 = $ 8%; and

(iii) a bank loan of £1.5m at an interest rate of 7.5%.

Then the total market value = £1m + £0.45m + £1.5m = £2.95m, and the *WACC* = (1M × 15% + 0.45m × 8% + 1,5m × 7.5%)/2.95m = 10.19%.

---

[2] An estimate of the return on equity for a firm can easily be obtained by looking at its dividend and share price movements over an historical period. The one-period return on equity at time t, R_t^e, is given as $R_t^e = (P_t - P_{t-1} + Div_t)/P_{t-1}$, where Div_t is the dividend during the period, and P_{t-1} and P_t are the ordinary share's prices at time $t-1$ and t, respectively. Thus, $P_t - P_{t-1}$ is the capital gain or loss; the return on equity comprises the dividend plus the capital gain over the period divided by the initial outlay of amount P_{t-1}.

[3] It is often argued that managers will also prefer to finance investment through retained earnings because new share issues or bank borrowing place the firm's plans under external scrutiny. Thus, managers may not like third parties scrutinizing their competency, and the use of retained earnings keeps everything 'in house'.

[4] There are a variety of intermediate forms of finance, such as 5 above, not discussed here; see e.g. Ross *et al.* (1996).

This would be referred to as a before-tax weighted average cost of capital. In fact, corporate taxes typically are important to the calculation of a *WACC*. This is so because the interest that a firm pays to investors is a tax-deductible expense (that is, interest is paid out of gross operating profits, before tax). This reduces the effective cost of paying interest. If the corporate tax rate is denoted τ_c (in the UK at present, $\tau_c = 0.33$, or 33%), the net cost of paying £1 of interest is only £$(1 - \tau_c)$ in after-tax cash flow (whilst paying £1 of dividend costs a full £1 of after-tax cash flow). Hence it is conventional to multiply the debt rates of interest by the factor $(1 - \tau_c)$ to obtain an after-tax[5] *WACC*:

Definition 7.3 The after-tax weighted average cost of capital. If a company has various types of finance, it is possible to calculate a *WACC* as follows. If there are n types of finance,

$$WACC = \frac{V_1 R_1 + (V_2 R_2 + \ldots + V_n R_n)(1 - \tau_c)}{\sum_{i=1}^{n} V_i R_i},$$

where denotes market value of equity plus retained earnings, R_1 is the return on equity, and $R_2, \ldots, R_n$ are the rates of interest and $V_2, \ldots, V_n$ the market values of various bonds and bank loans.

It is usually argued that the *WACC* is the appropriate discount rate for investments in the company's normal line of business. However, it can also be argued that it is an inappropriate rate for projects that are significantly riskier, or less risky, than the firm's usual business risk (the definition of risk also needs to be considered further). This point is discussed at greater length in section 7.4. It should also be noted that the *WACC* calculated here is a nominal or money discount rate, and not a real discount rate.

Debt typically looks cheaper because of the tax deductibility of interest. This **tax shield** on debt seems to suggest that firms ought to be entirely debt-financed. However, high levels of debt finance can make firms more vulnerable to financial distress, and for this reason it is usually argued that there is a limit to the advantages of debt finance. For an introduction to the complexities of choosing the financial mix (and whether it matters), see e.g. Ross *et al.* 1996, or Brealey and Myers 1996.

---

[5] This is an approximate adjustment factor, for the simple reason that tax is not paid instantaneously. A firm will delay tax payments if it is profitable to do so, and tax payments can be deferred by a year or so—the time value of money then reduces the effective tax rate (although the appropriate discount rate for discounting these cash flows also needs careful consideration).

7.3 Traditional Methods of Taking Account of Risk

In section 7.4, it is argued that risk in project appraisal can be taken into account through an adjustment in the discount rate used; riskier cash flows are more heavily discounted (although what counts as 'riskier' is not straightforward). Prior to this, two potentially useful practical ways in which risk can be taken into account in project appraisal are examined; sensitivity analysis, and simulation.

7.3.1 Sensitivity Analysis

Sensitivity analysis examines the impact of changes in the values of key variables (technological, financial, etc.) on the *NPV* (or *IRR* etc.) of a project. For example, the investment proposal can be re-evaluated using different discount rates (to investigate sensitivity of *NPV* to interest rates), different values for project life, etc. Several forms of sensitivity analysis can be conducted. In each case it typically involves changing the value of a single parameter and then re-evaluating the project performance criterion (which is assumed here to be net present value, *NPV*). For example, for each parameter (capital cost, project life, discount rate, inflation rate, etc.) one might consider calculations such as the following (a numerical example follows thereafter):

1. Vary by plus or minus 20% the variation in the input parameter and compute the absolute or percentage change in *NPV*.

2. Vary by plus or minus 1% the variation in the input parameter. Compute the percentage change in *NPV*. This gives an approximate value for the point elasticity for *NPV* with respect to the variable.

3. Calculate how far (in absolute or percentage terms) each parameter needs to be changed to make the *NPV* fall to zero. This gives some idea of how robust the project-accept decision is to variation in the parameter. Since the fall in *NPV* is 100%, the *NPV* arc elasticity is given as 100 divided by the percent change in the input parameter. This might also be calculated.

In the following example, the focus is on 3 above, the changes that make the project marginal. Following this there is an example which illustrates the calculation of elasticities.

EXAMPLE 7.2 $NPV = 0$ sensitivity calculations.
Consider the following project cash flow:

t	0	1	2	...	6
π_t	-100	24	24	...	24

Suppose these are real cash flows, and that the money rate of discount is $r_m = 0.12$, whilst inflation $f = 0.04$. Hence the real discount rate is given by $1 + r = 1.12/1.04 = 1.077 \Rightarrow r = 0.077$. The NPV of the project is thus

$$NPV_r = -100 + 24[1 - (1 + r)^{-T}]/r$$
$$= -100 + 24[1 - 1.077^{-6}]/0.077 = 11.99 \quad (i)$$

where T is the expected project life (6 years). Now consider the following parameter sensitivities:

Capital cost overrun
An increase of £1 in capital cost clearly reduces NPV by £1. Hence if capital costs overrun by £11.99, the $NPV = 0$ and the project is marginal. This amounts to an 11.99% cost overrun.

Operating benefits
Suppose benefits change to £X per year (in real terms). What value of X makes $NPV = 0$? First note that

$$[1 - (1 + r)^{-T}]/r = [1 - 1.077^{-6}]/0.077 = 4.6666. \quad (ii)$$

Hence (i) becomes

$$NPV_r = -100 + X*4.666. \quad (iii)$$

Hence if $NPV_{0.077} = 0$ if $X = 100/4.666 = 21.43$. Thus a fall in benefit per annum of £2.57 (from £24 to £21.34) makes the project marginal. This amounts to a 10.7% drop in benefits.

Real interest rate
This simply requires a calculation of the IRR (since this is the rate of interest that makes $NPV = 0$). This is 11.54%. Thus the real rate of interest can increase by 11.5%−7.7% = 3.8% before the project becomes marginal.

Inflation
Since a real rate $r = 0.1154$ makes the project marginal, the equation relating inflation, money, and real rates of interest can be used as follows: setting

$$(1 + r_m)(1 + f) = (1 + r) = 1.1154 \quad (iv)$$

gives values of r_m and f which make the project marginal. Fixing r_m at its original value, $r_m = 0.12$, (iv) gives the inflation rate at which the project would be marginal; that is, $1.12(1 + f) = 1.1154$. This gives $f = 0.004$.

Thus inflation can fall to 0.4% (i.e. by 3.6% from the original 4%).

Money rates of interest
Using (iv), and setting f at its original value $f = 0.04$, the money rate of interest at which the project becomes marginal is given by $(1 + r_m)$ $1.04 = 1.1154$; this gives the marginal money rate r_m as 7.25%. That is, the money rate can fall by 4.75% (from its original value of 12%).

Project life
It is possible to estimate in equation (i) above the project life, T, which makes the project marginal (either analytically, by rearranging (i) to make T the subject of the equation, or simply by using trial values for T and iterating to a solution using the same procedure as for calculating the IRR). Thus, evaluating for $T = 5$ and $T = 6$ gives $NPV_{T=5} = -3.39$ and $NPV_{T=6} = 11.99$. Using linear interpolation then gives the estimate $T=5.22$. Thus the project must last at least 5.2 years to be viable.[6]

Focusing on $NPV=0$ is useful as an indication of project robustness. However, the alternative of computing elasticities is also useful, since elasticity is a measure of sensitivity that has the nice property of being a dimensionless number.[7] It is thus possible to

---

[6] The annuity formula is based on a discrete number of years; using the formula to determine T as a continuous variable implies an assumption about how funds accumulate within the year, but it is unnecessary to get bogged down in such details here. Refinements make little difference to the answer obtained. Analytically, the problem is to solve $NPV_r = -100 + 24(1 - 1.077^{-T})/0.077 = 0$. Rearranging and taking logs, this gives

$$1.077^{-T} = 1 - [(100 \times 0.077)/24],$$

so

$$T = \frac{-\ln\left(1 - \dfrac{100 \times 0.077}{24}\right)}{\ln 1.077}.$$

In the more general case, the rearrangement gives

$$T = -\ln\left(1 - \frac{Kr}{B}\right)/\ln(1 + r),$$

where r is the real rate of interest, K the initial outlay, and B the per-period return. The formula may prove useful in tabulations in spreadsheet analysis, although many spreadsheets have a function for doing this job. In EXCEL, for example, the function NPER (*interestrate, payment, pv, fv, type*) returns the number of periods required to get *fv* (future value) at that time starting from an initial amount *pv* and constant payment of amount *payment* per period, for a specified *interestrate*.

[7] For students unfamiliar with the concept of an elasticity, a brief review can be found in sect. 8.6, where the primary focus is on the elasticity of demand.

compare across such elasticities to see with respect to which parameters the *NPV* is most sensitive.

EXAMPLE 7.3 Consider the project with cash flows as in Example 7.2.

1. The capital cost elasticity can be calculated by considering a small increment in K, of say 1%; i.e. £1, given that the initial outlay was £100. This decreases *NPV* by £1. Hence $\eta_K = (-1/1)(100/11.99) = -8.34$.

2. As for elasticity with respect to project life T: when $T = 6$, *NPV* = 11.99. Increasing T by 1%, to 6.06, and re-evaluating *NPV* gives *NPV* = 12.88. Hence

$$\eta_K = \frac{(12.88 - 11.99)}{(6.06 - 6.0)} \frac{6.0}{11.99} = 7.42.$$

Thus the project is slightly more sensitive to assumptions about capital cost than to project life.

It is also possible to vary more than one input parameter at the same time, of course. One useful idea is to take pessimistic values for all parameters and compute an *NPV*, and to take optimistic values and re-compute the *NPV*. This establishes a range for *NPV*. Sensitivity analyses are usually presented as tabulations showing the effect of parameter variation on *NPV*, tables of *NPV* elasticities, and/or graphs showing how *NPV* varies with different parameters. The details of the calculations involved are typically not reported.

The principle advantage of sensitivity analysis is its simplicity. It also lends itself to spreadsheet analysis. (One idea is to set out the net present value calculation in the spreadsheet, and then to tabulate *NPV* against variations in the various input values. It is then possible to use the chart facility to depict how *NPV* varies against input variations.[8]) The chief drawback of the technique is that it gives no idea of how likely the variations are, nor does it give any idea of how variations in input values are likely to interact.

7.3.2 Simulation Techniques

Simulation requires some degree of model building, and in particular the assignment of (usually subjective) probability distributions for key project variables (such as capital cost, interest rates, project life, etc.). The advantage of simulation over sensitivity analysis lies in the fact that it gives some information

on how the variables interact and also a probability picture for outcomes. Unfortunately, there are also several drawbacks to the use of simulation. This section briefly outlines the approach and then assesses its pros and cons.

Modern spreadsheets provide a facility for undertaking some limited forms of simulation analysis,[9] although more specialized software, and usually detailed programming, is required to set up a simulation model. The program (or spreadsheet) provides a procedure for taking a drawing from each of the input distributions and, on the basis of the values drawn, evaluates the cash flow for each year of the project life. The process is then repeated many times. Each time a new value for each year's cash flow can be calculated. It follows that the simulation process can be used to generate a distribution for each year's cash flow. From these distributions, the expected cash flow in each year can be estimated and, given an appropriate discount rate, the *NPV* can be calculated. Of course, when using this approach, there is a need to assess the appropriate rate of discount for risky cash flows—and this will depend upon the level of risk associated with the cash flow (see section 7.4).

Many of the early proponents of the simulation approach suggested a rather different use of the simulation methodology, and it is worth reviewing because it continues to be advocated by many writers.[10] This approach is illustrated in Figure 7.1. It advocates using, on each simulation run, the calculated cash flows to compute a net present value or internal rate of return. Repeating the simulation experiment many times then generates a distribution for net present value—or internal rate of return. Summary statistics (mean, variance, measures of skewness, etc.) can then be computed and the results also used in risk profile and even expected utility analysis. From the empirical distribution of *NPV* (or *IRR*), it is possible to construct an estimate of the distribution function and hence a **risk profile**, as in Figure 7.2. The risk profile is derived from the histogram of net present value (drawn in Figure 7.2 as a smooth density function). For example, the probability of getting an *NPV* > 0 (roughly 0.7 in the lower panel) corresponds to the area to the

---

[8] Dobbs (1996) illustrates some applications of these ideas.

[9] See e.g. Clarke and Low (1993).

[10] David Hertz (1964), (1968) has been the most influential proponent of simulation and the risk profile approach to project risk analysis. The approach is discussed in many managerial texts (for example, and at random, Reekie and Crook 1987, McGuigan and Moyer 1993, Pappas and Brigham 1995).

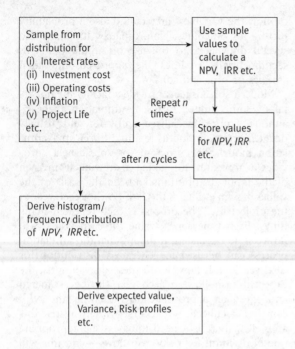

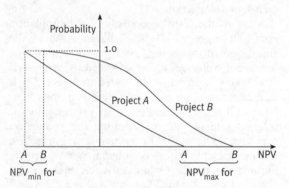

Fig. 7.1 Simulation

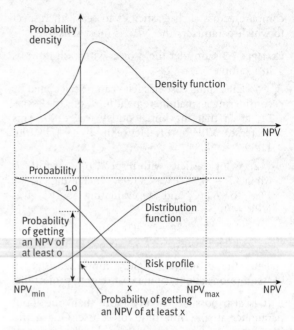

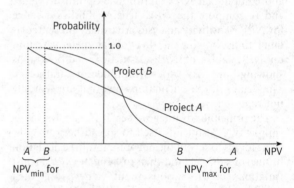

Fig. 7.2 Derivation of a risk profile

Fig. 7.3 A case of dominance

Fig. 7.4 A case with no clear ranking

right of zero under the density function in the upper panel of the Figure (recall that the total area under the density function equals unity).

The risk profile depicts the relationship between *NPV* and the probability that the project will earn at least this level of *NPV*. In principle, such risk profiles can be used to rank projects, as in Figure 7.3, where project *B* clearly dominates project *A* (for any given level of *NPV*, *B* has a higher probability of achieving at least this). However, it may be the case, in choosing between projects, that the risk profiles intersect, as in Figure 7.4. In this case, the risk profile analysis offers no clear-cut decision rule.

It may seem natural to extend the simulation approach to the computation of expected utility, particularly in cases where risk profile analysis does not give any clear-cut decision, as in Figure 7.4. If the decision-maker's utility function has been estimated using the methods of section 4.4, it is straightforward to extend the simulation model to evaluate not only NPV_i on the ith simulation run but also $U(NPV_i)$, the associated utility index. If there are n runs, an estimate of expected utility for the project is simply $\sum_{i=1}^{n} U(NPV_i)/n$. Using the expected utility criterion requires estimating expected utility for each project and choosing the project which has the largest expected utility. The estimated utility function automatically takes into account the way the individual trades off risk against expected return. Unfortunately, whilst this might prove attractive to some decision-makers, the criticisms levelled at a direct application of the expected utility approach, discussed in section 4.6, apply equally here. Essentially, the above forms of project appraisal are piecemeal and neglect the fact that projects form part of a portfolio, and that project-specific risk may not be relevant when viewed in this wider context. This point is addressed in section 7.4 below. This section concludes by briefly reviewing some of the other problems associated with the application of simulation methods.

An important drawback, from the viewpoint of would-be users of the simulation approach, lies in the fact that it tends to be 'black-box'. This means that if the decision-maker has not actually constructed the simulation model personally, it is difficult to know how well the work has been done, or to check whether the model is giving meaningful insights into the nature of the problem. Furthermore, it is difficult to know which of the subjective probability assumptions (and other assumptions) are primarily responsible for the outcomes.[11] It can also be argued that simulation is relatively complex and hence costly to implement. This criticism is weakening, at least for rudimentary forms of simulation modelling using spreadsheets, as more and more managers become comfortable with these forms of software. Furthermore, many projects have a similar structure, such that the modifications in the simulation programming from one problem to the next can be very straightforward.[12] The bottom line on the use of simulation, of course, is that not using probability assessments is throwing away the only information you have. Furthermore, a definite merit of the approach is that it forces the decision-maker to think at least about each of the key variables and the risk involved in each case.

As mentioned earlier, the simulation approach may be used to identify the distribution of cash flows; whether it is appropriate to translate these into distributions for NPV as outlined above is less clear. Brealey and Myers (1991), for example, argue forcefully that the NPV of a project should represent its value in a competitive market (clearly, the project would have a price if sold). The whole motivation for NPV is that it should reflect the value of the stream of (uncertain) cash flows. Hence, they argue, simulation is primarily useful as a method of identifying the distribution of cash flows from which a calculation of expected cash flow is possible (the expected cash flows can then be discounted at an appropriate rate to obtain the net present value of the project). On this view the calculation of NPVs on each run of the simulation process is undesirable (since such NPVs are not market values).

The author has some sympathy with both views, although for rather different reasons, as follows.

1. The Brealey and Myers line is that taken by most texts on corporate finance. The firm can be viewed as a diversified portfolio of projects (and the firm's shareholders also hold diversified portfolios; the share of the firm in their portfolios will also typically be small). A new project can thus be viewed as the addition of a new asset to the firm's portfolio (and hence to those of its owners). Hence it would seem natural to consider how such projects should be valued within the context of the financial market as a whole. This is a logical and coherent view in a world in which the objective of managers is taken to be that of acting in shareholders' interests (i.e. to maximize the value of the firm). This view is discussed in more detail in section 7.4.

2. Risk profile and expected utility analysis (utilizing the simulation approach) appear to have some value when project managers are motivated by personal rewards and job security. Often a manager's performance is evaluated on how the projects actually turn out. That is, the quality of a project is judged by the actual cash flows that have occurred, with the benefit of hindsight. In effect, this is a net present value calculation based on the actual cash flows that resulted. If so, then it would be rational for the project manager to be interested in exploring the distribution of such possible future NPVs. The picture of this distribution of NPVs (or IRRs) gives the decision-maker some feeling for the total risk (arising out of hindsight evaluation of project performance) associated with the project.[13] All of this invites the question whether managers should be

---

[11] Although in principle it is possible to investigate this by undertaking sensitivity analysis with respect to the parameters of the subjective probability distributions.

[12] Although the spreadsheet approach is increasingly being advocated, and this may be appealing for simple projects; see for example Clarke and Low (1993).

[13] It can be argued that the IRR avoids the problem of choosing the appropriate rate at which to discount cash flows in this kind of analysis—but the IRR suffers from a catalogue of defects of its own (see sect. 6.5).

evaluated with the benefit of hindsight. This complex question is explored further in Chapter 29 when we consider agency theory. However, as a matter of practice, given the evaluation procedures widely used, the risk profile methodology may make a lot of sense to decision-makers who have to operate in such far-from-ideal worlds. Indeed, the fact that many consultants have made a tidy living from selling such risk appraisal services, suggests that such analyses are perceived as having value.

7.4 The Asset-Pricing Approach to Risk Analysis

The primary criticism associated with the direct use of expected utility as an approach to decision-making lies in the fact that the firm is in fact a collection of (risky) projects. In attracting investment funds, it has to compete in the market place against alternative risky traded securities. In Chapter 4, it was suggested that managers might well be concerned with total project risk, especially if they are rewarded or evaluated on the basis of *ex post* returns, but that this was not necessarily something about which the firm should be concerned.[14] This section enlarges on this point and argues that, if managers are concerned with maximizing the wealth of shareholders, then the existence of a well-functioning capital market helps to simplify the project evaluation problem.

7.4.1 The Capital Asset Pricing Model

The capital asset pricing model (CAPM) has been (and still is) an influential theory seeking to explain asset prices in terms of the way their returns vary with the return on the overall market. The model can be rigorously derived under various assumption sets; these are all restrictive, albeit in different ways. A typical set of assumptions which enables a simple version of the model to be established is as follows:

1. Investors are risk-averse maximizers of end-of-period utility of wealth.

2. Investors are price-takers who all have the same expectations about asset returns.

3. Returns are normally distributed.

[14] See sect. 4.7 on portfolio effects.

4. There is a risk-free asset on which unlimited amounts can be borrowed/lent.

5. The quantities of assets are fixed, and all are marketed and are continuously divisible.

6. There are no transactions costs and information is costlessly available to all.

7. There are no taxes, regulations, or restrictions on short selling.[15]

More complex versions of the model incorporate transactions costs, taxes, restrictions on short selling, etc. and it is also possible to adopt a more general and intertemporal form of utility function. However, it remains the case that strong assumptions of the type given above also give rise to an appealingly simple form of advice for the appraisal of risky projects, and this is the focus of the present section.[16]

The CAPM is built on portfolio theory (and takes into account the fact that investors hold diversified portfolios and that diversification reduces risk). Space considerations preclude a formal derivation of the model;[17] here I focus on the key prediction of the model, namely that there is a simple linear relationship between the expected return on any traded asset and the covariance between the return on that asset and the return on the market as a whole. If there is a riskless asset offering a risk-free rate of interest R_f, then the CAPM states that

$$E(R_i) = R_f + [E(R_m) - R_f]\beta_i, \qquad (7.1)$$

where R_i denotes the return on the ith asset, R_m the return on the market as a whole, and $E(.)$ denotes the expectation operator; that is, $E(R_i)$ is the expected or 'average' return on the ith asset whilst $E(R_m)$ is the expected return on the market portfolio as a whole. Finally, β_i is defined as

$$\beta_i = (\sigma_{im}/\sigma_m^2), \qquad (7.2)$$

and is referred to as a security's **Beta** coefficient. Think of the term σ_m^2, the variance of the market return, as a fixed constant; the part of the beta

[15] 'Short selling' means selling an asset you do not have; mathematically, it simply means that an individual can have negative holdings of some assets.
[16] Furthermore, although the CAPM has been subject to considerable criticism in respect of its predictions for asset returns, it is arguably still the best available readily operational model for the practical implementation of risk analysis in project appraisal. The evidence is still being debated (see for example Ross *et al.* 1996).
[17] Brealey and Myers (1994) or Ross *et al.* (1996) give a sketch of the main elements. For a more formal derivation, see e.g. Huang and Litzenberger (1988) or Jarrow (1996).

coefficient which varies across assets is σ_{im}, the covariance of the ith asset's return with that of the market. Almost all asset returns are positively correlated with the market return; that is, the covariance is positive. The larger this covariance, the larger the asset's beta will be. Equation (7.1) is the essence of the CAPM; it says that the larger an asset's beta coefficient, the larger the average or expected return that the asset should achieve. The graph of expected return versus beta is referred to as the **security market line** (see Figure 7.5).

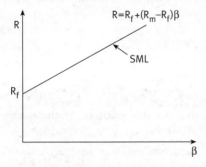

Fig. 7.5 CAPM - the security market line (SML)

The term $E(R_m) - R_f$ is the **market risk premium** (the excess average return on the market as a whole over and above what can be had by investing in a riskless asset[18]). That is, it is what investors expect over and above the risk-free rate by investing in the market portfolio. The beta coefficient, β_i, measures the extent to which the share moves with the market. A beta of zero, for example, means that the asset's return is uncorrelated with that of the market as a whole. Note that the correlation coefficient for the ith asset's return with that of the market, denoted ρ_{im}, is defined as

$$\rho_{im} = \sigma_{im}/(\sigma_i\sigma_m),^{19}$$

so beta can be also be written as

$$\beta_i = \rho_{im}(\sigma_i/\sigma_m).$$

That is, beta depends on the relative riskiness of the asset compared to the market (σ_i/σ_m) and the correlation of its return with the market return, ρ_{im}.

The more highly correlated an asset's return is with that of the market, the higher the expected return investors will require of the share. The CAPM is an equilibrium pricing model: given the covariance σ_{im} (or equivalently, its beta), this defines the expected return which the security should be offering. That is, the only risk that is priced is the one which covaries with the market as a whole.

Empirically, beta is the slope coefficient on a regression of an asset's return on that of the market (something which is extremely straightforward to estimate).[20] This regression can be run for any traded asset, using past observed return data. Sharpe (1964) proposed the appealingly simple OLS regression model,

$$R_{it} = \alpha_i + \beta_i R_{mt} + \varepsilon_{it}, \qquad (7.4)$$

where

R_{it} is the return for asset i in period t,

R_{mt} is the return on the market, and

α_i and β_i are constants associated with the i asset.

The principal drawback to the above approach to beta estimation is that the data are historic (the past is not necessarily a good guide to the future), and it is difficult to get very precise estimates of beta. The nature of the regression is indicated in Figure 7.6.

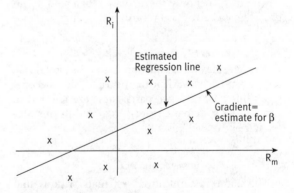

Fig. 7.6 Estimating β

---

[18] If there were no premium, no risk-averse investor would invest in risky assets! For risky assets to exist, they must be priced so that they offer a return which compensates for the systematic risk associated with them.

[19] For a pair of random variables, the correlation coefficient is defined as the covariance divided by the product of their standard deviations.

[20] There is a big issue regarding what the market return actually is. In practice, a proxy for the market is normally used. For example, for the UK market, an equities index such as the FT all share index, or the FT 100, is often used.

Considerable research has been undertaken on the CAPM prediction regarding asset returns being correlated with their beta coefficients, and the issue of whether beta is alive or dead is very much both a theoretical and empirically active question. The debate matters, since, if anything, the CAPM is the cornerstone of much practical financial policy. In practice there are undoubtedly other factors which help to explain expected returns (firm size, financial leverage, and other financial ratios such as book-to-market equity); see Ross *et al.* (1996) for further discussion of this issue.

7.4.2 Systematic and Unsystematic Risk in the CAPM

Having estimated each security's beta, it is straight-forward to calculate the beta of any portfolio of such assets. The beta of a portfolio is simply the value-weighted average of the betas of the individual assets:[21]

$$\beta_p = \sum_{i=1}^{n} w_i \beta_i. \tag{7.5}$$

The CAPM establishes the expected return on an asset. The actual return (i.e. return actually observed) may be written as expected return plus 'noise':

$$R_i^a = R_f + (R_m - R_f)\beta_i + \varepsilon_i, \tag{7.6}$$

where R_i^a denotes the actual return and ε_i an unsystematic error with zero mean and variance $\sigma_{\varepsilon_i}^2$. It follows that[22]

$$\sigma_i^2 = \beta_i^2 \sigma_m^2 + \sigma_{\varepsilon_i}^2. \tag{7.7}$$

The left side of this equation is an asset's **total risk** (as measured by variance); the right side decomposes this total into two parts: these are referred to as an asset's **systematic risk** ($\beta_i^2 \sigma_m^2$) and its **unsystematic risk** ($\sigma_{\varepsilon_i}^2$). Thus

Asset total risk = Asset systematic risk

+ Asset unsystematic risk (7.8)

The names are intuitive: systematic risk is that part of an asset's total return variance that is corre-

lated with the market return (note that it is zero if beta is zero); unsystematic risk is that part of the asset's total return variance which is uncorrelated with the market return, that is, variability that is peculiar to the asset itself. The idea is that macro-economic forces may move prices generally, which tends to give rise to systematic risk—whilst firm-specific factors (such as the CEO dying, or a new product discovery) lead to price movements which are uncorrelated with the market and show up as unsystematic risk.

The same equation, (7.7), holds for any portfolio of assets p:

$$\sigma_p^2 = \beta_p^2 \sigma_m^2 + \sigma_{\varepsilon_p}^2. \tag{7.9}$$

Suppose we create a portfolio of N assets with a value proportion $1/N$ in each asset: the portfolio beta is then given as

$$\beta_p = \sum_{i=1}^{N} w_i \beta_i = \sum_{i=1}^{N} (1/N)\beta_i = (\sum_{i=1}^{N} \beta_i)/N. \tag{7.10}$$

Thus β_p, the portfolio beta, tends to the average of the asset betas. Hence

Fact 7.1 Diversification leads to an averaging of systematic risk.

Let me re-emphasize this important point: the systematic risk associated with an asset is that associated with movements in the market as a whole (hence it is also referred to as 'market risk'), whilst the unsystematic risk is that which is independent of the market as a whole (i.e. it is unique to the firm; hence it is sometimes referred to as 'unique risk'). The unsystematic risk is $\sigma_{\varepsilon_p}^2$, where $\varepsilon_p = \sum_{i=1}^{N} (1/N)\varepsilon_i$. So

$$\sigma_{\varepsilon_p}^2 = \sum_{i=1}^{N} (1/N)^2 \sigma_{\varepsilon_i}^2 = (1/N)(\sum_{i=1}^{N} \sigma_{\varepsilon_i}^2/N), \tag{7.11}$$

where the second term on the right side is the average unsystematic risk. As N increases, this second term tends to a (finite) constant, but this is multiplied by $1/N$, so

$$\sigma_{\varepsilon_p}^2 \to 0 \text{ as } N \to \infty. \tag{7.12}$$

That is,

Fact 7.2 Diversification reduces unsystematic risk to (near) zero.

Notice that, if an investor holds a portfolio which is proportional to the overall market portfolio, then $\beta_p = 1$ and the total risk is reduced to σ_m^2, the market risk.

The above analysis provides the key to under-standing the CAPM. The essential insight in finance is that there is a trade-off between risk and return. Investors are risk-averse, and will only hold a riskier

---

[21] This follows from the definition of beta and the fact that, if a, b, and c are random variables, then $COV(a + b, c) = COV(a, c) + COV(b, c)$.

[22] Recall that, if a, b, c are constants and X, Y are independent random variables, then $Var(a + bX + cY) = b^2 Var(X) + c^2 Var(Y)$. Thus, since R_f and β_i are constants, and R_M and ε_i are independent, it follows that

$$Var(R_i) = Var[R_f + (R_M - R_f)\beta_i + \varepsilon_i]$$
$$= \beta_i^2 Var(R_M) + Var(\varepsilon_i),$$

or, in the usual notation, $\sigma_i^2 = \beta_i^2 \sigma_M^2 + \sigma_{\varepsilon_i}^2$.

asset if it offers a greater return. Hence, in equilibrium, a riskier asset must offer a higher return. However, what is the risk that counts? Essentially, because individual investors hold diversified portfolios, they diversify away the unsystematic risk associated with assets—hence this kind of risk is of no concern to them, and it is not priced in the market. By contrast, systematic risk cannot be diversified away and hence is of concern to investors—accordingly systematic risk *is* priced in the market; the higher the systematic risk (the more an asset return is correlated with the market return) the higher the average or expected return that asset will offer, as illustrated in Figure 7.5.

7.4.3 CAPM and Investment Appraisal

The firm's debt and equity are traded assets and hence have betas (in the UK, company debt is often not traded, but it is in principle possible to guesstimate the debt beta). Given equity and debt betas, the weighted average of these gives the beta for the firm as a whole, and the CAPM can then be used to compute the expected return for the firm (its *WACC*). However, the question arises as to whether the *WACC* is the appropriate rate to use as a discount rate for evaluating projects. In the CAPM framework, the *WACC* is all right as a discount rate if the project has similar beta risk to that of the firm as a whole—but if the project beta is significantly different from the firm's beta, then this is no longer the case. According to the CAPM, the correct discount rate is

$$R_{project} = R_f + (R_m - R_f)\beta_{project}. \qquad (7.13)$$

In practice, firms often do use a **risk-adjusted discount rate** to evaluate risky projects. Usually, some *ad hoc* adjustment to the discount rate is used. Equation (7.13) suggests a way of deciding how much of an increase in discount rate is appropriate. However, there remains the difficult problem of estimating $\beta_{project}$. (Probably the best one can do is to classify it broadly as low, medium, or high.[23]) The usefulness of the CAPM perspective is that it suggests the firm should be concerned with systematic rather than total risk. Figure 7.7 contrasts the use of the *WACC* with the recommended discount rate implied by the CAPM. According to the CAPM, if the firm uses a constant *WACC* discount rate to appraise projects, rather than varying the discount

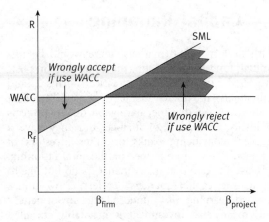

Fig. 7.7 CAPM and the discount rate

rate according to the projects' expected beta risk, it will make two kinds of mistakes. First, it will tend to accept too many high-beta-risk projects; second, it will reject too many low-beta-risk projects.

EXAMPLE 7.4 Suppose the risk-free rate is 5% and the market premium is 4%. Then the appropriate discount rate might vary as follows:

1. Cost-reducing projects: here the project returns may be completely independent of market movements; accordingly set $\beta_{project} = 0$ and use 5% as the discount rate.

2. Projects in the firm's usual line of business: suppose $\beta_{firm} = 0.9$ (note that this is computed by estimating debt and equity betas and forming a value weighted average); then the appropriate discount rate is $5 + (0.9 \times 4) = 8.6\%$.

3. Speculative projects whose success may depend on general market conditions: if project beta was guesstimated at, say, 3, then the discount rate would be $5 + (3 \times 4) = 17\%$.

The key point to understand from the above example is that quite different discount rates can be justified, depending upon the procedure for estimating the systematic risk (beta) of the project.

The CAPM perspective is highly logical, but it does assume that the object of managers is to run the firm in the interest of the shareholders. In practice, managers are more likely to be concerned with a project's total risk, especially if they are evaluated on the basis of actual returns. Thus a manager may be inclined to reject some projects that shareholders would like accepted, and accept some they would prefer not to be undertaken.

---

[23] Dobbs (1996) provides a simple illustration of this kind of pragmatic approach to the use of CAPM (in the context of a study of payback thresholds).

7.5 Capital Rationing

With perfect capital markets, there would be un-limited funds available for the financing of posi-tive-NPV projects. In practice firms (and individuals) often face financing constraints. That is, they may feel that they have good-quality projects to justify the supply of finance, but they have a problem convincing banks or other investors of this fact. This is often termed **hard capital rationing**. It is also the case that many managers do not like to go to the capital markets, preferring to utilize retained earning for undertaking investment.[24] This means that investment is inevitably curtailed by earnings currently available. Furthermore, most project managers are required to operate under investment budget constraints. That is, there is a limit to the amount of investment finance that an individual project manager can commit in a given period. These limits are imposed for control pur-poses, of course, and it can be claimed that they also motivate managers to assign priorities to their investment plans. This is often referred to as **soft capital rationing**.

In **hard capital rationing**, financial markets ration investment funds given to a firm by price (i.e. the interest rate or return that has to be paid). As a firm tries to raise more finance (through issues of equity or debt stock), the price required by the market may rise (perhaps because outside investors perceive there is an increasing risk associated with the company expanding its investment programme). This idea, that the cost of capital may vary as the volume of investment varies, does not create any conceptual problem; the problem is simply to deter-mine the firm's cost of capital at its current level of investment.[25]

Internal or soft capital rationing is widespread. It occurs whenever management imposes investment budgets independently of the ability of the firm to raise additional capital. There are at least two reasons for this:

1. For control purposes. If there is a scarcity of managerial talent within the firm (capable of overseeing the implementation of the new pro-jects), it may be important to restrain the volume of investment such that it is appropriate when account is taken of such skill shortages (naturally, this is a short-run argument; in the long run, such shortages should theoretically be remedied by an appropriate personnel recruitment policy).

2. To stimulate the search for new and higher-yielding project opportunities. Restraining invest-ment may serve to free scarce managerial talent for the quest for higher-yielding projects (rather than letting project managers get bogged down in acceptable but marginal investment projects which add little value).

Capital rationing may be for the present period, or may hold over several periods. These are consid-ered in turn below.

7.5.1 Single-Period Capital Rationing

Essentially, if there are no constraints on investment funds for projects, the problem for each project is simply whether to accept it or not, and the NPV criterion seems to be satisfactory for this purpose. However, with an investment budget constraint, there is a need to economize on the finance required per project. The net benefit–cost ratio (NBCR), or the benefit–cost ratio (BCR), give a measure of pre-sent value generated per pound of investment funds. Clearly then, more NPV will be tend to be generated in total if projects are selected in order of their NBCR until the budget is exhausted. Indeed, we can state this as

Fact 7.3 Assuming the budget is insufficient to undertake all positive-NPV projects, then

(i) if projects are infinitely divisible, and

(ii) if reducing the investment outlay in an individual project from a maximum of 100% reduces each of the future cash flows pro rata, and

(iii) if there is a single initial period when projects must be activated (if at all), and

(iv) if total project capital outlays must not exceed a given level,

then total NPV is maximized by undertaking projects in rank order according to NBCR until funds are exhausted.[26]

---

[24] Although it can be argued that using retained earnings is rational because it avoids issue costs etc., probably more cogent reasons for its use lies with the fact that it avoids external scrutiny and monitoring of the firm. To gain external finance, the firm has to convince external agencies (banks, investors) that the use of the funds is sound.

[25] The extreme form of hard capital rationing is where the firm is unable to raise finance at any price. This is fairly rare in practice, and is if anything a very short-run phenomenon (for example, when the firm is clearly going bankrupt).

[26] It can be argued that budget constraints have implications for the appropriate discount rate to be used. This is ignored here; it is simply assumed that NPV is calculated according to the principles discussed in sect. 7.4, where differences in risk are taken into account by using different values for the discount rate.

Notice that there are a lot of ifs here. Point (iii) is relaxed in section 7.6. Points (i) and (ii) are also significant. This approach to project selection when there is a budget constraint is theoretically inappropriate if projects can be increased in size—or are of a fixed size; in the first case it is clearly optimal to select the project with the highest *NBCR*, and expand it to the point where it exhausts the budget. By contrast, in the case where projects are of fixed size (often the most realistic case), it is really just a matter of examining all the possible collections of projects which satisfy the budget constraint, and selecting the collection which generates the largest total *NPV*. This case is worth spelling out a little more carefully:

Fact 7.4 Assuming the budget is insufficient to undertake all positive-*NPV* projects, then

(i) if projects are of fixed size, and

(ii) if there is a single initial period when projects must be activated (if at all), and

(iii) if total project capital outlays must not exceed a given level,

then the procedure involves first defining all possible collections of projects which satisfy the budget constraint; the optimal collection is then simply that which has maximum total *NPV*.

These procedures are illustrated in Example 7.5.

EXAMPLE 7.5. Optimal choice if budget = 1000 (£m)

Table 7.1 Projects

Project	Capital outlay K (£m)	NPV (£m)	NBCR = NPV/K
A	500	500	1.0
B	400	360	0.9
C	300	261	0.87
D	200	160	0.8
E	400	280	0.7
F	200	120	0.6
G	100	40	0.4

If projects can be downsized but not increased in scale, the solution is to choose $A + B + 1/3C$, giving total *NPV* of £947 (i.e. selecting projects in order of *NBCR*). Of course this assumes linearity: 1/3 of the investment in *C* yielding 1/3 of its original *NPV*. This will often not be a realistic assumption. Alternatively, if projects can be scaled up such that costs and benefits, and hence *NPV*, increase linearly, the optimal solution is to undertake 2 *A* projects, with total $NPV = 2 \times 500 = £1000$. Again, this is often not realistic. In many

cases it may be better to think of the projects as having a fixed size. In this case, following Fact 7.4, we consider all collections of projects which satisfy the budget constraint:

Projects selected:

	AB	ABG	ACD	BCDG	BDE	AEG	BEF	CDEG
∑*NPV*	860	900	921	821	800	820	760	741

Thus the optimal choice of fixed-size projects is to undertake $A + C + D$, with total *NPV* = 921.

The above analysis is only appropriate if there is a single budget constraint. In practice, if there is a constraint on investment funds in the current period, there is usually one in future periods too. The procedures discussed above no longer apply in this scenario. It is possible to extend the approach, however, through the use of linear programming. Furthermore, one can include the possibility that projects may also be deferred to future periods within a more sophisticated optimization structure. The major issues in setting up such an optimization problem are

(i) whether projects are divisible, or are of fixed size;

(ii) whether the cash flows generated by projects activated earlier can be utilized for investment purposes in later periods (often firms distinguish between operating cash flows and capital expenditure, so the contribution of operating cash flow to relaxing future investment budget constraints is not allowed).

7.5.2 Multi-Period Capital Rationing

This case is more realistic, since it recognizes that, if management impose budget constraints on investment at all, they will typically continue to do so over time. The problem in this case is that the firm may be able to scale or defer projects, and also use the cash flows from projects to alleviate the budget constraints in future periods. Formally, a programming approach is required, although the information requirement to implement such an approach is formidable and the technique is not widely used in practice. For further details see Lumby (1988: chap. 7), Trivol and McDaniel (1987), and, for an excellent assessment of the value of this approach, Weingartner (1977).

The assumptions are quite demanding; apart from the usual assumption that the discount rate is fixed over the future horizon (this can be relaxed to some extent), there is a substantial amount of information required to implement the approach (which may not be available) and, furthermore, some of the assumptions are unlikely to hold except very approximately; the most significant assumptions are that

1. there is a known set of projects, each with known future cash flows, and, given a known discount rate for valuing future cash flows, each project's NPV is known;

2. the cash flows of each project depend only on the time at which it is implemented; if a project is deferred one period, then this has the simple consequence of deferring its cash flows by one period at all points in the project's life;

3. the budget constraints on investment funds in each period are known at time 0 with certainty, and do not change as time evolves.

To illustrate the programming approach, let x_i, $i = 1, \ldots, n$ indicate the proportion of project i undertaken, NPV_i the NPV of the fully implemented ith project, π_{it} the cash flow for the ith project in time period t, and I_i the investment funds available in time period t. The linear programming problem can be written as

$$\text{Maximize } \sum_{i=1}^{n} NPV_i x_i \qquad (7.14)$$

subject to

$$\sum_{i=1}^{n} x_i \pi_{it} \leq I_t \quad t = 1, 2, \ldots \qquad (7.15)$$

$$0 \leq x_i \leq 1 \quad i = 1, \ldots, n. \qquad (7.16)$$

Before giving a simple example of this type of problem, the assumptions which underpin this formulation are worthy of further consideration. First, note that the choice variables are x_i, $i = 1, \ldots, n$; the other variables are simply assigned numerical values for a given problem. A linear programming formulation of this sort assumes that the x_is are continuous; hence there is the assumption that projects can be downsized (such that all cash flows are downsized pro rata). If some or all of the projects are better viewed as having a fixed size, then this would necessitate a more complex integer-programming approach. Secondly, it is assumed that projects are activated, if at all, at time 0. In practice it may be possible to defer investment; a project not activated at time period 0 may be activated at time period 1, and so on. The program would need to be adjusted to allow that projects can start at different points in time. Thirdly, it is assumed that cash flows relieve the budget constraints. Again,

it is possible to revise the analysis to exclude the possibility of operating cash flows relaxing a capital expenditure budget constraint.

The following example makes use of the graphical approach to analysing simple linear programming problems discussed in Chapter 3. The drawback of the graphical approach here is that it can only illustrate the principles in a rather stylized example (a consideration of two-period budget constraints, and a choice of only two projects). However, this should suffice to indicate how the approach can be generalized to much more complex problems (involving the possibility of projects being deferred, and also being of discrete size; standard linear programming software exists which can deal with large-scale problems of this type).

EXAMPLE 7.6

Table 7.2 Project Data

Project	NPV	Project outlays at	
		time 0	time 1
1	100	−50	−200
2	500	−200	−50
Budget constraints		100	100

The programming problem becomes

$$\text{Maximize } z = 100x_1 + 500x_2 \qquad (i)$$

subject to

$$50x_1 + 200x_2 \leq 100, \qquad (ii)$$

$$200x_1 + 50x_2 \leq 100, \qquad (iii)$$

$$0 \leq x_1 \leq 1, \qquad (iv)$$

and

$$0 \leq x_2 \leq 1. \qquad (v)$$

The reader is referred to section 3.6 for an exposition of how to construct the constraint set and the optimal solution for this problem. The constraints are depicted in figure 7.8 (not to scale) and the feasible set is shaded. Making x_2 the subject of equation (i) gives

$$x_2 = (z/500) - 0.2x_1. \qquad (vi)$$

For a fixed value of the objective function z, this is a line with negative slope and gradient -0.2. The higher up the line, the larger the value for z. Hence it is clear that the optimal solution occurs at the point where $x_2 = 1$, $x_1 = 0$ when the solution is simply to implement 50% of project 2.

A sensitivity analysis is revealing; suppose instead of NPVs of 100 and 500, we keep these as variables, and simply write them as NPV_1 and NPV_2. Then instead of (vi) we get

$$x_2 = (z/NPV_2) - (NPV_1/NPV_2)x_1. \qquad \text{(vii)}$$

Hence the gradient of the objective function level curve depends on the NPVs. As the gradient of constraint (ii) is $-1/4$ and that of (iii) is -4, it should be clear that the solution will change as follows:

If $NPV_1 < 0.25\ NPV_2$, choose to do 50% of project 2 (and none of project 1);

If $0.25\ NPV_2 < NPV_1 < 4 \times NPV_2$, then do 2/5 of each project;

If $NPV_1 > 4 \times NPV_2$, choose to do 50% of project 1 (and none of project 0).

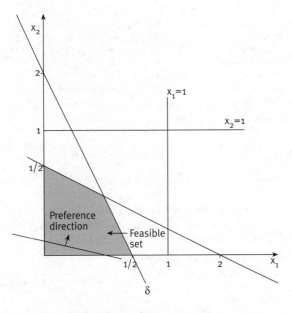

Fig. 7.8 Capital rationing

7.6 Economic Life, Deferment, and Abandonment Decisions

Much of the discussion of project appraisal so far presumes that the project must be implemented immediately, and that it has a fixed life. In practice, many projects have a long shelf life; that is, if they are not activated today, they can be activated next year or later. It is also often the case that the project

life is open; the project continues until a point is reached where it is no longer adding value, at which point it is abandoned. This section introduces some important ideas regarding the valuation of projects when the point of project termination can be chosen (section 7.6.1) and when it is possible to defer the start of a project (section 7.6.2).

7.6.1 Project Economic Life: The Abandonment Decision

If there is no learning or revision in expectations regarding future cash flows as time progresses, then the project life can be determined at the outset, and there will be no reason for this economic life to be revised as time progresses (the 'no-learning case' below). This should be contrasted with projects which involve change and revision to future expected cash flows as time progresses (the 'learning case'). For example, optimal abandonment of a coal mine depends upon the level and volatility of the price of coal. In this case, the choice of termination or temporary shutdown has to take into account the fact that future prices might rise again or, indeed, fall further.

(a) The No-Learning' Case

Suppose a single isolated project generates estimated cash flows $\{\pi_t;\ t = 0, 1, 2, \ldots \}$, where π_0 denotes the initial capital outlay. If the project is terminated at time T there will typically be a further cash flow S_t which arises (this could be positive or negative; positive for scrap or resale value, negative if, as in the case of mining, there are termination costs such as making good the site). Thus the net present value of keeping the project for T years, denoted $NPV(T)$, is given as

$$NPV(T) = \sum_{t=0}^{T} \frac{\pi_t}{(1 + r)^t} + \frac{S_t}{(1 + r)^T}. \qquad (7.17)$$

Optimal economic life can be determined by evaluating NPV for each value of T, and then simply choosing the value of T which gives a maximum value for this (the calculation is illustrated in Example 7.6 below).

A more complex case occurs if the project involves a replacement chain. For example, in forestry, harvesting a crop is normally followed by seeding a new crop. Thus, the longer the present crop is allowed to grow, the longer this defers future harvests. The same point applies to much equipment replacement (plant and machinery, cars, buses, lorries, etc.). In this case, the longer the equipment is made to last, the longer this defers the costs associated with future equipment purchases. The usual assumption for the replacement case is that the project, when replaced, is replaced by an identical project. Furthermore, whatever the optimal economic life of a single project, all future projects will also have this same economic life (since they have an identical set of cash flows).[27] Given this assumption, the cash flow looks as follows:

Time: 0   T   2T   3T   etc.
       NPV(T) NPV(T) NPV(T)   NPV(T)   etc.

Here, we have present-valued the individual cash flows involved in each individual project; this is denoted $NPV(T)$, indicating that the present value depends on how long the project is kept running, T. Thus $NPV(T)$ replaces the individual project cash flows for the first project (at time 0) whilst the cash flows for the next project are present-valued back to time T, the next project to time $2T$, and so on.

Let V denote the overall present value (at time 0) of the stream of cash flows associated with the replacement chain. Then it can be shown that this present value is given by the formula[28]

$$V = \frac{NPV(T)}{[1 - (1 + r)^{-T}]}. \quad (7.18)$$

The problem of determining optimal economic life for projects when there is a chain becomes one of evaluating for alternative values for T, in order to find the value which maximizes V. Example 7.6 illustrates the effect of changing the assumption that the project is a one-off to that where the project

is viewed as one in a chain; in the latter case, the economic life tends to be shorter.

EXAMPLE 7.6 A project involves the installation of a new drug manufacturing process. The initial investment cost is 15 (thousand pounds) new and the project has annual operating costs (labour, power, maintenance and repairs) which tend to rise with age. At the same time the resale value of the equipment falls. Total revenues from the sale of product are likely to be 10 (thousand pounds) in the first year. All cash flows are already adjusted to real terms, and the real interest rate is 5%, constant over time.

Table 7.3 Cash flow involving a replacement chain

	Time								
	0	1	2	3	4	5	6	7	8
Revenue		10	10	10	10	10	10	10	10
Operating costs		3	3	3	4	5	7	10	13
Operating profit		7	7	7	6	5	3	0	−3
Resale value	15	10	7	5	3	2	2	2	2

To illustrate the calculation involved: for $t = 3$, we have

$$NPV(3) = -15 + \frac{7}{1.05} + \frac{7}{1.05^2} + \frac{7+5}{1.05^3} = 8.38$$

and

$$V = \frac{8.38}{1 - 1.05^{-3}} = 61.56.$$

Tabulating these results gives the following: (note that this kind of table is easy to construct using the financial functions in EXCEL or LOTUS):

Table 7.4 Results for example 7.6

	T						
	2	3	4	5	6	7	8
NPV	4.37	8.38	11.47	14.48	16.65	15.87	13.10
V	46.95	61.56	64.68	66.91	65.60	54.84	40.51

Thus the optimal economic life is 6 years for a single plant, but only 5 years for a plant when there is a need for periodic replacement.

An interesting feature of the analysis conducted in Example 7.6 is that it also quantifies the cost of choosing a sub-optimal economic life. For example, a firm may choose to replace its car fleet every 2 years even though the optimal economic life is, say, 4

---

[27] Thus, for example, if fleet cars are replaced every 3 years, the assumption is that this policy continues into the future. The assumption turns out to be reasonably robust, so long as it is fairly true for the next plant in the chain (the present-value contribution of later plants being relatively small, changes in policy later on do not typically alter significantly the optimal economic life for the first plant).

[28] To see this, note that

$$V = NPV + \frac{NPV}{(1 + r)^T} + \frac{NPV}{(1 + r)^{2T}} + \frac{NPV}{(1 + r)^{3T}} + \cdots$$

Subtract NPV from both sides and multiply by the factor $(1 + r)^T$. This gives

$$(V - NPV)(1 + r)^T = NPV + \frac{NPV}{(1 + r)^T} + \frac{NPV}{(1 + r)^{2T}} + \cdots$$

The right side is simply V of course. Hence

$$(V - NPV)(1 + r)^T = V.$$

Rearranging this gives equation (7.18).

years. The difference in present values as between these two policies (2-year versus 4-year replacement policy) indicates the cost of projecting a more up-market image.

(b) The Learning Case

The optimal decision on abandonment is much more complex when the cash flows are uncertain and evolving through time in a way which means that the forecast of a price at time t improves the closer to t one gets. This is the case, for example, with a coal mine when the price of coal is volatile (and with many other types of mining, but also with any project in which prices are stochastic). In such a case, the decision to abandon has to take into account the possibility that price might rise in the future (so making the mine viable again). The problem is that, once the mine is abandoned, if prices rise in the future, the firm will have to incur the full set-up costs to restart production. Hence it is worth continuing with a mine even when prices are such as to make it unprofitable period by period, in order to take advantage of future possible price increases. Of course, if prices continue to fall, there will come a point beyond which it is sensible to abandon the project. The key point is that it is not necessarily optimal to abandon simply when operating profits turn negative. I omit detailed analysis of this case, as the analysis is rather complex, although section 7.6.2 explores the notion of option value a little further (for the case of project deferment). The interested reader is referred to Dixit and Pindyck (1994) for a detailed discussion of the issues that arise.

7.6.2 Project Deferment

The option to abandon a project has parallels in the option to defer implementation. To illustrate, suppose a firm has a design patent, the implementation of which requires an outlay of £10 million but yields a riskless return in one year's time of £11 million. The net present-value of this project is calculated for various interest rates in Table 7.5.

Suppose the current rate of interest is 9.99999% and hence the project has $NPV = £1$. This would normally be an indication that the project should be implemented: although it involves £10 million outlay it has positive NPV, and in Chapter 6 we saw that, so long as the money could be borrowed at the specified interest rate, the project should be implemented if it has positive NPV. But is this a correct valuation of the project if it is possible to defer

Table 7.5 Effect of change in interest rate on project NPV

Interest rate	Net present value
9%	+£91,740
9.99999%	+£1
10%	£0
11%	−£90,090

implementation? Or, to put it another way, would you be willing to sell the patent for any sum of money so long as it was greater than £1? The answer is a resounding 'not at all'! The value of the project is £1 only if the project must be implemented at once or not at all. If it is possible to defer the starting date, then if there is any volatility associated with interest rates, the value of having the right to implement the project is not given by the simple NPV calculation— and the value is likely to be considerably greater.

For concreteness, let us suppose the project has a shelf life of exactly one year. That is, if it is not implemented now, it must be implemented in exactly one year's time. Furthermore, let us suppose that whilst the current one-year interest rate is 9.99999%, next year's one-year interest rate is volatile, such that it might be 9%, 10%, or 11% in a year's time, with each outcome being equally likely. How much is it worth paying for the patent rights? Well, anyone purchasing this project will *not* choose to implement it immediately (even though it currently has positive NPV); if they are rational, they will wait until the next and final period. The value at this future point in time will be one of the values in the above table. If the interest rate goes to 9 or 10%, they will implement it, whilst if it increases to 11%, then they will let the option to implement lapse (giving a return of £0). The chance of each interest rate occurring is in 1/3 each case, so the expected return is thus

$$(1/3) \times £0 + (1/3) \times £0 + (1/3) \times £91,740 = £30,580.$$

This is a risky cash flow, and so would normally need to be discounted at an appropriate risky discount rate. However, using 10% will give some idea of the value of the option at time zero; discounting at 10% gives £30,580/1.1 = £27,800. Thus I would be willing to pay up to around £27,800 to buy the patent.[29] The patent is clearly much more valuable than the £1 originally indicated by the NPV criterion.

---

[29] Changing the discount rate, to reflect this being a risky cash flow, makes little difference to the NPV; try conducting a sensitivity analysis.

With multiple periods, or in continuous time, the analysis is much more complex. This is because the decision to implement has to take into account the fact that it renounces the option to defer to even later, when an even lower interest rate might occur. Increasing the time over which an option can be exercised tends to add value. The general point behind option value should now be clear: *NPV* underestimates the value of the project when it can be deferred, and the magnitude of the undervaluation can be substantial. The extra value added, over and above the simple calculation of value by *NPV*, is termed **option value**.

Unfortunately there is no simple decision rule for the general case of project appraisal when it is possible to defer implementation, although simulation model building can be used to explore the value of this option for particular applications (see e.g. Ingersoll and Ross 1983). It is possible to establish simple rules in simple cases, however. Ross (1995), for example, reports a rule of thumb for projects which involve an initial cash outlay in order to obtain a single cash flow at some future time *T*. If the internal rate of return for the project is denoted *IRR*, then the project should be undertaken only when the interest rate falls below the threshold rate r^*, defined by

$$r^* = IRR - (\sigma/\sqrt{2}), \qquad (7.19)$$

where $\sigma^2 r$ is the variance of the interest rate at level r (that is, the model assumes that variance of the interest rate is proportionate to its level). Thus the project is not activated just as the interest rate falls below the *IRR* (as conventional theory would indicate); it needs to fall further, by an amount which depends on the interest rate volatility. This is because project initiation forecloses the option to wait for an even more advantageously low interest rate in the future. The larger the volatility, the greater the chance of getting this lower rate at some time in the future and so the tougher the rule becomes. To put this another way, using the *NPV* criterion, the decision criterion is to wait to invest until the market rate of interest r is such that the project has a positive *NPV* at the discount rate

$$r^* + (\sigma/\sqrt{2}).$$

Since σ can be large relative to r, the discount rate can be considerably in excess of that conventionally used to evaluate projects.[30]

---

[30] Interestingly, the rule is independent of project duration, *T*, except in so far as the interest rate *r* chosen should be the spot rate holding over the same interval, $[0, T]$.

More realistic projects involve more complex cash flow profiles than the single-cash outflow, single-cash inflow example discussed above. However, in the absence of detailed modelling, it may be reasonable to adopt the above rule of thumb *faute de mieux*. (Certainly, a higher discount rate is appropriate, and the above analysis at least gives some idea of how high it should be.)

EXAMPLE 7.7 Suppose the one-year treasury bill rate is 6.64% whilst σ is estimated at 5% (typical values in practice). It thus follows that the discount rate is $0.0664 + (0.05/\sqrt{2}) = 0.0664 + 0.0353 = 0.102$ or 10.2%. That is, a project is worth implementing immediately if it has positive *NPV* at 10.2%; if not, the project must be deferred. For example, a project which has an *IRR* of 9% will not be implemented until the interest rate falls to $0.09 - 0.0353 = 0.0547$ or 5.47%.

The above analysis of project-deferral option value can be viewed as rationalizing the observation that managers in practice do often use quite high hurdle rates in evaluating projects (the other major reason being the imposition of soft capital rationing, discussed in section 7.5).

7.7 Summary

This chapter has covered a wide range of material; it began with section 7.2 in setting out how to calculate a firm's cost of capital, the discount rate for use in project evaluation, when the project is of a type similar to the firm's normal line of business. In section 7.3, some methods of taking account of risk were examined; it was argued that sensitivity analysis is easy to do, easy to understand, and easy to communicate to non-specialist managers in the firm, and hence is likely to be a useful form of analysis. Simulation, risk profile analysis, and expected utility were briefly considered; it was shown that they cannot easily be justified at the theoretical level, when project selection is supposed to contribute to the goal of value maximization although it may give some insight and have some value at the pragmatic level. Section 7.4 dealt with the asset pricing approach to project appraisal; this suggested that only a project's systematic risk really matters, and that the higher this is, the higher the risk-adjusted discount rate should be. Again, it was pointed out that this focus on systematic rather than total risk makes sense as policy advice when the concern is with value maximization. In practice, project managers may well be concerned about total project risk (since adverse project performance might adversely affect their job prospects and pay). Section 7.5 dealt with capital rationing and discussed some ideas that might prove useful in particular contexts, including the use of linear programming models for project selection. Finally, section 7.6 dealt with the question of when to terminate a project, and when to implement it. The major issue in the latter case was that implementation takes away the option to implement at a later stage (say, when interest rates are more favourable). It was shown that the possibility of project deferral, when interest rates are volatile (which they are), revises the present-value rule significantly: The analysis suggested that if there is an option to defer, the project has to offer a significantly higher rate of return than the current market rate of interest if it is to be activated immediately.

7.8 Review Questions

1. Reproduce the sensitivity analysis of the project discussed in examples 7.2 and 7.3 using EXCEL. Further to this, tabulate *NPV* for alternative values of project life and interest rates, and produce charts depicting the sensitivity of *NPV* to these variables.

2. The asset pricing approach to project appraisal suggests that only systematic risk really matters, and that the discount rate should be adjusted to reflect this.

   (*a*) How might you try to assess the beta of a project?

   (*b*) To what extent do you think that this approach, using the risk-adjusted discount rate, is valid? (List arguments in favour and arguments against.)

3. Consider the following problem of capital rationing.

   Assume that projects can be reduced in scale (in which case their outlays and future cash flows are

Table 7.6 Problem of capital rationing

| Project | NPV | Project outlay at | |
		time 0	time 1
1	100	−60	−70
2	130	−90	−60
Budget constraints		100	60

scaled down equally). Set up and solve this problem of project selection as a linear program. How sensitive is the solution to the value of project 2's *NPV*? (How does the solution change as the value for this *NPV* is changed?)

4. Set up the optimal economic life problem analysed in Example 7.6 as an EXCEL spreadsheet, i.e. explore how optimal economic life varies with the discount rate (set up a table in which the value function is tabulated against alternative economic life values and alternative interest rate values). Do this for both the case where the project is a one-off and the case where there is a replacement chain. Compare and contrast your results for the two cases.

7.9 Further Reading

It is hard to find satisfactory reading material on sensitivity analysis. The asset pricing approach to project appraisal is discussed in all of the intermediate texts in corporate finance (e.g. Brealey and Myers 1996 or Ross *et al.* 1996). Lewellen and Long (1972), Myers (1976), and Brealey and Myers (1996) put forward critiques of Hertz's (1968) risk profile analysis (Myers 1976 discusses some of Hertz's defences against these critiques). Ross (1993) and Ingersoll and Ross (1986) discuss the issue of project deferral in a reasonably elementary way. Dixit and Pindyck (1994) is a whole text wholly devoted to the options pricing (and related) approaches to investment decision analysis (deferral, temporary shutdown, mothballing, and abandonment decisions).

Part III

Demand and Cost Analysis

Part III deals with the information inputs of importance to a firm when it is concerned with developing its marketing (pricing, advertizing, etc.) and investment strategies. Chapter 8 presents the traditional neo-classical consumer theory, along with some interesting and useful extensions (such as the characteristics approach), and follows this with a coverage of demand analysis (the relationship between price, revenue and elasticity, etc.). Chapter 9 follows this by considering how it is possible to estimate demand functions (with a fairly extended discussion of the potential role which econometrics can play). This is followed by a parallel approach on the cost side: Chapter 10 deals with the traditional neo-classical theory of production and cost; Chapter 11 considers how it is possible to estimate cost functions (again with some emphasis on the potential use of econometrics). Chapter 12 finishes off this part by focusing on practical short-run revenue and cost analysis, with an extended case study designed to illustrate how the concepts of incremental and opportunity cost can prove helpful in such analysis.

8 Consumer Theory and Demand Analysis

Objectives This Chapter gives a practical introduction to demand analysis and the relevance of concepts such as income, own-price, and cross-price elasticity to the business economist. It also provides theoretical background on neo-classical and Lancaster's characteristics approaches to consumer theory.

Prerequisites None.

Keywords advertizing elasticity, arc elasticity, attributes, better set, brand loyalty, *ceteris paribus*, characteristics, compensating variation, complement, completeness, consumer surplus, continuity, cross-price elasticity, effi-ciency frontier, elasticity of demand, equivalent variation, Giffen good, greed, habit formation, homogeneous function, implicit price, income effect, income elasticity, indifference, inferior good, inverse demand function, life-cycle, marginal rate of substitution, marginal revenue, non-satiation, normal good, ordinal utility, point elasticity, preference, reflexivity, search, snob effect, status effect, strict convexity, substitute, substitution effect, superior good, transivity, trigger prices, utility function, Willig's Approximation Theorem.

8.1 Introduction

This Chapter has mixed objectives. In part it aims to achieve the traditional goal of providing an exposition of the theory of consumer behaviour (sections 8.2 and 8.3). It has to be admitted that this has little relevance or importance for the business economist, who is more concerned with estimating the price responsiveness of demand to changes in prices, income, advertizing, etc. However, a review of pure theory is of interest, as it explains the origin of restrictions often imposed in demand studies (such things as homogeneity or the Slutsky restriction). Thus it is useful to know what these are (Chapter 9 then discusses whether and when it is appropriate to impose such restrictions in demand estimation). The pure theory also provides further insight into the problem of measuring economic welfare (and in particular, what consumers gain or lose when prices change), something of considerable policy relevance (for example, in judging the merits of environmental or financial regulation of private enterprise).

The representation of preferences through the use of utility functions, also discussed in section 8.2, is widespread in economic modelling and applications;

again, an understanding of theory here deepens an understanding of the validity (or otherwise) of using utility functions in economic analysis. Finally, the pure (neo-classical) theory of consumer behaviour provides a direct lead in to Lancaster's characteristics approach (section 8.5), which can prove useful in the analysis of demand for new goods.

8.2 Neo-Classical Consumer Theory

This section begins with an account of consumer theory and the representation of consumer preferences through the use of utility functions. It ends with a brief review of the pros and cons of the theory.

8.2.1 Preferences and the Budget Constraint

The presentation of neo-classical consumer theory begins by outlining certain fundamental assumptions. The model should be regarded as a base model, as it is merely a starting point for the development of more sophisticated models (as in section

8.5, for example). The clear specification of assumptions facilitates empirical testing, and also illuminates some of the important causal relationships that undoubtedly do affect individual behaviour.[1]

The basic model assumes an atemporal one-shot choice in which the consumer has to choose a consumption bundle subject to the goods having a clearly defined price per unit and there being a fixed income or budget available for the purchases.[2] This implies that there is a feasible set of affordable consumption bundles. The individual is then assumed to pick a most preferred bundle from this feasible set. In introductory courses on economics, this choice is often described as one which maximizes the individual's utility level, where utility is understood as an index of happiness or satisfaction. Historically, this idea of a psychological utility index can be traced back to Bernoulli (1738) and Jevons (1871). By contrast, the modern approach begins with an analysis of what is termed an individual's preferences. Indeed, the neo-classical theory of consumer behaviour can be developed without any mention of the notion of utility. However, under certain assumptions regarding the structure of preferences, it turns out that it may be possible to represent an individual's preferences using a utility function, and that there are some advantages in doing this. The utility representation of a consumer's choice problem is thus discussed in section 8.2.2.

It is assumed that there are n goods available and that the individual must select a consumption bundle represented by a vector $\mathbf{x} = (x_1, \ldots, x_n)$, where x_1 represents the quantity of the first good (e.g. bread), x_2 the quantity of the second (e.g. beer), and so on. The quantities of each good within a bundle may be continuously divisible, or may be discrete. Discreteness is quite common in practice; 2.35 litres of petrol is no problem, but it is difficult to purchase 1.3 elephants. For simplicity, goods are assumed to be continuously divisible. The analysis can be extended to discrete goods, but this is rarely done in an introductory text. Two consumption bundles are different if they have a different quantity of at least one of the goods in them. If $\mathbf{x}$ and $\mathbf{y}$

represent two consumption vectors, then the vector notation $\mathbf{x} \geq \mathbf{y}$ indicates that $\mathbf{x}$ has at least as much of every good, and strictly more of at least one good, than the bundle $\mathbf{y}$.[3] When we come to practical demand analysis, it is also important to define the period over which consumption has to take place. For the present, I will leave this undefined.

There is a price vector $\mathbf{p} = (p_1, \ldots, p_n)$, where again p_1 represents the price per unit of the first good, p_2 of the second, and so on. Total expenditure is thus

$$\sum_{i=1}^{n} p_i x_i = p_1 x_1 + p_2 x_2 + \ldots + p_n x_n, \quad (8.1)$$

and it is conventional to view the consumer as choosing commodity bundles subject to a budget constraint.[4] Thus, it is simply assumed that there is a fixed amount of money available for the purchase of commodities now; this is referred to as the individual's income or budget. Hence the consumer's expenditure is limited by the budget available:

$$\sum_{i=1}^{n} p_i x_i \leq Y, \quad (8.2)$$

where Y is the income available. For the two-good case, we have

$$p_1 x_1 + p_2 x_2 \leq Y. \quad (8.3)$$

This budget constraint is illustrated in Figure 8.1.

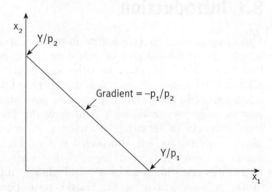

Fig. 8.1 The budget constraint

Preference for an individual is defined in terms of pairwise comparisons of consumption bundles. Loosely, the idea is that, in the absence of any prices for goods, an individual is able to say which of any pair of consumption bundles he or she would rather have. Let the vectors x, y, z, etc. represent three potentially different consumption bundles. Suppose the individual has to choose between two bundles, x or y; if the individual selects x, then we say that, for this individual, x is at least as good as y. A shorthand notation for this is to write x ⩾ y. If x ⩾ y holds, but not y ⩾ x, then we write x > y (x is **preferred** to y). If x ⩾ y and y ⩾ x, then we write x ~ y (x is **indifferent** to y).

The following axioms (or assumptions[5]) are standard; they are first stated, and then explained. For any consumption bundles x, y, z:

Axiom 1 (reflexivity): x ⩾ x.

Axiom 2 (completeness): Either x ⩾ y or y ⩾ x.

Axiom 3 (transitivity): For any consumption vectors x, y, z, if x ⩾ y and y ⩾ x then x ⩾ z.

Axiom 4 (non-satiation, or 'greed'): If x ⩾ y then x > y.

Axiom 5 (continuity): the graph of an indifference set is a continuous surface.

Axiom 6 (strict convexity): for any x, the better set B(x) is strictly convex.

The first axiom states that a bundle is as good as itself (this axiom has little empirical content and is included primarily for the formal development of theory—here we concentrate on the intuition behind the assumptions rather than the formal mathematics). The second, completeness, suggests that the individual can always decide whether one bundle is preferred to another or not. (Notice that this presumes there is no information uncertainty regarding what is obtained in purchasing a particular consumption bundle.[6]) Since it presumes that this is true for any arbitrary pair of consumption bundles, it clearly presumes that tastes are well formed even for goods the individual has never consumed or even

heard of. Axiom 3, transitivity, seems a plausible additional assumption; it presumes that, for example, if a consumer prefers bundle x to y, and y to z, then he or she also prefers x to z. This is a crucial assumption, and yet it is hard to think of a convincing counter-example, or a plausible reason why it might not hold.[7] Axiom 4, 'greed', suggests that bigger bundles are preferred to smaller ones. There are clearly exceptions to this; if we consider the number of bottles of wine consumed in (say) a day, it could be that a consumption bundle with 4 bottles is preferred to one with 12 (note that you have to consume within the specified period; satiation can occur in the short run!). Satiation does occur, particularly in the short term, for certain types of good. However, axiom 4 is generally viewed as a reasonable broad generalization. Finally, axioms 5 and 6 are purely for convenience (see later).

The **indifference set** $I(y)$ associated with a commodity bundle y is defined as

$$I(y) = \{\text{all } x \text{ such that } x \sim y\}. \qquad (8.4)$$

That is, for any bundle y, its indifference set comprises the bundle itself and all the other bundles which are indifferent to it. Clearly, if, for a pair of bundles x, y, it is the case that x ~ y then their indifference sets are identical; $I(x) = I(y)$. The associated **better set** $B(y)$ is given as

$$B(y) = \{\text{all } x \text{ such that } x \geqslant y\}. \qquad (8.5)$$

That is, the better set is the set of points which are as least as good as y (so it would be 'better', but more clumsy, to call it 'the at least as good as set'!). The axiom of continuity implies that commodity bundles can always be found, arbitrarily close in commodity space to any given bundle, between which the individual is indifferent.

The above axioms imply that indifference curves are non-thick and non-intersecting.[8] This can be shown by considering each possibility, and showing that it entails a contradiction of one or more of the axioms.

1. *Non-thick indifference curves.* Figure 8.2 illustrates the case of a thick indifference set in two-commodity space. Now, on any thick indifference

---

[5] An axiom is best thought of as a very simple form of assumption—ideally, one which is self-evidently true or unexceptionable. The preference 'axioms' are simple forms of assumption, but they are not self-evidently true—it is possible to dispute them all as being 'unrealistic'. However, this brings us back into the methodological mire—as to whether it matters whether assumptions are realistic or not (see Chap. 1). In general, it is the case that assumptions are never wholly 'realistic'—they are always abstractions from reality.

[6] Consider purchasing a second-hand car; you might not get the quality you expect, and the car may turn out to be a 'lemon'.

[7] Thresholds of perception are sometimes suggested as a potential source of intransitivity. That is, on pairwise comparisons differences might not be discernible, so that a ~ b, b ~ c, . . . , y ~ z but the accumulation of indiscernible differences leads to (say) a discernible preference for z over a.

[8] And these properties hold, suitably generalized, for indifference sets.

curve, it is always possible to select two points such that one lies north-east of the other. Thus in Figure 8.2, y has more than x of both the commodities—the axiom of non-satiation implies that y must be preferred to x, hence the two points cannot both be members of the same indifference set. Hence the graph of an indifference set must be non-thick or it will contradict non-satiation.

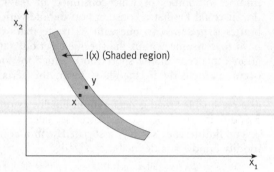

Fig. 8.2 Thick indifference sets?

2. *Indifference curves do not intersect.* Figure 8.3 illustrates this, again for the two-commodity case. If their indifference curves intersect, then it is always possible to prove a contradiction. For example, selecting commodity bundles x, y, z as in Figure 8.3, y ~ x (same indifference curve) and x ~ z (same indifference curve), hence, by transitivity (axiom 3), it must also be that y ~ z. However, z is clearly a larger bundle than x—which by non-satiation implies that z is preferred to x. Hence there is a contradiction. As a consequence it must be that indifference curves cannot intersect.

Figure 8.4 illustrates the axiom of strict convexity (the better set is shaded; note that it is unbounded to the north-east). A set is said to be strictly convex if all points on a line segment between any two points in the set lie strictly within the set. Hence the indifference curves (in the two-good case) must look something like that depicted in Figure 8.5; here the indifference curves are also superimposed on the feasible set (defined by the prices and the available budget, via equation (8.3)). The assumption of convexity is often motivated by the observation that individuals typically prefer averages to extremes; notice in Figure 8.4 that points on a line segment between any two points on an indifference curve involve quantities of each good somewhere in between the endpoints; these points lie above the indifference curve, indicating that they are preferred.

To sum up, instead of simply assuming that indifference curves exist (a typical ploy in introductory courses), the above discussion clarifies how more fundamental assumptions regarding preferences can be used to generate the idea more formally.

In view of axiom 4, non-satiation, it should be clear that the individual will select a point on the

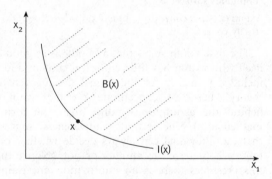

Fig. 8.4 Strict convexity of the better set

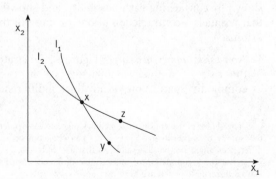

Fig. 8.3 Intersecting indifference curves?

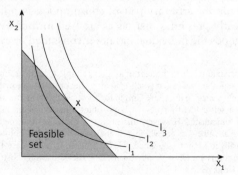

Fig. 8.5 Indifference curves and the feasible set

outer boundary of the feasible set, and on the highest indifference curve possible; furthermore, if the indifference curves are assumed to be smooth, this will occur at a point where the indifference curve is tangential to the budget line, as depicted in Figure 8.5. In this figure, I_1, I_2, and I_3 denote indifference curves and x denotes the consumer's optimal choice when faced with a given feasible set (which is defined by product prices and the available budget, as described in equation (8.2) and Figure 8.1).

8.2.2 The Utility Function

Given axioms 1–6, it can be shown that an individual's preferences can be represented by an ordinal utility function $U(\mathbf{x})$. This function assigns a utility number to every possible commodity vector x such that, for any pair of bundles, whichever is preferred is assigned a higher utility number. So long as indifference surfaces are smooth, it can also be shown that the individual's utility function is also smooth. Theorem 8.1 states this a little more formally:

Theorem 8.1 If axioms 1–6 hold for an individual, then there exists a utility function for that individual such that, for any pair of commodity bundles, x, y, if $\mathbf{x} \succcurlyeq \mathbf{y}$ then $U(\mathbf{x}) \geq U(\mathbf{y})$.[9]

It can also be shown that there are infinitely many functions which will correctly represent the individual's preferences in the way described in Theorem 8.1. This is illustrated in the following example.

EXAMPLE 8.1 Suppose there are only four possible commodity bundles available in the set of all possible consumption bundles, and these are denoted w, x, y, z. Suppose further that an individual expresses the following preferences: $\mathbf{w} > \mathbf{x} > \mathbf{y} > \mathbf{z}$. Then a utility function, U, is a function which assigns a number to each commodity bundle such that $U(\mathbf{w}) > U(\mathbf{x}) > U(\mathbf{y}) > U(\mathbf{z})$. Thus the functions U^a, U^b, U^c, U^d which assign numbers as in Table 8.1 below are all satisfactory utility functions; that is, they represent satisfactorily the individual's preferences.

The utility function is said to be 'unique up to an increasing monotonic transformation'; this merely means that, for an individual, any strictly increasing transformation of a utility function is also a utility function. This can be seen by considering the utility

[9] For a more formal presentation of this result, see e.g. Kreps (1991).

Table 8.1 Satisfactory utility functions

Commodity vector	U^a	U^b	U^c	U^d
w	4	64	0.40	3.2
x	3	27	0.39	−5.3
y	2	8	0.38	−40.1
z	1	1	0.37	−2222.9

functions in Example 8.1. If you plot (say) U^a on the vertical axis U^b and on the horizontal, then if you draw a smooth curve through the four points, you will see that the graph has positive slope. This is true for any pair of such utility functions; each utility function is a strictly increasing (albeit generally nonlinear) transformation of each of the other utility functions.[10] For a careful discussion of the meaning of ordinal utility, see e.g. Kreps (1991). The key point is very simple: the utility function assigns numbers to commodity bundles, but these utility numbers have no meaning other than that a bundle with a higher number is preferred to a bundle with a lower number.

The utility representation of an individual's preferences is useful because it allows a simple mathematical representation of the individual's choice problem. Essentially, the individual wants to select the most preferred bundle that is affordable; this amounts to choosing a bundle from the feasible set which has the largest utility number. This is the problem of maximizing utility.

$$\text{Maximize } U(\mathbf{x}) \qquad (8.6)$$
$$\text{subject to } \sum_{i=1}^{n} p_i x_i \leq Y, \qquad (8.7)$$

where the choice variables are the quantities of goods in the commodity bundle, $\mathbf{x} = (x_1, \ldots, x_n)$. We already know that the solution must be one which exhausts the budget available, so (8.7) will hold with equality at the optimum. Thus the problem can be treated as one of equality-constrained optimization. Since the Lagrange function is

$$L = U(\mathbf{x}) + \lambda[p_1 x_1 + p_2 x_2 + \ldots + p_n x_n - y], \qquad (8.8)$$

[10] The von Neumann–Morgenstern (VNM) utility function established in Chap. 4 for choice under uncertainty was cardinal rather than merely ordinal; recall that it was possible to transform a VNM utility function so that the new function was also a utility function (i.e. correctly represented the individual's preferences, in this case over risky choices), but the transformation in that case had to be linear.

the first order conditions are:[11]

$$\partial L/\partial x_i = \partial U(\mathbf{x})/\partial x_i + \lambda p_i = 0 \quad i = 1, \ldots, n.$$
(8.9)

Here, $\partial U(\mathbf{x})/\partial x_i$ is the rate at which utility increases as x_i is increased; this is referred to as **marginal utility** (with respect to good i). Rearranging (8.9) gives

$$\partial U(\mathbf{x})/\partial x_i / p_i = -\lambda \quad i = 1, \ldots, n.$$
(8.10)

That is, the ratio of marginal utility to price should be equalized across all the commodities, or, in other words, the consumption level of each commodity should be adjusted such that the higher a product's price, the proportionately higher the marginal utility associated with it.

Figure 8.5 illustrates the solution for the two-product case. Utility is constant at all points on an indifference curve (since the individual is indifferent between all such points). Consider the total differential for the utility function. This is

$$dU = [\partial U(\mathbf{x})/\partial x_1]dx_1 + [\partial U(\mathbf{x})/\partial x_2]dx_2.$$
(8.11)

The total differential measures how utility varies as x_1 is increased by the amount dx_1 and x_2 by the amount dx_2.[12] If dx_1 and dx_2 are chosen so as to move along an indifference curve, then clearly $dU = 0$; there is a zero change in utility. Thus, on an indifference curve, the choices of dx_1 and dx_2 must satisfy

$$dU = [\partial U(\mathbf{x})/\partial x_1]dx_1 + [\partial U(\mathbf{x})/\partial x_2]dx_2 = 0.$$
(8.12)

Rearranging this gives

$$dx_2/dx_1 = -[\partial U(\mathbf{x})/\partial x_1]/[\partial U(\mathbf{x})/\partial x_2].$$
(8.13)

This means that the gradient of an indifference curve is given by (minus) the ratio of the marginal utilities. The (absolute value of the) gradient of the indifference curve at a given point is known as the **marginal rate of substitution**, denoted MRS_{21} at that point; MRS_{21} is the rate at which good 2 must be substituted for good 1 such that the individual remains neither better nor worse off. Notice that

MRS_{21} is not constant; as one moves from left to right along an indifference curve, MRS_{21} decreases. This is the principle of the diminishing marginal rate of substitution. Thus strict convexity of the better set implies a diminishing marginal rate of substitution. The Axiom of Convexity was motivated by the observation that individuals tend to prefer averages to extremes. In Figure 8.5, at the optimum, the gradient of the indifference curve is equal to the gradient of the budget line, which is $-p_1/p_2$. Hence

$$MRS_{21} = [\partial U(\mathbf{x})/\partial x_1]/[\partial U(\mathbf{x})/\partial x_2] = p_1/p_2.$$
(8.14)

Thus the ratio of marginal utilities must be equal to the ratio of prices at the optimum, or equivalently, the ratio of marginal utility to price must be equal for both products, as was obtained in equation 8.10. Thus Figure 8.5 is a pictorial representation of the solution to the problem of constrained utility maximization.

The above analysis should make it clear why it is legitimate to replace the problem of choosing a most preferred bundle with that of maximizing a utility function. The individual's choices can be represented as those that arise out of utility maximization. In most of the applications in this text (and in economic analysis generally), it is simply assumed that the choice problem can be characterized as one of utility maximization.

8.2.3 Individual Demand Functions

It is either from Figure 8.5, that the individual's choice of how much to purchase of each good depends on the individual's preferences, but also on the prices of the goods and the income available. If prices or income change, then it can be expected that the consumption choices will change, simply because a change in any of these parameters implies a change in the shape of the feasible set. Note that small changes in price or income will lead to small changes in the feasible set and hence small changes in the demand for individual products. Intuitively, this suggests that the individual's demand for product i will vary smoothly with changes in price or income if the indifference curves are smooth and strictly convex, as depicted in Figure 8.5.[13] Hence there is a functional relationship between the optimal consumption choice and the independent

---

[11] Note that, in performing the differentiations, the prices p_1, $\ldots$, p_n and Y are simply constants, not choice variables. The consumer chooses quantities when faced with exogenously determined prices and a fixed budget. Thus, for example,

$$\partial(p_1 x_1)/\partial x_1 = p_1, \partial(p_1 x_1)/\partial x_2 = 0, \text{ and } \partial Y/\partial x_1 = 0.$$

[12] If you are unfamiliar with the concept of a total derivative, it is fairly intuitive; a move from a given point (x_1, x_2) to a new point $(x_1 + dx_1, x_2 + dx_2)$ causes a total change in the value of U (denoted dU) given by the distance moved in the x_1 direction, dx_1, times the rate at which utility increases in this direction, $\partial U/\partial x_1$, plus the further increment in the x_2 direction, dx_2, times the gradient in that direction, $\partial U/\partial x_2$.

[13] And this can be formally proved; see e.g. Beavis and Dobbs (1990).

variables (prices and the budget available). This can be written as

$$x_i = f^i(p_1, p_2, \ldots, p_n, Y) \quad i = 1, \ldots, n. \quad (8.15)$$

That is, the individual's demand for the ith product, denoted x_i, is a function of all the prices and the individual's budget.[14]

Now, the indifference map in Figure 8.5, and concepts such as marginal utility, do not constitute the stuff of testable propositions. However, the above analysis suggests one testable proposition:

Fact 8.1 Under axioms 1–6, demand functions exist and are homogeneous of degree 0 in money and prices. That is, there is no money illusion.

Before explaining this, I give a definition and a few examples of homogeneous functions:

Definition 8.1 A function $f(x_1, \ldots, x_n)$ is said to be **homogeneous** of degree k if, when each value for $x_1, \ldots, x_n$ is multiplied by a constant, λ, then the function simplifies in the following way: $f(\lambda x_1, \lambda x_2, \ldots, \lambda x_n) = \lambda^k f(x_1, x_2, \ldots, x_n)$.

EXAMPLE 8.2

1. If $f(x_1, x_2) = x_1^2 + x_2^2$, it is homogeneous of degree 2. Thus

$$f(\lambda x_1, \lambda x_2) = (\lambda x_1)^2 + (\lambda x_2)^2 = \lambda^2(x_1^2 + x_2^2)$$
$$= \lambda^2 f(x_1, x_2).$$

2. If $f(x_1, x_2) = x_1/x_2$, it is homogeneous of degree 0. Thus

$$f(\lambda x_1, \lambda x_2) = (\lambda x_1)/(\lambda x_2) = \lambda^0(x_1/x_2)$$
$$= \lambda^0 f(x_1, x_2).^{15}$$

3. The so-called Cobb–Douglas production function takes the form

$$f(K, L) = AK^\alpha L^\beta,$$

where K denotes capital input and L labour input. This is homogeneous of degree $(\alpha + \beta)$. Thus

$$f(\lambda K, \lambda L) = A(\lambda K)^\alpha(\lambda L)^\beta = \lambda^{\alpha+\beta}AK^\alpha L^\beta$$
$$= \lambda^{\alpha+\beta}f(K, L).$$

Thus, demand functions are homogeneous of degree zero if

$$f^i(\lambda p_1, \lambda p_2, \ldots, \lambda p_n, \lambda Y) = \lambda^0 f^i(p_1, p_2, \ldots, p_n, Y)$$
$$= f^i(p_1, p_2, \ldots, p_n, Y).$$
$$(8.16)$$

---

[14] The notation $f^i(.)$ is used to indicate that the functions are different for each of the products, $i = 1, \ldots, n$.

[15] Note that, focusing on the exponents, we have $\lambda/\lambda = \lambda^1/\lambda^1 = \lambda^1\lambda^{-1} = \lambda^0(= 1$, of course). $\lambda^0 = 1$; by definition, any function raised to the power 0 is equal to unity.

That is, if prices and income rise by the same factor, the individual continues to purchase exactly the same quantities of each good as before the change. Now utility is maximized subject to the constraint (8.7). If prices and income all change by the same factor λ, then the new constraint becomes

$$\sum_{i=1}^n (\lambda p_i)x_i = \lambda p_1 x_1 + \lambda p_2 x_2 + \ldots$$
$$+ \lambda p_n x_n \leq \lambda Y. \quad (8.17)$$

Clearly, λ cancels through in this constraint. That is, changing income and prices proportionately has no effect of the feasible set. It follows that the choice of consumption bundle does not change; hence for each good i, the individual's demand, x_i, does not change. Thus there is no money illusion

$$x_i = f^i(\lambda p_1, \lambda p_2, \ldots, \lambda p_n, \lambda Y)$$
$$= f^i(p_1, p_2, \ldots, p_n, Y). \quad (8.18)$$

8.3 Income and Substitution Effects and Measures of Economic Welfare

This section begins with an account of income and substitution effects, and links this analysis to the measurement of consumer's gain, via the concepts of ordinary and compensated demand curves. The reader who has taken a first course in economics will be familiar with income and substitution effects, but typically less familiar with the linkage to measures of economic welfare (consumer's surplus, compensating variation, equivalent variation).

In Figure 8.6, the quantity consumed by the individual of good 1 is measured on the horizontal axis. The vertical axis measures the individual's expenditure on all other goods (this could also be thought of as a single product with unit price). The individual starts out with budget Y_0 and faces a price p_1^a for product 1. Given this price, the budget line is drawn between the points marked Y_0 and A and the individual achieves an equilibrium at point E^a, involving the consumption of an amount q_1^a of good 1; the rest of the budget, $(Y_0 - p_1^a q_1^a)$, is then clearly spent on the other, composite commodity. Now consider a fall in the price of good 1; if this falls to some new level p_1^b, the budget line will swing out to a new position $(Y_0 B)$. The individual is encouraged by the lower price to re-optimize consumption, and so attains a new equilibrium at E^b, at which point consumption of good 1 is q_1^b. The individual is now

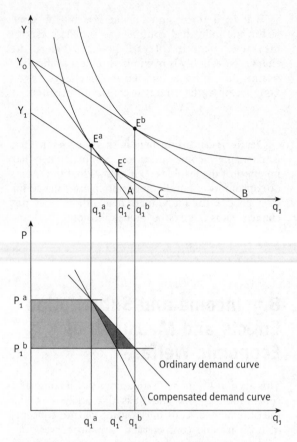

Fig. 8.6 Income and substitution effects

on a higher indifference curve and so is clearly better off as a consequence of the price fall.

The fall in price can be partitioned into two effects, termed the **income** and **substitution effects**. First consider the equilibrium point E^b. Suppose, starting from here, income is taken away from the individual. This causes the budget line to move parallel to itself and inwards. If sufficient income is taken away, the budget line eventually shifts parallel and inward to a point of tangency with the original indifference curve (at the point E^c). At this point, the individual is no better off than in the original situation (E^a). Now, the total effect of the change in price is the move from E^a to E^b. This total effect can be obtained by first moving from point E^a to E^c and then from E^c to E^b. The move from E^a to E^c is termed the substitution effect, in which the change in relative price changes the gradient of the budget line (whilst holding the individual on the same indifference curve), and the further move from E^c

to E^b is termed the income effect (since a change in the budget causes a parallel shift in the budget line). The idea is intuitive; a fall in price-makes the good relatively more attractive (the substitution effect), but also enables the individual to buy absolutely more of all goods if he or she so wishes (the income effect).

The income effect can be either positive or negative (or, indeed, zero). Figure 8.6 illustrates the case where an increase in income leads to an increase in demand for good 1 (compare the points E^c, E^b). This is a positive income effect, and a good that has a positive income effect is termed a **normal good**. However, consider moving the indifference curve which features a tangency at E^b in Figure 8.6 to a point further up the budget line Y_0B. It is clearly possible for the tangency point to occur to the left of the point E^c (without any crossing of indifference curves!). If the tangency at E^b on Y_0B had been to the left of E^c on the line Y_1A, then this would correspond to a case where an increase in income leads to the individual choosing to consume less of the good; this is the case of an **inferior good**. Inferior goods are typically low-quality goods for which there exist higher-quality alternatives but at higher prices. For example, people tend to eat absolutely less sliced bread and low-quality cuts of meat (mince etc.) as their income rises.

The substitution effect is, by contrast, always negative. A fall in the price of good 1 leads to an increase in demand for good 1 in the move from E^a to E^c (holding the individual on the same indifference curve, or equivalently, holding the utility level constant). This follows because of the strict convexity of the better set, which restricts the allowable shape of the indifference curves to the form depicted in Figure 8.6.

Notice that it is possible in Figure 8.6 for the tangency point E^b on Y_0B to be to the left of the point E^a. In this case, a fall in the price of good 1 leads to a fall in the quantity demanded of that good! This is the case of a **Giffen good**, a very inferior good indeed.[16] This theoretical possibility is extremely rare in practice; increasing price leading to increas-

---

[16] After Robert Giffen, an English statistician, who reportedly found that, in the 19th century, poor families actually increased their consumption of bread as the price of bread rose. As the price of bread rose, because all the other foodstuffs were still more expensive, in order to survive it was expenditure on these which was cut; the families ended up consuming even more bread in order to survive.

ing demand, if it arises at all, usually does so for other reasons (see section 8.4).

Figure 8.6 thus suggests another (in principle) testable proposition, as follows.

Fact 8.2 If an individual is observed to consume more of a good when income rises, then that individual must also consume less of the good if its price rises.

This follows from the fact that a positive income effect and a negative substitution effect reinforce each other to give a negative overall or total effect.

The lower panel in Figure 8.6 relates the indifference curve analysis to ordinary and compensated demand functions. The ordinary demand curve gives the demand the individual wishes to purchase as a function of own price. Thus this curve must pass through both points (p_1^a, q_1^a) and (p_1^b, q_1^b). The compensated demand function gives the demand under the condition that the individual is compensated so as to be no better or worse off. Thus starting from (p_1^a, q_1^a), this curve passes through the point (p_1^c, q_1^c).

A price fall gives the individual an increase in utility. If money is then taken away, this reduces utility, and if enough is taken away, the individual will eventually be brought back to the original level of utility (the original indifference curve). The money sum taken away is the **compensating variation**, denoted CV. It is a monetary measure of how much the price fall makes the individual better off (note that we do not actually take the money away). Although not proven here, it can be shown that an individual's compensating variation, or CV, is given as the (lightly shaded) area to the left of the compensated demand curve in Figure 8.6, whilst the gain in consumer surplus, CS, is measured as the sum of both the shaded areas to the left of the ordinary demand function.

The difference between CV and CS arises because of the income effect. It was argued in Chapter 2 that measurement of compensating variations might be useful in identifying whether a potential Pareto improvement existed, and that a reasonable approximation for compensating variation is consumer surplus. Figure 8.6 makes this clear; in particular, the diagram indicates that, where income effects are relatively small, consumer surplus is a good approximation for compensating variation. Indeed, this can be formalized in a theorem (the details of this theorem are less important than the observation that CS is usually a reasonable approximation for CV).

Theorem 8.2 (**Willig's Approximation Theorem**, Willig 1976). For a single price fall which induces a gain in consumer surplus of amount CS, so long as

$$\left| \frac{\eta_Y CS}{2Y} \right| \text{ is less than 5\%, then } \left| \frac{CS - CV}{CS} \right| \approx \left(\frac{\eta_Y}{2} \right) \left| \frac{CS}{Y} \right|.$$

Here, η_Y is the income elasticity in the region of the price change (see section 8.6 for more details of income and price elasticities). Income elasticities rarely significantly exceed 2 in absolute value (see Table 8.3, page 138, for some numerical estimates); for example, if $\eta_Y/2 = 1$, then theorem 8.2 indicates that so long as the change in consumer surplus is less than 5% of the individual's income, the discrepancy between CV and CS is also less than 5%. Thus, since most changes in practice are unlikely to have a major impact on an individual (CS/Y less than 5%), the errors involved in using consumer surplus rather than compensating variation are likely to be negligible.

Finally, it is possible to obtain a similar result at the aggregate level. That is, adding up the individual demands for a given product gives the market demand for that product. So long as all individuals face the same prices, the market demand will then logically be a function of prices and the incomes of the various individuals (hence the distribution of income will affect the demand for a given product). If, for each individual, the Willig approximation result holds, then the aggregate consumer surplus will be a good approximation to aggregate consumer variation.[17] Aggregate CS is measured simply as the area between the two prices to the left of the market demand curve (as illustrated in Chapter 2). In practice, any errors in approximating aggregate CV by aggregate CS are likely to be swamped by the errors associated with the estimation of demand functions. This theorem thus provides convincing motivation for using consumer plus producer surplus as a criterion for identifying (approximately) potential Pareto improvements.

---

[17] This is a sufficient condition for an approximation result at the aggregate level. It is clearly not necessary; that is, some individuals can have relatively large CS relative to income and the result can still hold.

8.4 Review of Neo-Classical Consumer Theory: Pros and Cons

The basic model of neo-classical consumer theory indicates some testable hypotheses (the existence of demand functions, no money illusion, negative substitution effect) and provides a foundation for welfare analysis. It also suggests the most important variables to consider in any empirical demand analysis (namely prices and incomes). However, the model also clearly omits many important features, for example:

1. *Search.* How do consumers come to find out about products? How do they decide when to stop searching and evaluating products? In the standard model, the consumer knows all there is to know about all actual and potential products. Hence there is no point in any firm incurring advertizing expenditure.

2. *Habit formation.* It is clear that individual consumption choices are as much about habit formation as anything else. Often a search ceases after a satisfactory outcome is achieved (e.g. when a beer drinker sticks to just one brew for his or her whole life). This appears more like satisficing rather than optimizing behaviour. In practice individuals often use rules of thumb to short-circuit the need for calculation.

3. *Preferences are often not independent of prices.* The model presumes that individuals have preferences, which define indifference curves. Variation in prices is assumed not to affect the position of the indifference curves. However, there is some evidence not only that individuals judge quality by price, but also that they may increasingly prefer a product the more highly priced that product is—because of the **status** or **snob effect**. Such effects lie outside the theory because the theory gives no predictions at all if preferences are allowed to shift as prices are changed.[18]

4. *New goods.* The model gives no idea what the likely demand for a new good might be—or why goods are substitutes or complements. These issues are addressed in a simple extension to the basic model in section 8.5.

Although all these observations are criticisms of the basic consumer theory, it has to be said that the optimizing framework is rather chameleonic. For example, searching, habit formation, satisficing behaviour, rules of thumb, etc. are all ideas which can be set within the optimizing framework in consumer theory. That is, such behaviours can be characterized simply by recognizing that there are costs associated with calculation, and hence there are optimal stopping rules and benefits to be had from using rules of thumb which may perform adequately. The gains from extended computation may be outweighed by the costs of undertaking it.

So is the above characterization of individuals as computational automatons fundamentally flawed? Many, particularly the behavioural economists (e.g. Earl 1995, Loasby 1976, Simon 1957), have argued that this is the case. Simon (1957: 198), for example, argues that 'the capacity of the human mind for formulating and solving complex problems is very small compared with the size of the problems whose solution is required for objectively rational behaviour in the real world', and, of course, it is well known, from the psychology literature, that individuals have difficulty in holding more than 5–7 separate ideas in their mind at the same time.

The issue regarding realism of assumptions is discussed in some detail in Chapter 1. It should be fairly obvious to anyone cognizant with work in the social sciences that these so-called 'sciences' are not in the business of discovering 'ultimate truth', but rather with the construction of alternative models aimed at approximately describing or predicting behaviour (of individuals, of organizations, of societies, etc.). Some descriptions and some assumptions may seem more appealing or more realistic than others, but it is generally difficult to test assumptions directly. Hence the emphasis on testing the predictions of models (Friedman 1953). The base model suggests that demand depends on prices and incomes, that there should be no money illusion, and that there should be a negative relationship between the price and the quantity demanded of a normal good (one with positive income effect). These are broadly verifiable, if rather limited, predictions. On the down side it also suggests that advertizing should not affect demand, and that there should be no habit formation or brand loyalty effect, but these effects are clearly of importance for some commodities (see section 8.5).

---

[18] See Leibenstein (1950) for an extended discussion of status, bandwagon, snob, and Veblen effects.

8.5 Lancaster's Characteristics Approach to Consumer Theory

8.5.1 Motivation and Basic Model

What are the fundamental objects of choice? Neo-classical consumer theory assumes it is the goods and services individuals actually purchase; that is, 'goods are goods'. However, Lancaster (1966a, 1966b) argued convincingly that consumer preferences are better defined not over goods, but rather over the **attributes** or **characteristics** of those goods. For example, a car is not purchased for its own sake, but rather for its attributes (load-carrying capacity, fuel economy, road handling, etc.). Thus products package characteristics in different quantities and proportions; a choice of product is thus a choice from one of the alternative available attribute bundles.

The standard theory developed in sections 8.2–8.4 provides a useful insight into the origins of demand functions (and welfare economics), but it is relatively weak in explaining the following:

(a) *The demand for new goods.* Neo-classical consumer theory assumes that preferences are defined over the whole of goods space. That is, one has to assume that preferences are defined over all goods, including all potential new goods. This is conceptually unsatisfactory, and in particular, it does not give any guidance on how to predict the likely level of demand for a new good. The characteristics approach, by contrast, does allow predictions regarding likely demand and also the sensible range within which selling price can feasibly be set. This is because new goods typically involve no new characteristics; they merely combine the existing characteristics in different quantities and proportions.

(b) *Why goods are substitutes.* (or complements). Neo-classical theory does not explain why goods are close substitutes. Indeed, it is completely silent on this; it makes no prediction regarding whether goods are likely to be close substitutes or complements or not. The characteristics approach explains that goods are likely to be substitutes if they combine characteristics in similar proportions.

(c) *The effect of advertizing.* Advertizing is discussed in more detail in Chapter 26. It appears to have no function in the neo-classical base model (since individuals have full information). The characteristics approach gets behind the goods and so is better able to determine the extent to which advertizing is informative (telling the consumer about product characteristics) and the extent to which it is persuasive.

The simplest version of the theory makes some (rather strong) assumptions, as follows:

1. The characteristics contained within any good can be given a numerical measure.

2. All consumers agree on the above objective measures; everyone agrees on what you get in terms of characteristics from each unit of a given product.

3. Linear additivity: two units of a given product give twice as much of each characteristic as one unit, and the units of a given characteristic provided by one commodity can be added to the quantity of that characteristic provided by other goods.

Each of these assumptions can be questioned. Measurability may be more problematic for some characteristics than for others (sweetness, hardness, comfort, . . .); individuals may not evaluate characteristics in the same way; and the last assumption, that of linearity, is especially dubious: what does it mean to say there is twice as much sweetness per unit in one toothpaste than another, twice as much comfort in one car compared to another, etc.? Measurability is not absolutely essential: some progress can be made simply through orderings; for example, cars can typically be ranked on various characteristics even if these characteristics are not given some form of cardinal measure (economy, comfort, etc.). However, it is convenient for expository purposes to stick with the simple theory, which assumes measurability and linear additivity.

The general formulation is set out first, and then simplified it to the two-characteristic case, for diagrammatic expository purposes. Suppose then there are m characteristics which any good may possess, and suppose that there are n goods. Let x_i be the quantity of the ith good purchased by the consumer at price p_i. Suppose each unit of good i contains a quantity a_{ij} of attribute j. Thus one unit of good i gives the consumer a bundle of characteristics defined by the vector $(a_{i1}, a_{i2}, \ldots a_{im})$. If $x = (x_1, x_2, \ldots, x_n)$ denotes the consumption vector chosen by the individual consumer, then this choice gives the consumer a total quantity a_j of characteristic j, defined as follows:

$$a_j = \sum_{i=1}^{n} a_{ij} x_i. \qquad (8.19)$$

It is assumed that the six axioms of consumer theory (section 8.2) apply now to characteristics of goods. This implies that there exists a utility function defined over characteristics rather than goods. Thus the consumer's choice problem can be written as

$$\text{Maximize } U(a_1, a_2, \ldots, a_m) \qquad (8.20)$$

subject to

$$\sum_{i=1}^{n} p_i x_i \le Y, \qquad (8.21)$$

$$a_j = \sum_{i=1}^{n} a_{ij} x_i \qquad j = 1, \ldots, m, \qquad (8.22)$$

and

$$x_j \ge 0 \qquad j = 1, \ldots n, \qquad (8.23)$$

where Y denotes the consumer's budget. Clearly, (8.21) is the individual's budget constraint, (8.23) is the restriction that goods must be consumed in non-negative quantities, and (8.22) defines how much of each characteristic is provided by the overall consumption of goods. Given the equality constraint, (8.22), it is possible to analyse the problem in goods space by directly substituting (8.22) into the objective function, so reducing the problem to one involving solely the choice variables x_j, $j = 1, \ldots n$. However, more insight can be extracted from a diagrammatic exposition which focuses on characteristics space. The exposition parallels that for neoclassical consumer theory, with two-characteristics replacing the two goods.

The initial focus in the ensuing analysis is on the establishment of what is termed the efficiency frontier in characteristics space. Notice that, for given prices and income, equation (8.21) limits the amount of goods that can be purchased, and hence there are limited attainable levels of characteristics, in view of (8.22) (note that the a_{ij}s are given positive constants, so finite quantities of goods give rise to finite quantities of characteristics). Thus, just as there is a feasible set in goods space, there is also a feasible set in characteristics space. The outer bound of this set is referred to as the efficiency frontier.

To illustrate the determination of the efficient frontier, and to show its value in the pricing of new products, consider the following illustrative example involving brands of cereals. By assumption these contain just two characteristics, namely calories (per kilo) and vitamins (e.g. vitamin A, milligrams per kilo). There are currently just three brands in the market, labelled 1, 2, and 3, and a firm is also considering whether to introduce a new good, labelled N, but is unsure about what price to set

Table 8.2 Lancaster's characteristics approach: an example

Brand	Price (/kilo)	a_1 (calories/kilo)	a_2 (vitamin content/kilo)
1	10	100	20
2	8	56	56
3	6	12	60
N	?	20	10

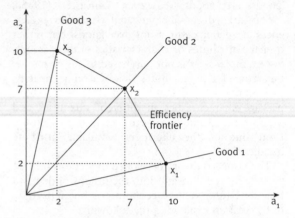

Fig. 8.7 The efficiency frontier

for it. For each good, the current selling price and the quantities of characteristics provided, per kilo are given in Table 8.2.

Given the linearity of the problem, and without loss of generality, consider an expenditure of $Y = £1$.[19] Ignoring the new good, then, and using the data in Table 8.2, equations (8.21) and (8.22) become

$$10x_1 + 8x_2 + 6x_3 = 1, \qquad (8.24)$$

$$a_1 = 100x_1 + 56x_2 + 12x_3, \qquad (8.25)$$

and

$$a_2 = 20x_1 + 56x_2 + 60x_3. \qquad (8.26)$$

Now, suppose that the whole £1 is spent on good 1: then $x_2 = x_3 = 0$ and so from (8.24), $10x_1 = 1$, so $x_1 = 1/10$ (simply divide the £1 by the price of the good and you get the quantity that can be purchased). This gives quantities

$$a_1 = 100(1/10) = 10$$

and

$$a_2 = 200(1/10) = 2.$$

That is, multiplying the quantity of characteristic

---

[19] Having a larger budget means that more can be purchased, but the analysis of which products are efficient etc. is unchanged.

per kilo times the number of kilos purchased gives the total quantity of characteristic. Thus, in Figure 8.7, purchasing exclusively good 1 gives a characteristic bundle somewhere along the ray labelled, appropriately enough, 'good 1'. The characteristics vector purchasable with £1 is marked up to the point (2,10) and labelled x_1. If the £1 is spent exclusively on good 2, then $x_2 = 1/8$ kilo is affordable and this buys quantities of characteristics

$$a_1 = 56 \times (1/8) = 7$$

and

$$a_2 = 56 \times (1/8) = 7$$

This is the point (7,7), marked x_2 in Figure 8.7. Finally, if the £1 is spent purely on good 3, it buys

$$a_1 = 12 \times (1/6) = 2$$

and

$$a_2 = 60 \times (1/6) = 10,$$

which corresponds to the point (2,10), marked x_3. Now, it can be shown that if the £1 is spent in part on good 1 and in part on good 2, the quantity of characteristics obtained plots at a point on the line segment between points x_1 and x_2 (and the more of the £1 is spent on good 1, the nearer the outcome will be to point x_1, etc.). So any combination of characteristics on this line is attainable by spending £1 on some particular combination of goods 1 and 2. Likewise, spending £1 on some combination of goods 2 and 3 can be used to reach any point on the line segment between x_2 and x_3. This outerbound line (marked in bold in Figure 8.7) is termed the **efficiency frontier**. Points inside the frontier are inefficient. Thus, consider spending £1 on a combination of goods 1 and 3. The attainable characteristics in this case plot on the straight line between points x_1 and x_3. These points lie inside the frontier. For any point on this line (except the endpoints), there exist points to the north-east on the efficiency frontier which, for the same expenditure, offer more of all characteristics. Since the individual prefers more to less, commodity bundles which plot at points inside the frontier will never be consumed by a rational consumer. Figure 8.7 plots the full efficiency frontier; note that since there are no goods more a_2-intensive than good 3, the frontier is horizontal to the axis from the point (2,10). Likewise, it is vertical from the point (10,2), as there are no goods more a_1-intensive.

8.5.2 Analysis of New-Good Pricing

The following discussion assumes that the prices of existing goods do not react as the new-good price is changed. As such, the analysis provides a benchmark; since the new good may drive other brands out of the market place, one might expect price competition to occur. Price competition is discussed in Chapter 16 (on oligopoly).

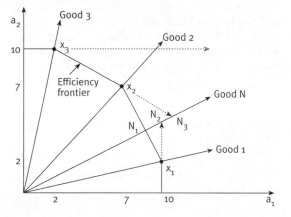

Fig. 8.8 New-good pricing

The introduction of the new good is illustrated in Figure 8.8. This makes clear the idea that a new good merely involves packaging up the existing characteristics in new proportions. The characteristic vector attainable by spending £1 on good N lies on the ray marked 'good N', but the length of the vector depends on the price of good N. At high prices, good N will plot at a point inside the frontier, and rational consumers will not purchase it. As price is reduced, the ray lengthens until it reaches N_1, at which point it becomes efficient. Here, it is just possible that some consumers might purchase the good. If price is decreased further, the ray lengthens to reach point N_2. At this point, good N offers (for £1) the same quantity of characteristic 1 and more of characteristic 2. Hence at this point it dominates good 1, and good 1 will disappear from the market. Since good 1 originally existed in the market, its market share can be observed; this market share will be captured entirely by the new good (which will also have captured some sales from good 2 as well). As price of N is reduced yet further, point N_3 is reached. At this point, a combination of goods 3 and N will offer more of both characteristics than good 2, so good 2 will cease to be purchased. Finally, as price is reduced yet further, a point N_4 is reached (actually off the graph in Figure 8.8) when good N offers 10 units of characteristic 2. At this point, good N offers a larger characteristic vector than good 3, and it disappears from the market (leaving the good N with the entire market).

The prices at which the new good knocks out competitors are referred to here as **trigger prices**. The prices correspond to the points $N_1, \ldots, N_4$, and can be calculated once the co-ordinates of these points are known. The co-ordinates can be established computationally or by constructing a scale diagram. I adopt the computational approach.

(a) Product Viability

First note that the ray 'good N' passes through the origin with gradient $^1/_2$. The equation of this ray is thus

$$a_2 = (1/2)a_1. \tag{8.27}$$

The equation of the line between points x_1 and x_2 takes the form

$$a_2 = \alpha + \beta a_1 \tag{8.28}$$

and passes through the points (10,2) and (7,7). Hence α, β must satisfy

$$2 = \alpha + \beta 10 \text{ and } 7 = \alpha + \beta 7.$$

Solving these equalities gives $\alpha = 56/3$ and $\beta = -5/3$, so the equation is

$$a_2 = (56/3) - (5/3)a_1. \tag{8.29}$$

At point N_1 both (8,28) and (8.29) hold. Solving these equations gives

$$a_1 = 8.6154, a_2 = 4.3077.$$

The price which gives at least these quantities of characteristic is determined by either

$$20(1/P_N) \geq 8.6154 \Rightarrow P_N \leq 2.3214$$

or

$$10(1/P_N) \geq 4.3077 \Rightarrow P_N \leq 2.3214$$

(recall $1/P_N$ is the quantity of good N purchasable with £1, so 20 times this is the quantity of the first characteristic obtained, and 10 times this is the quantity of the second characteristic). Notice that it suffices to make the calculation of price based on just one of the characteristics.[20] Thus a price of less than £2.32 is needed if there are to be any sales at all.

---

[20] Either calculation suffices to get the answer; the equations are not independent, and will give the same solution value.

(b) Price at Which Good N Dominates Good 1

The point N_2 clearly has co-ordinates (10,5). Hence good 1 becomes inefficient if the price of good N satisfies

$$20(1/P_N) \geq 10 \Rightarrow P_N \leq 2.0.$$

(c) Price at Which Good N Dominates Good 2

This is given by determining the co-ordinates of the point N_3. The line passing through points x_2, x_3 can be shown to have equation $a_2 = (56/5) - (3/5)a_1$. Solving this with equation (8.27) gives the co-ordinates of N_3 as (10.1818, 5.0909). Hence P_N must satisfy

$$20(1/P_N) \geq 10.1818 \Rightarrow P_N \leq 1.9643.$$

(d) Price at which good N dominates good 3:

At N_4, $a_2 = 10$. Hence P_N must satisfy

$$10(1/P_N) \geq 10 \Rightarrow P_N \leq 1.0.$$

The effect of the reduction in price on the efficiency frontier is illustrated in Figure 8.9. If the new good plots at a point inside the original frontier it has no effect (and gets no sales); as price is reduced, it moves outside the old frontier to create a new frontier. Thus the dotted line gets replaced by the fine line and this in turn moves out and up as the price of good N falls.

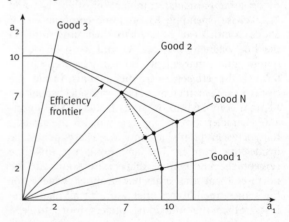

Fig. 8.9 Alterations in the efficiency frontier

8.5.3 Implicit Prices

In the conventional analysis, p_i represents the price to be paid to obtain an additional unit of product. It is also true that, since individuals will only select points which are on the efficient frontier, there is an implicit price to be paid to obtain an additional unit of characteristic. Thus, consider goods 1 and 2. On the efficient frontier between points x_1 and x_2 in Figure 8.7, the following equations hold:

Budget constraint: $p_1 x_1 + p_2 x_2 = Y$
$$\Rightarrow 10 x_1 + 8 x_2 = Y \qquad (8.30)$$

$$a_1 = a_{11} x_1 + a_{12} x_2$$
$$\Rightarrow a_1 = 100 x_1 + 20 x_2 \qquad (8.31)$$

$$a_2 = a_{21} x_1 + a_{22} x_2$$
$$\Rightarrow a_2 = 56 x_1 + 56 x_2. \qquad (8.32)$$

If we denote the **implicit prices** for characteristics 1 and 2 as π_1 and π_2, then the amounts of characteristics purchased must just exhaust the budget at these implicit prices: that is,

$$\pi_1 a_1 + \pi_2 a_2 = Y. \qquad (8.33)$$

As x_1 and x_2 are varied, so the quantities a_1 and a_2 vary; however, along the efficient frontier, (8.33) continues to hold, as do (8.30)–(8.32). Inverting equations (8.31) and (8.32) gives

$$x_1 = \frac{a_1 a_{22} - a_2 a_{12}}{a_{11} a_{22} - a_{21} a_{12}} \quad \text{and} \quad x_2 = \frac{a_2 a_{11} - a_1 a_{21}}{a_{11} a_{22} - a_{21} a_{12}}.$$

Substituting these into (8.30) and simplifying gives (8.33), in which

$$\pi_1 = \frac{p_1 a_{22} - p_2 a_{12}}{a_{11} a_{22} - a_{21} a_{12}} \quad \text{and} \quad \pi_2 = \frac{p_2 a_{11} - p_1 a_{21}}{a_{11} a_{22} - a_{21} a_{12}}.$$

In the numerical case given above, this implies that

$$\pi_1 = 1/40 \quad \text{and} \quad \pi_2 = 30/224.$$

A final point of interest is that, as in standard consumer theory, the relative implicit price π_2 / π_1 is given as the gradient of the efficient frontier. Thus the implicit prices change at corners in the efficient frontier.

8.5.4 Relevance of Pricing Analysis

Clearly, in a market where a set of brands compete against each other, firms are likely to pay close attention to the prices of the brands which are near-neighbours in characteristics space. Any change in price, or a new product entry, may induce near-neighbour firms to react.[21] However, the above analysis is of interest as it provides an initial benchmark for testing the viability of the new product. In particular, if the good cannot be profitably produced at a price which enlarges the efficiency frontier ($P_N \leq 2.32$ in the example in section 8.5.1),

[21] And this may induce a chain reaction in what has been termed a continuum of intersecting oligopoly markets.

there is little point in setting up the plant or process. Furthermore, an understanding of a product's characteristics is clearly vital to an understanding of what constitutes the nearest neighbours, and hence an understanding of where the competition is likely to come from.

8.5.5 Indifference Curve Analysis of Consumer Choice

So far, the focus has been on the 'technology' of consumption; there has been no discussion of individual preferences. Applying the axioms of consumer theory to characteristics rather than goods, it follows that an individual's preferences can be represented by a utility function, but also, in terms of the above diagrams, by the usual indifference curve map in characteristic space. Different individuals may have different preferences, and so different indifference curve maps. They may also have different budgets. However, the budget merely affects the scale of the efficient frontier; a bigger budget merely scales up the frontier depicted for £1 of expenditure. Thus for a given budget, an efficient frontier can be constructed. Given this, the individual will aim to attain the highest possible indifference curve by selecting a point on this frontier. Figure 8.10 illustrates the point that such an indifference curve will either pass through one of the corners of the frontier, or will be a tangency point between two goods. In the former case, the individual consumes only one brand; in the latter, two goods are consumed.

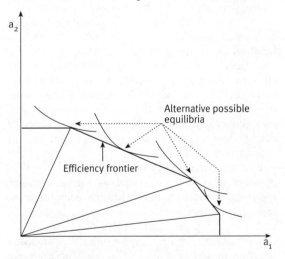

Fig. 8.10 Illustration of some alternative possible choices by individuals

Clearly, if there are just two characteristics, then an individual consumer will never consume more than two adjacent brands. This point can be generalized, and is worth reporting more formally:

Fact 8.1 Given the assumptions on preferences and the additional assumptions regarding additivity (etc.), if there are n characteristics, then an individual will consume at most n different goods.

As a corollary, if the theory is true and we observe an individual consuming n brands, then it can be concluded that these brands must have at least n distinguishable characteristics associated with them. Of course, although an individual can only consume one or two brands, if there are only two characteristics, different individuals can reach different tangency points on the efficient frontier, so heterogeneity of consumers suggests that there can be many brands in existence. By contrast, if individuals all had the same preferences, then the number of brands *would* be limited by the number of characteristics.

It is perhaps worth noting some other features regarding the above model of consumer choice. First, it suggests that there can often be non-smooth substitution. In the neo-classical theory, an increase in price leads to smooth substitution into other goods. Here, a change in price might change the shape of the frontier, but the consumer may continue to buy the same brand. This constitutes one notion of **brand loyalty**; it occurs to some extent when the consumer's choice occurs at a corner on the efficiency frontier (and the extent of the brand loyalty depends on the sharpness of the corner).

The extent to which goods are close substitutes for each other becomes, in the Lancaster approach, a function of the proportions of characteristics and also their relative prices. The structure of the efficient frontier is important in determining individual choices. Where the frontier features corners which are close to 180°, small changes in price may have significant impact on market shares of neighbouring goods (neighbouring, that is, in characteristics space).

Whilst the model presented above is not so widely directly applied in demand analysis, the basic insight regarding product characteristics has been incorporated fairly extensively in what is often termed the hedonic pricing literature. Often, these studies are concerned with determining the implicit prices associated with characteristics of goods (for example, estate agents and house builders might be interested in knowing how much value is added to a property by its characteristics—number of bedrooms, size of garden, accessibility variables, neighbourhood variables, environmental variables such as noise and pollution, etc.). Once the implicit prices associated with characteristics have been estimated, they may prove useful in the design of new products and so on (although there are many conceptual and technical difficulties). For interesting applications, see e.g. Hartman (1989) or Morey (1985).

8.6 Demand Analysis

8.6.1 Introduction and Motivation

Demand analysis is the study of how the quantity a firm is able to sell depends upon variables such as the product's own price, the prices of related products, and other market factors such as advertizing, income, etc. Section 8.2 set out the theory of individual consumer behaviour. An individual's demand function was shown to depend on the available budget and the set of prices faced. In principle, changes in the price of each and every product can affect the individual's demand for a given product. In practice, only the prices of close substitutes and complements are likely to matter. Aggregating over individual demand functions yields the market demand function. Again, in theory, for a given product this will depend on the prices of all goods and also the budgets of all consumers. However, if one thinks more generally about the determinants of demand for a product, it becomes clear that there are several potentially important factors which are not included in the neo-classical base model, in particular, advertizing, product quality, even the weather. Furthermore, it may not be only today's prices which affect sales today; expectations regarding future prices (of the product itself, of closely related products, and indeed, of other variables) may influence demand for product today.

Example 8.3

1. If there is a general expectation that the price of oil (or the government tax on oil products) is likely to rise in the near future, this will increase the demand for oil products today.

2. If a firm decides to introduce a new model, the release of information on the new car, and the date at which it is to be made available, may affect the demand for close-substitute models today.

If q_i^d denotes the quantity of good i demanded by consumers, the amount they wish to purchase (the superscript d denotes demand), then the demand function depicts a relationship of the form $q_i^d = f^i(v_1, v_2, v_3, \ldots, v_r)$, where $v_1, v_2, v_3, \ldots, v_r$ denote variables which affect the level of demand and the notation $f^i(.)$ stands for a particular function which relates demand to these variables; that is, different products will have different functional relationships, and the variables which are important determinants of the demand for one product may not be important for another. It is useful to consider in more detail the types of variable which are likely to influence demand, and to consider the extent to which these variables are controllable by the firm (since the firm will wish to choose values for controllable variables so as to maximize profitability or some other objective).

(A) Variables under the firm's control

 (i) The product's own price.

 (ii) The price of related products from the firm's product line (these are usually substitutes, but occasionally complements[22]).

(iii) Future prices for (i) and (ii).

(iv) Advertizing (and promotional expenditure generally) for the product.

 (v) Advertizing for the product line.

(vi) Product design characteristics (and those for products in the rest of the product line).

(B) Variables under competitors' control

 (i) Prices of competitor products which are close substitutes (or, less commonly, complements).

(ii) Advertizing (and promotional efforts) for these products.

(C) Environmental or macroeconomic factors

 (i) The level of income, or GDP (aggregate or per capita).

(ii) The weather (ice cream, beers, and carbonated drink sales are affected by temperature).

---

[22] Most firms produce a range of similar products; these tend to be near-neighbours in characteristics space. However, spare-part sales are generally a complementary product. Substitutes and complements are defined in sect. 8.6.7.

(iii) Government policy (e.g. through restrictions on advertizing of tobacco or alcohol).

(iv) Tastes and fads. Although firms may sometimes be able to create new fads and trends, most firms are not fashion leaders but followers.

In practice, in order to estimate a demand function, it is necessary to select a particular functional form. Typically this will be either linear or log-linear; the issues that arise regarding selection of functional form, and of demand estimation more generally, are discussed in Chapter 9. For example, the demand for a firm's specialist tea, EG Tea, might be specified as follows:

$$q_{EG\ Tea}^d = \alpha_0 + \alpha_1 p_{EG\ Tea} + \alpha_2 p_{other\ tea} + \alpha_3 p_{coffee} + \alpha_4 \text{GDP} + \alpha_5 T + \alpha_6 A,$$

$$(8.34)$$

where $q_{EG\ Tea}^d$ demand is specified as depending on own price, $p_{EG\ Tea}$, the price of a close competitor's make, $p_{other\ tea}$, the average price of coffee (another substitute), p_{coffee}, consumer wealth as measured by gross domestic product, GDP, some measure of temperature or season, T, and the level of advertizing expenditure on the product, A. Here $\alpha_1 - \alpha_6$ are simply constants (empirically, the task is to estimate the values for these constants). Note that (8.34) is a linear specification for the demand function; it focuses on the key variables (and necessarily omits a myriad of other less important determinants of demand), but also specifies the way in which they affect demand (i.e. linearly!). The true functional form for the demand function is unknown, and a variety of alternative demand specifications may be used in empirical analysis (specification issues are discussed in some detail in Chapter 9).

8.6.2 The Demand Curve or Schedule

Of all the factors affecting demand, the price of the product is focal; it is typically the most important influence on demand that is also within the firm's control. The demand curve depicts the relationship between quantity demanded and price, holding all other variables in the demand function constant. The term widely used in economics for holding all other things equal or constant is **ceteris paribus**. For this reason, the ordinary demand curve is often termed the ceteris paribus demand curve. In effect, the values of the other variables fix the position of the demand curve; any change in these variables will lead to a shift in the demand curve. The demand function takes the general form

$$q_i^d = g^i(p_i). \qquad (8.35)$$

That is, it states that quantity demanded depends solely on own price. In the linear EG-tea example, this function takes the form

$$q_{EG\ Tea}^d = \beta_0 + \beta_1 p_{EG\ Tea}, \qquad (8.36)$$

where

$$\beta_1 = \alpha_1 \qquad (8.37)$$

and

$$\beta_0 = \alpha_0 + \alpha_2 p_{other\ tea} + \alpha_3 p_{coffee} + \alpha_4 GDP$$
$$+ \alpha_5 T + \alpha_6 A. \qquad (8.38)$$

This should make it clear that any change in the values of other variables is equivalent to a change in the intercept of the demand curve, and hence induces a shift in it.

Now, if the standard form for an ordinary demand function is $q^d = \beta_0 + \beta_1 p$, it is possible to rearrange this to make price the subject of this equation:

$$p = (\beta_0 / \beta_1) + (1/\beta_1)q. \qquad (8.39)$$

Writing $b_0 = (\beta_0 / \beta_1)$ and $b_1 = (1/\beta_1)$, this gives the so-called **inverse demand function**,

$$p = b_0 + b_1 q, \qquad (3.40)$$

where again b_0 and b_1 are constants. Since there is usually a negative relationship between price and the quantity demanded, both β_1 and b_1 are typically negative. The graph of the demand curve is depicted in Figure 8.11 for the case of the specialist tea. The Figure also illustrates the effect of a change in any of the other determinants of the demand function. In

this case, a change in the price of coffee is considered. Assuming that coffee is a substitute, the coefficient α_3 is greater than 0, so an increase in α_3 will lead to a rightward shift in the demand function.

Normally, in any bivariate graph, the independent variable takes the horizontal axis whilst the dependent variable takes the vertical axis. Notice that Figure 8.11 has price on the vertical axis and quantity demanded on the horizontal axis. The modern neo-classical perspective is that price is the independent variable and that the quantity demanded depends on price. On this view, it would be more sensible to have price on the horizontal axis. However, for historical reasons it is conventional to draw the graph the 'wrong way round'.[23]

Most textbook diagrams are drawn under the assumption that the demand curve is linear. Whilst demand is generally non-linear in practice, the practice can be justified

(i) for pedagogical reasons: linearity reduces complexity; linear figures are easier to understand;

(ii) because it is a good approximation in the region of the current price; and given this,

(iii) because it also facilitates estimation and calculation.

The idea of linear approximation is very powerful, and is illustrated for the one-variable case in Figure 8.12, from which it should be clear that a linear function can always provide a useful approximation to a non-linear smooth function over some interval.[24] In the case of the demand curve, the linear approximation can be viewed as taken in the region of the existing price. However, having said this, alternative specifications (including the log-linear form) will often fit the data even better (see Chapter 9).

---

[23] This goes back to Marshall (1890). Marshall took the view that price, not quantity, was the dependent variable. In his view a point on an individual's demand curve depicts the maximum price per unit he or she would be willing to pay for the associated quantity. Walras, by contrast, took the view described here. For present purposes, the debate has little significance; however, the interested reader is referred to Blaug (1968) and Page (1980) for more details. In nearly all the applications in this text, firms will have scope to set price, and consumers then choose how much to buy, so quantity is the dependent variable. However, sometimes quantity supplied is fixed (as often happens with agricultural products, such as pigs or hogs); in such a case, it is price which adjusts to clear the market.

[24] This linear approximation idea generalizes to the case of a multivariate function. This and some related issues are discussed in more detail in sect. 9.4.

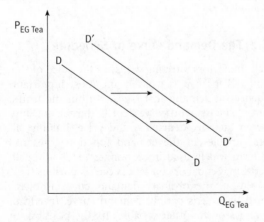

Fig. 8.11 Shift in the demand curve

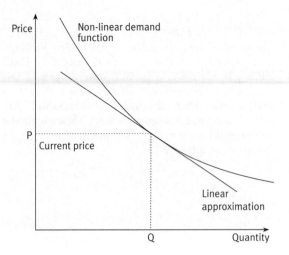

Fig. 8.12 Linear approximation

The following example, a numerical example of rudimentary demand estimation, illustrates some points about units of measurement.

EXAMPLE 8.4 Twelve months ago, the local swimming pool increased its pool prices by 10%. The average price had previously been £2.00, with an average number of swims per annum of 50,000. In the past year, only 45,000 swims have been recorded. Estimate a linear demand curve using this information.

Answer: The demand curve takes the form $q = \alpha_0 + \alpha_1 p$, where q denotes the number of swims per annum and p denotes the price per swim. This curve must satisfy two price–quantity pairs, namely (£2.00, 50,000) and (£2.20, 45,000). Thus

$$50{,}000 = \alpha_0 + 2.0\alpha_1 \qquad \text{(i)}$$

and

$$45{,}000 = \alpha_0 + 2.2\alpha_1. \qquad \text{(ii)}$$

Subtracting (ii) from (i) gives

$$5000 = -0.2\alpha_1 \Rightarrow \alpha_1 = -25{,}000. \qquad \text{(iii)}$$

Substituting this into (i) gives

$$50{,}000 = \alpha_0 - 2.0 \times 25{,}000 \Rightarrow \alpha_0$$
$$= 100{,}000. \qquad \text{(iv)}$$

Hence the ordinary demand curve is

$$q = 100{,}000 - 25{,}000p. \qquad \text{(v)}$$

Rearranging this gives the inverse demand function

$$p = 4.0 - (1/25{,}000)q = 4.0 - 0.00004q. \qquad \text{(vi)}$$

Notice that, if quantity had been measured in

thousands, the two points would have become (50,2.0) and (45, 2.2), and the ordinary demand function would have become

$$q = 100 - 25p. \qquad \text{(vii)}$$

Thus the choice of output measure (units or thousands of units) alters the parameters of the demand function in an obvious way (here simply by dividing the originals by 1000). The associated inverse demand function, when q is measured in thousands, is thus

$$p = 4.0 - (1/25)q = 4.0 - 0.04q. \qquad \text{(viii)}$$

Figure 8.13 illustrates this.

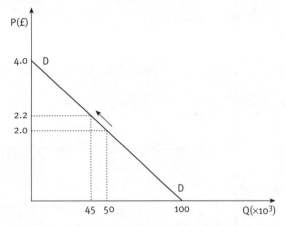

Fig. 8.13 A change in a good's own price involves a movement along, not a shift in, the curve

Figure 8.13 illustrates the important general point that changes in own price are movements along the demand curve, whilst changes in the values of other variables (prices of substitutes, income, advertizing, etc.) cause a shift in the curve itself.

8.6.3 Revenue and Demand

In general, the higher the price set by the firm for a given product, the less the firm is able to sell. At a very high price nothing at all will be sold, and no revenue raised. Equally, at zero price, demand may be massive, but again no revenue is raised. This suggests that, as price is raised from zero upwards, revenue is likely to rise for a while and then peak and finally fall back to zero. This is indeed the case for the linear demand function (although for non-linear demand functions, revenue may attain multiple local maxima; this is not discussed further here). To see this, consider the linear demand curve $p = $

$\alpha_0 - \alpha_1 q$, where α_0 and α_1 are positive constants (so the inverse demand curve has negative slope). Now revenue (R) is price times quantity, so

$$R = pq = (\alpha_0 - \alpha_1 q)q = \alpha_0 q - \alpha_1 q^2. \quad (8.41)$$

The revenue function associated with a linear demand function is thus quadratic. The relationship between linear demand and revenue is illustrated in Figure 8.14 (the figure also incorporates reference to elasticity and marginal revenue concepts; these are discussed below).

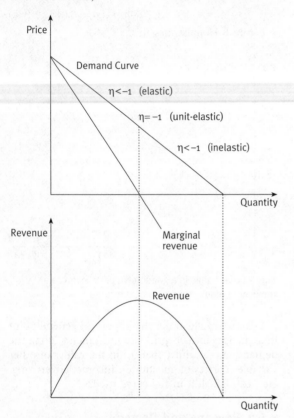

Fig. 8.14 Demand, elasticity, and revenue

8.6.4 Marginal Revenue

The concept of marginal revenue, defined below, proves to be of central importance in price theory, as we shall see.

Definition 8.12 If quantity is discrete, **marginal revenue** is defined as the change in revenue that arises when the quantity demanded increases by one unit. If quantity is a continuous variable, then marginal revenue is defined as the rate of change of revenue with respect to change in quantity demanded.

When the demand curve has negative slope, in order to increase the demand for the product (holding all other variables constant, i.e. ceteris paribus), it is necessary to reduce price slightly. Thus, although another unit is sold, some money is lost because all the existing units are now selling at a slightly lower price. This idea is illustrated in Figure 8.15. Notice that marginal revenue varies with the amount sold; both revenue and marginal revenue are functions of quantity.

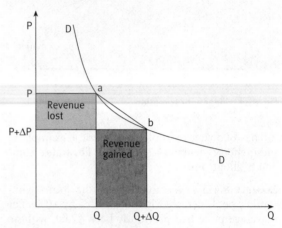

Fig. 8.15 Marginal revenue

In Figure 8.15, initial revenue is $R = PQ$; demand then increases by an amount ΔQ if the price is changed by amount ΔP (with downward-sloping demand, $\Delta P < 0$ if $\Delta Q > 0$). The revenue then changes to $R + \Delta R = (P + \Delta P)(Q + \Delta Q)$. The change in revenue, ΔR, is given as

$$\begin{aligned}\Delta R &= (R + \Delta R) - R = (P + \Delta P)(Q + \Delta Q) - PQ \\ &= (PQ + \Delta PQ + P\Delta Q + \Delta P\Delta Q) - PQ \\ &= \Delta PQ + \Delta Q(P + \Delta P). \quad (8.42)\end{aligned}$$

Now $\Delta P < 0$, so the first term here, ΔPQ, is negative; this is the revenue lost on original sales because the price had to be reduced, whilst the term $\Delta Q(P + \Delta P)$ is the gain in revenue from additional sales at the new price. These areas are shaded in Figure 8.15. It should be clear that the magnitude of the two areas depends on the starting point (P,Q), and the gradient of the inverse demand curve. Depending on which area is larger, marginal revenue can be either positive or negative.

The interpretation of marginal revenue is straightforward: assuming a negatively sloped demand curve, if marginal revenue is positive, then reducing price increases demand, and the additional units sold increases revenue. An increase of one unit in sales increases total revenue by the numerical magnitude of marginal revenue at that output level.

If output is continuously divisible, it is natural to define marginal revenue as the rate at which revenue changes as output increases. For example, in the case of linear demand, equation shows that revenue is a quadratic function of quantity sold ($R = \alpha_0 q - \alpha_1 q^2$). Differentiating this gives marginal revenue, MR, as

$$MR = \partial R / \partial q = \alpha_0 - 2\alpha_1 q. \qquad (8.43)$$

That is, for the straight-line demand curve, the marginal revenue curve has the same intercept on the vertical axis, and twice the gradient (so it cuts the horizontal axis midway between zero and the point where the demand function cuts it, as illustrated in Figure 8.14).

EXAMPLE 8.5 Taking the inverse demand curve in Example 8.4, $p = 4 - 0.04q$, it follows that marginal revenue is given as $MR = 4 - 0.08q$. Thus revenue is maximized when $MR = 0$, which occurs when $q = 4/0.08 = 50$, and hence when price $p = 4 - (0.04 \times 50) = 2.0$. Thus setting price at 2.0 maximizes revenue.

More generally, for the non-linear demand function, since $R = pq$ and since we can view p as a function of q (from the inverse demand function),[25]

$$MR = \frac{dR}{dq} = \frac{d[pq]}{dq} = p + q\frac{dp}{dq}. \qquad (3.44)$$

This states that marginal revenue, the rate at which revenue increases as sales are increased, is equal to price plus quantity times the gradient of the inverse demand function. Assuming the gradient of the inverse demand curve is negative ($dp/dq < 0$), then

$$MR < P. \qquad (8.45)$$

Marginal revenue is therefore less than price where demand is falling (and is equal to price when demand is flat, and greater than price if demand is rising).

----

[25] Mathematically, this is an application of the product rule for differentiation;

$$\frac{d[f(x)g(x)]}{dx} = f(x)\frac{dg(x)}{dx} + g(x)\frac{df(x)}{dx}.$$

Here,

$$\frac{d[pq]}{dq} = p\frac{dq}{dq} + q\frac{dp}{dq} = p + q\frac{dp}{dq}.$$

Note in Figure 8.14 the connection between the behaviour of the demand curve, the revenue function, and the marginal revenue function. Revenue is increasing so long as marginal revenue is positive, and decreasing when it is negative; the maximum point for revenue is attained at a point where marginal revenue is equal to zero. This makes sense; a necessary condition for maximizing revenue is that $dR/dQ = 0$; that is, the gradient of the revenue function must be zero; since marginal revenue is the gradient of the revenue function, this must be zero at the maximum.

8.6.5 Elasticity

One of the major inputs into decisions on selling price is the price sensitivity of sales. It follows that a very important component of demand analysis is that of measuring sensitivity. Now, it might appear that the slope of the inverse demand function provides a useful index of sensitivity. However, one of the points to note about Example 8.4 is that changing the units of measurement changes the parameter values associated with the demand function. Thus, if a linear demand curve has the equation $p = 4 - 0.04q$, as in Example 8.4, the gradient 0.04 does not immediately tell us very much about how responsive demand is to a change in price (since changing the units of measurement changes the value of this parameter). It is thus difficult to compare the price sensitivity of different demand curves (for different products) simply by focusing on the slope coefficient. The concept of elasticity resolves this problem.

Elasticity is a very general concept of how responsive a dependent variable is to variation in an independent variable. Consider the function

$$y = f(x_1, x_2, \ldots, x_n), \qquad (8.46)$$

in which the value of y, depends on the values of n independent variables, $(x_1, x_2, \ldots, x_n)$. Then the **elasticity** of y with respect to x_j, denoted η_{yx_j}, is defined simply as

$$\eta_{yx_j} = \frac{\text{percentage change in } y}{\text{percentage change in } x_j}, \qquad (8.47)$$

holding all other variables constant. Thus, if a 1% increase in x_j causes a 3% increase in y, then $\eta_{yx_j} = 3$, whilst if it causes a 2% fall in y, then $\eta_{yx_j} = -2$, and so on. One of the attractive features of the elasticity measure is that it is a dimensionless number; that is, it is invariant to changes in the units in which the variables are measured.

The elasticity of demand is thus defined as

$$\eta = \frac{\text{percentage change in quantity}}{\text{percentage change in price}} . \quad (8.48)$$

If quantity demanded falls by 5% when price is increased by 1%, then the elasticity is -5 and so on. Now, writing ΔP as a change in price, and ΔQ as a change in quantity caused by the change in price, then

percentage change in quantity $= (\Delta Q/Q) \times 100$

and

percentage change in price $= (\Delta P/P) \times 100$.

Putting these together gives

$$\eta = \frac{(\Delta Q/Q) \times 100}{(\Delta P/P) \times 100} = \frac{\Delta Q}{\Delta P} \times \frac{P}{Q} . \quad (8.49)$$

Now, in Figure 8.15, starting from the initial point (P, Q), $\Delta Q/\Delta P$ is the inverse of the gradient of the straight-line chord or arc drawn between points a and b. For obvious reasons, this definition of elasticity is termed **arc elasticity**. The size of the price change ΔP is something which can be arbitrarily chosen; once it is chosen, the magnitude of the arc elasticity is defined by the structure of the demand curve. Notice that as the magnitude of ΔP is reduced, the gradient of this chord converges on the gradient of the inverse demand curve at the point (P, Q) (i.e. at point a in Figure 8.15), that is, the derivative of the inverse demand curve at that point. Indeed, we can write

$$LIM_{\Delta P \to 0}(\Delta Q/\Delta P) = dQ/dP, \quad (8.50)$$

and define what is known as **point elasticity** as

$$\eta = \frac{dQ}{dP} \times \frac{P}{Q} . \quad (8.51)$$

Thus, to calculate a point elasticity of demand we simply need to know the point at which it is to be evaluated, (P, Q), and the gradient of the ordinary demand curve at that point, dQ/dP.

EXAMPLE 8.6 Taking the ordinary demand curve in Example 8.4, where $q = 100 - 25p$, what is the elasticity of demand at price $p = 3$?

Answer: At $p = 3$, $q = 100 - 25 \times 3 = 25$. Furthermore, the gradient is $dq/dp = -25$. Hence

$$\eta = (dq/dp)(p/q) = (-25)(3/25) = -3.$$

Similarly, at $p = 2$, $q = 100 - 25 \times 2 = 50$ and

$$\eta = (dq/dp)(p/q) = (-25)(2/50) = -1.$$

Notice that at price $p = 2$, revenue is at a maximum, elasticity equals -1, and $MR = 0$. This is a general point regarding any demand curve. At the revenue-maximizing point, it must be that demand elasticity is -1 and $MR = 0$. This example also illustrates the point that the elasticity varies along the length of a linear demand curve; the point is that the gradient remains constant but the value of (p/q) changes along its length.

In what follows, only point elasticities of demand will be considered.[26] It is conventional to classify a function at a given point as being elastic or inelastic, as indicated in Figure 8.16.

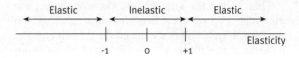

Fig. 8.16 Elasticity-classification

8.6.6 Elasticity and Revenue

A fundamental relationship, central to much of the pricing analysis discussed in this text, concerns the relationship between price, revenue, and the elasticity of demand. This is derived as follows. Given that

$$R = PQ, \quad (8.52)$$

it follows that marginal revenue can be written as

$$MR = \frac{dR}{dQ} = P + Q\frac{dP}{dQ} = P\left[1 + \frac{Q}{P}\frac{dP}{dQ}\right]. \quad (8.53)$$

as in equation (8.44) above. Now, notice that the term

$$\left[\frac{Q}{P}\frac{dP}{dQ}\right] = 1 \Big/ \left[\frac{P}{Q}\frac{dQ}{dP}\right] = \frac{1}{\eta} .$$

Inserting this into (8.53) gives

$$MR = P\left[1 + \frac{1}{\eta}\right]. \quad (8.54)$$

That is, marginal revenue equals price times one plus one over the elasticity of demand. This is hugely important for pricing analysis, as we shall see (in particular, in Chapters 14, 18, and 19). For the moment, I confine attention to the relationship between elasticity of demand and marginal revenue; from (8.54), since $P > 0$, it follows that

---

[26] Arc elasticities suffer from the fact that it is necessary to specify not only the point at which the elasticity is being measured, but also the magnitude of the change in price being considered. Point elasticity depends solely on the point selected.

$$MR > 0 \text{ if } \left[1 + \frac{1}{\eta}\right] > 0.$$

If we rearrange this formula, and note that with downward-sloping demand, the elasticity is negative (so the inequality reverses on cross-multiplying by η, then we can see that

$$\left[1 + \frac{1}{\eta}\right] > 0$$

is equivalent to the condition $\eta < -1$, so

$$MR > 0 \text{ if } \eta < -1 \text{ (and } MR < 0 \text{ if } \eta > -1).$$
(8.55)

Thus, whether revenue increases or decreases as output increases (equivalently, as price decreases, since a price decrease implies a quantity increase) depends on whether the elasticity is below or above -1 in value; or, in terms of the classification scheme in Figure 8.16, whether demand is elastic or not. To summarize, in words:

Fact 8.3 Assuming demand has downward slope, then

(i) if demand is inelastic ($-1 < \eta < 0$), an increase in price (hence a decrease in quantity) will lead to an increase in total revenue, whilst a fall in price (increase in quantity) will decrease total revenue;

(ii) if demand is elastic ($\eta < -1$), an increase in price (hence a decrease in quantity) will lead to a decrease in total revenue, whilst a fall in price (increase in quantity) will increase total revenue.

The demand curve is more inelastic the steeper it is at a given point. If the demand curve is flat, it has infinite elasticity, and zero elasticity corresponds to a vertical demand curve. A moment's reflection on Figure 8.15 should then make sense of the above statement; the steeper the demand curve in this Figure, the smaller the revenue-gain area and the larger the revenue-loss area; with a steep demand curve, a cut in price clearly loses revenue, whilst an increase in price gains revenue.

8.6.7 Cross-price and Other Elasticities of Demand

Just as the own-price elasticity of demand measures the sensitivity of quantity demanded to changes in the product's price, it is possible also to measure the sensitivity to changes in prices of other determinants of demand (in particular, other product prices, but also advertizing and consumer incomes). The point is that the price of close substitute goods may affect the demand for a given product significantly. The **cross-price elasticity** measures this sensitivity.

(a) Some Definitions of Elasticity

Consider the impact of the jth good's price on the demand for the ith product. If we denote the demand for the ith product as q_i, and the price of good j as p_j, then the cross-price elasticity for good i with respect to a change in price p_j is denoted $\eta q_i p_j$, or in a more compact notation, simply as η_{ij}, and is defined as

$$\eta_{ij} = \frac{\text{percentage change in demand for good } i}{\text{percentage change in price of good } j},$$
(8.56)

or, in an obvious parallel to (8.51),

$$\eta_{ij} = \frac{\partial q_i}{\partial p_j} \frac{p_j}{q_i}.$$
(8.57)

Substitutes are goods which have a positive cross-price elasticity. This means that an increase in the price of a substitute good leads to a positive increase in the demand for the product.

EXAMPLE 8.7 Suppose the price of brand 1 coffee increases by 2% and the demand for brand 3 coffee increases by 5% (all other things being equal). Then the cross-price elasticity is simply $\eta_{31} = 2.5$.

Likewise, two goods are **complements** if, when the price of one increases, ceteris paribus, the demand for the other product decreases (for example, petrol and cars with heavy fuel consumption).

Of course, for a given product, changes in the price of many other goods may have little impact on quantity demanded; that is, the cross-price elasticities may be close to zero. However, it is worth remarking that, even if goods are totally unrelated (in terms of characteristics space they are not close neighbours), the so-called income effect tends to make them appear related. This is because a decrease in the price of product A (say) has both substitution and income effects (see section 8.2) and the income effect allows the individual to purchase more of all products. So, for normal goods, there will tend to be an increase in demand when the price of A falls whilst inferior goods will tend to experience a fall in demand, even if these goods are unrelated to A tastewise.[27]

---

[27] A deeper analysis of this would distinguish between gross and net substitutes, to take account of the income effect; see e.g. Green (1965).

The **income elasticity** of demand is defined as

$$\eta_Y = \frac{\text{percentage increase in demand}}{\text{percentage increase in } Y}$$

where Y is some measure of consumer income or wealth, so the point elasticity is expressed mathematically as

$$\eta_Y = \frac{\partial q}{\partial Y} \frac{Y}{q}. \qquad (8.59)$$

EXAMPLE 8.8 Suppose that an increase of 1% in GDP decreases demand by 2%. Then the income elasticity is -2 and the good is an inferior good.

An **advertizing elasticity** of demand can also be defined; this is simply measured as

$$\eta_A = \frac{\text{percentage increase in demand}}{\text{percentage change in advertizing budget}}, \qquad (8.60)$$

or,

$$\eta_A = \frac{\partial q}{\partial A} \frac{A}{q}. \qquad (8.61)$$

EXAMPLE 8.9 If advertizing is increased by 1% and, ceteris paribus, sales increase by 0.5%, then the advertizing elasticity is 0.5.

Chapter 9 will explore in more detail how econometric analysis can be used to estimate elasticities such as the above. Own-price elasticities are of importance for price policy; this is indicated to some extent in the analysis of the relationship between elasticity and revenue above, and will be explored more deeply in Chapters 14, 18, 19, and 24. Cross-price elasticities are of interest since they allow the firm to assess the extent to which other firms products are competitive and also how much the firms' own products compete against each other (see also Chapter 20). Large cross-price elasticities suggest the firm is vulnerable to variations in competitors' product prices. The income elasticity, by contrast, indicates the extent to which the product is likely to be subject to the vagaries of the business cycle; it also gives a useful way of predicting long-term growth in sales (via forecasts of GDP growth etc.). That is, if a product has an income elasticity of, say, $+3$, and GDP grows at an average rate of, say, 2% per annum, then, ceteris paribus, demand will grow at 6% per annum. Conversely, if the good is an inferior good, this will have negative income elasticity. In this case, sales will tend to fall as the economy grows. Finally, the advertizing elasticity is of importance when it comes to deciding

Table 8.3 Some estimates of elasticities

Category of good or service	Income elasticity	Price elasticity
Foreign travel	3.32	−2.26
Clothing	1.47	−1.83
Car travel	1.23	−0.83
Books and magazines	0.95	−0.52
Cigarettes and tobacco	0.77	−0.26
Housing	0.54	−0.23
Vegetables	0.26	−0.26

Source: Deaton (1975: 176–80).

how much to spend on advertizing (see Chapter 26).

Notice in Table 8.3 that all the products cited are normal goods (have positive income elasticities). If a good has an income elasticity of greater than unity, it is sometimes referred to as a **superior good** (a good on which the individual spends proportionally more income as he or she gets wealthier). Thus, in the above example, foreign travel, clothing, and car travel would be classified as superior goods.

(b) Cross-price Elasticities and Product Line Pricing

Where a firm produces a product line, typically of substitute goods, economic theory, as we shall see later in the book, indicates that the profit-maximizing prices will depend not only on own-price elasticities, but also on cross-price elasticities. This is intuitive; changing the price of one product affects the sales of the other products—and vice versa—and these interdependencies should ideally be taken into account in determining prices.

EXAMPLE 8.10 The UK letters business: Recent econometric work on the UK post suggests that the own-price elasticity is between -0.1 and -0.3. The cross-price elasticity with telecommunications is between 0.0 and 0.1. Thus the letters business at current prices is inelastic (this means an increase in price leads to an increase in revenue) whilst a 1% fall in telecom prices leads to a small (circa 0.1%) fall in postal volumes. A more detailed analysis distinguished first- and second-class post. The elasticity estimates in recent work were $\eta_{11} = -1.9$; $\eta_{12} = 1.2$; $\eta_{21} = 0.95$; and $\eta_{22} = -1.25$, where η_{ij} denotes the elasticity of good i with respect to the price of good j (see Cuthbertson and Dobbs 1996).

In this postal example, it is clear that the relative volumes of first- and second-class post are sensitive to the two prices (and the differential between them). Thus any decision on changing the price of one product should take into account the impact of this on the demand for the other product (see Chapters 20 and 22 for more details). Demand analysis and estimates of elasticities can be very useful in developing pricing policy, either for profit maximization or, indeed, welfare maximization.

(c) Guesstimation of Elasticities

Whilst it is possible to estimate elasticities through the use of relatively sophisticated econometric procedures, for many smaller firms and businesses the expertise is lacking or the expense cannot be justified. However, it remains true that some idea of own-price, cross-price, income, and advertizing elasticities are of importance to product strategy (pricing, advertizing, etc. over the product life-cycle). In many cases, it is possible to make an educated guess at the elasticity under consideration. For example, for a relatively homogeneous product, it may be fairly clear that advertizing will not increase sales (hence the elasticity will be close to zero). Or, if there are close substitutes for a product, then it is likely to be fairly sensitive to price (and hence be elastic). Typically, a business person, posed the question of 'what per cent sales would you lose if price was increased by 10%?', would have *some* idea of the likely consequence. If the answer is, say, that you might lose 20% of sales, then the guesstimate of elasticity is simply $\eta = -20\%/10\% = -2$. Thinking explicitly about these sensitivities is likely to improve decision-making in the area of product strategy. It also helps to identify those products where the decision-maker feels vaguest regarding price sensitivity; often it is in such areas that further market research may prove worthwhile. Section 9.3 deals with ways in which market research may be undertaken to develop a better understanding of the elasticities discussed here.

(d) Short-run and Long-run Elasticity

For products like gas, electricity, etc., demand is less elastic in the short run than in the long run. This is simply because, in the short run, individuals have specific fuel-using appliances. Thus, if the price of gas goes up, individuals will economize to an extent on their use of gas, but they are stuck with their gas fires, cookers, etc. In the long run, individuals can also switch to appliances which run on other fuels.

Hence the long-run adjustment is greater than occurs in the short run (this short-run/long-run effect is true for most products, but is particularly the case for products such as electricity, gas, coal, etc.).

8.6.8 The Product Life-cycle

Much of the demand analysis discussed above is short run; that is, the elasticity estimates (even the long-run elasticities discussed above) measure quantity responses to price changes over the short to medium term. In the longer run, however, many (but not all) products go through what is termed a **life-cycle**. At product launch, few consumers know about the product; it is typically innovative and ahead of its rivals. Consumers take time to learn about the qualities of the new product; it takes time for new advertizing to bite. Hence there is a period of upswing in which individuals find out about the good and its characteristics. In this period, it is likely to gain market share rapidly at the expense of rival products. As this happens, competitor products will be squeezed by this added pressure in the market place (and they may try defensive strategies, in particular price discounts, although much depends on the type of market structure). As time passes (and newer products come into the market to compete), any technical advantages tend to fall away, and the product enters what is termed the mature phase. During this period, there is likely to be little gained from extensive further advertizing (although this is likely to depend on market structure; see Chapter 26). Finally, there is decline as the product is no longer at the cutting edge of technology (although its specification may have been improved, it no longer is really able to compete). Typically, in such a phase there is a need to cut margins in order to compensate for inferior performance levels.

To sum up, for products with a pronounced life-cycle, one would expect own-price and cross-price

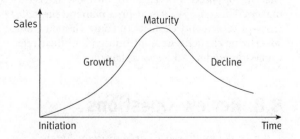

Fig. 8.17 The product life-cycle

elasticities, income elasticities, advertizing elasticities, etc. to change over time, and along with these, the choice of advertizing and pricing policy. The product life-cycle is likely to be pronounced for goods where there is considerable technical change (personal computers, automobiles, etc.), and to be relatively unimportant where there is little change (Stilton cheese, broccoli, etc.).

Recognition of the product life-cycle is clearly important when forecasting product demand—and this is essential for capacity planning and also for decisions on whether to put the product on (or take it off) the market place. It is also of importance in designing price and advertizing policy. Of course, all these decisions are interdependent, as the expected level of sales at each point in the product life-cycle is likely to be also influenced by the pricing and advertizing strategies (see Chapter 26).

8.7 Summary

This Chapter began with an analysis of the pure neo-classical theory of consumer behaviour, starting from assumptions on preferences and working through to properties of demand functions, the existence of a utility function which represents preferences (of central importance to so much economic theorizing), and the measurement of economic welfare when prices change (the motivation for the latter being that it is essential for policy purposes to have some idea of when a proposed policy change is in the public interest). Following this, the switch to making attributes of goods rather than the goods themselves the object of choice was explored. This provided some understanding of what makes goods substitutes (and hence what would be nearest neighbour competition), and also of how it is possible to make predictions regarding new-product demand. Finally, section 8.6 dealt with the kind of demand analysis of direct relevance to business decision-makers. The concepts of own-price demand elasticity, cross-price demand elasticity, income elasticity, and advertizing elasticity were introduced and their relevance for product strategy explained.

8.8 Review Questions

1. Draw the indifference curve diagram for the case where one of the goods is a Giffen good.

2. What properties does neo-classical consumer theory predict for an individual's demand functions?

3. A truck manufacturer is considering whether to introduce a new truck into the local market and wishes to assess whether it is commercially viable. Trucks have two essential characteristics: fuel economy (unladen) and load-carrying capacity. At present, there are three trucks available; their details are given in the following table.

Table 8.4 Entering the truck market

Truck	Price	Fuel economy (miles per litre)	Maximum load (tons)
A	£100,000	2.0	20
B	£90,000	1.75	30
C	£100,000	1.5	40
New	£?	1.85	35

Assuming the other truck prices are unchanged by the new entrant, estimate the price

(i) at which the new truck would just become viable,

(ii) the prices at which the new truck would dominate each of trucks A, B, and C. (Hint: assume that hauliers purchase a sufficiently large number of trucks, so the indivisibility of the product can reasonably be ignored in the analysis, and develop the efficiency frontier for some arbitrary expenditure level, such as £100,000.)

4. If demand is elastic and price is increased, what happens to total revenue?

5. If the demand for widgets is 10,000 at a price of £1 per widget, and 7,000 at a price of £1.40, estimate the parameters of a linear demand curve passing through these two points. What is the elasticity of demand at the price of £1.40? At what price does the demand curve have unit elasticity?

6. An estimated linear demand function for a specialist aromatic tea, called simply Tea, is as follows:

$$q_{Tea} = 10,000 - 1000p_{Tea} + 200p_{Sim\text{-}Tea} + 0.001A + 30\,GDP,$$

where SimTea is a rival product, A denotes advertizing expenditure on Tea, and GDP is gross domestic product. If the current levels for the independent variables are

$p_{Tea} = £1$, $p_{Sim\text{-}Tea} = £0.90$, $A = £10,000$, and GDP $= 100$,

calculate the own price, cross-price, advertizing, and income elasticities of demand at these values.

8.9 Further Reading

Green (1971) is hard to beat as an exposition of this type of material, but is unfortunately out of print. Gravelle and Rees (1991) gives a more thorough but also more technical analysis of both traditional and Lancaster's approaches to consumer theory; the same can be said of Kreps (1991). Earl (1995) offers a reasonable exposition, and also more material by way of critique of the neo-classical theory, along with some discussion of alternative (primarily behavioural) approaches. Most managerial economics texts do not give a serious treatment of consumer theory, preferring generally to stick to demand analysis (treated primarily in section 8.6 above); Douglas (1992) is probably the best of these, however.

9 Demand Estimation

Objective This Chapter examines direct and indirect methods for assessing the relationship between sales and its determinants (including price, advertizing, etc.).

Prerequisites Concepts of a random variable, random sample; some familiarity with distributions such as the normal, t, χ^2, and F distributions; basic understanding of bivariate and multiple regression analysis, including some appreciation of the consequences of breakdown in regression assumptions (autocorrelation, multicollinearity, etc.), hypothesis testing, confidence intervals.

Keywords autocorrelation, bias, Breusch–Pagan statistic, confidence interval, dependent variable, Durbin–Watson statistic, efficiency, endogenous variable, exogenous variable, F statistic, general-to-specific methodology, heteroscedasticity, homogeneity, homoscedasticity, identification, independent variable, misspecification, multicollinearity, omitted-variables bias, R square, simultaneous-equations bias, specification, standard error, testing down, test marketing, t-statistic, unbiasedness

9.1 Introduction

Many businesses get by with only rudimentary forms of demand assessment, whilst others invest substantial resources and utilize sophisticated techniques. According to the economists' old adage, it is worth investing in demand estimation up to the point where the marginal cost is equal to the marginal expected return. Logically, therefore, the amount of effort worth expending is likely to depend upon the nature of the product market. Demand analysis and forecasting using an econometric analysis of historical data is likely to work best in stable, well-developed markets where there is little change in consumer tastes, technology, or product design. By contrast, the formal modelling approach is less likely to work well in markets subject to rapid technological change (personal computers), or where new competitor products are continually being introduced (e.g. automobiles, fashion garments). In such markets, there is a greater need to try to predict what the competitors are likely to produce and when (investment in industrial espionage might be more appropriate here). Larger firms and organizations are more likely

to have the skill base for conducting formal demand estimation; however, whether the skills are in place or not, it is the nature of the product market which will determine whether the effort is likely to pay off.[1]

The object of the demand estimation exercise is to establish the relationship between expected sales and variables that are either under the firm's control (price, advertizing, prices of the firm's product line, etc.) and variables over which it may not have control (the weather, inflation, GDP, etc.). This type of demand information is of importance for any implementation of the marginal analysis so beloved by economists, and for the development of product strategy (pricing, advertizing, etc.).

Section 9.2 begins with a consideration of alternative sources of demand information (historic data, market surveys, direct market tests, etc.), section 9.3 reviews the econometric approach, and section 9.4 examines an extended case study which illustrates the general approach. All the analysis conducted in this Chapter can be replicated and checked using EXCEL (a recommended exercise for the reader; one of the best ways to acquire econometric modelling skills, and the confidence to use them, is by hands-on working through such case studies).

---

[1] Many large organizations do operate in the kind of markets which are likely to be amenable to formal analysis (e.g. electricity, gas, water, telecoms, rail, post, etc.).

9.2 Sources of Demand Information

There are basically four ways of obtaining demand information:

· qualitative demand information ('gut feelings'),
· historical data,
· market survey information,
· direct market experiments.

These are discussed in turn below.

9.2.1 Qualitative Demand Information

Even in the absence of any formal analysis, decision-makers often have some idea or 'gut feeling' for the likely impact of variations in price (and other variables, such as advertizing) on sales. In so far as guesstimates are based on an informal understanding of past behaviour of sales, it can be argued that it is useful to formalize the informal, since quantitative guesstimates of demand elasticity can prove quite useful in the development of pricing policy.[2] Elasticities can be guesstimated by simply posing to the decision-maker simple questions such as 'what do you think the percentage loss in sales would be if we raised prices by 10%?' An answer of, say, '5%' implies a guesstimate of an arc elasticity of demand of $\eta = -5/10 = -0.5$.

Such quick and easy assessments of elasticity are worth making even if more formal analysis, such as market research or direct market testing, is envisaged. This is because such preliminary estimates provide a benchmark for the assessment of estimates provided by more sophisticated approaches. If demand elasticities estimated using econometric procedures are in the same ballpark as prior guesstimates, this is reassuring. If they differ significantly, this warrants a pause for reflection; in such cases, particular care should be taken in checking the robustness of both types of estimate.

Guesstimates have at least two significant weaknesses:

1. Guesstimates are only as good as the judgement of the individual who makes them. Decision-makers implicitly process past information in

making such judgements regarding price sensitivity (although they may sometimes also be able intuitively to judge expected future market developments and how these may affect price sensitivity). In so far as guesstimates are based intuitively on how sales responded in the past to changes in price, a formal statistical analysis is likely to do a better job.

2. Guesstimates are often very imprecise. For example, the impact on sales of a 5% rise in price might be conjectured to be 'anywhere from 3 to 15%'; this is not a very helpful estimate!

9.2.2 Historical Data

The major source of information for demand analysis is the past; the firm will often have a fairly detailed history not only of its product prices, but also of customer sales. It will also have information regarding expenditure on advertizing and other expenses. Aggregate sales data by product, along with the above information, can be used to estimate aggregate demand for the firm's products, in the manner illustrated in section 9.3. However, firms can often do even better; this is so when they have access to information regarding individual sales data, as is available, for example, for most utilities (such as water, gas, electricity, telecoms); in such cases more detailed demand analysis and the fine-tuning of pricing policy (price discrimination) is possible. For further details, see Chapter 19 (and the references cited there).

Apart from firm-specific data, there is much publicly available information which may also prove useful in demand analysis. Most important in practice are measures for general inflation (the retail price index, or RPI), and measures of wealth or income (such as gross domestic product, GDP), although other factors can sometimes be relevant (in particular, environmental variables such as temperature, which can affect the demand for drinks and ices). In many countries there are also other sources of information available on individual consumption behaviour (for example, government-commissioned household surveys). All these sources are of interest in so far as they contain information on variables which may affect the demand for the firm's product. For further discussion and analysis of such data sources, see e.g. Deaton and Muellbauer (1980).

The principal weakness of historical data is that

[2] This is discussed in some detail in Chaps. 14, 18, 19, and 24—see especially sect. 24.4.

they are historical; they lie in the past, and any analysis of them will at best uncover relationships which seem to have held in the past. Relationships established on historical data may well continue to hold in the future, but on the other hand, they may not. Historical data are of greatest use in stable markets which feature little innovation or new-product competition; they are less likely to be useful where innovation is the name of the game (cars, fashion clothing, PCs, etc.).

9.2.3 Market Survey Information

The firm may also commission market research. Market research includes questionnaires, surveys, and interviews. These can be used to assess not only individual characteristics and past purchasing behaviour, but also how people might behave in different scenarios. For demand analysis, such studies attempt to discover how individual buying habits might be affected by changes in product price (and/or other characteristics of the product). Often, such information is gathered as part of a larger survey which might investigate a variety of aspects of individual lives and purchasing behaviour. From the firm's perspective, it is useful to gain a range of information regarding the characteristics of the household in conjunction with assessments of household purchasing behaviour (such as household income, car ownership, the number and age range of individuals in the household, etc.). Such information may provide useful dimensions on which the firm may practise price discrimination (see Chapters 18 and 19).

Of course, the market survey approach has its weaknesses. Getting at future intentions involves hypothetical questions such as 'Would you purchase our product if the price was £3?' The information produced by answers to such questions *can* be used to develop the demand function, but there remains the problem that the questions are hypothetical. Clearly, since customers do not always put their money where their mouth is, the questionnaire approach is less reliable than direct observation of actual market behaviour. For example, (a) individuals may be inclined to give answers they think the questioner wants to hear, (b) they may give a strategic answer (expressing an interest only at a low price might be seen as a way of increasing the likelihood that the firm would indeed launch the product at a lower price), and (c) self-image might affect responses; for example, if low income is

regarded as a social stigma, individuals may be inclined to exaggerate the truth as to their income level when filling in a survey form, or, if their true income has not been reported to the tax authorities, they may well underreport true income, just in case.

9.2.4 Direct Market Experiments

Whilst it is rarely the case that the firm will wish to experiment on the whole market, it is often possible to segment the market (particularly geographically), and to explore the consequences of actually changing price in a relatively small market segment. This kind of **test marketing** can be quite useful for discovering the sensitivity of sales to variations in selling price. In comparison with the consumer interview approach, it has the merit of featuring actual purchases by consumers (rather than hypothetical purchases). The same approach can be used for investigating other facets of the overall marketing mix. For example, the impact on sales can be explored for regional variations in product characteristics, or variations in the intensity of local advertizing.

As with the survey approach, there are several pitfalls and potential drawbacks to the test market approach, as follows:

1. Some care has to be taken regarding the drawing of inferences from direct local market tests. After all, local regions may be heterogeneous, and the response obtained in one region might not be observed elsewhere.

2. It is more risky than market research, and it can be expensive; the variations in price (or other variables) may lead to adverse profit consequences (and unlike the interview situation, the consequences have to be borne by the firm).

3. It is difficult to deal with variations in more than a small number of variables, given that there are likely to be a limited number of sales regions (effectively, a small number of independent observations).

4. Unless the experiment lasts a reasonable period of time, only the short-run effect will be revealed. Often, consumers are slow to adjust, and habit formation may be an important component in their behaviour. Such longer-term effects will not be captured by short-term experimentation. A good example of this delayed response is that to an increase in the price of petrol; in the short run,

demand is fairly inelastic, as individuals may economize on fuel by driving less, but continue to run fuel-inefficient cars. In the longer run, they have the option of choosing a more fuel-efficient car as well as economizing on the use to which it is put.

5. A single change in price merely gives two points on the demand curve (price and quantity before the change, and then after the change). This information may be enough to judge which price is preferred, but going beyond this requires assumptions regarding the functional form of the demand curve to be drawn through the two points. A large number of smooth curves can be drawn through just two data points; a linear curve may yield a reasonable approximation, but equally, may be inappropriate (much depends on how far apart the two points are; for a case study dealing with this point, in the context of cost plus pricing, see section 24.8.2). It follows that care needs to be taken in interpreting the outcome of such experiments, and implications for optimal pricing should not be extrapolated too far outside the price interval for which sales have actually been observed.

9.3 The Economic Approach to Demand Estimation

Whatever the source of demand data, there remains the problem of drawing inferences from them. Sometimes, as in section 9.2.1 above, the implications are fairly direct. However, more often there is a need for econometric or statistical modelling work. I begin in 9.3.1 with a (brief) review of the assumptions that underpin ordinary least squares (OLS) regression; 9.3.2 then discusses the choice of functional form and 9.3.3 examines a variety of econometric problems which can arise. Section 9.3.4 then deals with the testing of restrictions, whilst section 9.3.5 pulls all this material together in setting out a general approach to demand analysis. Section 9.4 then implements the suggested approach in an extended case study.[3]

9.3.1 The OLS Regression Model

This section briefly reviews the structure of the OLS regression model and the basic assumptions that underpin it.[4] The basic model is linear in its parameters (but not necessarily in the variables); it takes the general form

$$y_t = \alpha_0 + \alpha_1 x_{1t} + \alpha_2 x_{2t} + \ldots + \alpha_n x_{nt} + \varepsilon_t$$
$$t = 1, \ldots, n, \qquad (9.1)$$

where y_t denotes the value at time t of the **endogenous** or **dependent variable** (usually, in demand analysis, the quantity of product sold in time period t), and x_{it} denotes the value of the ith **exogenous** or **independent variable** at time t, whilst ε_t denotes a random error or disturbance term. By assumption, the values of each of the variables $y, x_1, x_2, \ldots x_n$ are available for a set of consecutive time periods $t = 1, \ldots, n$ (see Table 9.1 below, for example). The parameters $\alpha_0, \alpha_1, \ldots, \alpha_m$ are fixed (but unknown) constants.

Non-linearity in variables is permissible in the choice of functional form. For example, consider the demand equation

$$q_t = \alpha_0 + \alpha_1 p_t + \alpha_2 p_t^2 + \alpha_3 p_t^3 + \alpha_4 p_{sub,t}$$
$$+ \alpha_5 \text{GDP}_t + \varepsilon_t, \qquad (9.2)$$

where q_t, p_t denote sales and price of a given commodity in time period t, $p_{sub,t}$ denotes the price of a substitute good at time t, GDP_t is a measure of gross domestic product at time t, $\alpha_0, \ldots, \alpha_5$, are parameters (constants), and ε_t is the error term. This model suggests that sales depends linearly on GDP and on the price of the substitute good, but non-linearly on own price (since there is a quadratic and a cubic term in own price). This equation can be estimated using OLS; it illustrates not only that it is possible to include both a wide range of variables on the right side as determinants of demand, but also that variables can enter in a non-linear way. An important point to note is that this model contains, as a special case nested within it, a model which is linear in the variables; thus if we set $\alpha_2 = \alpha_3 = 0$ then sales depends linearly on own price. Apart from featuring higher-order polynomial terms, the other main form of linear-in-parameters model worth considering is the so-called log-linear (constant

---

[3] A competent approach to econometric analysis of demand really does require a full course and text on econometric analysis; hence the presumption in this Chapter of some prior acquaintance with the basics (provided in texts such as Griffiths *et al.* 1993 or Wonnacott and Wonnacott 1991).

[4] Some familiarity with this model is assumed; readers unfamiliar with it may find a more detailed discussion in texts such as Wonnacott and Wonnacott (1991) or Thomas (1997). Only OLS estimation applied to models which are linear in their parameters are discussed here.

elasticity) form. The log-linear Cobb–Douglas form is

$$y = Ax_{1t}^{\alpha_1} x_{2t}^{\alpha_2} x_{3t}^{\alpha_3} \ldots x_{mt}^{\alpha_m} e^{\varepsilon_t}. \qquad (9.3)$$

Taking logs here yields the log-linear specification

$$\begin{aligned}
\ln y &= \ln(Ax_{1t}^{\alpha_1} x_{2t}^{\alpha_2} x_{3t}^{\alpha_3} \ldots x_{mt}^{\alpha_m} e^{\varepsilon_t}) \\
&= \alpha_0 + \alpha_1 \ln x_{1t} + \alpha_2 \ln x_{2t} + \ldots \\
&\quad + \alpha_m \ln x_{mt} + \varepsilon_t, \qquad (9.4)
\end{aligned}$$

where we write $\alpha_0 = \ln A$. Equation (9.4) is linear in parameters $\alpha_0, \ldots \alpha_m$, and so can be estimated directly using ordinary least squares (see section 9.4 for a numerical example). The log-linear functional form is termed 'constant elasticity', simply because the value of the coefficient associated with a given variable gives the elasticity of demand with respect to that variable. Thus, with the log-linear form the elasticities are constants, independent of the values of the independent variables (unlike the linear functional form, where the elasticities systematically vary). Thus it can be shown that the elasticity of y with respect to variable x_j, denoted η_{yx_j}, satisfies[5]

$$\eta_{yx_j} = \frac{x_j}{y} \frac{\partial y}{\partial x_j} = \alpha_j. \qquad (9.5)$$

Thus, the estimate of parameter α_j ($j = 1, \ldots, m$) is a direct estimate of the associated elasticity of y with respect to the variable x_j.

Figure 9.1 illustrates a set of data points (indicated by crosses). Suppose that the following functions were estimated using this sample of data points:

$$q_t = \alpha_0 + \alpha_1 p_t + \varepsilon_t, \qquad (9.6)$$

$$q_t = \alpha_0 + \alpha_1 p_t + \alpha_2 p_t^2 + \varepsilon_t, \qquad (9.7)$$

and

$$\ln q_t = \alpha_0 + \alpha_1 \ln p_t + \varepsilon_t. \qquad (9.8)$$

The OLS procedure effectively estimates a line of best fit through the data points. The goodness of fit is then clearly restricted by the intrinsic flexibility of the functional form chosen. It can be seen that a quadratic model (equation (9.7)), or a log-linear one (equation (9.8)), is able to fit the data in Figure 9.1 rather better than that of a simple linear function of the form (9.6).

---

[5] To see this, first note that the derivative of $\ln x$ is $1/x$, and let the elasticity of demand with respect to variable x_j be denoted η_{qx_j}, defined as $\eta_{qx_j} = (\partial q/\partial x_j)(x_j/q)$. Thus, differentiating (9.3) with respect to a particular independent variable, x_j,

$$\frac{\partial \ln q}{\partial x_j} = \frac{1}{q} \frac{\partial q}{\partial x_j} = \alpha_j \frac{\partial \ln x_j}{\partial x_j} = \alpha_j \frac{1}{x_j}$$

which, on rearranging, gives (9.5).

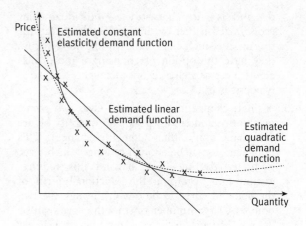

Fig. 9.1 Linear and constant elasticity demand curves

The quadratic functional form is more flexible than the linear form, and indeed, the higher the order of the polynomial fitted, the more closely it will tend to fit the data. Indeed, estimating an nth-degree polynomial will usually suffice to fit the data without any error at all. However, this does not mean that it is necessarily better to choose a higher-over a lower-degree polynomial. The problem is that the sample may not be representative of the underlying population. The goodness of fit achieved may be essentially spurious, and not robust to the introduction of additional observations (the problem is sometimes referred to as 'data mining'; see section 9.3.5 below). The cost of increasing the number of explanatory variables is that the number of parameters to be estimated increases, and the degrees of freedom associated with the regression falls. In general, the larger the number of parameters involved, the higher the variance of individual estimators is likely to be. A higher variance, for an unbiased estimator, means there is a greater probability of the estimate in a given sample taking a value further away from the true value. Section 9.3.3 deals in more detail with the trade-off involved here.

Figure 9.1 also illustrates the dangers associated with making forecasts outside the region for which the data was estimated. If either of the estimated demand functions (9.6) or (9.7) is extrapolated too far to the right, the predictions become decidedly dubious; thus the linear model has demand intersecting both axes (such that there is finite demand even when you pay people to take the product) and the quadratic form typically cuts the vertical axis and, in this example, eventually suggests that the demand curve turns upward. The log-linear model

(9.8) is well behaved with respect to the axes, but makes a dubious prediction that, no matter how high price is increased, there will still be positive sales. The point, of course, is that any significant extrapolation outside the region of estimation must be treated with caution. Policy prescription far outside the region of estimation can easily be nonsensical.

Economic theory often gives guidance as to what variables are likely to be important in determining demand, but it is largely silent on the details of what functional form is appropriate.[6] Hence the statistical analysis needs also to be concerned with the relative performance of alternative specifications of functional form. A variety of alternative functional forms have been used in econometric analysis of demand, production, and cost functions. The essential feature of all these forms is that they do not involve the estimation of too many parameters. For a fairly detailed discussion of these forms and their properties, in the context of demand analysis, see e.g. Deaton and Muellbauer (1980). For simplicity, in what follows only the linear and log-linear models will be considered.

Suppose (9.1) is the true but unknown data-generating process. The problem is then seen as one of estimating the values for $\alpha_0, \alpha_1, \ldots, \alpha_m$ on the basis of the data in a given sample. The OLS procedure generates OLS estimators of these parameters.[7] For a given sample, it generates particular numerical estimates, denoted $\hat{\alpha}_0, \hat{\alpha}_1, \ldots, \hat{\alpha}_m$. The focus is now on the properties of these estimators.

Establishing confidence intervals, or testing whether the OLS parameter estimates obtained in a given sample are significantly different from zero, requires certain assumptions regarding the distribution of the error term ε_t ($t = 1, \ldots, n$) in the multiple regression equation. In order for the OLS

regression parameter estimators to be BLUE (best linear unbiased estimators), it is necessary that[8]

1. the individual errors or disturbances, ε_t, $t = 1, \ldots, n$, are random variables with finite means, variances, and covariances

2. the errors all have zero expected value, independent of the values of the right-hand variables; that is, $E(x_{it}\varepsilon_t) = E(\varepsilon_t) = 0$ for all observation $t = 1, \ldots, n$

3. the variance of each error, ε_t, is a constant independent of t (**Homoscedasticity**). That is, var(ε_t) $= \sigma^2$, a constant

4. the error terms are distributed independently of each other (zero serial correlation). That is, cov($\varepsilon_i, \varepsilon_j$) $= 0$ for all observations i, j in the sample.

5. the error terms are normally distributed (normality); that is, $\varepsilon_t \sim N(0, \sigma^2)$ for $t = 1, \ldots, n$.

6. the exogenous variables are deterministic and linearly independent[9] (or stochastic, but suitably well behaved; for example, they must be uncorrelated with the error term; see e.g. Griffiths et al. (1993)).

In addition, for multiple regression (where there is more than one independent variable), it must also be the case that there is no exact linear relationship between variables in the set of dependent variables (such as would be the case, for example, if two of these variables were perfectly correlated in the sample). Intuitively, if there was such a relationship in the sample, then one of the explanatory variables is redundant. Fortunately, such a state of affairs is unlikely to happen, although the situation where the right-hand variables are highly correlated with each other is quite common (this is termed the problem of multicollinearity, discussed in section 9.3.2(b) below).

OLS parameter estimators have the following properties:

(a) **Unbiasedness.** A parameter estimator is said to be unbiased if the expected value of it is equal to

---

[6] This specification problem arises because the true demand function is unknown. A parameterized functional form (such as a linear function, a polynomial function, or a constant elasticity function) has to be chosen as an approximation for the underlying but unknown true functional form.

[7] The OLS parameter estimates of $\alpha_0, \alpha_1, \ldots, \alpha_m$ are denoted as those values $\hat{\alpha}_0, \hat{\alpha}_1, \ldots, \hat{\alpha}_m$ which minimize the sum of squared errors in a given sample. That is, for observation t, the predicted value is $\hat{\alpha}_0 + \hat{\alpha}_1 x_{1t} + \hat{\alpha}_2 x_{2t} + \ldots \hat{\alpha}_n x_{nt}$ and the observed value is y_t. Hence the parameter values $\alpha_0, \alpha_1, \ldots, \alpha_m$ are chosen such that $\sum_{i=1}^{n}(\hat{\alpha}_0 + \hat{\alpha}_1 x_{1t} + \hat{\alpha}_2 x_{2t} + \ldots \hat{\alpha}_n x_{nt} - y_t)^2$ is minimized. EXCEL provides a regression tool which gives OLS estimates; see sect. 9.4.

[8] In what follows, $E(x)$ denotes the expected value of a random variable x; cov(x,y) denotes the covariance between x and y, whilst $r(x,y)$ denotes the associated correlation coefficient.

[9] To be more precise, if there are k right-hand variables, for these to be linearly independent of each other, the $n \times k$ matrix formed from the observations on these variables should have rank k (it is assumed that $k < n$, the number of observations).

the true value.[10] OLS parameter estimators are unbiased so long as 1, 2 and 6 hold (the property of unbiasedness does not depend on 3, 4 or 5).

(b) **Efficiency.** The estimators are BLUE (best linear unbiased estimators) if assumptions 1–4, and 6 hold (but note that 5, normality, is not required). That is, the estimators have minimum variance amongst the class of linear estimators.

(c) **Inference.** For all the usual tests of significance, for establishing confidence intervals, etc., all the above assumptions 1–6 are required, including normality.

In applications to demand analysis, it is desirable that the parameter estimates have all these properties; unfortunately, it is often the case that some of the above assumptions do not seem to hold in the data. Accordingly, it becomes important to be aware of how to detect violations of these assumptions (and to be aware of ways of dealing with such violations). Section 9.3.2 addresses these issues.

9.3.2 Econometric Problems and Pitfalls

This section examines four important problems which may arise in undertaking a single-equation OLS estimation of a relationship (such as in demand or cost estimation). These are (1) violations of the assumption regarding the OLS error term, (2) multicollinearity, (3) the problems which arise when important explanatory variables are omitted from the analysis, and (4) the problems that may arise if the equation to be estimated is really part of a system of equations.

(a) Breakdown of the Assumptions Regarding the OLS Error Term

The major problems here concern assumptions 3 (homoscedasticity), 4 (zero correlation between errors), and 5 (normality). Most texts on econometrics tend to focus more on the first two of these, as they are the major sources of deviation.[11]

1. *Non-zero Serial Correlation.* The error for each observation t in the sample is assumed have an independent and normal distribution; that is, $\varepsilon_t \sim N(0, \sigma^2)$, where σ^2, the variance, is constant, independent of t. In particular, errors are assumed independent over time, so that the correlation coefficient $r(\varepsilon_i, \varepsilon_j) = 0$ (or equivalently, that the covariance, $\text{cov}(\varepsilon_i, \varepsilon_j) = 0$) for any pair of errors in time periods i, j.

Unfortunately, the above assumption may not hold. Serial autocorrelation occurs when the errors at different points in time have non-zero correlations. First-order autocorrelation is the case where each pair of consecutive errors are correlated; thus positive first-order autocorrelation occurs when $r(\varepsilon_{t-1}, \varepsilon_t) > 0$ (or $\text{cov}(\varepsilon_{t-1}, \varepsilon_t) > 0$). Thus first-order positive autocorrelation occurs if there is a tendency for there to be trends in the errors, such that a positive error tends to be followed by another positive error, a negative by another negative, and so on. In empirical work, positive autocorrelation is more likely than negative; Figure 9.2 illustrates for the case of bivariate regression (where there is just one independent variable) how the errors tend to be distributed around the regression line in such a case.

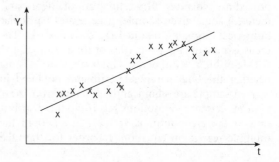

Fig. 9.2 Autocorrelation

Misspecification of functional form can give rise to positive autocorrelation; for example, consider the distribution of errors around the estimated linear demand function in Figure 9.1. At low prices, the

---

[10] An estimator is said to be unbiased if its expected value is equal to the true value of the parameter in the underlying data-generating process, and biased if it is not. The parameter estimator is a random variable. Thus, for different data samples, parameter estimates will vary (simply because samples will vary in the extent to which they are representative of the population from which they are taken). The expected value of an estimator can be thought of as the average value taken by it across the infinity of possible samples that could be taken.

[11] However, in principle it is also desirable to test the normality assumption as well, although space considerations preclude this here. For a discussion of test statistics (for tests of normality), and a discussion of the problems in applying them, see Davidson and MacKinnon (1993: sect. 16.7).

errors are all positive; they then turn negative for medium prices and then turn positive again for high prices. This is a manifestation of positive autocorrelation, which would tend to be eliminated by a change in the choice of functional form; for example, adding a quadratic term would largely eliminate this source of autocorrelation. Thus, it is worth inspecting the graph of the residuals to see whether it suggests a particular kind of functional form misspecification (a formal comparison of alternative functional specifications is conducted in the case study in section 9.4 below).

2. *Heteroscedasticity.* Heteroscedasticity occurs when the variance of the error term is not constant across observations (if it is constant, the errors are termed homoscedastic). Often heteroscedasticity manifests itself as an increasing variance from observation to observation, as illustrated in Figure 9.3, where the dispersion of the observations around the regression line increases from left to right (although more generally the form of heteroscedasticity could be non-linear). Heteroscedasticity is particularly likely if the variables themselves are trending over time, since the variance of a random variable often tends to increase as the level in the variable increases. For example, the variance of an interest rate is likely to be proportional to its level, with high volatility manifest when interest rates are high.

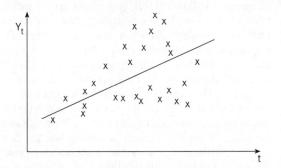

Fig. 9.3 Heterocedasticity

Most texts on econometrics deal with specific tests for autocorrelation (such as the use of the Durbin–Watson statistic) and heteroscedasticity (such as the Goldfeld–Quandt or Breusch–Pagan tests); see e.g. Griffiths *et al.* (1993) or Thomas (1993). It is recommended procedure to undertake such tests whenever a regression is performed; details of how to do this using EXCEL are given in the case study in section 9.4 below.

Parameter estimates in the presence of autocorre-

lation and/or heteroscedasticity are still unbiased, but are not efficient. In general, if these turn out to be serious problems in a particular application, then further model reformulation is required. Often, the presence of significant autocorrelation is an indicator of misspecification, so that a suitable reformulation eliminates the problem (as in Figure 9.1). However, apart from model reformulation, techniques for dealing with these problems are beyond the scope of the present text. (For more details, see Griffiths *et al.* 1993: chaps. 15 and 16.)

(b) Multicollinearity

Multicollinearity is a problem which arises only in multiple regression (and not bivariate regression). It occurs when some (or all) of the explanatory right-hand variables in the regression equations are highly correlated with each other. When this occurs, speaking loosely, it becomes difficult to disentangle the independent effects of the variables and the parameter estimates are no longer robust.[12] Multicollinearity is particularly likely to occur if the variables on the right side are trending over time. For example, in demand analysis, with prices as explanatory variables, this is likely to be a problem because inflation tends to cause all prices to rise over time. The consequences of multicollinearity are that estimates may deviate significantly across individual samples, with potentially large variances for the parameter estimators (possibly with high covariances between parameter estimators). The regression may manifest a lack of robustness, in the sense that dropping or adding a few observations may radically alter parameter estimates. Finally, in testing, the analyst may be led to drop the wrong variables (that is, variables may actually have an explanatory role, but their role is not manifest in the given sample). However, it is also worth remarking that, although no longer robust, the parameter estimators still remain BLUE (best linear unbiased estimators).

There are no formal tests for the presence of multicollinearity. However, the following observations may prove useful. First, the analyst should always compute the correlation matrix for the explanatory variables, and should inspect this to determine the extent to which these right-hand variables

---

[12] The extreme case is where the explanatory variables are not independent and there is an exact linear relationship between the right-hand variables: that is, if the matrix described in n. 9 has rank less than k. Johnston (1972) discusses this case in some detail.

are correlated with each other. Correlations in excess of (say) 0.9 are likely to indicate potential problems. However, even if there are fairly high correlations between regressors, so long as the regression as a whole has a high enough R^2 value, and so long as all the parameter estimates have relatively low standard errors (high t-values), multicollinearity is unlikely to be a problem.

(c) Omitted-Variables Bias

It is important to include all the important variables likely to influence the dependent variable; otherwise parameter estimates will be **biased**.[13] This in turn may prejudice the ability of the estimated equation to provide satisfactory forecasts. The following simple numerical example illustrates this point.

Table 9.1 Coffee Data

t	q_t^{coffee}	p_t^{coffee}	p_t^{tea}
1	10	1	2
2	7	2	1

EXAMPLE 9.1 Suppose that the true demand for a particular brand of coffee, denoted q_t^{coffee}, depends solely on its own price, p_t^{coffee}, and the price of a particular brand of tea, denoted p_t^{tea}, as follows:

$$q_t^{coffee} = \alpha_0 + \alpha_1 p_t^{coffee} + \alpha_2 p_t^{tea} \qquad \text{(i)}$$

(without any random error, for simplicity), where $\alpha_0 = 10$, $\alpha_1 = -2$, $\alpha_2 = 1$, and the data in Table 9.1 represent observations for just two time periods. Since there are only two data points this makes the estimation of parameters particularly transparent. Suppose that p_t^{tea} is omitted from the analysis, and the regression equation estimated is

$$q_t^{coffee} = \alpha_0 + \alpha_1 p_t^{coffee} + \mu_t. \qquad \text{(ii)}$$

Given there are only two data points, estimates of α_0, α_1, denoted $\hat{\alpha}_0$, $\hat{\alpha}_1$, can be obtained directly by solving the equations

$$10 = \hat{\alpha}_0 + \hat{\alpha}_1 \quad \text{and} \quad 7 = \hat{\alpha}_0 + 2\hat{\alpha}_1. \quad \text{(iii)}$$

(since the regression function will pass through both points with zero errors). Solving these equations gives $\hat{\alpha}_0 = 13$, $\hat{\alpha}_1 = -3$; the estimated demand forecasting equation is then that

$$q_t^{coffee} = 13 - 3p_t^{coffee}. \qquad \text{(iv)}$$

Thus $\hat{\alpha}_0 = 13$ when true $\hat{\alpha}_0 = 10$, and $\hat{\alpha}_1 = -3$

when true $\hat{\alpha}_2 = -2$. Given that there were no disturbances in the original data-generating process, a correctly specified regression model should have recovered the true parameter values without error. The misspecification (omitting an important determinant of demand, in this case) gives rise to bias in the parameter estimators and this bias is manifest in the sample estimates.

Note that the regression equation estimated in (iii) does actually perform satisfactorily in terms of 'predicting the historical data' precisely because it is fitted using this (indeed the regression gives a perfect fit!). Unfortunately, the omitted-variable bias will typically mean that the equation does not have good forecast performance. For example, if, in another period, $p_t^{coffee} = 3$ and $p_t^{tea} = 4$, then the actual demand for coffee will be, from (i), $q_t^{coffee} = 10 - (2 \times 3) + (1 \times 4) = 8$. The prediction using estimated equation (iv) is that $q_t^{coffee} = 13 - (3 \times 3) = 4$; a singularly poor prediction given that the out-turn is 8. Variations in the price of tea have an impact on coffee sales, but this is not picked up in equation (ii).

The key insight, regarding omitted-variable bias, is that, at the start of the analysis, careful consideration must be given to deciding which variables might conceivably be important in predicting the variable of interest. Following this, it is necessary to gather relevant data on all these variables. If a convenient numerical measure does not exist for a potentially important explanatory variable, this is not a good excuse for omitting it. The object in such cases should be to seek out or construct measures that can serve as proxies for the unobserved variable. For example, in capital asset pricing (see Chapter 7) the return on the market is an important explanatory variable, but one for which a perfect measure is impossible; the best that can be done is to construct a measurable proxy for this return (e.g. equity indices such as the S&P or the FT).[14] Every attempt should be made to include all potentially important variables in the analysis.

(d) Simultaneous-Equations Bias and the Identification Problem

In some applications, the equation to be estimated may be part of a system of equations. For example, suppose that

---

[13] It is possible to predict the direction of bias in simple models such as that discussed here; see e.g. Thomas (1997).

[14] Equity indices clearly omit many assets that are of importance to individual investors (bonds, artworks, antiques, housing, job, etc.). Still, using such an index may be better than using no variable at all.

$$q_t^d = \alpha_0 + \alpha_1 p_t + \alpha_2 p_t^{sub} + w_{1t}, \qquad (9.9)$$

$$q_t^s = \beta_0 + \beta_1 p_t + \beta_2 w_t + w_{2t}, \qquad (9.10)$$

and

$$q_t^d = q_t^s = q_t, \qquad (9.11)$$

where q_t^s, q_t^d, q_t, p_t, p_t^{sub}, and w_t denote, respectively, the quantity of some given product that individuals wish to supply, the quantity individuals wish to purchase, the quantity actually traded, the market price, the price of a substitute good, and a wage rate for labour used in production (and v_{1t} and v_{2t} denote random errors). Thus (9.11) indicates that price adjusts to clear the market in every period; it follows that price is not really an exogenous variable, but is endogenous, being determined within the system. It can be shown that the price variable is not independent of the error term in the equation (9.9), so violating assumption 2 of the OLS assumptions set.[15] It then follows that the parameter estimates are biased and inconsistent; hence the term **simultaneous-equations bias**.

Sometimes, as in the above example, it is possible to solve the simultaneous-equations estimation problem by first expressing the endogenous variables in terms of the exogenous variables, and then estimating these so-called reduced-form equations.[16] In other cases, more advanced systems methods are required (see Griffiths 1993).

Another problem that can arise in systems of equations such as that described above is the so-called **identification problem**. Suppose that equations

(9.9)–(9.11) describe the economic system, with the parameters α_2 and β_2 both equal to zero (i.e. demand depends solely on price, and supply likewise). In such a system it is not possible to estimate either the demand or the supply curve; they are unidentified. The easiest way to see this is through a diagram (Figure 9.4). Notice that, for given values of the parameters α_0, α_1, β_1 and β_2, particular values of the errors w_1 and w_2 fix the position of the demand and supply curves. Thus we can expect period by period that, as the errors fluctuate, the position of both supply and demand curves shift (and hence the observed equilibrium point shifts).

Panel (a) gives the observed data points. A simple bivariate regression of quantity on price would produce a line of best fit through these points. Such a fitted function would clearly look like a demand curve. Panel (b) illustrates how this just might be the truth. If the supply curve was shifting whilst the demand curve was fairly stable (with w_1 fairly constant and close to zero), the observed equilibrium points would indeed characterize a demand curve. Unfortunately, both the disturbances are likely to change from observation to observation as in panel, (c), causing supply and demand curves to shift; in such a case, the observed equilibrium points represent merely the intersections of such curves, and it is not possible to infer anything about the slope of the supply or the demand curve from them. Thus, a simple regression of quantity on price cannot be relied on to reveal anything about the structure of the demand function. It turns out that this type of problem depends on the structure of the problem; with other exogenous variables present, as in (9.9)–(9.11) above, the identification problem does not arise.

To sum up, if price and quantity are really endogenous variables, part of a system of equations, single-equation regression analysis can be seriously misleading. What the above discussion of simultaneous-equations bias and identification problems indicates is that our fitted equation could give a totally bogus indication of how demand is likely to vary as prices change. How then can we be sure whether the regression is meaningful or not? Certainly, the diagnostic analysis discussed in section 9.4 below cannot be relied on. The answer lies in thinking about the nature of the market structure:

1. When the firm is a price-taker, the data are determined simultaneously by supply and demand; simple regression of quantity on price cannot

---

[15] To see this, substitute (9.9) and (9.10) into (9.11) and rearrange to obtain

$$p_t = \left(\frac{\beta_0 - \alpha_0}{\alpha_1 - \beta_1}\right) + \left(\frac{-\alpha_2}{\alpha_1 - \beta_1}\right) p_t^{sub} + \left(\frac{\beta_2}{\alpha_1 - \beta_1}\right) w_t$$
$$+ \left(\frac{1}{\alpha_1 - \beta_1}\right)(v_{2t} - v_{1t})$$

The OLS assumption is that the error is independent of right-hand variables; that is, $E(p_t\, v_{1t}) = 0$. However,

$$E(p_t\, v_{1t}) = \left(\frac{1}{\alpha_1 - \beta_1}\right)^2 \text{var}(v_{1t}) > 0$$

(assuming v_{1t} is independent of v_{2t} and the exogenous variable w_t, as is reasonable).

[16] Thus equations (9.9)–(9.11) can be rearranged to obtain

$$q_t = \pi_{10} + \pi_{11} p_t^{sub} + \pi_{12} w_t + \varepsilon_{1t}$$

and

$$p_t = \pi_{20} + \pi_{21} p_t^{sub} + \pi_{22} w_t + \varepsilon_{2t},$$

where the parameters $\pi_{ij}(i = 1,2; j = 1,2,3)$ are simple functions of the parameters in (9.9)–(9.11). These equations have genuinely exogenous variables on the right sides, so there is no simultaneous-equations bias in estimation.

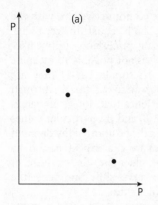
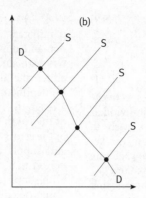
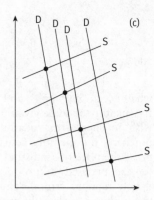

Fig. 9.4 Simultaneous-equations bias

be relied on to retrieve good estimates of either the demand or the supply function. (A more sophisticated approach is required, beyond the scope of this chapter.)

2. If the firm is a price-maker, such that it sets price and then customers decide on how much to purchase, the problem of simultaneous-equations bias usually does not usually arise.

The insight is thus simple. First check the nature of the market in which the firm is operating. If this is a market in which the firm is a price-setter, then the single-equation demand analysis of the type discussed above should prove satisfactory. However, if the firm operates in a competitive market in which it is a price-taker, then an analysis of the market demand and supply functions often requires more careful handling (and often simultaneous-equation estimation methods; see e.g. Griffiths *et al.* 1993: Chap. 18).

9.3.3 On Testing Restrictions

I shall discuss just two types of restrictions and their pros and cons, namely

1. the homogeneity restriction;
2. dropping variables: the zero-coefficient restriction.

The neo-classical theory of consumer choice (Chapter 8) suggests that prices and income are likely to affect demand, that individual demand curves are homogeneous of degree zero in money and prices, and that the substitution effect is negative. This is non-sample information which can be imposed in estimation. Equally, we may observe that several variables do not appear to make any significant explanatory contribution to the forecasting of demand. If we drop such a variable from the regression equation, this is equivalent to imposing the restriction that the value of the coefficient on this variable is equal to zero.

(a) The Pros and Cons of Imposing Restrictions

However, business economists are not usually concerned with testing economic theory, but rather with the more pragmatic objective of estimating a model that works. The concern is thus with

(i) forecasting demand, and

(ii) estimating how changes in variables are likely to feed through into aggregate sales.

Thus the question arises as to whether restrictions based on economic theory (particularly the homogeneity restriction) should be imposed or not. A similar issue arises with respect to the dropping of variables which do not appear to contribute to the explanation of the variation in the dependent variable; dropping a variable is equivalent to imposing the restriction that the coefficient on that variable is equal to zero. It can be shown that dropping a variable that does in fact have explanatory power (albeit not observed in the particular sample under consideration) implies bias in the estimators (section 9.5). On the other hand, including variables which do not in fact explain variation in the dependent variable can be shown to imply a loss of efficiency in the parameter estimates (essentially because of the loss of degrees of freedom). So there is a trade-off, and the trade-off tends to vary with the sample size. With large sample sizes, the problem over the loss of degrees of freedom is less important, and it is often reasonable to leave in potentially irrelevant variables when making forecasts. For small sample sizes,[17] the loss of degrees of freedom becomes more important, so it can be argued that the improvement in estimator efficiency is likely to be worth having. However, there is another reason for imposing homogeneity, as explained below.

(b) Homogeneity Restrictions

Consider the homogeneity restriction for the case of the constant elasticity demand function. Suppose the demand function takes the multiplicative (Cobb–Douglas form

$$q_{1t} = Ap_{1t}^{\alpha_1}p_{2t}^{\alpha_2}\text{RPI}_t^{\alpha_3}Y_t^{\alpha_4}e^{\varepsilon_t}, \tag{9.12}$$

where, during time period t, q_{1t} is the demand for product 1, p_{1t} is its price, p_{2t} is the price of a closely related good (a substitute, say), RPI_t is the retail price index (representing the prices of all other goods), Y_t is some measure of income, such as gross domestic product (GDP), and, finally, ε_t is a disturbance term which captures the effect of variables not included in the equation. The latter is assumed to enter exponentially, so that taking logs of both sides of (9.12) gives a model which is linear in its parameters and has an additive error term, and hence one which can be estimated using ordinary least squares: thus[18]

$$\ln q_{1t} = \alpha_0 + \alpha_1\ln p_{1t} + \alpha_2\ln p_{2t} + \alpha_3\ln \text{RPI}_t + \alpha_4\ln Y_t + \varepsilon_t, \tag{9.13}$$

where $\alpha_0 = \ln A$ is a constant. The demand function is homogeneous of degree zero if, when all prices and income rise by a constant factor, the level of demand for the product does not change. When the value of each variable is increased by the factor λ, if demand does not change, it must be that

$$A(\lambda p_{1t})^{\alpha_1}(\lambda p_{2t})^{\alpha_2}(\lambda\text{RPI}_t)^{\alpha_3}(\lambda Y_t)^{\alpha_4}e^{\varepsilon_t} = Ap_{1t}^{\alpha_1}p_{2t}^{\alpha_2}\text{RPI}_t^{\alpha_3}Y_t^{\alpha_4}e^{\varepsilon_t}. \tag{9.14}$$

That is, the value of the function is unaffected if all variables are altered by a constant factor λ. Now the left side of (9.14) can be expanded to give

$$A(\lambda p_{1t})^{\alpha_1}(\lambda p_{2t})^{\alpha_2}(\lambda\text{RPI}_t)^{\alpha_3}(\lambda Y_t)^{\alpha_4}e^{\varepsilon_t} = \lambda^{\alpha_1+\alpha_2+\alpha_3+\alpha_4}(Ap_{1t}^{\alpha_1}p_{2t}^{\alpha_2}\text{RPI}_t^{\alpha_3}Y_t^{\alpha_4}e^{\varepsilon_t}). \tag{9.15}$$

Compare this with the right side of (9.14): clearly (9.14) will hold only if $\lambda^{\alpha_1+\alpha_2+\alpha_3+\alpha_4} = 1$ for arbitrary values of λ—that is, if the exponents sum to zero:

$$\alpha_1 + \alpha_2 + \alpha_3 + \alpha_4 = 0. \tag{9.16}$$

This is the homogeneity restriction for the constant elasticity demand function. Standard statistical software packages can estimate models with restrictions, although I do not discuss the details here. Such procedures are generally beyond the present scope of the regression modules provided by most spreadsheet manufacturers. Since I wish to make use of the EXCEL software in the case study below, an alternative (and instructive) strategy is followed. This involves reformulating the estimation problem so that the restricted estimation problem reduces to an equivalent unrestricted model. Thus rearrange (9.16) to give

$$\alpha_3 = \alpha_1 - \alpha_2 - \alpha_4, \tag{9.17}$$

and use this to rewrite (9.12) as

$$q_{1t} = Ap_{1t}^{\alpha_1}p_{2t}^{\alpha_2}\text{RPI}_t^{-\alpha_1-\alpha_2-\alpha_4}Y_t^{\alpha_4}e^{\varepsilon_t} = A(p_{1t}/\text{RPI}_t)^{\alpha_1}(p_{2t}/\text{RPI}_t)^{\alpha_2}(Y_t/\text{RPI}_t)^{\alpha_4}e^{\varepsilon_t}. \tag{9.18}$$

Taking logs, this gives

$$\ln q_{1t} = \alpha_0 + \alpha_1\ln(p_{1t}/\text{RPI}_t) + \alpha_2\ln(p_{2t}/\text{RPI}_t) + \alpha_4\ln(Y_t/\text{RPI}_t) + \varepsilon_t. \tag{9.19}$$

Equation (9.19) indicates that imposing the homogeneity restriction allows the equation to be transformed into one involving relative prices. The variables in (9.19) (such as $\ln(p_{1t}/\text{RPI}_t)$, $\ln(p_{2t}/\text{RPI}_t)$, etc.) can easily be constructed, and the equation estimated directly as an OLS regression; this will give estimates for the parameters α_0, α_1, α_2, and α_4. The parameter α_3 can then be calculated from (9.17).

The parameter values $\alpha_0, \ldots, \alpha_4$ estimated under the restriction (9.16), or equivalently through estimating (9.19), will not in general be equal to the parameter values estimated by the simple regression (9.13). The latter, unrestricted model allows that the demand equation may manifest money illusion; (9.19) does not.

(c) Restrictions and Multicollinearity

In most econometric analyses of demand, real prices are used rather than nominal prices (it is common to use a general index of prices, such as the retail price index, to deflate nominal prices; if p_{it} denotes the nominal price of the ith good at time t, then

---

[17] Under 30 observations would count as a small sample, whilst a sample of 100 or more observations might be considered to be reasonably large.

[18] Recall that $\ln(x^a y^b) = a\ln x + b\ln y$. Also $\ln(e^x) = x$.

p_{it}/RPI_t gives a real price at time t).[19] The reason for this is that general inflationary pressure leads to all prices tending to rise over time. This means the right-hand variables are trending upwards and this in turn means that these variables will be positively (and often highly) correlated, so multicollinearity may be a problem. Using real prices helps to make the right-hand variables more stationary and this helps to reduce multicollinearity.

(d) Restrictions and Efficiency

Imposing a restriction increases the degrees of freedom by 1, and reduces the variance of the estimators (notice how the restriction reduces the number of parameters to be estimated from 5 in (9.13) to 4 in (9.19)). If the restriction is true then the restricted estimators are unbiased, and hence more efficient than the unrestricted estimators. That is, imposing the restriction, and so reducing the variance of the estimators, increases the probability that the observed estimates are close to the true parameter values. Unfortunately there is a down side to imposing a restriction, for if the restriction is false (does not hold in the underlying but unknown data-generation process), then imposing the restriction will make for biased estimators. For this reason it is important to test whether the restriction is supported by the data or not (this is illustrated in section 9.4). If so, imposing the restriction makes some sense, given that the concern of the business economist is to get more efficient estimates of response coefficients and elasticities.

9.3.4 General-to-Specific Methodology

It is often reasonable to assume that current prices determine current demand. However, it is possible to make out a case that lagged variables may also have an influence on demand (particularly if it takes time to learn about new prices, or if there is habit persistence, brand loyalty, etc.). Thus demand at time t, denoted q_t, might depend on current price, p_t, but also on past prices, $p_{t-1}, p_{t-2}, p_{t-3}, \ldots$). Unfortunately, economic theory usually provides

little guidance on whether there should be lags, or how many. Likewise, economic theory provides little guidance as to the processes by which adjustment to equilibrium may take place, nor does it generally indicate much detail about the functional form for demand functions (or production or cost functions, for that matter).

The above observations motivate what has sometimes been called the 'LSE tradition' (particularly identified with the influential work of David Hendry; see e.g. Spanos 1986). This involves a modelling process in which a fairly general model is specified, including many lags for all the candidate explanatory variables. Following this, a **testing-down** procedure is applied, in which variables which appear to have insignificant explanatory power are dropped from the equation. Formal tests are then conducted to see whether the data support the more parsimonious model.[20] This process continues until all the variables that remain in the equation have significant explanatory power. This methodology, termed 'general-to-specific', is well set out at the introductory level in Thomas (1993, 1996).[21] The main practical drawback to the approach is that because of lack of data, it is often not possible to include as many lagged values of the right-hand variables as one might like (as in the case study in section 9.4). That is, the general model cannot be very general if data are in short supply.

Even if the researcher has a particular model in mind for estimation and testing, the above approach can still be utilized; the point is that the model of

---

[19] It makes no difference to the parameter estimates of α_1, α_2, and α_4 whether one estimates (9.19) or the function based on real prices, namely

$$\ln q_{1t} = \alpha_0 + \alpha_1 \ln(p_{1t}\text{RPI}_0/\text{RPI}_t) + \alpha_2 \ln(p_{2t}\text{RPI}_0/\text{RPI}_t) + \alpha_4 \ln(Y_t\text{RPI}_0/\text{RPI}_t) + \varepsilon_t,$$

although the intercept will change. The equations have the same diagnostics and forecast performance. The reader can check this by expanding and inspecting the log terms in the above equation.

[20] A more parsimonious model is one which involves fewer variables, and hence fewer parameters to be estimated.

[21] The general-to-specific methodology has both advocates and critics. The critics typically prefer some version of the Popperian testing programme (see Chap. 1) and argue that a model should be fully specified at the outset, the hypothesis testing then being concerned with whether the model is rejected by the sample data. (For a critical assessment, see Darnell and Evans 1990), and for pro-Hendry views of the econometric methodological debate, see either Spanos (1986) or Thomas (1993, 1996). Both approaches are plagued by the problem of what is termed 'data mining' (on which, see Leamer 1978, 1983). Particularly in early work, many of the reported results in econometric analysis could rightly be viewed as the tip of an iceberg; that is, a model is presented and tested but there is little discussion of all the models discarded on the way. Analysts may have tried many different specifications before deciding on what to report. Often the process by which the final model is arrived at is not reported. Data mining is the problem that such *ad hoc* processes will tend to throw up regression results with a spuriously good fit. The general-to-specific approach is more open about the process by which it arrives at the final equation. However, the data mining critique also applies to some extent; for further discussion, see the above references.

interest can be embedded in a more general model (incorporating other variables and more lagged variables), the testing procedure then being utilized to see whether the data support the restriction to the particular case of interest. A case study in section 9.4 illustrates a simple form of general-to-specific modelling.

9.4 A Case Study: The Demand for UK Second-Class Mail

In this section, a simple case study is used to illustrate the process by which an econometric analysis of demand may be developed. Most of the issues discussed above will be addressed within this case study (multicollinearity, autocorrelation, heteroscedasticity, choice of functional form, etc.), and all the computations are undertaken using EXCEL (and in particular, the 'regression' tool, which is available in Data Analysis under the TOOLS pulldown menu). All the data for the case study are given in Table 9.2, so the reader can also reproduce the analysis described in parallel with a reading of this section (a highly recommended learning process).

The case study involves the estimation of the demand for second-class mail in the UK. Table 9.2 gives data for a measure of the volume of delivered second-class mail, denoted q_{st}, the prices of first- and second-class delivery p_{ft}, p_{st}, a price index for telecoms, TEL_t (basically an average price for a telephone call), and an index of retail prices, RPI_t.[22] Eventually a comparison of a linear and log-linear demand function will be considered. Prior to this, however, the general-to-specific methodology is applied to the log-linear specification. The starting point for the analysis is thus the equation

$$\ln q_{st} = \beta_0 + \beta_1 \ln p_{ft} + \beta_2 \ln p_{st} + \beta_3 \ln TEL_t + \beta_4 \ln RPI_t + \varepsilon_t. \quad (9.20)$$

Notice that this equation does not feature lagged

values on the right side. A more general formulation would take the form[23]

$$\begin{aligned}
\ln q_{st} = {} & \beta_0 + \beta_{11} \ln p_{ft} + \beta_{12} \ln p_{ft-1} + \beta_{13} \ln p_{ft-2} + \ldots \\
& + \beta_{21} \ln p_{st} + \beta_{22} \ln p_{st-1} + \beta_{23} \ln p_{st-2} + \ldots \\
& + \beta_{31} \ln TEL_t + \beta_{32} \ln TEL_{t-1} + \beta_{33} \ln TEL_{t-2} + \ldots \\
& + \beta_{41} \ln RPI_t + \beta_{42} \ln RPI_{t-1} + \beta_{43} \ln RPI_{t-2} + \ldots \\
& + \varepsilon_\tau
\end{aligned} \quad (9.21)$$

However, notice the proliferation of parameters to be estimated in this form. In this case study, we have just 13 observations, and it is necessary to keep the number of explanatory variables associated with the general model at significantly less than the number of observations. That is, we simply do not have enough data to estimate a more general form than that given in (9.20).[24] (However, a priori economic reasoning also suggests that, since we are dealing with annual data, lags are unlikely to play a major role.) The data and the full set of analytical results obtained in the modelling process are set out in Tables 9.2–9.9 below.

To perform log-linear regressions, it is first necessary to construct a data set as in Table 9.2 but in which the price variables are log-values. The appropriate data set is given in Table 9.3; Table 9.3 can be quickly constructed from Table 9.2 using the EXCEL Log function[25] and the Fill Down command.

Correlation matrices for the right-hand variables are given in Table 9.4 (these can be obtained using the EXCEL Correlation tool, available from the data analysis toolpack). The results of using the regression tool for the model in (9.20) are given in Table 9.5. The EXCEL Regression tool is menu-driven and straightforward to use; it is also possible, in addition to the output reported in these tables, to produce tables of residuals etc., and charts which plot these residuals in various ways (at the click of a mouse). The residuals so produced are used for diagnostic checking in what follows (testing for autocorrelation and heteroscedasticity).

---

[22] The data are actually abstracted from a quarterly data set analysed in Cuthbertson and Dobbs (1996); these data comprise the first-quarter figures for each year over a period of 13 years. Given that they are in effect annual data, there is no need to be concerned with seasonal effects; had the full data set been analysed, it would have been necessary to incorporate seasonal dummy variables (see e.g. Griffiths *et al.* 1993: Chap. 12 and Cuthbertson and Dobbs 1996 in the context of this example).

[23] It is also possible to introduce partial-adjustment or error-correction terms into this type of formulation. This is beyond the scope of the present chapter; an elementary exposition is given in Thomas (1996), whilst Cuthbertson and Richards (1991) estimate an error-correction model in the context of the UK letters business. On a priori grounds, with annual data such a refinement is unlikely to prove useful, but with quarterly or monthly data, adjustment effects are likely to be more prominent.

[24] Even introducing just one lag would lead to there being 9 parameters, and there are only 12 observations. Thus, the size of the data set has a significant impact on the possible complexity of the most general form of model that can be considered.

[25] If cell A3 contains a value for price, then typing '=ln(A3)' in cell D3 (say) puts the log value of price in cell D3, etc.

Table 9.2 Postal data

t	q_{st}	p_{ft}	p_{st}	TEL_t	RPI_t
1	19.87	8.50	6.50	193.90	149.43
2	19.14	8.50	6.50	193.10	174.10
3	18.39	9.00	7.00	191.70	190.63
4	19.47	9.00	7.00	191.70	208.90
5	18.11	11.33	9.33	237.50	248.77
6	17.61	13.33	11.00	299.90	280.37
7	18.52	15.00	12.17	348.50	311.57
8	18.33	15.50	12.50	337.50	327.03
9	18.45	16.00	12.50	346.40	343.90
10	19.54	17.00	13.00	370.00	362.87
11	20.23	17.00	12.00	391.70	380.80
12	21.10	18.00	13.00	400.60	395.82
13	22.27	18.00	13.00	404.60	409.10

(a) Some Comments on Reported and Non-Reported Statistics Using the Regression Tool in EXCEL

A basic familiarity with regression analysis is presumed. However, a brief review of the EXCEL regression output is given for the regression model (9.20), reported in Table 9.5, before proceeding to the process of testing down.

(1) REPORTED STATISTICS
(a) R-SQUARE
$R^2 = 0.78$; this indicates that 78% of the variation in the dependent variable is explained by variation in the independent variables.

(b) THE F-STATISTIC
The reported value of the F-statistic in Table 9.5 can be used to test the overall significance of the regression (that is, the null hypothesis is that $\beta_0 = \beta_1 = \beta_2 = \beta_3 = \beta_4 = 0$; the alternative hypothesis is that

at least one of these parameters is significantly different from zero). The formal test takes the form

$$H_0: \beta_0 = \beta_1 = \beta_2 = \beta_3 = \beta_4 = 0,$$

against the alternative hypothesis

H_1: at least one of the β_i is significantly different from zero.

The F-statistic to test this is given in the ANOVA (analysis of variance) section in Table 9.4; the reported value is $F^{calc} = 7.09$, whilst the critical value at the 5% level of significance, with $k - 1, n - k = 4,8$ degrees of freedom, is obtained from tables as $F_{4,8}^{crit,5\%} = 3.84$. Hence we reject H_0. However, a simpler way of arriving at the same answer is to note that the summary information actually reports the significance level of the F-statistic, at 0.9642%. This means that the null hypothesis would be rejected at both the usual 5% level and the more stringent 1% level (as a cross-check, if you look up the 1% critical level; it is $F_{4,8}^{crit,1\%} = 7.01$).

(c) STANDARD ERRORS AND t-STATISTICS
The standard errors reported for individual slope coefficients in Table 9.5 give an indication of how tightly they are estimated. The reported t-statistics can be used to test formally whether individual coefficients are significantly different from zero. For a non-zero null hypothesis, it is necessary to calculate the appropriate t-statistic. Thus, to test the null hypothesis $H_0: \beta_i = b$, where b is an arbitrary number, against the alternative hypothesis $H_1: \beta_i \neq b$, construct the t-statistic

$$t_{calc} = \frac{\hat{\beta}_i - b}{s.e._{\hat{\beta}_i}}, \qquad (9.22)$$

where $\hat{\beta}_i$ denotes the estimate of β_i, and $s.e._{\hat{\beta}_i}$ is its

Table 9.3 Postal data (log real prices)

t	q_{st}	$\ln p_{ft}$	$\ln p_{st}$	$\ln TEL_t$	$\ln RPI_t$	$\ln(p_{ft}/RPI_t)$	$\ln(p_{st}/RPI_t)$	$\ln(TEL_t/RPI_t)$
1	2.989	2.140	1.872	5.267	5.007	−2.867	−3.135	0.260
2	2.952	2.140	1.872	5.263	5.160	−3.020	−3.288	0.104
3	2.912	2.197	1.946	5.256	5.250	−3.053	−3.304	0.006
4	2.969	2.197	1.946	5.256	5.342	−3.145	−3.396	−0.086
5	2.897	2.428	2.234	5.470	5.517	−3.089	−3.283	−0.046
6	2.869	2.590	2.398	5.703	5.636	−3.046	−3.238	0.067
7	2.919	2.708	2.499	5.854	5.742	−3.034	−3.243	0.112
8	2.908	2.741	2.526	5.822	5.790	−3.049	−3.264	0.032
9	2.915	2.773	2.526	5.848	5.840	−3.068	−3.315	0.007
10	2.973	2.833	2.565	5.914	5.894	−3.061	−3.329	0.019
11	3.007	2.833	2.485	5.970	5.942	−3.109	−3.457	0.028
12	3.049	2.890	2.565	5.993	5.981	−3.091	−3.416	0.012
13	3.103	2.890	2.565	6.003	6.014	−3.124	−3.449	−0.011

Table 9.4 Correlation matrices

(a) Log nominal prices

	ln(PF)	ln(PS)	ln(TEL)	ln(RPI)
ln(PF)	1			
ln(PS)	0.986449	1		
ln(TEL)	0.994617	0.975905	1	
ln(RPI)	0.98338	0.96742	0.968386	1

(b) Log real prices

	ln(PF/RPI)	ln(PS/RPI)	ln(TEL/RPI)
ln(PF/RPI)	1		
ln(PS/RPI)	0.847664	1	
ln(PTEL/RPI)	0.933689	0.702045	1

(c) Real prices

	PF/RPI	PS/RPI	TEL/RPI
PF/RPI	1		
PS/RPI	0.857724	1	
TEL/RPI	0.943291	0.736949	1

standard error. If $|t_{calc}| > t_{crit}$, where t_{crit} is the critical value for the t-statistic (with $n-k$ degrees of freedom, where n is the sample size and k is the number of parameters being estimated in the regression as a whole), then the null hypothesis is rejected.

To illustrate using the results in Table 9.4, if the null hypothesis is that the coefficient on second-class mail ($\hat{\beta}_2 = -1.14$) is not significantly different from zero, then the calculated value of the t-statistic is

$$t_{calc} = \frac{\hat{\beta}_i - b}{s.e._{\hat{\beta}_i}} = \frac{-1.142 - 0}{0.2542} = -4.49, \quad (9.23)$$

as is also reported in the table. The critical value with $n-k=13-5=8$ degrees of freedom[26] is 2.306. Thus the absolute value of the calculated t-statistic is greater than this, so the null hypothesis can be rejected. However, if the null hypothesis had been that this coefficient was equal to -1 (unit elasticity), then the appropriate t-statistic calculation would have become

$$t_{calc} = \frac{\hat{\beta}_i - b}{s.e._{\hat{\beta}_i}} = \frac{-1.142 - (-1)}{0.2542} = -0.56,$$
$$(9.24)$$

---

[26] Recall that a 5% two-tailed significance test requires 2.5% of the area in each of the tails of the t-distribution (a one-tailed test would allocate 5% to the appropriate tail).

and this null hypothesis could not have been rejected.

To emphasize the point, the t-statistics reported in the summary statistics are appropriate only for testing the null hypothesis that the coefficient is zero.

A quicker way of checking whether a coefficient is significantly different from any given number is to examine the 95% **confidence interval**. This is also reported in Table 9.5 (the interval is defined for a given coefficient by following the row across from the coefficient name to the 'lower 95%' and 'upper 95%' columns). It thus suffices to check whether the value of the parameter under the null hypothesis is included within the confidence interval or not. If it is, then this means that the null hypothesis cannot be rejected. If it is not, the null is rejected. For example, in Table 9.5, if in each case the null is that the true value of the parameter is in fact zero, then this null hypothesis is rejected only for coefficient $\hat{\beta}_2 = -1.14$; the estimate, $\hat{\beta}_2$, is significantly different from zero since the associated confidence interval is $[-1.727, -0.556]$ and this does not include zero (notice that the null hypothesis that it is equal to -1 is not rejected, as this is within the confidence interval). By contrast, the intercept $\hat{\beta}_0 = 2.68$, is not significantly different from zero, since the confidence interval is $[-1.34, 6.71]$ (which includes zero); the same observation applies to all the coefficient estimates other than $\hat{\beta}_2$.

(d) OTHER INFORMATION

Other information of use in computing some test statistics in the ensuing analysis are as follows. The standard error of the regression is 0.038119; df stands for degrees of freedom (which equals 8 in Table 9.5, as there are 13 observations and 5 parameters estimated). In Table 9.5, SS stands for sum of squares and MS for mean square. For example, the sum of squared errors (or residuals), usually denoted in texts as SSE, is 0.011625 here. The portion of the total squared deviations explained by the regression, more usually denoted SSR, is 0.041229.

(2) NON-REPORTED STATISTICS

The EXCEL Regression tool gives only basic diagnostic output. For time-series analysis in particular, there are several other diagnostic statistics which it is desirable to compute. These are discussed below.

Table 9.5 Regression output: log-linear model, nominal prices, equation (9.20)

SUMMARY OUTPUT

Regression statistics

Multiple R	0.88321
R^2	0.780059
Adjusted R^2	0.670089
Standard error	0.038119
Observations	13

ANOVA

	df	SS	MS	F	Significance F
Regression	4	0.041229	0.010307	7.093349	0.009642
Residual	8	0.011625	0.001453		
Total	12	0.052853			

	Coefficients	Standard error	t-statistic	P-value	Lower 95%	Upper 95%
Intercept	2.681918	1.746391	1.535692	0.163164	−1.34527	6.709105
ln (*PF*)	1.173196	0.751794	1.560528	0.157257	−0.56045	2.906837
ln (*PS*)	−1.14161	0.254127	−4.49227	0.002023	−1.72763	−0.55559
ln (*TEL*)	−0.00496	0.437246	−0.01135	0.991219	−1.01326	1.003327
ln (*RPI*)	−0.01274	0.219759	−0.05799	0.955177	−0.51951	0.49402

RESIDUAL OUTPUT

Observation	Predicted q_{st}	Residuals
1	2.965813	0.023394
2	2.963887	−0.01213
3	2.945222	−0.03319
4	2.944056	0.025059
5	2.882796	0.013806
6	2.883211	−0.01448
7	2.904224	0.014661
8	2.911378	−0.00292
9	2.947856	−0.03259
10	2.973194	−0.00064
11	3.063674	−0.05635
12	3.03875	0.0103
13	3.03828	0.065068

(*a*) TESTING FOR AUTOCORRELATION: THE DURBIN–WATSON (DW) STATISTIC

The **Durbin–Watson statistic** d is a useful measure of the degree of first-order autocorrelation. It is defined as

$$d = \frac{\sum_{t=2}^{n}(e_t - e_{t-1})^2}{\sum_{t=1}^{n}e_t^2}. \qquad (9.25)$$

To calculate d using EXCEL, when using the Regression tool, take care to tick the box titled 'Residuals'. This ensures that the residuals are listed in a column directly under the 'summary' output tables; these residuals are reported in Table 9.5 (but omitted, to save space, in the other tables). Given the list of residuals, e_t, $t = 1, \ldots, 13$, it is straightforward to form a series which comprises the squared residuals, e_t^2, $t = 1, \ldots, 13$, and squared deviations, $(e_t - e_{t-1})^2$, $t = 2, \ldots, 13$. Each of these two series can then be summed (using the SUM function; note that the second sum is for observations 2 to 13) and hence the Durbin–Watson statistic d can be calculated.

It can be shown that the DW statistic lies in the range [0,4], and, under the null hypothesis of no autocorrelation, it takes the value $d \approx 2$. Positive autocorrelation is associated with a value for d of less than 2, and negative autocorrelation with a value greater than 2. Usually, time-series regressions will feature some degree of positive autocorrelation; the closer d is to 0, the more pronounced this is. Thus, in general, if the calculated value for d is in the region of 2, there will be no significant autocorrelation. Note that, if there is significant autocorrelation, then the parameter estimates remain unbiased, but the calculated standard errors, t-statistics, and tests based on such statistics are generally suspect.

The critical values for the DW statistic at the 5% level of significance are, when testing for positive autocorrelation[27], $d_L = 0.574$, $d_U = 2.094$, since there are 13 observations, and 5 parameters estimated (most econometrics texts give tabulations of the critical values for the Durbin–Watson statistic). If the value lies below d_L, there is significant positive first-order autocorrelation, whilst if it lies between d_L and d_U, the test is inconclusive; if it lies above d_U, there is no significant positive autocorrelation. In fact, for the model in Table 9.5, the DW statistic takes the value $d = 1.688$ (indeed, in all the regressions reported in the tables, the DW statistic lies in the region 1.6 to 1.8). The test is, formally, inconclusive; with such a small sample, the test lacks power, but values in the region of 2, as in these applications, indicate there is little problem from autocorrelation.

(b) Multicollinearity: Calculating the Correlation Matrix

The Regression tool does not give any indication of whether there is likely to be any problem with multicollinearity. One way of exploring this further is to generate the correlation matrix for the independent variables. This is found in EXCEL under the TOOLS menu, Data Analysis, and then Correlation. Correlation matrices for all the models discussed in this case study are presented in Table 9.4. Notice that, in the matrix in Table 9.4(a), the correlations between the log-variables in levels are all very high. This suggests that there may be a problem with multicollinearity in regression (9.20) (see later).

(b) Testing for Heteroscedasticity: the Breusch–Pagan (BP) statistic

Heteroscedasticity is the problem that the variance of the error term is not constant from observation to observation. There are a variety of tests available for examining this problem; some of these are large-sample tests, whilst others can be applied to the small-sample case.[28] For simplicity I discuss only one large sample test, using a version of the

Breusch–Pagan statistic. In order to implement this test, it is necessary to construct an hypothesis as to what the determinants of variance are. If we stick to linear models, a simple hypothesis is that some or all of the variables used to explain demand might also influence the variance of the error term. That is, for model (9.20), instead of assuming that the disturbance term has constant variance σ^2, it can be hypothesized that it varies across observations as[29]

$$\sigma_t^2 = \alpha_0 + \alpha_1 \ln p_{ft} + \alpha_2 \ln p_{st} + \alpha_3 \ln TEL_t + \alpha_4 \ln RPI_t. \tag{9.26}$$

That is, we simply use the same variables as in the estimating equation; these are log-variables in the case of (9.20). The null hypothesis is that the error variance is really constant. That is,

$$H_0:\ \alpha_1 = \alpha_2 = \alpha_3 = \alpha_4 = 0. \tag{9.27}$$

This is tested against the alternative hypothesis that at least one of these parameters is significantly different from zero. Now, under the null hypothesis (that variance is constant), the squared residuals give estimates for σ_t^2. Hence we simply take the residuals e_t, $t = 1, \ldots, n$ from the original regression equation (9.20) (given in Table 9.5), square them, and then run the regression

$$e_t^2 = \alpha_0 + \alpha_1 \ln p_{ft} + \alpha_2 \ln p_{st} + \alpha_3 \ln TEL_t + \alpha_4 \ln RPI_t + \mu_t. \tag{9.28}$$

The results for this regression are given in Table 9.6.

Essentially then, the problem becomes one of testing whether (9.27) holds. It can be shown that if μ_t has a normal distribution, then the Breusch–Pagan statistic

$$BP = \frac{SSR}{2(\sum_{i=1}^{n} e_t^2 / n)^2} \sim \chi_{(V)}^2 \tag{9.29}$$

(where SSR is the regression sum of squares calculated from (9.28)). That is, for large samples, the BP statistic has an approximate chi-square distribution with degrees of freedom V, where V is the number of variables in the estimating regression (9.28). Even

---

[27] See e.g. Griffiths *et al.* (1993) for tests for negative autocorrelation.

[28] See e.g. Griffiths *et al.* (1993).

[29] The model used here could be extended to include cross-product terms in the regression, to create a more flexible functional form for testing for non-linear heteroscedasticity (for details see e.g. Griffiths *et al.* 1993). This form of heteroscedasticity is not the only hypothesis one might make; for example, variance at time t might be viewed simply as a function of variance at time $t - 1$ and noise (this is termed an ARCH process—autoregressive conditional heteroscedasticity). However, such processes are beyond the scope of the present treatment.

Table 9.6 Regression output for equation (9.28): Analysis of Heteroscedasticity

SUMMARY OUTPUT   Dependent variable: e_t^2

Regression statistics

Multiple R	0.708611
R^2	0.50213
Adjusted R^2	0.253195
Standard error	0.001138
Observations	13

ANOVA

	df	SS	MS	F	Significance F
Regression	4	1.04E−05	2.61E−06	2.017115	0.184849
Residual	8	1.04E−05	1.29E−06		
Total	12	2.08E−05			

	Coefficients	Standard error	t-statistic	P-value	Lower 95%	Upper 95%
Intercept	−0.04734	0.05213	−0.90807	0.390375	−0.16755	0.072875
ln (*PF*)	−0.00122	0.022441	−0.0542	0.958106	−0.05297	0.050534
ln (*PS*)	−0.01352	0.007586	−1.7823	0.112555	−0.03101	0.003973
ln (*TEL*)	0.00803	0.013052	0.615238	0.55549	−0.02207	0.038128
ln (*RPI*)	0.006592	0.00656	1.00495	0.344346	−0.00853	0.021719

more straightforward, it turns out that, for large samples, the statistic

$$nR^2 \sim \chi^2_{(V)}. \tag{9.30}$$

That is, the simple statistic nR^2 (sample size times the R^2 obtained from the regression in (9.28)) has an approximate large-sample chi-square distribution, and this is true even if the errors are non-normally distributed. Now in fact, the sample involved here (13 observations) is small, so these tests do not formally hold. However, it is of interest to see how the calculations turn out; after all, the magnitude of the BP or nR^2 statistic still gives some idea of the extent of heteroscedasticity that may be present. The regression (9.28) and its results are presented in Table 9.6. In this table $nR^2 = 13 \times 0.502 = 6.53$. There are 4 variables in the estimating equation, so the critical value is $\chi^2_{(4)} = 9.49$ at the 95% level of significance. The calculated value would have to exceed 9.49 for there to be significant heteroscedasticity (the sample size would also need to be much larger for this test to be a formal test of significance;

[30] The BP statistic takes a similar value to nR^2 here, as the reader may care to verify.

here it at best merely gives some idea of whether there might be heteroscedasticity).[30]

In fact the values for the DW and the nR^2 statistics do not vary much across the various regressions dealt with here, so I omit reporting results for further regressions. This does not mean that, more generally, this kind of analysis should be ignored; good practice in undertaking econometric work involves checking the diagnostics fully for every regression run.

It is worth emphasizing that if autocorrelation and/or heteroscedasticity are present, then hypothesis testing of the type discussed below is no longer formally valid; resolving this kind of problem requires further explicit modelling, which is beyond the scope of this Chapter (see e.g. Griffiths *et al.* 1993).

(b) The Process of Testing Down

The process of testing down begins with the general equation (9.20), repeated here for convenience:

$$\ln q_{st} = \beta_0 + \beta_1 \ln p_{ft} + \beta_2 \ln p_{st} + \beta_3 \ln TEL_t + \beta_4 \ln RPI_t + \varepsilon_t. \tag{9.20}$$

(1) THE UNCONSTRAINED LOG-LINEAR MODEL (9.20): TABLE 9.5

Whilst the regression as a whole is significant (at 0.96%), 4 out of the 5 parameters are insignificantly different from zero, and the correlation matrix in Table 9.4(*a*) suggests fairly high correlations between the explanatory variables, this is often an indication that multicollinearity may be a problem. Furthermore, a general criticism of this model, which involves nominal prices on the right side, is that these variables are not stationary. A natural first step to consider in the process of testing down is the homogeneity condition. Imposing this in effect means that demand is modelled as a function of real rather than nominal prices. Real prices are more likely to be stationary (i.e. not trending over time), and this should help to reduce the level of correlation between the explanatory variables. The question now addressed is whether the sample data support the imposition of this restriction. The homogeneity restriction is that $\beta_1 + \beta_2 + \beta_3 + \beta_4 = 0$. In the unconstrained model,

$$\hat{\beta}_1 + \hat{\beta}_2 + \hat{\beta}_3 + \hat{\beta}_4$$
$$= 1.1732 - 1.1416 - 0.0049 - 0.0127$$
$$= 0.0139.$$

This is fairly close to zero, indicating approximate homogeneity in the unconstrained model, so the data do appear likely to support such a restriction (see below for the formal test).

(2) THE CONSTRAINED LOG-LINEAR MODEL: TABLE 9.7

To impose the homogeneity restriction, simply construct the real price variables and run the regression[31]

$$\ln q_{st} = \beta_0 + \beta_1 \ln(p_{ft}/\text{RPI}_t) + \beta_2 \ln(p_{st}/\text{RPI}_t)$$
$$+ \beta_3 \ln(TEL_t/\text{RPI}_t) + \varepsilon_t. \quad (9.31)$$

The results of the OLS estimation procedure are given in Table 9.7. Imposing the restriction increases the degrees of freedom (*df* in the tables) by one, from 8 to 9. Notice that this reduces the values of the correlation coefficients in Table 9.4(*b*); this sug-

gests that multicollinearity may be less of a problem here. The DW statistic d in this model takes the value $d = 1.721$, so there is no evidence of significant positive autocorrelation.[32]

I shall only consider the testing of linear restrictions on parameters, and indeed, only two types of linear constraint; namely the constraint of the type $\beta_i =$ a constant (usually zero) and a constraint of the type $\beta_i + 2\beta_j + 3\beta_k = 1$. (For an introductory discussion of non-linear restrictions, see Thomas 1993, 1996). An *F*-test can be used to test multiple linear restrictions on parameters; essentially, the sum of squared errors (*SSE*) measures the goodness of fit of the regression, and when a restriction is imposed, the goodness of fit falls and the *SSE* necessarily increases. However, the question is by how much; loosely, the restriction is satisfactory if the *SSE* does not increase too much. The *F*-statistic for simultaneously testing J equality restrictions amongst the parameters is

$$F = \frac{(SSE_R - SSE_U)/J}{SSE_U/(n - K)}, \quad (9.32)$$

where n is the number of observations, K the number of parameters estimated in the unrestricted regression, and SSE_U the unrestricted sum of squared residuals, whilst SSE_R denotes the restricted sum of squared residuals. Clearly, the worse the fit of the restricted model, the larger SSE_R will be, and so the larger the value of the calculated *F*-statistic. Under the null hypothesis that the restriction is true, this statistic has an *F*-distribution with $1, n - K$ degrees of freedom, and the restriction is rejected if the calculated *F*-statistic is larger than the critical value, denoted $F^{crit}_{1,n-K}$.

In the above case, there is just a single restriction and, from Table 9.5, $SSE_U = 0.011625$, whilst from Table 9.7, $SSE_R = 0.011764$. Hence

$$F = \frac{(0.011764 - 0.011625)/1}{0.011625/(13 - 5)} = 0.095656.$$

The critical value, at the 5% level of significance, is $F^{crit,5\%}_{1,8} = 5.32$ (at 1% it is 11.26). Here clearly the null hypothesis (homogeneity) can be accepted, since the calculated value is less than the critical value.

According to the confidence intervals for the parameters, the coefficient on $\ln(p_{st}/\text{RPI}_t)$, is still significant, but none of the others are. In particular, the telephone price variable, $\ln(TEL_t/\text{RPI}_t)$ appears to do very little work. It would seem natural to consider a further restriction on the model by setting this coefficient equal to zero, as below.

---

[31] It is possible to estimate model (9.20) subject to the restriction on the parameters—but not by using EXCEL. However, the reformulation in (9.31) is formally equivalent to imposing the restriction, and this can be estimated using simple OLS. Note: for simplicity, the same notation is used for the parameters in each of these equations; naturally, β_0, β_1, ... and ε_t are not the same across equations; in particular, estimates of the parameters will in general be different across equations!

[32] The critical values alter, since there are now only 4 estimated parameters; hence $d_L = 0.715$, $d_U = 1.816$; this can be checked from the tables of critical values for the Durbin–Watson statistic, which can be found at the back of any econometrics text.

Table 9.7 Regression output: log-linear model, real prices (homogeneity imposed), equation (9.31)

SUMMARY OUTPUT

Regression statistics

Multiple R	0.881712
R^2	0.777416
Adjusted R^2	0.703221
Standard error	0.036155
Observations	13

ANOVA

	df	SS	MS	F	Significance F
Regression	3	0.041089	0.013696	10.47803	0.002709
Residual	9	0.011764	0.001307		
Total	12	0.052853			

	Coefficients	Standard error	t-statistic	P-value	Lower 95%	Upper 95%
Intercept	2.454794	1.503654	1.632553	0.136997	−0.94671	5.856298
ln (*PF*/RPI)	1.079205	0.65252	1.653902	0.132535	−0.3969	2.55531
ln (*PS*/RPI)	−1.14638	0.240587	−4.76493	0.001023	−1.69062	−0.60213
ln (*TEL*/RPI)	0.045117	0.385381	0.11707	0.909375	−0.82668	0.91691

(3) IMPOSING HOMOGENEITY AND DROPPING *TEL*, LOG-LINEAR MODEL: TABLE 9.8

Using EXCEL, this restriction can be tested simply by dropping the variable *TEL*, rerunning the regression, and comparing the results. That is, the model to be estimated is

$$\ln q_{st} = \gamma_0 + \gamma_1 \ln(p_{ft}/\text{RPI}_t) + \gamma_2 \ln(p_{st}/\text{RPI}_t) + \varepsilon_t.$$
$$(9.33)$$

The results are reported in Table 9.8.

The *F*-test of the restriction (that the coefficient on $\ln(TEL_t/\text{RPI}_t)$ is zero) essentially examines the quality of fit (as measured by *SSE*) of the restricted model (9.33) in comparison with that of (9.31). The *F*-statistic is

$$F = \frac{(SSE_R - SSE_U)/J}{SSE_U/(n-K)} = \frac{(0.011782 - 0.011764)/1}{0.011764/(13-4)}$$
$$= 0.0138, \qquad (9.34)$$

whilst the critical value[33] at 5% is $F_{1,9}^{crit5\%} = 5.12$, so again, the restriction is not rejected (the fact that the calculated *F*-statistic is so small indicates that very little explanatory power is lost in setting the

coefficient on the *TEL* variable to zero); this, and the gain in degrees of freedom, is also manifest in the further increase in the adjusted *R*-square value in Table 9.8.

All the remaining variables are now highly significant (i.e. for each parameter, the null hypothesis that it is zero can be rejected not only at the 5% but also at the 1% level), although the estimated values have not shifted substantially.[34] If the process of imposing restrictions is continued, the zeroing of any other variable fails the *F*-test of that restriction.

The economic implications of the above model of the demand for second-class mail are quite interesting. The own-price elasticity of demand is elastic, estimated at −1.1596, as is the cross-price elasticity with respect to first-class price, at 1.147. Notice, however, that the impact of putting up both prices is fairly small; for example, if both first- and second-class prices are raised (simultaneously) by 1%, the net effect on sales is −1.1596% + 1.147% =

---

[33] Note the change in degrees of freedom in this test, as compared to the previous *F*-test.

[34] It is generally encouraging to note that the estimated parameters on first-class price and second-class price do not vary much in moving from regressions (9.31) to (9.33). This is an indication that the estimates obtained here may be reasonably robust.

Table 9.8 Regression output: log-linear model, real prices (homogeneity imposed), *PTEL*/RPI variable dropped, equation (9.33)

SUMMARY OUTPUT

Regression statistics

Multiple R	0.881519
R^2	0.777077
Adjusted R^2	0.732492
Standard error	0.034325
Observations	13

ANOVA

	df	SS	MS	F	Significance F
Regression	2	0.041071	0.020536	17.42923	0.000551
Residual	10	0.011782	0.001178		
Total	12	0.052853			

	Coefficients	Standard error	t-statistic	P-value	Lower 95%	Upper 95%
Intercept	2.621928	0.448173	5.850262	0.000162	1.623336	3.620519
ln (*PF*/RPI)	1.147666	0.274853	4.175567	0.001901	0.535256	1.760076
ln (*PS*/RPI)	−1.15963	0.201536	−5.75398	0.000184	−1.60868	−0.71058

−0.0126%. Thus the overall effect of putting up postal prices is that demand falls very little (this means that raising both prices will increase revenue taken from second-class mail). The fact that the own-price and cross-price elasticities are relatively large merely reflects the fact that raising the price of second-class mail, or reducing the price of first-class mail, narrows the price differential between first- and second-class mail and causes a shift in demand toward first class.

(4) Imposing Homogeneity and Dropping *TEL*, Linear Model: Table 9.9

The final point to be discussed in this section is that of functional form. Again, this is a large topic, and is merely touched on here in considering how it is possible to test the relative merits of linear versus log-linear functional forms. It seems useful to do this, since these remain fairly popular alternative specifications. Taking (9.33) as the log-linear model, an equivalent linear model is one which involves the same (but non-log) variables; that is,[35]

$$q_{st} = \gamma_0 + \gamma_1(p_{ft}/\mathrm{RPI}_t) + \gamma_2(p_{st}/\mathrm{RPI}_t) + \varepsilon_t. \quad (9.35)$$

Recall that the *SSE* is a measure of goodness of fit for a model. Denote the *SSE* from the log-linear model (9.33) as $SSE_{log\text{-}lin}$, and that from an equivalent linear model as SSE_{lin}. In order to compare models, it is intuitive to compare the *SSE*s of the alternative models. The problem with this is that the residuals are not really directly comparable. Box and Cox (1964), however, demonstrated that the *SSE*s are comparable if we calculate an adjusted sum of squared residuals for the linear model, defined as $SSE_{lin}/\overline{q}_G$, where $\overline{q}_G$ is the geometric mean of the independent variable in the linear model. Call this $SSE_{adj\ lin}$, the adjusted *SSE* of the linear model. This can now be compared to $SSE_{log\text{-}lin}$, the sum of squared residuals for the log-linear model. Essentially, whichever of these is smaller can be viewed as the *SSE* of the better model. However, one could be smaller than the other just as a matter of statistical chance, so the question is whether the

[35] A more complete presentation of the analysis would have included a set of procedures for the linear model parallel to those presented for the log-linear model. However, the main point of including linear and log-linear models here is simply to make the point that specification testing is not only important (a point made in sect. 9.1) but also possible.

Table 9.9 Regression output: linear model, real prices (homogeneity imposed), *PTEL*/RPI variable dropped, equation (9–35)

SUMMARY OUTPUT

Regression statistics

Multiple R	0.872442
R^2	0.761155
Adjusted R^2	0.713386
Standard error	0.703229
Observations	13

ANOVA

	df	SS	MS	F	Significance F
Regression	2	15.75982	7.879909	15.93411	0.000777
Residual	10	4.945308	0.494531		
Total	12	20.70513			

	Coefficients	Standard error	t-statistic	P-value	Lower 95%	Upper 95%
Intercept	19.99372	2.871884	6.961882	3.89E−05	13.59476	26.39267
PF/RPI	483.8005	116.7607	4.143523	0.002001	223.6415	743.9595
PS/RPI	−644.333	116.6195	−5.52509	0.000253	−904.178	−384.489

difference is statistically significant. Box and Cox showed that the following statistic is distributed as $\chi^2_{(1)}$ (chi-square with one degree of freedom):

$$\chi^2_{calc} = (n/2) \ln\left(\frac{\text{the larger } SSE}{\text{the smaller } SSE}\right). \qquad (9.36)$$

To apply this test in the above case, we need to calculate $\bar{q}_G$. This is defined as $\bar{q}_G = (q_1, q_2 \cdots q_{n-1}q_n)^{1/n}$ for n observations. This can be calculated directly using EXCEL. A small short-cut is to note that $\ln\bar{q}_G = (1/n)\sum_{i=1}^{n}\ln q_i$, which is simply the average value of the independent variable in the log-linear regression (Table 9.8). Hence $\bar{q}_G = \exp\{(1/n)\sum_{i=1}^{n}\ln q_i\}$. That is, compute the average value for the log-dependent variable and then take the exponential of this. For the postal data, this gives

$$(1/13)\sum_{i=1}^{n}\ln q_i = 2.9586,$$

so

$$\bar{q}_G = \exp\{2.9586\} = 19.27178.$$

The log-linear model's *SSE* is given in Table 9.8 as

$$SSE_{log\text{-}lin} = 0.011782.$$

The linear model's SSE_{lin} is 4.945308 (Table 9.9). The adjusted *SSE* is

$$SSE_{adj\text{-}lin} = SSE_{lin}/\bar{q}_G^2 = 4.9453/(19.2718)^2 = 0.01331526.$$

Thus the log-linear model fits the data slightly better. The test statistic χ^2_{calc} is, from (9.36), given as

$$\chi^2_{calc} = (13/2) \ln\left(\frac{0.0133153}{0.011782}\right) = 0.795125. \qquad (9.37)$$

Now, at the 5% level of significance, $\chi^2_{(1)} = 3.84$. To suggest that the difference in performance was a significant difference, we would need $\chi^2_{calc}(= 0.79) > \chi^2_{(1)}(= 3.84)$. Clearly then, on the basis of this data set, there is no significant difference in performance between the linear and log-linear model. This would suggest that, depending on the purpose at hand, either model could be used; on statistical grounds, there is little reason to prefer one to the other.

9.5 Summary

This Chapter began by considering alternative sources of data for the estimation of demand relationships; section 9.3 focused on econometrics and the application of econometrics to demand estimation (including issues such as testing the whole regression, testing individual parameters for significance, testing the choice of functional form, etc.), and also testing for violations of basic assumptions, such as autocorrelation and heteroscedasticity. A general-to-specific approach was recommended, and section 9.4 provided an extended case study to illustrate the approach in action.

9.6 Review Questions

1. Load the postal case study data in Table 9.2 into a spreadsheet. Use this to generate the log-data in Table 9.3, and then reproduce the correlation matrices and regression results obtained for the various models discussed in section 9.4. Make sure in using the EXCEL Regression tool that you produce not only the normal regression output, but also a listing of the residuals and plots of these residuals.

2. Use these residuals to run the tests for auto-correlation (calculate the Durbin–Watson statistic) and heteroscedasticity (calculate the Breusch–Pagan statistic) for each regression. Compare your results with the critical values in each case.

3. Work through the general-to-specific modelling analysis presented in section 9.4 and see whether you agree with the results obtained there.

4. Does it matter what value the Durbin–Watson statistic takes in 2 above? Discuss.

5. Do you think the regression analysis undertaken in the case study in section 9.4 is likely to suffer from omitted-variable bias or simultaneous-equations bias? Explain your answer.

9.7 Further Reading

For a basic introduction to econometric analysis, see Wonnacott and Wonnacott (1991). Griffiths *et al.* (1993) is somewhat more thorough and detailed, and particularly useful for those interested in actually doing econometrics, as it pays significant attention to many of the practical problems. Thomas (1993, 1996) deals in more detail with the particular problems which arise in time-series econometrics, and also discusses the 'LSE tradition' in econometric analysis (general-to-specific modelling, error-correction mechanisms, etc.), again in a very readable style. Darnell and Evans (1990) is worth reading as a critical commentary on current econometric practice (see also Leamer 1978, 1983, although this is somewhat less accessible).

10 Production and Cost Analysis

Objective This Chapter gives an account of the traditional neo-classical theory of production and cost analysis. The theory of production here is concerned with the relationship between inputs and outputs, whilst cost analysis is concerned with the minimization of the cost of producing a given output, and of how this cost varies with output.

Prerequisites None.

Keywords average cost, average fixed cost, average product, average variable cost, break-even point, break-even quantity, cost elasticity, economics of scale, elasticity of sale, excess capacity, expansion path, experience curve, factor of production, fixed cost, homogeneous function, isocost line, isoquant, law of diminishing returns, learning by doing, learning curve, long run, marginal cost, marginal product, marginal rate of technical substitution, production function, scale elasticity, short run, technical efficiency, variable cost, very short run.

10.1 Introduction

This Chapter deals with the neo-classical theory of production and cost whilst Chapter 11 deals with cost estimation, and Chapter 12 with cost analysis in short-run decision-making. The focus here is on how the firm should use its inputs in order to produce output in a cost-efficient (cost-minimizing) manner. Naturally, relative to best practice, not all firms are necessarily cost-efficient, either because they operate out-of-date technology and/or they operate it in an inefficient manner. There may also be incentives to operate systems in non-cost-minimizing ways, particularly if the firm is subject to regulatory constraint.[1] The reason for the focus on cost efficiency is simply that, if the firm does not cost-minimize, then it will not be profit-maximizing.

In describing production, the objective is not to get involved in the detail of actual production techniques (since these vary so much across the myriad processes that can be found in the real economy), but rather to capture the features which these production systems have in common; any account of production in general must necessarily abstract from the particularity of these processes.

Ultimately, the firm transforms inputs into outputs; the inputs are costly, and can often be used in a variable mix in order to produce a given level of output. The problem then is to determine the cost-minimizing mix, given the prices of the various inputs. Following this, it is of interest to give an account of how the optimal solution varies as the output to be produced is varied. This then forms an essential ingredient into the analysis of pricing and output choices by firms in different market structures.

Another preliminary point worth stressing is the time dimension associated with production. In general, inputs and outputs are flows per unit time. The unit of time might be the hour, day, week, month, or year, but this does not alter the fact that the relation between inputs and outputs is a relationship between rates of flow. A difficulty arises here in that capital input (land, buildings, machines of various types) does not appear to be a flow. Rather, capital appears to be a stock which facilitates flows, since it is used to transform material inputs into outputs. Such equipment forms part of the firm's asset base; in purchasing a piece of machinery, whilst it can be thought of as a stock of productive services, it is probably best thought of as the purchase of a capacity for productive services. Thus one lathe, for example, gives the firm a maximum possible output of 24 lathe-hours per day. If the lathe is set to turn widgets and can turn 10 per hour, then the lathe's capacity is 240 widgets per day.[2]

---

[1] See Chap. 28 for discussion of the so called Averch–Johnson effect.

[2] Ignoring maintenance and repair time, etc.

10.2 Production and Production Functions

Production is the process of transforming inputs into outputs. Such inputs are often also termed the **factors of production**. For a given set of input quantities, there is typically a limit to the amount of output that the firm can produce. At its simplest, this can be seen for the case of a single input being used to produce a single output, as illustrated in Figure 10.1.

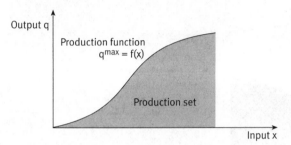

Fig. 10.1 The production function

The shaded area in Figure 10.1 indicates the feasible set of (q,x) combinations. For any given level of input x, clearly there is a maximum output q^{max} that can be produced; the functional relationship between maximum output and input is termed the **production function**. In Figure 10.1 it is denoted $q^{max} = f(\mathbf{x})$. Notice that this maximum level of output increases with the level of input x, but at a varying rate.

This idea of a production function can be generalized to the case where there are multiple inputs. Denote q as output and $\mathbf{x} = (x_1, x_2, \ldots, x_n)$ as a vector of inputs (such that x_i denotes the quantity used of the ith input). As discussed above, both output and inputs are understood as flow rates; that is, output is defined as output per period (hour, day, week, . . .) and likewise the inputs. Inputs are materials, fuels, labour, and, in the longer run, machinery, and even land and buildings.

Definition 10.1 The production function, written as $q^{max} = f(\mathbf{x})$, denotes the relationship between the maximum achievable output, q^{max}, and the input vector $\mathbf{x}$.

Actual output q might fall below the maximum achievable, q^{max}, from any given vector of inputs, either because of incompetence or because agents within the firm at some level have objectives other than that of achieving technical efficiency.

Definition 10.2 An input vector $\mathbf{x}$ which produces output level q is said to be **technically efficient** if there is no smaller input vector $\mathbf{x}'$ (i.e. such that $\mathbf{x}' \leq \mathbf{x}$) which can be used to produce that output level. An input vector $\mathbf{x}$ which produces output level q is said to be technically inefficient if there is a smaller input vector $\mathbf{x}'$ ($\mathbf{x}' < \mathbf{x}$) which can be used to produce that output level.

In what follows, it is simply assumed that the firm is technically efficient, so that actual output is always equal to maximum potential output; to avoid notational clutter, I will simply write q rather than q^{max}, it being understood that henceforward, q is the maximum attainable output.

Definition 10.3 An input x_i is termed essential if for all input vectors $\mathbf{x}$ with, $x_i = 0$, $f(\mathbf{x}) = 0$.

That is, no production is possible if an essential input is absent. Two common assumptions often made about the production function are that

1. $f(\mathbf{0}) = 0$: there is no output without some input;

2. it is a smooth function; that is, it is at least twice continuously differentiable.

(Assumption 2 is purely for expository convenience; a variety of commonly used production functions are not differentiable everywhere.[3])

The case where there are two inputs can also be represented diagrammatically, and is worth exploring in a little detail. For purposes of exposition, in illustrating the two-input case, the two inputs are typically described as capital, K, and labour, L, so the input vector $\mathbf{x}$ is written simply as (K, L). In discussing various production and cost concepts, I shall use the Cobb–Douglas production function as an illustrative case. For the case of two inputs, this takes the form

$$q = AK^{\alpha}L^{\beta} \qquad (10.1)$$

Notice that this functional form satisfies assumptions 1 and 2 above, and also note that all inputs are essential (set either input to zero and there is zero output). The parameters A, α, β in (10.1) are fixed positive constants. Table 10.1 and Figure 10.2 (both produced using EXCEL[4]) illustrate the case where $A = 1$ and $\alpha = \beta = 1/2$.

---

[3] The Leontief production function is a case in point; see e.g. Ferguson (1969).

[4] Using the Table command under TOOLS. For example, put the value for K in cell A1, for L in A2, and the formula for q in cell A3 by typing '=(A1^0.5)*(A2^0.5)' in that cell. A bivariate table can then be produced using A1 and A2 as input cells, and A3 as the output cell.

Table 10.1 Cobb–Douglas Production with $\alpha = \beta = 1/2$ (Output tabulated against alternative input levels)

Capital input	Labour input					
	1.00	2.00	3.00	4.00	5.00	6.00
1.00	1.00	1.41	1.73	2.00	2.24	2.45
2.00	1.41	2.00	2.45	2.83	3.16	3.46
3.00	1.73	2.45	3.00	3.46	3.87	4.24
4.00	2.00	2.83	3.46	4.00	4.47	4.90
5.00	2.24	3.16	3.87	4.47	5.00	5.48
6.00	2.45	3.46	4.24	4.90	5.48	6.00

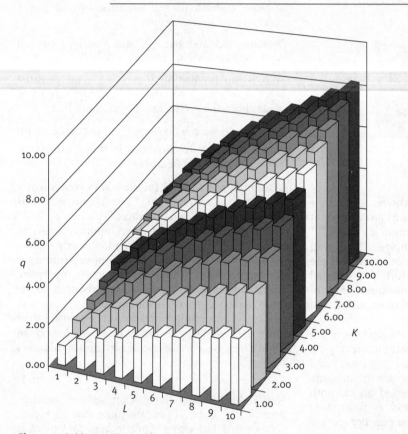

Fig. 10.2 Cobb–Douglas production

10.2.1 Marginal and Average Products

Typically, a firm can vary its input mix, and this will lead to variation in the maximum output which it can produce. From a given starting input configuration, the rate at which output varies as a single-factor input is increased is termed the marginal product associated with that factor.

Definition 10.4 The **marginal product** of factor input i, denoted MP_i, is defined as the rate of change of output with respect to change in the level of that input. Mathematically, it is the partial derivative of the production function with respect to that variable (thus $MP_i = \partial q / \partial x_i = f_i(\mathbf{x})$).

Definition 10.5 The **average product** of factor input i, denoted AP_i, is defined simply as the ratio of output to factor input: $AP_i = q/x_i$.

The marginal products feature significantly in the optimization of production (see section 10.3). In Table 10.1, the effect on output of increasing one input while holding the other constant can be seen; for example, starting with input vector (3,3), the effect on output of changing one of the inputs alone means a movement along either the column or the row.

EXAMPLE 10.1 For the Cobb–Douglas production function in equation (10.1), the marginal product of labour is

$$MP_L = \frac{\partial q}{\partial L} = \frac{\partial f(K,L)}{\partial L} = \frac{\partial}{\partial L}(AK^\alpha L^\beta) = \beta AK^\alpha L^{\beta-1}.$$

The marginal product is positive, since β, A, K, L > 0.

Marginal products are generally positive; however, it is usually argued that there are diminishing returns from adding more and more of one input whilst holding all the other input levels fixed. This is manifest in Table 10.1 (output increases at a diminishing rate as one moves vertically down a column, or horizontally across a row). Thus

Definition 10.6 The **law of diminishing returns** to a factor states that, eventually, as the level of an input is increased, holding all other inputs constant, the rate of increase of output declines.

This is an empirically based idea, often motivated by agricultural examples; for example, increasing the amount of fertilizer spread on a given area eventually leads to diminishing returns (smaller and smaller increases in yield).

EXAMPLE 10.2 For the Cobb–Douglas production function in equation, the rate of change of the marginal product of labour is the second derivative of the production function:

$$\frac{\partial}{\partial L}(MP_L) = \frac{\partial}{\partial L}\left(\frac{\partial q}{\partial L}\right) = \frac{\partial}{\partial L}(\beta AK^\alpha L^{\beta-1})$$
$$= \beta(\beta-1)AK^\alpha L^{\beta-2}.$$

Notice that $\beta, A > 0$ and, assuming positive levels of K and L, then K^α, $L^{\beta-2} > 0$. Hence if $\beta < 1$, $\beta(\beta-1)AK^\alpha L^{\beta-2} < 0$; that is, the marginal product gets smaller as L increases, holding K fixed. For example, tabulating the marginal product for the case where $A = 1$, $\alpha = \beta = 1/2$ and $K = 1$ gives Table 10.1.

Another natural question to ask of production is 'what happens if all inputs are increased pro rata?'

Table 10.2 Cobb–Douglas Production function: table for example 10.2

L	1	2	3	4	5
q	1.00	1.41	1.73	2.00	2.24
MPL	0.5	0.35	0.29	0.25	0.22

This is a question about economies of scale. Loosely speaking, if the output increases faster than the inputs, we say there are **economies of scale** (and if output increases by less than the inputs, we say there are diseconomies of scale). More formally, we have

Definition 10.7 Suppose, for a given vector of inputs at specified levels, $\mathbf{x}$, the output level is q. Suppose also that if all inputs are increased by the same factor, λ, such that $\mathbf{x} \to \lambda\mathbf{x}$ (i.e. such that $x_i \to \lambda x_i$ for each and every input i) where $\lambda > 1$ (but arbitrarily close to 1), this causes output to increase from q to γq. Then there are

locally increasing returns to scale (or scale economies) if $\gamma > \lambda$;

locally constant returns to scale if $\gamma = \lambda$; and

locally decreasing returns to scale (or scale diseconomies) if $\gamma < \lambda$.

If this holds for all feasible input vectors $\mathbf{x}$, then there are globally increasing/constant/decreasing economies of scale.

It is usually (loosely) suggested that economies of scale arise because of economies of specialization (the division of labour etc.), the reduction of indivisibility effects as output increases, and the naturally increasing efficiency of many types of machines as their scale is increased. Diseconomies of scale may arise at large levels of output from diseconomies associated with the increasing problems connected with co-ordination and organization of production. Whilst economies of scale is a useful concept, it should be noted that, in expanding output, the firm will not necessarily choose to expand output by expanding all inputs at the same rate (since this will not usually be a cost-minimizing strategy).

Definition 10.8 The **elasticity of scale**, η_s, is defined as

$$\eta_s = \frac{\text{percentage change in output}}{\text{percentage change in inputs}}$$

when all inputs are changed by the same percentage amount.

This is an arc-elasticity definition of scale elasticity; if we let the percentage change in inputs go to zero, we get the point elasticity. Given this definition, it follows that there are economies of scale if $\eta_s > 1$ and diseconomies of scale if $\eta_s < 1$.

If a production function is homogeneous, then it turns out that the degree of homogeneity indicates whether there are global economies or diseconomies of scale:

Definition 10.9 A function $f(\mathbf{x})$ is said to be **homogeneous** of degree k if, when the vector $\mathbf{x}$ is changed by a constant factor such that $\mathbf{x} \to \lambda\mathbf{x}$, the value of the function at this point can be simplified such that it can be written as

$$f(\lambda\mathbf{x}) = \lambda^k f(\mathbf{x}).$$

EXAMPLE 10.3 Examples of homogeneous functions.

(i) $f(\mathbf{x}) = 3x_1 + 4x_2$ is homogeneous of degree 1.

(ii) $f(\mathbf{x}) = x_1^2 + x_1 x_2 + x_2^2$ is homogeneous of degree 2.

(iii) $f(\mathbf{x}) = x_1^2 + x_1 x_2 + x_2^2 + 3$ is not a homogeneous function.

(iv) $f(\mathbf{x}) = A x_1^\alpha x_2^\beta$ is homogeneous of degree $\alpha + \beta$.

In order to test whether a function is homogeneous, simply write it out, replacing each variable x_i with the term λx_i. Then examine the function to see if it simplifies. For example, consider case (iv) above. Replacing x_1 with λx_1 and x_2 with λx_2, we get

$$f(\lambda\mathbf{x}) = A(\lambda x_1)^\alpha (\lambda x_2)^\beta = \lambda^{\alpha+\beta}(A x_1^\alpha x_2^\beta) = \lambda^{\alpha+\beta} f(\mathbf{x}),$$
(10.2)

so this function is homogeneous of degree $\alpha + \beta$. The reader is encouraged to check the other results. If $f(\mathbf{x})$ is a production function, then clearly output goes up by the factor $\lambda^{\alpha+\beta}$ when inputs are increased by the multiplicative $\lambda(>1)$; clearly, if $\alpha + \beta > 1$, $\lambda^{\alpha+\beta} > \lambda$ and there are economies of scale (and diseconomies if $\alpha + \beta < 1$).

The above analysis indicates that the Cobb–Douglas production function features economies of scale equal to the sum of the exponents of the inputs. Clearly, in Example 10.2, if $\alpha = \beta = 0.5$ the exponents sum to unity, and the function exhibits globally constant returns to scale (a 1% increase in inputs leads to a 1% increase in output).

10.2.2 Isoquants

In examining the problem of cost minimization, the concept of an isoquant plays a useful role.

Definition 10.10 An **isoquant** is the locus of input combinations which generate the same level of output.

Each different level of output will have a (different) isoquant associated with it. Consider the Cobb–Douglas production function $q = AK^{1/2}L^{1/2}$. Dividing through by $AL^{1/2}$ and then squaring both sides makes K the subject of this equation; that is,

$$q = AK^{1/2}L^{1/2} \Rightarrow K^{1/2} = \frac{q}{AL^{1/2}} \Rightarrow K = \frac{(q/A)^2}{L}.$$
(10.3)

The final equality is the equation of an isoquant; it specifies, for given q, what values of K and L give this output. Clearly, the higher the value of q, the further to the north-east the isoquant lies, as indicated in Figure 10.3.

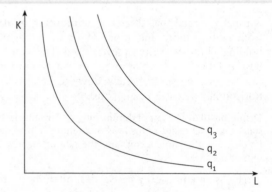

Fig. 10.3 Isoquants

Definition 10.11 The **marginal rate of technical substitution** of input i for input j, denoted $MRTS_{ij}$, is the rate at which input i may be reduced as input j is increased such that output is maintained constant.

$MRTS_{ij}$ varies, depending upon what the current input vector is. For the case where production involves just two inputs, the $MRTS_{ij}$ for given values of the input variables is (the absolute value of) the gradient of an isoquant at that point. Thus it is a measure of how substitutable the inputs are for each other. To show that the $MRTS_{ij}$ at a point in input space is equal to the gradient of the isoquant passing through that point, take the total differential of the production function and set it to zero. Thus, if $q = f(K, L)$, then

$$dq = (\partial f/\partial L)dL + (\partial f/\partial K)dK = 0. \quad (10.4)$$

Setting the total differential equal to zero in effect restricts attention to variations dK, dL which maintain output at the same level ($dq = 0$ means no variation in output is allowed); that is, to movements along an isoquant. Rearranging this, we get

$$MRTS_{KL} = -\frac{dK}{dL} = \frac{\partial f/\partial L}{\partial f/\partial K} = \frac{MP_L}{MP_K}. \quad (10.5)$$

where dK/dL is the gradient of the isoquant; note that the $MRTS$ is equal to the ratio of marginal products (this is a result parallel to that in consumer theory, where the marginal rate of substitution has been shown to be equal to the ratio of marginal utilities).

10.3 Cost Minimization and Cost Functions

The question addressed in this section is how to organize production given the production function and the prices of inputs. The focus here is exclusively on cost minimization. The rationale for this is that objectives such as welfare maximization or profit maximization require that whatever is produced should be produced at lowest cost.[5] To emphasize this, let us note:

Fact 10.1 A necessary condition for the firm to maximize profits is that it should be minimizing costs.

Fact 10.2 A necessary condition for the firm to maximize welfare (consumer surplus plus profits) is that it should be minimizing costs.

Fact 10.1 is established as follows. Profit is revenue minus costs. For selling a given level of output, the firm raises a given level of revenue and incurs a given level of cost. If the level of output can be produced at lower cost, it is clear that this will increase profit. Hence maximum profit can only be attained if, at that given level of output, the cost of producing it is minimized. The same reasoning applies to the welfare maximization case. Here, welfare is given as willingness to pay minus costs. For a given level of output, consumers have a given willingness to pay. If the cost of producing that level of output can be reduced, clearly economic welfare is increased. Hence, at the level of output at which welfare is maximized, it must also be the case that

the cost of producing that level of output must also be minimized.

Profit maximization is a major focus in this text, although on occasion alternative maximands are considered (see Chapter 17), whilst welfare maximization is of importance in discussing public utility pricing (Chapter 22) and state intervention in the mixed economy (Chapters 27 and 28).

10.3.1 Long-Run Cost Minimization: All Inputs Variable

To illustrate the basic ideas, it is traditional to restrict attention to the case where there is a single output and just two inputs. This permits a diagrammatic exposition. However, everything discussed below for this case can be generalized to the multi-input (>2) case (see (b) below).

(a) Long-run Cost Minimization With Two Variables

Call the two inputs capital, K, and labour, L, and let their prices per unit be w_K, w_L. As before, the production function is $q = f(K, L)$. The total cost C is simply the sum of inputs times their prices:

$$C = w_K K + w_L L. \quad (10.6)$$

It is instructive to rearrange this equation to make K its subject, giving

$$K = \left(\frac{C}{w_K}\right) - \left(\frac{w_L}{w_K}\right)L. \quad (10.7)$$

Fixing cost C as a constant, (10.7) is the equation of an **isocost line**. The isocost line gives the locus of points (K, L) which generate the same level of cost.

Figure 10.4 illustrates this; isocosts are straight lines with vertical intercept Cw_K and gradient

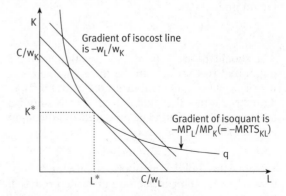

Fig. 10.4 Cost minimization

---

[5] There are of course circumstances in which firms do not run efficiently, either through incompetence, or because agents within the firm pursue their own objectives to the detriment of the firm's performance. These issues are addressed in Chap. 17, where alternative theories of the firm are considered, and in Chaps. 29–31, where the internal organization of the firm is addressed.

$-w_K/w_L$, the ratio of the input prices. Increasing C increases the intercept, and causes a parallel shift of the isocost function away from the origin. It follows that cost minimization requires the firm to choose a point (K, L) which is on the lowest feasible isocost line. For any given level of output q, there is an associated isoquant, defined by the equation $q = f(K, L)$. This is also depicted in Figure 10.4. Clearly the minimum-cost solution for producing this level of output q features a tangency between the isocost line and the isoquant. Since the gradient of an isoquant is equal to the ratio of the two marginal products, this solution features the condition

$$w_L/w_K = MP_L/MP_K, \qquad (10.8)$$

or, rearranging,

$$w_L/MP_L = w_K/MP_K. \qquad (10.9)$$

That is, the ratio of price to marginal product is equalized across all inputs. This is established more formally in section (b) below.

Notice in Figure 10.4 that cost minimization requires a particular choice of K and L; if the level of output q is changed (so shifting the position of the isoquant), or if the input prices are changed (so changing the gradient of the isocost line), the position of the equilibrium will change, and hence the optimal choice of K and L. Thus it is clear that the optimal choices of K and L are functions of these three parameters; if the optimal choices are written as K^* and L^*, then this relationship can be represented by writing

$$K^* = K^*(q, w_L, w_K) \qquad (10.10)$$

and

$$L^* = L^*(q, w_L, w_K). \qquad (10.11)$$

The optimal choices are depicted in Figure 10.4. Substituting these optimal choices into (10.6) gives the minimized cost C^* as

$$C^* = w_L L^*(q, w_L, w_K) + w_K K^*(q, w_L, w_K). \qquad (10.12)$$

It should be clear from this equation that the minimized cost varies with the three parameters q, w_L, w_K. This is referred to as the cost function; ultimately, it says that (minimized) cost is simply a function of the output to be produced and the input prices: that is, we can write

$$C^* = C^*(q, w_L, w_K). \qquad (10.13)$$

Notice that, holding input prices constant, (10.13) is purely a function of the output to be produced. For this reason, the cost function is often written simply as $C(q)$. However, it should be clear from the above that any change in an input price will affect the optimal choices of inputs and hence the minimized cost of production; this translates into a shift in the cost function. Thus, if the cost function is written simply as $C(q)$, changes in quantity represent a movement along the cost curve, whilst changes in input prices will cause a general structural shift (i.e. not simply a parallel shift) in the curve at all levels of output, as depicted in Figure 10.5.

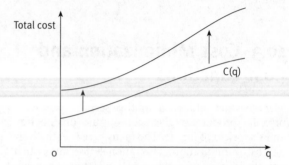

Fig. 10.5 Impact of a rise in an input price

(b) Long-Run Cost Minimization in the General Case

Let $\mathbf{x} = (x_1, \ldots, x_n)$ be a vector of input quantities, and $\mathbf{w} = (w_1, \ldots, w_n)$ the associated prices. Let the production function be $q = f(\mathbf{x})$. Clearly, variations in the quantity of inputs used changes the input vector, and this leads to a variation in the level of output produced. The cost minimization problem is then represented as

$$\text{Minimize } C = \sum_{i=1}^{n} w_i x_i \qquad (10.14)$$

$$\text{subject to } q = f(\mathbf{x}), \qquad (10.15)$$

where C denotes the overall cost of producing a target output q whilst the choice variables are the levels for the inputs, $\mathbf{x} = (x_1, \ldots, x_n)$. The input prices ($w_i$, $i = 1, \ldots, n$) and output q are simply constants as far as this optimization is concerned. Given the Lagrange function,

$$L(\mathbf{w}, \mathbf{x}, \lambda, q) = \sum_{i=1}^{n} w_i x_i + \lambda[q - f(\mathbf{x})], \quad (10.16)$$

the first-order conditions for a minimum are then given by differentiating (10.16) with respect to each of the choice variables x_j, $j = 1, \ldots, n$:

$$\partial L/\partial x_j = w_j - \lambda \partial f/\partial x_j = 0, \, j = 1, \ldots, n, \qquad (10.17)$$

In addition, naturally, equation (10.15) must

hold.[6] Rearranging (10.17) gives the following result (recall that $\partial f/\partial x_j = MP_j$, the marginal product with respect to input j):

$$1/\lambda = (\partial f/\partial x_j)/w_j = MP_j/w_j \text{ for } j = 1, \ldots, n.$$
(10.18)

That is, the ratio of marginal product MP_j to input price w_j must be equalized across all inputs (and set equal to the constant $1/\lambda$). This solution was illustrated in Figure 10.4 in the case of two inputs.

As in the two-input case, it can be shown that, given cost is minimized, the optimal level chosen for each input depends simply on the output required and the input prices. That is,

$$x_i{}^\star = x_i{}^\star(q, \mathbf{x}),$$
(10.19)

and hence (minimized) cost is simply a function of output and input prices:

$$C^\star = \sum_{i=1}^{n} w_i x_i{}^\star(q, \mathbf{w}) = C^\star(q, \mathbf{w}).$$
(10.20)

Thus, again, we get back to the idea that, if input prices remain constant, minimized costs are simply a function of q, the output level. So long as $\mathbf{w}$ is constant, the dependence of the cost function on $\mathbf{w}$ is usually suppressed, by writing the cost function as simply $C(q)$. The likely shape of this cost function (and related functions such as average and marginal cost) is discussed in section 10.4 below.

10.3.2 Short-Run Cost Functions: Some Inputs Fixed

The analysis so far indicates that a cost function exists when all inputs can be varied, and chosen so as to minimize the cost of production. However, in the short run, not all factors are variable. The contrast between what is termed the **short run** and the **long run** is only loosely related to real time; usually, the focus is on a time horizon for which some factors are fixed and others variable. Varying the time horizon will fix varying numbers of input variables. For example, in what Marshall (1890) termed the **very short run**, only materials, fuel, etc. are variable. In the short run, both materials and labour are variable, whilst in the long run, all factor inputs can be varied. In practice, things are more complex than this. For example, there is a variety of categories

of labour, and the time scale on which one can hire or fire may vary across categories. Also, the labour input can often be varied even in the very short run, through the use of overtime, short-time working, etc. The long run is also likely to vary depending on the type of manufacturing process involved; nuclear power capacity, reservoir capacity, bridge capacity, etc. often require much longer time-scales for capacity change than, say, baking or van hire.

What is the effect of having some factors in fixed supply on the costs of achieving any given level of output? Is the short-run cost function different from the long-run cost function? The answer is yes, of course, with short-run costs generally being greater than the long-run attainable levels. This is explained for the two-input case using a simple diagram. A more general analysis is possible, but adds little further insight and is therefore omitted.

Figure 10.6 illustrates the case where the quantity of capital is fixed, but labour is variable. The diagram illustrates several points. First, it indicates the long-run (*LR*) output **expansion path**. That is, it indicates what the optimal choices of labour and capital are for different levels of output (namely, the tangencies between the isocost and isoquant curves). In the short run, however, the firm has some particular level of capital, denoted $\overline{K}$ in Figure 10.6. There is a cost associated with this, per unit of amount r (think of this as rents, rates, lease payments per period, etc.). The payment $r\overline{K}$ runs on whether or not the firm chooses to use the capital. It follows that the only controllable cost is that of labour, and the objective ought to be that of minimizing the amount of labour utilized in producing any given level of output. To put this another way, the opportunity cost[7] of capital, when it is under-utilized, is zero; it pays to use the available equipment to the fullest extent possible.

Figure 10.7 illustrates how the solutions depicted in Figure 10.6 for cost minimization translate into a relationship between the short-run and long-run cost functions. In Figure 10.6, at output level q_1, the capital available in the short-run happens to be just right for this level of output. Thus long-run and short-run costs coincide. At q_0, short-run capital is, relative to long-run requirements, too much, whilst at q_2, it is too little; that is, if these levels of output were to persist, in the long run the firm would find it

---

[6] To spell this out, $\partial(\lambda q)/\partial x_i = 0$ since λq is a constant here, $\partial(\lambda f(\mathbf{x}))/\partial x_i = \lambda \partial f(\mathbf{x})/\partial x_i$ and $\sum_{i=1}^{n} w_i x_i = w_1 x_1 + w_2 x_2, + \ldots, + w_n x_n$, so, for example, $\partial(\sum_{i=1}^{n} w_i x_i)/\partial x_3 = w_3$ (only the term $w_3 x_3$ varies with x_3); likewise, in general, $\partial(\sum_{i=1}^{n} w_i x_i)/\partial x_j = w_j$.

[7] This concept should be familiar to students who have taken a first-level economics course; it is treated in some detail in the context of short-run decision-making in Chap. 12.

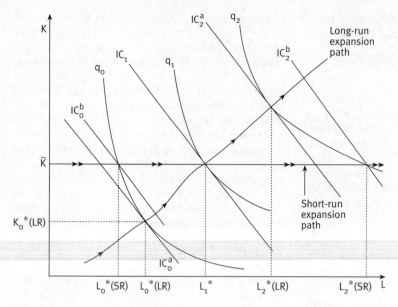

Fig. 10.6 Short-run and long-run cost solutions

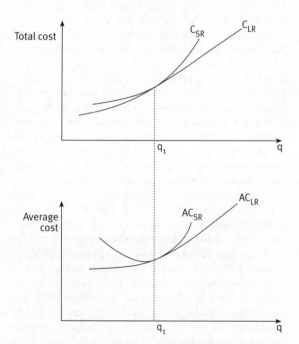

Fig. 10.7 Short-run and long-run cost curves

advantageous to adjust the level of capital input. Clearly costs are higher in the short run at q_0 and q_2; the short-run isocost lines lie to the right of the long-run isocost lines for these output levels; for example, for output q_0, short-run cost is given by

isocost line IC_0^b and long-run cost by isocost line IC_0^a, etc. This is depicted in the upper panel in Figure 10.7; the short-run cost curve lies above the long-run cost curve, except at the point of tangency at q_1.

Average cost, $AC(q)$, is defined simply as total cost divided by output,

$$AC(q) = C(q)/q, \tag{10.21}$$

so the tangency between the total cost functions in the short and long run translates into a tangency between long-run and short-run average cost functions, as shown in the lower panel in Figure 10.7.

If the level of $\overline{K}$ is changed, then the value of q for which $\overline{K}$ happens to be the right level for both the short and long run changes. For example, if $\overline{K}$ was set at the level $K_0^*(LR)$, this would imply a new short-run cost curve which would be tangential to the long-run cost curve at the point q_0.

Thus, for any given output level q, once capital input is fixed at its long-run optimal level in order to produce q, if output is then varied in the short run, the short-run cost curve lies above the long-run curve but is tangential to it at q. The same applies to average cost curves in the short and long run. This explains the standard result that the long-run cost curve is the envelope of short-run cost curves, and the **long-run average cost** (*LRAC*) curve is the envelope of **short-run average cost** (*SRAC*) curves, as depicted in Figure 10.8.

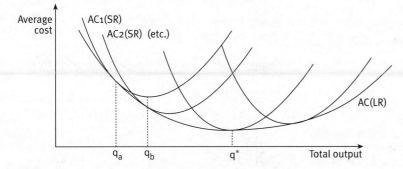

Fig. 10.8 Short-run and long-run average cost functions

Notice in Figure 10.8 that when the *LRAC* is falling, or rising, it is not optimal, even in the long run, to operate a plant at its design-optimum level of output (minimum average cost). If the *LRAC* is falling, it pays to purchase a larger plant and operate it at an output level below that which minimizes *SRAC*, whilst (as the reader can check) if *LRAC* is rising, it pays to purchase a smaller plant and to operate it at an output level above that which minimizes *SRAC*. For example, if, in Figure 10.8, a level of output q_b is desired, it is better to produce it with a plant having the short-run average cost curve $SRAC_2$ and to run this plant at an output level below that which minimizes its short-run average cost. Only if the firm wished to produce output level q^* would it choose a plant and operate it at minimum short-run average cost.

Of course, once a plant has been installed, in the short run the firm may experience significant fluctuations in demand, and may need to operate existing capacity at levels either above or below that which minimizes *SRAC*. However, there are various ways in which the firm will seek to keep the plant operating at around minimum short-run average cost. For example, at times of low demand it can maintain production and produce for inventory, or at times of high demand it can run down inventories and also introduce waiting lists (this approach is often adopted by small-output bespoke producers such as Morgan or TVR, the car manufacturers).

The smooth long-run average cost curve, depicted in Figure 10.8, presupposes that it is possible for the firm to select any plant size (any level of capital input $\overline{K}$ in terms of Figure 10.6). In practice, particularly for smaller levels of production, plant and machinery may only be available in fixed 'off the peg' sizes. The idea that the *LRAC* is the envelope of *SRAC*s still applies, but the *LRAC* is no longer smooth (it has some corners, as depicted in Figure 10.9).

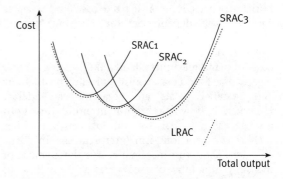

Fig. 10.9 Long-run average cost (discrete plant sizes)

10.4 Cost Analysis and Concepts

Section 10.3 established the idea that minimum cost is a function of the output level. This motivates the focus in this section on the cost curves themselves. The concepts discussed here find application throughout the rest of the text, when discussing models of how individual firms operate (pricing, output, advertizing, investment decisions, etc.) and how these are embedded in different market structures. I start with a set of definitions of basic concepts, and follow this with several diagrams which illustrate the interrelationships between these concepts.

Definition 10.12 Costs which do not vary as output is increased are termed **fixed costs** (denoted *FC*).

Definition 10.13 Average fixed cost (*AFC*) is simply fixed cost, *FC*, divided by output, *q*. That is, $AFC = FC/q$.

Definition 10.14 That part of total cost which varies with the output level is termed **variable cost** (*VC*).

Definition 10.15 **Average variable cost** (AVC) is defined as variable cost per unit of output; i.e. $AVC = VC/q$.

Definition 10.16 **Average total cost** (AC) is total cost (C) per unit output; i.e. $AC = C/q$.

Definition 10.17 **Marginal cost** (MC) at a given level of output is:

(*a*) (Discrete definition) the additional cost of producing one more unit of output, or

(*b*) (Continuous definition) the rate at which total cost increases as output is increased; it is thus the derivative or gradient of the cost function at that output level; i.e. $MC = dC/dq$.

The above definitions do not specify the time horizon; what counts as a fixed cost, and what as variable, will depend on the decision context involved. Here the concern is primarily with short-run variations in the level of output, so the rental costs of plant, machinery, land, and buildings are all regarded as fixed costs, whilst typically, most labour and materials costs are regarded as variable. However, it is worth bearing in mind that both average and marginal cost concepts can bear either a short-run or a long-run interpretation. In particular, the short-run marginal cost is the gradient of the short-run total cost curve at a given level of output, whilst long-run marginal cost is the gradient of the long-run total cost curve at that point.

10.4.1 Basic Relationships Between Cost Concepts

Total cost equals fixed plus variable costs,

$$C = FC + VC, \tag{10.22}$$

so it follows that, dividing through by output, average total cost equals average fixed plus average variable costs:

$$AC = (FC/q) + (VC/q) = AFC + AVC. \tag{10.23}$$

Since fixed costs are invariant with output, $dFC/dq = 0$. Hence it follows that

$$MC = \frac{dC}{dq} = \frac{d(FC + VC)}{dq} = \frac{dVC}{dq}. \tag{10.24}$$

That is, marginal cost, MC, is equal to the gradient of the total cost function, which, at the same output level, equals the gradient of the variable cost function.

Figure 10.10 illustrates the relationship between total cost, variable cost, and fixed cost (upper panel) whilst average fixed cost and the implied relationships between the marginal cost curve, the average

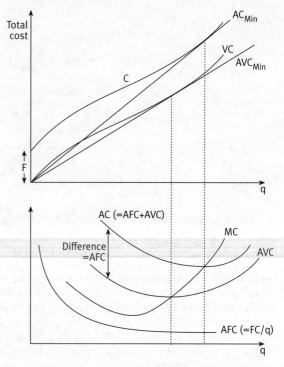

Fig. 10.10 Cost and average cost of curves (1)

variable cost curve, and the average total cost curve are depicted in the lower panel. Given (10.23), the difference in the levels of the AC and AVC curves is equal to AFC. The level of marginal cost is defined as the gradient of the total cost curve, or equivalently, the variable cost curve (in view of (10.24)). Hence the marginal cost is increasing if the slope of the total cost function is increasing, as can be verified in the figure. Notice also that, in the upper panel, average cost is graphically depicted as the gradient of a line from the origin to any point on the total cost function, and the gradient of a line from the origin to a point on the variable cost function gives average variable cost.[8] The lines drawn are those associated with minima for AC and AVC respectively.

Speaking loosely, with every unit increase in output, if marginal cost is greater than average cost, it is adding more than the average to total cost, and so this leads to the average cost increasing; equally, if marginal cost is below average cost, this means

---

[8] A line which passes from the origin to a point (x, y) clearly has gradient y/x. Thus here the gradient of the total cost function is $TC/q(=ATC)$ and the gradient of the variable cost function is VC/q ($=AVC$).

marginal cost pulls the average cost down as output increases, as depicted in Figure 10.10. The same argument applies to the relationship between marginal cost and average variable cost. These points can be demonstrated more formally. Thus the gradient of the average variable cost function is given as (applying the quotient rule for differentiating the ratio of two functions):

$$\frac{d}{dq}(AVC) = \frac{d}{dq}\left(\frac{VC}{q}\right) = \frac{q(dVC/dq) - VC}{q^2}$$
$$= (1/q)(MC - AVC) \qquad (10.25)$$

(noting that from (10.24) $dVC/dq = MC$, marginal cost). Since $q > 0$, the gradient of the AVC curve is positive if $MC > AVC$ and negative if $MC < AVC$. So, AVC has positive/negative gradient, depending on whether MC is above or below it. Similarly,

$$\frac{d}{dq}(AC) = \frac{d}{dq}\left(\frac{F + VC}{q}\right) = \frac{q(dVC/dq) - AC}{q^2}$$
$$= (1/q)(MC - AC), \qquad (10.26)$$

so that AC has positive/negative gradient, depending on whether MC is above or below it.[9]

As with demand elasticities, it is possible to speak of a cost elasticity:

Definition 10.18 The **cost elasticity** η_C is defined, for a discrete change in output, as the percentage change in output caused by the percentage change in the level of output:

$$\eta_C = \frac{\text{percentage change in cost}}{\text{percentage change in output}}.$$

The point elasticity is defined as $\eta_C = (\partial C/\partial q)(q/C) = MC/AC$ (since $AC = C/q$, and $MC = \partial C/\partial q$).

If the cost elasticity is unity, then a 1% increase in output leads to a 1% increase in costs. This means that average cost is flat, not changing at this output level; notice that this occurs when $MC = AC$. If the cost elasticity is greater than unity, then average cost is rising ($\eta_C > 1 \Rightarrow MC > AC$), whilst if it is less than unity, average cost is falling ($\eta_C < 1 \Rightarrow MC < AC$).

10.4.2 Elasticity of Scale Revisited

It was remarked that the elasticity of scale measures how output increases when inputs are increased pro rata, but that cost-minimizing behaviour would often require that, starting from an input configuration which is cost-minimizing, any move to another input configuration which was also cost-minimizing would be unlikely to feature a pro rata expansion in the level of all inputs. However, notwithstanding this, it turns out that, at points in input space which are cost-minimizing ways of producing output, the following simple relation between cost elasticity and scale elasticity, marginal cost, and average cost holds:

$$\eta_s = 1/\eta_C = AC/MC \qquad (10.27)$$

(a formal proof is beyond the scope of this text; see e.g. Varian 1978 or Silberberg 1978). Thus, at any given level of output, a local economy of scale greater than unity ($\eta_s > 1$) implies a cost elasticity of less than unity ($\eta_C < 1$) and $MC < AC$ (which means average cost is falling with output); equally, if there are diseconomies of scale, the inequalities reverse (and the average cost curve is rising). And the argument applies in reverse too; falling average cost at a given output level implies local economies of scale associated with the (cost-minimizing) input vector used to produce that level of output.

EXAMPLE 10.4 A crude estimate of the UK Royal Mail cost elasticity gave a figure of around 0.6 (see Dobbs and Richards 1992). This implies, if production is cost-efficient, a scale elasticity of $1/0.6 = 1.66$; that is, production features economies of scale at current output levels. (Of course, this is an aggregate measure, which ignores the fact that there are multiple products: first- and second-class post, parcels, etc.)

10.4.3 Definitions of Plant Capacity

Empirically, for many types of manufacture, the technology of production is such that over quite a wide range of output, average variable cost and marginal cost do not vary much, as indicated in Figure 10.11.[10]

It is conventional to term the point at which marginal cost and average variable cost start to increase as the point of full capacity (which, as indicated, is typically significantly less than the maximum attainable output level). The difference between the actual output level at any point in time and full capacity is referred to as spare capacity. Firms often install plant with full capacity in excess of current production needs, to allow for expansion of demand in the future (especially in the case of new products), or to cope with demand fluctuations

---

[9] Note that $dC/dq = d(F + VC)/dq = dVC/dq = MC$.

[10] Note that a flat AVC implies $dAVC/dq = 0$; hence $MC = AVC$, in view of (10.25).

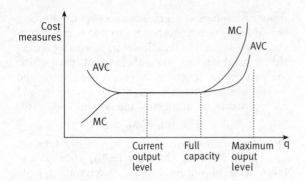

Fig. 10.11 Cost and average cost curves (2)

and uncertainty (particularly if storage of product is costly, as in the case of electricity). Installing excess capacity can also help when there are problems in production (machine outage, labour disputes, etc.), since it means that inventory can be rebuilt more quickly when production does eventually get back on stream.

10.5 Multi-Plant Operation

In practice, many firms operate multiple plants. These may be located on the same site, or on different sites. The discussion of cost curves above implicitly assumed that the firm would select a single plant size, and that the plant would have a particular optimal scale depending on the output the firm wished to produce. Capacity planning is a topic discussed in Chapter 23. Here, the issue of how to plan production when there are several plants able to contribute to overall output is discussed.

10.5.1 Pros and Cons of Multi-Plant Operation

The adavantages of multi-plant over single-plant operation are:

1. Reliability; if there is a positive probability of a plant not being able to run, because of technical failure, disputes, etc., then having several plants, possibly in different countries, can at least maintain some level of output. In addition, those plants that remain in operation can often, in the short run, cover the shortfall in production. The analogy with single- versus multi-engined aeroplanes holds good; the latter are intrinsically

safer, because they can remain airborne even if units fail.

2. Multi-plant operation facilitates routine maintenance; maintenance on a single production unit would typically necessitate total shutdown. With several plants, the loss of output by one unit being out for maintenance can be covered by higher output from the remaining units.

3. Multiple-plant operation may allow plants to be located closer to local demand, and this may reduce transportation or transmission costs.

4. If output fluctuates, plants can be put into or taken out of production, such that those remaining in operation can be maintained at close to minimum average variable cost. With just a single plant, unless inventory can take the strain, the plant may have to be operated at significantly above minimum average variable cost.

The disadvantages of multi-plant operation vis-à-vis single-plant operation lie in

1. Increased complexity in co-ordinating production (operational and administrative costs).

2. Possible loss of economies of scale; larger plants may be able to operate at lower average cost.

Electricity generators and combined heat and power plants typically operate with multiple units; these are examples where it is more costly to meet fluctuations in demand from inventory, and where there are likely to be high costs of plant outage (breakdown). Multi-plant operation protects against these risks.

10.5.2 Cost Minimization and Multi-Plant Production

Given that a certain total output is required, then, assuming it is rational to run all the plants,[11] cost minimization involves operating each plant at a level such that all plant marginal costs are equalized. To see this, suppose there are two plants, labelled 1 and 2, and their costs of production are $C_1(q_1)$ and $C_2(q_2)$, where q_1 and q_2 are the output levels of the two plants. Thus total output, q, is given as the sum of these:

$$q = q_1 + q_2. \qquad (10.28)$$

---

[11] An important assumption; it may be rational to operate only a subset of plants (see below).

The problem is to minimize total costs, $C_1(q_1) + C_2(q_2)$, subject to producing output q. Thus, the choice variables are q_1, q_2, whilst q is a fixed constant as far as the optimization is concerned. Given the Lagrangian,

$$L = C_1(q_1) + C_2(q_2) + \lambda[q - q_1 - q_2], \quad (10.29)$$

the first-order conditions are that

$$\partial L/\partial q_1 = \partial C_1/\partial q_1 - \lambda = 0 \quad (10.30)$$

and

$$\partial L/\partial q_2 = \partial C_2/\partial q_2 - \lambda = 0. \quad (10.31)$$

Note that $\partial C_i/\partial q_i = MC_i$, the marginal cost of producing output from the ith plant, and λ is a constant. Hence, from these equations,

$$MC_1 = MC_2 (= \lambda). \quad (10.32)$$

That is, marginal costs should be equalized. The idea can easily be extended to any number of plants. The solution is illustrated in Figure 10.12.

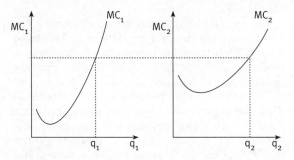

Fig. 10.12 Multi-plant operation (1)

The intuition for this result is straightforward. To see that marginal costs must be equalized as a necessary condition for cost minimization, suppose that they have not been. For example, suppose that at the chosen levels of output q_1 and q_2, it is the case that $MC_1(q_1) > MC_2(q_2)$. Then total output can be maintained if output in plant 1 is decreased by one unit (with a cost saving of MC_1) whilst output in plant 2 is increased by one unit (incurring additional cost MC_2). The overall cost saving is $MC_1 - MC_2$. If marginal costs are still different, the process should be repeated, and so on. Eventually, a point is reached where the two plants have the same marginal cost.

The above analysis does, however, presume that all plants are to be used in the final solution. In practice, this may not be the case; depending on the level of demand, it may be preferable to operate with only a subset of the available plants. If the plants have the usual U-shaped marginal cost curves, the analysis is quite complex; basically, it involves computing the optimal solution for how you would operate n plants (this entails equalizing their marginal costs), for $n = 1, 2, 3, \ldots, n$, and then asking the question 'what number of plants gives the lowest overall cost, given we wish to produce a particular level of total output q?' As q is increased, it becomes optimal to operate more and more plants, and each plant gets to be operated at nearer and nearer its minimum average cost. What we can say is that, for the subset of plants that are used, their marginal costs should be equalized. Figure 10.13 illustrates the optimal production plan (for the case where all plants have identical U-shaped marginal cost curves

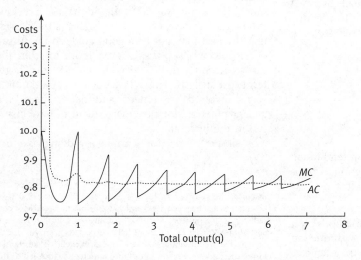

Fig. 10.13 Multi-plant operation (2)

of the form $MC_i(q_i) = \alpha - \beta q_i + \gamma q_i^2$, where α, β, γ > 0 are constants).

The optimal solution in the above case is that, as output increases from zero, it is satisfied by just one plant; this continues until marginal cost has increased well past the minimum of the average cost curve; suddenly, it becomes optimal to introduce a new plant; at this point, output of the first plant drops by a half, and both plants produce this new output level. As the required output increases, production at both plants expands equally; eventually it becomes optimal to switch to three-plant operation; again, outputs in the original two plants drop (to 2/3 the previous level); . . . and so on. It is possible to prove all this (although it is tedious, and is left as an exercise for the interested reader in section 10.10, question 7).

An important feature of multi-plant production is that, as indicated in Figure 10.13, it is clear that average cost tends to flatten out, as does marginal cost, to a constant level. It is often assumed that long-run average costs of production are fairly flat; one motivation for this is that, once economies of scale at the individual plant level are exhausted, firms will simply use multiple plants, with the consequence that the long-run average cost should never rise, as depicted in Figure 10.8; that is, it should fall, and eventually level off. However, this argument forgets that, with increasing total output and increasing numbers of plants, the problems of co-ordinating and managing production may start to increase. Thus, the possibility that long-run average costs for the firm as a whole (as opposed to the individual plant) might rise is usually ascribed to these reasons rather than to any intrinsic diseconomies of scale in production in itself (see e.g. Baumol 1982).

10.6 The Learning or Experience Curve

In certain industries, costs of production tend to fall as the firm gains experience in production. This is particularly notable in the aerospace industry. Costs fall because

1. labour productivity improves: methods get streamlined, the organization of production improves, fewer mistakes are made, maintenance schedules get refined, and so on;

2. defective process elements are eliminated, subprocesses get redesigned, etc.

In order to price contracts appropriately (a topic discussed in some detail in Chapter 25), the firm needs to try to make some assessment of how costs are likely to change as production proceeds. If costs fall substantially with the magnitude of the order (or with repeat or future orders), it may be worth while setting a price below unit cost for the first units of production. Setting initial prices below cost may help to secure orders; the increased level of production then leads to lower unit costs for future production such that the initial losses can be recouped from later sales. This is a kind of virtuous circle; certainly, failure to recognize the learning curve may lead to initial production being too highly priced, with tender prices set at uncompetitive rates; at its worst, this can then lead to low or zero orders for the product, with disastrous consequences (see Chapter 25).

The general idea is that, if the rate of learning can be estimated from an analysis of the past, this can be used as a predictor for how costs will fall for new products of similar type. The estimation problem involved here is discussed in section 11.5.

The learning curve model does not examine in detail the reasons why costs tend to fall in certain types of manufacturing process as cumulative output increases. Certainly, the cost reductions do not simply happen; the learning process is active, and the cost reductions have to be actively sought. The idea is that this pursuit of increased efficiency can be expected to continue for new products in pretty much the same way as it has done for previous products. The caveat that there is always the danger that the past may not be a good guide to the future does, however, apply with even more force in the case of learning curve effects than it does for short-term cost analysis. This is because, typically, the time spans involved are longer, and hence there is a greater potential for the environment to have changed in the interval.[12]

A simple model for learning by doing assumes

[12] See Mansfield (1996) for a discussion of examples: for instance, the price of a Model T Ford fell from over $3000 to less than $1000 between 1908 and 1923, primarily because of cost reductions arising from learning by doing. By contrast, the unit cost of the Douglas DC9 did not fall as expected (primarily due to unexpectedly tight labour markets); the firm incurred substantial losses and ended up being forced into a merger (which led to the creation of McDonnell-Douglas).

that average cost per period falls at a constant percentage rate.[13] Let q_t denote output in period t, and Q_t the cumulative amount produced up to and including period t, i.e. since the product was launched; C_t denotes either total cost or, more usually, variable cost incurred in period t. The constant-percentage learning curve postulates that average variable cost (or average cost), C_t/q_t, falls at a constant rate, i.e. exponentially. That is,

$$C_t/q_t = AQ_{t-1}^{-b}. \tag{10.33}$$

Multiplying through by q_t, this implies

$$C_t = Aq_tQ_{t-1}^{-b}. \tag{10.34}$$

For example, the commonly quoted 80% learning curve suggests that if total cumulative production doubles, average cost, for any given period output level, will fall by 20%. That is, comparing average cost AQ^{-b} at a given cumulative output level Q with that at cumulative output level $2Q$, namely $A(2Q)^{-b}$, we get

$$A(2Q)^{-b}/AQ^{-b} = 2^{-b}.$$

If $b = -0.3219$ then $2^{-0.3219} = 0.8$ and average cost falls by 20% for each doubling of cumulative output. That is, the 80% learning curve corresponds to a parameter value $b = -0.3219$. More generally, an L% learning curve corresponds to the value

$$b = \ln(L/100)/\ln(2)$$

(since $2^b = (L/100)$). It is thus straightforward to move from estimates of b to the percentage rate and vice versa. Estimation of the learning curve coefficient is fairly straightforward in principle; see section 11.4. The typical structure of the effect is depicted in Figure 10.14.

10.7 Multi-Product Cost Functions

Most firms actually produce more than one product. This has implications for the issue of what constitutes a natural monopoly and also leads to complexity in the formal analysis of product costing and the determination of optimal selling prices. Chapter 14 introduces the issue of natural monopoly, and discusses the role of cost structures in this context,

[13] Various similar models can be formulated here; for a slightly more detailed exposition, see Kaplan (1982) or Horngren (1986), whilst Belkaoui (1986) gives a detailed analysis and many applications.

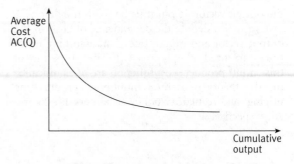

Fig. 10.14 The experience curve

whilst Chapter 20 examines cost and demand structures when the firm sells a set of interrelated products, a product line. Finally, Chapter 28 deals with the various measures that the state has used to try to restrain such monopoly power: competition policy, merger policy, regulatory constraints, antitrust measures, etc. It is more appropriate to discuss the relevant multi-product cost concepts, such as cost subadditivity, economies of scale and scope, etc., at those points in the text rather than here. Accordingly, this section explains the idea that the multi-product cost function is established as a cost-minimizing solution to the problem of organizing production in order to produce a given output vector (instead of a single output).

Define the output vector, for a firm which produces m products, as $\mathbf{q} = (q_1, \ldots, q_m)$, and the vector of inputs (as before) as $\mathbf{x} = (x_1, \ldots, x_n)$. The single-product production function, written in explicit form as $q = f(\mathbf{x})$, could equally be written in implicit form as the function $f(q, \mathbf{x}) = 0$; the multi-product production function, which relates how technically efficient production can produce outputs from inputs, can likewise be written in the implicit form

$$f(\mathbf{q}, \mathbf{x}) = 0. \tag{10.35}$$

The problem of producing $\mathbf{q}$ at minimum cost involves choosing input vector $\mathbf{x}$ so as to minimize $C = \sum_{i=1}^{n} w_i x_i$ subject to (10.35). I omit formal analysis, but note that, for a given vector of outputs $\mathbf{q}$, the optimization leads to optimal levels for each of the inputs, such that these are functions of the output vector (given input prices are fixed). That is, we can write $x_i^* = x_i^*(\mathbf{q}, \mathbf{x})$ for $i = 1, \ldots, n$ (to indicate that the optimal choice of each input level is a function of the output vector and the input prices); hence minimized cost is $C = \sum_{i=1}^{n} w_i x_i^*(\mathbf{q}, \mathbf{w})$. Thus minimized cost depends solely on input prices and the output vector. It can thus be written either as $C = C(\mathbf{q}, \mathbf{w})$ (to denote the dependence of cost on the output vector and input prices), or, assuming input prices are fixed, simply as $C(\mathbf{q})$. The properties of this (multi-product) cost function are of significance for the theory of natural monopoly, product-line pricing, and regulatory policy (Chapters 14, 20 and 28, respectively).

10.8 Cost–Volume–Profit (Break-even) Analysis

The competitive firm facing a fixed market price, and the firm with monopoly power, once it has chosen price, are both in a similar position. They are both concerned with how much needs to be sold of any given product in order for that product to make a profit contribution to the business. Thus, in the very short run, the idea is that input prices and selling prices are fixed, and variation in sales naturally leads to a variation in profit contribution. A useful statistic to calculate is the product's **break-even quantity**. This is particularly straightforward if it is assumed that costs vary linearly with output (accountants often simply *assume* that costs have a linear structure).[14] If q stands for output and C for total cost, the linear cost function can be written as

$$C = \alpha + \beta q, \tag{10.36}$$

where α and β are positive constants. Given a fixed price p, then profit π is given as

$$\pi = pq - (\alpha + \beta q) = -\alpha + (p - \beta)q. \tag{10.37}$$

Hence the profit function is a straight line with intercept $-\alpha$ and gradient $(p - \beta)$, as depicted in Figure 10.15.

If we fix profit equal to zero in (10.37), the break-even quantity is given as

$$\pi = -\alpha + (p - \beta)q_{BE} = 0. \tag{10.38}$$

Rearranging this gives

$$q_{BE} = \frac{\alpha}{p - \beta}. \tag{10.39}$$

If a positive target level of profit is set, then the quantity that achieves this profit level, denoted q_π, is found by rearranging (10.37) to give

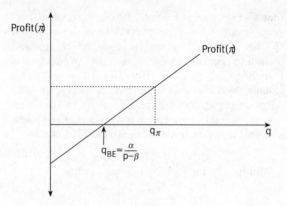

Fig. 10.15 Break-even analysis

$$q_\pi = \frac{\alpha + \pi}{p - \beta}. \tag{10.40}$$

That is, an increase in the profit target merely shifts the quantity required, as illustrated in Figure 10.15. The break-even quantity is a useful statistic to calculate, as it gives the product manager a minimum target to focus on; often it will be clear whether or not there is likely to be a problem in reaching this minimum break-even sales figure (even if there has been no formal analysis of demand).

The limitation of break-even analysis as described above lies in the assumption of linear costs and a fixed selling price. A natural extension is to refine the cost function; if there are significant non-linearities in production cost, it may be possible to estimate a non-linear cost function.[15] It is then straightforward to incorporate such a non-linear cost function into the break-even analysis. It is also possible to consider the relationship between price and sales (or to plot the profit contribution and break-even point for a set of different selling prices, by way of sensitivity analysis). This is omitted here, as it takes us close to the analysis of profit-maximizing pricing, a topic treated in detail in Chapter 14 (and Chapters 18 and 19, in the context of price discrimination).

Another extension to traditional break-even analysis that is sometimes considered by accountants (see e.g. Kaplan 1982) is to recognize that sales fluctuate by the day, week, month, season, etc. If data are gathered on sales over time, it is possible to estimate not only the average level of sales, but also the higher moments of the sales distribution. The

---

[14] It is worth noting that such a linear function can give a reasonable approximation to a smooth non-linear function, at least in the neighbourhood of the normal level of output—see sect. 11.4 for more details of this in the context of cost estimation.

[15] Chap. 11 discusses the estimation of polynomial and constant-elasticity cost functions.

following example elucidates this idea for the simple case where sales have a normal distribution with a given mean and standard deviation. It illustrates the point that it is possible to calculate the probability not only of breaking even, but of attaining any given target level of profitability.

EXAMPLE 10.5 Suppose that sales are approximately normally distributed, with average sales of 100 units per period, and a standard deviation of 20, when the price is £12 per unit. Suppose the costs of production are approximated by the function $C = 100 + 10q$, where q denotes actual sales in the period. What is (a) the probability of the firm breaking even, and (b) the probability of it attaining a profit contribution of at least £100 from this product in the coming period?

To answer these questions, write sales as $100 + \varepsilon$, where $\varepsilon \sim N(0, \sigma^2) = N(0, 20^2)$. Equation (10.37) for this application is

$$\pi = -\alpha + (p - \beta)(\bar{q} + \varepsilon) = -100$$
$$+ (12 - 10)(100 + \varepsilon)$$
$$= 100 + 2\varepsilon. \tag{i}$$

Answer to (a): Given (i), for profit to be at least equal to zero we must have

$$100 + 2\varepsilon \geq 0 \text{ or } \varepsilon \geq -50.$$

Now, $\Pr[\varepsilon \geq -50] = \Pr[z \geq -^{50}/_{20}] = \Pr[z \geq -2.5] = 0.9938$ (note that for a normal variate x with mean μ and standard deviation σ,

$$z = \frac{x - \mu}{\sigma}$$

is distributed as $N(0, 1)$; z is the standard normal variate; according to the normal tables, the probability of exceeding z when its value is -2.5 is around 0.993, i.e. over 99%.

Answer to (b): By contrast, the probability of making at least £100 is given by requiring profit in (i) to exceed 100:

$$100 + 2\varepsilon \geq 100 \text{ or } \varepsilon \geq 0.$$

Now, $\Pr[\varepsilon \geq 0] = \Pr[z \geq 0] = 0.5$, so there is a 50% chance of making at least £100.

Whilst this sort of extension might seem of interest, one should beware of using it without due care and attention. Sales undoubtedly will fluctuate from period to period. However, the fluctuations will often have a systematic seasonal component; that is, there may be some degree of systematic variation, for example across weekends, or from month to month (e.g. December, with Christmas, is often a predictable outlier). Time-series analysis of sales can

help to identify the systematic components in sales over time; such an analysis may be used to refine the above probabilistic analysis (but this is beyond the scope of this text).

10.9 Summary

This Chapter explained all the key cost concepts used in discussing pricing and output decisions later in the text; in particular, it dealt with the concepts of average cost, average variable cost, and marginal cost, and examined the problem of attaining technical efficiency and cost efficiency, including the case where the firm needs to organize production utilizing several plants. It also considered how the time dimension can play an important role in cost analysis, not only in drawing a distinction between what are termed short-run and long-run costs, but also because, for new products and programmes, there can be significant cost reductions arising from learning by doing.

10.10 Review Questions

1. (a) If the marginal cost curve lies below the average cost curve, the latter is falling. Why is this?
   (b) Why is the minimum of the average variable cost curve usually depicted as lying to the left of the minimum for the average total cost curve?

2. For a single-product firm, what is the relationship between the scale elasticity, the cost elasticity, and economies/diseconomies of scale?

3. If a single-product firm features economies of scale at all levels of output, what does this imply for the average cost curve and the marginal cost curve? Sketch the two curves on the same graph. Attempt to justify the structure of your sketch.

4. Is it necessary for a multi-plant firm to choose outputs such that all plant marginal costs are the same? Discuss.

5. A firm's production function is $q = K^{1/2}L^{1/2}$, and its input prices are denoted w_K, w_L. Show that the production function has diminishing marginal products and also manifests constant returns to scale.

6. Set up the cost minimization problem for question 4 (see equations (10.13), (10.14) and (10.15)

above), and solve the first-order conditions ((10.18) plus (10.15)) to obtain the input demand functions (solutions for the levels of L and K in terms of the required output level q and the input prices) and hence determine that the analytic form of the firm's cost function, from (10.20), is $C(q, w_K, w_L) = w_K^{1/2} w_L^{1/2} q$.

7. Suppose a firm has two plants which have identical total cost functions taking the form

$$C_i(q_i) = 100q_i - 10q_i^2 + q_i^3 \quad i = 1, 2.$$

Explain how the firm should operate these plants in order to minimize costs. In particular, establish the total output level at which the firm will switch from operating with just one plant to operating with both plants. (Hint: analyse the two-plant solution and determine how costs vary for this case; compare the solution with operating just one plant.)

10.11 Further Reading

Ferguson (1969) is a seminal (if somewhat traditional) approach to the neo-classical theory of production and cost. More modern presentations, at a more demanding level than this book, can be found in Varian (1978) and Silberberg (1978)). Texts such as Kaplan (1982) or Horngren (1987) give more detail on cost–volume profit analysis, and also on experience curves. Belkaoui (1986) goes into considerably more detail on the latter and also gives many applications. For discussion of the implications of learning by doing on pricing (in the context of chemical processing) see Lieberman (1984).

11 Cost Estimation

Objective To outline some alternative ways of estimating the relationship between cost and output, with some emphasis on the econometric approach.

Prerequisites Section 9.4 gives an outline of the econometric modelling and testing procedures involved in estimating relationships; this is essential background to section 11.3 below. An understanding of basic cost concepts is given in Chapter 10.

Keywords cross-section analysis, data envelopment analysis, experience curve, learning by doing, learning curves, net realizable value.

11.1 Introduction

This chapter is concerned with the estimation of cost functions. Once estimated, such functions can be used as a basis for cost forecasting (predicting what costs will be in the future) and for the analysis of price, output, and advertizing decisions (since the estimate of marginal cost is a key element in such decisions). The neo-classical theory of production and cost presented in Chapter 10 presumed that the production function was known, and hence that cost minimization would lead to a cost function known with certainty. In practice, firms often have an extremely imprecise understanding of the production function (how inputs relate to output) or the cost function (how costs vary with output).

As a general proposition, and ceteris paribus, more information about production and cost functions is preferred to less. Unfortunately, obtaining such information is rarely costless. It follows that a preliminary judgement is required as to the likely benefits and costs of undertaking such an analysis. The net benefit arising from formal analysis is perhaps more pronounced when the firm has market power and the capacity to set product price, since in theory the estimate of marginal cost affects this choice. However, even in competitive markets, price-takers have to decide how much to produce, and according to marginalist theory, should expand production to the point where marginal cost equals price, so again a knowledge of how marginal cost varies with output is helpful for this decision.

Various types of production and cost analysis can be distinguished; in short-run analysis, plant capacity is fixed and the problem is to understand how input requirements, and hence costs, vary with output. This type of analysis makes use primarily of firm-specific data (although data across several plants within the same firm might usefully be pooled, particularly if the plants are of similar vintage and technology). Estimating the function relating cost to output is attractive, since it allows marginal cost to be expressed as an explicit function of output. This facilitates analysis of optimal output and pricing. (Recall that profit maximization requires choosing an output such that marginal revenue equals marginal cost—this is made particularly straightforward if we have **analytic** functions for both marginal revenue and marginal cost.)

Long-run cost analysis, by contrast, focuses on how plant costs vary with variations in installed capacity, and often, where firms operate multiple plants, how cost varies with aggregate firm output. This type of analysis is useful for capacity planning, the long-run decision on the size and timing of plant installation. Estimation usually involves **cross-sectional analysis**, looking at costs and outputs of different firm/plant sizes across an industry. Such an analysis can hope to determine the structure of the long-run average cost curve, and hence how economies of scale vary with firm or plant output. Long-run cost analysis is fraught with difficulties, since firms often operate plants of different vintages and technologies, and may operate in different geographical areas and face different environmental and technical demands and input prices (labour costs often vary significantly from region to region).

This type of analysis is complex, and there is a variety of statistical problems which need to be dealt with.[1]

Long-run analysis is beyond the scope of this chapter, which concentrates on firm-specific forms of short-run cost analysis. The motivation for this is that, in managerial economics, firm-specific costs are of primary concern for firm-specific decisions on price, output, advertizing, etc. Whilst I focus here exclusively on the cost function, it should also be noted that the firm also has to decide how to organize production in an efficient (cost-minimizing) way. In undertaking cost estimation, the issue of how to organize production is not addressed. In many cases, this is not a problem since, with capacity already installed, the level of output often uniquely determines the inputs required to produce it; that is, there is little scope for varying the input mix.

However, there are many processes where alternative combinations of inputs can be used to produce the same level of output. In such cases, the firm will also be concerned to choose the input combination that minimizes costs; to this end, it is desirable to try to estimate the underlying production function (and then to optimize production in the way described in Chapter 10).[2]

The other estimation problem covered in this chapter is that of the learning or experience curve. For some products, particularly new products, there are likely to be significant cost reductions as the firm builds experience and refines the production process. Section 11–5 gives an example to illustrate this point, and shows how it is possible to estimate the learning curve effect.

Finally, before proceeding, it is worth emphasizing that in this chapter, the analysis is exclusively concerned with production and costing for a single product. In practice, most firms produce several products. Theoretically, the analysis presented here is satisfactory so long as the cost function is additively separable. This is so if the marginal cost of producing the product under consideration is independent of the output levels of all the other products. If the cost function is interdependent (because products often use common facilities, or because one product is a by-product of another, etc.), the problem of cost estimation requires a global approach in that the impact of all outputs on cost must be studied simultaneously. This point is explored in more detail in Chapter 20, which explicitly addresses the problem of setting prices for a product range.

11.2 Overview of Alternative Methods of Cost Estimation

Although the principal focus in this chapter is on statistical cost estimation, a simple calculation of average variable cost can often be adequate, whilst engineering analysis may prove a fruitful alternative approach to the determination of the cost function. These three methods are briefly reviewed here. They should not be viewed as mutually exclusive; single-point calculations are well worth making even if more detailed statistical and/or engineering analysis is envisaged, and likewise, engineering analysis not only may be used to estimate the cost function directly, but also may prove helpful in revealing the key variables likely to be of importance in a statistical analysis.

11.2.1 Point Estimation

Simple extrapolation from the past can give a rudimentary assessment of costs of production. For example, managers responsible for particular aspects of the overall production process may be asked to make direct cost estimates for a specified level of output; such estimates would typically be based on these managers' experience of historic costs, and on their expectations of how any imminent changes (in the nature of production, or in input prices, etc.) might filter through into costs. Such predictions are often based on simple calculations of average variable cost, with the prediction being that the new level of output will be produced either at the same level of *AVC*, or at this level plus or minus some

---

[1] A brief outline of the nature of the difficulties is given in Thomas (1993: Chap. 11); see also Varian (1992). Johnson (1960) is a seminal application of this type of statistical cost analysis. For a useful survey of alternative and more sophisticated techniques for the measurement of efficiency (such as data envelopment analysis and stochastic frontier methods), and a major international application to the electricity industry, see Pollitt (1995).

[2] There is of course a close relationship between cost functions and production functions, as is made clear in Chap. 10 (the structure of the production function determines the structure of the cost function, via the cost minimization process described in section 10.3). However, it can be shown that pretty much all the economically relevant information concerning the structure of the underlying production function can be recovered from the estimated cost function (see Chambers 1988: Chaps. 2 and 3 for formal analysis of this issue).

amount. Such simple cost estimates are often suffi-cient, particularly when the new level of output is not dissimilar to what has already been produced. Often firms have average variable cost (and hence marginal cost) fairly constant over quite wide ranges of output. Thus a rough calculation of AVC based on past figures may well suffice. Example 11.1 illustrates the calculation.

EXAMPLE 11.1 If total variable cost (VC) of £500 has been observed at an output level of 20 units, then at this output level, $AVC = 500/20 = 25$. If it is assumed that AVC is constant with output, the prediction of AVC at any other output level is then also simply 25.

Of course, the firm will usually have experience of historical variations in output; repeating the above calculation at different output levels will give alter-native estimates of average variable cost. If such estimates appear uncorrelated with output, this lends support to the hypothesis that AVC is constant as output varies. If, however, there appears to be a systematic variation in the AVC estimate as output varies, then this variation can be explicitly modelled (see sections 11.2.3 and 11.4).

Another benefit of estimating a constant level, such as that described in Example 11.1, is that it lends itself to sensitivity analysis; thus, in consider-ing pricing, it is possible to consider variations in the (assumed constant) level of AVC.[3] With multiple observations, and especially when it is suspected that the cost function is non-linear, cost estimation and forecasts are better developed using more formal statistical methods (as in section 11.4 below).

11.2.2 Engineering Analysis

This engineering analysis is conceptually straight-forward. It consists of two or three stages (depend-ing on whether there is a choice of process in the short run), namely:

1. establishing the input–output relationship for each process,
2. pricing the inputs, and
3. optimizing production to derive the cost function.

[3] Dobbs and Cuthbertson (1996) undertake this type of sensi-tivity analysis for the Ramsey pricing of postal services (Ramsey pricing is discussed in Chap. 22 below).

In the short run, the production process will often fix how the inputs required (man-hours, materials, fuel and maintenance, etc.) vary as output is increased. To some extent, the inputs required will depend on chemical or physical laws, and to some extent on spoilage and wastage rates etc. associated with the production process. Often relationships will be approximately linear; for example, material inputs may increase pro rata with output. However, some elements may be non-linear: for example, fuel efficiency and spoilage rates.

The second stage simply involves determining the price of inputs. Note that, if the object is to estimate a current or future cost function, the need is to estimate current or future input prices. This is usually straightforward, although there may be com-plications for some inputs; for example, labour costs may be aggregated despite the fact that labour is heterogeneous and has heterogeneous prices. (Apart from occupational wage variations, there are varia-tions arising from overtime and higher rates for shift work; such variations can affect whether production should be concentrated during the day or run over-night, and so on.)

Finally, if it is possible to vary the input mix and/ or use alternative processes to generate output, the production process needs to be optimized. For example, in biscuit manufacture, there is usually a range of tolerances for input ingredients (a little more sugar, a little less salt); in such a case it is often possible to set up the problem of minimizing cost subject to satisfying certain restrictions on input mix (often this type of production planning problem can be modelled using linear programming; see e.g. Taha 1992). A more detailed discussion of how this gen-erates the cost function is beyond the scope of the present chapter, however.

The chief drawbacks of the engineering approach are as follows:

1. Often, there is no explicit consideration of input optimization. In such a case, the calculated engi-neering cost–output relationship may be based on inefficient process and input use.

2. With complex, highly interdependent production processes, where there are many inputs used in common to produce many outputs, it may be difficult to construct analytically the mathemat-ical relationship between inputs and outputs, and a statistical approach to estimating the relation-ship becomes necessary (for example, in oil refining).

3. The pure engineering approach has nothing to say about how distribution, selling, and administration costs are likely to vary with output; thus estimation of the relationship between these categories of cost and output has to proceed by other means (for example, via the statistical approach).

11.2.3 Statistical Analysis

Statistical modelling becomes appropriate whenever there are multiple observations of cost and output. At its simplest it involves the regression of the cost category under investigation against output (and other variables, possibly including input prices). Detailed applications are discussed in sections 11.4 and 11.5. The statistical approach can be applied to historical data, to data generated through direct experimentation, or even to quasi-data generated from engineering analysis (if one desires a simpler approximation to what may be a complex analytical engineering cost function).

The statistical approach to cost estimation is often used in experimental situations, but much less so on historical data, where more rudimentary (usually linear) cost models of the type described in section 11.2.1 are more commonly found. Since historical data are often the only data that are available, section 11.3 discusses in some detail the issues and problems which can arise in constructing an appropriate data set for cost analysis. The problems that arise in utilizing historic cost data may explain why it is rarely used as a basis for the 'sophisticated' statistical approach. However, the simple calculations used in practice may be viewed as special cases of more general statistical models, and the accusation of 'low-quality data' is not appropriately levelled at the statistical approach (particularly when, given the power of spreadsheet and statistical software, it is almost as quick and easy to estimate a 'more sophisticated' cost model as it is to undertake the single-point estimation described in section 11.2.1 above). If historic data manifest low quality, this merely suggests that there should be further investment in improving the quality of that data (and in controlled experiment, in some circumstances). Section 11.4 gives a case study in which the general-to-specific methodology described in Chapter 9 is used to explore the extent to which a linear cost model is supported by the data.

11.3 Data for Statistical Cost Estimation

Statistical cost estimation involves the following steps;

1. identification of variables likely to affect cost (usually, and primarily, the level of output),
2. collection of data on all these variables, and
3. analysis of the relationship between these variables.

Once the variables of interest have been identified, the next task is to collect data on these variables. Essentially, data can be generated either through direct experimentation or through an examination of the firm's past experience of production. Section 11.3.1 briefly deals with the experimental approach. However, more usually, the only source of data is the past history of actual production. The issues that arise in constructing a data set from this past history is reviewed in some detail in section 11.3.2.

11.3.1 Experimental Data

In some circumstances, the firm may be able to set up a controlled experiment to explore how inputs and outputs are related. For example, in farming, there have been many studies exploring how input of fertilizer affects the output of particular crops. Likewise, pharmaceutical R&D often involves controlled experimentation to study dose-response curves etc. Obviously, controlled experiment is not costless, but it can offer data of much higher quality (and a satisfactory quantity of data; this should be the case if the experimental design is well chosen). Many issues arise in the design of experiments such as this; for example, the number and choice of dose levels depends on the range to be investigated, and on the cost of generating each observation. Experimental design is, however, beyond the scope of the present chapter.[4]

11.3.2 Historic (Accounts-Based) Data

The naive accounting approach typically involves classifying inputs as either fixed, variable, or semi-

---

[4] See Griffiths *et al.* (1993: sect. 11.8) for examples of estimation in experimental contexts. For a discussion of the design of experiments, see Mead (1988).

variable. I do not discuss accounting details here, but rather focus on general considerations, pitfalls, and problems which can arise with historical data. The reader can, however, find an extended and more detailed consideration of how relevant costs can be derived from the costs thrown up by the typical accounting system in section 12.4.2, where an analysis of historical accounts is used as the basis for a branch closure decision. That case study illustrates many of the practical issues that arise in translating account-based figures into relevant costs for cost estimation.

The approach from historical accounting data clearly ignores any possible future changes in plant operations, procedures, or input mix, and uses historic costs (or, at best, current costs) and not expected future or opportunity costs. It typically also factors in average levels of wastage/maintenance/idle time from the past. In each case, the past may not be a good guide to the future; any cost estimation exercise based on historic data is of relevance only if the values estimated in the past continue to hold good in the future.

Some of the more important considerations, in selecting (and judging the relevance of) historic data, are as follows:

1. *Stable production processes.* There should be no major changes in the production process within the estimation period chosen. This consideration can often severely limit the length of the data-run which can be used. Ignoring such changes implies the model estimated will be misspecified, and the cost function so obtained will be likely to have poor predictive performance. The problem is illustrated in the context of learning curves in section 11.5 below.

2. *Period choice and the problem of spillovers.* A reasonable run of data is required, and these data must feature significant variation in output levels across periods. A longer sample period with more observations is, ceteris paribus, statistically desirable; unfortunately, the longer the time series, the more likely it is that ceteris are not paribus; input prices change, processes get re-optimized, refined, or replaced, etc. Clearly, shortening the length of each individual period (years → months → weeks, etc.) increases the number of data points. Shortening the measurement period may increase the data set, but unfortunately, the problem of spillovers and measurement error tends to increase. In practice, the frequency of internal reporting can be used as a

guide for the choice of data frequency. Typically, this is monthly, although some variables may be weekly or biweekly (e.g. some types of labour). Spillovers can occur when there are misalignments (end of calendar months not coinciding with weekends, etc.). In addition to non-alignments, spillovers occur whenever a cost incurred in a period is not actually recorded in that period. Thus late billing, variation in inventory, or assignment of maintenance charges can lead to overspills across periods. Maintenance, for example, may well be proportional to usage, but is often scheduled for slack periods; this leads to the danger that too much is allocated to the slack periods (and too little to the peak periods).

3. *Overhead cost allocations.* Overhead costs often vary to some extent with output. The question is how much. If the firm produces a single product, it may be possible to study how overhead costs vary with output, with the hope of identifying that portion of the overhead which is genuinely fixed. At its simplest, this might involve examining in detail each element of overhead cost, and making a judgement as to whether it would vary or not. Graphing the level of total overhead cost against output might also be helpful. Finally, it is possible to analyse the problem statistically, by simply regressing overhead cost against output (or a polynomial function of output). The intercept of such a regression might then be construed as an estimate of fixed costs—of overheads which are fixed, independent of output. However, there are some difficulties with such an interpretation. This is discussed in more detail in section 11.4 (see, in particular, Figure 11.1).

More generally, firms often produce several products. The multi-product production and pricing problem is examined in Chapter 20. However, even if individual products are effectively produced separately (so the costs of producing each product are unaffected by the levels of output of the other products), often the way overheads are treated can make overheads appear to be variable. The following example illustrates this.

EXAMPLE 11.2 A firm produces two products, labelled 1 and 2. Each of them has a constant average variable cost of £10 per unit, while their constant selling prices are £20 and £15 respectively. Suppose there is fixed overhead of £10,000. This means that the true cost function can be written as $C(q_1, q_2) = 10{,}000 + 10q_1 + 10q_2$. Thus, holding q_2 fixed, variable costs for product 1 are simply $VC = 10q_1$. What is termed the **net realizable value** method of allocating joint fixed costs involves allocating the overhead in proportion to net realizable value, calculated as the difference between revenue and attributable costs. This is illustrated in Table 11.1, which gives illustrative sales in two periods, and the associated revenues and costs in lines (ii) and (iii). The net realizable value (NRV) is given in line (iv) and hence the percentage fixed cost allocation in line (v), which determines the allocation of the £10,000 fixed cost across products in line (vi). Product full cost, according to NRV, is then given in line (vii).

Table 11.1 illustrates how an allocation rule can make things look variable when they are in fact fixed, and how this can infect a calculation of how costs respond to output. For example, suppose that the analyst hypothesizes a linear cost function of the form $C = \alpha_0 + \alpha_1 q_1$; if the total product cost figures for product 1 are taken (uncritically), then the two period full cost estimates could be used to estimate α_0 and α_1 as follows:

at output 1000: $C = 17{,}142 = \alpha_0 + \alpha_1 1000$;

at output 900: $C = 17{,}182 = \alpha_0 + \alpha_1 900$.

Solving for α_0 and α_1 gives $\alpha_1 = -0.4$ and $\alpha_0 = 17{,}582$. This is clearly a nonsense; the estimates indicate that average variable cost for product 1 is −£0.40 per unit, when it is really £10 per unit. This occurs because the cost allocation rule causes an overhead spillover from one product to the other. The fall in output of product 2 makes product 1 take a larger share of the total overhead (through the arbitrary net realizable value allocation rule), and this makes it appear that, although product 1 sales fell, the cost of producing the lower output was actually higher! The same point applies to product 2, as the reader may care to verify.

The moral behind the above example is that in examining cost data, any allocation rules must be undone prior to the analysis. There is no harm in including total overhead costs in a cost estimation exercise; the point is not to include only a portion of overhead based on an accounting allocation rule. If total overhead is included, the statistical exercise will reveal the portion of the overhead which does vary with output.

4. *Adjusting for inflation and relative price changes.* So long as there is

(i) no significant flexibility in the use of inputs, and

(ii) no change in input prices,

then it is appropriate to model cost simply as a function of output. If input prices change because of general inflation, or because some inputs become relatively more expensive than others, then so long as (i) continues to hold, it can be shown that it is still possible to model cost simply as a function of output, but that all the elements of cost used in the cost estimation exercise should be adjusted to constant prices. This is in fact the standard recipe recommended in most accounting texts (see e.g. Horngren and Foster 1988 or Kaplan 1972). Often, individual

Table 11.1 Joint cost allocations

Period 1		Product	Product 2	Total
(i)	Sales quantity	1000	800	
(ii)	Revenues	20,000	12,000	32,000
(iii)	Production and finishing costs	10,000	8000	18,000
(iv)	NRV (= (ii) − (iii))	10,000	4000	14,000
(v)	% NRV of total NRV	71.42	28.58	100
(vi)	Joint cost allocation	7142	2858	10,000
(vii)	Product 'apparent' total cost (= (iii) + (vi))	17,142	10,858	28,000

Period 2				
(i)	Sales quantity	900	400	
(ii)	Revenues	18,000	6000	24,000
(iii)	Production and finishing costs	9000	4000	13,000
(iv)	NRA	9000	2000	11,000
(v)	% NRA of total NRA	81.82	18.18	100
(vi)	Joint cost allocation	8182	1818	10,000
(vii)	Product 'apparent' total cost (= (iii) + (vi))	17,182	5818	23,000

Time period	1	2	3	4
Actual labour cost	120	110	130	140
Average earning index	73.9	86.3	97.8	113
Real labour cost	120 × (113 / 73.9) = 183.49	110 × (113 / 86.3) = 144.03	130 × (113 / 97.8) = 150.20	140

Fig. 11.1 Labour costs and the index of labour costs

prices are not available, or the cost category under consideration involves a large number of different individual products (such as stationery). In such cases, the usual approach is to use a cost index for each particular cost category (if such cost indices are available).[5] If the intention is to predict cost in the immediate future, it can also be shown that the best way to adjust costs is to revalue them at present-day prices. That is, if the data span a period $t = t_1, \ldots, t_2$, where t_2 is the current period, and if the nominal (i.e. actual historic) cost in a particular category i at time t is denoted C_{it}, the real cost, in terms of today's (t_2's) prices, is calculated as

$$RC_{it} = C_{it}(I_{t_2}/I_t), \qquad (11.1)$$

where I_t represents the value of the appropriate cost index at time t. This calculation is illustrated in Figure 11.1.

In the absence of any individual cost indices, it is desirable to adjust at least for general inflation. This involves the same calculation as in Equation (11.1), except that the cost index associated with a particular cost category, I_t, is replaced with an index of price inflation, such as the retail price index, RPI_t.

If there is significant flexibility in the choice of inputs required to produce any given level of output, then simply modelling cost as a function of output will involve a misspecification, and it may be necessary to adopt a more sophisticated approach which includes prices as explanatory variables (see e.g. Thomas 1993).

Large firms may have several plants producing the same product. When the processes involved are similar, this can help to increase the amount of data available for estimation and help mitigate the problem of short data-runs. When such data are available, it is also possible to undertake (long-run) comparative efficiency analysis, using more

advanced techniques such as data envelopment analysis, parametric programming, or stochastic frontier methods.[6]

11.4 Statistical Cost Estimation

Section 11.3 discussed the conditions under which it is reasonable to estimate simple cost functions, in which some measure of cost (which may be total cost, variable cost, total overhead cost, or some category of overhead cost) is modelled as simply depending on output in some way. This section examines the type of analysis involved. In what follows, I shall work through a simple case study based on the raw data provided in Table 11.2. This table gives a set of cost figures associated with outputs for 12 months. The origin of the cost figures is not discussed here; the type of accounts analysis required is discussed in section 12.4.2 (in a case study concerned with branch closure based on historical data[7]).

The general approach to the analysis of these data is given in section 9.4. As in the case of demand estimation, specification is again an issue in cost estimation. This is because economic theory does not suggest any particular function form for the cost function. The simplest forms of cost function typically estimated are the log-linear (Cobb–Douglas) form

$$\ln C_t = \alpha_0 + \alpha_1 \ln q_t + \varepsilon_t, \qquad (11.2)$$

where q_t is the level of output in period t and C_t, the magnitude of cost under investigation (as previously mentioned, this could be total cost, variable cost, or

---

[5] The *Annual Abstract of Statistics* provides a variety of price and cost indices. Some journals, such as *Process Engineering*, publish their own cost indices for use in specialist applications.

[6] A useful review and applications of some of these more advanced techniques are given in Pollitt (1995).

[7] The case study in sect. 12.4.2 gives an analysis of accounting data for a single month, in the context of a branch closure decision; clearly, this analysis could be repeated for several months.

Table 11.2 Data for Cost Estimation

Month	Cost (£ooo)	Output (ooo)			
t	C_t	q_t	q_t^2	q_t^3	q_t^4
1	400	200	40000	8000000	1.6E+09
2	370	190	36100	6859000	1.3E+09
3	360	210	44100	9261000	1.94E+09
4	440	220	48400	10648000	2.34E+09
5	420	200	40000	8000000	1.6E+09
6	480	240	57600	13824000	3.32E+09
7	470	250	62500	15625000	3.91E+09
8	500	260	67600	17576000	4.57E+09
9	480	240	57600	13824000	3.32E+09
10	380	200	40000	8000000	1.6E+09
11	400	180	32400	5832000	1.05E+09
12	430	230	52900	12167000	2.8E+09

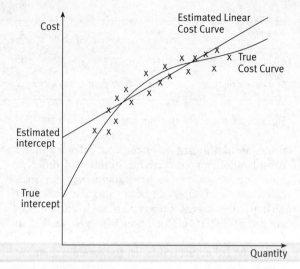

Fig. 11.2 Interpreting the intercept

indeed some other subcategory of cost—for example overhead or a subcategory of overhead), and the polynomial form

$$C_t = \alpha_0 + \alpha_1 q_t + \alpha_2 q_t^2 \, \alpha_3 q_t^3 + \ldots + \varepsilon_t, \quad (11.3)$$

of which the linear form

$$C_t = \alpha_0 + \alpha_1 q_t + \varepsilon_t \quad (11.4)$$

is an important special case (accountants in particular tend to focus on the case where costs vary linearly with output).

In what follows, the polynomial specification (11.3) is examined (the reader is then asked to undertake a comparison of linear and log-linear models in question 3 at the end of the chapter). The question addressed is that of whether the data support the more parsimonious linear model (11.4). Before doing this, it is worth remarking on the interpretation of the fitted cost equation. Figure 11.1 illustrates a true (but unknown) cost function and some observed data points (clearly there is measurement error or all points would lie on the cost function), along with a fitted linear cost function.

A general point is that the intercept of the regression function (whether it is a linear function or a higher-order polynomial) should *not* be interpreted as an estimate of fixed cost; this is because the fitted equation can only be regarded as an approximation to the true function in the region of estimation. Since very low levels of output are unusual, there are few if any data points near to the vertical axis. As a consequence, the value of the intercept of the estimated cost fuinction gives little information as

to what the true fixed costs are likely to be. This point is illustrated in Figure 11.1.[8]

Suppose then we begin with a general model of the cost function based on (11.3), in which variables up to the power level 4 are included on the right side; that is,

$$C_t = \alpha_0 + \alpha_1 q_t + \alpha_2 q_t^2 \, \alpha_3 q_t^3 + \alpha_4 q_t^4 + \varepsilon_t. \quad (11.5)$$

The results of such a regression are reported in Table 11.3, whilst Table 11.4 reports the results of the simple regression of cost against output, equation (11.4).

For brevity, I omit any diagnostic testing of either equation (the reader is encouraged to conduct the more detailed analysis of the type described in section 9.4 for these models), although it is worth noting that, although the regression (11.5) as a whole is highly significant (the F-statistic for the regression is significant at 0.9%), the individual coefficients on the explanatory variables all have low t-statistics. This is suggestive of the fact that the higher-order powers of q are not adding much explanatory power.

In general, the idea of testing down is to simplify the equation systematically in order to find the most parsimonious model supported by the data.[9] For

[8] For those of a mathematical persuasion, the slope and gradient of the fitted line should also not be interpreted as giving estimates of the coefficients of a linear Taylor-series approximation to the cost function. See White (1980) for a careful analysis of the nature of the approximation involved.

[9] i.e. the model with fewest parameters; the object is to explain much, from as little as possible.

Table 11.3 Regression (11.5): C_t on q_t, q_t^2, q_t^3, and q_t^4

SUMMARY OUTPUT

Regression statistics

Multiple R	0.907
R^2	0.823
Adjusted R^2	0.723
Standard error	24.82
Observations	12

ANOVA

	df	SS	MS	F	Significance F
Regression	4	20113.22	5028.30	8.163	0.008973
Residual	7	4311.783	615.96		
Total	11	24425			

	Coefficients	Standard error	t-statistic	P-value	Lower 95%	Upper 95%
Intercept	1720.71	68967.61	0.0250	0.988	−161362	164803.1
q_t	10.98	1275.51	0.0086	0.993	−3005.13	3027.08
q_t^2	−0.32	8.798	−0.0365	0.972	−21.12	20.48
q_t^3	0.0017	0.0268	0.0635	0.951	−0.0617	0.065
q_t^4	−2.7E−06	3.05E−05	−0.088	0.932	−7.5E−05	6.94E−05

Table 11.4 Regression (11.4): C_t on q_t

SUMMARY OUTPUT

Regression statistics

Multiple R	0.865
R^2	0.748
Adjusted R^2	0.723
Standard error	24.76
Observations	12

ANOVA

	df	SS	MS	F	Significance F
Regression	1	18293	18293	29.834	0.000276
Residual	10	6131	613.16		
Total	11	24425			

	Coefficients	Standard error	t-statistic	P-value	Lower 95%	Upper 95%
Intercept	78.67	64.26	1.224	0.249	−64.5	221.9
q_t	1.598	0.292	5.462	0.00028	0.946	2.249

brevity, only the test of moving from the general model, (11.5), to the linear specification, (11.4), is presented. This involves a test of the null hypothesis that, in (11.5),

$$H_0: \alpha_2 = \alpha_3 = \alpha_4 = 0. \qquad (11.6)$$

This involves the imposition of three restrictions relative to the unconstrained model. As in Chapter 9, I do not explicitly impose the restrictions on the parameters, but simply drop the variables and run regression (11.4). The sum of squared residuals obtained from this model is identical to what would be obtained if one imposed the restriction on model (11.5) and computed the restricted least-squares regression. As in section 9.4, the restriction can be checked using an F-test. Letting SSE_R and SSE_U denote the restricted and unrestricted sum of squared residuals obtained from the regressions in Tables 11.3 and 11.2, respectively, the appropriate F-statistic is defined as

$$F^{calc} = \frac{(SSE_R - SSE_U)/J}{SSE_U/(n - k)} = \frac{(6131.63 - 4311.78)/3}{4311.78/(12 - 5)}$$

$$= 0.9848, \qquad (11.7)$$

where J is the number of restrictions imposed (3), n is the number of observations in the sample (12), and k the number of parameters estimated in the unrestricted model (5). (Compare with similar tests in section 9.4.) The critical value of the F-statistic with $(h, n - k) = (3, 7)$ degrees of freedom at the 5% level of significance is $F_{3,7}^{crit,5\%} = 4.35$ (whilst $F_{3,7}^{crit,1\%} = 8.45$). The null hypothesis is accepted, since $F^{calc} = 0.9848 < F_{3,7}^{crit,5\%} = 4.35$ (note that it is accepted at both the 5% and 1% significance levels).

The above analysis suggests that the simple linear model is an adequate characterization of how costs vary with output. More generally, the testing-down procedure can proceed sequentially, by systematically dropping variables until the data no longer support any further simplification.[10]

---

[10] As one simplifies the model, the significance tests are not strictly independent, and the process can be accused of being susceptible to data mining. However, it has the enormous merit of being an open process. See Chap. 9 for further discussion of methodological issues.

11.5 Estimating Learning Curves

As new products bed in and production teething problems are eliminated, unit costs of production may fall: such an effect is referred to as the **learning curve** or the **experience curve**. If there are significant learning effects, cost functions such as (11.2) or (11.3) are misspecified; the estimated function obtained from performing such regressions can be seriously misleading when predicting how costs vary with output. In what follows, the basic learning curve theory is recapitualted and a case study is presented which illustrates the misspecification impact on a standard cost-regression model; this is followed by the estimation of the learning curve effect.

Chapter 10 outlined a simple model for **learning by doing** in which average cost fell at a constant percentage rate as cumulative production increased.[11] Let q_t denote output in period t, and Q_t the cumulative amount produced up to and including period t (since the product was launched); C_t denotes either total cost or, more usually, variable cost (or often the component of variable cost specifically associated with the learning effect, namely, labour costs) incurred in period t. In what follows, it is assumed that we are dealing with product variable cost. The constant percentage learning curve postulates that average variable cost, C_t/q_t, falls at a constant rate, i.e. exponentially. That is,

$$(C_t/q_t) = AQ_{t-1}^{-b}. \qquad (11.8)$$

Multiplying through by q_t, this implies that

$$C_t = Aq_t Q_{t-1}^{-b}. \qquad (11.9)$$

This is a pure learning curve model, as it presumes that variations in output within the period do not affect average variable cost. In practice, in the absence of the learning curve effect, average (variable) costs could well be influenced by the output per period; indeed, if we adopt the same constant elasticity formulation, the standard form of cost function in which there is no learning effect would be $C_t = Aq_t^\alpha$. Thus a natural relaxation of the pure learning curve model is to write $C_t = Aq_t^{\alpha_1}Q_{t-1}^{\alpha_2}$, so that average variable cost is $C_t/q_t = Aq_t^{\alpha_1 - 1}Q_{t-1}^{\alpha_2}$.

---

[11] As mentioned in Chap. 10, there are also other (similar but not identical) types of learning curve model which can be used for estimating the learning effect. For further details see e.g. Kaplan (1982) or Belkaoui (1986).

This model allows that average variable costs may vary within the period (as a function of output), and from period to period (as cumulative output increases). Then we can examine whether there is decreasing ($\alpha_1 < 1$) or constant ($\alpha_1 = 1$) or increasing ($\alpha_1 > 1$) average variable cost, and whether $\alpha_2 < 0$ (i.e. whether there is a significant learning effect). Taking logs and adding an error term, the model to be tested is

$$\ln C_t = \alpha_0 + \alpha_1 \ln q_t + \alpha_2 \ln Q_{t-1} + \varepsilon_t, \quad (11.10)$$

where $\alpha_0 = \ln A$. The estimate of the learning curve coefficient, α_2, implies that each doubling of output leads to a fall in average variable cost by the factor 2^{α_2} (see section 10.6). Thus, if $\alpha_2 = -0.3$, this corresponds to an 81% learning curve ($2^{-0.3} = 0.81$).

Table 11.5 gives cost and output figures for Novowidgets, a new product developed by Widgewood plc.

The first three columns in Table 11.5 represent the raw data; the other columns are computed on the basis of this information. First, I illustrate in Table 11.6 the consequences of not explicitly modelling learning effects when they are significant; that is, Table 11.6 reports the results of running the ordinary least-squares regression.

$$\ln C_t = \alpha_0 + \alpha_1 \ln q_t + \varepsilon_t. \quad (11.11)$$

The regression has a low R^2 and shows little explanatory power (examine the F-statistic). This shows how the misspecification (omitted learning effects) leads to a poor fit; if such a model is used to forecast future costs, it is likely to have poor predictive performance.

Table 11.7 reports the regression (11.10). This equation has high R^2 and the F-statistic indicates

it is highly significant (significant at the 0.0026% level). All the individual parameter estimates are also significant. Note that the 95% confidence interval associated with α_2 is $(-0.342, -0.214)$. This indicates that we can reject the null hypothesis of no learning effect at the 5% level of significance: that is, there is a significant learning effect. The estimate, $\alpha_2 = -0.278$, implies that every doubling in cumulative output reduces average variable costs by the factor $2^{-0.278} = 0.757$: that is, there is an estimated 76% learning curve effect. The next question is whether average variable cost is affected by the amount produced within a period, i.e. whether there are economies of scale. In fact the estimated parameter is $\hat{\alpha}_1 = 1.03$, which suggests that the hypothesis that average costs are constant with period output cannot be rejected. Indeed, this is indicated by the 95% confidence interval for this parameter, $(0.786, 1.293)$. It is possible to impose the restriction that $\alpha_1 = 1$ and to re-estimate the learning curve coefficient α_2; this is set as an exercise in section 11.7.

11.6 Summary

This chapter reviewed alternative techniques for cost estimation, emphasizing the importance of the engineering approach and the statistical approach, and noting the complementarities between these approaches. It followed this by exploring the major weaknesses of the data used in typical cost studies (mainly arising from changing technology and input prices). Following this, the econometric approach to

Table 11.5 Data for Cost Estimation with learning effects

Month t	Cost per period C_t	Output per period q_t	ln (C_t)	Cumulative output Q_t	ln (q_t)	ln (Q_t)
1.00	12.50	10.00	2.53	10.00	2.30	2.30
2.00	13.78	11.00	2.62	21.00	2.40	3.04
3.00	11.86	12.00	2.47	33.00	2.48	3.50
4.00	10.18	11.00	2.32	44.00	2.40	3.78
5.00	11.98	14.00	2.48	58.00	2.64	4.06
6.00	11.81	15.00	2.47	73.00	2.71	4.29
7.00	11.99	17.00	2.48	90.00	2.83	4.50
8.00	11.04	16.00	2.40	106.00	2.77	4.66
9.00	8.17	13.00	2.10	119.00	2.56	4.78
10.00	11.61	17.00	2.45	136.00	2.83	4.91
11.00	11.16	19.00	2.41	155.00	2.94	5.04
12.00	12.86	21.00	2.55	176.00	3.04	5.17

Table 11.6 Regression (11.11): $\ln C_t$ on $\ln q_t$

SUMMARY OUTPUT

Regression statistics

Multiple R	0.183
R^2	0.034
Adjusted R^2	−0.074
Standard error	0.141
Observations	11

ANOVA

	df	SS	MS	F	Significance F
Regression	1	0.006	0.006	0.313	0.590
Residual	9	0.178	0.020		
Total	10	0.184			

	Coefficients	Standard error	t-statistic	P-value	Lower 95%	Upper 95%
Intercept	2.125	0.554	3.832	0.004	0.870	3.379
$\ln q_t$	0.115	0.205	0.559	0.590	−0.350	0.579

Table 11.7 Regression (11.10): $\ln C_t$ on $\ln q_t$ and $\ln Q_{t-1}$

SUMMARY OUTPUT

Regression statistics

Multiple R	0.964
R^2	0.928
Adjusted R^2	0.910
Standard error	0.041
Observations	11

ANOVA

	df	SS	MS	F	Significance F
Regression	2	0.171	0.086	51.840	2.63E−05
Residual	8	0.013	0.002		
Total	10	0.184			

	Coefficients	Standard error	t-statistic	P-value	Lower 95%	Upper 95%
Intercept	0.768	0.210	3.658	0.006	0.284	1.252
$\ln q_t$	1.040	0.110	9.462	0.000	0.786	1.293
$\ln (Q_t - 1)$	−0.278	0.028	−9.997	0.000	−0.342	−0.214

modelling cost behaviour was discussed, with an extended case study on short-run cost estimation. Finally, estimation in the presence of learning effects was explored.

11.7 Review Questions

1. What difficulties is the analyst likely to face in implementing a statistical analysis of the cost function?

2. To what extent is engineering analysis an improvement on statistical analysis as a basis for cost estimation?

3. In the case study presented in section 11.4 (using the data presented in Table 11.1), a polynomial cost function was used to estimate the relationship between cost and output. For brevity, diagnostic testing was omitted. Extend the analysis of the statistical validity of these models by examining in detail the usual battery of diagnostic tests (use section 9.4 as a template).

4. Again, for the case study presented in section 11.4, use the analysis presented in section 9.4 to compare the performance of a linear and a log-linear cost model for this data set.

5. Using the data presented in Table 11.5, estimate the restricted model in which average variable cost is a constant within the period: that is, model (11.10) with the restriction $\alpha_1 = 1$. The equivalent of imposing the restriction and estimating a restricted least-squares model is to restructure the model as follows. Notice that, if $\alpha_1 = 1$, then from (11.10) we can write $(\ln C_t - \ln q_t) = \alpha_0 + \alpha_2 \ln Q_{t-1} + \varepsilon_t$. Use the data on C_t and q_t to construct the left-hand variable in this equation and hence run this unrestricted ordinary least-squares regression. Compare the results for this equation with those for (11.10). The restricted estimate should turn out to be $\hat{\alpha}_2 = -0.270$, compared to $\hat{\alpha}_2 = -0.278$ in the unrestricted case. Apply the F-test for the restriction.

11.8 Further Reading

Thomas (1993) devotes a chapter on the problems and pitfalls of the estimation of production functions, and there are simple examples in Griffiths et al. (1993). Johnston (1960) is a classic reference for cost estimation studies. Belkaoui (1986) discusses theory and gives learning curve several applications of learning curve models. Pollitt (1995) provides a useful survey of some more sophisticated techniques, such as data envelopment analysis, parametric programming, and stochastic frontier models (plus many further references for applications of these techniques), and presents an extended case study, an international analysis of the efficiency of electricity generation.

12 Short-Run Benefit and Cost Analysis

Objectives To define key concepts used in short-run decision-making — relevant costs, opportunity costs, incremental costs, fixed costs, sunk costs, historic costs — and to illustrate the pros and cons of using these concepts in practice.

Prerequisites None, although Chapter 10 introduces some of the concepts discussed in this chapter.

Keywords contribution, economic depreciation, explicit opportunity cost, fixed cost, historic cost, implicit opportunity cost, incremental cost, incremental profit, incremental revenue, marginal profit, mutually exclusive choice, net sunk cost, opportunity cost, overhead, relevant cost, sunk cost, variable cost.

12.1 Introduction

Chapter 10 focused on neo-classical cost analysis, emphasizing the optimization processes which go into determining the least-cost way of producing any given level of output. It introduced various cost concepts (marginal cost, average cost, average variable cost, etc.) useful in the analysis of pricing, output, and capacity decisions. However, many decisions within the firm are not concerned with price or output and, indeed, may not be concerned with these variables at all. For example, the question of whether the firm should switch to an alternative telecom carrier will depend upon an analysis of the firm's telephone usage rate and the tariffs on offer by alternative carriers. For these types of decision, the focus is typically on what changes in taking one course of action in comparison with taking another.

Economists traditionally emphasize the role of incremental and opportunity cost in decision-making. Section 12.2 gives definitions and examples, whilst section 12.3 examines the concepts in more detail. Section 12.4 then gives two extended examples which illustrate the use of opportunity cost and related concepts in a practical context. This section prefaces all this by discussing some of the more philosophical aspects of the concept of opportunity cost.

Suppose we define an accounting cost as one which gets recorded in the firm's books; that is, it is an actual cash flow. Such cash flows will ultimately feed into a calculation of the firm's profit (or loss) and also its corporate tax liability etc. Thus the accounting cash flows are obviously the **relevant cash flows** for these purposes. However, if the purpose is to choose one of several competing courses of action, the accounting costs may in fact be irrelevant. This is the case whatever the decision, whether it be a plant location decision, an equipment investment decision, an advertizing campaign decison, etc. One simple reason why accounting costs may be irrelevant is that they are historic costs. That is, they are cash flows that have already occurred. In well-worn proverbs, we can say that 'it's no good crying over spilt milk', that 'history is history', or 'that's water under the bridge'. For short-run decision-making the general principle is to forget the past. The objective is thus to make the best decision given one's current situation (however good or bad that situation may be). This in turn suggests that one should focus on things that can be changed. As a logical consequence, anything which cannot be changed can be ignored. Thus historic costs are cash flows which occurred in the past and so, for decision-making purposes, can be ignored. Likewise, costs to which one is wholly committed can also be ignored. Such costs are often referred to as sunk costs.

The opportunity cost of a given resource is simply defined as its value in the next best alternative use. Opportunity cost is what the decision-maker sacrifices in selecting one course of action in preference to the next best. Section 12.2 defines the concept more precisely; however, before proceeding, it is worth noting some of its characteristics.

Opportunity cost

· is subjective (to the decision-maker);

· is a forward-looking concept. What is past is past; only the future is open and affected by choice, i.e. opportunity cost is based on anticipations of the future consequences which flow from alternative courses of action;

· is inherently linked to choice. What the decision-maker gives up in selecting one alternative over the others depends on the range of alternatives considered (this emphasizes the need to define carefully the full set of alternatives);

· is never explicitly realized. The alternatives, once rejected, are not undertaken and hence are not directly experienced;

· incorporates a degree of optimization. It is only defined once the alternatives have been ranked and the next best alternative identified.

The following example illustrates these points:

EXAMPLE 12.1 The author's university car park features a variety of parking lots and on-campus street parking. The author would like to park as close to the office as possible. He sees a vacant space on entering the campus, but it is 800 yards from the office. If he passes up this space, he may lose it and end up parking even further away. Or he may get lucky and find a place nearer the office. If he takes the space, he may never know whether he could have improved on it because, by the time he gets to the office, the parking situation will be different from what existed at the time he was in the car and looking for a parking place.

This example emphasizes the subjectivity of cost, how it is personal to the decision-maker, how it is based on the information available at the point of decision, of how the anticipated outcomes from alternative choices, once these have not been taken, are not experienced, and how in choosing one thing, you may have to give up on other things.

12.2 Essential Cost Concepts

This section briefly reviews the main cost concepts likely to prove useful in short-run decision analysis. The concepts are introduced fairly briefly because a fuller understanding is best obtained by studying their use in the examples discussed in detail in section 12.4.

12.2.1 Opportunity Cost

Definition 12.1 For decision-making purposes, **opportunity cost** is the value forgone when a decision-maker chooses one course of action in preference to others.

It follows that the opportunity cost of using a resource in a given project is its value in the next best alternative use. For marketed products, the opportunity cost for an item you do not have is simply the purchase price (this represents the value to other potential users of the product). For an item in stock, the opportunity cost depends upon the alternative possible uses for the item. If the only alternative to using the item in a given project is to resell it, then the opportunity cost is simply the price it would command on resale. Sometimes an opportunity cost corresponds to an actual cash flow, but not always; accordingly, it is useful to distinguish explicit from implicit opportunity cost:

Definition 12.2 An **explicit opportunity cost** is one for which there is an actual cash flow.

Definition 12.3 An **implicit opportunity cost** is one for which there may be no actual cash flow involved.

Implicit opportunity costs generally arise where there are mutually exclusive choices or courses of action; that is, where choosing any one option rules out all the others (as in the examples below).

EXAMPLE 12.2 Implicit opportunity cost: You win a vintage Austin Healey 3000 in a lottery. The prize includes free petrol insurance and maintenance costs for 12 months. Having received the car, if you choose to keep it for the year, there is no cash outlay involved, but there is an opportunity cost, since there is an alternative—to sell the car. For example, suppose the market value is currently £15,000, and it is still £15,000 after one year. There is thus no (nominal) depreciation, yet there is still an opportunity cost associated with keeping it, namely the interest forgone on the £15,000.

EXAMPLE 12.3 (Implicit opportunity cost): A firm has an inventory of widgets; the price paid last year for each of these was £1000 (historic cost). Inflation has increased the market price for widgets to £2000. If the widgets can be sold on the open market at this price, then the opportunity cost of using the widgets held in inventory in an internal project by the firm is £2000 each. (This assumes that the only alternative for the widgets is to sell them off; there may be other alternatives, as in Example 12.4 below.)

Why do mutually exclusive choices occur? For example, if the firm has three investment projects under consideration, why can't it choose to do all three? There are, of course, a variety of possible reasons. For example, the managers of the firm may lack the skilled personnel, or the expertise to handle the volume of business implied by undertaking all the projects, or they may be subject to budget constraints (if the firm is part of a group, the volume of investment in any firm may be controlled by the head office). It would thus appear that, in practice, mutually exclusive choices tend to arise because of constraints of one form or another.

Fact 12.1 Mutually exclusive choices can arise in two ways:
1. as a consequence of scarce resources (budget or financial constraints, skill shortages, etc. which prevent more than one course of action being selected);
2. for technical reasons (which can also often be traced to some physical or financial constraint). For example, the choice of location for a bridge or motorway may physically rule out alternative sites, although more often, it is the level of demand which will rule out a multiplicity of motorways or bridges performing essentially the same or a similar function.

Thus, when such constraints are seen to be operating, one can expect to find implicit opportunity costs arising in the decision analysis.

12.2.2 Incremental Cost

Definition 12.4 Incremental cost is the change in cost between undertaking a course of action and not undertaking it. It is a special case of opportunity cost in which the next best alternative is defined as doing nothing.

Thus, given the current position, or status quo, incremental cost is defined simply as the change in cost which occurs when an action is implemented. It is useful to contrast the concept of incremental cost with the more familiar concept of marginal cost.

Fact 12.2 Marginal cost is a special case of incremental cost.

Marginal cost is the change in cost incurred when output is incremented by one unit (or, if output is a continuous variable, it is the rate at which cost increases as output increases). However, incremental cost applies to any change in cost consequent on taking a course of action; thus the incremental cost of increasing output by one unit is simply the marginal cost at that output level. However, one can also consider non-marginal output changes, such as the incremental cost of increasing output by, say, 20%. Furthermore, incremental cost need not relate to the firm's output level at all, such as the incremental costs of the firm upgrading a particular department's photocopier.

The following definitions of some concepts related to incremental cost are pretty much self-explanatory; accordingly, I omit further commentary.

Definition 12.5 Incremental revenue is the change in revenue incurred in undertaking a course of action as compared to not undertaking it.

For the same reasons as discussed under Fact 12.2, we have:

Fact 12.3 Marginal revenue is a special case of incremental revenue.

The cost concepts thus have their counterparts on the revenue side, and can also be defined for profitability:

Definition 12.5 Incremental profit is the change in profit which occurs in implementing a course of action, in comparison with the status quo.

Fact 12.4 Marginal profit is a special case of incremental profit.

Definition 12.6 Incremental profit is what accountants conventionally call **contribution**.

Fact 12.5 Incremental profit equals incremental revenue minus incremental cost.

An action is worth undertaking if the incremental revenues exceed the incremental costs; equivalently, it is worth undertaking if it makes an incremental profit, or a contribution.

12.2.3 Relevant/Irrelevant Costs

All transactions/accounting costs which are unaffected by the choice are irrelevant costs and may be ignored for the purposes of decision-making.

Definition 12.7 Any cost which cannot be altered by the decision is termed a **sunk cost**.

Definition 12.8 Any cost which happened in the past is termed an **historic cost**.

A sunk cost can lie in the future; for example, a binding agreement may require you to take a shipment of product and pay a price for it. If there is no right to cancel the shipment, then for the purposes of decision-making, the payment is a sunk cost. It clearly follows that

Fact 12.6 All historic costs are sunk costs (but not all sunk costs are historic costs).

Since nothing can be done about sunk costs, it follows that they can be ignored. It is possible to include sunk costs in a cost analysis, but they will enter into the costing for every alternative under consideration, and so will not alter the decision as to which is the best alternative to choose (this point is made explicitly in Example 12.4 below). The choice problem, correctly interpreted, is to do the best you can from now (by selecting the best amongst the available alternatives) using what you happen to have inherited from the past.

However, perhaps it is overstating the case somewhat to suggest that historic costs are completely irrelevant for decision-making purposes. Looking at past costs and revenues may provide a useful forecast of what the future profit performance is likely to be. Indeed, the whole edifice of econometrics is founded upon estimating relationships using historic data. However, historic cost is at best only a guide to future cost; whether it is likely to be a good guide is an empirical question which the decision-maker will need to judge on a case-by-case basis. For example, if the item in question is subject to significant price volatility (the prices of commodities, such as coffee, tea, and metals, and of raw materials, such as platinum and oil, can fluctuate considerably), or if the company is operating in an inflationary economy, historic costs may be a poor guide to future costs, and a more sophisticated cost estimation procedure may be required. For example, in an inflationary environment, a bookseller would be foolish to assume that the books on the shelves can be replaced at historic cost.

In considering the buildings, plant and machinery, etc. required by a firm to enter a new business, if, after purchase, the resale price is still close to the purchase price, economists often refer to the industry as one featuring low sunk costs, whilst if the assets, once purchased, are hard to resell at any price, this is a case where sunk costs are large. This notion of sunk cost is best related to that given in Definition 12.7 by thinking of it as a **net sunk cost**. In considering the purchase of an item of equipment, the decision-maker can have in mind the price she can get if she wishes to undo the purchase. If the resale price after purchase is the same as the purchase price, the buyer can undo the action at zero net cost; hence the term 'zero sunk cost'. By contrast, if there is no resale value after purchase, the whole of the purchase price will become a sunk cost. Whether there are large or small net sunk costs is of importance for firms considering entry into new markets, and hence it is an important determinant of market structure (see Chapter 13).

The following concepts were introduced in Chapter 10, but are briefly considered here in relation to the foregoing concepts.

Definition 12.9 **Fixed cost** is that part of the total cost of production that does not vary with output. That is, it is the cost associated with services of fixed factors.

Definition 12.10 **Variable cost** is that part of total cost which varies with output.

It was suggested in Chapter 10 that what is a fixed factor and what is variable depends upon the decision context and the time horizon associated with that decision context. For example, in the very short run, capital equipment, land and buildings, and labour may be regarded as fixed factors, whilst material costs are variable (for many organizations, labour costs will also be variable, since hours worked can often be varied from day to day without recourse to hiring and firing workers). In the short run, labour becomes a variable factor, whilst in the long run, everything, including plant capacity, becomes variable. Now, it might be supposed that once land, buildings, plant, and machinery are installed, there is no fixed cost associated with them. However, this is not so, for there is usually an opportunity cost. That is, even if the land, buildings, and equipment are wholly owned, in using these the firm forgoes the rent it could receive from hiring out the space and equipment. This is often referred to as a rental cost. Of course, this rental cost might be zero (for example, this would be the case if, in the period under consideration, no potential user can be found at any positive price).

12.2.4 Depreciation

Economic depreciation is simply the decline in market value of an item with age. Accounting definitions (such as straight line, reducing balance, etc.) are principally concerned with writing off the original (i.e. historic, and hence sunk) cost of an item. For short-run decision-making, the decision-maker needs to know the sacrifice involved in using the item for the project, compared to its use in the next best alternative. Accounting definitions of depreciation may prove to be useful proxies or estimates of economic depreciation but can in some cases prove seriously deficient as predictors of changes in economic (resale or salvage) value. In any short-run decision problem, the simplest way to think about depreciation is to simply ask the following question: by how much will the resale value of the equipment be affected by its use in the project?

12.2.5 Overheads

Many items which come into the category of **overhead** are independent of, or do not vary across, the alternatives under consideration. If so, there is a zero incremental cost associated with this category, and such costs can be ignored in deciding between alternative courses of action. However, not all the items typically categorized as overheads are necessarily invariant. If some items do vary across alternatives, then these must be included in the analysis. Furthermore, there can be complications when there are centrally provided services which relate to usage and capacity constraints. For example, suppose a firm has spare installed capacity which is currently lying idle. Then it is conventional to assign an opportunity cost of zero to using some or all of the capacity available (that is, if a project makes use of the capacity, any material inputs and perhaps labour would be costed, but there would be no capacity charge). Assigning an opportunity cost of zero is correct so long as there is no imminent prospect of the spare capacity running out. However, if the capacity constraint is likely to bind, using the spare capacity for this project might preclude its use for some other project. Theoretically, in such a case one would want a 'shadow price' for the value of capacity to these other projects. In the short run, this shadow price could even exceed the market price for expanding capacity. The concept of shadow price finds application in the analysis of peak load

pricing and related types of capacity constraint in Chapter 23.

Accounting cost classifications (in particular, overhead classifications) are not always helpful for decision-making. A critical attitude is desirable in studying such cost allocations. The inappropriate allocation of overhead can easily lead to the rejection of projects which would actually make a positive incremental profit for the firm (or contribution to the firm, as accountants like to say). That is, projects are rejected which would increase the firm's profitability. The case studies in section 12.4 illustrate this point (amongst others).

12.3 The Usefulness of Opportunity Cost Analysis

Consider the following (apparent) paradox. Most economists regard opportunity cost as a central concept in decision analysis—yet it is only defined once the best choice and the next best alternative have been decided on. The best and the next best can only be decided on once all the alternatives have somehow been assessed. Thus the best choice is already known before the concept can be used. How then can it be useful?

The answer to this apparent conundrum lies in the observation that any complex decision problem typically involves a myriad of sub-decisions. The concept of opportunity cost really only comes into play in complex decision problems; there is no need for it in trivial decision problems. Thus, each opportunity cost embodies the solution to a sub-decision, and in so doing, it facilitates a compact presentation of the cost analysis.

In fact, incremental reasoning and opportunity cost analysis are not absolutely essential to correct decision analysis, but the concepts do help to simplify analysis and also the presentation of analysis. A cash budgeting approach *can* be used to obtain correct answers, but such an approach rapidly becomes unwieldy when the projects under consideration become at all complex. The following highly stylized example illustrates how, despite the fact that different approaches, correctly undertaken, give the same (correct) answer to a choice problem, incremental reasoning and opportunity costing facilitate the presentation of results. It also illustrates the point that the interpretation of 'profit' in each case is different.

EXAMPLE 12.4 There is just one project for the firm to consider; if it is not taken up, everything remains idle next period. Rent for the period is £1000 and employee wages are also £1000. These occur whatever happens. The project *p* promises sales revenue of £1200 and utilizes all the labour and factory space. It requires inputs of (*a*) widget-nuts: these are in stock, historic cost £750, and (*b*) widget-bolts: these are on order for £900. There is a cancellation fee of £300 on the widget bolts if they are not taken, and if taken, they have no resale value. The widget nuts, by contrast, can be sold for £500. The firm has no foreseeable future use for widget nuts or bolts, other than in this project.

1 A CASH BUDGETING APPROACH

Although the main concern is with the decision to undertake project *p*, there are five alternative courses of action to consider; these are

*A*0. do nothing;

*A*1. sell widget nuts;

*A*2. cancel widget bolts;

*A*3. sell widget nuts and cancel widget bolts;

*A*4. undertake project *p*.

Alternative *A*4 (undertaking the project) is clearly the best choice, even though the business runs at a loss in this period (−2450). By assumption, closure is not an option under consideration.

2 THE INCREMENTAL APPROACH

*A*0 is taken as the benchmark; incremental reasoning focuses on the things that change; things which do not change are ignored.

Again, as Table 12.2 indicates, *A*4 is the best choice, with an incremental profit of £1200. The interpretation is that *A*4 increases profit by £1200 relative to doing nothing at all.

3 THE OPPORTUNITY COST APPROACH

This examines the project *A*4 in relation to what will be done if it is not undertaken. There are two

Table 12.1 A cash budgeting approach

	Alternative *A*0	*A*1	*A*2	*A*3	*A*4
	Do nothing	Sell nuts	Cancel bolts	Sell nuts and cancel bolts	undertake *p*
Revenue from *p*	n/a	n/a	n/a	n/a	£1200
Rent	£−1000	£−1000	£−1000	£−1000	−1000
Wages	−1000	−1000	−1000	−1000	−1000
Historic cost of nuts	−750	−750	−750	−750	−750
Sell nuts	n/a	500	n/a	500	n/a
Cost or cancellation cost of bolts	−900	−900	−300	−300	−900
Profit	£−3650	£−3150	£−3050	£−2550	£−2450

n/a = not applicable.

Table 12.2 Incremental costing

	Alternative *A*1	*A*2	*A*3	*A*4
	Sell nuts	Cancel bolts	Sell nuts and cancel bolts	Undertake *p*
Revenue	n/a	n/a	n/a	£1200
Sell nuts	£500	n/a	£500	n/a
Cancel bolts (incremental benefit)	n/a	£600	600	n/a
Incremental Profit	£500	£600	£1100	£1200

n/a = not applicable.

items to consider: the next best use for the widget nuts is to sell them (opportunity cost, OC, is the lost revenue, £500), whilst the next best alternative use for the widget bolts is to cancel the order (net OC = £900 − £300 = £600). The resultant opportunity costing is displayed in Table 12.3.

Table 12.3 Opportunity costing

Revenue	£1200
Sell nuts: OC	−500
Cancel bolts: OC	−600
Profit	£100

The interpretation of profit in this opportunity cost analysis is that $A4$ increases the firm's profit by £100 relative to implementing the next best alternatives. It is thus worth implementing.

Example 12.4 illustrates the general point that as the complexity of projects increases, the cash budgeting approach rapidly becomes unwieldy when compared to the opportunity cost approach (note that the decision problem discussed above is very simple compared to most real-world applications). The general insight to be drawn from the above example is that, although it is possible to use the cash budgeting approach to obtain the correct decision, when there are many sub-decisions it is necessary to examine every combination of alternative decisions, something which rapidly becomes unwieldy. The opportunity cost approach keeps the analysis more under control and facilitates a single-column presentation of costs and benefits associated with any given project. A further point to note is that all items which remain the same across all the alternatives can be ignored. This is an important key principle which greatly simplifies analysis. Example 12.4 makes it clear that it is legitimate to ignore both fixed and sunk costs.

12.4 Opportunity Cost Reasoning: Case Studies

This section presents two case studies, examples which illustrate many of the above cost concepts in action. The first is an assessment of whether or not to accept a contract; the second, of whether to close down part of a firm's operations (akin to a branch closure decision). The first remains a fairly stylized example, in which the classification of costs is unproblematic; it thus provides a straightforward illustration of the application of different cost concepts. The second case study is much closer to being a description of a real-world situation—in which the decision-maker has to think hard about what the alternatives are, and what the correct classifications might be.

12.4.1 Rejecting or Accepting a Contract[1]

A customer has offered to pay a maximum of £100,000 for your firm to undertake a specialized (and probably one-off) widget project.

(a) Accounting Information for the Project

The following traditional costing has come from the Accounts Department. This shows a contract cost of £132,800, and the recommendation is that the firm reject the offer. In the final column of Table 12.4, an opportunity cost analysis is added, based on additional information and the ensuing analysis of this material. An explanation of these figures follows the analysis.

Further investigation reveals the following information:

(b) Additional Information for the Project

1. Material A, if not used in the above project, will either be sold for £6,000 or used as a substitute input in another project. The latter project requires a conversion expenditure of £2500 but replaces an input which would cost £9000.

2. As for material B, there is no need to take this contracted shipment, although it is estimated that the cancellation costs will amount to £2000. If taken and not used in this project, it is unlikely to be used in the foreseeable future. Its (net of selling costs) second-hand value is around £6000.

3. The labour has to be hired in for the project except for the foreman. He would be transferred to the project (his wage cost = £10,000). However, someone would have to be hired to do the foreman's current job (estimated cost £5000).

4. The equipment, when new, cost £120,000; depreciation has been allocated over 6 years on a straight-line basis. Hence the contract, in utilizing

---

[1] This is an much abbreviated and amended version of a case study originally discussed in Arnold (1973).

Table 12.4 Costs and revenues for the laundry business

			Revenues	'Accounting' costs	Opportunity costs
1	Contract offer price		£100,000		
2	Materials	A (in stock)		£8,000	£6,500
3		B (contracted)		9,000	7,000
4	Labour			35,000	30,000
5	Capital equipment	C (leased)		25,000	25,000
6		D (owned)		20,000	10,000
7	Overheads			30,000	0
8	Total costs			127,000	78,500
9	Profit on contract			−£27,000	£21,500

the equipment for the best part of 1 year, has been assigned 1 year's depreciation, £20,000. However, the equipment's current second-hand value (net of selling costs) is £30,000 and, if not used on the contract, will be sold. If used on the project, this second-hand value would reduce to £20,000, the equipment being sold once the contract is complete.

(c) Analysis of the Project Cashflows

Whether the above project is worth taking depends on what the firm will do if it does not accept the contract. There are seven sub-decisions here, one for each of rows 1–7 in Table 12.4, which are now analysed sequentially. The results of the analysis are presented in the final column of Table 12.4.

Row 1 The contract offer price of **£10,000** is an incremental revenue, and thus can be entered unchanged.

Row 2 For material A, the figure entered in the table, £8000, is an historic cost, and is thus not relevant to the analysis. It can be sold for £6000; if this were the only alternative, the opportunity cost of using the material for the contract would simply be that the firm misses out on selling it, so the opportunity cost would be £6000. However, there is the alternative of utilizing the material as a substitute input. This saves the firm an expenditure of £9000, but they must incur a conversion cost of £2500; thus, if used in this way, the net saving to the firm would be £6500. Clearly this is a better use of the material than simply selling it for £6000. Hence using it as a substitute input is the next best alternative, and hence the opportunity cost for using A in the project is **£6500**.

Row 3 If the material B could be cancelled costlessly, then the opportunity cost would simply be the mar-

ket price of £9,000, as indicated in the table. If the material could not be cancelled at all, the £9,000 in Table 12.4 would be a sunk cost and hence could be totally ignored. However, the actual alternatives to taking the material and using it for the contract are:

(i) to take the material and then sell it. The net cost to the firm is the purchase price, £9000, minus the revenue raised by resale, £6000. Thus the net cost is £3000;

(ii) to cancel the order. This costs the firm £2000.

Hence the next best alternative for the firm (to taking the material and using it in the contract) is to cancel the order. Therefore, if the firm takes the order, it pays out £9000 for material B; if it rejects the order, it cancels B and pays out £2000. Thus the net opportunity cost of using B for the contract is the difference, i.e. £9000 − £2000 = £7000. Another way of looking at this is to note that the agreement to purchase material B means that the firm must hand over £2000 whatever else it does. This makes the £2000 a sunk cost. If the firm chooses to take the material, it incurs a further incremental cost of £7000; thus **£6000** is the opportunity cost for this material.

Row 4 Of the £35,000 labour charge, £25,000 is for labour which will be hired only if the contract is taken. Clearly the opportunity cost of this labour is its market price, £25,000. However, the foreman is not hired in, but is transferred from another job. His wage over the period of the contract would be £10,000, but the incremental cost to the firm of moving him to this new job is simply the fact that someone else needs to be hired to perform his old job, a cost of £5000. Hence the cost to the firm of using the foreman on this project is simply £5000. (Note that, if the firm can freely hire and fire employees, it would seem rational to simply fire the foreman and hire someone else at only £5000 even if the contract is not taken, since apparently the price of £5000 secures someone competent to do the foreman's current job. However, firing an employee can be politically sensitive, difficult, and/or expensive for the firm so this is probably not an option, and certainly not one discussed in the additional information provided above.) So, the overall opportunity cost for labour is £25,000 + £5000 = **£30,000**.

Row 5 There is no information provided regarding the lease on equipment C. Presumably it costs £25,000 over the period required for the contract. If the lease can be costlessly cancelled, then this is the money sum the firm would save if the equipment was not used for the contract. At the other extreme, if there is no possibility of cancellation, and the equipment C would lie idle if not used on this contract, the opportunity cost of using it would be zero. Equally, if there was a cancellation fee associated with the lease, then the opportunity cost would be £25,000 minus the cancellation fee (cf. material B above; the opportunity cost of £7000 there was £9000 minus the cancellation charge of £2000). Given there is no information, we take the pessimistic case (that least favourable to the acceptance of the contract); this is to assume that the lease can be costlessly cancelled, in which case, there is no change: opportunity cost = **£25,000**.

Row 6 Capital equipment D is owned by the firm and is currently being depreciated by £20,000 per annum. However, the effect of using the equipment in this project is an economic depreciation of £10,000. This arises because, if the contract is not taken, the equipment will be sold for an expected £30,000, whilst if it is used, it is expected that it will be sold at the end of the contract for only £20,000. Ignoring the timing differences[2] of these cash flows, the depreciation is £30,000 − £20,000 = £10,000. Hence the opportunity cost is **£10,000**.

Row 7 Overheads are logged at £30,000. No information is given regarding whether there will be any incremental overhead costs if the contract is accepted. If it is assumed that these overheads come from central office and are costs totally independent of the contract, then they can be ignored. In this case, there is a zero incremental

overhead cost associated with the contract, so opportunity cost = **£0**.

(d) Conclusion

The opportunity costs highlighted in bold above are gathered together in Table 12.4.

Using the accounting costs, the contract appears to cost £127,000 and hence makes a loss of £27,000. Using the opportunity cost figures, the project costs £78,500 and makes a profit for the firm of £21,500. The opportunity cost analysis indicates the project should be undertaken. It is worth emphasizing the interpretation to be placed on this 'profit' of £21,500. According to this analysis, the firm makes £21,500 more profit if it takes this contract than it will do if it rejects the contract, and activates all the next best alternatives. (It goes without saying that the firm's profitability will be even worse if it does not activate the next best alternatives.)

MBA students confronting this case study for the first time often remark that, if you do not recover overhead, you might go bankrupt. However, this misses the point of the analysis. Imagine that your company is invited to tender for the above project. Then the analysis of costs indicates that any price above £78,500 increases the profitability of the firm relative to its next best alternatives. This does not imply that the tender should go in at £78,500! Clearly, the firm wishes to maximize its profit; it thus needs to assess the chances of it getting the contract—and of how this probability varies as the asking price is increased. Where there is little competition, the tender price could be considerably in excess of £78,500. Naturally, the firm will wish to charge what the market will bear. The point is that this analysis requires an understanding of how profit varies as the tender price is varied. This means the firm needs to know the real (i.e. opportunity) cost of the project. Note, especially, that if it tried to 'cover overhead allocation' and set a price of £127,000 or more, this might lose it the order—and leave it worse off as a consequence. (For example, if the best price the firm can get is £100,000, this makes the firm better off by £21,500; if it bids higher—because of the concern to cover overheads—and loses the contract, it is then worse off than it need have been by that £21,500.)

Finally, in any bidding or tender process, it should be clear that having used opportunity cost reasoning to establish the price at which to tender, it may then be politically astute to massage the costing through a

---

[2] With longer-term projects, cash flows which occur at different points in time would need to be appropriately valued; see Chaps. 6 and 7 for detailed discussion of the issues involved.

judicious allocation of overhead in order to justify to the client the price offered. After all, if there is little competition, there may be considerable profit in the contract—but it is not usually in the firm's interest to let the client know this. The creative use of overhead allocation can thus be useful as a presentational device (to hide the true profitability of the project). The key point, however, is that the overhead allocation comes into play only after the price has been determined by opportunity cost reasoning. The problem of tendering for contracts is discussed in rather more detail in Chapter 25 (the above case is taken up again in Example 25.6 as a problem of determining the optimal tender price).

12.4.2 Closing Down a Line of Business[3]

Agamemnon B. Shipley is the local manager of the Oldcastle branch of Cato's Cleaners. In March, the ratio of wages and salaries of the Oldcastle branch to sales was 46%, whilst the company guideline was that this ratio should not generally exceed 30%. Cato's CEO had recently recommended that Mr Shipley keep the dry cleaning business going, but that he should discontinue the laundry service in order to bring labour costs more into line.

(a) Accounting Information for the Firm

Mr Shipley consulted the March accounting reports (from central office) in considering the closure decision. He made an estimate of costs and revenues resulting from the laundry for that month, and also gathered data on labour costs and supplies. In addition, he consulted Mrs Robinson, an accountant friend, who suggested the basis for allocating overhead. Table 12.5 shows that under the full cost allocation, the laundry made a £50 monthly loss. Table 12.6 shows how the costing in Table 12.5 was arrived at. Table 12.7 gives the net income report for the business as a whole.

   Since Table 12.5 showed a small loss on the laundry business, it seemed the CEO might be right in suggesting closure.

(b) Marginal Income Accounting

However, Mrs Robinson also suggested that such a full costing might be misleading. She suggested that some form of marginal income accounting might be

[3] This is a revised and shortened version of a case reported (but not analysed) in Haynes (1969).

Table 12.5 Costs and revenues of the laundry business

Revenue	£7400
Full cost	£7450
Loss	(£ 50)

Table 12.6 Laundry costings: March (including a brief explanation of the overhead allocation basis)

Indirect costs		
Manager's salary: average time spent in the department	£1470	
Advertizing in proportion to sales	400	
Telephone in proportion to sales	140	
Heat, light, power: ratio of departmental heat, light, power costs	150	
Employer's payroll tax: ratio of departmental salary costs	180	
Rent in proportion to floor space	160	
Insurance in proportion to sales	200	
Total indirect costs		£2700
Direct costs		
Salaries	£2000	
Supplies	1400	
Heat, light, power	250	
Payroll tax	100	
Depreciation	1000	
Total direct costs		£4750
Total cost		£7450

Table 12.7 Net income statement for March

Sales		£35,400
Expenses		
Salaries	£16,400	
Supplies	9000	
Heat, light, power	2100	
Employer's payroll tax	890	
Advertizing	1880	
Telephone	660	
Rent	1400	
Depreciation	4830	
Insurance	950	
Total expenses		£38,110
Net loss		(£2710)

more appropriate. This involves, in drawing up the accounts,

1. segmentation of the business into dry cleaning and shirt laundry;
2. segregation of costs into fixed and variable (qualitative judgements might be necessary as to which costs were fixed and which were variable);
3. assignment of costs to each segment. Variable costs are easy to attribute to each segment. Fixed costs also need to be classified as either assigned or unassigned. The assigned fixed costs for a segment are those which are fixed for short-period fluctuations in activity but which are avoidable if the segment is permanently discontinued (e.g. equipment depreciation and salaries in the particular segment). The unassigned fixed costs are those which do not vary with output and which could not be avoided by discontinuing of any one segment.

This analysis is presented in Table 12.8. The data are divided into four categories: revenue, variable costs, assigned fixed costs, and unassigned fixed costs, and these are reported for the two segments of the business. The table thus indicates the contribution each segment made in March to the assigned and unassigned fixed costs and to profits.

Note that some expenses in Table 12.7 overlap several categories, requiring judgement as to what is genuinely attributable to each segment in Table 12.8. For example, heat, light, and power falls into both the variable cost and unassigned fixed cost categories. Mr Shipley also needs to determine which labour costs will in fact vary with output, which will be fixed as long as the segment is maintained, and which will be attributable only to the total operation.

(c) Questions on the Case Study

You may find it helpful to consider the following questions before reading the ensuing analysis of the case (which discusses them in turn).

1. Table 12.8 separates unassigned fixed costs, assigned fixed costs, and variable costs. Which are relevant to the decision on whether to close the laundry segment of the business?
2. Are there any problems or pitfalls associated with

Table 12.8 Marginal income report

	Dry Cleaning		Laundry		
Sales		£28,000		£7400	
Variable costs					
Salaries	£7900		£2000		
Supplies	7600		1400		
Heat, light, power	1500		250		
Employer's payroll tax	430		100		
Variable cost totals		£17,430		£3750	
Contribution to assigned and unassigned fixed cost		£10,570		£3650	
Depreciation		2000		1000	
Contribution to unassigned fixed cost		£8570		£2650	
Total contribution					£11,220
Unassigned Fixed Costs (UFC)					
Salaries				£6500	
Advertizing				1880	
Telephone				660	
Heat, light, power				350	
Employer's payroll tax				360	
Rent				1400	
Depreciation				1830	
Insurance				950	
Total UFC					£13,930
Net loss for period					£(2710)

basing the closure decision on the data given in Table 12.8? Try listing any that come to mind.

3. What is the correct decision on the laundry business?

It may also be helpful to consider these two ancillary questions:

4. Is it a good idea to use rules of thumb?

5. Are the allocation bases in Table 12.6 useful for any purpose? Do they contribute to decision-making in this firm?

(d) Analysis and Answers to Questions on the Case Study

Lets now take the questions in sequence:

QUESTION 1 For the sake of this question, it is assumed that the figures are expected to hold in the future, month on month. Separating out variable costs from assigned and unassigned fixed costs tells the decision-maker what the benefit of a temporary cessation of production would save the firm. The contribution of the laundry is £3650. Hence the firm would be £3650 per month worse off if the laundry was temporarily shut down. Separating out the assigned from the unassigned fixed costs is important to the decision whether to close down the laundry side of the business on a permanent basis. The point is that the equipment could be sold; if the depreciation figure of £1000 in the right column can be used as an appropriate measure of the monthly cost, selling the machinery reduces the contribution to unassigned fixed costs to £2650 per month. Even so, on these figures, the business would be worse off by £2650 per month if the firm shuts down the laundry business permanently.

QUESTION 2 On the face of it, the marginal income analysis in Table 12.8 gives the relevant incremental costs and benefits necessary to make a correct decision on the laundry business. However, it is unsatisfactory on several counts, as follows:

1. The figures are for one month only (and are historic costs). The principles discussed in sections 12.1–12.3 counselled that we should ignore historic costs except in so far as they provide good forecasts for future costs. This business is likely to vary significantly from month to month, and may well manifest a seasonal pattern. Any judgement should therefore be made only after consulting a time series of such accounts (perhaps a whole year's worth of monthly figures if these can be made available) and making forecasts of the likely future cash flows. This one month's figures may be representative of the likely future—but they may not.

2. The figures for depreciation are not discussed anywhere. We cannot tell what the second-hand value of the plant and machinery is from the case study, but this is what is required. It seems quite likely that the equipment will have negligible resale value; if so, the depreciation figure, which may be simply a notional value concerned with recovery of the original cost of the equipment, may well be irrelevant. If we set the value at zero, the monthly contribution of the laundry rises to £3650.

3. Some of the unassigned fixed costs may well be assignable; for example, advertizing and phone bills may well change when the laundry is closed.

4. Product interdependence is likely to be a major consideration. It is assumed that closure of the laundry will not have any adverse effects upon sales of the dry cleaning part of the business. However, customers may well wish to have the full range of services under one roof rather than having to expend time and effort in seeking separate laundry facilities. Thus closure of one part of the business could lead to a fall in revenues (and some variable costs too) on the dry cleaning side.

5. It does not include an opportunity costing of the space which would be released by closure. For example, could it be used in other projects by the firm, or rented out to other organizations? Likewise, the closure might release some managerial time; could this be used productively elsewhere?

The key idea behind any cost–benefit analysis is to think hard about the alternatives that are available; if some alternatives are omitted, this may lead to an underestimate of the opportunity costs associated with using resources. Brainstorming sessions may well have value in expanding the set of alternatives for each sub-decision involved in a major decision problem. Likewise, it pays to adopt a critical attitude in assessing cost figures; they should never be taken at face value.

QUESTION 3 Clearly it can be argued that there is insufficient evidence. However, if the one month's results given in Table 12.8 were to continue, then it would be clearly incorrect to close the laundry segment. The same argument can be made regarding the dry cleaning business (since it also makes a contribution). The problem is that the contributions in total do not cover full costs; although there are questions regarding the costings, taking the figures at face value, the best decision would be to close the entire business!

QUESTION 4 Rules of thumb can be helpful. For example, it may be the case that best-practice, efficiently run laundry and dry cleaning premises operate with a 25% labour-to-sales ratio. Noting that the ratio is out of line with best practice may alert head office to the fact that maybe the operation needs to be investigated. However, it should also be noted that it is not a good idea to focus on just one single measure of performance like this. The labour-to-sales ratio can be driven to target in a very cost-inefficient way. For example, the ratio could be driven down to (or close to) zero by investing in expert systems and robot technology; however, depending upon the relative price of such technology and labour etc., this may not be the cost-efficient solution.

QUESTION 5 The allocation bases in Table 12.6 might be reasonable for *some* purpose, but clearly not for the decision on whether to keep the laundry or not. In fact, on the basis of Table 12.6, we get the erroneous idea that the laundry made a loss of £50 per month in Table 12.5. Thus, allocating overheads gives the impression that closing the laundry is a good idea when, on the basis of the figures, this would reduce the firm's monthly profits by £2650 (or, more exactly, would increase the firm's loss by £2650 per month). Arbitrary overhead allocations can clearly lead to incorrect decision-making.

12.5 Business Practice: When is a Sunk Cost Really Sunk?

If the objective is to maximize profits, then decisions at any point in time should be based exclusively on future (expected) costs and benefits which can be affected by the choice made. The past should be ignored along with all those things which may lie in the present or future but over which one has no influence or control. In practice, business decision-makers very often allocate overheads (as in the case study in section 12.4.1) and do not ignore sunk costs.

I have already commented that such behaviour might be rational and in the firm's interests. For example, it is rational to assign a shadow price to capacity, even when there is spare capacity, if there is a risk of that spare capacity being exhausted and

precluding better projects in the future (see section 12.2 on overheads). Equally, there may be significant switching or termination costs involved, or a learning curve effect (that is, a project may be incurring losses, but be worth pursuing further because it will reduce the costs of undertaking projects in the future).

However, putting to one side this set of reasons, there does seem to be a tendency for managers not to want to let the past go, not to view sunk costs as really sunk. As a consequence, there is an observable tendency for them to throw good money after bad. Why is this? It could be a purely psychological problem, of course,[4] but economists usually prefer to seek economic explanations for such phenomena. One such explanation is that there are inappropriate managerial incentives; the idea here is that, if a project is failing, this is likely to be private knowledge held by the project manager and not the CEO or owners of the firm (there is an asymmetry of information). Such a project manager may be able to prolong the project and move on to another job before it becomes clear to others that the project is failing. There may also be a reputation effect, in that abandoning projects is seen as weakness whilst persevering against the odds is seen as heroic (such that, if the project is pulled round there will be considerable kudos involved, whilst final failure is rationalized by the excuse that 'you tried every which way').

12.6 Summary

This chapter defined a variety of cost concepts of use in decision-making: in particular, incremental cost and opportunity cost. It then discussed the apparently paradoxical nature of the concept of opportunity cost (that it requires a ranking of alternatives in order to decide what is next best—how then does the concept of opportunity costs help us to choose the best?) and demonstrated the usefulness of opportunity cost through the presentation and analysis of two extended case studies.

---

[4] Authors, in writing texts, constantly confront this problem. All the effort so far is a sunk cost. So it should not affect the decision whether to abandon or to complete the book. However, it is hard to think of all the effort put in so far as going to waste! This often affects the decision to carry on (and on . . . and on . . .).

12.7 Review Questions

1. What is the difference between incremental cost and opportunity cost?

2. 'Incremental and opportunity cost reasoning tells us to ignore overheads—but if you ignore overheads you could go bust.' Should overheads be ignored? Assess the pausibility of this statement.

3. The following case study illustrates the problems that can arise in overhead cost allocation (the questions are at the end):

What Price Progress?[5]

EFFICIENCY EXPERT   Joe, you said you put this rack of peanuts in your restaurant because some people ask for them, but do you realize what this rack of peanuts is costing you?

JOE   It ain't gonna cost. It's gonna be a profit. Sure, I hadda pay £25 for a fancy rack to hold the bags, but the peanuts cost 20p a bag and I sell 'em for 30p. Figger I sell 50 bags a week to start. It'll take 5 weeks to cover the cost of the rack. After that I gotta clear profit of 10p a bag. The more I sell, the more I make.

EFFICIENCY EXPERT   That is an antiquated and completely unrealistic approach, Joe. Fortunately, modern accounting procedures permit a more accurate picture which reveals the complexities involved.

JOE   Huh?

EFFICIENCY EXPERT   To be precise, those peanuts must be integrated into your entire operation and be allocated their appropriate share of business overhead. They must share a proportionate part of your expenditures for rent, heat, light, equipment depreciation, decorating, salaries for your waitresses, cook—

JOE   The cook? What's he got to do with the nuts? He don' even know I got 'em.

EFFICIENCY EXPERT   Look Joe, the cook is in the kitchen, the kitchen prepares the food, the food is what brings people in here, and the people ask for peanuts. That's why you must charge a portion of the cook's wages, as well as a part of your own salary, to peanut sales. This sheet contains a carefully calculated cost analysis which indicates the peanut operation should pay exactly £1360 per year toward these general overhead costs.

JOE   The peanuts? £1360 a year for overhead? The nuts?

EFFICIENCY EXPERT   It's really a little more than that. You also spend money each week to have the windows washed, to have the place swept out in the mornings, to keep soap

in the washroom and provide free teas to the police. That raises the total to £1574 per year.

JOE (thoughtfully)   But the peanut salesman said I'd make money. Put 'em on the end of the counter, he said, and get 10p a bag profit—

EFFICIENCY EXPERT (with a sniff)   He's not an accountant. Do you actually know what the portion of the counter occupied by the peanut rack is worth to you?

JOE   It ain't worth nothing. There ain't no stool there—just a dead spot at the end.

EFFICIENCY EXPERT   The modern cost picture permits no dead spots. Your counter contains 60 square feet and your counter business grosses £15,000 a year. Consequently, the square foot of space occupied by the peanut rack is worth £250 per year. Since you have taken that area away from general counter use, you must charge the value of the space to the occupant.

JOE   You mean I gotta add £250 a year more to the peanuts?

EFFICIENCY EXPERT   Right. That raises their share of the general operating costs to a grand total of £1829 per year. Now then, if you sell 50 bags of peanuts per week, these allocated costs will amount to 60 pence per bag.

JOE   What?

EFFICIENCY EXPERT   Obviously, to that must be added your purchase price of 6 pence per bag, which brings the total to 66 pence. So you see, by selling peanuts at 10 pence per bag, you are losing 56 pence on every sale.

JOE   Somethin's crazy!

EFFICIENCY EXPERT   Not at all! Here are the figures. They prove that your peanuts operation cannot stand on its own feet.

JOE (brightening)   Suppose I sell a lotta peanuts—a thousand bags a week instead of 50.

EFFICIENCY EXPERT (tolerantly)   Joe, you don't understand the problem. If the volume of peanut sales increases, your operating costs will go up—you'll have to handle more bags, with more time, more depreciation, more everything. The basic principle of accounting is firm on that subject: 'The Bigger the Operation, the More General Overhead Costs that Must Be Allocated'. No, increasing the volume of sales won't help.

JOE   Okay, if you're so smart, you tell me what I gotta do.

EFFICIENCY EXPERT (condescendingly)   Well . . . you could first reduce operating expenses.

JOE   How?

EFFICIENCY EXPERT   Move to a building with cheaper rent. Cut salaries. Wash the windows biweekly. Have the floor swept only on Thursday. Remove the soap from the washrooms. Decrease the square-foot value of your counter. For example, if you can cut your expenses 50 per cent, that will reduce the amount allocated to peanuts from

---

[5] This case study was originally published anonymous in the *Lybrand Journal*, and can be found in various sources (e.g. Haynes 1969).

£1563 to £781.50 per year, reducing the cost to 36 pence per bag.

JOE (*slowly*) That's better?

EFFICIENCY EXPERT Much, much better. However, even then you would lose 26 pence per bag if you only charge 10 pence. Therefore, you must also raise your selling price. If you want a net profit of 4 pence per bag you would have to charge 40 pence.

JOE (*flabbergasted*) You mean even after I cut operating costs 50 per cent I still gotta charge 40p for a 10p bag of peanuts? Nobody's that nuts about nuts! Who'd buy 'em?

EFFICIENCY EXPERT That's a secondary consideration. The point is, at 40 pence you'd be selling at a price based upon a true and proper evaluation of your then-reduced costs.

JOE (*eagerly*) Look! I got a better idea. Why don't I just throw the nuts out—put 'em in a dustbin?

EFFICIENCY EXPERT Can you afford it?

JOE Sure. All I got is about 50 bags of peanuts. They cost about three quid—so I lose £25 on the rack, but I'm outa this nuts business and no more grief.

EFFICIENCY EXPERT (*shaking his head*) Joe, it isn't that simple. You are in the peanut business! The minute you throw those peanuts out you are adding £1,563 of annual overhead to the rest of your operation. Joe, be realistic—can you afford to do that?

JOE (*completely crushed*) It's unbelievable! Last week I was makin' money. Now I'm in trouble, just because I think peanuts on a counter is gonna bring me some extra profit—just because I believe 50 bags of peanuts a week is easy.

EFFICIENCY EXPERT (*raising one eyebrow*) That is the object of modern cost studies, Joe . . . to dispel those false illusions.

(*a*) Italian Joe's reasoning is, in much of the above discussion, fairly rational; that is, he displays, intuitively, the rudiments of opportunity cost reasoning. Give examples of this fact from the text.

(*b*) What is wrong with the efficiency expert's reasoning?

12.8 Further Reading

Buchanan (1969*a*) and the readings in the text edited by Buchanan and Thirlby (1973) give an extended conceptual discussion of the nature of the opportunity cost concept. The more recent texts in managerial economics often give this important topic a rather cursory treatment. However, further applications can be found in Douglas (1994), whilst earlier texts such as Arnold (1973), Haynes (1969), and Horngren and Foster (1987) also discuss the basic concepts.

Part IV

Market Structure and Theories of the Firm

Part IV presents some of the traditional microeconomic models of market structure; after an introduction which outlines the range of market structures which exist (Chapter 13), the ensuing chapters treat each structure in turn (with the exception of perfect competition, for reasons discussed in Chapter 13). Thus Chapter 14 deals with monopoly (single-seller markets), 15 with monopolistic competition (many sellers, differentiated products), and 16 with oligopoly (where there are small numbers of sellers in the industry). Finally, Chapter 17 takes a step back and considers whether the assumption of profit maximization is an appropriate one; it first looks at the fundamental question (why are there firms at all?), and then moves on to a consideration of alternative objectives that firms might be considered to pursue (managerial discretion and related models).

13 Introduction to Market Structure

Objective This Chapter gives a very brief overview of the principal determinants of market structure and an outline of the four major types; competition, monopoly, monopolistic competition, and oligopoly.

Prerequisites None.

Keywords competitive market, conduct, monopolistic competition, monopoly, oligopoly, performance, structure.

13.1 Introduction

This chapter provides a quick review of the key points regarding market structure, along with a listing of the salient characteristics of these market structures. The idea is to give the reader an overview of the nature of market structure and its relevance prior to the deeper analysis of particular market structures in the following chapters.

This discussion takes firms largely as given and focuses on the different types of market structure within which they operate. The interesting, and more fundamental question that can be posed is 'Why are there firms?' The firm is an organizational structure which internalizes many forms of exchange transaction; why is it that these are not dealt with by markets? This question is addressed in Chapter 17 (which discusses alternative theories of the firm) and Chapters 29, 30, and 31 (where organizational considerations are discussed in some detail).

13.2 The Structure–Conduct–Performance Paradigm

A central idea in discussing the theory of the firm is that the firm is embedded in a particular market structure and this market structure has implications for the firm's conduct and performance. Figure 13.1 illustrates what is referred to as the **structure–conduct–performance** (SCP) **paradigm** (this was also briefly reviewed in Chapter 1). Early work (pre-circa 1970) suggested that the direction of causation was principally in the direction $S \rightarrow C \rightarrow P$, with some idea that the origins of structure had to do with the technology of production (for example, that networks gave rise to economies of scale and this seemed to lead to monopoly power in such industries as electricity, gas, etc.).

The modern view is that the directions of causation are complex (see e.g. Tirole 1993) and that critical to what is observed in the way of SCP is the nature of the technology in production, denoted T (in a way, it might be better to refer to the overall set of relationships as the TSCP—the 'technology–structure–conduct–performance paradigm'). Accordingly, in figure 13.1, the arrows indicating directions of influence go both ways; this indicates that there are influences in one direction but also feed back influences. Thus the conditions of production T influence market structure S, which in turn affects the possible conduct C and performance P of firms; however, it is also true that conduct C and performance P can feed back and affect market structure. Thus predatory pricing or a firm's merger policy are forms of conduct which will affect the numbers of firms in the industry and hence the extent of competition in that industry.

An additional box has been added in Figure 13.1 for the impact of government policy (G). The idea is that the state can choose to influence S, C, and P. In the UK, the government, through privatization and regulation policy, has substantially changed the structure of industries such as water and electricity, the way they are able to conduct their affairs, and their economic performance. Again there are feed back effects; it is clear that the structure, S, of an industry has in some cases motivated particular

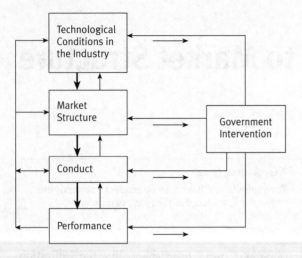

Fig. 13.1 The SCP paradigm

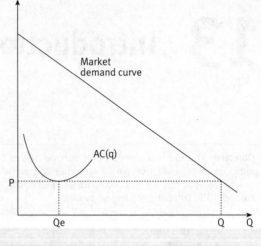

Fig. 13.2 Firm numbers

privatizations. Also conduct, C, has been scruti-nized (for example, when British Telecom wanted tariff rebalancing), and what were deemed to be excess profits in the water and electricity indus-tries, P, led the regulators to tighten the price caps in those industries. Thus the arrows again go both ways; government intervention influences S, C, and P, but equally, S, C, and P may influence policy, G.

As we shall see, the SCP view of the world is a useful way of organizing preliminary thinking about the problems facing an individual firm within an industry. It is of even more relevance for state inter-vention in the mixed economy—the appropriate-ness of different forms of competition policy and regulation of private sector enterprise.

The structure–conduct–performance paradigm suggests that the determinants of market structure are complex, featuring the interplay of a variety of forces. However, the primary force in Figure 13.1 is clearly the intrinsic nature of production. At its most naïve, the argument is that, if there is free entry, plant-efficient scale is the key determinant of market structure. The argument is illustrated in Figure 13.2.

Suppose that potential firms have access to the same technology, a technology which gives rise to an average cost curve as depicted in Figure 13.2, having a minimum average cost AC_{min} at an output q_E (the efficient scale of plant output). Given the position of the market demand curve, if the firms just break even and operate at minimum average cost (as

would occur in a perfectly competitive market equilibrium), the number of firms, n, is given simply by

$$n = Q/q_E. \qquad (13.1)$$

This gives only a rough idea of the likely numbers in the industry, since in imperfect competition, price may be above average cost, and the firm may not choose to produce the efficient level of output (although it can be argued that, with free entry, firms will not be able to stray very far from the efficient scale, or market price will be sufficiently high to allow scope for further entry[1]). If q_E is small relative to Q, then there will be a large number of firms in the industry, whilst if q_E is large relative to Q, this tends to make for monopoly or oligopoly.

The above argument is too naive, as it ignores the details of how firms compete (or collude) in markets, and how this is affected by the number already in the industry. It likewise assumes free entry; barriers to entry other than those implicit in the cost structure are often significant in practice. However, the above analysis gives a simple starting point for thinking about the structure of a given

---

[1] Deviation from efficient scale means that price must be in excess of AC_{min}, which suggests an entrant could undercut the existing market price and make a profit by producing at the level q_E. This is only a very approximate argument in view of the so-called 'integer problem'—an entrant into a monopoly doubles the number of firms; it may be that the monopolist can deviate significantly from efficient-scale output without making it possible for another firm to enter the market profitably. This discrete-ness effect tends to diminish as the number of firms increases.

industry. Chapters 14–16 elaborate on the complications for each market structure in turn.

13.3 Market Structures

This section gives a very brief listing of the essential characteristics of the four primary forms of market structure, whilst Table 13.1 sets these out in a schematic outline. Chapters 14 through 17 then deal with these market forms in some detail (other than that of perfect competition, for the reasons stated in section 13.2 above).

13.3.1 Competition

I do not discuss what constitutes perfect or pure competition, but confine attention to the broad characteristics of what would generally be considered an approximately **competitive market**:

1. *Buyers and sellers should be small and numerous.* Here, small means small relative to the overall market size. The idea is that their production and purchase decisions are sufficiently small to have a negligible effect on the market price.
2. *The product must be homogeneous in all its characteristics.* If a good is sold in a different place, or at a different time, or is differentiated in terms of some detailed characteristic (e.g. baked beans by the type of sauce), then the product is not truly homogeneous; indeed it can be viewed as a different product. Only if the product is completely homogeneous will there necessarily be a single market price for the good.
3. *There should be free exit and entry into the market by producers.* In particular, there should be no

sunk costs. Zero sunk costs means that once a firm sets up in the business, if it then decides to close down, it is able to recover the full value of the productive assets it originally purchased (assuming the plant has not been used, aged, or physically depreciated in any way). If, once purchased, assets have a much lower resale value, then this can affect an entrepreneur's decision as to whether to enter in the first place.

4. *There should be perfect knowledge,* i.e. complete and perfect knowledge of the technology that is available, and of the prevailing market price.

The firm in the competitive industry has only the decision of whether to produce, and if so, how much. Clearly, with a homogeneous product, there is little point in advertizing and no scope for price policy.

How many markets even approximately match up to this specification of what counts as a competitive market? Financial, commodity and agricultural markets often approximate the textbook paradigm of a perfectly competitive market. However, the bulk of industrial and retail products do not fall into this category. For such products, typically, the product is differentiated (think of the automobile market) and often produced by a relatively small number of producers (at least some of whom are not small relative to market size—think of Ford, Microsoft, General Electric, etc.).

13.3.2 Monopoly

Monopoly is treated in detail in Chapters 14 (and also in Chapters 18 and 19, where the focus is on pricing policy) it has the following characteristics:

1. *Single supplier, many buyers.* The buyers are all

Table 13.1 Categories of Market Structure

	Market structure			
	Perfect competition	Monopoly	Monopolistic competition	Oligopoly
Number of Sellers	Large	One	Large	Few
Product homogeneous or heterogeneous?	Homogeneous	Homogeneous	Heterogeneous	Either
Entry/exit costs	Zero	Zero or positive	Zero	Zero or Positive

small relative to the overall market size, but there is just one supplier of the good.

2. *Homogeneous product.* The monopolist is the only seller of the product. Of course, monopolists may proliferate several variations of their basic monopoly product; this is the case of multi-product monopoly, dealt with in Chapter 23.

3. *Barriers to entry and/or exit*; these can arise either for peculiar reasons, such as in the case of a legal monopoly or a natural resource monopoly (oil, diamonds), or because of the nature of the technology (the so-called natural monopoly).

13.3.3 Monopolistic Competition

Monopolistic competition is treated in detail in Chapter 15. In monopolistic competition,

1. *Buyers and sellers are small and numerous* (relative to the overall market size).

2. *Products are differentiated but similar.* An industry characterized as monopolistically competitive features a large number of products each of which is distinct but is a close substitute to each of the others; that is, the products are all close to each other in characteristics space (see Chapter 8 on Lancaster's characteristics approach to consumer theory).

3. *There is free exit and entry into the market by producers* (conditions identical to those for perfect competition).

13.3.4 Oligopoly

Oligopoly is treated in detail in Chapter 17. Oligopolies have the following characteristics:

1. *There are many buyers but few sellers.* More than one seller is involved, but only a relatively small number, such that the pricing, output, advertizing, etc. decisions of one firm have discernible impacts on the profits and sales of the other competitors. Such firms are thus likely to monitor each other's behaviour closely; any change in policy may provoke competitive reactions.

2. *The product may be homogeneous or differentiated.* The case of homogeneous product oligopoly clearly maximizes the interdependent nature of the market structure. However, differentiated oligopoly is more common in practice.

3. *There may be free entry and exit—or there may be entry or exit costs for producers.*

13.4 Further Reading

Little is required here. However, Scherer (1980) provides useful background discussion of the nature of the structure–conduct–performance paradigm, whilst the introductory chapters of Martin (1994) and Tirole (1993) place this paradigm in the context of recent developments.

14 Monopoly

Objectives To examine the conditions under which a market is likely to be monopolized, and to explore the characteristics of price and output decisions within this market structure.

Prerequisites None.

Keywords accommodated entry, backward, induction, barrier to entry, blockaded entry, Coase conjecture, common knowledge, complete information, contestability, cost-subadditivity, deadweight welfare loss, deterred entry, dominant firm, durable goods monopoly, economies of scale, endogenous barrier to entry, endongenous sunk cost, entrant, entry, excess capability, exogenous barrier to entry, exogenous sunk cost, incumbent, learning by doing, licence, limit pricing, monopoly, natural monopoly, patent, potential entrant, potential Pareto improvement, price-skimming policy, rent seeking, reputation building, subadditivity, Sylos postulate.

14.1 Introduction

Section 14.2 gives a brief overview of the essential characteristics of the monopoly market structure. The key feature is that a single firm is the sole seller of a product for which there is no close substitute. This is, apparently, a simpler form of market structure than those in which firms vie with each other for dominance and survival (oligopoly, monopolistic competition, or, indeed, perfect competition). The absence of competition suggests the firm need merely concern itself with the organization of production and the choice of marketing mix, as dealt with in section 14.3. However, unless the firm's product is protected by patents or law, there is always the possibility that other firms might try to enter the market. Entry typically leads to competition and a reduction in profitability. The question then arises whether the incumbent firm can profitably modify its behaviour so as to deter entry. This is examined in section 14.4. Since entry naturally leads to oligopolistic competition, the decision to enter depends on what the nature of this competition is likely to be; Chapter 16, on oligopoly, gives further insight into this (and considers the entry decision in slightly more detail). Section 14.5 extends the analysis of monopoly to the more common form in which it occurs in practice, namely that of the dominant firm (one faced with competition from myriad small firms, the so-called competitive

fringe). Finally, section 14.6 deals with monopoly welfare loss and the problem of how to measure it.

14.2 Characteristics of Monopoly

This section gives a brief overview of the essential features of monopoly, prior to discussing issues such as pricing, entry deterrence, etc. in greater detail.

14.2.1 A Single Producer

Monopoly is characterized as a market structure in which there is a single producer in the industry. Thus there are no other firms in the same line of business. It would thus appear that the firm can choose its marketing strategy (price, output, advertizing, etc.) without regard to the behaviour or reactions of other firms. However, if there are other firms who produce substitute products, then the firm is really in a differentiated oligopoly, and may have to consider the possible reaction of such firms to changes in its prices and outputs. Obviously, in practice, and for any product, there are always substitutes,[1] so the question is always one of how close

---

[1] Even if you own the only diamond mine in the world, there are still substitute products (including artificial diamonds for use in cutting processes, and alternative gemstones for use in jewellery).

these substitutes are and whether a reaction by these other firms is likely?'. To sum up, a firm is said to be a monopoly if it is a price-maker rather than a price-taker and if its choice of price/output is unlikely to induce competitive reaction.

14.2.2 Barriers to Entry

If there are no competitors, it might appear that the firm is free to exploit its monopoly power. However, the exercise of such power may be limited by the threat of potential entrants. The question then arises as to what prevents firms from entering a monopoly industry. It is conventional to assume that new firms will be attracted into industries in which incumbent firms are earning super-normal profits. The things which prevent firms muscling in on profitable markets are termed barriers to entry. Some of these can be described as exogenous to the firm whilst others are endogenous:

Definition 14.1 A barrier to entry is anything that prevents entry into an industry in which incumbents are earning super-normal profits. An exogenous barrier to entry is one which is outside the firm's control, whilst an endogenous barrier to entry is one whose size and extent can be controlled by the firm's choice of strategic variables (price, capacity, advertizing, etc.).

(a) Exogenous Barriers to Entry

(1) CONTROL OF A NATURAL RESOURCE/ABSOLUTE COST ADVANTAGES

Perhaps the best of the barriers to entry is where the firm secures control of the only available source of supply. Perrier, for example, has control over (what it claims to be) a unique source of mineral water. Water supply is often a (local) monopoly in this sense. Incumbent firms may have natural or locational advantages (lower transport and distribution costs etc.) over potential competitors which give rise to absolute cost advantages. A sufficiently large absolute cost advantage can preclude entry simply because of the threat that post-entry competition with a more efficient incumbent would not give a positive profit to the entrant.

(2) STATE- OR LEGALLY-CREATED MONOPOLY

Industries may have their monopoly status protected by the state. Thus, electricity supply in the UK used to be publicly provided, it being illegal for any firm to sell (or resell) electricity. Postal services in many countries are likewise legally protected monopolies.

More generally, the granting of patents or licences[2] is widespread and these create monopoly power (although often power of a temporary nature). State intervention through specific import taxes or import quotas is also common; such intervention helps protect indigenous industries from external competition.

(3) ECONOMIES OF SCALE

If the technology is such that the minimum efficient scale (the output level at which long-run average cost first attains its minimum value—see Chapter 10) is large relative to product demand, then it will not be possible for new firms to enter and earn positive profits.

(4) IMPERFECT CAPITAL MARKETS

New entrants may be perceived by those who finance them to face higher risks of failure than incumbents. Since new entrants have no track record of production in the industry, there is greater uncertainty regarding whether they will be as efficient as the incumbent. The consequence is that the cost of capital for such ventures is likely to be higher.

(5) MARKET RESEARCH COSTS

The decision whether or not to enter a market requires that the market be investigated in considerable detail. A potential entrant needs to acquire the information in order to assess whether entry is likely to be profitable. Thus it needs to explore the overall market demand and the market shares of the firms already in the industry. It also needs to explore what the likely responses will be to entry. These costs have already been sunk by incumbents (and are not recoverable on exit).

(b) Endogenous Barriers to Entry

(1) ENDOGENOUS COST ADVANTAGES

Cost advantages can arise because of the behaviour of the incumbent. These are described as endogenous. For example, there may be learning by doing; the experience curve[3] may give incumbents a cost advantage over any potential entrant. Research and development may also give rise to new technologies which are not available to potential entrants (because of complexity, or skill shortages, or simply because new processes are protected by patent law).

(2) ENDOGENOUS SUNK COSTS

The incumbent may choose to incur significant sunk costs as an entry deterrent. For example investment,

---

[2] Pollution permits, taxi and bus licences, etc.
[3] See Chaps. 10 and 11 for a discussion of the experience curve.

in excess capacity, R&D, and advertizing[4] (which builds brand loyalty) are all costly, and to a greater or lesser extent, sunk costs. A sunk cost is one which, once incurred, cannot be recovered (through resale in second-hand markets). For example, most advertizing expenditure is product-specific, and if the firm exits the business, much of the value of this advertizing is lost. The same is true of many types of equipment; they can only be resold at values considerably below the new price. The deterrent value of sunk costs is explored further in section 14.4.1.

(c) Natural Monopoly

Natural monopoly arises when, despite all potential firms having access to the same technology etc., the efficient scale of production is such that the market is most efficiently supplied by a single plant. In particular, an industry is said to be a natural monopoly if the technology associated with producing a product features cost-subadditivity.

Definition 14.3 A cost function is **subadditive** if, for any given output q, it is cheaper to produce it in a single batch rather than in smaller batches. If $C(q)$ denotes the cost of producing an output level of q, then, for any $n > 1$ and any $q > 0$, the cost function $C(q)$ is subadditive if $C(q) \leq C(q_1) + C(q_2) + \ldots + C(q_n)$ for all $q_1, \ldots, q_n > 0$ such that $q = q_1 + q_2 + \ldots + q_n$. It is strictly subadditive if $C(q) < C(q_1) + C(q_2) + \ldots + C(q_n)$.

It can be shown that a cost function that features global economies of scale is in fact cost-subadditive (although the converse is not necessarily the case). So, any technology featuring economies of scale gives rise to natural monopoly. The key idea, worth highlighting, is

Fact 14.1 If the technology implies that costs are subadditive, then no competitive equilibrium exists.

Hence we also have

Fact 14.2 If the technology features global economies of scale, then no competitive equilibrium exists.

Fact 14.1 can be explained as follows. First note that a competitive long-run equilibrium features

(i) identical price-taking firms (since all firms have access to the same technology), and

(ii) each firm earning zero profit.

If firms were earning positive profit, this would signal profitable new firm entry, whilst losses would induce firms to exit the industry. For an individual firm producing output q, profit is given as

$$\pi = (p - AC(q))q, \tag{14.1}$$

where $AC(q)$ denotes the average cost of producing output q. Suppose there are n such firms. Then industry output is nq. Now, from Definition 14.3, (strict) cost-subadditivity implies that $C(nq) < nC(q)$, hence

$$AC(nq) = \frac{C(nq)}{nq} < \frac{nC(q)}{nq} = \frac{C(q)}{q} = AC(q). \tag{14.2}$$

Thus at any given market price p, each firm has the incentive to expand output, reduce average cost, and so make a positive profit (by supplying the whole market). Thus no competitive equilibrium can exist. The prediction is thus that industries in which the technology is cost-subadditive will end up as monopolies.

Many industries, particularly network industries (electricity, post, telecoms, railways, gas, water, etc.) feature economies of scale and cost-subadditivity. Such industries are termed natural monopolies. However, it is worth noting that often such industries have cost-subadditivity only in some aspects of their operations. This means that there may be scope for competition in those areas where there is an approximately constant return to scale technology.

EXAMPLE 14.1 In the UK electricity supply, there are economies of scale in distribution (via the national grid network). However, economies of scale in generation are more limited, and it has proved possible to introduce some degree of competition amongst generators (whilst the distribution network is retained as a natural monopoly subject to regulatory control).

Clearly, the nature of the technology is crucial to any assessment of whether it is desirable to privatize, regulate, or try to promote workable competition in such firms—and the assessment could well be different for different parts of the business.

---

[4] Advertizing as a barrier to entry is discussed in more detail in Chap. 26.

14.3 Price and Output Decisions I: No Potential Entry

This section examines the case where the firm does not face any threat of entry. Section 14.4 follows this by examining the case where there is such a threat.

14.3.1 The One-Period Price and Output Decision

The simplest model of the monopoly firm assumes the firm produces just one product for just one time period. The firm faces a deterministic demand function for this product which is known, smooth, and downward-sloping. This means that a choice of price determines the level of sales—and that a choice of the quantity to sell entails a price which will sell it. That is, we can choose price or quantity—but not both independently.[5]

(a) The Marginalist Pricing Rule

Traditionally, economics texts tend to focus on choosing the optimal quantity (and hence only implicitly on the price that will sell this quantity). At its simplest then, we have

$$\pi(q) = R(q) - C(q), \tag{14.3}$$

where π denotes profit, $R = pq$ is total revenue (p is price and q is quantity) and C is total cost. In equation (14.3) these are viewed as varying, depending upon the level of output produced and sold.[6] The first-order condition for a profit maximum is thus that

$$\frac{d\pi(q)}{dq} = \frac{dR(q)}{dq} - \frac{dC(q)}{dq} = MR(q) - MC(q) = 0, \tag{14.4}$$

where MR (dR/dq) denotes marginal revenue, the rate at which revenue increases as quantity is increased, whilst MC denotes marginal cost (dR/dq), the rate at which cost increases as output increases. Both marginal revenue and marginal cost typically vary with output (hence they are both written as functions of q in equation (14.4)).

[5] Assuming the firm, when it does set a price, is committed to satisfying all demand at that price (it does not wish to ration consumers' quantity, behaviour which is not usually conducive to customer goodwill).

[6] In this one-period problem, the amount produced is always equal to that sold. There is no purpose in producing for inventory, for there is no future period in which it can be sold.

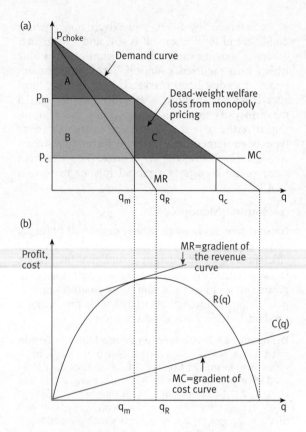

Fig. 14.1 Monopoly pricing

Figure 14.1 illustrates the monopoly pricing solution for the case where the demand curve is linear and marginal cost is constant, independent of output. Recall that, for the linear demand function, the marginal revenue curve has the same intercept on the vertical axis, and then drops at twice the rate (bisecting the horizontal axis exactly halfway between the origin and the point where the demand function cuts it in panel (a)).[7] The intuition behind equating marginal revenue and marginal cost is straightforward. For each unit to the left of q_m, the profit-maximizing monopoly level of output, marginal revenue exceeds marginal cost, whilst for each

[7] This is explained in some detail in sect. 8.6. Basically, a linear inverse-demand function takes the form $p = a - bq$. Hence revenue is given as $R = pq = (a - bq)q = aq - bq^2$. After differentiating, marginal revenue is then given as $MR = \partial R/\partial q = a - 2bq$. Hence both the demand function and the marginal revenue function have the same intercept on the vertical price axis (at a) with the marginal revenue function falling twice as fast (gradient $-2b$, as compared to gradient $-b$ for the demand curve).

unit beyond this output level, marginal revenue is less than marginal cost. Clearly, any unit which generates more additional revenue than it costs to produce is worth producing and selling; hence it pays to expand output up to the level q_m, but not beyond this point. This can also be seen in panel (b), where profit at a given output level is given as the vertical difference between the revenue curve and the cost curve. This is at a maximum when the gradients of the revenue and cost curves are equal. Panel (a) also illustrates the point that a choice of output simultaneously implies a choice of price. Associated with the optimal quantity q_m, reading off the demand curve, we have the optimal price p_m. Finally, area C in this figure represents monopoly welfare loss; this is discussed in more detail in section 14.6 below.

Section 8.6 explained a fundamental relationship between the concepts of marginal revenue (MR), elasticity of demand (η), and price (p). It is a fundamental relationship, and one worth restating:[8]

$$MR = p(1 + 1/\eta) \qquad (14.5)$$

(where $\eta < 0$ if the demand curve has negative slope). Now, the first-order condition (14.4) requires $MR = MC$, so

$$MR = p(1 + 1/\eta) = MC. \qquad (14.6)$$

Since $MC > 0$, and $p > 0$, this implies that, at the optimum, $(1 + 1/\eta) > 0$. Simplifying this, we get

$$\eta < -1. \qquad (14.7)$$

That is, the profit-maximizing firm will choose to operate at a point on the demand curve where demand is elastic. This is worth some emphasis:

Fact 14.3 A single-product, single-period profit-maximizing monopolist operates at a point on the demand curve at which demand is elastic.

Fact 14.4 If, at current prices, demand is inelastic, then profits are not being maximized (some increase in prices will increase profit).

EXAMPLE 14.2 The UK letter business, at current prices, has an estimated demand elasticity of around −0.1 to −0.3. This is in the inelastic range of demand, hence we may conclude that the UK postal service is a long way from setting profit-maximizing prices. It also suggests that increasing

postal prices will lead to higher levels of profitability for the service (Cuthbertson and Richards 1990).

(b) A Pricing Rule of Thumb

A further rearrangement of equation (14.6) gives the rule

$$\left(\frac{P - MC}{P}\right) = -\frac{1}{\eta}. \qquad (14.8)$$

That is, the price-marginal cost mark-up should be set equal to (minus) the inverse of the demand elasticity. Thus, a more inelastic demand commands a higher mark-up; a more elastic demand implies a lower mark-up. Equation (14.8) can be rearranged as a mark-up pricing rule:

$$P = (1 + m)MC, \qquad (14.9)$$

where

$$m = -\left(\frac{1}{1 + \eta}\right). \qquad (14.10)$$

Thus the optimal mark-up should be related to the elasticity of demand. The idea is that if you have a notion of what the elasticity is at the current price, you can use this to estimate the optimal price.

EXAMPLE 14.3 If $\eta = -2$, then $m = -1/(1 - 2) = 1$; the optimal mark-up is thus 100%. By contrast, if $\eta = -5$, then $m = -1/(1 - 5) = 0.25$, a 25% mark-up. Notice that the more elastic the demand, the lower the optimal mark-up.

The rule can also be used to test the rationality of existing pricing practices, as in the following example:

EXAMPLE 14.4 Suppose that the firm currently sells a product at a price of £2 when marginal cost of production at this level of output is £1. Then

$$\left(\frac{P - MC}{P}\right) = \frac{2 - 1}{2} = 0.5.$$

For this mark-up to be profit-maximizing, it would have to be the case that $0.5 = -(1/\eta) \Rightarrow \eta = -2$. That is, the price is right only if the elasticity is equal to $(-)2$. It is then possible to ask the individual responsible for pricing whether he or she believes that a 1% increase in price would lose 2% of sales. A response of, say, 'No, it would lose more' would indicate that a reduction in price was warranted, whilst a response of 'No, it would lose less' would indicate that a price increase was desirable.

---

[8] $R = pq$, so $MR = \dfrac{dR}{dq} = \left(p + q\dfrac{dp}{dq}\right) = p\left(1 + \dfrac{q}{p}\dfrac{dp}{dq}\right)$

$= p\left(1 + \dfrac{1}{\eta}\right)$ since $\eta = \dfrac{dq}{dp}\dfrac{p}{q}$.

(c) Caveat on the Mark-up Rule

It is worth noting that changing price can also change the elasticity of demand. (For example, with a linear demand, elasticity changes continuously as price and quantity are changed.) Starting with an estimate or guess for the elasticity at the current price, a calculation of a new price using equation (14.8) involves a move to a new point on the demand curve which will have a different elasticity of demand. In theory, an iterative process could be used to home in on the optimal price.[9] However, in practice, elasticity is often approximately constant; no iteration is required when demand is iso-elastic, or approximately iso-elastic.

As previously mentioned, it makes no difference whether one thinks of the problem as choosing the optimal price or choosing the optimal output level. Thus, if we treat price as the choice variable, the first-order condition is that[10]

$$\frac{d\pi}{dp} = \frac{d}{dp}(pq - c(q)) = q + p\frac{dq}{dp} - \frac{dc(q)}{dq}\frac{dq}{dp} = 0,$$

$$(14.11)$$

so that

$$(p - MC)\frac{dq}{dp} = -q. \qquad (14.12)$$

Dividing both sides by $p(dq/dp)$ gives

$$\frac{p - MC}{p} = -\frac{q}{p}\frac{dp}{dq} = -\frac{1}{\eta} \qquad (14.13)$$

as before.

Apart from the inverse elasticity formula, it is perhaps worth mentioning that analytic problems can generally be tackled directly, as in the following example.

EXAMPLE 14.5 Suppose demand is linear, e.g.

$$q = 100 - p, \qquad (i)$$

and that the cost function is quadratic, e.g.

$$C = 100 + 2q + q. \qquad (ii)$$

From (i), the inverse demand function is clearly

$q = 100 - p$. The profit function can thus be written as

$$\pi = pq - C$$
$$= (100 - q)q - 100 - 2q - q^2. \qquad (iii)$$

Here profit is written as a function of q. Differentiating, the first-order condition is that

$$\partial\pi/\partial q = 100 - 2q - 2 - 2q = 0, \qquad (iv)$$

and so solving for q gives

$$4q = 98 \Rightarrow q = 24.5. \qquad (v)$$

(Notice that the second-order sufficient condition for a local maximum is satisfied; $\partial^2\pi/\partial^2q = -4 < 0$). The optimal price is computed using the inverse demand function: to sell $q = 24.5$, price p is given by

$$p = 100 - q = 100 - 24.5 = 75.5. \qquad (vi)$$

Finally, total profit is given by substituting $q = 24.5$ into (iii); this gives $\pi = 1100.5$.

It is also worth mentioning that a monopolist does not generally operate at efficient scale. To see this, consider Figure 14.2.

Panel (a) indicates an equilibrium in which the firm chooses to operate at a point of falling average cost (increasing returns to scale) whilst panel (b) indicates the case in which it operates at a point where average cost is rising. Which is the case in practice depends on the technology and the level of demand, since the former determines the point at which the average cost curve attains its minimum, q_e, and the latter then determines whether $q_m > q_e$ or $q_m < q_e$.

14.3.2 Erosion of the Monopoly Price? Bargaining and the Coase Conjecture

The essential insight of the above pricing analysis is that a monopolist will set a price above marginal cost. This entails a monopoly welfare loss (see section 14.6 below). There are two interesting arguments which run counter to the proposition that the monopolist prices above marginal cost, even in the absence of any threat of entry (entry might induce the monopolist to set a lower price—see section 14.4 below). The first of these involves a bargain between consumers and the firm, of a type similar in spirit to that discussed at greater length in Chapter 27 (which deals with externalities). The Coase conjecture is a somewhat different argument, applicable in the case of a monopolist who manufactures durable goods. Both arguments suggest that a

---

[9] That is, using the new elasticity, compute a further estimate of price using the elasticity formula, and then a further elasticity at this new price, and so on. Under reasonable assumptions regarding the structure of the demand function, such a process would converge. However, this computation is clearly cumbersome, and with a non-constant elasticity demand function, solving for the optimal price is best effected directly, as in Ex. 14.5 below.

[10] Using the product rule and the chain rule in performing the differentiations.

(a)

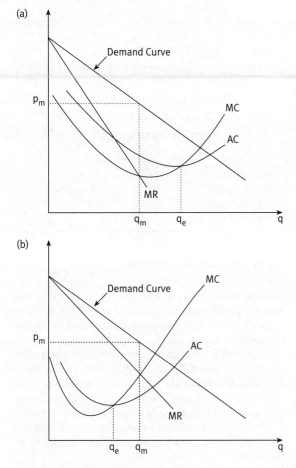

(b)

Fig. 14.2 Monopoly and efficient scale

monopolist has to set price equal to marginal cost (so there is no monopoly welfare loss). I explore these ideas in turn.

(a) The Bargaining Solution

There are two versions of this. The first goes as follows. By assumption, the monopolist sets a price and says to the customers, 'Take what you want at this price.' Now consider an individual customer. Suppose she says, 'I'll give you your marginal cost, plus 10 pence—or I won't buy anything at all.' Why wouldn't the monopolist accept such an offer? After all, any contribution above marginal cost increases his profit. If each individual customer is able to bargain bilaterally with the monopolist, it would appear that the monopolist might find it difficult to exploit his supposed monopoly power. One counter to this view lies in the observation that there

are many customers and only one monopolist; that is, the monopolist can do without any one customer, but the customer is going to find it harder to do without the product. There may be some truth in this argument, but perhaps a more compelling reason for why the monopolist will refuse to bargain lies in the concept of **reputation building**.

EXAMPLE 14.6 Many pubs and wine bars sell sandwiches which go into the dustbin if unsold at closing time. Just before closing time, try offering the barperson the following deal: 'I'll give you half price for the sandwich; after all, you're only going to throw it away!' On the face of it, incremental reasoning suggests that the bar should agree to the deal—but they rarely do.

The idea is that it can be rational to refuse to enter into such deals because refusal builds reputation (for not giving in to negotiation). The problem for the monopolist is that if word gets around that deals can be done, then everyone will start to press harder for such deals, and try to drive harder bargains. Furthermore, it can lead to shifts in the timing of demand. In the case of sandwiches, demand might shift heavily toward eating at closing time! If demand proves to be flexible in this way, the practice of discounting this can actually lead to a fall in the firm's profit.

An alternative bargaining solution involves all the customers banding together. Refer to Figure 14.1, consider the move from monopoly pricing to marginal cost pricing (price p_c). In this simple model where there are no fixed costs and marginal cost is constant, under monopoly pricing (p_m) the firm earns profit equal to area B whilst consumers earn consumer surplus equal to area A. Under marginal cost pricing, p_c, the firm loses all its super-normal profit, and just breaks even in selling output q_c, whilst the consumers gain consumer surplus equal to area $A + B + C$. Thus, relative to monopoly pricing, setting marginal cost prices leads to consumers gaining (by amount $B + C$) more than the firm loses (area B). It follows that there is a **potential Pareto improvement**. That is, if the consumers can costlessly come together and agree, they can offer a mutually beneficial contract to the firm. In exchange for, say, the consumers handing over a money sum equal to $B + \frac{1}{2}C$ to the firm, the firm has to agree to set price equal to marginal cost. Relative to monopoly pricing, the contract makes the firm $\frac{1}{2}C$ better off. Moving to marginal cost pricing makes the consumers better off by $B + C$, but they hand back $B + \frac{1}{2}C$, so leaving them also better off by $\frac{1}{2}C$. Thus, relative to monopoly pricing, the contract would make all parties better off. It follows that, if only there was full information about what was to be negotiated over, and negotiating, contracting, and policing the contract were costless activities,[11] monopoly welfare loss would not exist; prices would be equal to marginal cost everywhere. Of course, in the real world, with a large number of consumers, all small relative to the total market, the transactions costs associated with setting up and enforcing such deals are prohibitive. Thus the bargaining solution fails, and prices remain above marginal cost.

(b) Durable Goods Monopoly and the Coase Conjecture

Many firms with market power sell what can be described as durable goods (such as cars and washing machines). Typically, for such goods, a consumer only wishes to purchase one item, and having purchased, drops out of the market. Coase (1972) suggested that, if consumers were rational, a firm in such a market would not be able to sell any product except at marginal cost. That is, the firm's monopoly power is illusory. The argument is straightforward. Suppose the firm sets a price, any price, above marginal cost. For example, suppose it sets the monopoly price. On the face of it, as in Figure 14.3, it would then sell a quantity of product (equal to q_m). Apparently, in this durable goods market, everyone who was willing to pay the price now has their washing machine (or whatever). No further purchases occur. However, once these customers have made their purchase, the firm then has a powerful incentive to reduce price a little. Thus, in Figure 14.3, after selling q_m at price p_m, if the price is reduced to p, this gets extra sales $(q - q_m)$, giving extra profit equal to the shaded area in that figure. Having done this, the firm has an incentive to reduce price further, so as to sell some more product at a profit. The process continues until price reaches p_c, the marginal cost price.

Coase's idea is that rational consumers will know the firm will eventually reduce price to p_c. It follows that, although they may be willing to pay above the current price p_c, they will refuse to buy until the price falls to p_c. Thus if the firm sets any price above marginal cost, it will sell nothing at all. By contrast, if it

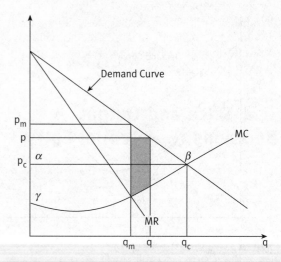

Fig. 14.3 Durable-goods monopoly

sets the price at p_c, it will sell the amount q_c and make a profit equal to the area $\alpha\beta\gamma$.[12] Coase thus argues that the firm will immediately do this. So the monopoly price is simply marginal cost.

In practice, customers are impatient (have discount rates generally larger than that of the firm) and may not know the marginal cost price p_c, and there may also be new demand continually adding to the market (durable goods do physically depreciate). These factors mean that, in practice, what is called a price-skimming policy may still prove attractive to the firm:

Definition 14.4 A **price-skimming policy** is one in which the price is systematically reduced over time.

If customers are naive, the price-skimming policy extracts all the consumer surplus under the demand curve. Thus, as the price falls to the level of a customer's willingness to pay, that customer makes the purchase. Being naive, she does not realize that it is possible to wait for a lower price. If customers are not totally naive, then the price-skimming policy works less effectively because some customers will wait for lower prices. However, so long as the rate of price discount is not too rapid, the monopolist can still exploit the individual customer's impatience. The firm's problem becomes one of maximizing net present value by optimizing the

---

[11] And no game playing that might upset the bargaining process.

[12] Note that this is a positive profit, given the structure of the marginal cost function. Coase originally assumed constant marginal cost. What do you think are the consequences if there are global economies of scale?

rate at which price is lowered: too fast, and too many customers spot the trend and become willing to wait; too slow, and it takes too long to capture the whole market.

14.4 Price and Output Decisions II: Potential Entry

In both monopoly and oligopoly, the firms already in the industry may well be concerned about the possibility of further entry. I shall refer to a firm already in the industry as an **incumbent**, and a new firm as an **entrant**. Section 14.4.1 introduces the idea of limit pricing by the incumbent; this involves setting a lower price in order to deter entry. Section 14.4.2 then criticizes this view and develops a more refined, game-theoretic view of entry. Section 14.4.3 then examines contestability theory, which basically looks for conditions under which entry deterrence is impossible. Finally, section 14.4.4 briefly reviews the empirical evidence on entry.

14.4.1 Limit Pricing

The key question an entrant has to pose is—what happens post-entry? The point is that entry into a monopolized industry creates an oligopoly, and the entrant needs to consider what kind of oligopolistic competition is likely post-entry. The early limit-price models (e.g. Bain 1956, Sylos-Labini 1962) were based on the following assumptions.

(i) The market demand curve is known by both the incumbent and the entrant.

(ii) The entrant's average cost function is known to both the incumbent and the entrant.

(iii) The entrant assumes that prior to entry, the incumbent chooses price and output. Post-entry, the incumbent it maintains its output level (even if the price changes)— this is the so-called **Sylos postulate**.

(iv) The incumbent knows that the entrant assumes (iii), and takes in this into account in setting a price and output so as to deter entry (the so called **limit price** and output levels).

Figure 14.4 illustrates the limit-pricing story. The idea is that p_m, q_m represent price and output under monopoly profit maximization ignoring the threat of entry, whilst p_L, q_L represent the incumbent's

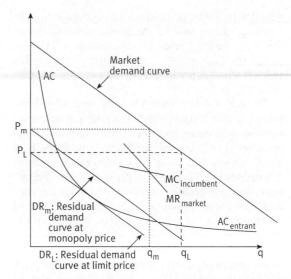

Fig. 14.4 Limit pricing

'limit price and output', choices which take into account the entry threat. First consider what happens if the monopolist sets price p_m. The entrant sees the monopoly output q_m, and assumes this will continue to be the incumbent's choice of output after entry. The entrant thus sees a residual demand curve, DR_m (the market demand curve shifted to the left by the amount q_m). It then reckons that, as it produces additional output, this will depress price according to this residual demand curve. Noting that the entrant's average cost curve lies below the residual demand curve DR_m over a range of output, it is clear that the entrant can find an output level such that it can earn positive profit. It will therefore enter.[13]

Now, if the incumbent wishes to deter entry, it needs to set a lower price than p_m—how much lower can be computed by simply shifting the residual demand curve leftward to the point where it becomes tangential to the entrant's average cost curve. Thus, if the incumbent chooses an output level just above q_L, this shifts the residual demand curve sufficiently far to the left that there is no point on it at which the entrant can earn a positive profit (since the entrant's average cost curve lies everywhere above the residual demand curve). Entry is

[13] The entrant's optimal choice is given where the MR curve associated with the residual demand curve cuts the entrant's marginal cost curve—to avoid cluttering the diagram, these curves are not depicted.

thus deterred. The price which allows the incumbent to sell q_L can be read off the market demand curve; this is p_L, the limit price. The incumbent will choose to set the limit price if (as is often possible) this yields it a higher profit level than by setting a higher price which allows entry and competition.

The major defect with this early version of limit pricing is that it starts with a price-setting monopolist who, post-entry, abdicates any influence over the price set (in the model, the incumbent keeps to a fixed output, and as a consequence, the entrant determines price on entry). In practice, the incumbent does not need to maintain output at the pre-entry level, nor would this generally be a rational strategy for it. Clearly a more realistic model of post-entry competition is required; section 14.4.2 examines a model in which the incumbent chooses either to accommodate entry or to fight it through price and advertizing wars, etc. (further discussion of entry can be found in Chapter 16).

14.4.2 Entry Deterrence and Endogenous Sunk Costs

Bain (1956) suggested the following entry classification:

Definition 14.5 Blockaded entry occurs when the strategic choices made by the incumbent (price, output, capacity, advertizing, etc.) ignore the threat of entry yet these choices still preclude profitable entry. **Deterred entry** occurs when the firm does take account of the threat of entry in setting price, output, etc. Finally, **accommodated entry** occurs when the incumbent does not try to prevent entry (because it is more profitable to allow entry than to try to prevent it).

A good way of thinking about entry is as a game. Figure 14.5 illustrates a simple entry game in which the entrant chooses at node I either to enter or not, and then the incumbent chooses to accommodate

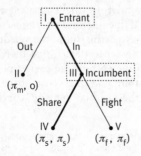

Fig. 14.5 An entry game

entry (strategy Share) or contest it via price wars etc. (strategy Fight). The possible outcomes are depicted in brackets at each of nodes II, IV, and V (with the pay-off to the incumbent on the left, to the entrant on the right). At node II there is monopoly profit $\pi_m > 0$ to the incumbent and 0 to the entrant (since there is no entry). Equal profits go to incumbent and entrant if they share the market, of amount π_s, and equal but lower profits if they fight (price wars etc.), of amount π_f. Thus

$$\pi_m > \pi_s > \pi_f. \qquad (14.14)$$

It is supposed that both players are rational and know the structure of the game and its payoffs; in particular they make the same assessments (π_m, π_s, π_f) about the consequences of different strategic choices. This is the **common knowledge** assumption (that is, it is a game of **complete information** in which both players know that all players are rational and can be relied on to behave rationally).

The game is solved using **backward induction**.[14] Thus at node III, the incumbent will rationally choose to share the market rather than fight (since $\pi_s > \pi_f$). The entrant therefore knows this, and compares her outcome from entering (ending at node V with π_s) to staying out and getting zero (node II). Clearly, if $0 > \pi_s > \pi_f$, entry will be blockaded; whatever the post-entry game there can be no profitable entry. This is the case where the industry is a natural monopoly. However, let us assume that sharing the market allows both firms to be profitable, so that

$$\pi_s > 0. \qquad (14.15)$$

In this case, the outcome is accommodated entry. Any threat by the incumbent that he will fight if there is entry is not credible because it is not rational. (Note that the rational choice at a node is indicated by a thickened line.)

Naturally, different behaviour is possible if we introduce uncertainty or asymmetric information (about who knows what etc.). However, rather than taking this tack, let us consider whether there is anything the incumbent might do before the entry stage that might deter entry (as in the limit-pricing model). Figure 14.6 illustrates such an extended

---

[14] For useful background, see Chap. 5. Backward induction, using dominance, gives the solution, which is also a subgame-perfect equilibrium. The normal or strategic form of this game is discussed in question 6 in sect. 14.8.

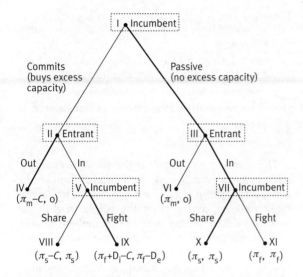

Fig. 14.6 Deterrence in the entry game

game, in which the incumbent may try a preemptive strategy.[15]

At node I, the incumbent has the option of undertaking an action which may help to deter entry. For the sake of argument, suppose this is an investment in **excess capacity**. The idea of holding excess capacity is that it makes fighting a price war cheaper and more effective. By assumption, the investment in excess capacity is irreversible; it is a sunk cost. Recall that the idea of sunk cost here is that the asset, once purchased, cannot be resold at full value.[16] It is crucial that a significant part of the investment is a sunk cost, as we shall see. The incumbent's strategies are either to commit itself to excess capacity (Committed), or to take no action (Passive). At the next stage, the entrant has to decide whether or not to enter (strategies In or Out). Finally, if it does enter, the incumbent has to decide whether to fight entry or whether to accommodate it (strategies Fight or Share).

Payoffs are again as in (14.14), with $\pi_s > 0$ and π_f either positive or negative (depending on how much the fight hurts). It is assumed that the purchase of excess capacity, which involves an investment cost $C > 0$, reduces the incumbent's net profitability in

all states. However, if there is entry, the excess capacity makes the incumbent more effective if it chooses to fight. Let's assume this strategy adds to its profit from a fight an amount D_i and also reduces the entrant's profit from a fight by an amount D_e, where $D_i, D_e > 0$ as indicated at node IX in figure 14.6.

Again we apply backwards induction. Consider the subgame at node VII. Since $\pi_s > \pi_f$ it is clear that the incumbent will accommodate entry and will not fight (this choice is indicated by the thickened line from node VII to node X). At node III, it is then clear that the payoff to the entrant from staying out is 0, whilst that from entering is that of ending up at node X and getting $\pi_s > 0$. Hence the choice here is to enter (indicated by the thickened line from node III to VII).

On the other side of the tree, at node V, the incumbent's choice is to choose Fight if

$$\pi_f + D_i - C > \pi_s - C. \tag{14.16}$$

Originally we had $\pi_f < \pi_s$ and the incumbent could not credibly threaten to fight the entrant if it chose to enter. However, by assumption the investment in capacity improves the incumbent's performance in a pricing war (by D_i). If it does so sufficiently (D_i is sufficiently large), it may be that (14.16) holds; in such a case the excess capacity, a committed sunk cost, leads the incumbent to choose to fight if there is entry (thickened arrow between nodes V and IX). Now consider the entrant's choice at node II. She gets 0 if she stays out, and gets $\pi_f - D_e$ if she enters (since she knows it will come to a fight). Entry is thus deterred if

$$\pi_f - D_e < 0. \tag{14.17}$$

Let us suppose this is the case. Then the entrant stays out (thickened arrow from II to IV). Finally we are in a position to consider the incumbent's action at stage I. If it chooses Passive, the entrant enters and the incumbent will then share the market, getting payoff π_s. If it chooses the committed path (node I to II), the entrant stays out and the incumbent gets $\pi_m - C$. It will therefore choose to invest in excess capacity as an entry deterrent if

$$\pi_m - C > \pi_s. \tag{14.18}$$

To sum up, if all of (14.16)–(14.18) hold, then investing in excess capacity is optimal; otherwise, the incumbent will not try to deter entry. Notice the importance of the excess capacity being a sunk cost. The point is that if it could be sold on, then this would eliminate the pay-off of $-C$ at nodes IV and VIII; it would then be much less likely that the

---

[15] This is sometimes termed the Spence–Dixit entry game (see e.g. Spence 1982, Dixit 1980, and the review in Dixit 1982).

[16] The difference between purchase price and immediate resale price represents the magnitude of the sunk cost. If the asset cannot be sold at any positive price, then the whole of the investment is a sunk cost.

excess capacity would act as a deterrent (since at node V, it is more likely that $\pi_s > \pi_f + D_i - C$ and hence there would be no fight, and hence no point in buying the excess capacity).

To recapitulate, if we ignore the possibility of pre-commitment to excess capacity by the incumbent, it may huff and puff and threaten entrants with a price war if they dare to enter—but its threat is not credible because it will earn greater profit by sharing the market. However, by adding an initial stage in which the incumbent can choose to invest in excess capacity, there are circumstances where this will be an optimal strategy for the incumbent. Of course it is possible for the inequalities in either of (14.17) or (14.18) to be reversed (everything depends on the specific numbers for π_m, π_f, π_s, D_e, etc.; the reader may care to explore the alternative solutions). Depending on the numbers, it may be that the investment is ineffective as a deterrent (in which case it will not be chosen, and entry will be accommodated).

Thus the game in Figure 14.6 is rich enough to capture the idea that in some markets entry is blockaded (there is no entry deterrence and yet no entry), in others entry may be accommodated (no deterrence, with entry and market sharing), whilst in others there may be entry deterrence (and no entry). Of course, in the real world, players may also have to cope with the possibility that players may not be rational, they may make mistakes (such as investing in entry deterrence, only to find that it does not deter entry), or they may have incomplete and/or asymmetric information. However, the above analysis does offer the key insight that there is an incentive to try to protect monopoly power, once it has been acquired. Thus a monopolist may practice monopoly pricing, which entails a welfare loss—but worse than this, it may expend resources (on excess capacity and advertizing, for example) in order to protect itself from entry; much of this additional expenditure is a further welfare loss.

14.4.3 Contestability

The nature of entry, described in section 14.4.2, suggests that sunk costs may be important in entry games. This also suggests that, if there are no sunk costs, maybe entry will be facilitated. The (highly influential) theory of contestability, developed by Baumol et al. (1982), looks precisely for the conditions where entry deterrence is impossible.

Definition 14.8 A market is said to be **contestable** if
 (i) all potential producers have access to the same technology;
 (ii) this technology may feature economies of scale, fixed costs, etc. but must not feature sunk costs;[17]
 (iii) consumers respond to prices instantaneously; but
 (iv) incumbents cannot change prices instantaneously.

Fact 14.5 In a contestable market, the incumbent will set price equal to average cost.

The idea is very simple. If the incumbent sets a price p above average cost, then another firm could enter, set a price $p - \varepsilon$, where $\varepsilon > 0$ is an arbitrarily small number, and capture the whole market, so making positive profits until the incumbent is able to react. Furthermore, the entrant can costlessly exit from the industry because there are no sunk costs; that is, it can sell its purchased capacity on second-hand markets at the price originally paid. In order to prevent this form of 'hit and run' entry, the incumbent is forced to set a pre-entry price equal to average cost; only with price equal to average cost is an entrant prevented from profitably capturing the whole market.

Thus, in a contestable market, the firm has little monopoly power. It sets an average cost price, so the welfare loss is much reduced (and so the need to regulate such an industry), as illustrated in Figure 14.7 (the measure of welfare loss is discussed further in section 14.6). Airline and rail operators are often cited as examples of near-contestable markets. The idea is that the major investment (aeroplanes, trains, and carriages) can be sold on at near-purchase price in competitive second-hand markets.[18]

The primary criticism of contestable market theory is that it assumes that entry and exit can be undertaken instantaneously, or, at least, in a shorter period of time than it takes to adjust prices. In practice, even in industries for which sunk costs are relatively low, it is almost always the case that prices can be adjusted more rapidly than firms can set up and enter markets. Hence it follows that

---

[17] Fixed costs are costs independent of scale, but are locked in as necessary for production in any given period. However, fixed costs need not be sunk; if capacity is shut down, this equipment may be sold on. If the full purchase price can be obtained, the sunk cost is zero.

[18] Note that the size of sunk cost is not necessarily related to the specificity of the asset involved; aeroplanes may only be used to fly particular sorts of cargo (people, mail, freight, etc.) but can be easily resold at prices not so dissimilar to their purchase price.

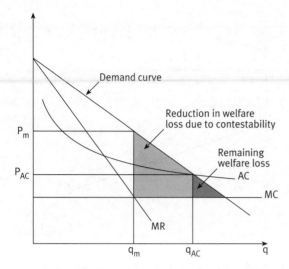

Fig. 14.7 Contestability

before entry, incumbents can price as they like (reacting promptly only if entry occurs).

However, contestability *can* be made to bite if the legal framework prevents firms from making a predatory response to entry. If the legislature regards any reduction in price by an incumbent, post-entry, as evidence of unfair competition (and imposes restraints or fines for such behaviour), then the incumbent will be forced to take into account (to some extent) the threat of potential entry by keeping pre-entry price lower than the monopoly level so as to deter entry. This point is discussed further in Chapter 28.

14.4.4 Entry: Some Empirical Facts

Entry can be by completely new firms, but in practice, entry is more likely to occur by firms which operate in related industries, including those upstream or downstream in the 'river of production'. Entry may require the building of new plant, or it may be that relatively small modifications to existing plant allows a firm to produce new products. Entry may simply be the commencement of exports from firms who have already established themselves in the same product line in other countries. Multi-product firms may be able to piggy-back production on pre-existing lines of business, and because of this may even have lower costs of production than other potential entrants, or indeed incumbents in the industry. Geroski (1995) provides an excellent survey of the stylized facts about entry. These are sum-

marized here (see also Martin (1993) and Dunne *et al.* 1988):

(i) Entry is common, but much of it is short-lived; that is, most entrants exit within a short space of time (entry and exit are highly correlated), and find it hard to gain significant market share. It is hard to enter at large scale, or to grow successfully and quickly to capture significant market share.

(ii) New entry is more common, but entry by diversification is more successful.

(iii) Entry has similar characteristics across many industries. However, it varies with the maturity of the industry.[19]

Geroski then draws the following conclusions:

1. Entry seems slow to react to high profit rates. Equally, entry does not significantly dissipate industry profitability.

2. Differences in profitability between industries seem to be stable and persistent.

3. Differences in profitability between firms within the same industry are also persistent.

4. Empirical work suggests high entry barriers.

5. Given entry barriers and profit rates, it is hard to explain entry rates.

6. High rates of entry are associated with high rates of innovation and rapid changes in production efficiency.

7. The response to entry by incumbents is selective.[20]

8. Price is not usually used to block entry. If anything is used as an entry deterrent, it is advertising.[21]

Geroski therefore argues that entry is not a significant mechanism for promoting competition within an industry. Although the theoretical work (in particular on contestability) has shifted the emphasis of anti-trust policy to an examination of entry barriers and a focus on the promotion of

---

[19] Individual products may have a life-cycle, but often, so too do whole industries. Think of the personal computer market, for example.

[20] Many do not react at all (on any dimension). Some in advertizing-intensive industries react by intensifying advertizing, but again, many do not react.

[21] The idea that advertizing is a barrier to entry, because it increases the fixed costs associated with gaining entry into a market, has a long pedigree (see Chap. 26).

workable competition, it suggests that intervention which reduces entry barriers (such as curbs on allowable advertizing expense etc.), at least from an empirical perspective, is suspect (since such intervention is likely to have little short- or long-term impact). On this view, then, it is more important to focus on the behaviour of the incumbent firms that already exist, and to focus on the control of their profit rates (see Chapter 28).

14.5 Dominant Firms and Monopoly Power

Many industries are characterized by a **dominant firm** which faces a competitive fringe of much smaller firms. Companies like Microsoft and Intel, or Campbell Soups (US), are international players who face some degree of competition from local rivals. A supermarket may have a dominant position, but may face competition from myriad corner shops. The dominant firm, in setting price, needs to consider the behaviour of the fringe. Raising price will tend to induce customers to switch to fringe suppliers and it may also encourage further new small-firm entry. Thus the extent and vigour of such a fringe may limit the ability of the dominant firm to exert its monopoly power.

Perhaps the simplest model is that of a dominant firm which shares the market with a price-taking fringe. In this model, the fringe firms act as price followers, but tend to produce more output if the price set by the dominant firm is higher. The dominant firm supplies that part of the market not supplied by the fringe. In Figure 14.8, at prices below p_1, there is no fringe supply and the dominant firm faces the market demand curve. By contrast, at price p_2 the whole market is supplied by fringe production. Thus the dominant firm faces a residual demand curve, labelled DDD, which is given as the horizontal difference between the market demand curve and the supply curve of fringe firms; this residual demand curve is more elastic than the original market demand (for price above p_1). The dominant firm thus sets the standard monopoly price, treating the residual demand curve as the demand curve in this calculation. This analysis is identical to that presented in section 14.3, and so is omitted here. Clearly, the dominant firm will equate marginal revenue with marginal cost and so determine its own output, the price it wishes to set;

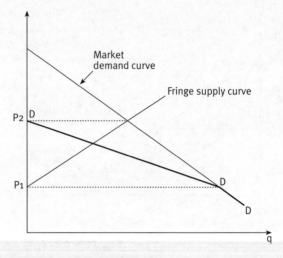

Fig. 14.8 The dominant-firm model

this in turn will determine the quantity produced by the fringe (the reader may care to complete this analysis using Figure 14.8 as a starting point).

Dominant firms, according to this model, still exert monopoly power and charge price above marginal cost. It follows that there is still a monopoly welfare loss. The policy question is one of judging when a firm is significantly dominant—and if so, of judging the type of regulation, if any, most appropriate for controlling such a firm (see Chapter 28).

14.6 Monopoly Welfare Loss

This section discusses the notion that profit-maximizing monopoly involves setting price above marginal cost and that this leads to welfare losses. This question is then discussed in more general terms in Chapter 28, where the issue of what is to be done about the exploitation of monopoly power is addressed.

14.6.1 The Welfare-Loss Triangle

Monopoly welfare loss has already been discussed in Chapter 2. Here the analysis is taken somewhat further.

(a) **The Linear Marginal Cost/Linear Demand Case:**

First consider the simple case where there is linear demand and constant marginal cost, as depicted in

Figure 14.1 (page 222). The area under the demand curve and above the price line represents consumer surplus (area A), and profit is given as the area B (price minus marginal cost multiplied by the quantity sold). So monopoly pricing yields total economic welfare of $W = CS + \pi = A + B$. By contrast, marginal cost pricing would lead to the firm just breaking even ($\pi = 0$), with output q_c, and with consumers getting consumer surplus equal to area $A + B + C$. Total welfare in this case is simply $W = A + B + C$. For this reason, the area C has been identified as the dead-weight welfare loss associated with profit-maximizing monopoly pricing. The geometry of the figure is such that areas A and C are equal, and equal to one half of area B. For this reason, it has often jokingly been commented that the answer to the question 'what is monopoly welfare loss?' is the answer 'one quarter!' ($C/(A + B + C =$ one quarter). Since, $\pi = B$, we also have for this rather special-case model that

$$\Delta W = -\tfrac{1}{2}\pi. \tag{14.19}$$

This is of interest, since welfare is less readily observable than firm profit levels. That is, it would appear that firm profitability gives an indication of the level of welfare loss present in the economy (if this naive model were to represent reality correctly!).

(b) The More General Case

In practice, demand curves are not necessarily linear and marginal costs may likewise not be constant. For example, if the situation is as depicted in Figure 14.1, but the firm has fixed costs F as well as constant marginal costs, then profit falls to $B - F$, monopoly welfare to $A + B - F$, and the proportionate welfare loss, $C/(A + B + C - F)$, is greater than one quarter. This might suggest that a welfare loss of 25% of observed industry profits is a conservative estimate of welfare loss. However, if the functions involved are non-linear, then the welfare loss could be more—or less—than the naive measure of 25%.

Interestingly, it is still possible to derive a simple measure of welfare loss, so long as it is reasonable to assume that, on the interval between the monopoly output level and the competitive (marginal cost pricing) output level, economies of scale are largely exhausted (so the marginal cost curve is flat) and demand is approximately linear. The point is that the behaviour of demand and marginal cost curves to the left of the monopoly output is of no importance to the following result. In Figure 14.9, the

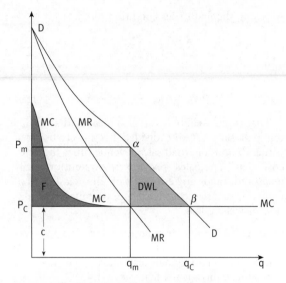

Fig. 14.9 Monopoly welfare loss

demand, marginal revenue, and marginal cost curve are non-linear to the left of q_m but linear to the right. This means that, on the interval $[q_m, q_c]$, the total cost function can be modelled as

$$C(q) = F + cq, \tag{14.20}$$

where c denotes the (constant) marginal cost on this interval. The first-order condition for profit maximization (for arbitrary demand and cost functions) requires that (14.8) holds. That is,

$$\frac{p - MC}{p} = -\frac{1}{\eta}. \tag{14.21}$$

where η is the elasticity of demand. Finally, the dead-weight loss is measured as the triangle DWL (area = one-half base times height):

$$DWL = \tfrac{1}{2}(p_m - c)(q_c - q_m). \tag{14.22}$$

Now, the elasticity of demand at the monopoly price/output level is given as $\eta = (dq/dp)(p_m/q_m)$. In Figure 14.9, for linear demand on this interval, the gradient (dq/dp) of the inverse demand curve at the point α is also by assumption equal to the gradient of the line $\alpha\beta$. Thus

$$\frac{dp}{dq} = \frac{1}{\eta}\frac{p_m}{q_m} = -\frac{(p_m - C)}{(q_c - q_m)}. \tag{14.23}$$

Hence

$$\begin{aligned} DWL &= \tfrac{1}{2}(p_m - c)(q_c - q_m) \\ &= -\tfrac{1}{2}\frac{(p_m - c)^2}{p_m}\eta q_m, \end{aligned} \tag{14.24}$$

so, using the first order condition, (14.21),

$$DWL = \tfrac{1}{2}\frac{R_m}{\eta}, \qquad (14.25)$$

or

$$DWL = \tfrac{1}{2}R_m\left(\frac{p_m - MC}{p_m}\right). \qquad (14.26)$$

That is, the welfare loss is also measured as minus one-half sales revenue divided by the elasticity of demand, or as one-half sales revenue times the price cost mark-up. Sales revenue is straightforwardly measured, and an estimate of the elasticity of demand, or price cost mark-up, permits a calculation of welfare loss.

EXAMPLE 14.7 Sales revenue for Glaxo in 1993 was £4930m (m = million). If we assume an average mark-up on marginal cost of, say, 40% for its products, this means that $p_m = 1.4MC$, so

$$\left(\frac{p_m - MC}{p_m}\right) = \left(\frac{1.4MC - MC}{1.4MC}\right) = 0.286$$

Hence from (14.26), this gives an estimate of welfare loss of £$(\tfrac{1}{2} \times 4930 \times 0.286)$m = £704m. Expressed as a percentage of 1993 GDP this is about 0.1%.

Naturally, one can vary the mark-up and the estimate changes; the above calculation is illustrative only. Furthermore, there are many caveats on the interpretation of such measures of welfare loss, and whether such measures are in fact meaningful or useful from a policy perspective.[22] Perhaps the most important is examined in section 14.6.2 (rent-seeking behaviour). However, a fuller discussion of welfare loss, and its policy relevance, is deferred to Chapter 28, which deals in more detail with state intervention in the market economy.

14.6.2 Rent-Seeking Effects

In a dynamic economy, individual agents can be viewed as continually in pursuit of super-normal profit opportunities; the general term for this behaviour is **rent seeking**. Monopoly power is worth having because it would appear to give the opportunity to realize super-normal profit. It follows that individuals will expend resources on seeking ways of

finding, developing (through R&D), and protecting (through advertizing etc.) such monopoly power. If there is competitive pressure in the rent-seeking market, these protection costs could rise all the way up to the full present value of the super-normal profits that the monopoly power is expected to return. On this view, the profit indicated as area B in Figure 14.1 should not be regarded as a social benefit (to the owners of the firm) but rather as an index of resources already expended in acquiring the monopoly power. Posner (1975) argues that, if all this effort is competitive, the whole of the monopoly profit is an index of social costs incurred in getting it. On this view, the social benefits under monopoly are simply measured in Figure 14.1 by the consumer surplus, area A (since area B no longer counts). Given the maximum welfare attainable (through marginal cost pricing) is A + B + C, the welfare loss increases to area B + C. That is, the welfare loss is not 25% but 75% of the maximum level of welfare attainable.

Clearly this argument does not hold if the rent-seeking activity is imperfectly competitive (since then agents get rents from their rent-seeking behaviour) and in so far as their activities have some independent value (for example, since rent-seeking also tends to lead to increased product differentiation, new products, new technologies, etc.). However, there is clearly a kernel of truth in the argument that rent-seeking is a fact of life, and that resources are expended in such activities— and that this will tend to increase the level of welfare loss relative to the naive marginal cost benchmark.

Apart from welfare loss (the size of which can be debated), there is also an equity aspect to monopoly pricing: high prices shift wealth from consumers to the owners (shareholders) of the monopoly. The long-term effect can be substantial, and although some might wish to argue that most individuals in the modern economy are both consumers and owners, the fact is that many customers have no or few shares in any companies, and clearly there are significant distributional effects.

14.7 Summary

The basic characteristics of monopoly—and the critical role of barriers to entry (exogenous or endogenous)—were explored first. Following this, profit-maximizing pricing was examined (notably

---

[22] Estimates made of the dead-weight loss to the US economy range from 0.1% to 13% of GDP. See Cowling and Mueller (1978) for this type of loss calculation, and the further debate regarding its validity by Littlechild (1981) and Cowling and Mueller (1981).

the relationship between price, marginal cost, and elasticity of demand),[23] including some arguments for why monopolists may not always be able to exploit their monopoly power (bargaining and the Coase conjecture). Following this, the question of how entry might influence incumbent behaviour was explored both in theory (limit pricing, entry deterrence strategies, contestability theory) and in practice. The general conclusion was that the state probably cannot rely on entry to keep incumbents from exploiting their monopoly power. Finally, the problem of measuring the extent to which monopoly pricing leads to welfare loss was explored (including the idea that rent-seeking behaviour might actually increase the level of welfare loss). Further consideration of the strategic decisions faced by the firm with monopoly power are to be found in Chapters 18–26 and 28.

14.8 Review Questions

1. Explain the difference between endogenous and exogenous barriers to entry, and give three examples of each.

2. If a single-product firm operates with price set at 50% above marginal cost, what elasticity of demand would validate this as a profit-maximizing choice of mark-up?

3. Construct a dominant-firm model in which market demand is linear (draw the demand curve so that it reaches both vertical and horizontal axes) and fringe supply is also linear, with positive slope and passing through the origin. If the dominant firm has constant marginal cost, show that its price must be less than if the firm had the whole market to itself. Compare monopoly welfare loss for these two cases.

4. If a single-product firm operates with price at £2 (50% above marginal cost), and sells 200,000 units per annum at this price, estimate the magnitude of the dead-weight welfare loss.

5. Explain the concepts of blockaded entry, accommodated entry, and entry deterrence.

6. The entry game discussed in section 14.4.2 (see Figure 14.5) can be set up in strategic form as in Figure 14.10 (see section 14.4.2 for the interpretation of the game and pay-offs).

		Incumbent	
		Share	Fight
Entrant	Enter	(π_s, π_s)	(π_f, π_f)
	Stay out	$0, \pi_m$	$0, \pi_m$

Fig. 14.10 The entry game revisited

Here, the left element in a cell is the payoff to the entrant, the right being the payoff to the incumbent. Assume $\pi_m > \pi_s > 0 > \pi_f$. Show that both Enter/Share and Stay out/Fight are Nash equilibria, but that the latter is not a subgame-perfect equilibrium. That is, under Stay out/Fight, the entrant is being dissuaded from entering by an incumbent strategy, Fight, which, if the entrant did enter, the incumbent would have no incentive actually to choose. That is, the incumbent's threat to fight is not credible. Thus No entry/Fight may be a Nash equilibrium, but it is not a good prediction regarding how the game would or should be played. For more on this in a general context, see the discussion of extensive-form games in Chapter 5.

14.9 Further Reading

Sharkey (1982) gives a general analysis of monopoly, including a more extensive discussion of the multi-product case. Martin (1993, 1994) also provides useful additional material, especially on dominant-firm models. Kreps (1993) considers some thought-provoking ideas regarding the ability of monopolists to exploit their monopoly power (as discussed in section 14.3.2). Dixit (1982) is a very readable and commendably brief review of some key game-theoretic ideas in entry theory. Geroski (1995) gives an excellent and readable survey of the empirical evidence on entry.

---

[23] Many extensions to the marketing strategy of the firm are explored in further detail in later chapters, notably Chaps. 18 and 19 (on price discrimination), 20 (on multiple products), and 26 (on advertizing).

15 Monopolistic Competition

Objective To examine the characteristics of markets where there are a large number of firms and free entry, but where each firm is able to produce a slightly differentiated product.

Prerequisites Lancaster's characteristics approach to consumer theory (utilized in section 15.3) is presented in

Chapter 8. Chapter 14, on monopoly pricing, also gives useful background on pricing formulae.

Keywords brands, monopolistic competition, product differentiation, product positioning, unexhausted economies of scale.

15.1 Introduction

Many industries seem to be characterized by brand proliferation and product differentiation, and yet there appears to be free entry, a large number of firms in competition, and, because of the product differentiation, some scope for the individual firm to choose its own price level.[1] This is because, although each firm faces fairly close substitutes, product demand curves still have some negative slope.

Chamberlin (1933) argued that, when there are many firms all taking a small market share, each firm will be able to set price without being concerned about other firms reacting. A version of this model is examined in section 15.2. Unfortunately, it is hard to see how products can be similar and yet firms need not be concerned about competitor reaction. Section 15.3, argues that in almost any market which at first glance looks like monopolistic competition, firms will typically be concerned about a relatively small number of near-neighbour products; on this view, firms in monopolistic competition are really in a small numbers, or oligopolistic, situation, whilst the market as a whole is characterized as a set of free-entry intersecting oligopolies. The truth of this argument becomes clear when one considers any market which might appear to be a candidate for being called monopolistically competitive. For

example, there are many corner shops in a city conurbation, but each is really only in direct competition with a small number in the local area. City restaurants bars and night clubs arguably come closest to fitting the Chamberlin view of monopolistic competition, but it is hard to think of many examples that are not better characterized as oligopolies.

15.2 Chamberlin's Large-Numbers Analysis

This section presents a version of Chamberlin's (1933) large-numbers model of monopolistic competition. The object of this model was to explain certain stylized facts about such markets which were not captured by the models in existence at that time (namely perfect competition, oligopoly, and monopoly). Thus monopoly and oligopoly dealt only with markets having a small number of firms, whilst the competitive model failed to address the stylized facts which were apparently manifest in so many markets. In particular, the two key stylized facts that competition did not address were:

1. **Product differentiation.** Perfect competition assumed homogeneous product, whilst in these markets, there were typically many closely related brands competing against each other. As a result, firms engaged in advertizing and marketing strategies (with homogeneity, this would be pointless).

---

[1] Chamberlin (1933) tends to get most of the credit for first characterizing this type of market, although there were several contributions of significance at around the same time, notably by Robinson (1933) and Sraffa (1926).

2. **Unexhausted economies of scale.** Firms often seemed to remain small relative to market size despite operating under economies of scale. In the long run, economic theory seemed to predict that market structure depended on plant-efficient scale. With efficient scale large relative to market demand, one would expect to see monopoly or oligopoly. With efficient scale small, one would expect to see competition, and, in the long run, firms operating at an output level corresponding to the minimum of the long-run (and short-run) average cost curve. In these monopolistically competitive industries, so it was argued, firms were observed to be operating at output levels at which there were unexhausted economies of scale.

The Chamberlin large-numbers model is constructed using the following basic assumptions:

(i) There are large numbers of buyers and sellers, each small relative to market size.

(ii) There is free entry and exit for firms (with positive profit inducing entry to, and negative profit inducing exit from the industry).

(iii) Each firm produces a single product or brand.

(iv) All firms face identical cost and demand functions.

(v) Firms, in setting prices, ignore the behaviour of other firms (i.e. take other firms' prices as fixed).

A discussion of the validity of these assumptions is deferred to section 15.3. The concern here is merely to explain how the model functions. The presentation is in two stages: first, the short-run situation, where the number of firms is fixed, and following this, the long run, in which the number of firms is allowed to be variable.

15.2.1 Short-Run (*SR*) Equilibrium

Consider Figure 15.1. This illustrates the situation facing an individual firm in the short run, when the number of firms is fixed. The problem the firm faces is to set a price, given that it faces a downward-sloping demand curve D for its product. The exact position of the individual demand curve depends on the number of competitors and the prices they set. However, the number of competitors is fixed, and their prices are also assumed fixed; the demand curve is thus fixed—although note that it will shift

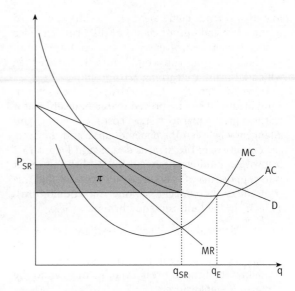

Fig. 15.1 Monopolistic competition: short-run equilibrium

if any other firm alters price, or if there is new firm entry into the market as a whole.

The short-run (*SR*) solution is simply that of monopoly pricing, in which the firm chooses a price such that marginal revenue is equal to marginal cost. Figure 15.1 is drawn such that, at the optimal price p_{SR}, there are positive profits. It is also drawn with the traditional U-shaped marginal and average cost curves.[2] With a U-shaped average cost curve, there is a unique level of output, q_E, at which average cost is minimized. This is sometimes referred to as the efficient scale for the firm. In the short run, the firm's actual choice of output, q_{SR}, could be above or below the efficient scale q_E. In Figure 15.1, it is drawn such that $q_{SR} < q_E$. Clearly, if the figure had been drawn with the *MR* curve intersecting the *MC* curve to the right of q_E, then $q_{SR} > q_E$.

15.2.2 Long-Run (*LR*) Equilibrium

Positive profit, as in Figure 15.1, is assumed to attract entry into the market (and as a corollary, negative profit induces exit). New firm entry increases the competitive pressure on existing firms, and causes each existing firm's demand curve to shift to the left and/or down. The shift in the demand curve naturally induces a corresponding shift in the

---

[2] Note that the solution holds even if the marginal and average cost curves are continuously falling with output, as the reader may care to verify.

marginal revenue curve and hence a shift downward in the price and output choice of the firm. The idea is that the process of entry or exit continues until eventually a long-run equilibrium is reached in which all firms are earning zero profit.

What then are the characteristics of the long-run equilibrium? It can be proved mathematically that it features price equal to average cost (zero profit) and a tangency between the demand curve and the average cost curve of the firm, as depicted in Figure 15.2 below.[3] An intuitive argument to establish this result is to suppose that it is not true (and to show that this contradicts the concept of long-run equilibrium). Thus if, in the long-run equilibrium,

(a) the demand curve lay everywhere below the average cost curve, then clearly in this case, no choice of price/output configuration would allow the firm to break even, so this cannot be an *LR* equilibrium;

(b) the demand curve lay above the average cost curve for some levels of output (as in Figure 15.1), then it is clear that the firm could always select a price/quantity configuration which would allow it to earn positive profit (i.e. to sell some given quantity at a price above average cost for that quantity). Again, this is inconsistent with long-run equilibrium, because it suggests the firm (or a new entrant) can make positive profit.[4]

The long-run equilibrium thus occurs when entry has driven the demand curve to the point where price equals average cost (zero profit), a point at which the demand and average cost curves touch. The curves touch only at such an equilibrium point; at all other outputs, the average cost curve must lie

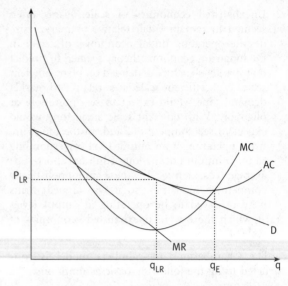

Fig. 15.2 Monopolistic competition: long-run equilibrium

above the demand curve. It then follows, because the curves are assumed to be smooth, that any such equilibrium point is a point of tangency between the two curves (see Figure 15.2).[5]

Because the demand curve is downward-sloping, the fact that it is tangential to the average cost curve means that the average cost curve has negative slope at this point, so the firm operates at a point of **unexhausted economies of scale**, an output level q_{LR} which is less than q_E, the unit cost minimizing output level.[6] Downward-sloping demand also implies that (since the equilibrium features $MR = MC$, and downward sloping demand implies $MR < P_{LR}$) price is above marginal cost, as in the case of pure monopoly. The reason for the apparently welfare 'sub-optimal' output level q_{LR} is the standard monopoly one, namely that a falling demand curve limits the desire for output expansion.

In practice, since products are likely to be close substitutes, the demand curve facing the individual firm is likely to be fairly elastic, so it can be argued that the output q_E at which minimum average cost is attained may not be much less than q_{LR}, the output predicted by the above model. However, whilst this may be true in a particular case, it certainly does *not* follow from theory; indeed it is perfectly possible for

---

[3] A proof of the tangency result is as follows. Monopoly pricing requires marginal revenue equal to marginal cost, so

$$dR/dq = d(pq)/dq = p + q(dp/dq) = MC, \qquad \text{(i)}$$

where p and q denote the optimal choice of price and output, respectively, so the gradient of the demand curve at the point (p, q) is given, by rearranging (i), as

$$dp/dq = [MC - p]/q. \qquad \text{(ii)}$$

Let $C(q)$ denote total cost and $C'(q) = MC$ denote marginal cost. Now, the gradient of the average cost curve is given, using the quotient rule for differentiation, as

$$dAC/dq = [qC'(q) - C(q)]/q^2 = [MC - AC]/q. \quad \text{(iii)}$$

However, at the optimum, we also have price equal to average cost: $p = C(q)/q = AC$. Hence, comparing (ii) and (iii), we see that the gradients are equal at the long-run equilibrium point (p, q).

[4] Recall that each individual firm is atomistic, or small relative to market size.

[5] This would be true even if there were multiple long-run equilibria, as the reader can verify by sketching such possibilities.

[6] Since by assumption all firms are identical, in equilibrium they all charge the same price p and produce the same quantity q.

Table 15.1 Characteristics of alternative market structures

Perfect Competition	Monopolistic Competition	Monopoly
$P = MR = MC$	$P > MR = MC$	$P > MR = MC$
$P = AC$	$P = AC$	$P > AC$
$Q = Q_{MES}$	$Q < Q_{MES}$	Q may be above or below Q_{MES}
$\pi = 0$	$\pi = 0$	$\pi > 0$

the firm's cost curve to continue to decline for all positive output.[7]

Table 15.1 provides a summary comparison of the principal features of monopolistic competition à la Chamberlin vis-à-vis the models of perfect competition and monopoly.

15.2.3 Socially Inefficient Production?

In Chapter 14, it was shown that, if a firm sets price above marginal cost, this implies a social welfare loss.[8] From Figure 15.2, it should be clear that this is necessarily the case here too; at the long-run equilibrium point, $p > MC$. An omniscient and omnipotent social planner (an OOP for short) could force the firms to produce output levels such that price equalled marginal cost. If the firms featured extensive economies of scale, this would leave them earning financial losses, but these could be rectified by the planner levying lump-sum taxes on consumers (in an appropriate way) to finance these losses.[9] Carefully arranged, everyone could be made better off. Unfortunately, OOPs are mythical creatures and the gain is simply not realizable.[10]

---

[7] Chamberlin (1933) assumed the U-shaped average cost curve without much consideration of whether this assumption was realistic. Furthermore, even if the AC curve is U-shaped, the argument does not work, simply because AC could still be falling over quite a large range of output (so the difference between q_{LR} and q_E could also be large).

[8] In the absence of other distortions in the economy. Marginal cost pricing is no longer necessarily welfare-desirable if there are other distortions (monopoly power, non-lump-sum taxes, and externalities all count as distortions). See Chap. 22 for a discussion of the theory of the second best.

[9] Recall that lump-sum transfers are welfare-neutral; that is, such redistributions do not alter the value of the welfare index (see Chap. 2). The problem of economies of scale is discussed under public utility pricing in Chap. 22.

[10] A Coasian solution would involve consumers bargaining with the firms and agreeing the socially optimal outputs. Again, if negotiations could be undertaken costlessly, the outcome that everyone is made better off is possible. This idea is discussed in Chap. 14, and also in Chaps. 27 and 28. Unfortunately, bargaining and contracting are not costless activities.

Chamberlin (1933) argued that the loss should not even be thought of as a welfare loss, although it *is* a welfare loss in the same sense that there is monopoly welfare loss in the single-firm monopoly case. That is, it is a welfare loss relative to a benchmark (albeit an unattainable benchmark). The welfare loss is a natural outcome of consumers' taste for variety.

15.3 More Modern Views

A useful starting point is the set of assumptions underpinning the model set out in section 15.2. The first two assumptions are descriptive and unproblematic, but all the others can be disputed; they are first restated (for convenience):

(iii) Each firm produces a single product or brand.

(iv) All firms face identical cost and demand functions.

(v) Firms, in setting prices, ignore the behaviour of other firms (i.e. take other firms' prices as fixed).

Assumption (iii) is questionable; in theory and in practice, incumbent firms are likely to find a greater incentive in the development of new brands closely related to their existing brands (see Tirole 1993: chap. 7). Assumption (iv) is based on the idea that product differentiation is limited, so all firms will have roughly the same cost and demand curves. Chamberlin (1933) regarded this as merely a simplification, in order to present a simple model (and he discussed further the consequences of relaxing the assumption). With firms having heterogeneous cost structures, one might expect at least some firms to earn inframarginal super-normal profits; clearly it becomes necessary to characterize more completely how firms choose what products to produce and where to enter. The early models provide little detail on these issues. Assumption (v) is even more problematic. The idea behind (v) is that each firm, in setting price, can ignore all the other firms because the impact of its decision on the sales of any other firm is negligible. In practice, firms are likely to face competition from nearest-neighbour products, and it can be argued that the type of competition that this induces is a particular type of differentiated free-entry oligopoly. This argument is developed in more detail below.

Lancaster's 'characteristics approach' (after

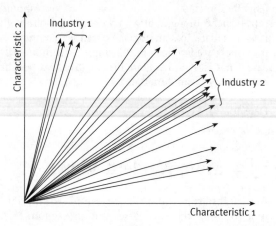

Fig. 15.3 Goods in characteristics space

Lancaster 1962*a*; see Chapter 8) provides a good way to think about products in monopolistic competition. The point is that goods are only similar if they have similar characteristics, if they cluster in characteristics space. It follows that each product will always have a set of nearest neighbours in characteristics space. This is illustrated in Figure 15.3, for the case where there are just two characteristics. In this special case, each product has at most two neighbours (which may or may not be near neighbours). Clearly, with three or more characteristics, the number of near neighbours can increase substantially. However, the point remains that it is only the nearest neighbours which are of any significance; a reduction in price will, in the first instance, only steal market share from nearest neighbours (see Chapter 8 for a full explanation).[11] Given that a change in price may have a significant impact on the sales of nearest-neighbour products, it is unreasonable to assume that the firm will ignore this interdependence. The implication is that nearest neighbours will behave as oligopolists. Thus even if firms ignore products which

are not near in characteristics space, it would appear that monopolistic competition looks more like a web of intersecting oligopolies.

In fact things are still more complex, since there is also free entry, and hence presumably free choice as to **product positioning** within characteristics space. If the choice of product characteristics did not significantly affect the cost of production, and if consumer demand is reasonably uniform over characteristics space, one might predict a fairly uniform coverage by firms of the whole characteristics space. The number of products, and the extent of differences between them, would then be largely dictated by the density of demand and the extent of economies of scale in production. With constant economies of scale, one might expect a continuum of products, whilst with fixed costs or other sources of economies of scale, a discrete number of products might be expected. Discreteness may also arise because brand names, trade marks, and patents are protected by law from being too closely mimicked.

If products with certain combinations of characteristics are significantly more costly to produce, then we might expect gaps in the provision in characteristics space. Likewise, gaps in demand across characteristics space induce gaps in provision. As a consequence some degree of bunching of products in characteristics space might be expected, as depicted in Figure 15.3. Conceptually, we can think of a bunching in characteristics space as an industry. Naturally, an industry may be fairly tightly defined (large gaps around the bunch, as with industry 1 in Figure 15.3), or may be rather fuzzy at the edges (if product density falls away more gradually, as with industry 2 in the figure).

The above criticisms of Chamberlin's early ideas have been around in the literature for some time (see Robinson 1933). Indeed, the criticism seems so powerful that one might take the view that there really is no distinct market form termed monopolistic competition. Kreps (1990: 346), for example, challenges the reader to think of any observable market behaviour which even remotely conforms to the description given in section 15.2. The modern argument is that monopolistic competition is really a particular type of oligopolistic spatial competition (where 'spatial' can be interpreted as either geographical space or more generally as characteristics space). Models of this type have been around for a while, but it is only recently that models which address the issue of free entry into a product characteristics space (and oligopolistic competition

[11] In Lancaster's model, small changes in price have no impact on distant neighbours (see Chap. 8).

between firms) have been significantly developed. Unfortunately, the models tend to be fairly complex technically, and a presentation is beyond the scope of this chapter.[12]

15.4 Summary

Although the simple model discussed in section 15.2 seems appealing at first sight, it was noted that most of the markets where there are many firms producing differentiated products are better described as intersecting free-entry oligopolies. That is, in practice, firms typically face a relatively small number of near neighbours (in product characteristics space); these near neighbours are quite likely to be concerned about and reactive to changes in the firm's pricing and marketing policy.

15.5 Review Questions

1. List three types of market which might be described as 'monopolistically competitive' and

consider to what extent the assumptions listed in section 15.2 are satisfied for such markets.

2. Explain what is meant by the term 'unexhausted economies of scale' and why this is a characteristic of the long-run equilibrium in monopolistic competition. Is it a characteristic in the short run?

3. What factors are likely to influence the degree of product differentiation manifest in a given market?

15.6 Further Reading

Koutsoyiannis (1979) gives an excellent review and survey of early models of monopolistic competition. Tirole (1993) gives some more recent spatial models (and further references) for models of monopolistic competition which recognize that, whilst there is free entry, firms are typically faced with competition from a limited number of near neighbours.

---

[12] Tirole (1993) gives some illustrative simple models of spatial competition. Pascoa (1997) gives a model with a continuum of differentiated products in which it is shown that free entry is compatible with product differentiation, contrary to Chamberlin's (1937) claim that these assumptions are really incompatible.

16 Oligopoly

Objective This Chapter examines markets which involve a small number of firms, where the behaviour of any firm has significant implications for the sales and profits of the other firms in the industry.

Prerequisites Chapter 8, on demand analysis, and Chapter 14, on the basic theory of Monopoly pricing, and for the extended discussion of limit pricing and entry.

Keywords accommodated entry, barometric price leadership, Bertrand equilibrium, Bertrand model, blockaded entry, cartels, concentration, conscious parallelism, Cournot equilibrium, Cournot model, deterred entry, duopoly, entry deterrence, explicit collusion, first-mover advantage, focal point, Herfindahl index, implicit collusion, kinked demand curve model, limit pricing, price leadership, price setting, price watching, prisoner's dilemma, quantity setting, reaction function, refund guarantee, resale price maintenance, satisficing, Stackelberg equilibrium, Stackelberg model, Sylos postulate, tacit collusion.

16.1 Introduction

Oligopoly is concerned with markets which involve a relatively small number of firms. In such a market, the levels chosen by one firm for strategic variables such as advertizing, pricing, output, and investment decisions can have a significant impact on the sales, profits, and long-term viability of other firms in the industry. It follows that, in such an industry, firms will keep a careful watch on competitor behaviour and will also take account of potential reactions when considering any change in policy.

The initial focus is on competitive oligopoly and the firm's price and output decisions (advertizing is examined separately in Chapter 26). Behaviour is usually modelled as either

1. **quantity setting**, or
2. **price setting**.

In the former, the firms decide (independently) how much to produce, their outputs are brought to market and, following this, the price adjusts to clear the market. In the latter, the firms set price, and then simply produce for the demand that turns up at the price offered. Clearly, the nature of the manufacturing and distribution processes will have a major influence on whether it is price or quantity setting that prevails (see Dixon 1986). Quantity setting is typical of products for which production involves set-up costs and/or relatively long lead times in production; many agricultural products fall into this category.[1] Price setting occurs when quantity is quick and easy to adjust relative to price; for example, in many types of retailing and service industry, car/van hire, hotel accommodation and holiday packages, etc.

Although we focus here exclusively on price and quantity, there are of course many other decisions where a firm's choices affect other firms; each of these may have a different time horizon on which they can be regarded as fixed or variable—for example, entry/exit, capacity expansion, R&D, advertizing, and promotional effort decisions may all involve a longer time horizon than the price and quantity decisions discussed here. The capacity decision is touched on in section 16.2.5, whilst advertizing is addressed in Chapter 26.

Section 16.2 examines a variety of models in which firms behave competitively in the absence of potential entry; 16.3 discusses the relationship between firm numbers (concentration), industry prices, and profits; 16.4 then examines entry and barriers to entry (but see also the extended discussion of entry in Chapter 14), whilst 16.5 offers a short case study. Finally, section 16.6 discusses co-operative oligopoly, in which firms seek to collude rather than compete; it examines the incentive to

---

[1] Transport costs can make for local oligopolistic markets.

form cartel agreements, and also the incentives to cheat on such agreements.

16.2 Competitive Oligopoly: No Potential Entry

This section examines models of oligopolistic competition with a fixed number of firms. As will become clear, the difference between these models revolves around assumptions regarding what firms expect in the way of competitor reaction (so-called conjectural variations) and what variables the firms control—in particular, prices and/or quantities.

16.2.1 The Kinked Demand Curve

The **kinked demand curve** (Sweezy 1939, Hall and Hitch 1939) offers an explanation of the supposed stylized fact that oligopolistic markets feature greater price stability than other market forms.

(a) The Basic Model

The essence of the kinked demand curve model is that

Assumption 16.1 Each firm assumes its competitors will follow a reduction in price, but will not follow a price rise.

The simplest version of the theory supposes there are a number of similar-sized firms producing a homogeneous product. All firms set the same price and have similar market shares. Naturally, if they all set a high price they sell relatively little, whilst at low price, consumers buy more in total. Thus, the relationship between a firm's sales and price, when all firms set the same price, has downward slope; this demand curve is referred to as the *mutatis mutandis* or *pari passu* demand curve, indicated by the line D_1D_2 in Figure 16.1.

Given that all firms are currently setting a price p, then according to Assumption 16.1, the individual firm conjectures that if it were to reduce price, all competitors would immediately match the price reduction. Thus its sales, for a price reduction, are given by the curve D_1D_2 for prices below p. By contrast, if the firm unilaterally increases price, the firm conjectures that no one will follow. With a homogeneous product, this is something of a disaster; customers switch to other, lower-price suppliers, and so if price is increased above p, the firm loses sales much faster than is indicated by the curve

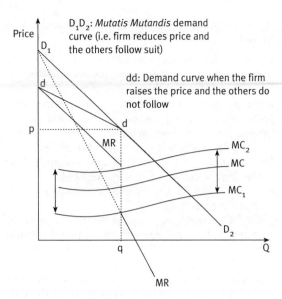

Fig. 16.1 The kinked demand curve

D_1D_2. This is suggested by drawing a much flatter demand curve, *dd*. The idea is that a small increase in price will lead to a large fall in sales.[2]

The above discussion implies that the demand curve is steeper for price reductions than for price increases, with a kink at the current price p. Thus the demand curve perceived by the individual oligopolist is labelled ddD_2 in Figure 16.1. This in turn implies there is a discontinuity in the MR schedule, as indicated in the figure. That is, for prices above p, the relevant marginal revenue is that associated with *dd*, whilst for price reductions, it is that associated with D_1D_2.[3] Now, marginal reasoning tells us that output should be increased whenever $MR > MC$ and decreased whenever $MR < MC$. Suppose the marginal cost curve is the one indicated as MC. Clearly, to the left of q it is worth expanding output, since $MR > MC$ here, whilst to the right it is worth contracting output, since $MR < MC$. Thus the current level of output and current price are perceived by the firm as optimal.

---

[2] With a perfectly homogeneous product and rational consumers, the demand curve to the left of the kink would be completely flat. The diagram is drawn for the case where the firm may still be able to sell some product at slightly higher prices. The story is essentially the same, of course.

[3] If you doubt the discontinuity at the output level q, try drawing a straight-line demand curve and its associated marginal revenue curve (recall that the latter intersects the horizontal axis at half the quantity at which the demand curve intersects the axis). Then do the same for *dd*.

(b) Price Stickiness in the Kinked Demand Curve Model

Clearly, so long as *MC* passes through the gap in the *MR* curve, the current price and output is optimal. It follows that costs can fluctuate to some extent, illustrated in Figure 16.1 as the range from curve MC_1 up to curve MC_2 (say because of fluctuations in raw material prices due to exchange rate fluctuations). For fluctuations which stay within the *MR* gap, the firm will not be drawn into changing its price. This is the first argument for why oligopolies feature more stable prices; they have an incentive to absorb changes in costs.[4]

The argument also applies to fluctuations in demand; that is, so long as fluctuations are not too substantial, the firm will not be induced to change price. This is illustrated in Figure 16.2. The idea here is that a sudden increase in demand shifts the curve to the right. However, the kink remains at the current price. So long as the marginal cost curve continues to pass through the new discontinuity (in *MR′* at output level *q′*), there will be no change in price. Hence, this suggests the second prediction, that fluctuations in demand also may not induce a shift in price.

To sum up, firms in oligopoly, subject to fluctuations in either demand or cost, are more inclined to maintain stable prices. By contrast, in competition or monopoly, theory suggests that any such shifts will tend to lead to a change in the profit-maximizing price.[5]

The kinked demand curve theory is often regarded by students as fairly realistic, and there is a reasonable amount of evidence that oligopolistic prices are rather more sticky than in competitive or monopolistic markets.[6] However, this theory does not tell us much about price determination in such markets. The most important point to understand about the kinked demand curve theory is that

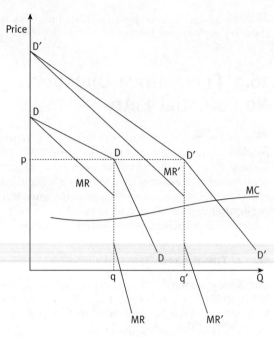

Fig. 16.2 The kinked demand curve: demand fluctuations

it is *not* a theory of price determination; that is, it does not explain why the current price happens to be what it is. It merely argues that, whatever the current price, this price will be sticky; that is, demand and cost fluctuations will often not induce any variation in price.

Thus the tacit collusion (on sticking with the current price) gives us no guidance as to how firms arrive at the current price. Tirole (1993), for example, suggests that the monopoly price is a natural **focal point** on which firms might try to coordinate (in the case where firms are similar, and so agree on what this is; in Figure 16.1, this corresponds to the price such that the *mutatis mutandis* marginal revenue curve intersects the marginal cost curve; thus *p* would be focal if MC_1 happened to be the true marginal cost curve). This invites further questions, of course (such as how the focal point shifts when demand and cost curves shift . . . and what happens then).

It has been argued that kinked demand is unlikely to apply when there are industry-wide cost fluctuations, simply because everyone knows that they are similarly affected. That is, if costs rise, so that each firm faces a higher marginal cost curve, then the focal price will also increase. Firms will wish to coordinate on this higher focal price:

---

[4] It should be clear that, if the cost curve was to shift so far that it intersected the marginal revenue curve either to the left or the right of the discontinuity point, then the standard monopoly pricing rule applies; the firm would change price to bring *MR = MC*.

[5] Of course there may be reasons why a monopolist will maintain relatively stable prices (for example, brand loyalty may be dissipated if consumers perceive exploitative behaviour, or regulators may intervene if the monopolist is viewed as overly exploiting the market).

[6] There is some debate, however; Earl (1995: 228–30) gives a review of some of the early exchanges, such as those between Stigler (1947) and Efroymson (1955). See also Scherer (1980).

Definition 16.1 The adjustment of price, with the expectation that all rivals will simultaneously follow suit, is termed **conscious parallelism** (see e.g. Hamburger 1967).

The idea is that price stickiness is more likely to be observed with regard to firm-specific cost fluctuations (such as moving premises, or investing in new production technology), whilst industry-wide effects are more likely to meet with co-ordinated price adjustments (this is closely related to the concept of price leadership; see section 16.6).

16.2.2 Cournot Quantity Competition

This section focuses on Cournot's model of quantity-setting competition.

(a) The Basic Model

The key assumption is that

Assumption 16.2 (Cournot model): Firms decide independently how much to produce. Output is brought to market, and the price adjusts to clear the market.

In the Cournot (1838) model, as an individual firm expands output, it conjectures that this is independent of the outputs chosen by the other firms, so that each unit of its production adds one unit to the total output of the industry. This increment in output depresses the market price, something the firm takes into account in deciding how much to produce. I choose, for expository simplicity, to focus on the extreme form of oligopoly known as **duopoly** (where the interdependence between firms is at its most severe). In this, there are just two firms (imaginatively labelled 1 and 2).[7] The market price is denoted as p and the firms produce outputs q_1 and q_2 respectively, so total industry output is $q = q_1 + q_2$.

Figure 16.3 illustrates the problem faced by firm 1. There is a fixed industry demand curve, whose position is, by assumption, known to both firms. For a given output q_2 by firm 2, firm 1 can calculate how price p varies with q_1. In effect, firm 1 faces a residual demand curve equal to industry demand minus firm 2's output level (labelled D_1 in Figure 16.3). The optimal choice of q_1 by firm 1 corresponds to the intersection of its marginal revenue, MR_1, with its marginal cost curve, MC_1. Notice how the magnitude of q_2 affects firm 1's optimal choice of output; a larger value for q_2 shifts the residual demand curve to the left, and so shifts the $MR_1 =$

[7] The Cournot model can easily be generalized to the case where there are more than two firms, as we shall see.

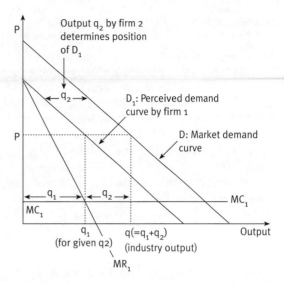

Fig. 16.3 Cournot model: choice of output

MC_1 intersection point to the left. Thus a larger q_2 implies a smaller choice of q_1 by firm 1.

Definition 16.2 The (negatively sloped) relationship between the amount firm 1 wishes to produce, given the amount produced by firm 2, is termed firm 1's **reaction function**.

Clearly, parallel reasoning applies to firm 2, and, given the amount produced by firm 1, there is an optimal choice of output for firm 2. The relationship between the optimal choice of q_2, given q_1, is termed firm 2's reaction function. These reaction functions are illustrated in Figure 16.4, with Example 16.1 below showing how, given analytic functions for

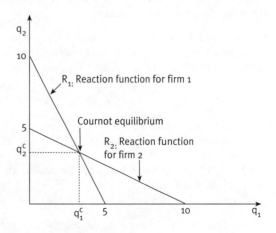

Fig. 16.4 Cournot equilibrium

demand and cost functions of the firms, it is straightforward to compute these reaction functions.

EXAMPLE 16.1 Suppose the inverse industry demand curve is $p = 12 - q$, where q is total output, made up of q_1 by firm 1 and q_2 by firm 2 (so $q = q_1 + q_2$). Further, suppose the firms are identical, and have marginal cost of 2 per unit, with zero fixed cost. Firm 1 thus makes profit

$$\pi_1 = (p - 2)q_1 = (10 - q)q_1 = (10 - q_1 - q_2)q_1$$
$$= 10q_1 - q_1^2 - q_2q_1.$$

It maximizes profits by choosing q_1. A necessary condition is thus that

$$\partial \pi_1 / \partial q_1 = 0.$$

That is,

$$\partial \pi_1 / \partial q_1 = 10 - 2q_1 - q_2 = 0.$$

Rearranging this gives firm 1's choice of q_1 as a function of q_2:

$$2q_1 = 10 - q_2$$

or, making q_2 the subject of the equation, that

$$q_2 = 10 - 2q_1. \tag{R1}$$

A similar analysis establishes that firm 2's choice of q_2 depends on q_1:

$$q_2 = 5 - (1/2)q_1. \tag{R2}$$

Equations $(R1)$ and $(R2)$ are the reaction functions for firms 1 and 2 respectively, as depicted in Figure 16.4.

The intersection point (q_1^c, q_2^c) of the reaction functions is referred to as the **Cournot equilibrium**. It is an equilibrium because at this point, if firm 1 chooses q_1^c, firm 2 wishes to choose q_2^c, and if 2 chooses q_2^c, then 1 wants to choose q_1^c. The output levels are thus mutually consistent.

EXAMPLE 16.2 In Example 16.1, the Cournot equilibrium is given as the simultaneous solution to the two reaction function equations; that is

$$q_2 = 10 - 2q_1. \tag{R1}$$

and

$$q_2 = 5 - (1/2)q_1. \tag{R2}$$

The solution involves $q_1 = q_2 = 3^1/_3$. The implied market price is thus $p = 12 - q = 12 - 2 \times 3^1/_3 = 5^1/_3$. The individual-firm profits at this equilibrium are thus $\pi_1 = \pi_2 = (p - 2)q_i = (5^1/_3 - 2)3^1/_3 = 100/9$.

In general, reaction functions do not always intersect at positive output levels as depicted in Figure

16.4; for example, one of the reaction functions could lie above the other (for example, if $(R2)$ was above $(R1)$, then firm 2 would be a monopoly, and firm 1 would exit the industry). In fact, marginal costs can differ significantly and yet there can still be such an intersection point; thus Cournot competition is not excessively fierce, and it allows inefficient firms to survive in the long run.

(b) Stability in the Cournot Model

It is possible to discuss how the firms might arrive at such an equilibrium. Cournot originally gave an account in which the two firms observed each other's output in one period, and assumed that this would be repeated in the next period. On the basis of this assumption, they calculated their next-period outputs and brought these to market, and so on. This is illustrated in Figure 16.5. Thus suppose for example that initially firm 1 is an incumbent, producing the monopoly level of profit q_1^m. Then firm 2 would wish to enter, and in the next period produce output level q_2^1 (read this off reaction function $(R2)$), whilst 1 would continue with q_1^m. Thus we are now at point a in the figure. In the following period, firm 2 would continue with q_1^2 (expecting 1 to maintain q_1^m), but 1 in fact chooses q_1^2 (read this off $(R1)$). We thus arrive at point b in the figure (and then d, and so on). The process converges to the Cournot equilibrium, given the fact that $(R1)$ is steeper than $(R2)$ (this is necessarily the case with a linear model, as described in Example 16.1). A similar process would apply had we initially started at, say, q_2^m. Notice that this dynamic process pro-

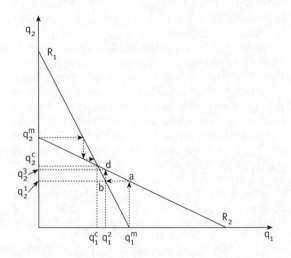

Fig. 16.5 Cournot dynamics

vides some rationale for calling the functions ($R1$ and $R2$) 'reaction functions'. By contrast, if there is only a single period to the game, reactions are necessarily hypothetical; there is no future period in which to react to present behaviour.

The above dynamic process envisages each firm conjecturing that the other will maintain output at its previous level, and in each period this conjecture is falsified since in each period one or other of the firms changes its output choice and this contradicts the assumption by each firm that the other will maintain output period by period. The firms never learn from past experience.

It is possible to try to patch up the adjustment model, to try to make each firm's conjectures in some sense more rational. However, this is difficult to do[8] and is not pursued here. Instead, I stick with the account of the game as an atemporal or one-shot game. In the one-shot game, the Cournot equilibrium is a **Nash equilibrium**. Given that both firms know the market demand curve and each other's cost functions, and assuming that they both know that each is a rational profit maximizer, then each can calculate that the only rational choice is the Cournot output level—so these will be chosen. Thus the equilibrium choices (q_1^c and q_2^c) are such that q_1^c is the profit-maximizing choice for firm 1 given firm 2 chooses q_2^c, and vice versa. That is,

$$\pi_1(q_1^c, q_2^c) > \pi_1(q_1, q_2^c) \quad \text{for all } q_1 \geq 0, \, q_1 \neq q_1^c;$$
$$(16.1)$$

$$\pi_2(q_1^c, q_2^c) > \pi_2(q_1, q_2^c) \quad \text{for all } q_2 \geq 0, \, q_2 \neq q_2^c.$$
$$(16.2)$$

This is of course a definition of a Nash equilibrium (see Chapter 5): no one can unilaterally get a higher payoff by deviating from the equilibrium.[9]

[8] See Tirole (1993: 244) for a short discussion of the logical problems that this tends to engender.

[9] If one firm considers that the other will choose some output other than the Cournot output, this can be shown to involve some degree of irrationality. For example, in Figure 16.5, if firm 1 conjectures that firm 2 might choose some other output, such as q_2^1, it would calculate that it ought to produce q_1^2; but firm 1 also knows that if this was the case and firm 2 was considering producing q_2^1, firm 2 would also know that this would induce 1 to want to produce q_1^2 and then 2 would prefer to choose q_2^3, and so on, *ad infinitum*. That is, the only conjectures regarding what the other will produce that are mutually rational and consistent are the Cournot outputs; anything other than the Cournot output involves irrational conjectures, which contradicts the assumption that each player is rational and knows the other is too. Hence they must both choose the Cournot output levels. In experimental play, this prediction is far from realized; most players simply are not that rational.

(c) Isoprofit Curve Analysis

Each point (q_1, q_2) in Figure 16.6 naturally corresponds to a particular level of profit for each firm. Lines of constant profit to firm 1 are denoted π_{1_1}, π_{1_2}, π_{1_3}, etc., where $\pi_{1_1} < \pi_{1_2} < \pi_{1_3}$, etc. (Note that q_1^m is the monopoly output point, and thus corresponds to firm 1 earning maximum attainable profit, whilst point M_1 corresponds to it exiting the market with zero profit.)[10] Likewise, the curves depicted π_{2_1}, π_{2_2}, π_{2_3}, etc. ($\pi_{2_1} < \pi_{2_2} < \pi_{2_3}$) depict loci of constant profit to firm 2. Note that, in drawing these isoprofit curves, those for firm 1 reach their peak as they cross the reaction function ($R1$), whilst those for firm 2 reach a maximum in the q_1-direction as they cross ($R2$).

It should be clear from Figure 16.6 that if the two firms were able to collude in co-ordinating their production plans so as to move from the Cournot equilibrium to a point in the shaded region (so restricting output and raising market price), both would be better off; that is, a move into the shaded region would move each firm onto a higher isoprofit curve. Indeed, if the two firms were to bargain, they would be able to reach a point where the two firms' isoprofit curves are mutually tangential. Such points correspond to the joint-profit-maximizing output level.[11]

Thus Cournot competition leads to an equilibrium in which the firms earn less profit than if they collude and achieve the monopoly (joint-profit maximum) outcome. The essential reason Cournot equilibrium features a lower than monopoly price is that, although each firm takes into account the effect its choice of quantity has on depressing market price, it ignores the effect that this then has on the other firms. It would appear that, if the firms understand the structure of the market, they will have an incentive to collude or bargain with each other. This is true; if a contractually binding agreement can be reached, the firms can be made better off. In principle, such a bargain will realize a point on the locus

[10] It is straightforward to compute these iso-profit loci for Ex. 16.1. Thus, setting firm 1's profit level at the constant level π_{1_1}, we get

$$\pi_{1_1} = (p - 2)q_1 = (10 - q_1 - q_2)q_1,$$

so rewriting this gives

$$q_2 = 10 - q_1 - (\pi_{1_1}/q_1).$$

This plots a curve like that in Fig. 16.6; that is, hills which reach their maximum values as they cross the reaction function $R1$.

[11] Those familiar with the Edgeworth box may note the parallels with that analysis.

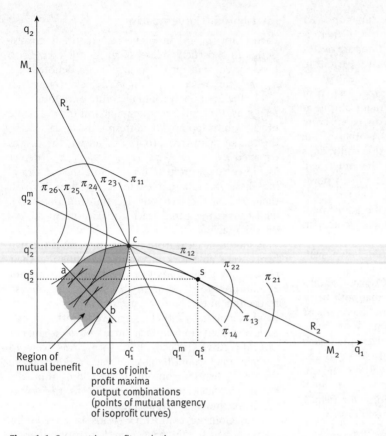

Fig. 16.6 Cournot isoprofit analysis

ab (with the actual position depending on bargaining skills; at *a*, firm 2 has made all the gains, whilst at *b*, it is firm 1—midway between *a* and *b*, in this symmetric model, corresponds to the equal-shares bargain). To illustrate:

EXAMPLE 16.3 (Joint-Profit Maximization). If the firms collude in Example 16.1, then given market demand is $p = 12 - q$ and firms have marginal cost of 2, joint profits are given simply as $\Pi = (p - 2)q = (10 - q)q$, so the joint-profit-maximizing output is given as $\partial\Pi/\partial q = 10 - 2q = 0 \Rightarrow q = 5$. An equal-profit-sharing agreement would thus involve $q_1 = q_2 = 2.5$, price $p = 12 - 5 = 7$ and profit to each of $\pi_1 = \pi_2 = (7 - 2)2.5 = 12.5$ (compared to $100/9 \approx 11$ each in the Cournot equilibrium).

Unfortunately, whilst there is an incentive to bargain, if this is not contractually binding there is also an incentive to cheat (the prisoners' dilemma!) and such a solution is not sustainable (in the one-shot game described here); this is discussed in some detail in section 16.5 below. Only in the Cournot–Nash equilibrium is there no incentive to cheat.

16.2.3 The Stackelberg Leader–Follower Model

One of the appealing things about the Cournot model is that it lends itself to a variety of extensions. In this section, the model is extended to explore the effects of giving one firm a **first-mover advantage**. This is Stackelberg's (1934) extension to the Cournot model, the key difference being that firms no longer make simultaneous moves:

Assumption 16.3 (**Stackelberg model**): Firm 1 (the market leader) announces (or actually produces) her output first, and is committed to bringing this to market. Firm 2 observes this, and chooses output accordingly.

Thus firm 2 remains a Cournot firm in that it takes firm 1's output as given and then chooses output so as to maximize its own profit level. It follows that, in Figure 16.6, firm 2's output choice, for a given q_1, can be read off its reaction function ($R2$). Now, given that it is assumed that firm 1 knows firm 2's cost function, and so is also able to compute firm 2's reaction function, it will pay firm 1 to select an output level that maximizes its profit, given the knowledge that its choice will call forth an output from 2 as given by ($R2$). It will therefore choose a point on ($R2$) which corresponds to the highest attainable iso-profit curve for itself. In Figure 16.6, the highest attainable profit for firm 1 on ($R2$) is π_{1_3}, and this is obtained by choosing the output level q_1^s. Thus the point s in Figure 16.6 is the **Stackelberg equilibrium** point.

The Stackelberg equilibrium involves the market leader choosing an output higher than the Cournot level, and this induces the follower to produce less. The leader increases its profit, and this has an adverse effect on the follower's profitability. Given the new structure of the game, in which the leader first announces its decision (or actually produces the output) and is committed to selling it on the market, the Stackelberg equilibrium is also a Nash equilibrium. Note that the quantity q_1 needs to be committed—commitment is important, since, having induced q_2^s from firm 2, firm 1 would like to renege on its announcement (so as to choose the point on ($R1$) where it intersects the line from q_2^s to s). This idea, of output being committed, will be important when I discuss entry in section 16.4 below.

Stackelberg analytics are illustrated in the following example:

EXAMPLE 16.4 (The Stackelberg solution to the model outlined in Example 16.1): Market demand is $p = 12 - q = 12 - q_1 - q_2$ and each firm has a marginal cost of 2, with no fixed costs. The reaction function for firm 2 (the Cournot follower) is ($R2$): $q_2 = 5 - (1/2)q_1$. The leader's profit is given as

$$\pi_1 = (p - 2)q_1 = (10 - q_1 - q_2)q_1$$
$$= \{10 - q_1 - [5 - (1/2)q_1]\}q_1$$
$$= (5 - \tfrac{1}{2}q_1)q_1. \qquad \text{(i)}$$

Notice that I have replaced q_2 using the reaction function ($R2$); the point is that firm 1 takes into account the impact its choice q_1 of has on firm 2's choice, q_2. Equation (i) is a quadratic in q_1; the first-order condition for a maximum involves

$$\partial \pi_1 / \partial q_1 = 5 - q_1 = 0 \Rightarrow q_1 = 5,$$

so from ($R2$), $q_2 = 5 - (1/2)q_1 = 2.5$. Total output is thus 7.5 and price $p = 12 - q = 4.5$. Recall that the Cournot solution had each producing $3\tfrac{1}{3}$ each. Thus, the leader produces more and makes a higher profit, with the follower producing less, with a lower profit. Total output is higher and market price lower.

This leader–follower model is utilized in section 16.4.2 below to discuss incumbent entry-prevention strategies.

16.2.4 Bertrand Price Competition

This section examines the case of price-setting oligopolistic behaviour.

Assumption 16.4 (Bertrand model): Firms decide independently and simultaneously what price to set for their product. The demand functions they face then determine how much they are able to sell at these prices.

The original Bertrand (1883) price-setting model involves the two firms producing a homogeneous product at the same constant marginal cost c. The two firms simultaneously and non-co-operatively choose price. By assumption, if they set the same price, they get an equal share of the overall market demand. If one firm sets a lower price, it captures the whole of the market, the other firm selling nothing at all. In this model, the **Bertrand equilibrium** involves both firms setting price equal to marginal cost and earning zero profit (i.e. a quasi-competitive outcome, even though there are only two firms). The idea is that, if any firm sets price $p > c$, the other firm can always profitably capture the entire market by setting a price $p - \varepsilon > c$ for some arbitrarily small $\varepsilon > 0$. Thus no price above marginal cost can be an equilibrium.

This suggests that Bertrand competition is extremely fierce (and thus is good for consumers). The homogeneous-product case, however, is rather extreme. A more realistic case in practice is where the industry involves several firms producing differentiated products. In this case, the equilibrium features prices above marginal costs, although competition tends to remain more vigorous than is the case in Cournot equilibrium. Naturally enough, the Bertrand equilibrium, denoted (p_1^B, p_2^B) and illustrated in Figure 16.7, is a Nash equilibrium. (neither firm has an incentive to deviate from the choice of the Bertrand price given that the other chooses its Bertrand price). The basic ideas are captured in the following extended numerical example, which also compares the Bertrand and Cournot equilibria in a differentiated-product duopoly.

EXAMPLE 16.5 There are (as in Cournot's original example) two mineral-water sellers (labelled 1 and 2) who extract water at zero cost. Each product is regarded by consumers as differentiated, with ordinary demand curves $q_1 = 1 - p_1 + \frac{1}{2} p_2$ and $q_2 = 1 - p_2 + \frac{1}{2} p_1$. Thus the goods are substitutes for each other (an increase in the price of one increases the demand for the other).

THE BERTRAND SOLUTION

In this case, firms choose prices. Firm 1's profit is

$$\pi_1 = p_1 q_1 = p_1(1 - p_1 + \tfrac{1}{2} p_2),$$

whilst firm 2's is

$$\pi_2 = p_2 q_2 = p_2(1 - p_2 + \tfrac{1}{2} p_1).$$

Each firm takes the competitor's price as fixed, and chooses its own price so as to maximize its profit. For firm 1, the first-order condition is thus

$$\partial \pi_1 / \partial p_1 = 1 - 2p_1 + \tfrac{1}{2} p_2 = 0, \qquad (R1)$$

whilst for firm 2 it is

$$\partial \pi_2 / \partial p_2 = 1 - 2p_2 + \tfrac{1}{2} p_1 = 0. \qquad (R2)$$

Equation $(R1)$ constitutes the reaction function for firm 1; it tells us what the optimal choice of price is for firm 1 conditional on a given price for firm 2. The higher firm 2's price, the higher the optimal price chosen by firm 1. Likewise, $(R2)$ is firm 2's reaction function. These are depicted in Figure 16.7. The point where the two reaction curves intersect is the Bertrand equilibrium point. Solving equations $(R1)$ and $(R2)$, we get the

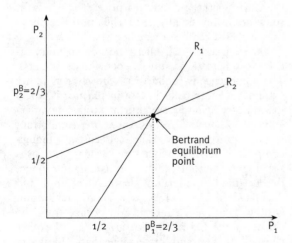

Fig. 16.7 Bertrand equilibrium

Bertrand equilibrium prices $p_1^B = p_2^B = 2/3$ (prices are the same because the costs of production are the same and the demand functions are symmetric). Substituting back into the demand functions gives $q_1^B = q_2^B = (1 - \frac{2}{3}) + (\frac{1}{2} \times \frac{2}{3}) = \frac{2}{3}$ and into the profit functions gives $\pi_1^B = \pi_2^B = (\frac{2}{3})(\frac{2}{3}) = \frac{4}{9}$.

THE COURNOT SOLUTION

If we invert the demand equations, we get

$$p_1 = 2 - \tfrac{2}{3} q_2 - \tfrac{4}{3} q_1$$

and

$$p_2 = 2 - \tfrac{2}{3} q_1 - \tfrac{4}{3} q_2.$$

First, let's express profits in terms of quantities, since there are the choice variables in Cournot; thus, $\pi_1 = p_1 q_1 = (2 - \frac{2}{3} q_2 - \frac{4}{3} q_1) q_1$ and the first-order condition is $(R1)$: $\partial \pi_1 / \partial q_1 = 2 - \frac{2}{3} q_2 - \frac{8}{3} q_1 = 0$ (this gives firm 1's reaction function, which has the usual structure, as in Figure 16.4). Results for firm 2 are symmetric, so a quick way to solve for the Cournot outputs is to set $q_1 = q_2$ in $(R1)$. Hence $2 - \frac{2}{3} q_1 - \frac{8}{3} q_2 = 0 \Rightarrow q_1^c (= q_2^c) = \frac{3}{5}$. Given these outputs, we can use the demand functions to calculate the implied prices: $p_1^c = p_2^c = 2 - (\frac{2}{3})(\frac{3}{5}) - (\frac{4}{3})(\frac{3}{5}) = \frac{4}{5}$. Profits are then $\pi_1^c = \pi_2^c = (\frac{4}{5})(\frac{3}{5}) = \frac{12}{25}$.

As we would expect, the Bertrand solution results in lower profits, lower prices, and higher levels of output.

As discussed in section 16.1, which form of competition (quantity or price, Cournot or Bertrand) is regarded as more realistic is likely to depend upon the structure of the market, and the speed with which different variables can be adjusted. However, section 16.2.5 notes that, even if there is apparent price competition, Cournot-like outcomes may still result.

16.2.5 The Kreps–Scheinkman Argument

On the face of it, many oligopolistic markets seem to look more like Bertrand than Cournot competition. In an interesting paper, however, Kreps and Scheinkman (1983) show that, in a two-stage model in which firms at the first stage simultaneously choose how much capacity to install, followed by a second stage in which they simultaneously choose prices as in the Bertrand model, then the outcome is precisely as if the game is a one-shot game of choosing capacity; since in equilibrium output equals capacity, the outcome is quite simply Cournot outputs and market price. The Kreps–Scheinkman argument is intriguing, since it suggests that the Cournot model can be thought of as a kind of reduced form or shorthand for this multi-stage type of model; Cournot analysis may give a reasonable prediction of market outcomes even where there does appear to be significant price competition.[12] That is, price competition may not be as vigorous as might be predicted in the naive Bertrand model.

16.3 Concentration and Price–Cost Margins

Here, the theoretical relationship between firm numbers and price–cost margins is examined (section 16.4 then examines what determines the number of firms). The basic result is due to Cowling and Waterson (1976). This model supposes there are N firms competing in a Cournot oligopoly, with each having a marginal cost c_i and fixed cost $F_i (i = 1, \ldots, N)$; these might be different across firms. The individual firm's profit is thus

$$\pi_i = (p - c_i)q_i - F_i, \quad (16.3)$$

where $p = f(Q)$ is the market demand function ($df(Q)/dq < 0$; demand has negative slope) and $Q = q_1 + q_2 + \ldots + q_n$ is the total industry output. The ith firm takes a market share $s_i = q_i/Q$, such that $\sum_{i=1}^{N} s_i = 1$. The ith firm chooses its output level taking the other firms' outputs as fixed; this implies

$$\partial \pi_i / \partial q_i = (p - c_i) + q_i \frac{dP}{dQ}\frac{dQ}{dq_i} = 0 \quad i = 1, \ldots, N. \quad (16.4)$$

Now, under the Cournot conjecture, the firm assumes that, as it changes its output level, the other firms' outputs remain fixed, so a one-unit increment in its own output increases Q by one unit; that is, $dQ/dq_i = 1$. Furthermore, the elasticity of demand is given as

$$\eta = \frac{dQ}{dP}\frac{P}{Q},$$

so, dividing (16.4) by p and substituting for η and s_i, we get[13]

$$\frac{p - c_i}{p} = -\frac{s_i}{\eta} \quad i = 1, \ldots, N. \quad (16.5)$$

The Cournot equilibrium is defined by the simultaneous solution of these first-order conditions; in the two-firm case this can be illustrated diagrammatically, corresponding as it does to the point at which the reaction functions intersect in quantity space (as in Figure 16.4).

Equation (16.5) tells us that the individual firm's price–cost margin is inversely related to the elasticity of demand, and is positively related to its market share. In the extreme case of monopoly, $s = 1$ and we get the familiar inverse elasticity result. Another simple result can be obtained by supposing that the elasticity of demand is a constant, and that all firms are identical, having common marginal cost c. In this case, given there are N firms, the market share is clearly $s_i = 1/N$. In this case, (16.5) simplifies to give

$$\frac{p - c}{p} = -\frac{1}{N\eta}. \quad (16.6)$$

That is, the price–cost mark-up varies with the demand elasticity η and the number of firms N. For $N = 1$, it is at its largest; that is, the standard monopoly result of $-1/\eta$. As $N \to \infty$, so $p \to c$, the marginal cost price of the competitive industry.[14] This suggests that price increases, ceteris paribus, with concentration. For example, the **Herfindahl index** of industry concentration, H (see Chapter 28 for more details), is defined as the sum of squared market shares: $H = \sum_{i=1}^{N} s_i^2$. This takes the value 0 for perfect competition and 1 for monopoly. Thus the larger the Herfindahl index, the more concentrated the industry. Here, with equal shares, $H = 1/N$. Hence, we could also write (16.6) as

$$\frac{p - c}{p} = -\frac{H}{\eta}, \quad (16.7)$$

[12] The robustness of the result can be debated. First, there are problems regarding the rationing assumptions in the homogeneous case (although this criticism disappears in the case of differentiated goods). Secondly, the model is not robust to other modifications (uncertainty, inventories, etc.).

[13] $\dfrac{p - c_i}{P} = -\dfrac{q_i}{P}\dfrac{dP}{dQ} = -\dfrac{q_i}{Q}\dfrac{Q}{P}\dfrac{dP}{dQ} = -\dfrac{s_i}{\eta}.$

[14] More care has to be taken in developing this type of insight if elasticity is endogenous (rather than constant) and firms are heterogeneous.

thus indicating that price–cost margin increases with concentration.[15] Hence the Cournot model gives the nice prediction that there is a market structure continuum moving from competition on the one hand through increasing levels of oligopolistic interdependence to monopoly at the other.

16.4 Entry and Barriers to Entry

The models discussed in sections 16.2 and 16.3 assume that the number of firms in the oligopoly is fixed, but there is no discussion of what determines that number. The number might be fixed by technical or physical barriers to entry (as, say, with natural diamond or bauxite supplies), or by legal barriers (as, say, with the postal businesses across Europe, where each firm has a local national monopoly, but competes internationally with others). However, in the absence of these artificial factors, the presumption is usually that barriers to entry arise out of the nature of the technology, in conjunction with the overall level of demand. If the minimum efficient scale for production is reasonably large relative to the overall market demand, then just as one can get a natural monopoly, so too one can get a natural oligopoly, in which there is free entry but further entry is unattractive (because the entrant assesses that, post-entry, it would be unable to earn positive profit). Of course, this is perfectly consistent with incumbents currently earning positive profits; a further entrant can depress equilibrium price sufficiently for that entrant to be unable to make a positive profit.

Section 16.4.1 briefly examines a simple model of free-entry oligopoly. Following this, section 16.4.2 illustrates how the Cournot isoprofit curve analysis introduced in section 16.2 can be used to address the issue of entry barriers.

16.4.1 A Free-Entry Cournot Oligopoly

This section relaxes the assumption that the number of firms is fixed and exogenous. The usual free-entry assumption is that entry occurs when potential entrants perceive that entry will be profitable; it ceases when this is no longer the case. If we assume that incumbent and potential entrant firms have access to the same technology and operate efficiently, etc., then a long-run Cournot equilibrium will feature all firms in the industry earning zero profit.[16] This long-run equilibrium is characterized by the first-order conditions (16.4) all holding, and in addition, a zero-profit condition. In a long-run equilibrium, the number of firms in the industry will tend to reflect the level of demand (higher demand means more firms, ceteris paribus) and the structure of costs (for example, higher fixed costs tend to reduce the equilibrium number of firms).

To illustrate what such a solution might look like, I consider a highly simplified model in which all firms are identical, each with constant marginal cost c and fixed cost F, whilst the demand curve features constant elasticity of -1. This means the market demand function takes the form

$$Q = A/p, \qquad (16.8)$$

where $A > 0$ parameterizes the overall level of demand (increase in A shifts the demand curve up and to the right). The individual Cournot firm chooses its output such that (16.6) holds; in this special case, since $\eta = -1$, this takes the simple form

$$\frac{p - c}{p} = -\frac{1}{N}. \qquad (16.9)$$

In long-run equilibrium, each firm earns zero profit.[17] Thus

$$\pi_i = (p - c)q_i - F = 0. \qquad (16.10)$$

All firms are identical, and so produce the same output level: $q_i = q$, constant for all i, so total output is $Q = Nq$. Hence, given $Q = A/p$,

$$q_i = q = \frac{Q}{N} = \frac{A}{Np}. \qquad (16.11)$$

---

[15] Cowling and Waterson (1976) show, in the absence of fixed costs, but with firms having different but constant marginal costs, that industry profits, Π, are given by

$$\Pi \equiv \sum_{i=1}^{n} \pi_i = -RH/\eta,$$

where R is total revenue earned in the industry and H is the Herfindahl index of industrial concentration. This suggests that, ceteris paribus, an industry's profitability is positively related to its concentration level.

[16] Naturally, if there are different cost structures, some firms will earn positive profits in long-run equilibrium.

[17] Ignoring the so-called integer problem. Clearly, the actual number of firms is likely to make some strictly positive level of profit, with the addition of one further firm turning all firms' profits negative.

Using this in (16.10) gives

$$\frac{p - c}{p} = \frac{F}{A}. \tag{16.12}$$

This states that the price–cost mark-up in a free-entry equilibrium increases with the magnitude of fixed costs F, and decreases with the overall level of demand A.[18] Comparing (16.9) and (16.12), we see that

$$N = A / F. \tag{16.13}$$

That is, higher fixed costs reduce the equilibrium number of firms and more demand increases it, as one would expect. Using the above, we can also obtain

$$p = \frac{Ac}{A - F} \tag{16.14}$$

$$q = \frac{A - F}{c} \tag{16.15}$$

$$Q = \frac{A}{p} = \frac{A - F}{c}. \tag{16.16}$$

These tell us that, in the long-run equilibrium, an increase in marginal cost c or fixed cost F, or a decrease in demand A, leads to an increase in price and a decrease in firm and industry output.

The above model serves only to illustrate some ideas; naturally, the detailed comparative statics results are specific to this model specification. However, the analysis illustrates how easily the Cournot model can be extended to incorporate free entry, and highlights some of the factors that are likely to influence the level of competition in such an industry. The reader is referred to Chapter 14 for a more extended discussion of the empirical evidence on the extent to which entry actually affects the level of profitability in an industry.

16.4.2 Barriers to Entry and Entry Deterrence

A game-theoretic approach to entry was discussed in Chapter 14, to which the reader is referred. The following classification was used there (reproduced here for convenience):

Definition 14.5 Blockaded entry occurs when the strategic choices made by the incumbent (price, output, capacity, advertizing, etc.) ignore the threat of entry yet these choices still preclude profitable entry. **Deterred entry** occurs when the firm does take account of the threat of

entry in setting price, output, etc. Finally, **accommodated entry** occurs when the incumbent does not try to prevent entry (because it is more profitable to allow entry than to try to prevent it).

The key question an entrant has to pose is: what happens post-entry? The point is that entry into a monopolized industry creates an oligopoly, so the entrant needs to consider what kind of oligopolistic competition is likely post-entry. The early limit-price models (e.g. Bain 1956, Sylos-Labini 1962) assumed that the incumbent sets a pre-entry price and produces an output level consistent with this. Post-entry, the incumbent is assumed to maintain the same level of output as before. This is termed the **Sylos postulate**.

Clearly, the incumbent needs to choose whether to ignore, deter, or accommodate entry. In Chapter 14, a limit price was calculated, but there was no assessment of whether the incumbent would find it rational actually to choose to implement it. Here, this question is explored in a simple model (first discussed in Dixit 1982). It particularly emphasizes the role of fixed costs (and economies of scale), and how these can create barriers to entry (and induce limit-pricing behaviour).

As in section 16.2, it is assumed that demand is linear and that firms have constant marginal costs, so their reaction functions are straight lines. Positive fixed costs plus constant marginal costs induce a falling average cost curve, in rather similar fashion to the way economies of scale in general do, and it is useful to keep in mind the idea that, in effect, the larger the fixed costs, the greater the extent of economies of scale (the more average costs fall with output). In the absence of fixed costs, the reaction functions stretch all the way from one axis to the other, as depicted in figure 16.5. However, if we introduce fixed costs, this creates a discontinuity in the firm's reaction function. This is because a firm only produces positive output if this earns positive profit. Otherwise, it shuts down and earns zero profit.[19] Thus, consider firm 1 in Figure 16.8; at point $m1$, the firm is a monopolist, and by assumption is earning relatively high profits. As we move up the reaction function, firm 1's profit falls, reaching zero at point α_1. At this point the firm shuts down

---

[18] By contrast, in the fixed-numbers case as examined in sect. 16.3, a change in fixed costs has no effect on equilibrium price.

[19] The nice thing about fixed costs is that they reduce profit without in any way altering the shape or position of the reaction functions (since these are defined by the first-order conditions; fixed costs drop output on differentiation, and thus play no role in determining the equations).

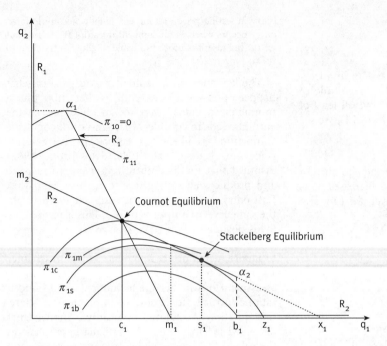

Fig. 16.8 Entry analysis

production; hence the discontinuity in the reaction function ($R1$), which coincides with the vertical axis above point α_1. Naturally, the same idea applies to firm 2, which shuts down at point α_2. Note that, if we increase fixed cost for firm 2, the discontinuity at point α_2 occurs further to the left on its reaction function.

In Figure 16.8, firm 1 is taken to be the incumbent, and firm 2 a potential entrant. Firm 1 has to decide on what output level to produce. Once it has committed itself to this, firm 2 decides whether or not to enter. The idea is that firm 1 may choose an initial output that keeps firm 2 out of the market.

Thus, suppose firm 1 chose the monopoly output level $m1$; then firm 2 would enter and firm 1 would get the profit level π_{1m}. If firm 1 chose the Cournot output level, $c1$, 2 would enter and 1 would get profit level π_{1c}. If firm 1 chose the Stackelberg leader output, $s1$, firm 2 would enter and firm 1 would get profit π_{1s}, whilst if firm 1 produced an output level just greater than $b1$, this would keep firm 2 out of the market, and firm 1 would earn profit π_{1b}. Firm 1 wishes to maximize profit, so, with the diagram as drawn, it will produce output level $q_1 = b1$, and get π_{1b} (since $\pi_{1b} > \pi_{1s} > \pi_{1m} > \pi_{1c}$). This prevents firm 2 from entering; hence $q_2 = 0$. Thus, given the

way the diagram has been drawn, entry is deterred; that is, the incumbent produces more output than if it had simply ignored the threat of entry (in which case it would have produced $m1$).

A little thought should reveal that the outcome depends on the structure of the diagram; in particular, it depends on the size of firm 2's fixed cost, and hence the position of the point α_2. For example, suppose we reduce firm 2's fixed cost; this extends the reaction function along the fine dotted line toward the point x_1; this moves the point $b1$ (and the associated isoprofit line[20]) toward $z1$. When $b1$ becomes greater than $z1$, $\pi_{1b} < \pi_{1s}$ and firm 1 would prefer to choose output level $s1$, the Stackelberg leader output. In such a case, the incumbent is taking into account potential entry, but is accommodating it. Finally, suppose we increase fixed costs for firm 2; this moves point α_2 up the reaction function toward $m2$, and so moves point $b1$ to the left (and so too its isoprofit curve). If $b1$ goes to the left of $m1$, then of course firm 1 does not need to worry about firm 2; firm 1 can choose the monopoly

[20] Note that when firm 1 isoprofit curves move, they must continue to attain a maximum as they cross the reaction function $R1$. Thus a move to the right of point $b1$ also means that curve π_{1b} moves upward everywhere.

output $m1$ and firm 2 stays out (in this case, note that the two reaction functions intersect at the point $m1$, since in this case ($R2$) coincides with the horizontal axis through this point).

To sum up:

Higher fixed cost	$b1 < m1$:	entry blockaded (monopoly pricing)
↕	$m1 < b1 < z1$:	entry deterred (limit pricing)
Lower fixed cost	$b1 > z1$:	entry is accommodated (leader chooses Stackelberg output level)

Thus, the behaviour of incumbents is predicted to depend on the cost structure of the potential entrant. With low fixed cost (low economies of scale), there are low barriers to entry and entry is accommodated (Stackelberg solution). As entrant fixed cost increases, it becomes more likely that entry will be deterred (with a limit price and output being chosen). With still higher fixed costs (still greater economies of scale), it becomes likely that entry will be blockaded; that is, the monopolist can completely ignore potential entry and simply charge the monopoly price.

Naturally there is much more that can be said about entry; much of this concerns the extent to which the incumbent can be pro-active in deterring entry (by investing in excess capacity etc.). These more general issues are discussed in Chapter 14.[21]

16.5 A Case Study: The Oil Industry — Full of Prune Juice?

This section presents a short case study[22] about the trials and tribulations of behaving competitively (and applying 'good incremental reasoning') in oligopolistic markets. This is followed by a discussion of key insights provided by the case.

[21] All the discussion here, and in Chap. 14, on the theory of entry presupposes that the entrants are rational players. One explanation for the observed high failure rates of new entrants is that they are simply not rational. That is, they do not take properly into account the likely consequences of their own behaviour (see Chap. 14 for further discussion).

[22] I seem to have lost track of the origin of this case study.

16.5.1 The Case Study

Bob Plumtree was in the prune juice business. He had his own prune orchard, which produced about half the prunes he needed. He bought the rest and shipped them all to his plant, where he put them through his squeezer, bottled the juice, and sold it for 25p a bottle. He sold the pulp for fertilizer.

Bob liked the prune juice business. Sure, he had competition. There were four other prune juice squeezers in Bob's area. But each had his steady customers, they all charged a fair price, and all were making a good living. And each was getting his share of new business as demand increased. Yes, Bob was happy to be in the prune business. It was a good industry.

One day one of Bob's boys came into his office. 'Look, boss,' he said, 'we're not operating that new squeezer we built a couple of years ago at full capacity.' This wasn't news to Bob. He was a smart businessman. When he had been obliged to expand his facilities to keep up with growing demand, he had looked ahead and provided for future growth by putting in a bigger squeezer than he needed right then. It was more economical to do it that way.

So Bob said, 'I know, but we're meeting our demand, aren't we?'

The boy admitted they were. 'But, boss,' he said, 'I've been doing some figuring,' and he laid a piece of paper on Bob's desk. 'It won't cost us hardly anything to turn out more juice. We won't need any more men at the plant, the same salesmen can handle it. It won't have to carry any overhead. It'll be marginal. We can make it for 15p a bottle instead of the 20p the regular stuff costs us.'

Bob checked the figures, thought a moment, then nodded. 'Yes, I guess at 5p off, the boys ought to be able to get rid of it. Go ahead, speed her up.'

The boys got rid of it—by taking a couple of accounts away from one of Bob's competitors. When the competitor got the news that two of his customers had switched to Bob because his price was 5p lower, he banged his desk and said, 'We can't let Bob run us out of business. Pass the word to all our customers that our price is down 5p as of right now. If Bob can do it, so can we.'

It didn't take long for Bob to learn that the market was down 5p. He silently cursed the stupidity of his competitors and lowered his price to meet the competition.

The next day Bob went out to the plant to see whether there wasn't some way to cut costs. The first thing he noticed was a big pile of prune pulp. 'What's this doing here?' he wanted to know.

'That's the pulp from that marginal-cost stuff we're making,' the boys replied. 'We don't seem to have a market for it.'

Bob was getting annoyed. 'Well, we can't just let it pile up here. Find a market for it.'

The boys found a market for it at a pound a ton off. In a day or two Bob cursed his competitors again, and spent an evening at the office figuring out how he could meet their reduction in the price of pulp and still sell the juice for 15p a bottle. It didn't work out very well.

Everybody in Bob's organization was worried about the state of the prune juice industry generally and about Bob's situation in particular. Everybody wanted to find some way to get into the profit column.

One day, one of Bob's boys came bursting into his office. 'Boss, I think I've got the answer. I've found a prune grower with a big surplus on his hands. He's willing to sell 'em for peanuts.'

'But we've got contracts for all the prunes we need' Bob explained patiently.

'I thought of that, too, boss. But we've still got some spare capacity in that new squeezer. We can buy this distress raw material and put it through our spare capacity. Everything will be marginal and we can make ourselves a nice sweet profit.'

Bob gave the idea a little thought, then said: 'I suppose we'll have to sell this marginal stuff at something off the regular price to dispose of it.'

'Oh, sure,' said the boy. 'I've figured it all out. We can go as low as 12p a bottle on the marginal stuff and still make enough on it to pull us out of the red.'

Time passes. Bob gets called in by his bank.

'Bob,' said the banker, 'it isn't just that you're not paying on the principal, it's that you're not paying the interest either. I'm sorry, but I'm afraid we're going to have to foreclose.'

'Go ahead,' said Bob. 'Nobody can be expected to meet expenses when he has to buck the kind of stupid competition you find in this industry.'

16.5.2 Comments on the Case

On the face of it, this case study illustrates the problem with marginal reasoning. The boys have learned some sound economic principles. They adopt the principle that, if the incremental revenue of an action exceeds the incremental cost of implementing it, then it is worth doing. Apparently, if everybody adopts marginal reasoning, there is simply too much competition, and everyone goes out of business.

So, does this mean that marginal reasoning is fallacious? At a theoretical level, the answer must be an emphatic 'no'; properly carried out, incremental reasoning gives the right answers. If you take account of all the possible ramifications which may ensue from a change, and if the expected incremental revenues outweigh the expected incremental costs, then the decision to go ahead must be sound.[23] The problem in this case study is that the boys did not take into account, in their ex ante calculations, all the effects that arose after the decisions were made. Basically, they did the computation correctly on the cost side, but did not consider the full impact on the revenue side. That is, they focused on the 'marginal stuff' but forgot that there might be a knock-on effect on the rest of the firm's business. Reducing price and stealing a few clients induced a reaction; the reaction led to increased competition on the core business.

One could argue that a properly conducted incremental analysis would have arrived at the correct decision (namely not to go down the price-cutting route). The proper analysis would have weighed the probability of competitor reaction, and judged the revenue and cost consequences of that reaction. This reasoning would have required Bob and the boys to assess the probability of competitor reaction. In effect, the implicit assumption in the case study was that the probability of reaction was zero. In fact, in this type of market, if the boys had asked Bob, he would probably have replied that the likelihood of reaction was close to one. Taking this into account, we can see that the expected loss on the core business would have more than outweighed any potential benefit on the 'marginal stuff'.

However, whilst it is comforting to conclude that incremental reasoning, appropriately specified, always gets the right decision, this is not so comforting in practice. The problem is that half-digested theory can be a dangerous thing. One could argue that incremental reasoning is a dangerous technique—simply because there is a greater probability of making serious errors in the analysis. On the other hand, one could equally argue that not undertaking incremental analysis, and blind adherence to cost-plus philosophy, can equally lead the firm into

---

[23] To be more precise, there are always caveats. Here, risk neutrality is assumed.

bankruptcy. Firms that carry substantial fixed/sunk costs need to understand thoroughly the need to keep the order book ticking over during recessions. This often means going below full cost when tendering for contracts. Refusal to do so can mean an empty order book and foreclosure.[24]

16.6 Co-Operative Oligopoly

A simple-minded oligopoly story that explains why firms collude, and how they collude, goes something like the following:

1. If firms behave competitively, they earn less profit than if they collude.
2. Hence there is an incentive to to do one of the following:
   (a) integrate (vertically or horizontally). Unfortunately, in most developed countries, the state attempts to to control monopoly power by (amongst other things) setting restrictions on allowable mergers and types of integration.
   (b) aim for joint-profit-maximizing collusion (by restraining output and holding price high), either explicitly or tacitly. Unfortunately the state also typically rules out as illegal any form of contractually binding collusive practice. Tacit collusion can be made to work to an extent (despite being illegal), although there is the problem that individual members of the cartel have some incentive to chisel (to agree on the collusive high price, but then discount below this). Naturally, chiselling destroys cartel trust and cohesiveness, and hence its ability to hold prices up.
3. If profit-maximizing collusion proves difficult, firms will often practise some form of non-profit-maximizing collusion. This is typically described as **satisficing** behaviour. Various forms of informal or tacit agreement, usually involving some form of **price leadership**, come under this category.

The first point was established in section 16.1, whilst I discuss in more detail later the ways in which the state tries to intervene (Chapter 28). Accordingly, in what follows, I first focus, in section 16.6.1, on the incentives to set up profit-maximizing collusive (but illegal, hence not contractually binding!) agreements, and the problems that may arise in trying to sustain them. Following this, section 16.6.2 focuses on various forms of (satisficing) price-leadership behaviour.

16.6.1 Cartels

Chamberlin (1929) was one of the first to suggest that, even if **explicit collusion** was made illegal, the repeating nature of the oligopoly game meant that firms could still practice **tacit collusion** so and co-ordinate on higher prices than would be indicated in the above competitive oligopoly models.[25] The point, of course, is that making collusion illegal is likely to be ineffective since it would merely drive it underground. However, if collusion were legal, cartels could form contractually binding agreements. By contrast, with collusion illegal, the agreements have no legal force and may prove unstable.

Essentially, the question whether to remain in a cartel, or cheat on it, amounts to a cost–benefit calculation for the individual firm. Cartel instability turns out to be a strong prediction in the single-period case; in this case, collusion can only be made to stick if it is contractually binding. An individual firm, by secretly reducing price below that agreed by the cartel, will be able to steal market share from the others. Chiselling is, formally, a dominant strategy in a prisoners' dilemma game, as is illustrated in the following numerical example of Cournot duopoly (the incentive to cheat tends to be even greater in a one-shot Bertrand model):

EXAMPLE 16.6 Given the market demand $p = 12 - q$ and two firms, each with a marginal cost of 2 and zero fixed cost, Example 16.3 established that equal-shares, joint-profit-maximizing profits were $\pi_1 = \pi_2 = 12.5$, obtained when each produces $q_1 = q_2 = 2.5$. However, each firm has an incentive to cheat on this agreement (to produce 2.5 each). For example, if firm 2 produces 2.5, then from the reaction function (see Example 16.1), the optimal choice for firm 1 is given as $q_1 = 5 - \frac{1}{2}q_2 = 5 - \frac{1}{2}(2.5) = 3.75$. Total output is then $q = 3.75 + 2.5 = 6.25$ and so price is

---

[24] To put it another way, when seeking the exit from the Labyrinth, and without a thread of Ariadne in your hand, does it pay to snuff out the only candle you happen to have with you?

[25] Prior to this, US anti-trust policy had tended to focus on rendering explicit or contractually binding collusion illegal.

$p = 12 - q = 12 - 6.25 = 5.75$. Firm 1 then makes profit $\pi_1 = (5.75 - 2)3.75 \approx 14.1$ whilst firm 2 earns $\pi_2 = (5.75 - 2)2.5 \approx 9.4$. If both firms cheat and produce 3.75, then $q = 7.5$, $p = 12 - 7.5 = 4.5$, and $\pi_1 = \pi_2 = (4.5 - 2) 3.75 \approx 9.4$. Table 16.1 gives the game strategy tableau associated with these outcomes. It should be clear that this is a classic example of the prisoners' dilemma—each firm has a dominant strategy; whatever the other player does, it is better to cheat and produce 3.75 than to stick to the joint-profit-maximizing agreement of producing 2.5. The consequence is that each cheats and produces 3.75. The outcome is that each only gets 9.4.

Table 16.1 Cartel Instability: The 'Prisoners' Dilemma'

		Firm 2	
		Stick to agreement $q_1 = 2.5$	Cheat on agreement $q_1 = 3.75$
Firm 1	Stick to agreement $q_1 = 2.5$	$\pi_1 = 12.5$, $\pi_2 = 12.5$	$\pi_1 = 9.4$, $\pi_2 = 14.0$
	Cheat on agreement $q_1 = 3.75$	$\pi_1 = 14.0$, $\pi_2 = 9.4$	$\pi_1 = 9.4$, $\pi_2 = 9.4$

Thus it can be argued that cartels are inherently unstable, as there is always an incentive for the members to cheat on the cartel agreement, and, because such agreements are illegal, there can be no legal redress from such chiselling behaviour.

Although one can point to famous instances of such chiselling behaviour (OPEC, in recent years), in practice, tacit collusion is often successfully sustained over considerable periods of time. So what is wrong with the above account of cartel instability? One of the major defects undoubtedly lies in the assumption that there is just one period. In practice, the cartel game involves a longer and uncertain time horizon. It was argued in Chapter 5 that in this case, non-cheating strategies can also be equilibrium strategies. In practice, a richer variety of factors are likely to influence the degree to which cartel price may be sustained in the longer term, as follows.

1. The kinked demand curve theory suggests that oligopolists will co-ordinate on the monopoly price, and then have no incentive to deviate from this (given the conjectures, that no one follows a price rise and everyone follows a price fall).

2. The extent to which price changes can be kept secret clearly matters. There is usually a time period before cheating or chiselling is likely to be discovered; the extent of this is clearly important. Profit taken by chiselling is a function of the time it lasts before discovery. It may be that sufficient profit can be taken from chiselling to more than compensate for any reprisal or punishment by cartel members once they discover the practice.

3. Monitoring is costly. However, increasing the level of monitoring of individual-firm behaviour, by reducing the scope for profitable chiselling, will clearly help to increase cartel stability. This suggests that the cartel may seek organizational structures which improve the ability of monitoring individual behaviour. For example, information may be generated by firms creating trade associations and trade publications (so promoting information about pricing practices).

4. Cartel members may also try to impose **resale price maintenance** to improve price transparency, or to offer **refund guarantees**. Thus the promise to customers that 'if you find the same item cheaper elsewhere, we will refund the difference' (or some multiple of the difference) is a technique by which firms can enlist customers in the **price watch** monitoring of rivals—and it simultaneously reduces other cartel members' incentive to reduce price, given that they will be quickly found out and hence make few additional sales. Thus, what appears to be a benevolent and competitive strategy by the firm can be an integral part of a profoundly anti-competitive practice (a means of sustaining a tacit cartel and monopoly price).

5. Asymmetries between firms make it harder for firms to co-ordinate on price and output shares:

(a) Consider differential costs (say, differential transport costs). It may not be clear what the monopoly price ought to be if different firms have different costs, and this is exacerbated if each firm is unsure of the others' cost structures. Typically, firms may know their own cost structures but will have a poor understanding of that of their competitors. In any bargaining, firms may have incentives to misreport their true costs of production.

(b) Product differentiation also makes chiselling harder to identify, since prices will naturally deviate to some extent to reflect quality differences. Furthermore, cartel members, once a price has been agreed, have an incentive to try to steal market share by offering variations on other (quality) dimensions.

6. The number of firms in the industry naturally may make a difference. Typically, monitoring and enforcement costs (of punishing deviant members) increase and the size of the cartel may need to be large for it to have significant market muscle with the size of the cartel. Cartels with a large number of firms are likely to prove more difficult to sustain over time.

7. Cartel members may not be well modelled as the neo-classical *homo economicus*. Self-interested agents may rationally co-operate, but it can be argued that, empirically, human beings co-operate to a greater extent and manifest a greater sense of fairness (on the average!) than might be predicted by game-theoretic models (see Kagel and Roth 1995). Co-operation is positively correlated with familiarity—and various institutions exist to promote the level of bonding between 'competitors' (trade associations, Rotary clubs, the Masons, etc.). These institutions clearly increase the likelihood that firms will be able to sustain collusive practices.

In practice, cartels are often sustainable, but they are far from profit-maximizing. The most common forms appear to be largely satisficing, involving some form of price leadership, to which I now turn.

16.6.2 Price Leadership

Whilst profit-maximizing collusive practices are difficult to organize, it appears that, in many industries, some level of tacit collusion does exist. In the kinked demand curve theory, each firm considers that, if it were to reduce price, it would lead the industry to reduce prices (as all the others would follow it in order to maintain market share), although no one would follow a price increase. However, I also discussed the case where there were industry-wide cost or demand impacts, when some form of simultaneous adjustment in price might take place (conscious parallelism). In practice, such adjustments typically take place by one firm moving first, and the others following shortly afterwards. This is termed price leadership. Three models of price leadership are typically identified, and I shall briefly discuss each case in turn.

1. *Barometric price leadership.* When firms are of similar size and cost-efficiency, leadership tends to be exercised by a firm which has tacit acceptance within the industry as being good at forecasting industry trends, of having good judgement as to when the time is right for a change in price. This firm is the 'barometer' for the industry (see Markham 1951). Naturally, such leadership can involve some degree of give and take; if the followers think the leader has, say, over-estimated the scope for a price increase, they may only follow partially; in such a case, the leader will be forced to shade back its price. This has happened on several occasions in petrol and cigarette markets for example, (see Earl 1995 for discussion of some interesting cases). It is also true that leadership may be to some extent up for grabs, with different firms taking the lead at different times. The main point is that, when firms are reasonably similar, they will tend to be in relative agreement as to what the best collusive price is likely to be. So long as there is a reasonable degree of transparency regarding individual-firm prices (so reducing the incentive to chisel), the prospects for tacit collusion are probably quite good.

2. *The low-cost producer as price leader.* Less efficient firms are perhaps less likely to wish to provoke a price war (being relatively more vulnerable to getting into financial distress). It follows that the lowest-cost producer can act as a price leader, using the implicit threat of a price war to back up its position. For example, Saudi Arabia has often used this tactic over the years when trying to discipline members of the OPEC cartel. Carrying out the threat of entering into a price war has the benefit of establishing a reputation that the firm means business. In terms of a model, effectively the other, higher-cost firms perceive that they face a kinked demand curve. They expect that, if they charge a higher price, no one will follow and they will simply lose market share, whilst a price reduction will be followed, and possibly worse, an even lower price might be imposed on them. Referring to Figure 16.1, we can interpret MC_1 as the marginal cost curve of the low-cost leader, with other firms having a higher MC curve. The low-cost leader perceives that it faces the *mutatis mutandis* demand curve D_1D_2, and maximizes profit by setting $MR = MC_1$. This determines the market price as p. The other firms, perceiving the kink, are happy to go along with this price. Clearly, if the leader suffers a fluctuation in cost (or demand), it will adjust its price to maintain $MR = MC_1$; the other firms will simply follow.

3. *The dominant-firm model.* When there is a

dominant firm in competition, with a set of small price-taking firms, the dominant firm sets a price, taking into account that, the higher the price it sets, the larger the output of the competitive fringe will be, and so the smaller the residual demand for its own sales will be. This model is discussed in Chapter 14.

All the above models suggest that at least one of the firms is approximately maximizing profits. However, in practice, the adjustments are typically much more approximate, and much of the price behaviour in these forms of price leadership can be described as satisficing. That is, given the difficulties of optimizing responses, firms merely aim for a satisfactory performance level and some degree of market stability.

16.7 Summary

This chapter has attempted to give an overview of some of the more basic models which seek to explain firm behaviour in oligopolistic industries. I began in section 16.2 with an outline of the kinked demand curve theory (which suggests that prices may be more stable in such industries, relative to other market structures). This was followed by an extended discussion of Cournot, Bertrand, and Stackelberg models. The general insight from these was that competition erodes profitability; furthermore, as revealed in the analysis in section 16.3, the greater the number of firms involved, the more competitive the industry tends to be. Section 16.4 looked at the determinants of the number of firms in an oligopolistic industry, and also at barriers to entry and entry-limiting behaviour by incumbents (it was suggested that fixed costs or economies of scale tend to increase entry barriers). Section 16.5 examined a case study (illustrating the dangers of an uncritical use of incremental reasoning), whilst 16.6 explored the incentives toward, and difficulties in maintaining, cartels and tacit collusion to restrain output and support higher prices.

16.8 Review Questions

1. Examine the interrelationship between the kinked demand curve theory and price leadership.

2. Show that, given the assumptions in the model, the Stackelberg equilibrium is in fact a Nash equilibrium. Examine the importance of commitment in this model.

3. Suppose, in a two-firm duopoly, that market demand is given as $p = 20 - 3q$, firm 1 has a marginal cost of 4 and a fixed cost of 10, whilst firm 2 has a marginal cost of 8 and a fixed cost of 1. Is there a Cournot equilibrium? (Hint: check whether the firms earn non-negative profits in equilibrium.) Now suppose firm 1 is an incumbent monopolist, whilst firm 2 is a potential entrant, as in the model described in section 16.4.2. What output (and price) will the incumbent choose, and what kind of strategy is this? (Hint: study firm's 1 and firm 2's profit levels as firm 1 chooses the monopoly, Stackelberg, or entry-preventing output levels, etc.).

4. 'Cartels are inherently unstable.' Are they? Examine the factors that are likely to affect cartel stability.

16.9 Further Reading

Koutsoyiannis (1979) gives a fairly detailed discussion of traditional oligopoly models (Cournot, Bertrand, and Stackelberg), whilst Tirole (1993) and Kreps (1990) are excellent though rather more advanced (but still very readable) references on game theory, oligopoly, and entry. Dixit's (1979, 1982) papers on entry in oligopoly are both short and highly readable. See also Utton (1970) on concentration in industry and Scherer (1980) on price leadership. For further discussion and references on the empirical side of entry in oligopoly, see Chapter 14 and the further reading discussed there.

17 Some Alternative Theories of the Firm

Objectives To review alternatives to the profit-maximization hypothesis and to consider the determinants of the structure and boundaries of the firm.

Prerequisites None.

Keywords agency costs, agent, asymmetry of information, control, economies of scope, expense preference, explicit contracts, free riding, hierarchy, implicit contracts, managerial discretion, minimum acceptable level of profit, ownership, principal, principal–agent problem, quality uncertainty, reward structure, sales revenue maximization, shirking, teams, teamwork, transactions costs.

17.1 Introduction

Early neo-classical theory characterized the firm as a 'black box', an entity which transforms inputs into outputs in the pursuit of maximum profit. This is a convenient characterization when tackling issues such as pricing, output, entry, etc., since it sidesteps unnecessary detail regarding the firm's internal structure and its contractual and organizational foundations. Neo-classical theory suggests that the optimal size of the firm is determined simultaneously with the number of firms in an industry; in a free-entry equilibrium, size and number are determined by the extent of demand for the product on the one hand, and the structure of the technology involved on the other. That is the extent to which the firm features economies of scale and scope. I have discussed the role of economies of scale in the context of single-product firms in Chapter 14. **Economies of scope** occur when it proves cheaper to produce several products in an integrated process rather than producing those products separately.[1] The existence of economies of scale creates a drive toward larger production units, whilst economies of scope create pressure toward integrated multi-product production. The quest for monopoly rents also gives an impetus toward such integration. Multi-product firms have greater capacity for cross-subsidizing products, and this can increase their capacity to practice predatory pricing, as well as other monopolistic practices such as product bundling where two products can only be purchased together and not separately (as, for example, with telephone line rental; directory books come as part of the overall telecom package). Neo-classical theory also suggests that the internalization of externalities may give some impetus to firm integration (externalities are discussed in some detail in Chapter 27). An externality occurs when the actions of one agent or firm have spillover effects on other agents or firms (pollution is a classic example). In such cases the market outcome is often inefficient. Integration can be beneficial because it internalizes the externality (it makes the polluter consider the impact of the pollution, since this now has impacts on another part of the same organization).

If we ask what limits the size of the firm, the above focus on technology, demand, externalities,

---

[1] If $C(q_1, q_2)$ denotes the total cost of producing output levels q_1, q_2, then the cost function is said to manifest economies of scope if $C(q_1, q_2) < C(q_1, 0) + C(0, q_2)$ for any $q_1, q_2 > 0$. This simply means that any two stand-alone firms could increase their total profit by merging. Notice that economies of scope are a special case of the general definition of cost subadditivity; a cost function is strictly subadditive if $C(\mathbf{q}) < C(\mathbf{q_1}) + C(\mathbf{q_2}) + \ldots +$ $C(\mathbf{q_n})$ for $q_1, q_2, \ldots, q_n > 0$ where $q_1, q_2, \ldots, q_n$ are output vectors and $\mathbf{q} = \mathbf{q_1} + \ldots + \mathbf{q_n}$ (see Chap. 14). That is, for the two-product case, $\mathbf{q_i} = (q_{i1}, q_{i2})$, where q_{ij} is the ith plant's output of product $j = 1, 2$. Subadditivity merely means that it is cheaper to produce all the multi-product output in a lump than in smaller combinations.

etc. suggests no obvious reason why the firm cannot monopolize the market. After all, if there are technological diseconomies of scale associated with a single plant, there is nothing to stop the firm from simply choosing multi-plant operation. Clearly, it is necessary to look inside the black box to see if there are organizational diseconomies associated with scale which ultimately limit firm size.

The idea that economic analysis can be brought to bear on the internal organization of production has arguably been one of the more exciting developments in the last twenty years or so, as the neo-classical methodology has sought to 'open the box' (for example, with the development of game theory and agency models and with the incorporation and systematization of earlier ideas from a variety of sources, notably behavioural and transactions-cost theories') regarding organizational architecture. Consider the following questions:

1. Given the observed organizational structure of firms, what goals would we expect them to pursue, and with what consequences?

2. What constitutes optimal organizational design and how does this relate to the firm's overall choice of corporate strategy?

3. Why do the firms have the organizational structure and boundaries that are observed to be prevalent in practice?

Early work on **managerial discretion** (Baumol 1959, Marris 1964, Williamson 1964) focused on question 1. It recognized the divorce of **ownership** from **control** in much of corporate enterprise, and constructed models in which management (meaning top management, or the chief executive officer, the CEO) had goals which were not necessarily aligned with those of the owners (the shareholders). Because in practice the control exerted by owners was weak, managers had discretion to pursue their own goals.

However, this early work on managerial discretion can still be characterized as black-box economics. That is, the objective function of the firm is changed from one of profit maximization to something else, but there is no analysis of the processes that occur within the box. Question 2 is more fundamental; it asks whether economic analysis can be brought to bear on the design of organizational architecture. Naturally, the answer to this is 'yes', and in section 17.2 I give a sketch of the general principles involved here (this is a prelude to a more detailed study of organizational architecture in Chapters 29–31).

Finally, question 3 asks why we observe what we observe. The neo-classical story (particularly associated with the 'Chicago school'[2]) tends to focus on the idea of a competitive evolutionary process which ultimately weeds out the weak and allows only the strong (the more efficient) to survive. To the extent that this is true, it follows that what we observe in the market place must be efficient. Thus the observed organizational architecture and boundary of the firm exist because they are the most efficient economically. If this evolutionary theory holds, it suggests that our answers to question 2 ought to explain why the organizational forms observed in practice are in fact the most efficient.[3]

Section 17.2 begins with an overview of the modern approach to organizational architecture and optimal firm size. This approach focuses on the pros and cons of integration versus outsourcing, and of teams versus hierarchies within a transactions and agency costs framework. (A more detailed treatment of this type of analysis will be given in Part VII, i.e. Chapters 29–32.) Section 17.3 then gives a brief review of earlier work on managerial discretion and related theories whilst section 17.4 reconsiders the traditional profit maximization hypothesis.

17.2 The Modern Theory of the Firm

What is a firm? The traditional neo-classical model took it to be simply a black box that transforms inputs into outputs. The more modern view still reduces *homo sapiens* to *homo economicus* (that is, it believes that the best model of individuals views them as creative individuals concerned with maximizing their own utility) but now takes the position that it is worth looking inside the box to see how such agents are likely to interact with each other.

A typical economic process uses factors of

---

[2] In this context, writers such as Armen Alchian, Ronald Coase, and Harold Demsetz; see sect. 17.8 for references.

[3] The Chicago view is often criticized as 'Panglossian'; that is, much of their work can be seen as trying to find explanations for why the present arrangement is the most efficient of all possible arrangements (otherwise, competition would have weeded it out). However, there is clearly much merit in trying to explain why a present arrangement works. This of course is what management gurus do all the time; they observe that a particular practice is highly successful and then seek to explain why it is—with a view to showing others how they can profitably follow. Management gurus rarely invent completely novel organizational ideas.

production (land, labour, capital goods, etc.) to transform raw materials through intermediate goods into finished goods, which are then distributed to the final customer.[4] Now if every transformation required only one person to undertake it, then it would be possible to produce everything without the need for firms. Markets would suffice; all necessary inputs for any given product or service could be purchased and assembled by some given individual. However, in practice,

1. Some things require **teamwork** to be produced at all, and some things are simply more efficiently produced using teamwork (because of the economies associated with specialization etc.).

2. Markets are not for free. Although the market is a powerful co-ordinating device, there are a range of **transactions costs** associated with market transactions.

These observations suggest that the firm exists to foster teamwork and the reduction of transactions costs. The firm is viewed as an administrative and multi-layered complex involving both hierarchy and teamwork. A central feature of the firm is that it is an independent legal entity which is the nexus for a whole range of bilateral contractual relations (between the firm and its owners, managers, workers, suppliers, etc.).

17.2.1 Transactions Cost Minimization

Coase (1937) argued that the firm exists in order to internalize what otherwise would be arm's length market transactions, and that this would occur whenever internalization reduced the associated transactions costs. Thus, whether it is the market or the firm that is the more efficient transactional form, depends on the nature of the transaction. These forms are discussed in turn.

(a) Why Markets?

The price mechanism, Adam Smith's 'invisible hand', is an impressive method for the organization of production and distribution in itself, as illustrated by the following example.

EXAMPLE 17.1 In the competitive market economy, decentralized decision-makers are co-ordinated by

the price mechanism. The idea is that the 'invisible hand' cheaply and effectively guides these decision-makers to make the most of their own specific knowledge. Hayek (1945) memorably wrote about the co-ordinating power of the price mechanism; in one example, he considers the impact of the loss of a supply of tin, or the development of a new use for tin. As a consequence, the forces of demand and supply (contraction of supply in the former case, expansion of demand in the latter) lead to a rise in the price of tin. This then motivates the search for new sources and supplies (including recycling), whilst simultaneously, existing users are encouraged to economize on the use of tin. All these efforts re-establish a new equilibrium price such that this price again represents the marginal value to buyers and marginal cost to sellers. As Hayek emphasizes, only necessary information is imparted; no one needs to know why the price has moved; it suffices only to know that it has moved.

The power of the market lies in its ability to harness the specific and local knowledge of individuals operating at the sharp end. In the above example, the market stimulates creativity in the search for new supplies, new technologies for recycling, and so on. By contrast, a central planner has great difficulty in making the most of specific knowledge and local creativity. The administrative/planning processes tend to stifle creativity, impair motivation, and induce sclerosis. This explains, so the story goes, the demise of the old USSR (and the increasing marketization of China).

(b) Why Firms?

Of course, if internalization and planning processes were as ineffective at the firm level as they appear to have been at the level of the nation state, one might wonder why there are any firms at all. Yet, as a matter of empirical fact, substantially more economic activity takes place within firms than in arm's length market transactions. According to transactions cost theory, the rationale for this internalization is that it avoids the transactions costs of arm's length trading. Thus, arm's length exchange requires that the firm has personnel to effect the buying and selling and the managing of both debtors and creditors; in addition to this there are the extra costs when exchange goes wrong—markets have to be underpinned by a judicial or legal system (the law of contract etc.). Some portion of these latter costs

---

[4] One might think that some services hardly use any raw materials, but this is usually a matter of degree. For example, a massage requires premises, oils, a bench, etc. as well as a labour input.

may be funded through the public purse (from funds ultimately obtained through taxation etc.) and hence will not be viewed by the firm as relevant to its decisions—however, many legal processes are in part or in whole funded by the parties involved, and these are clearly decision-relevant costs (to be avoided if possible). Through internalizing transactions, the associated transactions costs are reduced or avoided.

Coase's (1937) insight was that transactions, whether internal or arm's length (market transactions), involve contracting costs, and that the firm exists to reduce these:

1. *By simplifying the contracts involved.* The firm exists as an independent legal entity; it becomes the *nexus of bilateral contractual relationships* (between itself and its employees, shareholders, suppliers etc.). The bilateral nature of these contracts simplifies things; without the firm, production and distribution would typically require complex contracts involving several (more than 2) parties.

2. *By allowing incomplete contracting.* The existence of firms avoids the need for extensive formal contract development and enforcement, as would be required if all production and distribution was done through markets. The firm internalizes the transactions costs involved in having to draw up, monitor, and enforce explicit contracts. A market contract involves a specification of the various conditions of exchange (price, quantity, time, place, etc.), the rights of the parties on either side of the transaction, and so on. For many of the transactions taking place within an organization, there is no written **explicit contract**; however, there are still unwritten or **implicit contracts**. Explicit contracts are costly to write, monitor, and enforce; with implicit contracts, many of these costs are reduced (although there is still a need for monitoring and control—some transactions costs still exist). Coase (1937) argued that whether we observe exchange at arm's length or within an organizational structure depends on which method has lower transactions costs.

The above discussion might suggest that internalization always reduces transactions costs. However, this is not necessarily the case. As noted in example 17.1, the price mechanism is good at motivating individuals to make the most of their creativity and specific knowledge. Internalization means that information has to flow through hierarchies. This in itself creates costs, in that (i) mechanisms are required for such information flows (meetings etc.), (ii) there are problems with giving individuals incentives to pass on truthful and timely information, and (iii) there are implementation costs associated with decisions. So, for some decisions, the price mechanism may be preferable. The optimal boundary of the firm is then defined as that which minimizes overall transactions costs; activities and exchanges are drawn into the firm, the organization, only to the extent that this reduces the associated transactions cost.

(c) What Determines Which is Best: Internal or Market-based Transactions?

Both parties to a transaction have specific information concerning that transaction; what they know and do not know will often influence whether the transaction is more efficiently dealt with at arm's length, as a market transaction, or inside an organization. When the product quality and characteristics can easily be observed, arm's length market transactions are likely to be the most efficient way of organizing the transaction. This is especially the case in perfect competition, where the product is homogeneous, entirely standardized. However, if there is **quality uncertainty**, there may be benefits from internalizing the transaction.[5] A classic example of quality uncertainty is that of the second-hand car trade. The seller may know that her car has been driven carefully, been fully serviced and garaged, etc., but has the problem of convincing the buyer that these things are in fact true; the buyer cannot easily judge the quality of the car. Where there is an **asymmetry of information**, as in this case, there can be a gain in efficiency from bringing both parties into the same organization (for example, as when parents give their offspring the second car). The problems associated with arm's length trading of such products is discussed in more detail in Chapter 29.

---

[5] Although arm's length buyers and sellers do have an incentive to attempt to reduce the uncertainty involved—for example, with fresh fruit and vegetables, the product is typically shown for sale in an unpackaged form (or in see-through forms of packaging), so that the purchaser can actually inspect the quality of the product. In such a case there is good reason for not packaging, although there is a trade-off; the cost to the retailer of not packaging is that packaging usually helps in stacking materials in a given space, thus reducing storage costs and damage from handling etc.

17.2.2 Teams and Hierarchies

The firm may be a complex structure, but its fundamental building blocks are **teams** and **hierarchies** (whilst the cement is the specification of decision authority at each level and of the mechanisms used for motivating and monitoring individual performance). The pros and cons of these are discussed in turn.

(a) Teamwork

Team membership may be non-hierarchical; that is, membership of equals, peers, although hierarchy can exist, and certainly it often does at an informal level. The essence of teamwork is not so much that it is conducted by a set of peers or equals, but that the productivity of each individual member of the team is hard to define.

Definition 17.1 Teamwork is a mode of operation in which the individual outputs of team members cannot be separately identified.

In principle, it might seem possible to divide up any manufacturing process into its smallest component parts; if each part can be produced by an individual, it would seem possible for these components to be traded in markets, with anyone who wishes to combine such components simply buying them on the open market. Each transaction here is simply a contract between a buyer and a seller, and there is no obvious need for a firm or team. However, whilst individuals can produce some goods (notably services, such as gardening, hairdressing, and doing the books), many goods benefit from— or require—teamwork.

1. *Teamwork required.* Component production may be simply beyond the scope of the individual. The minimum size of a team required to undertake a particular task would thus appear to define the minimum size of a firm.
2. *Teamwork beneficial.* With many types of technology, a larger output can be had from teamwork than from individuals working independently (in particular, because of the economies that arise out of specialization and integrated production; see Chapter 10). This simply suggests that the optimal size of the team may correspond to some notion of efficient scale (that is, the scale at which average cost is minimized).

The economics of teams revolves around the following trade-off: teamwork, ceteris paribus, often generates proportionately greater output, but also gives greater opportunities for shirking and free riding. The problem is that, since in team production the concept of individual output is not meaningful, it is relatively difficult to assess how much reward is due to each team member. If team members are rewarded equally, or get a fixed share of the team's total output, then each has some incentive to **shirk** or **free ride** (this problem is discussed in greater detail below in section 17.2.3).[6] The point is that small teams can engender team spirit, with all parties pulling for the good of the team; however, this form of moral suasion works only to an extent, and is rapidly dissipated as the team gets larger.

(b) Hierarchy

In comparison with teamwork, a hierarchy necessarily involves a boss–subordinate relationship:

Definition 17.2 A simple **hierarchy** exists when each subordinate has a single boss. The authority wielded by a boss over her subordinates is typically specified through the job descriptions and employment contracts of the parties involved.

Hierarchy is the mode of operation favoured by the military, for the simple reason that it offers rapid response in decision-making and also a greater degree of accountability than the alternative of decision-making by team or committee (where by definition no one individual is responsible for the decision). Greater accountability allows for more direct incentive schemes, and hence greater commitment from the individuals involved. Shirking and free riding can, of course, occur in hierarchical structures, just as in teams; subordinates do not necessarily pursue wholeheartedly the goals their superiors set for them. However, the problems of motivation and efficiency are probably less severe in this type of structure. Hierarchical decision-making, when compared with team decision-making, may prove faster, more responsive, and less costly to implement (fewer personnel required), but there are potential drawbacks. Committees are more likely to consider a wider range of alternatives, and to appraise more carefully and securely the pros and cons of each alternative (because teams bring a range

---

[6] Undergraduate students may not have much experience of the world of work, but with the increasing use of group assignments, they quickly become aware of just how much like *homo economicus* their fellow-students can be. Team selection then becomes the issue. (Students in one department at our university appealed when they were given team allocations they didn't like.)

of skills to the process). Broadly speaking, one might expect committees or teams to be involved in decision-making when getting the decision right is critical (as for example when the board of directors debates the future strategy of the firm).

(c) The Origins of Hierarchy and the Role of the Owner or Entrepreneur

Alchian and Demsetz (1972) argue that the problem of free riding in teams explains the existence of hierarchy in organizations. The point is that since an individual's contribution to team output cannot easily be measured, there is a need to try to monitor the individual's input, or effort. Whilst it is possible to elect a monitor from existing team members, there is the problem that this member still has an incentive to shirk; the question remains of who monitors the monitors. Alchian and Demsetz suggest that giving an individual ownership of the residual income from the team's productivity (after payments to team members) gives that individual the motivation to monitor the team members efficiently. The team as a whole can then benefit from the ensuing increase in overall productivity. The idea still makes sense if there are several layers of hierarchy (in which individuals at each level are responsible for monitoring those of the level below), although there are potential agency problems at each intermediate level (see section 17.2.3).

17.2.3 Agency Costs

The so-called **Principal–agent problem** concerns the bilateral relationship between a boss (**principal**) and a subordinate (**agent**) when one (or both) individuals have imperfect information. Usually, the agent has specific and more detailed knowledge than the principal about the task the principal wishes the agent to do, and the principal can only partially observe the effort or output produced by the agent. Given the assumption that individuals are self-interested utility maximizers, if the agent is offered a flat rate of pay, independent of inputs or outputs, the agent will have an incentive to shirk or free ride (just as in teamwork). The principal–agent problem is viewed as that of designing a **reward structure**, based on those elements which it is possible for the principal to observe, so as to induce the agent to be more productive (from the perspective of the principal). The general idea is that individuals only work hard or productively when they perceive

some reward for it.[7] In the case where output is some form of physical product or service, incentive pay can be based on the amount produced. Likewise, if owners want managers to act in their interests, reward structures which incorporate elements of profit-related pay or share options can prove helpful. There is still the question of how much of an individual's overall pay is a fixed sum, and how much is incentive pay or piece rate. Incentive pay is risky (since the pay can fluctuate with performance and often also external factors); agents are typically more risk-averse than principals, so risk sharing also has to be considered (risk sharing involves reducing the extent of incentive pay—see Chapter 29 for an explicit analysis of this idea).

Managers typically are unable to monitor fully the activities of subordinates (both on the input and output side), and the same applies to shareholders; a firm's top management has greater specific knowledge regarding how well the firm could have performed vis-à-vis its actual performance. Thus at each level in the hierarchy, the agency problem is one which involves monitoring effort, efficiency, productivity, etc. and trying to induce 'good behaviour' by designing appropriate reward systems based on what can in fact be observed. Clearly, there is a cost–benefit analysis required; monitoring is costly, and the benefits that then flow from introducing incentives based on monitoring have to be balanced against the costs of that level of monitoring. (In practice, this type of design cost–benefit analysis is not typically conducted using specific monetary figures, but rather qualitatively, using orders of magnitude; that is, judgements can often be made that X is larger than Y.)

The above discussion has been very much at the overview level; further consideration of this modern theory of the firm is given in Part VII, which focuses in detail on the design of organizational architecture. Of course, it is worth emphasizing that transactions and agency cost considerations are not the only considerations; as mentioned in section 17.1, there are also plant economies of scale and the quest for monopoly rents (through integration and expansion of the product range) to take into account when considering the boundaries of the firm and how it should be structured.

---

[7] There is of course much debate as to whether incentives work or not—or indeed, whether they work too well. See Chap. 29.

17.3 Some Earlier Theories of the Firm

This section briefly reviews the early work on managerial-discretion and behavioural theories of the firm. The discussion in section 17.2.3 suggested that there was a natural role for an owner of a firm as the individual who then has an interest in motivating and monitoring the monitors. However, it would appear that transactions-costs minimization and efficient-scale considerations often make for very large units; as a consequence, ownership is rarely by a single individual. So, whilst the idea of ownership being a motivational device is appealing, ownership in practice is more typically by a group of shareholders who usually play no active part in the day-to-day business of the firm; that is, ownership is divorced from control.

For many firms, the number of shareholders is large, with many holding only a very small percentage of the overall value of the firm's equity. Although they own the firm, they do not control it; control is delegated to a board of directors, typically fronted by a CEO (chief executive officer) or MD (managing director). This managerial team takes all the major strategic decisions for the firm, there being a hierarchical structure of management from top management through middle management down to the 'shop floor'. The key feature of such chains of command is asymmetric and imperfect information. At each level in the hierarchy, bosses face a principal–agent control problem. In the managerial discretion models, the focus is purely on the agency problem arising at the interface between owners (shareholders) and top management (there is no consideration of the problem further down the hierarchy).

It is conventional to argue that shareholders want top management to maximize profit and hence to maximize the market value of the company. Management, by contrast, want other things (high salaries, 'perks', on-the-job leisure, job security, etc.) and have the scope to pursue these things because of

(i) *Imperfect and asymmetric information*: managers typically know much more than shareholders about the firm's operations and its performance capabilities. It is difficult for shareholders to monitor performance (it is possible to observe past performance, but it is more difficult to know how well the firm could have done if it had been managed to achieve its full potential).

(ii) *Transactions costs*: even if shareholders can see that management is under-performing, it remains difficult and costly for them to do much about it (as a consequence, managerial incompetence or under-performance has to be fairly radical before shareholders are likely to be motivated to undertake any action).[8]

The upshot of this is that managers have some leeway or discretion to pursue their own goals rather than those of shareholders.[9] This observation led to the development of a variety of managerial-discretion and related models[10] in the 1960s and 70s, in which it was postulated that managers aimed to maximize their own utility subject to the constraint of not damaging profits too much (since this might trigger a take-over, or shareholder action to oust the board). These models did not explicitly model the sources of the control problem or of how owners might try to deal with it (for example, by setting incentive pay); the separation of ownership from control was simply taken as an observed or stylized fact. (By contrast, the modern theory uses the principal–agent perspective to explore the ways in which owners can create reward structures and remuneration packages to motivate managers to operate more in the interests of shareholders.)

17.3.1 Baumol's Sales Revenue Maximization Hypothesis

Baumol (1958) argues that the goals supposedly pursued by managers (salaries, status, power, prestige, security, etc.) are all highly correlated with sales revenue. As a consequence, he suggested firms behave as if they have the objective of **sales revenue maximization**. Clearly, a firm which aims to maximize sales revenue will set a lower price and produce a greater output than would be the case under profit maximization.[11] The lower the realized

---

[8] It is often argued that the threat of take-over is more relevant than the threat from existing shareholders—but even take-over raiders need to make a significant investment (of time and effort) in studying the company's performance and in assessing its potential performance—and in trying to buy up a sufficient shareholding etc.

[9] Leech and Leahy (1991) give some empirical evidence on just how substantial the divorce of ownership from control actually is.

[10] There has been a variety of extensions to the basic models in which the objective is seen as that of maximizing managerial utility; see e.g. Gravelle and Katz (1976), Yarrow (1976).

[11] In the extension to advertizing (a major element in Baumol's original work; discussed in Chap. 26), it is shown that there is also a tendency for such firms to spend more on advertizing.

level of profit, the greater the extent to which a firm is visibly under-performing, and the greater the incentive to do something about it. The idea is that management is increasingly at risk from either shareholder action, or take-over raiders, if the firm earns below a certain **minimum acceptable level of profit**, or *MALP*. Thus the pursuit of sales is tempered by the need to earn enough profit.

The model supposes that the *MALP* is a clear-cut value. That is, the Baumol model supposes that there is a knife-edge figure such that if profit is above this figure there is no chance of intervention, whilst if profit is below it then intervention is certain. This is clearly not realistic; in practice management are more likely to believe that the probability of take-over or shareholder intervention continuously decreases as profit performance is improved; that is, there is no sudden intervention-determining profit level. This point is reconsidered at the end of section 17.3.1.

In the absence of any profit constraint, the firm maximizes revenue by choosing price p_R and output q_R such that $MR = 0$, as depicted in Figure 17.1.[12] This maximizes revenue but pays no attention to the resulting profit (which could even be negative at this combination of price and quantity). In the figure, at price p_R the firm actually earns a profit level π_R. If we denote the *MALP* as $\bar{\pi}$, then the firm is modelled as choosing p, q so as to maximize revenue R, subject to profit $\pi \geq \bar{\pi}$.

If the *MALP* happened to be at a level such as $\bar{\pi}_2$, for example, then clearly the unconstrained solution (p_R, q_R) applies; that is, revenue is maximized by setting $MR = 0$, at which point $\pi_R > \bar{\pi}_2$ and the profit constraint does not bind. However, if the *MALP* is higher, at say $\bar{\pi}_1$, then the firm needs to raise price (to p_1), thus restricting output (to q_1) in order to achieve this level of profit. However, so long as the *MALP* is less than the maximum attainable profit, the Baumol firm sets a price below the profit-maximizing level.

The Baumol sales-revenue-maximizing firm and the profit-maximizing firm behave rather differently when environmental variables change; some simple cases are illustrated in Figure 17.2. Panel (*a*) gives the consequence of an increase in fixed costs, or an increase in lump-sum profit tax (a windfall tax?); such a change causes the profit curve to fall everywhere by the amount of the increase. Panel (*b*) gives the effect of an increase in the corporate tax rate (an

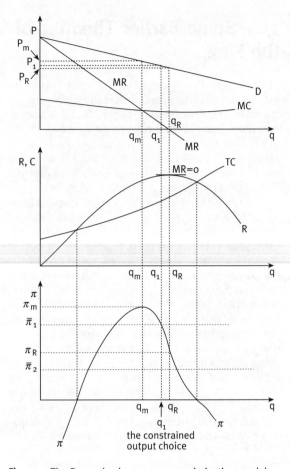

Fig. 17.1 The Baumol sales revenue maximization model

increase in the tax rate reduces profit proportionately). In both cases (*a*) and (*b*), the Baumol firm reduces output (and increases price) whilst a monopolist would change neither price nor output. Panel (*c*) illustrates the effect of the imposition of a per unit sales tax (or VAT); this causes a fall in the net profit function which is proportional to the level of output (a larger drop as output increases, as indicated in the figure); the impact of this is to induce a change in output of both the Baumol firm and the profit maximizer; however, it is fairly clear that the Baumol firm is more sensitive to a change in such a tax.

If the *MALP* constraint binds, then, because profit is now of concern, the firm will be cost-efficient. However, notice that in this simple version of the Baumol model,[13] if the *MALP* constraint does not

---

[12] The structure of this diagram should be readily understandable; if not, consult Fig. 8.14.

[13] Baumol focused more on sales revenue maximization in the presence of advertizing; this is discussed in Chap. 26.

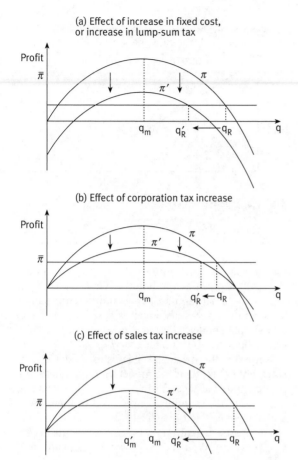

(a) Effect of increase in fixed cost, or increase in lump-sum tax

(b) Effect of corporation tax increase

(c) Effect of sales tax increase

Fig. 17.2 The Baumol firm: some comparative statics results

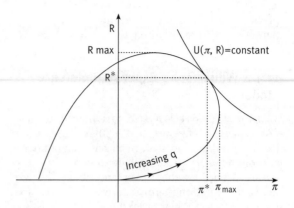

Fig. 17.3 Alternative version of the Baumol model

welfare loss associated with such a firm (and hence less reason for intervention, a point discussed further in Chapter 28).[14]

One of the weaknesses of the original model is that it suggests management prefers more sales to less, and cares nothing for profit—until the latter falls below the *MALP*, when suddenly profit is all-important. In practice one would expect management to be concerned about both profit and revenue; the former because it reduces the risk of take-over and loss of a job, the latter for all the reasons Baumol cites (see above). Thus a natural way to improve the modelling of the sales-revenue-maximization hypothesis is to assume that managers behave as if they maximize a managerial utility function of the form $U(\pi, R)$, where utility is increasing in both and R, with indifference curves in space having the usual form (convex to the origin; see Chapter 8). This model is illustrated in Figure 17.3. In this figure, the locus of attainable combinations of π and R is derived from Figure 17.1. That is, when output is zero, both π and R are zero. As output is increased, both π and R increase, until π reaches a maximum (whilst R is still increasing). As output is further increased, π starts to fall whilst R increases to reach its maximum value. Further increases in output lead to both π and R falling (with π going negative as R approaches zero). The optimum is characterized by the usual tangency solution; it clearly involves less than maximum revenue and less than maximum profit; output is thus clearly higher, and hence price lower than for the pure

bind, then the firm has no incentive to be cost-efficient (since it is by assumption solely concerned with sales when the profit constraint does not bind); that is, the firm could be cost-inefficient in an unconstrained equilibrium. This is clearly not very realistic; as mentioned earlier, ceteris paribus, managers will always have some preference for more profit rather than less (since increasing profit reduces the probability of intervention), so it might be reasonable to conclude that the firm is cost-efficient even in the unconstrained solution.

The above discussion is of some significance from a welfare perspective (and hence, a perspective of regulatory intervention); the point is that the Baumol firm is likely to be cost-efficient and is likely to set a price below that of the profit-maximizing level. This means there is a lower level of monopoly

---

[14] The reduction in welfare loss clearly depends on the level of *MALP* set, which in turn depends on the state of competition in the industry, the concentration of shareholder power, etc.

profit maximizer. Thus the essential features of the Baumol thesis remain intact, as one would expect.

17.3.2 Williamson's Expense Preference Model

Williamson (1964) suggested that managers manifest **expense preference**; that is they derive utility from expenditure on staff, managerial emoluments, and discretionary profits (where discretionary profits are defined as those over and above the level necessary for long-term survival). Profits may matter because a higher level reduces the risk of management being embarrassed either by adverse environmental fluctuations (fall in product demand etc.) or risk of take-over, or because of the presence of profit-related pay. Excess staffing may be attractive in part because it increases the dimensions of the managerial pyramid (and hence salaries at the upper end), but also because extra staff can help to reduce the pressure on the manager concerned, who then has more time for on-the-job leisure. Managerial perquisites, such as company cars, executive washrooms, the Van Gogh in the boardroom, are self-evidently attractive.

The essential properties of Williamson's model can be presented very compactly by focusing simply on profit and expenses S (where S can be interpreted as the catch-all expenditure on perquisites, non-line staffing, etc.); we shall ignore the Williamson constraint that there is a minimum acceptable level of profit ($MALP$) necessary for survival, and also ignore the possibility that some minimum staff expenditure may be necessary (and indeed may be functionally related to the level of output). Such constraints add complexity without greatly adding to the central message—which is, quite simply, that firms may well be cost-inefficient.

The managerial utility function is denoted $U(\pi, S)$; it is assumed to give rise to the usual form of indifference curves in (π, S) space, as depicted in Figure 17.4. If we write gross profits (before deducting staff and related expenses S) as $\pi_g = R(q) - C(q)$, where $R(q)$ denotes the revenue and $C(q)$ denotes the cost of efficiently producing q, then clearly there will be a profit-maximizing price and output level such that the firm attains a maximum level of gross profit. This is denoted π_m in Figure 17.4. Actual net profit depends on how much is dissipated in staff and related expenses:

$$\pi = \pi_m - S. \tag{17.1}$$

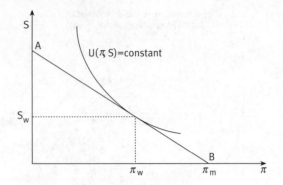

Fig. 17.4 Expense preference

Given that π_m is a constant, the graph of attainable combinations of (π, S) constitutes the straight line labelled AB in Figure 17.4. The optimal choice, (π_w, S_w), is given as the point of tangency with the highest attainable managerial indifference curve. This solution necessary involves cost inefficiency in our simple model, since the expenditures on staff etc. are positive but 'unnecessary'.

Naturally, the original Williamson model is considerably richer, than the model presented here, but the central message is the same. Managers get utility out of spending resources on themselves, and this makes it quite likely that such firms will not be cost-efficient. (For more details, the reader is referred to Williamson 1964 and Koutsoyiannis 1979).

Although the Williamson firm tends to be cost-inefficient, and hence not profit-maximizing, the welfare implications are more difficult to assess than in the Baumol case. This is because the resources spent on excessive staffing, emoluments, etc. do have value for those to whom these payments are made. For example, if S consists solely of staff perks and emoluments (and not additional staffing), then this represents a simple transfer of monies from shareholders to managers, the consequence of which is welfare-neutral. That is, the firm efficiently makes gross profit π_m; managers then choose how much to hand over to shareholders and how much to keep for themselves. An increase in S of £1 in this case increases managers' welfare by £1 but reduces shareholders' welfare by £1; aggregate welfare is unaffected by such a transfer (see Chapter 2 for a general discussion of this point). In this case welfare for the Williamson firm is identical to that of the profit-maximizing firm. However, if S includes the employment of excess staff, this involves welfare loss (although it will also confer greater utility and on-the-job leisure on the manager, which offsets this welfare loss to an extent). Given that excess staffing is quite likely, the overall welfare assessment would appear to be that welfare loss is rather larger than would be the case for the pure profit maximizer (so suggesting a greater reason for regulatory intervention than under the profit maximization hypothesis).

17.3.3 Marris's Growth Maximization Hypothesis

Marris (1963, 1964) developed a dynamic model of the firm in which he proposed that managers are concerned with growth maximization, with expanding product demand (and product variety etc.) over time. Empirical evidence suggests that managers tend to prefer internal to external promotions, simply because external promotion means having to learn new working practices and modes of operation and can reduce job security (LIFO, 'last in first out', often applies when it comes to redundancy). Marris's focus on growth is thus motivated by the observation that a growing firm gives managers greater opportunity for internal promotion, career development, and job security. The Marris model also examines how the problem of financing growth can play a role in observed behaviour.[15]

Although of some interest, this model is not only somewhat complex, but can also be criticized for making rather too many *ad hoc* assumptions (in particular with respect to pricing and product demand, and in presuming that owners' and managers' interests are aligned, when much of the thrust of modern agency theory suggests that this is unlikely to be the case), so a detailed exposition is omitted. Its main merit lies primarily in its focus on dynamic factors (which is often overlooked— most textbook models have a static focus). Dynamic elements can often be of importance in organizational architecture and design (see Chapters 29–31; for example, the incentives embodied in age-

for-wage salary schemes are discussed in Chapter 31).

17.3.4 Behavioural Theories

Behavioural theory (see e.g. Simon 1957, Cyert and March 1963) views the firm as a coalition of participants, or groups of participants (shareholders, suppliers, creditors, and consumers, plus the various categories of worker and manager in the organization) who work in the interests of the firm in exchange for a variety of rewards. The goals of the firm originate in an implicit bargain between these various interested parties. The influence these parties have on the overall direction of the firm is seen to depend on their bargaining power.

Now these elements are entirely consistent with the game-theoretic/agency treatment of the firm described in section 17.2, in which individuals are viewed as self-interested utility maximizers. However, behavioural theories usually disagree with the neo-classical paradigm of *homo economicus* in that they tend to emphasize satisficing and bounded rationality in decision-making. For example, employees are not viewed as having a definitive reservation wage, but rather as having aspiration levels. Aspiration levels can increase upward as employees build up experience, and if they see job opportunities elsewhere offering higher wages. However, there is no active job-seeking until the current wage is sufficiently below the aspiration level (because there are substantial transactions costs associated with seeking alternative employment— the costs of searching for jobs, of making applications, of going through interview procedures, not to mention the disappointment when not offered the post, etc.[16]). The same behavioural idea applies to consumer behaviour; in effect brand loyalty allows some degree of mismatch over price vis-à-vis competitors before change takes place. Again there may be some ignorance as to what the other product prices are, and this further reduces consumer responsiveness.

The difference between payments required to keep factors in their posts and the total possible revenues of the organization is termed organizational slack. In a stable environment, it might be

---

[15] Marris suggested that growth is limited by the availability of finance, but his modelling of this aspect is fairly crude. The modern perspective on financing emphasizes the principal–agent characteristics associated with the financing decision; for an introductory exposition, see Jensen (1986) or Ross *et al.* (1986). As mentioned in sect. 17.2, this merely reflects how neo-classical economics is developing from game-theoretic foundations a systematic approach to the analysis of such problems.

[16] Chap. 4 briefly discusses how the possibility of regret and disappointment may influence individual behaviour (and gives references).

thought that wages should converge on aspiration levels and competitive pressure might lead firms close to zero organizational slack—but in practice it is clear that the environment is not stationary. Not only are there business cycles, but there is the onward surge of technological progress, which ensures that firms must continue to strive to maintain themselves on an ever-moving best-practice frontier. Given this flux, it is possible for inefficient firms to survive in the long run (so long as they are not too inefficient; competition does tend to weed out the very weak).

To sum up the main features of behavioural theory:

(i) it argues that only individuals have goals (not firms);

(ii) it argues agents that have bounded rationality (and satisfice rather than optimize);

(iii) it recognizes that information is costly;

(iv) it views the firm as a coalition of agents (or participants).

Many of the (better) ideas suggested by so-called behavioural theories have now been incorporated into the 'optimizing perspective' of neo-classical economics. Thus (i) is, of course, a fundamental tenet of neo-classical economics, whilst (iii) and (iv) are actively incorporated through the use of game-theoretic, transactions-cost, and agency ideas (see section 17.2 and Chapters 29–31). The idea of search being costly, and hence that ignorance is rational, has also been extensively studied. Indeed, there has been a long tradition in economics of seeking to explain the apparently irrational as a rational and optimizing process. For example, there has been increasing interest by economists in developing models of bounded rationality; early behavioural work (e.g. Simon 1957) suggested that individuals do not optimize, they satisfice and simplify complex decision problems through the use of more or less arbitrary rules of thumb. However, neo-classical economics is often able to explain the rationality of many of these apparently satisficing rules of thumb (such as cost plus pricing—see Baumol and Quandt 1964) as optimizing solutions to the higher-level problem of how to deal efficiently with a large number of decisions when there are costs associated with information-gathering and calculation. That is, taken in isolation, the rule of thumb does not appear to be an optimization procedure—but the rule can be viewed as the optimal solution to the problem of choosing a cost-effective decision rule.

17.4 The Profit Maximization Thesis Revisited

The idea of managerial discretion (and the various models of it) suggests that firms do not maximize profit. The modern theory of the firm still retains the idea that individual agents are self-interested utility-maximizing agents, but recognizes that information is often imperfect (and often asymmetric)—and that this gives agents scope to pursue their own goals even when these goals are not in the interests of their superiors. Whilst the focus on agency and transactions costs gives a pleasingly coherent approach to the study of organizations and the design of organizational architecture, it is natural to ask whether the old idea of the profit-maximizing firm ought to be totally abandoned. This is an important question, not only because most elementary and intermediate texts still utilize for the most part the idea of profit maximization as the primary goal of the firm—but also because a great deal of public policy (on regulation, nationalization, privatization, etc.) is motivated by concern over the welfare loss which arises out of firms' quest for monopoly profit.

So why then might it be of interest to study firms' decisions, and market outcomes, under the assumption that firms aim to maximize profits? Some possible answers are as follows.

1. The owners of firms typically do want the firm to maximize profits. It follows that they will be interested in calculating prices, outputs, advertizing, etc. that yield maximum profit—in order to test whether the firm's behaviour is reasonably consistent with such calculations.

2. The managerial discretion theories discussed in this chapter suggest that firms may operate in cost-inefficient ways, and may also set prices which promote sales revenue or firm growth rather than profit. However, the two types of effect tend to work in opposite directions: revenue and growth maximization suggest lower prices, but cost-inefficiency suggests higher prices, relative to those which promote profit maximization. Furthermore, the discipline of the market is recognized in all theories; profit must not deviate too much from what is

attainable. Thus, in practice, outcomes may be consistent with approximate profit maximization. Profit maximization continues to retain its dominance in applied economics research primarily because of its predictive success.[17] These alternative theories do not perform appreciably better, in terms of predictions, when it comes to the study of markets and firm's decisions on prices, quantities, advertizing, etc.

3. The modern theory of the firm recognizes that imperfect and asymmetric information creates agency problems—but it also suggests that at each stage in the hierarchy from owners on down, there is an incentive to try to create reward structures that will help to align the interests of subordinates with their bosses. Well-designed organizational structures can bring the firm closer to behaving like a profit maximizer.

Significant deviations from profit maximization are predicted to arise where managerial discretion is large and where managerial reward structures are not aligned with profit performance. However, in such cases there is a large payoff to owners from designing incentive schemes which align to get managers' interests with their own. It is also clearly the case that the more competitive the industry, the smaller the difference between maximum and satisfactory profit performance is likely to be. As a consequence, profit maximization as a model of the firm is often a reasonable predictor of market outcomes. It is thus hardly surprising that it remains the primary assumption regarding firm's objectives in much empirical work in industrial economics.

17.5 Summary

This chapter has provided a review of some alternative views on the nature of the firm and the determinants of the way firms are likely to be seen to behave. It was suggested that recognizing the existence of transactions costs and agency costs is central to the problem of organizational design (which can be viewed as the search for organizational structures which maximize productivity and minimize these costs). Various alternatives were considered (sales revenue, expense preference, growth

maximization) as alternatives to the profit maximization hypothesis. Finally, section 17.4 reviewed the status of the profit maximization hypothesis in the light of the discussion of these alternative theoretical ideas.

17.6 Review Questions

1. Consider a simple single-product firm for which the demand function is given as $p = 100 - q$ and total costs are $C(q) = q^2$.

   (a) What is the profit-maximizing price, output, and profitability for the firm?

   (b) If the firm is a Baumol sales revenue maximizer, what is its choice of price and output if the minimum acceptable level of profit is $\bar{\pi} = 450$? Does the profit constraint bind in the optimal solution? (Hint: compute the unconstrained solution and check if it earns greater than the *MALP*; if not, solve by finding the level of output q which generates profit of 450).

   (c) What is the difference in economic welfare between the solutions in (a) and (b)? (Hint: recall that welfare is consumer surplus plus firm profit; consumer surplus is measured as the area of the triangle above the price line, one-half base times height).

2. Compare and contrast the transactions costs associated with arm's length trading on markets with those incurred in internal firm transactions. Give three examples of transactions which are likely to occur as market transactions, and three that are more likely to be internal to the firm.

3. Are teams and hierarchies simply alternative ways of organizing production? Discuss.

4. How do managerial-discretion ideas affect the incentive to regulate firms?

5. To what extent do the ideas discussed in this chapter invalidate the use of the profit maximization hypothesis as a basic assumption in economic theorizing?

17.7 Further Reading

The whole of Part VII of this text is devoted to detailing the use of transactions-costs and agency

---

[17] It typically gives clear-cut predictions, which can be confronted with the evidence. It also yields results which are relatively simple and elegant. See Chap. 1 for a discussion of criteria by which models may be judged.

theory in the economic analysis of organizational design. However, there are some excellent texts which give a thorough coverage of this field, notably Milgrom and Roberts (1992) and Brickley *et al.* (1997). For a detailed exposition and critical assessment of the earlier managerial and behavioural theories of the firm (apart from the original texts), the reader is referred to Koutsoyiannis (1982).

Part V

Pricing and Related Decisions

Part V provides a fairly extended discussion of various pricing strategies. It begins by examining the problem of price discrimination (the practice of charging different customers different prices) in Chapter 18 and this is continued in Chapter 19, where the use of non-linear pricing schedules (such as two-part tariffs) is considered as a form of price discrimination. Multi-product firms and the problem of multi-product pricing are examined in Chapter 20, pricing under uncertainty in Chapter 21, and pricing over time in Chapter 23. Chapter 22 examines the problem of setting prices in the public sector, where in theory the objective is no longer to maximize profits, but rather economic welfare. Chapter 24 gives an examination of the old debate regarding marginalist versus cost-plus pricing, whilst Chapter 25 discusses various cases where buyer(s) have market power. Finally, Chapter 26 examines how advertizing relates to market structure and how it can be used by the firm as a strategic variable.

18 Price Discrimination

Objectives This Chapter introduces the concept of profit-maximizing price discrimination (the practice of charging different customers different prices), the conditions under which it is possible, and the principles by which profit-maximizing prices may be determined. Finally, it discusses the welfare implications of such practices.

Prerequisites Chapter 8, on demand analysis, and Chapter 14, on the basic theory of monopoly pricing.

Keywords arbitrage, first-degree price discrimination, inverse elasticity rule, market segmentation, price discrimination, secondary market, secondary trading, second-degree price discrimination, third-degree price discrimination, transactions costs, uniform price.

18.1 Introduction

A profit-maximizing firm may find it advantageous to charge different prices to different customers. This is because different individuals have different tastes and different income/wealth levels; they can thus be expected to have a different willingness to pay for a given product. If the firm can identify and somehow segregate customers according to their willingness to pay, then it may be able to improve its profit potential compared to a uniform pricing policy. Typically, the firm does not observe the individual's willingness to pay, but can often identify some general characteristics of particular individuals. For example, individuals living in Belgium may have significantly and systematically different tastes to those living in the UK. This may lead a profit-maximizing firm rationally to charge different prices for the same product in these two countries (say, for example, with particular brands of beer). Likewise, working adults may have systematically greater willingness to pay as compared to children, the unemployed, or pensioners. If observable individual characteristics can be used to distinguish customer types, these may provide a basis for charging different prices.

18.1.1 Definitions of Price Discrimination

What is **price discrimination**? Here are a few possible definitions:

Definition 18.1 Alternative definitions of price discrimination:

(i) Price discrimination is said to exist if prices vary across market segments.

(ii) Price discrimination is said to exist if the absolute price–cost margin of a product or service varies across market segments.

(iii) Price discrimination is said to exist if the proportionate price–cost margin of a product or service varies across market segments.

In each case, an absence of variation across segments indicates there is *no* price discrimination.

Price discrimination in (i) is defined simply as the sale of a product at different prices to different customers. This has the merit of being a simple test, one which can be easily assessed by agencies external to the firm.[1] However, the cost of delivery of a product may vary by time (as with electricity by night and day) and place (e.g. because of varying transport costs). Thus it can be argued that a definition which takes into account the variations in cost is more appropriate (as in definitions (ii) and (iii)). In competitive markets, prices reflect long-run marginal costs of production; if marginal cost of delivery varies across segments, this would be manifest in the prices observed in such markets. Hence it makes some sense to argue that the definition of price discrimination should be based on whether the

---

[1] In the UK, the Monopolies and Mergers Commission has often been involved in assessing cases of price discrimination.

price–cost differential varies across different market segments; the idea is that, if it is shown to vary across segments, this is evidence of monopoly power being exploited.[2]

The drawback with any definition that involves some measure of cost is that it becomes more difficult for agencies external to the firm to assess whether the firm is in fact practising price discrimination (firms themselves often have a poor understanding of marginal costs; external observers are in an even weaker position). This is of some significance, since it is only those external to the firm who are likely to be concerned with whether or not the firm is practising price discrimination.[3]

If there were to be regulatory intervention to control price discrimination, the choice of definition of what constitutes price discrimination would clearly matter. The point is that prices which pass the test of 'no price discrimination' on one definition will generally fail on the other two definitions. This is illustrated in the following example.

Example 18.1 Suppose that the overall marginal cost of manufacturing and getting product to market segment A is £1000, whilst to market segment B it is £1100 (say because of differential transport costs). Then if the firm sets prices above marginal costs, any choice of prices which satisfies one of the above definitions of 'no price discrimination' fails according to the other two definitions. For example, setting the same price in each segment implies no price discrimination on definition (i) but fails this test under (ii) and (iii); a price of £1200, for instance, implies price–cost margins of £200 and £100 respectively, and proportional mark-ups of 16.7% and 8.3%, hence there is price discrimination under (ii) or (iii). If the firm satisfies the test of price discrimination under (ii), then it fails on definitions (i) and (iii); for example, a mark-up of £100 on each segment implies prices of £1100 and £1200 and proportional mark-ups of 9.1% and 8.3%. Finally, if the firm satisfies the test of no price discrimination (iii), then it fails on definitions (i) and (ii); for example, a 10% mark-up on each segment implies prices of £1111 and £1222 and absolute mark-ups of £111 and £122.

Is there an issue here? Why do we want a definition of price discrimination? The answer is that, where firms possess some degree of monopoly power, it may be that profit-maximizing price discrimination is against the public interest. In a sense, there is no need to provide a definition of price discrimination unless the aim is to use the definition as a test or a benchmark for regulating prices. If it can be shown that particular forms of price variation are in fact against the public interest, then this will motivate the choice of definition of price discrimination. In fact, in terms of economic welfare (consumer plus producer surplus), it can be shown that price discrimination has a generally ambiguous impact on economic welfare (see section 18.4).

18.1.2 The Three Degrees of Price Discrimination

Following Pigou (1923), it has become conventional to refer to three types of price discrimination, as follows:

First-degree price discrimination: Where it is possible to extract the whole of each and every individual's willingness to pay.

Second-degree price discrimination: Where consumers pay a different price depending upon the quantity they choose to buy (two-part tariffs, quantity discounts, etc.).

Third-degree price discrimination: Where customers are categorized by type (e.g. sex, age, nationality), and prices vary by type (but price does not vary by quantity, as in the second-degree case).

Naturally, one could also envisage a mixed second- and third-degree price discrimination, where price varies with the quantity purchased, but also varies with other characteristics of the individual customer.

Figure 18.1 depicts an individual's demand curve for the case of a discrete product; it shows a case where the individual's reservation price or marginal willingness to pay (WTP) for the item in question declines with the volume purchased. The price schedule B (a horizontal line) is that of a **uniform price** of the type used in third-degree price discrimination. At the level indicated, the individual purchases 6 units of the good and the consumer gains a

---

[2] Lott and Roberts (1991) suggest that many instances of what have been commonly assumed to be price discrimination are simply cases where the costs of providing the good have not been properly assessed.

[3] By assumption, the firm itself is concerned only with maximizing profits, and so has no interest whatsoever in definitions per se (except in so far as regulators might choose to use particular definitions to regulate, or threaten to regulate, the firm).

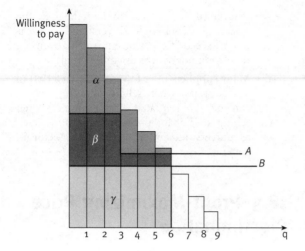

Fig. 18.1 Types of price discrimination

consumer surplus equal to the area $\alpha + \beta$ in the figure, whilst the firm earns revenue equal to the area γ. By contrast, price schedule A features second-degree price discrimination; the individual still chooses 6 units, but in this case the price schedule extracts some consumer surplus and transfers it to the firm; the individual gets consumer surplus whilst the firm gets $\beta + \gamma$. First-degree price discrimination would occur if the firm could extract all the willingness to pay; for example, if it knew the individual's demand function, it could offer 6 units to the individual on a 'take it or leave it' basis for a payment of $\alpha + \beta + \gamma$, in which case the firm would make revenue of $\alpha + \beta + \gamma$ and the consumer would get zero consumer surplus. However, the firm is rarely in such a privileged position (of knowing individuals' demand functions). In practice, first-degree price discrimination is not often a feasible option, and so is not discussed further here.[4]

The relatively more complex case of second-degree price discrimination is considered in detail in Chapter 19, whilst this chapter confines its attention to third-degree price discrimination. A variety of other selling strategies are often classified as examples of price discrimination, in particular, product bundling and tie-in sales; these are considered in Chapter 19.

---

[4] Although price-policies skimming have something in common with first-degree price discrimination; see sect. 23.2.

18.2 Conditions Facilitating Price Discrimination

When does a firm have scope to practise price discrimination? The following are necessary conditions for third-degree price discrimination:

1. the firm must have market power (be a price-maker);
2. it must be possible to segment the market so that some customers face a higher price than others, with
3. the higher-priced customers somehow prevented from purchasing at the lower price.

Condition 1 is self-evident. Consider the ways in which condition 2 might come to pass. Segmentation requires that customers can be identified. That is, they must be distinguished by some characteristic. In Chapter 19, it is shown that with non-linear pricing, customers distinguish themselves by the quantity they choose to purchase. With uniform prices, the distinguishing features must lie elsewhere, as follows:

· geographic (prices in different countries or regions may diverge);

· age (children and pensioners often pay a lower price);

· employment status, occupation or club membership, etc.

However, to be able to distinguish customers is only half the battle. Whenever prices for the same good diverge, there will be an incentive to set up **secondary markets** (in which individuals who qualify to buy at the cheaper rates sell the product on to those who would otherwise have to pay the full price). These riskless **arbitrage** operations, if extensive would lead, from the firm's viewpoint, to the effective price being simply the price in the cheapest segment of the market. If there are no barriers to secondary trading, no increase in profit can be obtained by practising price discrimination.

Barriers to secondary trading may arise, or be created:

(A) BY LAW

Until fairly recently in the UK it was illegal to resell electricity, and the UK Post Office still has a legal monopoly over the letters business at prices less than

£1 (that is, competitors are not allowed to offer a competing service at any price below £1).

(B) THROUGH POLICING USAGE

Given a definition of type (OAPs, children, the unemployed, etc.) club affiliation (student union), etc., the customer can be required to submit some form of documentary proof of their eligibility for the cheaper rate.

(C) BECAUSE OF TRANSACTIONS COSTS

Significant costs of transportation, time, and effort (of conveying goods to the cheaper market and then actually making sales there) may outweigh the profits to be obtained by secondary trading (i.e. purchasing at the lower rate and selling on to the higher-priced market segment at some intermediate price).

Cases (a) and (b), of course, could also be interpreted as particular sources of transactions costs, as in (c). That is, if secondary trading is not possible, this can be interpreted as an infinite transactions cost, whilst if secondary trading can be undertaken, but at some risk, the transactions cost can be interpreted as the expected cost of getting caught and punished. The magnitude of transactions costs limits the extent to which the firm can profit by differentiating prices across market segments. The more the price differential exceeds the transactions cost differential, the greater the expected leakage between the market segments. Transactions costs tend to be high for products which are perishable or difficult to store (such as electricity) or to transport (such as water). Note also that, apart from things that are normally thought of as perishable, anything with an expiry date is in a sense perishable; airline tickets, for example.

EXAMPLE 18.2 Examples of price discrimination

(i) Air, rail, and bus travel all feature mark-ups which vary according to market segment (business class, tourist class, senior citizen, child, time of day, season, etc.). Leakage is prevented by the perishable nature of the product (it is supplied at a particular time) and by the firm's ability to identify and police different market segments.

(ii) Car prices in the UK tend to be higher than in Europe.[5] This is geographic price discrim-

ination (it is also true that in the UK, the prices of diesel-engined versions of a car often exceed the petrol equivalent by more than the underlying cost differential).

(iii) Many suppliers offer lower prices (referred to as discounts) when selling to sectors which can be differentiated; for example, when selling to not-for-profit organizations such as universities and the education sector in general.

18.3 Profit-Maximizing Price Discrimination

This section deals with third-degree profit-maximizing price discrimination; in this type of price discrimination, the firm charges a uniform price, but a different uniform price to different market segments. The basic attraction of this form of price discrimination is that for any given total output by the firm, more revenue can be raised by segmenting the market than by simply charging the same price to all customers.

18.3.1 The Basic Model

The simplifying assumptions under which it is straightforward to characterize the optimum profit-maximizing solution are as follows:[6]

(i) there is a single period;

(ii) the market is divided into n segments, and no secondary trade is possible between segments;

(iii) demand and cost curves are assumed to be known with certainty.

Suppose the market is divided into n segments and the firm charges prices $p_1, p_2, \ldots, p_n$ and sells quantities $q_1, q_2, \ldots, q_n$ in segments $1, 2, \ldots, n$. Denoting the inverse demand functions for the segments as $p_i = P_i(q_i)$, $i = 1, \ldots, n$, revenues for each segment are $R_i(q_i) = q_i P_i(q_i)$, $i = 1, \ldots, n$. Thus, the revenue raised in market segment i depends on how much is sold (this is controlled by the firm indirectly, through its choice of price for that segment). Suppose the total cost c of producing total

---

[5] See for example Locke *et al.* (1991) and Dobbs (1995) for an assessment of the extent of price discrimination and a consideration of possible reasons for this.

[6] Some discussion of the problems that arise in multi-period pricing, where brand loyalty may be a factor, can be found in Chap. 23, whilst pricing under uncertainty is treated in Chap. 21.

output q is given by the total cost function $c = C(q)$. Then the firm's profit can be written as the sum of revenues from the market segments, minus the total cost of production:[7]

$$\pi = (\textstyle\sum_{i=1}^{n} R_i(q_i)) - C(q), \qquad (18.1)$$

where the total output q is sold to the n market segments; this implies the constraint

$$q = \textstyle\sum_{i=1}^{n} q_i. \qquad (18.2)$$

The standard approach involves analysing the first-order conditions for a constrained maximum. The choice variables are q, q_1, q_2, ..., q_n. The Lagrangian is thus

$$L = \pi + \lambda(\textstyle\sum_{i=1}^{n} q_i - q) = (\textstyle\sum_{i=1}^{n} R_i(q_i) - C(q))$$
$$+ \lambda(\textstyle\sum_{i=1}^{n} q_i - q), \qquad (18.3)$$

so the first-order conditions are that

$$\partial L / \partial q = 0 \qquad (18.4)$$

and

$$\partial L / \partial q_j = 0 \quad j = 1, \ldots, n. \qquad (18.5)$$

Thus, differentiating (18.3) with respect to q and q_i gives[8]

$$\partial L / \partial q = -\partial C(q) / \partial q - \lambda = 0, \qquad (18.6)$$
$$\partial L / \partial q_j = -\partial R_j(q) / \partial q_j + \lambda = 0 \quad j = 1, \ldots, n. \qquad (18.7)$$

From (18.6),

$$-\lambda = \partial C(q) / \partial q \quad (= MC), \qquad (18.8)$$

where MC denotes the marginal cost associated with a total output level of q, and (18.7) gives

$$-\lambda = \partial R(q_j) / \partial q_j \quad (= MR_j), \qquad (18.9)$$

the marginal revenue for the jth market segment. Hence, putting these together,

$$MR_j = \partial R_j(q_j) / \partial q_j = \partial C(q) / \partial q = MC \quad j = 1, \ldots, n, \qquad (18.10)$$

which is the familiar rule that

$$MR_1 = MR_2 = \ldots MR_n = MC. \qquad (18.11)$$

---

[7] Both demand and total cost functions are assumed to be continuously differentiable, with the inverse demand functions having negative slope ($dP_j(q_j)/dq_j < 0$) and the total cost function featuring positive marginal cost ($MC(q) = dC(q)/dq > 0$).

[8] Written out,

$$L = [R_1(q_1) + R_2(q_2) + \ldots + R_n(q_n)] - C(q)$$
$$+ \lambda[(q_1 + q_2 + \ldots + q_n) - q],$$

so

$$\partial L / \partial q = -\partial C / \partial q - \lambda,$$

and, for example, for $i = 2$,

$$\partial L / \partial q_2 = \partial R_2 / \partial q_2 + \lambda.$$

That is,

Fact 18.1 A necessary condition for profit-maximizing price discrimination is that the marginal revenues are equalized across market segments and are set equal to the marginal cost of the last unit produced.[9]

The intuition for this result is straightforward. First, for any given output level, if marginal revenues differ across any two market segments, then profits can be increased, without changing the level of production, by transferring a unit sold in a market with lower MR to one in which MR is higher. The profit gain is equal to the difference in marginal revenues. Secondly, it pays to expand output so long as marginal revenue is greater than marginal cost (and to contract output if marginal revenue is less than marginal cost). This process of transferring production proceeds until the marginal revenues across all segments are equalized (and set equal to the marginal cost of production).

The above analysis is illustrated in Figure 18.2 for the case where there are just two market segments (and the diagram could clearly be extended to several segments if space permitted this). The third panel in the figure features the horizontal summation of the marginal revenue curves for the two segments. The point at which the horizontally summed MR schedule cuts the marginal cost curve determines the optimal level for marginal cost and marginal revenue in each of the two market segments. If we track back to the first two panels of the figure, the prices in the two segments can now be read off the demand curves. Notice that the third panel also features the aggregate demand curve (formed by summing horizontally the demand curves of the two segments). Thus, a monopolist applying a uniform price would merely choose the output at which aggregate marginal revenue equals marginal cost (note that this is also the same as the output level under price discrimination). Under uniform pricing, the price is then read off the aggregate demand curve (cf. section 14.2). Thus it can be seen that price discrimination in the case where there are two market segments will feature one segment with price above and one with price below that of the uniform price. More generally, when there are several segments, the optimal discriminatory prices

---

[9] The convention in most intermediate texts is simply to assume that analysis of first-order conditions will identify a unique global maximum for the function. A sufficient condition here is that the objective function is strictly concave. The reader is referred to Chap. 3 for more details.

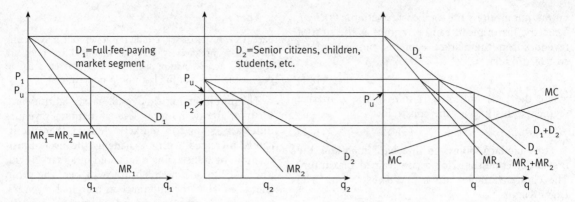

Fig. 18.2 Uniform and discriminatory prices

will form a constellation centred around the profit-maximizing uniform price.

If marginal costs vary across market segments, the above result needs to be amended; in this case, the rule is simply to produce an output and set prices such that, for each market segment, the marginal revenue in that segment is equal to the marginal cost of producing and selling to that segment.

18.3.2 The Inverse Elasticity Rule

Equalizing marginal revenues is done by adjusting prices, of course.[10] The marginal revenue/marginal cost rule in can be converted into a pricing rule for profit-maximizing price discrimination. This follows from one of the business economist's favourite formulae, namely that[11]

$$MR_i = P_i(1 + 1/\eta_i), \qquad (18.12)$$

where η_i (<-1) is the elasticity of demand in the ith market segment (recall that I established in section 14.3 that a profit-maximizing monopolist always chooses price and output such that demand is elastic). Thus, taking any pair of markets labelled i and j, since from (18.11) $MR_i = MR_j$ is a necessary condition for profit maximization, this implies that

$$P_i(1 + 1/\eta_i) = P_j(1 + 1/\eta_j), \qquad (18.13)$$

or

$$P_i/P_j = (1 + 1/\eta_j)/(1 + 1/\eta_i). \qquad (18.14)$$

This formula indicates that prices are relatively

higher in market segments where demand is more inelastic. Indeed, this becomes even clearer if the first-order condition (18.11), that $MR_i = MC$, is used in conjunction with (18.12) to give $MR_i = P_i(1 + 1/\eta_i) = MC$. This can be rearranged to obtain a pricing rule[12]

$$P_i = \left(\frac{\eta_i}{1 + \eta_i}\right)MC \quad i = 1, \ldots, n, \qquad (18.15)$$

or, more famously, the eponymous 'inverse elasticity rule':

Fact 18.2 (**The Inverse Elasticity Rule**): For profit maximization, the price–marginal cost mark-up for each segment should be set equal to the inverse of that segment's demand elasticity. That is,

$$\frac{(P_i - MC)}{P_i} = \frac{-1}{\eta_i} \quad i = 1, \ldots, n. \qquad (18.16)$$

This pricing rule is just common sense; profit maximization requires that higher mark-ups are applied to market segments which are more inelastic, and lower mark-ups where demand is relatively elastic.[13] It should be noted that a profit-maximizing monopolist will rationally charge lower prices to consumer groups who are more price-sensitive (such as senior citizens, children, students, etc.). Thus price discrimination at least fits fairly well with notions of equity (since the richer segments tend to face the higher prices). This can be a useful argument for those who wish to claim that price

---

[10] For each market segment, marginal revenue varies with quantity and hence also with price (via the segment's demand curve).

[11] A derivation is given, for the case where there is just a single market, in sect. 14.2. The only difference is that the rule applies to the ith market segment, hence the subscripts.

[12] See Chap. 14.

[13] Lerner (1934) proposed the observed mark-up, $(p - MC)/p$, as an index of monopoly power. One can see why: for a single-product monopolist setting a profit-maximizing price, this gives an indication of the demand elasticity faced by the firm; a high mark-up corresponds to relatively inelastic demand and considerable monopoly power. See Chap.14 for further discussion.

discrimination is not necessarily against the public interest (see section 18.4). Indeed, it can be shown that welfare maximization (subject to the firm breaking even) leads to a pattern of prices over market segments similar to that which arises through profit maximization (i.e. more inelastic demands face higher prices; see Chapter 22). The only difference is that the welfare maximizer sets a generally lower level of prices (but note that the prices could be significantly lower).

EXAMPLE 18.3 Suppose marginal cost is £10 per unit and there are three market segments with elasticities of -1.5, -2, and -3 (assumed not to vary as the firm varies its prices, as would be the case with constant-elasticity demand functions). This implies price–cost margins, and prices, as follows:

$$(p_1 - 10)/p_1 = -1/\eta_1 = -1/-1.5 = 2/3 \Rightarrow p_1 = 30,$$

$$(p_2 - 10)/p_2 = -1/\eta_2 = -1/-2 \Rightarrow p_2 = 20,$$

and

$$(p_3 - 10)/p_3 = -1/\eta_3 = -1/-3 \Rightarrow p_3 = 15.$$

Clearly, the more elastic the segment demand, the lower the mark-up.

On the face of it, the inverse elasticity rule looks as though it might be quite useful in developing a pricing policy; all that seems to be required is some idea of the demand elasticities for different market segments and some idea of marginal cost, and the optimal prices can be calculated straightforwardly. Furthermore, the rule can be helpful even where only rough guesstimates of demand elasticities are available (this idea is discussed in further detail in section 24.4). The idea is to judge which market segments are relatively less/more price-sensitive, and to set higher/lower mark-ups as appropriate.

Indeed, one can turn the profit-maximizing rule around to provide a test of the rationality of a firm's existing prices. Thus rearranging (18.16) gives

$$\eta_i = \left(\frac{p_i}{p_i + MC}\right). \qquad (18.17)$$

Most business decision-makers who practise some degree of price discrimination do not follow marginalistic principles. However, given that prices have already been set, it is possible to calculate, using equation (18.17), what the demand elasticities would have to be in order to validate the prices as profit-maximizing.

EXAMPLE 18.4 Suppose marginal cost is £10 per unit, there are three market segments, and the firm

currently sets prices for the segments of £30, £20, and £15 (cf. Example 18.3). By equation (18.17), these prices imply elasticities of -1.5, -2, and -3. The following question can then be posed to the decision-maker responsible for setting prices: 'Do you believe these segment-demand elasticities— do you believe that (say) a 10% increase in price will reduce sales by 15%, 20%, and 30% respectively?' The point is that gut feelings regarding the price sensitivity of sales can be used to adjust prices. For example, if the decision-maker suggested that, for segment 3, the volume loss would be more like 50%, then this implies an elasticity which can be used in pricing formula (18.16) to give a recommended price of £12.5.

Often, the decision maker may be rather vague about how price-sensitive sales really are. However, it will usually be the case that judgement or gut feeling will suffice at least to rank-order the elasticities, so the firm can at least get the segment prices in the correct rank order. In addition, if price–volume information is very vague, this is always an indication that more time and effort should be spent on firming up this knowledge (through econometric analysis or other forms of market research—see Chapter 9).

However, it is also worth emphasizing that rule (18.16) provides a simple method of calculating optimal prices only in the case where segment-demand elasticity can be assumed constant as price is varied. Often, this will be a reasonable assumption; that is, a constant-elasticity demand function will be a reasonable approximation to the true but unknown demand curve. However, it is at best an approximation. More generally, the elasticity varies with price, and the optimal price and the associated elasticity have to be solved for simultaneously. The linear demand curve is a case in point; it features a varying elasticity along its length.[14] Now it may be the case that, from an empirical econometric perspective, a log-linear functional form is supported by the data. In such a case, the estimated functional form imposes constant elasticity in the pricing calculation (see Chapter 9) and the pricing calculation is then trivial. However, if the functional form does not feature constant elasticity, a more direct approach to the computation of optimal prices is likely to be more appropriate. Example 18.5 below

---

[14] By contrast, constant-elasticity demand curves are convex functions (rectangular hyperbolas, in fact).

illustrates the pricing analysis for the case where demands and costs are linear.

The computation of discriminatory prices requires estimation or guesstimation of

(i) the demand functions for all segments (Chapter 9), and

(ii) the cost function (Chapter 11), such that, for any given output, the marginal cost of production can be computed.

It should be noted that whilst estimating demand functions on the basis of historical data is reasonably straightforward, it is very much an empirical question whether the analysis generates parameter estimates which are economically meaningful and stable. It is also worth bearing in mind that relationships estimated on historic data are often not very robust and may not always be a good guide to the future. Likewise, reliable estimates on the cost side can often be difficult to obtain. This is particularly true when the firm produces multiple products using common facilities and processes (see Chapter 20).[15] Finally, one is likely to have less confidence in the calculated prices if they lie far away for the price range on which the demand function was estimated.[16]

EXAMPLE 18.5 (Calculation of profit-maximizing prices for the case of linear demands and linear costs). Suppose the demand functions (and inverse demand functions) for three market segments are

$$q_1 = 1000 - 100p_1 \Rightarrow p_1 = 10 - \frac{1}{100}q_1, \quad \text{(i)}$$

$$q_2 = 1000 - 50p_2 \Rightarrow p_2 = 20 - \frac{1}{50}q_2, \quad \text{(ii)}$$

and

$$q_3 = 1000 - 20p_3 \Rightarrow p_3 = 50 - \frac{1}{20}q_3, \quad \text{(iii)}$$

and costs are, for output q,

$$C(q) = 1000 + 5q. \quad \text{(iv)}$$

[15] Firms often adopt arbitrary cost allocation procedures, and if these are used uncritically, a poor estimate of the variable costs associated with any particular product may result.

[16] For example, if the demand information developed in recent work on the UK letters business (Cuthbertson and Dobbs 1996) was used to determine profit-maximizing prices for first- and second-class mail, the calculated prices would be well over double the prices used in the estimation of the functions. Any extrapolation of prices beyond the region for which the functions were estimated is clearly very risky (although such analysis does indicate the way to go if increased profits are an objective).

The firm only produces enough to supply the three markets, hence

$$q = q_1 + q_2 + q_3. \quad \text{(v)}$$

The firm's profit function is thus

$$\pi = p_1q_1 + p_2q_2 + p_3q_3 - C(q). \quad \text{(vi)}$$

The procedure is (*a*) to use the demand functions to substitute for p_1, p_2, and p_3 and (*b*) use (v) to substitute for q to obtain a function in the three variables q_1, q_2, and q_3. Thus, substituting for prices using (i), (ii), and (iii), and for cost using (iv), equation (vi) can be written as

$$\pi = \left(10 - \frac{1}{100}q_1\right)q_1 + \left(20 - \frac{1}{50}q_2\right)q_2$$
$$+ \left(50 - \frac{1}{20}q_3\right)q_3 - 1000 - 5(q_1 + q_2 + q_3). \quad \text{(vii)}$$

The first-order conditions involve setting $\partial\pi/\partial q_1$, $\partial\pi/\partial q_2$, and $\partial\pi/\partial q_3 = 0$. This gives the three first-order conditions as

$$\partial\pi/\partial q_1 = 10 - \frac{1}{50}q_1 - 5 = 0 \quad \text{(viii)}$$

$$\partial\pi/\partial q_2 = 20 - \frac{1}{25}q_2 - 5 = 0 \quad \text{(ix)}$$

$$\partial\pi/\partial q_3 = 50 - \frac{1}{10}q_3 - 5 = 0. \quad \text{(x)}$$

Hence $q_1 = 250$, $q_2 = 375$, and $q_3 = 450$. Substituting these values back into the demand functions (i), (ii), and (iii), we obtain the prices as

$$p_1 = 7.5, \ p_2 = 12.5, \ p_3 = 27.5,$$

and substituting the quantities into (vii), we obtain the firm's profit level as

$$\pi = 7.5 \times 250 + 12.5 \times 375 + 27.5 \times 450 - 1000$$
$$- 5 \times (250 + 375 + 450) = 15,437.5.$$

It is also possible to calculate economic welfare and to compare this with what would result under some form of uniform pricing. However, this is dealt with in the next section (see Example 18.4).

18.4 The Welfare Consequences of Profit-Maximizing Price Discrimination

This section addresses the question whether profit-maximizing third-degree price discrimination reduces economic welfare (relative to the alternative of uniform pricing, where all customers face the same price; see definition 18.1(i)). The broad conclusions of the discussion can be summarized as follows:

1. If there is no exclusion (no customers priced out of the market by a uniform price), and the marginal cost of supply is the same to all customers, then price discrimination tends to reduce welfare.
2. If the cost of supply varies across customers the result is ambiguous.
3. If some customers are priced out of the market by a uniform price, the result is ambiguous.
4. Price discrimination may also be judged desirable on equity grounds.

Thus, it would appear that there is no prima facie case for legislating against price discrimination; it could be that ruling it out would be, overall, beneficial to welfare, but the matter is essentially an empirical one. Indeed, one could well argue that, if one wishes to improve economic welfare (consumer surplus plus profits), every case should be treated on its merits.

If price discrimination was in general against the public interest, it would seem useful to have a definition of price discrimination, a rule of thumb for identifying instances of it. The question addressed here is 'does it matter whether a firm charges different prices to different individuals?' Clearly it matters to the firm, as it is a means of increasing its profit level; by differentiating consumers, the firm is able to extract more of what consumers would otherwise retain as their consumer surplus. It thus looks as though consumers must lose out. However, whilst this is true in aggregate, it turns out that, relative to uniform pricing, some consumers will gain and some will lose. Furthermore, aggregate welfare (sum of consumer surplus plus profits) may rise or fall, depending on the particular market situation. That is, in aggregate consumers lose, but the firm gains; it is possible for the firm to gain more (or less) than the consumers lose.

Figure 18.3 illustrates the case where there are two market segments with identical demand curves (for clarity, the demand curves are plotted to the left and the right of the vertical axis), but with different marginal costs of supplying the two segments. In Figure 18.3, q_1^u and q_2^u denote the outputs in the two segments under uniform price p^u, whilst (q_1, p_1)

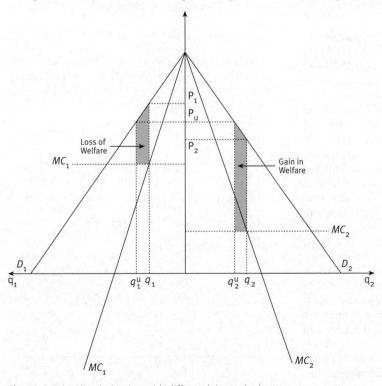

Fig. 18.3 Price discrimination with differential marginal costs

and (q_2, p_2) denote the output and price for each segment under price discrimination. It can be shown that with linear demand, output does not change when the firm practises price discrimination, and that, when there are two market segments, the uniform price lies between the discriminatory prices. Figure 18.3 reflects these facts; in this particular case, where demand is symmetric, the uniform price lies midway between the discriminatory prices. It should be clear that there is a welfare gain from allowing the firm to charge profit-maximizing prices which differ across market segments if there is an underlying difference in marginal costs (compare the shaded areas of welfare gain and loss).

However, by contrast, if marginal cost is the same across segments, but demand curves are different, it can be shown that uniform pricing yields higher economic welfare than if profit-maximizing price discrimination is allowed; in particular, when the demand curves are linear, it can be shown that the change in welfare, ΔW, which arises in moving from profit-maximizing uniform pricing to profit-maximizing discriminatory prices is related to the firm's increase in profits from the change, $\Delta \pi$ (>0), by the equation

$$\Delta W = -\Delta\pi/2. \qquad (18.18)$$

The overall loss in welfare is half the increase in the firm's profit. Since $\Delta W = \Delta CS + \Delta\pi$, it follows that $\Delta CS = -3\Delta\pi/2$; consumers in aggregate lose one and a half times what the firm gains by being allowed to practise price discrimination.

The result stated in (18.18)—price discrimination has a negative welfare impact—holds when the marginal costs of supply do not vary across segments and where no customers are priced out of the market. It has already been noted that profit-maximizing price discrimination could be beneficial to welfare if marginal costs vary across segments. It is also true that it can be beneficial to welfare in the case where it allows customer groups who were previously excluded from the market to participate. This point is straightforward: if the uniform price forces a consumer group out of the market, then if the firm is allowed to identify groups and discriminate its prices, it will have an incentive to offer the group a lower price; so long as this lower price is in excess of the firm's marginal cost of supply, the firm will increase its profits; and as the group is now participating in the market, it too must be better off, since previously, the group obtained no consumer surplus, and now it must be getting some (consumers only

choose to buy if they get non-negative consumer surplus from their purchases). Thus in this case, profits and consumer surplus increase, so price discrimination is clearly beneficial to welfare.

A further argument in favour of price discrimination has also been alluded to, namely that it may tend to lead to lower prices for disadvantaged groups (senior citizens, the unemployed, etc.), because these groups tend to be more price-sensitive. Our economic welfare criterion is distributionally neutral (see Chapter 2): that is, a gain of £1 by a wealthy person is counted just the same as a £1 gain by someone at the other end of the distribution of income and wealth. It can be argued that equity ought to lead to a heavier weighting being given to those who are less well off; if this is the case, price discrimination will again tend to appear more welfare-beneficial.

The following simple example illustrates some of these ideas and also some of the technical aspects associated with computing profit-maximizing prices and evaluating the associated levels of economic welfare.

EXAMPLE 18.6 (Comparing welfare impacts): There are two segments with demands

$$p_1 = 100 - q_1 \qquad (i)$$

and

$$p_2 = a - q_2. \qquad (ii)$$

In segment 2, the linear inverse demand curve has an intercept on the price axis at the level a. Leaving this as a parameter allows us to consider demands when they are the same (by setting $a = 100$) or

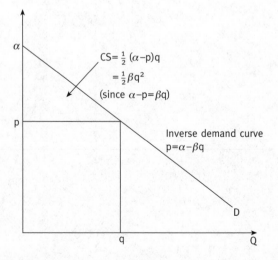

Fig. 18.4 Consumer surplus for linear demand

when segment 2 has higher or lower demand ($a >$ 100 or $a < 100$, respectively). The firm's cost of production is

$$C = bq_2. \qquad \text{(iii)}$$

That is, good 1 is costless to produce whilst good 2 has constant marginal cost of b. Introducing the parameter b allows us to explore the effect of differential marginal cost; as a special case, marginal costs for the two products are identical if we set $b = 0$. The firm's profit function is given by

$$\begin{aligned} \pi &= p_1 q_1 + p_2 q_2 - C \\ &= (100 - q_1)q_1 + (a - q_2)q_2 - bq_2. \end{aligned} \qquad \text{(iv)}$$

(A) WELFARE UNDER PRICE DISCRIMINATION

Optimal outputs can be deduced from the first-order conditions; that is, differentiating with respect to q_1 and q_2 in turn, we get

$$\partial\pi/\partial q_1 = 100 - 2q_1 = 0 \Rightarrow q_1 = 50 \qquad \text{(v)}$$

and

$$\partial\pi/\partial q_2 = a - 2q_2 - b = 0 \Rightarrow q_2 = \frac{(a-b)}{2}. \qquad \text{(vi)}$$

Substituting these results back into the demand equations gives the prices as

$$p_1 = 100 - q_1 = 100 - 50 = 50 \qquad \text{(vii)}$$

and

$$p_2 = a - q_2 = a - \frac{(a-b)}{2} = \frac{(a+b)}{2}. \qquad \text{(viii)}$$

Using (v) to (viii) for prices and quantities in the firm's profit function, and simplifying, yields

$$\pi = 2500 + 0.25(a-b)^2. \qquad \text{(ix)}$$

Consumers' surplus (CS_2) for segment 2 is given as the area under the inverse demand curve and above the price line (the triangle has an area equal to half its base times its height). For a linear demand curve, this is depicted in Figure 18.4. Thus, for both segments, $\beta = 1$ in Figure 18.4. We therefore have

$$CS_2 = q_2^2/2 \qquad \text{(x)}$$

and similarly for segment 1:

$$CS_1 = q_1^2/2. \qquad \text{(xi)}$$

Welfare, W, is given as

$$W = CS_1 + CS_2 + \pi. \qquad \text{(xii)}$$

Substituting in (xii) using (ix), (x), and (xi) and simplifying gives

$$W = 3750 + 0.375(a-b)^2. \qquad \text{(xiii)}$$

(B) WELFARE UNDER UNIFORM PRICING

Here the constraint that prices across segments must be uniform is imposed. Thus prices are constrained such that

$$p_1 = p_2 = p_u, \qquad \text{(xiv)}$$

where denotes the uniform price. In this case, it is most convenient to analyse the problem in price space (refer to section 15.2 for a discussion of this).[17] The profit function in this case is

$$\begin{aligned} \pi^u &= p_1 q_1 + p_2 q_2 - C = p_u(100 - p_u) \\ &+ p_u(a - p_u) - b(a - p_u), \end{aligned} \qquad \text{(xv)}$$

where $q_1 = 100 - p_u$ and $q_2 = a - p_u$ and π^u denotes that this is the profit obtained under uniform pricing. The optimal price can be found from the first-order condition that

$$\partial\pi^u/\partial p_u = 100 - 2p_u + a - 2p_u + b = 0. \qquad \text{(xvi)}$$

Thus

$$p_u = (a + b + 100)/4. \qquad \text{(xvii)}$$

Clearly, we can repeat the analysis as for the price discrimination case; that is, substitute back into (i) and (ii) to obtain q_1 and q_2, then into (iv) to obtain profits, and finally into (x) and (xi) for the consumer surplus values. Doing all this gives welfare under uniform pricing, denoted W^u, as

$$\begin{aligned} W^u &= 0.0625[7a^2 - 2a(7b + 100) + 3b^2 + 200b \\ &+ 70{,}000]. \end{aligned} \qquad \text{(xviii)}$$

Computing the difference in profits, $\Delta\pi$, and welfare, ΔW, between the uniform pricing and price discrimination cases gives

$$\Delta\pi = \pi - \pi^u = 0.125(a + b - 100)^2 \qquad \text{(xix)}$$

and

$$\begin{aligned} \Delta W &= W - W^u = -0.0625(a - 3b - 100) \\ &(a + b - 100). \end{aligned} \qquad \text{(xx)}$$

Thus, whether price discrimination reduces or increases welfare is generally ambiguous. This is particularly easy to see if the following special cases are considered.

(I) SAME DEMAND IN EACH SEGMENT: $a = 100$

Then ΔW simplifies to give

$$\Delta W = 0.1875b^2 \quad (> 0 \text{ if } b > 0)$$

---

[17] It is possible, but slightly more awkward, to solve the problem in quantity space. This involves maximizing (iv), where profits are expressed as a function of quantities, subject to the restriction from equatons (i) and (ii) that, since $p_1 = p_2$ in the final solution, $100 - q_1 = a - q_2$. The problem can then be solved using the Lagrange function in the usual way.

and

$$\Delta\pi = 0.125b^2 \quad (> 0 \text{ if } b > 0).$$

(II) SAME MARGINAL COSTS: $b = 0$

Then ΔW simplifies to give

$$\Delta W = -0.0625(a - 100)^2 \quad (< 0 \text{ if } a \neq 100).$$

and

$$\Delta\pi = 0.125(a - 100)^2 \quad (> 0 \text{ if } a \neq 100).$$

Thus with the same demand levels, if costs are different and the firm is allowed to discriminate prices, consumers gain (overall) and the firm gains, so economic welfare increases. By contrast, if marginal costs are the same but demand levels are different, then welfare falls (the firm gains, but consumers lose 50% more than the firm gains); notice that this result is an illustration of equation (18.18) above. In the more general case, where both demand and cost conditions are different across market segments, the results can go either way, depending upon the magnitudes of a and b.

This rather tedious example[18] illustrates the idea that it can be desirable to allow the firm to discriminate prices if the costs of supply differ across individuals. As mentioned in section 18.1, a better test of price discrimination might be to ask if the price–cost differential should be made uniform across market segments. In the above example, replacing the benchmark of uniform pricing with a benchmark of uniform price–cost margins (the restriction that $p_1 - MC_1 = p_2 - MC_2$), and then moving from this benchmark to that of profit-maximizing price discrimination, always involves a welfare loss. This suggests that restricting price–cost differentials is more likely to be welfare-beneficial than simply restricting prices so that they are uniform across segments.

In practice, the cost of supply of a product often varies across different consumer segments. First, the time of delivery and the place at which it is delivered can be viewed as part of what constitutes a product or service, and both may affect the cost of production. For example, electricity generated at night is produced by more efficient units than during the day (because there is lower demand and electricity companies utilize their power stations in rank order by marginal cost), and so the marginal cost is lower

at night. Transport costs can be significant; for a producer in Oxford, say, selling product in London is likely to incur much lower transport costs in comparison with sales to Land's End or John o'Groats. Furthermore, it may be useful to be able to apply the concept of price discrimination when the product is not entirely homogeneous. Firms often produce several closely related products or varieties; for example, the same model of car can often be purchased with different detailed specifications (engine size, radio-cassette, sunroof, . . .). Again, costs of production will vary. All this suggests that, if a definition is to be used at all, a more appropriate definition of price discrimination is one which takes into account the variation in the cost of supply, as in Definition 18.1.

The above discussion provides some motivation for using Definition 18.1(ii) for price discrimination rather than benchmark definition 18.1(i); that is, under 18.1(ii), there is no price discrimination if prices simply reflect variations in underlying costs of supply. It is by no means an ideal test for price discrimination; it remains true that if some groups are excluded under this new version, it is still possible that moving to free profit-maximizing prices could still be welfare-improving (though, empirically, there are likely to be fewer cases where this is true). Furthermore, there are the arguments pertaining to equity, and there remains the serious difficulty for external observers of accurately measuring marginal costs.

18.5 Summary

This chapter began by outlining the market conditions under which a firm with market power could practise price discrimination; the principal requirements were seen to be the ability to segment the market and the ability to prevent secondary trading by those able to purchase in the cheaper-priced sectors. Following this, the relationship between profit-maximizing market segment prices and the associated segment elasticities was established. Finally, the consequences of a profit-maximizing firm being allowed to discriminate prices were explored. It was noted that third-degree price discrimination often has adverse welfare consequences, but that this is not a general result; it is possible for profit-maximizing firms actually to increase economic welfare if they are allowed to discriminate

---

[18] Software such as DERIVE, which performs simple calculus and algebra, facilitates rapid manipulation and solution for these types of problem; this particular example took about 5 minutes to set up and solve.

prices. The consequences of state intervention are thus in general ambiguous.[19]

18.6 Review Questions

1. Under what conditions is a firm able to practise third-degree price discrimination?

2. To what extent do economic principles provide a basis for designing a policy of price discrimination?

3. Consider whether the following are examples of price discrimination (discuss each case in turn):

   (a) There are cheaper bus prices for senior citizens and children.

   (b) Theatres charge different prices for seats in different positions vis-à-vis the stage.

   (c) Players No. 6 (a type of cigarette) is the same price whether bought in John O'Groats, Land's End, or Piccadilly Circus.

   (d) Night tariffs for electricity are cheaper than day tariffs.

   (e) Rover cars (whatever the model) are more expensive in the UK than on the Continent.

4. A firm has two (geographically) segmented markets. The demand curves for these market segments are, respectively:

$$q_1 = 1000 - p_1$$

and

$$q_2 = 1600 - 2p_2,$$

where q_i and p_i, $i = 1, 2$, are the outputs and

---

[19] This issue is taken up again in Chap. 28.

prices (in £/unit) for segments 1 and 2 respectively. Suppose the firm has a constant marginal cost of £100 per unit (and no fixed costs).

(a) What are the profit-maximizing prices and outputs in the two market segments, and hence the firm's profits?

(b) Suppose the monopolist is constrained to charge the same price in both market segments. What is the profit-maximizing price and the firm's profit level in this case? Does total output change in moving from price discrimination to uniform pricing?

(c) Is economic welfare, as measured by the sum of consumer surplus plus firm's profits, greater under uniform pricing or under profit-maximizing price discrimination in this case, and if so, by how much? (Hint: recall that economic welfare is the sum of consumer surplus plus firm's profits, and that with linear demand, consumer surplus is measured as the triangle above the price line in each market segment).

18.7 Further Reading

Phlips (1983) gives a thorough coverage of price discrimination, whilst Varian (1989) reviews recent academic work on this topic, in particular on the relationship between profitability under price discrimination and its consequences for economic welfare.

19 Non-Linear Pricing

Objective This Chapter examines the practice of second-degree price discrimination, in which the marginal price paid varies depending on how much is purchased.

Prerequisites Chapter 8, on demand analysis, Chapter 14, on the basic theory of monopoly pricing, and Chapter 18, on the basics of price discrimination.

Keywords block tariff, bundling, demand profile, general outlay schedule, inverse elasticity rule, marginal price, multi-part tariff, outlay schedule, pure commodity bundling, quantity discounts, quantity premium, self-selection, tie-in sales, two-part tariff.

19.1 Introduction

Uniform pricing is the practice of charging the same price per unit, no matter how many units the consumer purchases. Non-uniform (or non-linear) pricing, by contrast, is the practice of allowing the price per unit to vary depending upon the quantity the consumer purchases. The **marginal price** at a consumption level q is the extra money paid for purchasing $q + 1$ units compared to buying q units. Thus uniform pricing is the case where the marginal price is a constant and does not vary with the amount purchased, and this is clearly a special case of non-uniform pricing. If the marginal price falls as the volume purchased increases, this is termed **quantity discounting**, whilst if the marginal price rises, this is called a **quantity premium**. Clearly, quantity discounting encourages the individual to buy in bulk whilst quantity premia encourages individuals to purchase repeatedly at the smallest level possible. The firm, in designing this type of policy, has to try to take into account the effect of these incentives on individual consumers. In particular, it is worth noting that firms generally find it difficult to prevent repeat purchasing; it follows that a schedule as in Figure 19.1 which features quantity premia will tend to see consumers repeatedly purchasing a single unit[1]

and so this tends to rule out quantity premia in the choice of the price schedule.[2]

In choosing a non-uniform pricing schedule so as to maximize the firm's profits, the optimal choice will at worst turn out to be that of uniform pricing. However, much more commonly, a non-uniform price schedule can be found which will increase the firm's profitability. It turns out that the non-uniform pricing schedule provides a mechanism by which individuals can be charged different prices. In doing this it allows the firm to capture more of what would otherwise have ended up as consumer surplus.

The focus here is exclusively on profit-maximizing choices for price schedules. However, organizations in the public sector may rationally practise both second- and third-degree price discrimination with the objective of maximizing economic welfare. These forms of price discrimination are explored in sections 22.4 and 22.5 in the chapter on public sector pricing.

Before proceeding to the analysis of optimal pricing policy, it is useful to contrast second- and third-degree price discrimination. In non-linear (or non-uniform) pricing, the firm offers an outlay schedule which specifies how much an individual must pay to consume any given amount.

Definition 19.1 An **outlay schedule**, $R(q)$, specifies the payment required to purchase q units (for any given purchase level $q \geq 0$).

---

[1] That is, if I wish to buy 5 units, it is cheaper for me to buy one unit five times in quick succession.

[2] Any schedule with quantity premia is thus effectively the same as a uniform price scheme in which the uniform price is equal to the price of the first unit.

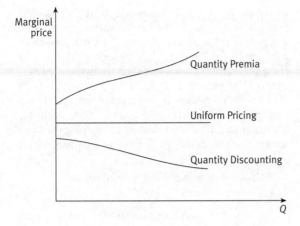

Fig. 19.1 Non-linear pricing

Definition 19.2 The marginal price, $p(q)$, if q is discrete, is the extra payment required to purchase q units over and above that required to purchase $q - 1$ units. Thus $p(q) = R(q) - R(q - 1)$. If q is continuous, and $R(q)$ is differentiable at q, then $p(q) = dR(q)/dq$.

19.1.1 Types of Outlay Schedule

As previously mentioned, uniform pricing is the case where the marginal price p is constant and the revenue schedule, $R(q) = pq$, is linear in q. The following types of outlay schedule are categorized as types of second-degree price discrimination (illustrated in Figure 19.2):

The general outlay schedule Here, the marginal price paid per unit can vary from unit to unit (although there may be intervals on which it is constant).

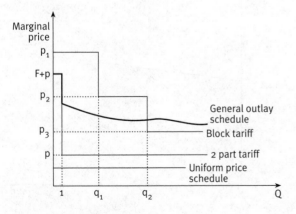

Fig. 19.2 Outlay schedules

Block tariffs (or quantity discounts) This is a special case of the general schedule where the marginal price paid varies only a relatively small number of times. Thus in Figure 19.2, there is a constant price p_1 per unit for consumption in the interval $[0, q_1]$; thereafter, there is a different (usually lower) but again constant price p_2 for each unit lying in the interval $[q_1, q_2]$. There may be further blocks and falls in the unit price; in Figure 19.2, the price p_3 is paid per unit for units greater than q_2.

Two-part tariffs Here, the consumer is required to pay a licence fee F (or fixed charge) and then pays a constant marginal price p per unit for consumption. Thus $R(q) = F + pq$.

Multi-part tariffs As in the two-part tariff, there is a fixed charge or licence fee. The unit price may then vary across products and by quantity.

The two-part tariff can of course be viewed as a special case of a block tariff in which the first 'block' is just the first unit of consumption; that is, in order to consume one unit, the licence fee has to be paid and also the marginal price for one unit. Thus the marginal price for the first unit is $F + p$ and then simply p per unit thereafter (Figure 19.2).

Other variations in tariffs, particularly with respect to time of consumption are also possible, as with telephone and electricity tariffs.

EXAMPLE 19.1 Many chocolate bars can be purchased singly or in multi-packs. If 'Chocolot' bars can be purchased at £0.20 each or in a pack of 4 for £0.70, then the unit price for 1, 2, and 3 bars is £0.20, but the marginal price paid to obtain the fourth bar is £0.70 − (3 × 0.20) = £0.10. This is an example of a quantity discount.

EXAMPLE 19.2 In most countries, a phone bill consists of a quarterly charge (which must be paid before any call can be made) and the unit rates, which vary by time of day and sometimes non-linearly with the length of the call. Such a schedule is termed a multi-part tariff.

EXAMPLE 19.3 Suppose that quantity is discrete and that the monopolist offers the following outlay schedule:

1 for £20, 2 for £38, 3 for £54, 4 for £66, etc.

The marginal prices are $P(1) = 20$, $P(2) = 18$, $P(3) = 16$, $P(4) = 12$. The marginal price is the extra money the consumer needs to pay to increase his/her purchase by one unit. This is an example of a general outlay schedule, where the marginal price may vary from unit to unit.

Clearly, the block tariff and the multi-part tariff are special cases of the general outlay schedule (since they constrain the marginal price to be constant over ranges of demand). If the firm chooses to restrict the class of outlay schedules from which it can select, then this will tend to reduce the maximum attainable level of profit. Thus, assuming that outlay schedules are optimally adjusted, a general outlay schedule will usually yield greater profit than one which is restricted to a block tariff with, say, three blocks, which will in turn outperform a two-part tariff, which in turn will outperform a uniform price. However, it is often the case empirically that a simple block tariff or two-part tariff will do almost as well as a general outlay schedule, and the simpler forms of second-degree price discrimination (two-part tariffs, simple block tariffs, and quantity discounts) have the merit of simplifying the optimization process (slightly) and, more importantly, of being more easily understood by the customer. Consumers are only likely to respond rationally to prices if they fully understand the nature of the prices they face. Almost certainly, a two-part tariff is easier to comprehend than a general outlay schedule. Indeed, if customers are actually put off purchasing by the complexity of the tariff, it could well be the case that an optimal design is one which features relative simplicity.

Second-degree price discrimination, just like first- and third-degree price discrimination, aims to increase profit by capturing more of what would otherwise be consumer surplus. One of the differences between third-degree and second-degree price discrimination lies in the fact that third-degree price discrimination is often imposed on different classes of consumer (e.g. consumers face different prices because they are under or over 16 years of age, or live in Britain or Belgium, etc.). With second-degree price discrimination, a different marginal price is paid depending upon how much is consumed; consumers are left to choose for themselves what marginal price they pay.

19.1.2 The Offer of a Choice of Schedules

Sometimes, companies offer a menu or selection of tariffs between which the consumer can choose. For example, it is not so uncommon to be offered alternative two-part or block tariffs for gas or electricity.

Interestingly, it can be shown that the multi-part tariff structure is formally equivalent to offering the consumer a choice amongst a variety of two-part tariffs (so long as they efficiently choose the cheapest tariff, given their consumption preferences). For example, consider a multi-part tariff (MT) which involves a £10 licence fee, £0.20 per unit for the first 100 units, and £0.10 each for further units. This is equivalent to offering the consumer the choice of the following two-part tariffs (TPTs):

TPT(i)　　£10 licence fee plus £0.20 per unit

and

TPT(ii)　　£20 licence fee plus £0.10 per unit.

This can easily be seen by plotting the total outlay costs for the three schedules, as in Figure 19.3. Given a choice of the two-part tariffs (i) and (ii), a rational consumer would select (i) if consumption was expected to be less than 100 units, and (ii) if greater than 100 units. Thus offering the choice of two-part tariffs is equivalent to offering a single multi-part tariff. In algebraic terms, the total revenue R_{MT} raised through the multi-part tariff, as a function of quantity purchased, q, is

$$R_{MT} = 10 + 0.2q \quad \text{for } 0 \leq q \leq 100 \quad (19.1)$$

and

$$R_{MT} = 10 + 0.2 \times 100 + 0.1(q - 100)$$
$$= 20 + 0.1q \quad \text{for } q > 100, \quad (19.2)$$

whilst for the two-part tariffs (i) and (ii),

$$R_{TPT(i)} = 10 + 0.2q \quad \text{for } q \geq 0 \quad (19.3)$$

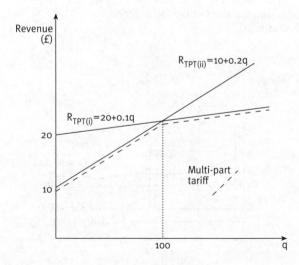

Fig. 19.3 Two part and multi-part tariffs

and

$$R_{TPT(ii)} = 20 + 0.1q \quad \text{for } q \geq 0. \qquad (19.4)$$

It was noted in section 19.1 that the multi-part tariff, optimally set, will generally earn more profit for the firm than a single two-part tariff. The above discussion suggests that the firm can do better than offering a single two-part tariff by offering a selection of two-part tariffs. Carefully designed, such a menu will raise more profit. The public relations aspect of such a policy is also attractive to the firm. Consumers, in being offered greater variety and choice by the firm, naturally feel as though they are being cared for by the firm.

19.2 Conditions for Second-Degree Price Discrimination

When does a firm have scope for practising second-degree price discrimination? Recall the following necessary conditions for third-degree price discrimination (from section 18.2):

1. the firm must have market power (be a price-maker);
2. it must be possible to segment the market so that some customers face a higher price than others, with
3. the higher-priced customers somehow prevented from purchasing at the lower price.

In essence these remain the conditions necessary for the practice of second-degree price discrimination. With third-degree price discrimination, there has to be some characteristic(s) associated with an individual that can be used to define his/her market segment and hence the price to be paid. The characteristic(s) must be such that individuals whose characteristics(s) define them as high-price consumers can somehow be prevented from buying at lower prices (characteristics such as geography, age, or club affiliation). In second-degree price discrimination, it is again a characteristic of the individual, but this time it is simply that individual's willingness to pay (WTP). If willingness to pay varies across individuals (because their income or tastes vary) then this creates the possibility for the firm to vary its charge depending on the amount purchased. So conditions 1 and 2 continue to hold. What about 3? In the case of third-degree price discrimination, it is

often possible to separate the markets physically, or to police the market segments so that it is not possible to resell the product or service (e.g. an under-16 or senior citizen bus ticket). Clearly this is not possible in the case of second-degree price discrimination. Thus, in third-degree price discrimination, the firm often imposes on the individual which price he or she will face; with second-degree price discrimination the customer self-selects the marginal price paid. That is, variation in tastes, income, etc. leads each customer voluntarily to choose a different consumption level, total outlay, and marginal price.

19.3 Potential Problems with Quantity Discounts and Premia

Section 19.1 noted that quantity premia could be problematic; this is also true for quantity discounts. Any departure from uniform pricing has to take into account the incentives it creates for the consumer to undertake secondary trading, storage, etc.

19.3.1 Quantity Discounts

With quantity discounting, the marginal (and average) price is falling; in this case, ceteris paribus, it is in the consumer's interest to buy in bulk:

(i) in order to sell on to other consumers (the bulk purchaser can sell on at a profit to consumers who would otherwise have purchased smaller quantities at the higher prices);
(ii) in order to store for future consumption (in effect setting up an internal trade in which the consumer sells on to his/her future self).

What prevents this? As in the uniform pricing case, the answer lies in transaction costs. Buying in bulk and then selling on takes time and effort (and the investment cost of first buying in bulk). In particular, storage costs may be substantial. Thus electricity can be stored (through batteries of various types) but there is a need to purchase this equipment (which is also less than 100% storage-efficient). Clearly, then, in many cases it will be possible for the seller to offer quantity discounts, since these transaction costs help to prevent significant levels of storage/reselling.

19.3.2 Quantity Premia

Quantity premia would appear in most cases to be a less than sensible option for the seller. With an upward-sloping marginal price schedule, the consumer has an incentive to buy the minimum order quantity repeatedly in order to get the desired demand, as in the following example.

EXAMPLE 19.4 Suppose the firm sets an outlay schedule which requires an outlay of $R(1) = £10$, $R(2) = £25$, and $R(3) = £45$ for purchasing 1, 2, and 3 units respectively. This implies marginal prices of $P(1) = £10$, $P(2) = £15$, and $P(3) = £20$, respectively. An individual wishing to purchase 3 units could do so by purchasing one unit three times (cost $3 \times £10 = £30$) rather than a single purchase of 3 units (cost £45).

Thus, assuming consumer rationality, the firm will in general be unable to improve its profitability by choosing a price schedule which is everywhere increasing. However, the schedule *can* have some portions on which marginal price is increasing. In fact, to prevent the kind of repeat purchasing discussed above, the firm needs to select a general outlay schedule which satisfies subadditivity; that is, an outlay schedule which satisfies, for any q, the condition

$$R(q) \le R(q_1) + R(q_2) + \ldots + R(q_n) \text{ for all } q_1, \ldots, q_n \ge 0$$
$$\text{satisfying } q = q_1 + q_2 + \ldots + q_n \text{ (for arbitrary } n > 1).$$
$$(19.5)$$

Only if this condition is satisfied will the rational consumer choose to buy q in a lump rather than buying in smaller quantities that add up to the desired q. (For a discussion of the concept of subadditivity, see Chapter 14). Whilst subadditivity does not rule out the outlay function having some regions which feature quantity premia, it

does rule out the case where the marginal price schedule is increasing everywhere, and it certainly limits the extent to which the schedule can feature quantity premia.

EXAMPLE 19.5 Consider the outlay schedules in Table 19.1. Both schedules feature quantity premia at unit $q = 3$. Thus the functions *may* violate subadditivity at this point. In fact, schedule A violates subadditivity, whilst B is subadditive. To see this, apply the test, equation (19.5). Thus for A, $R(3) = 60 > R(1) + R(2) = 55$, which violates (19.5). An individual would never buy 3 units in one purchase. For schedule B, on the other hand, the marginal price at $q = 3$ is reduced to 20, and this (just) makes the function subadditive. To see this, consider the cost for all the possible ways of purchasing 3 units: $R(3) = 55$, $3R(1) = 60$, and $R(1) + R(2) = 55$. Thus $R(3) \le R(1) + R(2)$ and $R(3) \le R(1) + R(1) + R(1)$. Of course, schedule B has only passed the test at $q = 3$ and the function is only subadditive if (19.5) holds for all q. In principle, all the other output levels need to be checked. However, these feature constant or declining marginal prices, and so will not contradict subadditivity, as the reader may care to verify.

Of course, if the firm could identify individual customers so as to prevent them from making repeat purchases, then the above restriction (that the choice of outlay schedule is effectively restricted to the class of subadditive outlay schedules) would not apply. However, even in this case, whilst quantity premia would then be feasible, in practice it turns out they are not likely to feature widely; profit maximization will usually involve quantity discounts (see section 19.6).

Table 19.1 Examples of outlay schedules

		quantity q				
		1	2	3	4	5 or more
Schedule A	mgl price $p(q)$	20	15	25	15	10
	Total outlay $R(q)$	20	35	60	75	85
Shedule B	mgl price $p(q)$	20	15	20	15	10
	Total outlay $R(q)$	20	35	55	70	80

19.4 Psychological Aspects of Quantity Discounts

The psychology associated with quantity discounting is highly seductive. It looks as though the firm is in fact doing the consumer a favour. Consumers may even perceive the quantity discount as arising because the firm is passing on economies of scale in selling at higher volumes; they are thus likely to perceive it as equitable or fair. The firm presents quantity discounts as price reductions relative to the product's 'normal' price. In fact, non-linear pricing schedules featuring quantity discounts will generally feature a marginal price for small levels of consumption which is higher than would have been the case had the firm been constrained to maximize profits using a uniform price. However, the 'exploitation' of the small-volume consumer is not observed because the counterfactual uniform price is not available for comparison. Small-volume consumers do not feel exploited because they do not know what they are missing.

Two-part and multi-part tariffs are widespread in industries such as electricity, gas, and telecommunications. In many cases, the firm has to make a customer-specific investment in equipment in order to supply the product (the lines, pipework into the customer's property, etc.). The fixed-fee part of tariff schedules is often explained to the customer as covering costs of this type. However, in practice, the licence fee or fixed charge can be considerably in excess of that required to cover such costs (a good example of this being the high price for hiring telephone handsets in the UK prior to the privatization of British Telecom). Tariff rebalancing following privatization has been a major and contentious area for firms and their regulators in the UK. Tariff rebalancing involves changing the marginal price and the licence fee in such a way that the firm's overall revenue does not change significantly.[3]

---

[3] Regulators may want the marginal price to be aligned with the marginal cost of supply (i.e. getting the proper cost signals across to the customer) but this often comes up against distributional problems. For example, disadvantaged consumer groups (senior citizens, the unemployed etc.) tend to use the telephone sparingly but are relatively expensive to supply; such users tend to be cross-subsidized by heavy users, and realignment to reflect more closely the costs of provision would tend to make them worse off.

19.5 Exclusion

Consider the case of the two-part tariff (TPT). The revenue raised by such a tariff is given by

$$R_{TPT} = F + pq, \qquad (19.6)$$

where F is the licence fee (for telecoms or most public utilities, a quarterly charge independent of how much is consumed), p is the marginal price (constant), and q is the quantity purchased by the consumer. In the absence of the licence fee, a consumer gets consumer surplus $CS(q)$, equal to the area denoted in Figure 19.4. With the licence fee, the individual gets only $CS(q) = S(q) - F$. The consumer chooses q so as to maximize consumer surplus; accordingly, the choice of q is determined by the intersection of the individual's demand curve with the marginal price line, and this is generally unaffected by the magnitude of the licence fee F.

It would seem that for any given price p, the firm can increase its profits by increasing F. Increasing F simply transfers consumer surplus from the individual to the firm. Indeed, so long as there is no exclusion, this is correct; the firm does increase its profits. However, as F increases, more and more individuals are likely to be priced out of the market completely. Thus, if F is so large that there is an individual for whom $S(q) - F < 0$ in Figure 19.4, that individual will choose $q = 0$ and exit from the market. That is, consumers only enter the market if

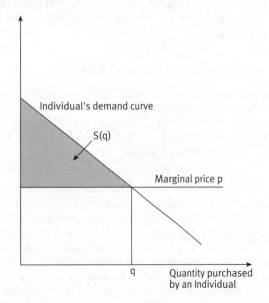

Fig. 19.4 Two-part tariffs and exclusion

they can get positive consumer surplus. Thus profit maximization involves trading off the gains to be had from increasing F (and so gaining revenue from those who remain in the market) against the fact that increasing F increases the number excluded from the market. That is, profit maximization will generally involve setting an optimal level of exclusion.. The mathematics of optimizing tariffs (and determining the level of exclusion) is beyond the scope of this text (see Dobbs 1995 or Lockwood 1993 for relatively simple examples which involve determining optimal exclusion levels).

19.6 Calculating the Optimal Non-Linear Price Schedule

In choosing a profit-maximizing uniform price for a single product, all that is required is estimation of the demand function, a relation between price and the quantity sellable at that price. The design of more complex tariffs requires greater demand information; this is because the advantage to the firm of the more sophisticated tariffs derives from the fact that individuals respond differently to changes in price. The approach adopted here is first to introduce ideas in terms of individual demand curves (since these are relatively familiar). It is then shown how this information can be transposed into what is termed a 'demand profile'; it is the demand profile which forms the basis for optimizing price schedules.

19.6.1 Individual Demand Functions

A very common way of modelling demand is to assume that individual demand curves have the same downward slope, differing only in respect of the vertical intercept. A simple example of this is the linear demand specification:

$$\rho(q, \theta) = \alpha_0 = \alpha_1 q + \theta. \qquad (19.7)$$

Here $\alpha_0, \alpha_1 > 0$ are constants and $\rho(q, \theta)$ denotes an individual's marginal willingness to pay for q units of the good. θ can be interpreted as some defining characteristic of the individual; thus a given value for θ defines a particular individual's demand curve (see Figure 19.5). It is assumed that $\partial \rho / \partial q < 0$ (demand curves all have the same negative slope) and that $\partial p / \partial \theta > 0$ (thus a larger individual characteristic θ implies a higher intercept for that indi-

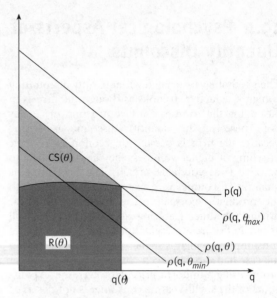

Fig. 19.5 The θ-individual's choice

vidual's demand curve). θ could be interpreted as a taste variable (see e.g. Goldman *et al.* 1984, Dobbs 1993) or as the individual's income level (see e.g. Roberts 1979). The value of the taste or income parameter of each individual is of course unobservable by the firm (it is known only to the individual) although the firm is assumed to know the distribution of tastes or income across the population of potential consumers.

Figure 19.5 illustrates the idea that there is a distribution for θ, and hence a distribution of individual customer demand curves, lying between the lowest (associated with θ_{min}) and the highest (associated with θ_{max}). A specimen intermediate demand function is depicted, and given the choice by the firm of the price schedule $P(q)$, the consumer makes the choice $q(\theta)$ such that marginal willingness to pay at this consumption level is just equal to the price paid; that is,

$$\rho(q(\theta), \theta) = p(q(\theta)). \qquad (19.8)$$

The consumer gains consumer surplus $CS(\theta)$ equal to the shaded region (the area $R(\theta)$ under the price schedule represents the sum paid over by the θ-consumer to the monopolist).

19.6.2 The Demand Profile

It is possible to analyse the problem of maximizing profits in the context of the above description of individual demand curves (see e.g. Goldman *et al.*

1984). However, at an introductory level it is easier to discuss such ideas by using what is termed the demand profile.

Definition 19.3 The demand profile specifies the number of consumers x who are willing to pay (at least) the marginal price P for the qth unit. Thus x will normally be a declining function of P and q: $x = X(q, P)$.

Given the distribution of individual demand curves, it is possible to estimate the demand profile. The approach is illustrated in Figure 19.6.

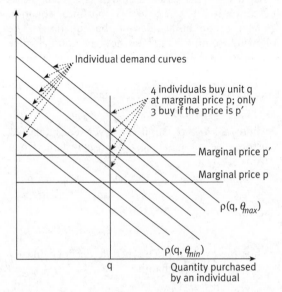

Fig. 19.6 From individual demand curves to the demand profile

For each level of sales q (to a customer, not in aggregate), given a marginal price $p = P(q)$ at that sales level, x is given by the number of demand curves which lie immediately above the point (p, q). Clearly, given the full set of demand curves, it is possible to compute the value of x for all values of p and $q > 0$.

19.6.3 The Optimal Non-Uniform Pricing Schedule

For simplicity, the case where there is exclusion is not considered (no one is priced out of the market). Let $x = X(q, P)$ denote the number of individuals who buy at least the amount q when there is a uniform price P. The function $X(q, P)$ is assumed to be differentiable and strictly decreasing in both q

and P. For simplicity, let c be the constant marginal cost of production. Fixed costs are ignored; they do not alter the optimal pricing policy, of course.

The firm can choose a different price for each unit; it follows that it should maximize the marginal profitability, or profit contribution, from each level of sales to consumers. The marginal profit contribution from all those who buy at least q units is, for the qth unit they purchase, denoted $M\pi(q, P)$. This is given as

$$M\pi(q, P) = (P - c)X(q, P), \qquad (19.9)$$

where P denotes the marginal price paid for the qth unit purchased by a consumer. Thus in (19.9), $(P - c)$ is the profit margin and $X(q, P)$ is the number of individuals who buy a qth unit. Two cases are now considered: First, the one in which p and q are restricted to discrete values, and, following this, the one in which p and q are both continuous.

(a) The Discrete Case

In the case where p and q are discrete, optimal prices can be determined by direct enumeration of the marginal profitability condition (19.9). Table 19.1 gives the type of information required (only a small number of discrete prices and quantities are considered, but the approach can easily be extended to a finer grid of prices and quantities).

Table 19.2 Consumer demand at different prices

Price, P	Quantity, Q			
	1	2	3	4
£1.1	1000	900	800	700
£1.2	900	700	500	300
£1.3	700	400	300	200
£1.4	400	100	50	0

At £1.10, at least 1000 people buy 1 unit of product, 900 buy at least 2, and so on. Notice that this implies that at price £1.10, 100 people bought exactly 1 unit (i.e. 1000–900). Suppose every unit costs just £1 to produce. Then it is straightforward to determine an optimal non-uniform price schedule by direct enumeration of profit. The firm chooses a price $P(1)$ to be paid for the first unit, $P(2)$ for the second, and so on. Each is chosen separately. By assumption, each price is restricted to £1.10, £1.20, £1.30, or £1.40. The profit raised on the first unit at each of these prices is shown in Table 19.3

Thus the optimal price for $P(1)$ is £1.30 (indicated

Table 19.3 Finding the price to set for the first unit

Price P(1)	Revenue
1.10	(1.10 − 1.00) × 1000 = 100
1.20	(1.20 − 1.00) × 900 = 180
1.30*	(1.30 − 1.00) × 700 = 210
1.40	(1.40 − 1.00) × 400 = 160

by * in the table). For the second unit, the optimal price for $P(2)$ is £1.20 (see Table 19.4).

Continuing on in the same fashion gives $P(3) =$ £1.20 and $P(4) =$ £1.10.[4]

Table 19.4 Finding the price to set for the second unit

Price P(2)	Revenue
1.10	(1.10 − 1.00) × 900 = 90
1.20*	(1.20 − 1.00) × 700 = 140
1.30	(1.30 − 1.00) × 400 = 120
1.40	(1.40 − 1.00) × 100 = 40

(b) The Continuous Case

In this case, p and q are both continuous variables. It follows that the standard approach of analysing first-order conditions is appropriate here. Thus the object is to maximize the profit contribution coming to the firm from the qth unit, $M\pi(q, P)$, by choosing the price P for this unit. Optimal P is thus given from the first-order condition,

$$\partial M\pi(q)/\partial P = X(q, P) + (P - c)\partial X(q, P)/\partial p = 0. \tag{19.10}$$

Making $(P - c)$ the subject of the equation and dividing both sides by P gives

$$\left(\frac{P - c}{P}\right) = -\left(\frac{X(q, P)}{P[\partial X(q, P)/\partial P]}\right)$$

$$= -\left(\frac{1}{\eta(q, P)}\right), \tag{19.11}$$

where the elasticity is defined as $\eta(q, P) = [\partial X(q, P)/\partial P][P/[X(q, P)]$. Just as in the single-product monopoly case and the uniform price discrimin-

[4] This example features a declining price schedule. Had the calculations led to any part of the schedule having upward slope, there might have been an incentive for consumers to make multiple orders of smaller quantities (the problem of quantity premia mentioned earlier). A more sophisticated analysis is required if the naive approach discussed above leads to the suggestion that there should be quantity premia.

ation case, this is an **inverse elasticity rule**. However, the interpretation is slightly different. Here P denotes marginal price and it varies with q, the number of units sold to the customer; indeed equation (19.11) indicates it should vary with the elasticity of demand associated with that level of sales. The intuition is that the more inelastic the consumer, the greater the marginal price mark-up. (e.g. in the discrete case, if the number of consumers buying at least 3 units hardly varies with $P(3)$ when its value is changed, then it makes sense to set $P(3)$ higher).

As in the other cases, although (19.11) is pleasingly intuitive, it is in general a non-linear equation (P features on both sides of the equation). The following example illustrates how an optimal price schedule can be calculated if $X(q, P)$ is a given analytic function.

EXAMPLE 19.6 (The linear case). Let

$$X(q, P) = \alpha_0 - \alpha_1 P - \alpha_2 q,$$

where α_0, α_1, $\alpha_2 > 0$ are given constants. As before, let marginal cost be c, constant. Then from (19.11),

$$\partial M\pi(q)/\partial P = X(q, P) + (P - c)\partial X(q, P)/\partial P$$
$$= (\alpha_0 - \alpha_1 P - \alpha_2 q) - (P - c)\alpha_1 = 0,$$

so that

$$p = (\alpha_0 + \alpha_1 c - \alpha_2 q)/(2\alpha_1).$$

Thus the optimal price schedule declines linearly with q, the order quantity.

19.7 Estimating Demand Profiles

The types of firms which are likely to find second-degree price discrimination feasible are often in a position of having detailed customer records over a considerable period of time. It is also often the case that they are relatively mature industries for which demand is relatively stable (e.g. electricity, gas, water) although there are some industries where the pace of change is rather more rapid (e.g. telecommunications). With relatively stable individual demand and detailed records, the kind of optimization discussed above is quite feasible, because it is usually possible to estimate the demand profile. The profile can be estimated directly; however, it has already been shown in section 19.5 that, given individual demand functions, it is a straightforward procedure to compute the demand profile. In principle, it is possible to estimate a demand equation of type (19.7) for each and every individual. This would allow slopes and intercepts to vary across individuals. However, with large numbers of customers, a more aggregated analysis is typical; for example, one might assume that all individuals have the same slope coefficient, so that (19.7) characterizes all individuals (they only differ by the individual characteristic, or error term, θ). First, note that any consumer who enters the market chooses to consume up to the point where marginal willingness to pay equals the marginal price. For simplicity, suppose the firm has in the past charged a uniform price p (or a simple two-part tariff for which there is a constant marginal price p). Then, from (19.7),

$$\rho(q, \theta) = \alpha_1 q + \theta = p. \qquad (19.12)$$

Solving for q, this gives

$$q = (\alpha_0/\alpha_1) + (-1/\alpha_1)p + (1/\alpha_1). \qquad (19.13)$$

This is an equation of the form

$$q = \beta_0 + \beta_1 p + \mu. \qquad (19.14)$$

Thus it would appear that a simple regression of individual consumption levels on price would reveal the coefficients β_0 and β_1 and hence give estimates for α_0 and α_1 (since $\alpha_1 = -1/\beta_1$ and $\alpha_0 = \beta_0/\beta_1$) and the estimated distribution for μ would give information about the distribution for θ. Unfortunately things are not so straightforward on the estimation side; for example, it can be shown that the estimates β_0 and β_1 in a simple regression of the type described by (19.14) are inconsistent and there is a problem in that some consumers are excluded—what is termed sample truncation (which, in particular, will affect the estimated distribution for θ). Nonetheless, econometric theory has developed to the point where such complexities can be dealt with almost routinely. The econometric difficulties, however, are beyond the scope of the present chapter.[5]

19.8 Commodity Bundling and Tie-in Sales

Commodity bundling is really a feature of the multi-product firm, which is discussed at length

in Chapter 20. However, it is convenient to treat the topic here.

Definition 19.4 Mixed commodity bundling occurs when a multi-product firm bundles some of its products together; that is, the consumer can purchase the collection of goods, usually at a price below that of purchasing the goods separately.

Definition 19.5 If a multi-product firm bundles some of its products and offers only the package (and not the goods separately), this is referred to as **pure commodity bundling** (or **tie-in** sales).

Mixed commodity bundling is rather similar in its effect to that of second-degree price discrimination, where the unit price can vary depending on how much is purchased. For example, most drinks companies (Pepsi, Coca-Cola, etc.) offer their drinks in different-sized bottles. One can view a family-size bottle as a bundle of smaller-size bottles, and of course, the family size is offered at a price discount relative to purchasing the equivalent multiple of standard-size bottles. Thus, when it is the same product, bundling is formally equivalent to a form of non-linear pricing or second-degree price discrimination. More usually, the term 'product bundling' refers to the case where the products are not identical.

19.8.1 Pure Bundling (Tie-in Sales)

Stigler (1963) gave an example where pure bundling might be beneficial to a monopolist. A film distributor has two films $F1$ and $F2$ to distribute and two exhibitors (cinema chains) $C1,C2$ are willing to pay (*WTP*) the amounts in Table 19.5 for the rights to show these films.

The distributor is unable to discriminate between the two exhibitors on price; accordingly the most revenue he can raise in selling the two films separately is to set $P(F1)$ at £7 million (so both buy it) and $P(F2)$ at £2.5 million (again so both buy it).

Table 19.5 Example of pure bundling

WTP	F1	F2	F1 + F2
		Films	
C1	£8m	£2.5m	£10.5m
C2	£7m	£3m	£10m

m = million

[5] See Wilson (1993) for a discussion of the econometric methods used for demand estimating in the presence of non-linear pricing by firms.

The distributor sells both films to both exhibitors and gets 2 × (£7 million + £2.5 million) = £19 million. If the distributor had bundled the films together, he/she could have charged £10 million so both exhibitors would have been induced to buy, the distributor thus making £20m.

This example shows that pure bundling can in some circumstances be advantageous. More generally, pure bundling or tie-in sales can sometimes be used as a form of **monopoly leverage**. That is, when a firm has a monopoly over one product, and produces a second for which there are (possibly many) competitors, it can sometimes manage to obtain a degree of market power in the competitive market by tying in sales of the two products (as Microsoft has recently done with its Internet browser and Windows software). Since this carries us further away from the area of non-linear pricing, and into that of multi-product firm pricing strategy, explanation and examples of such processes is deferred to section 20.2.

19.8.2 Mixed Bundling

Would mixed bundling enable the firm to increase its profits even further? As a general proposition, mixed bundling can never be worse than pure bundling, since pure bundling is merely a special case where the prices set for the products on their own are so high that no one purchases them. Mixed bundling is economically much more important than pure bundling, and it works in essentially the same way as second-degree price discrimination (non-uniform pricing, quantity discounts, etc.); namely, by offering the bundle of individual products at a price which is less than one can get by buying all of the individual items separately, the firm is able to discriminate between those willing to pay more and those willing to pay less—obviously, the discrimination is more complex in character but the effect is the same.

As with quantity discounts, the approach has the same highly attractive psychology; it appears to the consumer that they are being offered a bargain with the bundle—just as with the quantity discount, it appears to be the case that buying more gives a better bargain ('the more you buy, the more you save'). Appearances can be deceptive, however; here, the counterfactual is not observed by the consumer—customers do not know what they are missing. If the firm was forced to charge a uniform price or a price for the bundle that equalled the sum

of the prices of the component parts, it would probably be the case that the profit-maximizing prices for individual units would then be lower. Product bundling allows the firm to charge higher prices for the units sold separately.

The bottom line on all forms of effective price discrimination (second-degree pricing or product bundling) is that aggregate consumer surplus is reduced relative to the non-discriminatory alternative (and the firm's profits are increased). It is an interesting observation that, whilst second-degree price discrimination often falls foul of regulators, product bundling is a strategy which has, until recently, largely escaped all forms of regulation. However, the 1998 lawsuits against Microsoft's bundling strategies suggest an increasing awareness of this type of problem (see section 20.2).

19.9 Summary

Non-linear pricing is a form of price discrimination in which the price varies with the amount that is bought. Individuals who choose different quantities end up paying different prices; typically, this involves quantity discounts—the more you buy, the cheaper the unit price becomes. This has an appealing psychology to it; the firm increases its profitability despite the fact that the consumer appears to be offered a beneficial deal (in practice, this is not so, as the price set for the first units is higher than it would be if the firm was restricted to setting a constant price per unit). Ways of estimating/calculating profit-maximizing price schedules were discussed, including the issue of customer exclusion. Finally, the related idea of product bundling was considered as a type of non-linear pricing.

19.10 Review Questions

1. Under what market conditions will a firm be able to practise non-linear pricing (second-degree price discrimination)?

2. Why is it unlikely that a firm will set a non-linear price schedule which involves quantity premia?

3. Consider Table 19.6, which depicts the number of individuals who are expected to purchase a given quantity at given prices.

Table 19.6 Consumer demand at different prices

Price, P	Quantity, Q			
	1	2	3	4
£2.00	3000	2600	2400	2100
£2.20	2600	2200	1600	900
£2.40	2200	1300	1000	600
£2.60	1300	300	150	0

At £2.00, at least 3000 people buy 1 unit of product, 2600 buy at least 2, and so on (so at price £2.00, 400 people buy exactly 1 unit (i.e. 3000–2600). Suppose every unit costs just £1.90 to produce. Assuming that the firm has decided to price in steps of £0.20, determine the optimal pricing schedule on the range 1–4 units.

4. Suppose the demand profile takes the form

$$X(q, P) = 100 - P - q$$

and that marginal cost is £1 per unit (constant with output).

(a) What is the structure of the optimal price schedule?

(b) What is the marginal price for someone who buys 4 units?

(c) How much would an individual have to hand over to buy 4 units?

19.11 Further Reading

Wilson (1993) gives a thorough treatment of all aspects of non-linear pricing and an extensive bibliography. Despite the fact that firms make extensive use of quantity discounts and related non-linear pricing structures, few managerial, business, or intermediate microeconomics texts treat the topic in any detail.

20 Multi-Product Firms and Multi-Product Pricing

Objective This Chapter examines why multi-product firms are so prevalent and then explores the problem of profit-maximizing multi-product pricing.

Prerequisites Chapter 3 gives the necessary background in optimization; Chapter 8 introduces the concepts of own-price and cross-price elasticities used here.

Keywords cost independence, cost inter-dependence, cost subadditivity, demand interdependence, economies of scope, monopoly leveraging, technically competitive, technically complementary.

20.1 Introduction

Although economics texts at elementary and intermediate levels tend to focus on the single-product firm, in practice most firms produce more than one product. The reasons for this can usually be traced to either technological or organizational economies; these are addressed in section 20.2. Following this, the rest of this chapter focuses on the problem of pricing in the multi-product firm. Conglomerate firms may produce products which bear little relationship to one another, and whose production processes may be largely independent. In such cases, where products are genuinely independent of each other on both the demand side and the production side, the problem of pricing and marketing products is no different from that of the single-product firm. However, in practice, most firms produce a product line in which the individual products are either substitutes (often strong substitutes) or complements.

EXAMPLE 20.1 Most car manufacturers offer not only a range of models (substitutes), but also a range of variations for any given model type (close substitutes). That is, these products will feature positive cross-price elasticities (increasing one car's price will increases sales of the other models). They also manufacture spare parts for the cars they offer to the public. Spares are typically complements, having negative cross-price elasticity

(increasing the price of spares decreases the demand for the associated car).

It follows that most of the products sold by the firm will be demand-interdependent. Furthermore, there is the possibility that there are cost interdependencies too. These arise when the marginal cost of manufacturing one product is affected not only by its own output level, but also by the output of the other products produced by the firm. This typically happens when products utilize common production processes, common inputs, common inventory, etc.

These interdependencies imply, theoretically at least, that it is no longer possible to determine the profit-maximizing price of each product in isolation. Pricing of the whole range of the firm's products needs to be undertaken simultaneously, in a system-wide solution. The formal analysis is given in section 20.4. However, it is worth remarking that in practice most firms use ad hoc rules of thumb (often simple mark-up pricing rules) which take little account of the interdependencies discussed here. Section 20.5 discusses what insights the formal analysis of section 20.4 gives for those who wish to take some account of interaction effects, and points out the dangers of ignoring interdependencies. Of course, some firms do practise the sophisticated multi-product analysis of the type described here. Large firms and public utilities blessed with fairly stable demand functions are most likely to fall into this category, since the approach does rely on the statistical estimation of demand functions. Thus electricity, gas, telecoms, and posts are more amenable to this type of analysis.[1]

20.2 Why Multi-Product Firms?

Essentially, products are likely to be produced within a single organizational structure if it is more profitable to do so than to produce the goods separately. The issue of what determines the internal structure and external boundaries of the firm is discussed in much greater detail in Part VII so the treatment here is accordingly brief. The reasons can be loosely categorized as demand-related, cost-related, or financial. I deal with each in turn.

20.2.1 Demand-Related Reasons for Multi-Product Firms

The argument here is that drawing products under the umbrella of a single firm may help to facilitate price discrimination, to create barriers to entry, and to leverage monopoly power.

(a) Price Discrimination

Chapter 19 demonstrated that a firm with monopoly power could improve its profitability by designing a non-linear pricing schedule by which it sells its product. Typically, this involves quantity discounts. Firms routinely apply this type of pricing when they bundle products. Thus, a car manufacturer will typically offer a model with a wide range of specifications, such that a higher-specification model is cheaper than the cost of buying a lower-specification model and buying separately the additional specification. If we imagine separate firms providing each item of specification, each with a monopoly over its item, and ask what the benefits are of putting these firms together in a single unit, the answer is that, if there are no cost-side savings, the gain can only be in organizational economies. That is, the pricing of different commodity bundles is something which is likely to be better co-ordinated and controlled within a single firm than by a larger number of firms. Whilst it is possible in principle for individual

firms to negotiate and co-ordinate their pricing policies to achieve the same outcome, this is likely to be difficult and costly relative to that of internalizing the problem, making it into a multi-product firm pricing problem.

(b) Barriers to Entry and Monopoly Leveraging

It is also sometimes possible through what is termed monopoly leveraging, to exploit monopoly power in one market either to prevent others being able to enter, or to achieve a dominant position in another market. This is perhaps most likely to occur in markets where there is a degree of lock-in to the monopoly product. A famous example of lock-in is the QWERTY keyboard. Apparently faster layouts exist, but they cannot get into the market because of the huge installed base; everyone knows how to use QWERTY and all this asset-specific human capital would be lost in a switch to an alternative layout (see David 1985). A similar argument applies to Microsoft's dominant position regarding its Windows software.

> **EXAMPLE 20.2** Microsoft was indicted in the US for anti-competitive practices (*Financial Times*, 19 May 1998: 8). The US Justice Department (and 20 US states) charged in their anti-trust lawsuits against Microsoft that (amongst other anti-competitive practices) Microsoft forced PC manufacturers to install its Internet browser software (Microsoft Explorer) as a condition of obtaining licences for the Windows 95 operating system.

The point behind Microsoft's behaviour is that its Internet browser is not a superior product to those of the competition—but, because Microsoft has a stranglehold over the market for operating systems, it is able to leverage a significant market share for that product.

Does such leveraging benefit the firm? A simple argument that it does can be given, based upon the dominant-firm model presented in section 14.5. The idea is that the dominant firm (here Microsoft, selling its Internet browser) sets the market price, and other firms, acting as a competitive fringe, match this price. If so, then the dominant firm faces a residual demand curve, and sets price such that the marginal revenue from this residual demand curve is equal to the marginal cost of production. The price set is then matched by the other manufacturers. The point is that the dominant firm leads the market, and in particular, is able to set a price above its marginal production cost (and a price

---

[1] For applications, see Brown and Sibley (1985), Oren *et al.* (1987), or Cuthbertson and Dobbs (1996).

above that which would result if no firm had a dominant position). The dominant firm gains additional profit from the market (and this entails the usual monopoly welfare loss). Thus, tying products together may be beneficial for the multi-product firm—in that tying may earn greater profit than if the products were produced separately.

Of course, in principle, separate firms can also tie their products too, and such practices are not uncommon:

EXAMPLE 20.3 Microsoft also entered into anti-competitive agreements with the largest online services, such as America Online, as well as with Internet providers. In return for promoting these services on Windows, these companies agreed not to promote Netscape's browser software—Netscape being an Internet browser competitor to Microsoft Explorer. (For more details, see *Financial Times*, 19 May 1998: 8.)

Inter-firm collusive agreements of this type are typically illegal and so are subject to government intervention (as in the above examples). It is somewhat more difficult for the state to track such processes if they occur within a firm, so this suggests a further rationale, alongside the usual organizational economies,[2] for the multi-product firm.[3]

20.2.2 Cost-Related Reasons for Multi-Product Firms

The cost-based rationale for the multi-product firm is based on the concept of economies of scope, which is in fact merely a special case of cost-subadditivity. Cost-subadditivity was defined in Chapter 14 (see Definition 14.3, page 221: loosely, a cost function is subadditive if it is cheaper to produce any given output vector in one batch rather than in a set of smaller batches). Thus, suppose the multi-product firm produces n products, such that $\mathbf{q} = (q_1, \ldots, q_n)$ denotes its output vector, where q_i represents the quantity produced of the ith output, and that $C(\mathbf{q})$ represents the cost function (the minimum cost of producing output $\mathbf{q}$).

Definition 20.1 A cost function $C(q)$ is said to manifest

economies of scope if $C(\mathbf{q}^a + \mathbf{q}^b) < C(\mathbf{q}^a) + C(\mathbf{q}^b)$, where $\mathbf{q}^a$, $\mathbf{q}^b$ are disjoint output vectors (that is, if $q_i^a > 0$ then $q_i^b = 0$, and if $q_i^b > 0$ then $q_i^a = 0$ for all $i = 1, \ldots, n$).[4]

In the two-product case this simply means that $C(q_1, q_2) < C(q_1, 0) + C(0, q_2)$. Here, $C(q_1, q_2)$ represents the cost of multi-product output vector (q_1, q_2), whilst $C(q_1, 0)$ represents the cost of producing output q_1 in a single-product firm etc.

The argument is very simple. If the cost function displays economies of scope, then it costs more to produce products separately rather than jointly, and so it pays to produce them in a multi-product firm. As a corollary, if there are diseconomies of scope (i.e. the inequality in the definition is reversed), then it pays to produce outputs in separate firms. If an equality holds in Definition 20.1 ($C(\mathbf{q}^a + \mathbf{q}^b) = C(\mathbf{q}^a) + C(\mathbf{q}^b)$), then it is a matter of indifference whether there is joint or separate production.

What are the sources of economies of scope? In general, economies of scope arise because input resources have the characteristics of a public good. A public input is one in which the use of the input does not deplete its availability for other uses. Thus a database, once set up, can be used by many; use by one individual does not deplete it in any significant way (although there may be access congestion, of course). Shared facilities often give rise to this type of effect; production of one item often creates spare capacity which can be utilized for the production of other items more cheaply than if they are produced in a stand-alone mode. Thus, once capacity for day-time electricity demand is installed, it is available for the provision of night-time electricity. Whilst it may be possible in principle to offer to sell the use of spare capacity to other producers, there are usually organizational economies for multi-product firms in bringing these products in-house. Of course there are many famous cases where there are natural economies of scope associated with production, such as beef and hides, mutton and sheep, wheat and straw, and the refining of oil into a multiplicity of products. It is clearly cheaper to produce these jointly rather than separately (in these cases, single-product production would simply throw away a nearly finished additional product). Multi-product production thus tends to facilitate a fuller asset (capacity) utilization over time by reducing indivisibilities or lumpiness in the production process. For

---

[2] See Chaps. 29 and 30 for an extended discussion of how transactions costs can be reduced by taking transactions inside the firm.

[3] Monopoly leveraging is a fairly contentious area; for a discussion of it in the context of the Microsoft case, see Lopatka and Page (1995), and especially Blair and Esquibel (1995).

[4] To see that this is a special case of subadditivity, compare this with Def. 14.3.

example, when a product's demand is seasonal, it pays the firm to try to find other products which can utilize the capacity at other times.

It is useful to distinguish technological or plant economies of scope from overall firm economies of scope. Technological economies of scope are those associated with the production process itself (as in the hides and beef example) whilst firm economies of scope include these, but additionally involve organizational economies of scope. Organizational economies of scope are common; the point, and not a new one (see e.g. Hicks 1935), is that it often requires very little addition in overhead (managerial resources) in order to add a new product to the product range. Baumol et al. (1982) describe overhead and capital services as quasi-public inputs, since the services that flow from overhead are either non-congestible or only partially congestible (see Chapter 27). Thus inputs such as technical and managerial expertise and experience are quasi-public inputs; ideas and information developed in one context can often be cheaply mobilized to good effect in other applications.

20.2.3 Financial Reasons for Multi-Product Firms

It is sometimes argued that, by diversification and producing a wider range of products, the firm spreads its risks, particularly if the products are not close substitutes and therefore less likely to be affected by the same environmental factors and market movements. Basic finance theory suggests this argument is fallacious, on the grounds that diversification of this type does not add value to the company. This is because shareholders are already diversified, so they get no further advantage from the firm itself diversifying (they can, relatively costlessly, do or undo any action of this type taken by the firm, simply by readjusting their portfolios). The no-advantage argument can be found in most finance texts (see e.g. Ross et al. 1996: chap, 15). When real-world complexity (managerial discretion, taxes, asymmetric information, etc.) is introduced, the picture is considerably less clear. Thus:

(i) in practice there may be some tax advantages associated with such diversification, with the possibility that the firm may benefit from the particular ways that tax authorities deal with tax losses (more products means greater scope for offsetting tax losses);

(ii) diversification may also facilitate dividend smoothing, again something which does seems to be of interest to both managers and shareholders (Ross et al. 1996: chap. 18);

(iii) managerial discretion theory suggests that managers' concerns also count—and fairly clearly, diversification is of benefit to managers, as it reduces the company's total risk, and hence the risk to their jobs. Thus one would expect some pressure for diversification from managers, even if this does not particularly advance the interests of the firm's owners;

(iv) in practice, there may also be benefits in that the larger the enterprise, the lower the costs of raising finance (equity, debt issues, etc.) may be reduced.

Thus there is an assorted range of financial pressures which tend to encourage the formation of multi-product firms.

20.2.4 Limits to Diversification?

All the above discussion suggests there may be benefits to increasing the size of the firm—to increasing the number of products produced under one umbrella. So why is there not a single global firm? What limits the boundaries of the firm? The answer is usually that there are also diseconomies associated with organization, and these eventually become significant as size increases. This issue is discussed in more detail in section 17.2 and in Part VII (in particular, Chapters 30 and 31).

20.3 Cost and Demand Categorization

Section 20.2 emphasized that, when there are economies of scope, there is an incentive to set up a multi-product firm. With common provision and use of common facilities, it is quite likely that the cost function will feature some degree of interdependency in the sense that the marginal cost of producing each product may be affected not only by its own output level, but also by that of the other products in the product range. Likewise, because products in the product range are often related and hence substitutes, demand interdependence is also common. Whenever there is interdependence on the cost or demand sides, profit-maximizing

Table 20.1 The multi-product pricing problem

		Demand	
		Independent (zero cross-price elasticities)	Interdependent (non-zero cross price elasticities)
Cost	Independent (marginal cost independent of other product outputs)	Price each product separately	System solution required
	Interdependent (marginal cost varies with other product outputs)	System solution required	System solution required

prices cannot be determined for products independently. Table 20.1 emphasizes this point.

The rest of section 20.3 explores in more detail the ideas of independence and interdependence.

20.3.1 Cost Dependence or Independence

Two products are cost-independent if, as the output of the first product is varied, the marginal cost of the second does not change. A set of products is said to be cost-independent if, when each output is varied, this variation does not affect the marginal costs of producing any of the other products in the set.

Suppose there are n products, and the output vector is written as $\mathbf{q} = (q_1, \ldots q_n)$. Let the cost function be $C(\mathbf{q})$; this merely expresses the idea that total cost depends on how much is produced of each of the individual outputs q_1, q_2 etc. Assuming a smooth cost function, the marginal cost for the ith product is defined as $MC_i = \partial C(\mathbf{q})/\partial q_i$, the rate at which cost increases when q_i increases. The idea is that MC_i is a function of all the outputs $\mathbf{q}$, and so in general will vary whenever any one of the elements of $\mathbf{q}$ is varied.

Definition 20.2 Two products i, j are said to be **cost-independent** if MC_i is unaffected by q_j and MC_j is unaffected by q_i.

Definition 20.3 Two products i, j are **cost-interdependent** if $\partial MC_i/\partial q_j \neq 0$. They are said to be **technically complementary** if $\partial MC_i/\partial q_j < 0$ and **technically competitive** if $\partial MC_i/\partial q_j > 0$.

These definitions are entirely intuitive; technically complementary products have the property that increasing the output of one reduces the marginal cost of producing the other, whilst technically com-

petitive products are such that increasing the output of one increases the marginal cost of producing the other. Note that the effect is always symmetric; that is, if increasing q_1 increases MC_i then it follows that increasing q_j increases MC_i. This is because[5]

$$\partial MC_i/\partial q_j = \partial^2 C/\partial q_i \partial q_j = \partial^2 C/\partial q_j \partial q_i$$
$$= \partial MC_j/\partial q_i \qquad (20.1)$$

Thus $\partial MC_i/\partial q_j = \partial MC_j/\partial q_i$, so if one is positive (or negative or zero) so is the other.

A set of products is cost-interdependent if for each product in the set, its marginal cost depends on the output of at least one other product in the set. Two (non-overlapping) sets of products A, B are said to be cost-independent if $\partial MC_i/\partial q_j = 0$ for all $i \in A, j \in B$.

EXAMPLE 20.4 Consider the following cost functions:

(i) $C(q_1, q_2) = 10 + 2q_1 + 3q_2^2$. This features cost independence, since $\partial^2 C/\partial q_1 q_2 = 0$.

(ii) $C(q_1, q_2) = 2q_1 q_2^2$. This features cost interdependence, since $\partial C/\partial q_1 = 2q_2^2 =$, so $\partial^2 C/\partial q_1 q_2 = \partial[\partial C/\partial q_1]/\partial q_2 = \partial[2q_2^2] = 4q_2$. This is positive for positive q_2, indicating that in this case the products are technically competitive.

20.3.2 Demand Dependence and Independence

The firm's products are often substitutes (and occasionally are complements) for each other, and hence have non-zero cross-price elasticities. Whenever the cross-price elasticity is non-zero, we say there is demand interdependence. First, the cross-price elasticity of demand (as in Chapter 8) is defined as

$$\eta_{ij} = \frac{\partial q_i}{\partial p_j}\frac{p_j}{q_i}. \qquad (20.2)$$

For example, $\eta_{ij} = 3$ means an increase of 1% in the price of good 2 increases the demand for good 1 by 3%; likewise $\eta_{44} = -2$ means an increase in the price of good 4 decreases the demand for good 4 by 2%; and so on. Notice that η_{ii} denotes the own-price elasticity of demand for good i. Given this definition of cross-price demand elasticity, we have:

Definition 20.4 Two products i and j are demand-independent if $\eta_{ij} = (\partial q_i/\partial p_j)(p_j/q_i) = 0$, or equivalently

[5] According to Young's Theorem, for a smooth function, the second-order cross-partial derivatives $\partial^2 C(\mathbf{q})/\partial q_i \partial q_j$ and $\partial^2 C(\mathbf{q})/\partial q_j \partial q_i$ are equal; the order of differentiation does not matter.

$\partial q_i / \partial p_j = 0$. They are demand-interdependent if $\eta_{ij} \neq 0$ (equivalently, $\partial q_i / \partial p_j \neq 0$). They are substitutes if $\eta_{ij} > 0$ ($\partial q_i / \partial p_j > 0$), and complements if $\eta_{ij} < 0$ ($\partial q_i / \partial p_j < 0$).

As with cost dependence-interdependence, a set of products is demand interdependent if each product in the set has at least one non-zero-cross price elasticity with respect to the price of another good in the set. The sets of products A and B are demand-independent if $\eta_{ij} = 0$ for all $i \in A, j \in B$.

20.4 The *n*-Product Pricing Problem

If there is interdependence either on the cost or on the demand side, then the theoretical problem of setting prices in order to maximize profits requires the solution of a set of simultaneous equations (equal to the number of products). It is not possible to identify this optimum by setting prices for the various products either sequentially or independently. However, if there is independence on both the cost and demand side, then the products may be priced in isolation. To see this, we examine the mathematics of the problem; although diagrams can give some insight into special cases,[6] they give little insight into the general problem.

The necessary ingredients for optimizing prices for multiple products are estimates of the demand functions for each product and the cost function which describes how cost varies as the output mix and volume is varied. Chapters 9 and 11 discuss various approaches to these problems. Here, it is assumed that demand and cost functions are known with certainty.[7]

---

[6] A diagram can be used to illustrate the (rather special) fixed-proportions case. A classic of this type is the production of hides and beef, joint products supposedly produced in fixed proportions. However, even here there is some variability in the quantity of each produced. If a cow were a sphere, its volume would increase in proportion to the radius cubed, its surface area in proportion to the radius squared—so in the case of spherical cows, letting the cattle grow larger means more meat relative to hide! Some might argue that cattle are not well approximated as spherical. Whether the argument holds in the case of 'cow-shaped' cows clearly requires further analysis!

The point being made here is that it is hard to think of many cases where there is no possibility of varying the proportions of the output mix of products. Accordingly, the text treats this general case.

[7] Chap. 21 discusses the effect of uncertainty on pricing (and establishes conditions under which it is valid simply to use expected demand curves).

Suppose the firm manufactures n products. Ordinary demand functions (assumed to be differentiable functions) for these take the form

$$q_i = f_i(\mathbf{p}), \quad i = 1, \ldots, n, \quad (20.3)$$

where $q_i, i = 1, \ldots, n$ are the quantities demanded and

$$\mathbf{p} = (p_1, p_2, \ldots, p_n) \quad (20.4)$$

are the prices set by the firm. The formulation in (20.3) indicates that the prices of each of the firm's n products may have an influence on the sales of each product (although typically the own price will be the major determinant of an individual product's sales). The total cost of producing output $\mathbf{q} = (q_1, q_2, \ldots, q_n)$ is assumed to be a smooth function $C(\mathbf{q})$. The firm's profits are thus given as

$$\pi = (\textstyle\sum_{i=1}^{n} p_i q_i) - C(\mathbf{q}). \quad (20.5)$$

Given the ordinary demand function (20.3), the first-order necessary conditions for maximum profits are most easily obtained through analysis in price space. This treats the n prices as choice variables; the first-order conditions are thus[8]

$$\partial \pi / \partial p_j = q_j + \textstyle\sum_{i=1}^{n}(p_i - \partial C(\mathbf{q}) / \partial p_i)(\partial q_i / \partial p_j)$$
$$= 0 \quad j = 1, \ldots, n. \quad (20.6)$$

In fact, so long as the demand and cost functions are reasonably well behaved, these n equations, in conjunction with the demand equation (20.3), suffice to identify the optimum prices, outputs, and attainable profit for the firm. However, this may not be immediately obvious; the following numerical example illustrates the solution process.

EXAMPLE 20.5 Consider a simple two-product firm whose cost function takes the simple linear form

$$C(q_1, q_2) = 100 + 10q_1 + 20q_2 \quad (i)$$

(so costs are independent) and whose demand functions are also linear and given as

$$q_1 = 100 - p_1 + p_2 \quad (ii)$$
$$q_1 = 50 + p_1 - 2p_2. \quad (iii)$$

The profit function can then be written as

$$\pi = (p_1 q_1 + p_2 q_2 - 100 - 10q_1 - 20q_2. \quad (iv)$$

Using (ii) and (iii), this can be written as

$$\pi = (p_1 - 10)(100 - p_1 + p_2)$$
$$+ (p_2 - 20)(50 + p_1 - 2p_2) - 100. \quad (v)$$

Differentiating this with respect to the two choice

---

[8] Since, by the chain rule, $\partial[C(\mathbf{q})] / \partial p_j = \sum_{i=1}^{n} [\partial C(\mathbf{q}) / \partial q_i](\partial q_i / \partial p_j)$. The point is that in the light of (20.3), each element of $\mathbf{q}$ is affected by the change in price p_j.

variables gives the first-order conditions as follows (expand (v) first if you find it easier to then perform the differentiation):

$$\partial \pi / \partial p_1 = (100 + p_1 - p_2) - (p_1 - 10) + 2(p_2 - 20)$$
$$= 90 - 2p_1 + 24p_2 = 0 \qquad \text{(vi)}$$

$$\partial \pi / \partial p_2 = (p_1 - 10) + (50 + p_1 - 2p_2) - 2(p_2 - 20)$$
$$= 80 - 2p_1 + 4p_2 = 0. \qquad \text{(vii)}$$

Solving this pair of equations gives optimal prices $p_1 = 130$ and $p_2 = 85$. Substituting these values into (ii) and (iii) gives quantities $q_1 = 55$ and $q_2 = 10$, and substituting the prices into (v) gives profit level 7150.

Notice in Example 20.5 that, with two products, the first-order conditions generate two equations in the two unknowns p_1 and p_2. This observation can be generalized; with n products, there are n equations which, if well behaved, can be solved for the n prices $p_1, \ldots p_n$. The simple linear form of the cost and demand functions makes the analytic solution process fairly straightforward in the above example (and linear systems such as this can always be viewed as approximations to more complex non-linear systems in the region of the optimum). More generally, however, the equations obtained may be non-linear and complex in structure. In such cases, a variety of algorithms exist which can be used to obtain the optimal solution.[9]

20.5 The Elasticity Rule, Substitutes and Complements

The first-order conditions can be rearranged to construct an elasticity rule. Recall that in the single-product case, the elasticity rule was that

$$\frac{p - MC}{p} = -\frac{1}{\eta}, \text{ or, equivalently, } \left(\frac{p - MC}{p} \right) \eta = -1.$$
$$\text{(20.7)}$$

That is, the optimal mark-up is related to the inverse of the own-price elasticity of demand η. When product demand is elastic (e.g. -10), the

---

mark-up is low (10%) whilst if demand is relatively inelastic (e.g. -2), the mark-up is much higher (50%).

Writing $MC_i = \partial C(\mathbf{q}) / \partial q_i$ as the marginal cost of the ith product, and using this and dividing through by q_j in equation (20.6), gives

$$1 + \sum_{i=1}^{n} (p_i - MC_i)(\partial q_i / \partial p_j)(1 / q_j) = 0$$
$$j = 1, \ldots, n. \qquad \text{(20.8)}$$

This can be rewritten as

$$\sum_{i=1}^{n} \left(\frac{p_i - MC_i}{p_i} \right) \left(\frac{p_j}{q_i} \frac{\partial q_i}{\partial p_j} \right) \left(\frac{p_i q_i}{p_j q_j} \right) = -1 \quad j = 1, \ldots, n.$$
$$\text{(20.9)}$$

Notice that (20.9) is obtained from (20.8) by taking 1 to the other side and then multiplying both denominator and numerator of the left-hand sum by the term $p_i q_i p_j$. The equation can then be arranged as in (20.9) so that the first term in the left-hand sum is a price mark-up, the middle term is a cross-price elasticity η_{ij}, and the third term is a ratio of revenues taken from products i and j. Hence (20.9) is written more compactly as

$$\sum_{i=1}^{n} \left(\frac{p_i - MC_i}{p_i} \right) \eta_{ij} \left(\frac{R_i}{R_j} \right) = -1 \quad j = 1, \ldots, n.$$
$$\text{(20.10)}$$

Unfortunately, although this looks a little like the single-product elasticity result (20.7), it is in fact considerably more complex (each of the equations in (20.10) involves all of the product mark-ups). It is possible to re-express (20.10) by splitting off the term $i = j$ from the sum on the left, and taking all the other terms to the other side, to give:[10]

$$\left(\frac{p_j - MC_j}{p_j} \right) \left(\frac{R_j}{R_j} \right) \eta_{jj} = -1 - \sum_{\substack{i=1 \\ i \neq j}}^{n} \left(\frac{p_i - MC_i}{p_i} \right) \eta_{ij} \left(\frac{R_i}{R_j} \right)$$

$$j = 1, \ldots, n. \qquad \text{(20.11)}$$

Noticing $R_j / R_j = 1$ and dividing through by η_{jj}, we obtain

$$\left(\frac{p_j - MC_j}{p_j} \right) = -\left(\frac{1}{\eta_{jj}} \right) - \sum_{\substack{i=1 \\ i \neq j}}^{n} \left(\frac{p_i - MC_i}{P_i} \right) \left(\frac{\eta_{ij}}{\eta_{jj}} \right) \left(\frac{R_i}{R_j} \right)$$

$$j = 1, \ldots, n. \qquad \text{(20.12)}$$

If we forget about the summation term on the right side, this is precisely the result that is obtained in third-degree price discrimination (namely that each mark-up $(p_j - MC_j) / p_j$ is set equal to the inverse of the associated demand elasticity η_{jj}). Indeed, one can think of third-degree price discri-

---

[9] Spreadsheets such as EXCEL possess such optimization algorithms. Of course, numerical solutions may only determine local optima. Whether a global optimum is found by such algorithms depends on whether or not the profit function is well behaved; see Chap. 3 for further discussion.

[10] A trick used in Tirole (1993).

mination as a special case of multi-product pricing, since in this case the market is segmented and the cross-price elasticities are indeed zero; since $\eta_{ij} = 0$ when $i \neq j$, the summation term in (20.12) does collapse to zero.

However, in the general multi-product pricing problem, the cross-price elasticities are usually non-zero; what (20.12) suggests is that the simple price–cost mark-up $(1/\eta_{ii})$ has to be further adjusted in order to take account of the spillover effects; that is, to take account of the fact that an increase in one product's price not only alters the sales of that product but also the sales of all products in the range.

It is possible to extract a little further insight from (20.12). Thus, note that the following summation term is the product of terms some of which have a known sign:

$$- \sum_{\substack{i=1 \\ i \neq j}}^{n} \left(\frac{p_i - MC_i}{p_i} \right) \left(\frac{\eta_{ij}}{\eta_{jj}} \right) \left(\frac{R_i}{R_j} \right). \qquad (20.13)$$
$$(-) \qquad\quad (+) \qquad (?)\ (+)$$

In (20.13) I have indicated that the price–cost margins are all positive, which is usually the case (it is possible for some to go negative, but only if there are strong complement effects in demand). The revenue terms are all positive and $\eta_{jj} < 0$, since this is the own-price elasticity of demand (an increase in own price reduces demand). Now, suppose that all the products are substitutes; this implies that all the $\eta_{ij} > 0$ when $i \neq j$. Hence the sign of η_{ij}/η_{jj} becomes the ratio of a positive to a negative, and so is negative. This makes the overall expression in (20.13) positive (the product of two negatives and two positives). As a corollary, if all the goods are complements to the good in question (a less likely occurrence of course), the expression in (20.13) becomes negative. This discussion suggests the following conclusions:

1. when all the other goods are substitutes, then the price of a good should be higher than that indicated by the simple inverse elasticity rule, and

2. when all the other goods are complements, then the price of a good should be lower than that indicated by the simple inverse elasticity rule.

How much higher or lower is of course a more complex question; it requires an analytic or numerical solution to the optimization problem of the type illustrated in Example 20.5.

20.6 Multiple Products and Organizational Structure

Typically, multi-product firms, particularly large firms, may be organized such that individual sections or divisions of the firm are responsible for individual products, or subsets of the total set of products manufactured by the firm. There are many reasons for this. The advantages are discussed in some detail in Chapter 30 (which considers general organizational issues within the firm) and Chapter 31 (which considers divisionalization and transfer pricing). Divisionalization helps to keep jobs manageable and can stimulate competition amongst managers or divisions, leading to improvements in the productivity of both production and marketing practices. However, there is a potential problem when the products being sold by the divisions are related in demand (either as substitutes or as complements): if a manager is concerned only with her own profit, she will ignore the spillover effects of the pricing decision for this product on the other products manufactured by the firm (and the same point applies to related decisions, such as advertizing and marketing decisions generally). Thus, the manager of the division selling the jth product, if concerned only with her own performance, will compute a price using the mark-up rule

$$\left(\frac{p_j - MC_j}{p_j} \right) = - \left(\frac{1}{\eta_{jj}} \right). \qquad (20.14)$$

Compared with (20.12), this takes no account of the spillover term (20.13). If the products are substitutes, as is usually the case for a product line of similar goods, then this suggests that individual managers/divisions will tend to set their prices too low.

The danger is thus that product managers get drawn into competing against each other, while the firm as a whole benefits only if they co-operate. Each product manager sees the demand for their product as relatively elastic (because of the presence of competition from the rest of the product line) and is inclined to set too low a price. This ignores the fact that although raising price does lose sales, it also increases the sales of other managers/divisions.[11]

---

[11] This is an externality (when one agent's actions affect the welfare or profit level of another agent and the effect is unpriced in the market). Externalities tend to imply sub-optimal outcomes (see Chap. 27).

In principle it is organizationally possible to overcome this type of problem, so long as managers meet, exchange the relevant information, and agree on an overall set of prices which maximizes the firm's profits as a whole. Indeed, if one argues that bargaining (etc.) costs are small, it can be argued that the divisions will take into account spillover effects, and will come to some form of agreement.[12] In practice, however, such agreements are costly to implement; there is considerable asymmetry of information and much scope for game-playing. For example, there are elements of a prisoners' dilemma[13] about the pricing situation. Individual product managers may initially agree to setting higher prices, but will then have an incentive to cheat on that agreement. That is, once the agreement has been reached, individual managers will have an incentive to sell more product by (secretly) offering discounts and price reductions to customers. This may be individually rational but can lead to a general erosion of prices and adverse profit consequences for the firm as a whole.[14]

Organizationally, therefore, it would appear beneficial to choose product groupings such that products within a group manifest demand and/or cost interdependency, whilst between groupings there are relatively low-order demand and/or cost interdependencies. Managers looking after such product groups would then be motivated to internalize the form of within-group externality described above. However, if the product groupings turn out to be too large for a single decision-maker to manage, then the communication problems of the type described above may need to be faced. This suggests that, quite apart from any other considerations, cost and demand interdependencies give rise to organizational trade-offs in the choice of product groupings.

20.7 Summary

This chapter argued that most firms produce multiple products and that these products are typically related in demand; final products are often similar in type and hence to some extent substitutes, whilst spare parts might be expected to be complements.

At the same time, there are often interdependencies on the cost side (arising out of products utilizing common processes). Whenever there are demand and/or cost interdependencies, optimal pricing needs to take account of spillover effects. Spillovers occur when the increase in price of one product affects the level of sales and/or the marginal cost of production of other products in the firm's product line. Finally, it was noted that there is a potential organizational problem in that, whilst there are undoubted merits in divisionalization, if products are the responsibility of different divisions there may be a tendency for the divisions not to act in the interests of the firm as a whole (because divisional managers may ignore spillover effects).

20.8 Review Questions

1. Explain the relationship between economies of scope and cost subadditivity.

2. 'Whether products are produced by a single firm, or by separate single-product firms, depends solely on whether there are economies of scope or not.' According to theory, is this true? Discuss.

3. A monopolist produces two goods labelled a and b. The cost of producing quantities q_a and q_b of a and b is given by $C = (q_a + q_b)^2$. The inverse demand schedules are estimated to be $p_a = 10 - q_a$ and $p_b = 20 - 2q_b$ respectively.

   (a) If the firm wishes to maximize profits, what prices and output levels should it adopt? What is the attainable level of profit?

   (b) If the firm faces a per unit tax of τ on good a, how does this affect its price and output choices? (Hint: first write down an expression for the firm's after-tax profits; the tax payment is simply τq).

   (c) There is an impact on both product prices of imposing the tax in (b). Explain intuitively the direction of the impact of the tax on product prices. (Hint: consider the type of product interdependence involved in this model.)

4. 'Price discrimination is simply a special case of multi-product pricing.' True or false? Discuss.

5. Suppose a firm is organized such that product managers are each responsible for a single pro-

[12] This type of bargaining solution is often termed the 'Coasian solution' (after Coase 1937). Chap. 27 discusses this in detail.
[13] See Chap. 5 for an exposition of this game.
[14] These same issues arise in dealing with the problem of transfer pricing (see Chap. 31).

duct (production, marketing, and sales). To motivate these managers, they are rewarded in proportion to the profit earned on their product. Is such a scheme likely to lead to maximum profitability for the firm as a whole? Discuss.

20.9 Further Reading

Sharkey (1982) gives a useful review at an accessible level of concepts such as cost subadditivity and economies of scope. Most managerial, business, and intermediate microeconomics texts give a cursory treatment of multi-product pricing, if they consider it at all. Often they confine attention to the problem of pricing in the case where outputs are fixed proportions (hides and beef, etc.), which is a rather special case of limited interest (see e.g. Haynes 1969). Nagel (1984) and Rao (1984) provide useful reviews of theory and practice. Oren *et al.* (1987) provides an application to multi-product electricity pricing.

21 Pricing Under Uncertainty

Objective This Chapter offers a brief exploration of the problem of setting prices when uncertainty enters into some aspect of the decision-maker's problem. The primary focus is on noting conditions under which uncertainty does not matter.

Prerequisites the concepts of expected value and variance.

Keywords price setting, price and quantity setting, quantity setting.

21.1 Introduction

Firms operate in an uncertain environment, and the sources of uncertainty are many and varied; for example,

(i) Uncertainty in demand: at a fixed price, the level of sales will usually vary from day to day and feature weekly and seasonal variations.

(ii) Uncertainty in production: for the same level of factor inputs, agricultural output of agricultural products will often vary depending upon seasonal conditions; industrial production may also feature randomness (for example, in wastage rates).

(iii) Uncertainty over input prices: factor prices may fluctuate; wage negotiations may have an uncertain outcome; imported raw materials and intermediate goods may be subject to exchange rate fluctuations in the price to be paid; etc.

These sources of uncertainty can be largely thought of as depending on the 'state of nature'. Another source of uncertainty primarily manifest in oligopolistic markets lies in the behaviour of competitors, since their choices of prices, outputs, and advertizing may have significant effects on the firm (and these choices may not be predictable with certainty). This chapter focuses on natural uncertainty rather than competitor uncertainty; the latter is discussed in Chapter 16.

Most elementary or intermediate texts examine the pricing problem under the assumption that demand and cost curves are known with certainty. However, we know from Chapter 9 that the estimated demand function is one which relates expected demand to price (and other variables under the firm's control, such as advertizing). That is, actual demand may deviate from expectation period by period. Chapters 22 and 23 discuss the case where these deviations are systematic, as in the case of demand for electricity, which has a daily profile in which demand is systematically higher during the day than at night. This chapter, by contrast, considers the case where the fluctuations are random rather than systematic.

Given the predilection for deterministic analysis in most texts, a natural question arises: to what extent is it valid to use the expected demand curve for price determination? Section 21.2 shows that sufficient conditions for using the expected demand curve as a deterministic demand curve in pricing analysis are that

(i) the firm is a risk-neutral price-setter,

(ii) uncertainty enters demand additively, and

(iii) the cost function is linear or quadratic.

By contrast, with more general specifications for demand and cost functions, and/or with risk aversion, theory suggests that uncertainty does matter. This is illustrated in section 21.2 with a specific example (cubic cost function) and in section 21.3, where the decision-maker is risk-averse. However, it is worth emphasizing that the certainty analysis of pricing so popular in most texts is not totally invalidated by the observation that uncertainty is a fact of life. The sufficient conditions for validity are fairly plausible; it can be argued that firms are not significantly risk-averse[1] and that costs can often be modelled to good approximation as linear (or quadratic) functions of output. Actually, the most restrictive of the above assumptions is that the uncertainty enters demand and cost functions additively. Additive uncertainty *is* a somewhat restrictive assumption (it means that fluctuations are constrained to shift the whole of the demand, or cost, functions parallel to themselves), but is not wholly unpalatable. Indeed, it is a standard assumption in demand and cost estimation (see Chapters 9 and 11).

The key to studying the impact of uncertainty on pricing and output decisions lies in determining which choice variables need to have their levels set in advance of the uncertainty being resolved, and which after. Farmers selling to competitive markets typically have to decide on the level of production far in advance of knowing what the selling price will be; in this case they are choosing quantity (although with uncertain weather etc. there may be some uncertainty over final quantity), with the uncertainty over price resolved later. In markets with monopoly power, prices are often fixed, with sales fluctuating from day to day; in this case it is price that is set before the uncertainty over quantity is resolved.

Storage, as with the holding of inventories for input materials, considerably complicates the analysis. Even in a certain world, stockholding can be advantageous if there are economies of scale, since it may pay to produce in batches larger than the individual-period demand if the economies of scale outweigh the holding costs. The same point applies in the presence of uncertainty. The general effect of stockholding is that it breaks the direct link between production and sales and allows the firm to choose either batch production or production smoothing over time. However, many products are of a perishable nature, so that stockholding is either impossible or too costly. For simplicity, only the perishable good problem is examined here.[2]

21.2 Does Uncertainty Matter?

There is an extensive literature on pricing under uncertainty in different market settings.[3] In general, uncertainty often has a theoretical impact on the optimal choices of firm variables under the firm's control (such as prices, advertizing, etc.), but the impact is typically complex and highly dependent on the way the model is set up. The observation that

1. uncertainty does usually affect firm-specific decisions (in theory at least), but that

2. any conclusions are highly model-dependent

is disappointing since it suggests that theory offers little in the way of practical guidance for policy.

The object of this section (after some preliminaries) is to set out conditions under which the uncertainty washes out, that is, conditions under which the firm chooses price as if it faces a certain demand function.

Let p, q_p, and q denote price, production, and sales respectively. Then the following types of behaviour are in principle possible:

(i) **Quantity setting**: choose production q_p ex ante, price p and sales q being resolved when production is brought to market.

(ii) **Price setting**: choose p ex ante, sales q being determined ex post by demand, production q_p instantaneously adjusting to sales.

(iii) **Price and quantity setting**: set price p and production level q_p ex ante, and then see what gets sold in the market.

Price- and quantity-setting in (iii) above is perhaps more likely when there is the possibility of storage, since in the case of a perishable (non-storable) product it could on occasion lead to wasted production or a stockout situation. The quantity-setting scenario in (i) seems more likely in competitive markets. Uncertainty of type (ii) typically occurs when products are perishable in imperfectly competitive markets. For brevity and simplicity, only the price-setting form is considered further.

As mentioned in section 21.1, most texts (including this one, for the most part) treat the pricing

---

[1] Although in practice, of course, managers do not always act in the shareholders' interest, and often manifest a greater degree of risk aversion than the owners would ideally like. Much depends upon the details of the decision-maker's remuneration package; for example, a flat salary gives little incentive to take risks when there is the slightest chance of losing one's job if things turn out badly. The problem of designing remuneration packages to induce agents, in this case managers, to act in the interests of owners (shareholders) is discussed in Chap. 29.

[2] For some simple models of inventory and stockholding behaviour, see Anderson *et al.* (1982) or Taha (1992).

[3] Leland (1972) is a seminal work; see also Hey (1979) for a review of this topic.

problem as a deterministic problem. The following analysis will show that:

Fact 21.1   If

(i) the firm is a price-setting monopolist,

(ii) demand and cost uncertainty enters additively, and

(iii) the cost function is either linear or quadratic in form,

then taking the expected demand and cost curves as deterministic functions and choosing price such that marginal revenue equals marginal cost for these, the price so obtained will in fact also maximize expected profit.

Hence if the firm aims to maximize expected profit, it can use the estimated cost and demand functions as if they are deterministic and compute price in the standard way.

To keep the analysis as straightforward as possible, I establish the result for the case where the cost function is quadratic, and then consider the case where costs are cubic. Thus initially the cost function is

$$C(\tilde{q}) = F + c_1\tilde{q} + c_2\tilde{q}^2 + \tilde{v}, \qquad (21.1)$$

where F denotes fixed cost, c_1 and c_2 are positive constants, $\tilde{q}$ denotes output demanded (which by assumption the firm produces instantaneously), and $\tilde{v}$ is a random variable with an expected value of zero; i.e. $E(\tilde{v}) = 0$. Thus the cost function is quadratic and is subject to additive shocks. Demand depends on price but also suffers random fluctuations. By assumption price is set in advance of the uncertainty being resolved:

$$\tilde{q} = f(p) + \tilde{\varepsilon}, \qquad (21.2)$$

where p denotes price and $\tilde{\varepsilon}$ is a random variable, with $E(\tilde{\varepsilon}) = 0$ and variance $\mathrm{var}(\tilde{\varepsilon}) = \sigma^2$. The function $f(p)$ is positive-valued, with a negative derivative; i.e. $f'(p) < 0$. Thus the demand curve has downward slope but is subject to random shocks, $\tilde{\varepsilon}$, which shift its position. Expected sales are

$$E(\tilde{q}) = E(f(p) + \tilde{\varepsilon}) = f(p). \qquad (21.3)$$

Writing expected sales simply as q, so that $q = E(\tilde{q})$, then

$$q = f(p). \qquad (21.4)$$

This simply says that expected sales is a function of price. If there was no uncertainty in demand, then q would be actual sales, and the graph of (21.4) would be the deterministic demand curve. Now, if the uncertainty is simply ignored, and we treat expected sales as actual sales, we would get an as-if deterministic profit function of the form

$$\pi = pq - C(q) = pq - F - c_1q - c_2q^2, \quad (21.5)$$

where π denotes the as-if profits (that is, the profit that would be had if only there were no uncertainty). By contrast, because there is uncertainty present, the firm's actual realized profit depends on the random errors $\tilde{\varepsilon}$ and $\tilde{v}$, and is given as

$$\tilde{\pi} = p\tilde{q} - C(\tilde{q})$$
$$= p\tilde{q} - F - c_1\tilde{q} - c_2\tilde{q}^2 - \tilde{v} \qquad (21.6)$$

where $\tilde{q}$ is given by (21.2). Since $E(\tilde{\varepsilon})$ and $E(\tilde{v}) = 0$, expected profit $E(\tilde{\pi})$ is given as

$$E(\tilde{\pi}) = E(p\tilde{q} - C(\tilde{q}))$$
$$= pE(\tilde{q}) - F - c_1E(\tilde{q}) - c_2E(\tilde{q}^2). \quad (21.7)$$

Now, from (21.2),

$$E(\tilde{q}^2) = E([f(p) + \tilde{\varepsilon}]^2 = E([f(p)^2 + 2\tilde{\varepsilon}f(p) + \tilde{\varepsilon}^2)$$
$$= (f(p)^2 + \sigma^2 = q^2 + \sigma^2 \qquad (21.8)$$

(since $E(\tilde{\varepsilon}) = 0$, $E(\tilde{\varepsilon}^2) = \sigma^2$, and $q = f(p)$. Substituting these results into (21.7) gives

$$E(\tilde{\pi}) = E(p\tilde{q} - C(\tilde{q}))$$
$$= pq - F - c_1q - c_2q^2 - \sigma^2. \qquad (21.9)$$

Now, compare the true expected profits given in (21.9) with the calculated as-if deterministic profit function (21.5). The difference is simply the term σ^2, which is a constant; hence we can write

$$E(\tilde{\pi}) = \pi - \sigma^2. \qquad (21.10)$$

It follows that if we choose price to maximize as-if profit in (21.5), we get the same answer for the optimal price as if we chose price to maximize the true expected profit function (21.9). Hence the uncertainty washes out and does not affect the optimal pricing decision. That is, we can simply take the expected demand and cost curves and treat them as deterministic in deciding what price to charge; the answer so obtained is in fact the price which maximizes the true expected profit level of the firm.

If the firm is risk-averse, then this result (that certainty analysis is acceptable) no longer holds, and uncertainty will affect the choice of price; this is illustrated section 21.3. However, other deviations can also mean that the result breaks down. To illustrate this, in what follows I extend the analysis to the case where the cost function is cubic rather than quadratic. Thus we now have

$$C(\tilde{q}) = F + c_1\tilde{q} + c_2\tilde{q}^2 + c_3\tilde{q}^3 + \tilde{v}. \quad (21.11)$$

The effect on (21.5) is that it becomes

$$\pi = pq - C(q)$$
$$= pq - F - c_1q - c_2q^2 - c_3q^3, \quad (21.12)$$

whilst (21.9) becomes

$$E(\tilde{\pi}) = pq - F - c_1q - c_2q^2 - \sigma^2$$
$$- E(c_3\tilde{q}^3). \qquad (21.13)$$

That is, the cost uncertainty disappears, but now, even if we assume that the distribution for the demand uncertainty $\tilde{\varepsilon}$ is symmetrical (as in the case of the normal distribution) so that, $E(\tilde{\varepsilon}^3) = 0$, uncertainty still has an effect on the pricing rule. Thus

$$\begin{aligned}
E(c_3 \tilde{q}^3) &= c_3 E([f(p) + \tilde{\varepsilon}]^3) \\
&= c_3 E([f(p)^3 + 3f(p)^2 \tilde{\varepsilon} + 3f(p)\tilde{\varepsilon}^2 + \tilde{\varepsilon}^3) \\
&= c_3 (f(p)^3 + 3f(p)\sigma^2) = c_3 (q^3 + 3f(p)\sigma^2).
\end{aligned}$$
(21.14)

If we compare (21.12) and (21.13) (in the light of (21.14)), it is clear that

$$E(\tilde{\pi}) = \pi - \sigma^2 - c_3 \sigma^2 f(p).$$
(21.15)

The final term involves $f(p)$, and this implies that the maxima of the two functions, $E(\tilde{\pi})$ and π, cannot be the same. The point is illustrated in Figure 21.1 (assuming that both functions are in fact strictly concave). The idea is that

$$\frac{\partial E(\tilde{\pi})}{\partial p} = \frac{\partial \pi}{\partial p} - c_3 \sigma^2 f'(p),$$
(21.16)

so, at the price which maximizes π, where, $\partial \pi / \partial p = 0$, since $f'(p) < 0$, $\partial E(\tilde{\pi})/\partial p > 0$. That is, the expected profit function is still increasing. It follows that in this case the optimal price is actually higher than that indicated by a deterministic analysis. Thus, in this case (with a cubic cost function), uncertainty does matter. The deterministic analysis leads one to choose too low a price.

Before passing on to the risk-averse case, it is worth mentioning that the above analysis can also be extended to the type of multi-product pricing discussed in Chapter 20. Essentially, the same result holds: if uncertainty enters the cost function and each of the demand functions additively, and if the

cost function is linear or quadratic in form, then the analysis can be conducted using the expected cost and demand functions as deterministic functions; the uncertainty does not affect the solution. This is true even if the random fluctuations in demand for the firm's different products are interrelated, as is often the case in practice.[4]

21.3 Optimal Pricing Under Risk Aversion

Within the neo-classical framework, the general approach to decision-making is that of a von Neumann–Morgenstern agent maximizing the expected utility of profits, as presented in Chapter 4 of this book (see also Leland 1972). To illustrate how risk aversion affects the pricing decision, consider the simple case where the cost function is linear and deterministic, and where demand is linear and subject to additive uncertainty. To simplify the analysis further, suppose the agent has mean-variance preferences; that is,

$$V = E(\tilde{\pi}) - \gamma \operatorname{var}(\tilde{\pi}),$$
(21.17)

where γ is a positive constant. Thus V represents the decision-maker's valuation of the firm's profits; V increases linearly with expected profit and decreases linearly (at the rate γ) with the variance of profit. Finally, and again for simplicity, assume linear cost and demand functions: thus, in an obvious notation, let

$$\tilde{q} = \alpha - \beta p + \tilde{\varepsilon}$$
(21.18)

and

$$C(\tilde{q}) = F + c\tilde{q}.$$
(21.19)

The expected demand curve is thus given by

$$E(\tilde{q}) = \alpha - \beta p,$$
(21.20)

where α, β, and c are positive constants. Realized profit is given as

$$\begin{aligned}
\tilde{\pi} &= (p - c)\tilde{q} - F = (p - c)(\alpha - \beta p + \tilde{\varepsilon}) - F \\
&= (p - c)(\alpha - \beta p) - F + (p - c)\tilde{\varepsilon}.
\end{aligned}$$
(21.21)

Since $E(\tilde{\varepsilon}) = 0$, expected profit is thus given as

$$E(\tilde{\pi}) = (p - c)(\alpha - \beta p) - F,$$
(21.22)

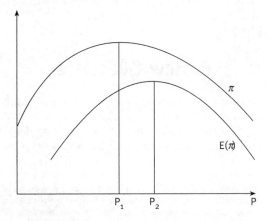

Fig. 21.1 Optimal pricing under uncertainty

---

[4] That is, demand shocks which adversely affect one product in the range often adversely affect all the firm's products to some extent and in the same direction; this is because many of the random effects stem from economy-wide shocks.

whilst the variance of profit, $var(\tilde{\pi})$, is given by

$$var(\tilde{\pi}) = E([\tilde{\pi} - E(\tilde{\pi})]^2). \qquad (21.23)$$

Inspection of (21.21) and (21.22) reveals that the difference between $\tilde{\pi}$ and $E(\tilde{\pi})$ is simply $(p - c)\tilde{\varepsilon}$, so (21.23) simplifies to

$$
\begin{aligned}
var(\tilde{\pi}) &= E([(p - c)\tilde{\varepsilon}]^2) = (p - c)^2 E(\tilde{\varepsilon}^2) \\
&= (p - c)^2 \sigma^2. \qquad (21.24)
\end{aligned}
$$

Thus the objective function becomes

$$
\begin{aligned}
V &= [(p - c)(\alpha - \beta p) - F] \\
&\quad - \gamma(p - c)^2 \sigma^2. \qquad (21.25)
\end{aligned}
$$

Choosing price p to maximize V, the first-order condition is that

$$
\begin{aligned}
\partial V / \partial p &= [-\beta(p - c) + (\alpha - \beta p)] \\
&\quad - \gamma 2(p - c)\sigma^2 = 0. \qquad (21.26)
\end{aligned}
$$

Collecting terms in p and rearranging gives the pricing rule as

$$p = c + \frac{\alpha - \beta c}{2(\beta + \gamma\sigma^2)}. \qquad (21.27)$$

Under certainty, or risk neutrality, the optimal price is simply given by (21.27), with σ^2 set equal to zero. Price has to be greater than marginal cost c if the firm is to make a positive profit; it follows that $(\alpha - \beta c)/[2(\beta + \gamma\sigma^2)] > 0$, which implies that $\alpha - \beta c > 0$ (since the denominator is positive), and hence that both an increase in risk (increase in σ^2) and an increase in risk aversion (increase in γ) lead to a decrease in the optimal price. The intuition for this is that a higher price implies a larger value of $(p - c)$, and hence, from (21.24), a higher variance for profit. Since the decision-maker is risk-averse, this encourages the setting of a lower price.

Clearly, ignoring uncertainty will not maximize the decision-maker's utility function; notice that, in the absence of uncertainty, the optimal price is

$$p = c + \frac{\alpha - \beta c}{2\beta} = \frac{c + \alpha}{2}. \qquad (21.28)$$

In this case, basing the pricing rule on the expected demand curve as-if demand is deterministic leads to setting a price that is too high.

The idea that a risk-averse firm tends to charge a lower price than if it were risk-neutral in fact holds so long as the demand curve has an additive random error and so long as marginal cost is non-decreasing (Leland 1972). However, more generally, risk aversion can lead to either a higher or lower price being set (relative to the case where the firm is risk-neutral); relatively few concrete predictions are possible. All that can be said is that it is likely to have some effect.

Whilst it is in principle possible to envisage a firm estimating the distribution of demand and making use of an explicit utility function, there is little evidence that many firms do in fact take any systematic account of risk in their pricing decisions. Indeed, even the idea of formally taking into account the notion that there is any kind of price–quantity relationship at all is far from widespread. These effects, in so far as they are considered at all, are usually taken into account in a very informal way. This point is addressed further and in more detail in Chapter 24 (which deals with cost-plus and mark-up pricing).

21.4 Summary

This chapter has shown that, when the firm is an expected-value maximizer, if uncertainty enters demand additively, and if costs are linear or quadratic, the pricing results obtained from a deterministic analysis of the firm's price decision (of the type presented in the rest of this text, and in most elementary and intermediate texts) gives results identical to those obtained by conducting an analysis which explicitly takes account of the uncertainty involved. It follows that in many situations, the deterministic analysis presented in the average managerial economics text is reasonably adequate; that is, taking the estimated demand function and using this as a deterministic function in computing optimal prices is likely to give a reasonably satisfactory solution.[5]

However, it was also shown that divergences from these assumptions (such as more complex cost structures, or risk aversion) imply that the firm's optimal pricing decision *is* affected by the extent and type of uncertainty involved.

21.5 Review Questions

1. Select a production process with which you have some degree of familiarity and then identify potential sources of uncertainty regarding the cost of producing a given output level using that process.

---

[5] Naturally, the results are only as good as the estimates of the expected cost and demand functions. If these are significantly in error (say because of unrepresentative sample data or incorrect model specification), then so too will be the calculated prices.

2. If there are systematic variations in demand, it may be possible to vary price systematically—but this is not possible if there is no underlying systematic pattern. For a product for which you have some degree of familiarity, identify factors which are likely to lead to systematic fluctuations in demand, and factors which may lead to essentially random or unforecastable fluctuations in demand.

3. Most intermediate textbooks totally ignore uncertainty when they consider the problem of price setting. To what extent is it valid to do so in the case of a product that is difficult/costly to store?

4. If the product is relatively easy to store, how might this affect your answer to question 3?

5. Example 20.5 illustrated how it is possible to solve a simple two-product pricing problem. Suppose that in this example the two demand functions have additive random errors $\tilde{\varepsilon}_1$ and $\tilde{\varepsilon}_2$ attached to them, whilst the cost function has an additive random error $\tilde{v}$ (where these random variables have the same properties as those in the models discussed in section 21.2). If the firm is an expected profit maximizer, and these random errors are all independent of each other, show that the optimal prices are unaffected by the introduction of this type of uncertainty. Does it make any difference to your answer if the three random variables are positively correlated with each other?

21.6 Further Reading

Hey (1979) provides a more detailed survey and analysis of uncertainty as it affects both firms and consumer decisions.

22 Public Sector Pricing

Objective This Chapter begins with an outline and critique of the idea that marginal cost pricing maximizes social welfare. It then examines Ramsey pricing (a type of third-degree price discrimination) and the use of non-uniform in pricing tariffs (second-degree price discrimination) to maximize economic welfare.

Prerequisites The concept of economic welfare is presented in Chapter 2. The derivations in the Appendix make use of optimization techniques discussed in Chapter 3.

Keywords marginal cost pricing, piecemeal social policy, Ramsey pricing, Ramsey pricing rule, second best.

22.1 Introduction

The concept of natural monopoly was discussed in detail in Chapter 14. For industries that are natural monopolies, a question which remains very much alive in policy debate is that of whether it is better to place such industries

(i) in the public sector and to run them not for profit, but for maximum economic welfare, or

(ii) in the private sector, either unfettered, or regulated in some way.

A prerequisite for a proper assessment of this question is knowing how an industry within the public sector should be run. This chapter examines public sector pricing, an issue of considerable practical significance wherever goods or services are publicly provided. This list often includes power (electricity, gas, coal), communications (telecoms, post), and transport (rail, roads, buses, coaches, etc.) industries, as well as health and education. Although privatization programmes have taken many industries back into the private sector across the globe, significant areas remain publicly provided (in the UK, postal services, health, education, and roads, for example).

Chapter 2 set out a simple criterion for measuring economic welfare, namely consumer plus producer surplus. It also demonstrated that, ceteris paribus, monopoly pricing leads to lower economic welfare than marginal cost pricing (with linear demand and marginal cost functions, the welfare loss amounts to 25% of achievable welfare). Section 22.2 reprises this argument for the case of a single-product monopoly; the difference introduced here, in comparison to Chapter 2, is that the case where there are economies of scale is outlined. It is shown that, with economies of scale, marginal cost pricing leads to maximum welfare, but the firm fails to break even. Financial losses usually lead to further welfare losses since financial losses, are typically financed by distortionary taxation.

This suggests that the problem of public utility pricing is one of **second best**, in which different and interdependent sources of welfare loss have to be taken into account simultaneously. Section 22.3 demonstrates this point—that marginal cost pricing is no longer desirable if there are distortions elsewhere in the economy—in a simple example of second-best optimization. Section 22.4 takes a different tack, namely of asking what public utility prices would look like if the firm was asked to maximize welfare subject to attaining a given target level of financial performance (such as to break even). This is the so-called **Ramsey pricing** problem.[1] Finally, section 22.5 examines the extent to which second-degree price discrimination can help to maintain the ideal of marginal cost pricing without inducing the firm to make losses.

---

[1] After Frank Ramsey's (1923) early and seminal contribution.

22.2 Marginal Cost Pricing Under Economies of Scale

As mentioned in section 22.1, according to the welfare criterion of maximizing consumer surplus plus firm profits, it appears that setting price equal to marginal cost will maximize welfare. This is illustrated in Figure 22.1 for the case of a single-product natural monopoly in which economies of scale imply that the marginal cost curve is continuously falling to the right.[2]

In Figure 22.1, consider first the effect of setting an arbitrary price p_1; consumers choose to purchase q_1, and clearly at this output level, price is not equal to marginal cost. Consumer surplus is the area above the price line (area ace) and firm revenues are the area $cekj$, whilst its costs are the area under the marginal cost line ($bfkj$). So profit, i.e. revenue minus costs, is the area def minus the area bcd. Summing profit plus consumer surplus gives the area $aefb$. That is, economic welfare amounts to the difference between willingness to pay (WTP, the area below the demand curve—area $aekj$) and costs (the area under the marginal cost curve, area $bfkj$). Thus, welfare can be expressed either as willingness to pay minus costs, or as consumer surplus plus profits:

$$W = CS + \Pi = WTP - \text{costs}. \qquad (22.1)$$

It should be clear that economic welfare is maximized if the quantity q_c is sold, as this maximizes the difference between willingness to pay, the area below the demand curve, and costs, given as the area under the marginal cost curve. Thus maximum attainable welfare is given as the area aib. To get this level of welfare requires the firm to charge the price p_c (the marginal cost price). It should also be clear that consumers do very well out of this marginal cost pricing solution, gaining consumer surplus $CS = aig$, whilst the firm makes a loss equal to area big, a big loss indeed (revenue is the area $gilj$ whilst costs are $bilj$).

There is, in principle, no problem with this solution so long as either

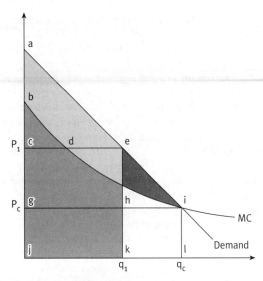

Fig. 22.1 Marginal cost pricing

(i) transaction costs are zero, or

(ii) the state can costlessly levy lump-sum taxes.

For example, in comparison with any higher-price solution, such as (p_1, q_1) in Figure 22.1, it should be clear that there is a potential Pareto improvement in moving to marginal cost pricing. That is, in dropping the price from p_1 (where p_1 is any price above the marginal cost price) to p_c, consumers get an increase in consumer surplus of amount $ceig$ whilst the firm's profits drop only by the amount $cehg$ (the loss of revenue on pre-existing sales) plus fih (the loss incurred on the extra sales). Summing the consumer gains and the firm losses, the overall gain is simply the area eif. The point is that, in moving to marginal cost pricing, p_c, the consumers can compensate the firm and still have some gains left over. For example, the consumers could offer to pay the amount $cehg$ plus fih to cover the firm's fall in profit, and give it an additional amount of, say, half of efi, thus making the firm better off relative to the original position (when the firm was charging p_1) by the amount $\frac{1}{2}efi$. This would also still leave consumers better off by $\frac{1}{2}efi$ relative to the original position. Thus, in moving from any initial price higher than the marginal cost price p_c, everyone can be made better off (through appropriate lump-sum transfers).

Now, if there are zero transactions costs to bargaining, negotiating, and contracting,[3] we might

---

[2] The reader can check that the argument applies equally for the case where marginal costs are constant or indeed of a more traditional U-shape. However, the falling marginal cost case illustrated in Fig. 22.1 is more appropriate when discussing an industry that is a natural monopoly; see Chap. 14 for further discussion of this point.

[3] And that would include the opportunity cost of the time taken to reach a settlement; i.e. the deal would need to be instantaneous.

expect this actually to happen; agreements ought to be reachable if all parties can be made better off. Unfortunately, in practise there are usually significant transactions costs which prevent the myriad consumers from getting together with the firm and negotiating the change to marginal cost pricing.

However, even in the presence of transactions costs, if lump-sum taxes can be levied on the gainers (such that they still have a net gain overall) in order to finance the losses, then again, an actual Pareto improvement can be realized. Unfortunately, such taxation is not in practise costless (intervention is always costly, and the information required to effect such taxes is particularly difficult to acquire). Furthermore, if lump-sum transfers are widely percieved as arbitrary, they tend to be politically unpopular and difficult to collect.[4] Thus, politically feasible taxation tends to be distortionary (usually involving per unit or percentage rate taxes either on income or on commodities). It was shown in Chapter 2 (Figure 2.4) that these types of distortionary tax lead to welfare loss. Matters are much more complex when all incomes and many products are taxed in various ways, but the general point remains: non-lump-sum taxes distort individual choices (on how much of each product to purchase, on how much labour to supply, and so on) and this tends to lead to welfare loss.

The idea that the optimal price to set for the firm needs to take into account in detail how losses will be financed is termed one of second-best optimization, because it recognizes that a simple first-best solution (marginal cost pricing) ignores spillover distortionary effects. In fact the problem of second-best optimization is much more complex than that of simply taking tax distortions into account. It can be shown that, because all markets in the economic system are to a lesser or greater degree interdependent, any distortions elsewhere in the system have implications for the optimal pricing of the firm's product. In particular, monopoly power and external effects (Chapter 29) as well as taxes affect prices throughout the economy. Optimal second-best pricing for a publicly provided good or service requires these distortions to be taken into account, in particular as they affect the substitutes and complements associated with the publicly provided good.[5]

22.3 Second-Best Effects in Pricing

This section provides a simple example to illustrate the idea that, in an interdependent economy, optimal second-best pricing requires that distortions elsewhere in the economy be taken into account. The example involves an electricity producer (a public utility) selling power to a private sector monopoly manufacturer who uses this power in the manufacture of its monopoly product.[6] For simplicity, all other distortions in the economy are ignored.

For the sake of further simplicity, it is assumed that each unit of electricity is transformed by the monopolist into exactly one unit of product at no extra cost. Hence in Figure 22.2, both electricity sold and the monopolist's sales of final product are measured on the horizontal axis. The marginal cost of production for the monopolist is simply the price she has to pay for electricity. Let p denote the price chosen by the monopolist for selling her final product, and p_E the price charged by the public utility for electricity. Again for simplicity, assume there are no fixed costs associated with electricity production, and that the marginal cost of generation of electricity is simply a constant, denoted MC_e, per unit (so marginal cost equals average variable cost equals average cost for each and every unit). In what follows, the welfare consequences of marginal cost pricing by the electricity generator are considered first, and then this is contrasted with the optimal second-best pricing solution.

22.3.1 Marginal Cost Pricing

In this example, the public utility will just break even if it sets price equal to marginal cost. However, the final-good monopoly is a market distortion in

---

[4] The UK (Thatcher) government's ill-fated attempt to implement a poll tax to pay for local government services was eventually abandoned in 1994.

[5] See Harberger (1977) for a more general treatment of the welfare loss arising in distorted markets. The theory of second-best pricing is treated in many standard texts on what is termed 'public utility pricing' (see e.g. Rees 1984) and, more generally, in the analysis of tax effects in 'public economics' (see e.g. Atkinson and Stiglitz 1980, Starrett 1988).

[6] The electricity industry in the UK was, until quite recently, in the public sector, and the industry remains in public hands in several European and Scandinavian countries.

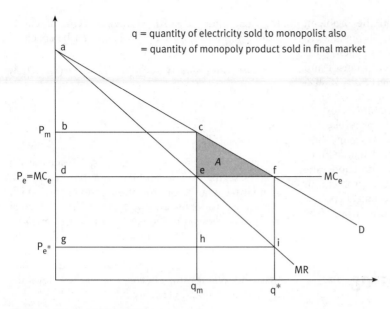

Fig. 22.2 Second-best pricing: an example

the sense that a monopolist will set price above marginal cost. This distortion implies that setting price equal to marginal cost for electricity will not yield maximum economic welfare. Thus, in Figure 22.2, if the utility sets the price $p_e = MC_e$, this will become the marginal cost curve for the monopolist, who will then set marginal revenue equal to marginal cost, choose an output q_m (of output, and hence of purchase of the electricity to produce this output), and charge a price p_m. Total welfare is given as the sum of profits to the public utility, the monopolist, and consumers; the utility makes zero profit, the monopolist makes a profit equal to area *bced*, and consumers gain consumer surplus equal to the area *abc*. Total welfare is thus *aced*, and this is simply the area to the left of q_m, below the demand curve and above the marginal cost curve.

22.3.2 Second-Best Pricing

Contrast the above marginal cost pricing solution with the case where the public utility sets a price $p_e{}^*$ (well below marginal cost) such that the cheap electricity induces the monopolist to produce the output q^* (recall that the monopolist takes the electricity price $p_e{}^*$ as marginal cost, and equates this with marginal revenue in deciding on the output to produce). In Figure 22.2, total welfare from second-best pricing is the area *adf*, and there is a gain in welfare relative to marginal cost pricing equal to the triangle *cef*.

The point is that a monopoly producer tends to charge too high a price and sell too little product. The second-best pricing solution involves subsidizing the final-good monopolist in order to induce her to sell the socially optimal quantity of final product. The public utility runs at a loss (equal to area *dgif*) whilst the monopolist gains a higher level of profit (also *dgif*) which exactly offsets the utility's loss, whilst consumers gain surplus equal to *adf*. Thus the second-best price has to deviate from marginal cost because of a distortion elsewhere in the economy; in this case, monopoly power in the final-good market.

Notice that, in the above example (which ignores all other possible deviations, including how the losses of the electric utility would be financed etc.), the price is set so as to correct for other sources of deviation from a global welfare optimum. The pricing problem takes the rest of the economy as fixed. The second-best pricing solution thus ignores the possibility that it may be preferable to tackle these other deviations directly. For example, if the final-good monopolist was price-regulated and forced to set a marginal cost price, it would then become optimal (in this simple setting) for the electricity utility also to set marginal cost pricing.

The above discussion suggests that significant policy issues arise over what is often termed **piecemeal social policy**. Here, the reason for having to set the low price for electricity is that the problem of monopoly in the final-goods market has not been tackled. Is it better to work around the problem, through second-best pricing—or is it possible to fix the distortions? Clearly the answer to such questions is likely to depend on the circumstances and real-world details of each individual case. It also tends to depend on a lot of information which is either poorly known or not known at all (for example, estimates of own-price and cross-price elasticities of demand are often crucial to second-best pricing analysis; for many products, demand functions are insufficiently stable to provide good estimates of such parameters). Thus the problem of how to go about undertaking piecemeal policy, when there are so many deviations from first best, is clearly complex.[7]

22.4 Welfare-Maximizing Third-Degree Price Discrimination: Ramsey Pricing

In section 22.1, it was noted that there might be some merit in setting prices above marginal costs in order to reduce the financial losses which would otherwise have to be financed through distortionary taxation. This section considers how a price-discriminating monopolist might set prices in order to maximize economic welfare (consumer plus producer surplus) subject to the firm attaining a particular profit level (for example, the break-even profit level). The conditions necessary for a monopolist to be able to practise third-degree price discrimination of the type described below are reviewed in detail in section 18.2.

Suppose the utility can segment the market n ways, and sells quantities $q_1, q_2, \ldots, q_n$ by charging prices $p_1, p_2, \ldots, p_n$ in segments $1, 2, \ldots, n$. The firm produces total output q, so

$$q = q_1 + q_2 + \ldots + q_n. \quad (22.2)$$

The firm's objective is to maximize welfare, W, equal to aggregate willingness to pay across all the segments minus the cost of production $C(q)$. This has to be done subject to the firm attaining a given level of profit, $\bar{\pi}$ (a constant). The ith segment's willingness to pay, denoted WTP_i, is measured as

[7] For early work on the second best, see Lipsey and Lancaster 1958, and Davis and Whinston 1965.

the area under the ith segment's demand curve. Thus the Ramsey pricing problem can be specified as

$$\text{Maximize } W = (\textstyle\sum_{i=1}^{n} WTP_i) - C(q) \quad (22.3)$$

subject to

$$\pi = (\textstyle\sum_{i=1}^{n} R_i) - C(q) \geq \bar{\pi} \quad (22.4)$$

and

$$q = q_1 + q_2 + \ldots + q_n, \quad (22.5)$$

where $R_i = p_i q_i$ is the revenue raised from the ith market segment. The problem can be set up as a standard Lagrange optimization problem in which the choice variables are $q_1, q_2, \ldots, q_n$; a formal analysis of these conditions is given in the appendix to this chaapter. Denoting $\partial C(q)/\partial q = MC$ as the marginal cost of producing another unit of output (defined at the total output level q), and recalling that the relationship between marginal revenue, price, and demand elasticity is

$$MR_k = p_k\left(1 + \frac{1}{\eta_k}\right), \quad (22.6)$$

where η_k is the elasticity of demand of the kth segment (see section 14.3), it can be shown that the first-order conditions associated with the above optimization problem entail the so-called **Ramsey pricing rule**, that

$$\frac{p_k - MC}{p_k} = -\frac{\theta}{\eta_k} \quad k = 1, \ldots, n, \quad (22.7)$$

where θ is a constant lying between 0 and 1.

Notice that if $\theta = 0$, then $p_k = MC$ for all k. This is the marginal cost pricing solution in which all segments face the same (marginal cost) price. Basically, this would be optimal in this model if, at this price, the firm earned a profit level above the target level $\bar{\pi}$. By assumption, however, this is not the case (because of economies of scale; see section 22.2). Notice also that, if $\theta = 1$, then (22.7) is identical to the profit-maximizing third-degree price discrimination rule (see section 18.3). If we assume that profit maximization more than achieves the profit target, then clearly the optimal level of the constant θ will lie strictly between zero and unity. It follows that the optimal Ramsey prices will lie between marginal cost and the profit-maximizing price discrimination level.

Thus Ramsey prices which maximize welfare subject to attaining the target profit level feature a similar pattern to the prices that a profit maximizer would charge. That is, the highest mark-ups are on the more inelastic (least price-sensitive) products, whilst low prices are charged to the elastic (price-sensitive) segments. Thus a utility practising price discrimination could be consistent with that firm actually pursuing an objective of welfare maximization (subject to financial constraints) *or* of profit maximization. Clearly, price discrimination in itself is not evidence of exploitation and profit maximization. However, to test whether the firm is indeed maximizing profits, or is setting prices below such levels, would require a considerable amount of information regarding not only demand elasticities across the market segments, but also the firm's marginal costs of production.

EXAMPLE 22.1 A whole range of services are made available to juniors at rates below the adult price (bus tickets, swimming pools, cinema tickets, etc.), when the cost of provision is pretty much identical. Some of these price differentials are undoubtedly motivated by the objective of profit maximization (as in the case of private sector cinemas), but the publicly provided service prices may be more motivated by the concern with economic welfare (as in swimming prices). However, it is not always easy to know how much profit and welfare-maximizing prices are likely to differ. If demand is weak, welfare-optimal prices may well be close to profit-maximizing prices (as in the case of swimming and rail travel).

EXAMPLE 22.2 Ramsey pricing can also be applied even if the products are differentiated. For example, the UK letters business involves first- and second-class delivery (with different average speeds of delivery). The products are thus not identical. A recent study (Dobbs and Cuthbertson 1996) suggested that the price differential applied in recent years could be justified from the perspective of Ramsey pricing.

22.5 Welfare-Maximizing Second-Degree Price Discrimination

Chapter 19 examines how firms can utilize non-uniform pricing in order to maximize profits. However, second-degree price discrimination can often also be utilized in the pursuit of economic welfare (the conditions necessary for a monopolist to be able to practise second-degree price discrimination are

reviewed in section 19.2). Since uniform pricing is a special case of non-uniform pricing, it follows that, whatever the objective (welfare or profit), a well-chosen non-uniform pricing structure will usually improve performance and should never do worse.

22.5.1 The Theory—Assuming the Absence of Exclusion

In section 22.2, the idea that welfare maximization required marginal cost pricing was examined. A major problem noted with marginal cost pricing was that, in the presence of economies of scale, the firm would fail to break even and would require financing, and the politically acceptable ways of funding such losses also lead to welfare loss.[8] One way of tackling this is through Ramsey pricing (third-degree price discrimination; see section 22.4). However, an important alternative is to use non-uniform pricing (second-degree price discrimination). Essentially, if the conditions required for the practise of second-degree price discrimination are satisfied (see section 19.2), the solution involves setting marginal prices equal to marginal costs, whilst infra-marginal prices can deviate and be set above marginal cost.

For example, Figure 22.3 illustrates the case of a two-part or block tariff; the first block of units (up to a consumption level q_1 per period) costs a price p_1, but additional units can be purchased at price $p_2 = MC$, where the marginal cost of supply to the individual is assumed constant.[9] Given the position of an individual demand curve such as D_i, clearly the individual will choose to purchase quantity $\hat{q}$. However, notice that exactly the same quantity would have been chosen if a purely uniform price $p_2 = MC$ had been set for all units. With a uniform price set at p_2, the revenue taken from the individual just covers the marginal cost at the firm's current level of output (and so this makes no contribution to the firm's fixed costs and higher costs of infra-marginal units). If this pricing rule was adopted

---

[8] In addition, there are other problems of a second-best nature (monopoly power and externalities) which might need to be taken into account.

[9] Although the firm may exhibit economies of scale, it is often reasonable to assume that, in the region of total output, the economies of scale have largely been realized, such that marginal cost is fairly constant. Furthermore, even if there are still persistent economies of scale, at the level of the individual consumer constant marginal cost is a reasonable assumption simply because individual consumption is small relative to overall total demand.

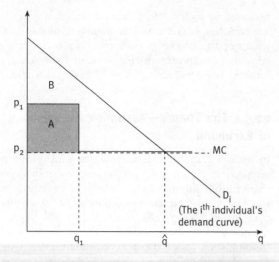

Fig.22.3 Block tariff

not so straightforward as it might appear. This is because individuals may not always choose to consume at the marginal cost price associated with the block tariff for consumption levels greater than q_1 in Figure 22.3. Some individuals may end up consuming less than q_1, and, furthermore, some individuals may be excluded from the market altogether. When this happens some welfare loss is entailed.

The problem arises because the position of each individual's demand curve is likely to be different (in level, in slope, etc.). Figure 22.4 illustrates the kinds of possible solution depending on the position of an individual's demand function; thus individual 1 with demand curve D_1 takes the same quantity q_1 under the block tariff as she would if there was uniform marginal cost pricing (hence there is no welfare loss in moving to the block tariff). However, an individual with demand curve D_2 would not choose the level q_2' but would prefer to choose quantity q_2 at the higher price of p_1, whilst individual 3 would be excluded from the market altogether by the block tariff when, under marginal cost pricing, she would have entered and consumed the amount q_3'. There is a clear loss of welfare associated with individual 3's choice (area A in Figure 22.4), and it can also be shown that there is a loss of welfare associated with individual 2's choice (equal to the diagonal shaded area B in the

for all consumers, the firm would suffer a loss, as described in section 22.2. By introducing a block tariff in which there is an infra-marginal block of units $[0, q_1]$ at a higher price p_1, the same total quantity of welfare is obtained (since the same quantity is purchased); all that happens is that there is a transfer (equal to $(p_1 - p_2)q_1$, the area A in Figure 22.3) from the consumer to the firm. That is, at a pure uniform price of p_2 the contributions to aggregate welfare are consumer surplus, given as area $A + B$, and a zero profit contribution. With the block tariff, by contrast, consumer surplus is the area above the block tariff price line, and is equal to area B, whilst the firm gets a profit contribution of amount A. Clearly in both cases the welfare contribution is the same, but the profit contributions generated by the block tariff can help the firm to break even.

Thus, if p_2 is set at an appropriate level, the block tariff can be constructed to just cover the losses that would otherwise have arisen. Apparently then, if second-degree price discrimination is possible, it can be superior to the Ramsey pricing approach (since the latter involves raising prices above marginal cost and this leads to a loss of economic welfare, ceteris paribus).

22.5.2 Infra-Marginal Units and the Exclusion Problem

Unfortunately, the second-degree price discrimination solution to the public utility pricing problem is

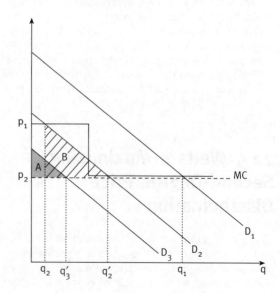

Fig. 22.4 Block tariff: inefficient consumption and exclusion

figure).[10] Thus, whenever individuals do not purchase at a marginal price equal to marginal cost, there will be some loss of economic welfare. If the same block tariff has to be set for all customers (as is usually the case), this means that there will usually be some welfare loss in setting the block tariff, simply because some individual's will be of type 2 or 3 above. The problem of setting the price p_1 and quantity q_1 of the first block thus involves the same type of trade-off as that involved in Ramsey pricing (namely, that a higher block price will usually raise more revenue, and so make a greater profit contribution, but will also tend to lead to greater exclusion, and hence a greater loss of economic welfare).

However, it is worth emphasizing that non-uniform pricing structures, if well chosen, will always be able to dominate uniform pricing structures (whether the objective is to pursue profit, or, as here, to pursue welfare). This makes sense, since uniform pricing is simply a special case of non-uniform pricing. Thus, for any Ramsey pricing solution, if it is possible to operate with a non-uniform price policy in each and every market segment, this in principle creates an opportunity for increasing welfare whilst still allowing the firm to achieve its profit target (to break even, for example).

In practice many public and private utilities operate non-uniform price policies (telecoms, electricity, gas, water, etc.). Particularly popular is the two-part or multi-part tariff. The two-part tariff involves a fixed charge, or licence fee, which has to be paid before any units can be consumed, followed by a uniform per unit charge. The two-part tariff is a special case of the block tariff (in which the first block is simply the first unit), and both are special cases of the general non-uniform pricing schedule. These price structures are described in more detail in Chapter 19 (along with some details on the optimal design of such pricing policies, in the context of profit maximization). Whether the utilities operate this form of second-degree price discrimination in the public interest, or as a means of increasing private profit, is an issue of great interest to the regulators of such firms (where such regulators exist). Typically, regulators like to see marginal prices well aligned with marginal supply costs, for the reasons outlined above.

---

[10] Recall that welfare is measured as the difference between willingness to pay (the area under the demand curve) and the marginal cost curve.

EXAMPLE 22.3 The 1990s have witnessed a continuing debate between British Telecom and the regulator (OFTEL) on BT's pricing policy regarding the issue of tariff rebalancing. The cost per minute of a telephone call has fallen considerably with technical advances over the years, and the per minute price charged often exceeds marginal cost. Rebalancing involves offering the consumer a lower rate per unit, the lost revenue being recovered through higher fixed charges or line rentals.

22.6 Summary

This chapter introduced the idea that in the public sector, prices should be chosen so as to maximize welfare rather than profits. It was shown that marginal cost pricing is unlikely to be welfare-optimal, either because it leads to deficits which need financing, or because of other distortions in the economy. Second-best theory suggests that if the other distortions are endemic and cannot be resolved by more direct means, then prices of publicly provided goods and services should deviate from marginal cost in order to compensate for the spillover effects which arise from such distortions. The idea of Ramsey pricing was then considered; this focuses on the problem of financing public utility losses arising under marginal cost pricing, and suggests how prices should be adjusted so as to contribute a maximum level of welfare subject to the firm earning a given target level of profitability. Finally, non-uniform (second-degree) price discrimination was considered. Where non-uniform pricing is operational, it is a superior way of dealing with the problem of getting public enterprise into profitability than the Ramsey third-degree price discrimination approach. However, it is worth remarking further that market segmentation followed by non-uniform pricing individually tailored for each market segment will perform even better (if well designed).

22.7 Review Questions

1. To what extent is it desirable for publicly provided goods to be priced at marginal cost?

2. 'It is a paradox that price discrimination is often regarded as reducing economic welfare, yet price discrimination is required if economic welfare is

to be maximized.' Is it a paradox? Explain and discuss.

3. Suppose, for the model described in section 22.3, that the marginal cost of electricity production is £10 per unit, and that the monopolist's inverse demand curve for the final product is $p = 1000 - 10q$ (where p is in pounds and q is in units of output). Calculate

   (a) the optimal second-best price for electricity and

   (b) the welfare loss (relative to the solution in (a)) if the electric utility sets price equal to marginal cost.

4. (a) What economic conditions must be present for the firm to be able to implement a Ramsey pricing solution to the public utility pricing problem?

   (b) What economic conditions must be present for the firm to be able to implement a non-uniform pricing solution to the public utility pricing problem?

   (Note: for a detailed discussion of these points, see Chapters 18 and 19, respectively.)

22.8 Further Reading

Brown and Sibley (1986) gives a thorough account of Ramsey pricing (third-degree price discrimination) but also examines in some detail the use of non-uniform pricing (second-degree price discrimination) in public utility pricing; it is also fairly accessible. It has relatively little to say about marginal cost pricing, or about the problem of second best. Rees (1984) covers these topics in more detail, and also looks at peak-load pricing and the relationship between investment and pricing (covered in Chapter 23 of this book).

Appendix: Derivation of the Ramsey Pricing Rule

The derivation of the Ramsey pricing solution is as follows. The utility can segment the market n ways, and sells quantities $q_1, q_2, \ldots, q_n$ by charging prices $p_1, p_2, \ldots, p_n$ in segments $1, 2, \ldots, n$. The firm produces total output q, so

$$q = q_1 + q_2 + \ldots + q_n. \tag{A1}$$

If we write $p_i(q_i)$ to indicate that the price charged in the ith segment is a function of the amount q_i the firm wishes to sell in that market (more can be sold only if the price is reduced; $p_i(q_i)$ denotes the inverse demand function for the ith segment), the ith-segment consumer aggregate willingness to pay, denoted WTP_i, is measured as the area under this demand curve; see Figure 22.5.

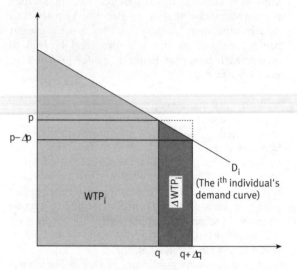

Fig. 22.5 Willingness to pay

Notice that if initially the price is p_i and demand is q_i, then if q_i is increased by the amount Δq (by reducing price slightly), willingness to pay increases by the amount $\Delta WTP_i \approx p_i \Delta q$. Hence $\Delta WTP_i / \Delta q \approx p_i$. In fact, it can be formally shown that $dWTP_i / dq_i = p_i$.[11] That is, the rate at which WTP_i changes with quantity is measured simply by the price.

The Ramsey problem can be set up as a standard Lagrange optimization problem in which the choice variables are $q_1, q_2, \ldots, q_n$. The Lagrangian is

$$L = (\textstyle\sum_{i=1}^{n} WTP_i) - C(q) + \lambda_1[(\textstyle\sum_{i=1}^{n} R_i) - C(q) - \overline{\pi}] + \lambda_2[q_1 + q_2 + \ldots + q_n - q]. \tag{A2}$$

The first of these constraints is an inequality ($\pi \geq \overline{\pi}$), whilst the second is an equality ($q_1 + q_2 + \ldots + q_n = q$). Since $\partial R_i / \partial q_i = MR_i$, the marginal revenue of the ith market segment, the Kuhn–Tucker conditions are that

---

[11] Thus $WTP_i = \int_0^{q_i} p_i(q)dq$. Differentiating with respect to the upper limit of the integral gives $dWTP_i / dq_i = p_i(q_i)$.

$$\frac{\partial L}{\partial q_k} = p_k + \lambda_1 MR_k + \lambda_2 = 0 \quad k = 1, \ldots, n,$$

$$(A3)$$

$$\frac{\partial L}{\partial q} = -\frac{\partial C(q)}{\partial q} - \lambda_1 \frac{\partial C(q)}{\partial q} - \lambda_2 = 0, \quad (A4)$$

and for the inequality constraint $\lambda_1 \geq 0$, and the complementary slackness condition, $\lambda_1(\pi - \overline{\pi}) = 0$, must hold (see section 3.5). Finally, of course, the constraints must also be satisfied.

Now $\partial C(q)/\partial q = MC$, the marginal cost of producing another unit of output, and we can also write

$$MR_k = p_k\left(1 + \frac{1}{\eta_k}\right), \quad (A5)$$

where η_k is the elasticity of demand of the kth segment (see section 14.3). Using (A5) to replace the marginal revenue terms in (A3), and rearranging the equation a little, it is possible to obtain the Ramsey pricing rule, that

$$\frac{p_k - MC}{p_k} = -\frac{\theta}{\eta_k} \quad k = 1, \ldots, n, \quad (A6)$$

where $\theta = \lambda_1/1 + \lambda_1$. As $\lambda_1 \geq 0$, clearly $0 \leq \theta \leq 1$. Now, suppose the profit constraint does not bind ($\pi > \overline{\pi}$). Then by complementary slackness [$\lambda_1(\pi -$ $\overline{\pi}) = 0$], it must be that $\lambda_1 = 0$, and so it follows that $\theta = 0$ and hence, from (A6), that $p_k = MC$ for all k. This is the marginal cost pricing solution. It states that if the profit level, when prices are set at marginal cost, is satisfactory, then this is an optimal solution. However, when there are economies of scale, this solution will not usually hold, as has already been remarked. If prices equal to marginal cost gives a negative profit level, then prices must be set above marginal cost. Equation (A6) then describes how this should be done. Essentially, the larger the value of θ, the higher the prices in (A6) and so the higher the level of profit will be. Notice that if we increase θ up to its maximum value of 1, this corresponds exactly to the profit-maximizing price discrimination solution (see section 18.3), and by assumption, a profit-maximizing mark-up will yield more than the target level of profit. Hence it follows that the optimal level of θ will lie somewhere strictly between 0 and 1. It follows that the optimal Ramsey prices will lie strictly between marginal cost and the profit-maximizing price discrimination level, and will have a similar pattern to profit-maximizing prices (that is, higher prices in more inelastic market segments).

23 Intertemporal Pricing

Objective To examine how the firm can adjust prices over time in the pursuit of profit, and to show how pricing and capacity choices are interdependent.

Prerequisites Chapter 14 gives some useful background on single-period pricing, and Chapter 18 gives information on price discrimination: in particular, the conditions that prevent secondary trading. Both are of relevance here.

Keywords Coase conjecture, firm peak, peak, off-peak, peak-load pricing, perishable goods, price-skimming policy, shifting peak.

23.1 Introduction

This chapter considers some of the issues that arise in pricing over time. Section 23.2 discusses the idea of price skimming, a form of intertemporal price discrimination in which price is reduced period by period in order to capture a greater revenue than can be obtained by setting a single fixed uniform price over time. Section 23.3 then deals with peak-load pricing. This occurs when demand fluctuates in predictable cycles over time and where the firm has to, or chooses to, operate a just-in-time production policy. With systematically fluctuating demand, it can pay the firm to set a price structure in which price also systematically varies over time. This is again a form of price discrimination, and one which is practised widely (bus, train, and airline ticket prices systematically vary by time of departure and return, electricity price varies by day and night, etc.). Finally, section 23.4 deals with the issue of capacity planning and its relationship to pricing policy. The problem described here is how the choice of capacity is contingent on the estimation of demand and demand growth over time, and of the expected pricing policy over a future project life. It also considers pricing once capacity has been installed (since realized demand may diverge above or below the previously expected growth in demand).

23.2 Price-Skimming Strategies

For a monopoly product which has the characteristic of a durable good, a price-skimming strategy involves setting an initially high price and then systematically reducing this price over time. Classic price-skimming examples are the biro and the Polaroid Land camera, which initially entered the market place at prices considerably higher than later in their life cycle.

23.2.1 Skimming with Naive Consumers

Suppose, for simplicity, that each individual desires only one unit of product (as is usually the case with, say, a camera or a washing machine). Different individuals are willing to pay different amounts (because of variations in individual preferences, income, and wealth); that is, they have different reservation prices. Only if the price is set below an individual's willingness to pay, or reservation price, does he or she purchase the good. The excess of reservation price (willingness to pay) over the actual price is, of course, consumer surplus. In Figure 23.1, individuals are rank-ordered by their willingness to pay (highest first and so on); these are labelled w_1, w_2, and so on for individuals 1, 2, etc. If the firm sets a price p, it will sell a quantity $q = 5$ and obtain a revenue $R = pq = 5p$, the shaded area B in the figure. The ith consumer who buys gets consumer's surplus CS_i equal to willingness to pay w_i minus the

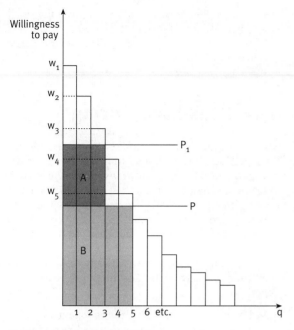

Fig. 23.1 Price-skimming strategy

price they actually have to pay; that is, $CS_i = w_i - p$. Contrast this with the case where the firm first sets a price p_1 and later the price p. In this case, at p_1, the firm will sell $q = 3$ units, and then, once these 3 consumers have dropped out of the market, if the firm reduces price to p, it will sell a further 2 units. Thus, the firm again ends up selling 5 units, but gains an increase in revenue (equal to area A in Figure 23.1).

The idea can be extended; if the initial price is set just below the first individual's reservation price or willingness to pay, she will just be induced to purchase (and the firm will capture revenue equal to w_1). If the price is then slowly decreased, it will eventually fall below the second person's reservation price and she will be induced to purchase, and so on. By continuously reducing the price, each consumer is drawn to pay their full reservation price, and the firm captures the whole of the consumers' willingness to pay for the product (all of $w_1 + w_2 + w_3 + \ldots$). This then is the essence of the price-skimming policy. It involves initially setting a high price, and then continuously reducing price as time passes. So long as consumers behave as described above, such a process will maximize the (undiscounted) revenue taken from the market. The process terminates when price finally falls to marginal

cost (since there is no point in selling units at price below marginal cost).

23.2.2 The Coase Conjecture: Sophisticated Consumers

Consider a monopolized durable goods market where there is no depreciation and no technical progress or product development. Suppose further the firm produces output at constant marginal (equals average) cost. Now, suppose that the firm sets a single price p and sticks to this over time. If it does so, it will make some level of sales immediately (in Figure 23.1, sales of 5 units), but none thereafter. It follows that, having sold the initial quantity at a price above marginal cost, the firm has a strong incentive to reduce price in the next period in order to sell further units at further profit. Indeed, the incentive is such that one would expect the monopolist to keep on reducing price period by period until price eventually falls to marginal cost.

Now consider this price process from the perspective of a consumer. Even if she has high willingness to pay for the product, a rational consumer will understand that the monopolist will eventually end up reducing price to marginal cost. It follows that rational consumers would refuse to pay any price above marginal cost for the product. As a consequence, the firm, if it wishes to sell at all, has to set price equal to marginal cost straightaway. This idea, originally proposed by Ronald Coase, suggests that price-skimming strategies are simply unworkable.

Definition 23.1 The **Coase conjecture** (after Coase 1972): A durable-goods monopolist (supplying an infinitely durable good at constant marginal cost) will sell her product instantaneously at marginal cost.

Thus, according to the Coase conjecture, a durable-goods monopolist cannot exploit her monopoly power, but must set price equal to marginal cost, a prediction which would indicate that, at least for the durable-good case, monopoly power does not lead to monopoly welfare loss. This is a prediction of potential policy significance since it suggests that there is no need for the state to protect consumers in such markets. Unfortunately, the Coase conjecture only seems to hold in rather special circumstances; as soon as real-world considerations are introduced, it becomes clear that price skimming can actually work (at least to some extent).

First, the Coase conjecture relies on consumer rationality. If consumers are myopic, a skimming policy will work. The extent to which it will is limited by the extent to which consumers in practice pick up on the price-skimming trend and respond by deferring purchases. The practicability of price skimming is probably best understood by recognizing that there is considerable noise or ignorance regarding what constitutes marginal cost (consumers lack the information for knowing when the monopolist is actually setting a price equal to marginal cost), that products are continuously being developed and improved, and that durable goods do physically depreciate. Furthermore, consumers are mortal and impatient, typically having time preference and discount rates which are higher than those of the firm.[1] In such circumstances, some rational consumers will buy at the initially higher prices: a price-skimming strategy can thus reap some reward.

The above considerations suggest that price-skimming policy requires a carefully judged rate of price discount. If the rate of price discount is sufficiently slow, those with high willingness to pay will become impatient and hence still buy at the higher prices. However, a slow rate of price fall means it takes longer to draw in consumers with lower willingness to pay; a longer process might give a higher total for undiscounted profits over time, but in taking longer to secure profits, it is possible for the present value of these profits to be lower.

EXAMPLE 23.1 A Newcastle retailer used to purchase job lots of discontinued lines (primarily clothing and fashion garments). New stocks were entered into the 'Red' section of the store. Thereafter, each week, unsold garments were moved to the 'Blue' section, the 'Green' section, and so on (and tagged accordingly). Each section represented a percentage price reduction on the marked price. Thus after each week, prices were cut a further 10%, and if a customer waited 5 weeks, a 50% reduction in price was on offer. The only drawback was that no garments might be available (or, more often, no garments in your size); the bigger the price reduction, the less likely it became that you would get anything at all. This is clearly an example of a workable price-skimming strategy. As time passes, an individual with high willingness to pay gets more and more consumer surplus (as the price falls)—but risks getting no consumer

surplus at all because of stock-out. Given the small numbers of initial stock, this means consumers tend to be drawn in at fairly close to their true valuation of the good.[2]

23.3 Peak-Load Pricing

Many firms face a systematically varying demand for their product: for example, utilities, such as electricity, gas, and telecoms, and transport services, such as trains, airlines, buses, coaches, and taxis. Demand may fluctuate over a daily or weekly cycle, and may also fluctuate over an annual (seasonal) cycle. This suggests that it may pay the firm to vary price systematically over time as well.

The extent to which systematically varying prices over time is likely to be advantageous is likely to depend on

(i) substitutability of demand: the extent to which consumers can substitute demand at one point in time to another;

(ii) the extent to which the firm has to produce for demand just in time (rather than through the accumulation of inventory).

To illustrate, consider the case of electricity, where demand during the day is considerably higher than at night. Consumers generally find it hard (expensive) to store electricity; if the firm charges a lower price for electricity at night (the so-called off-peak rate), this gives consumers an incentive to purchase at night for use in the higher-priced day period.[3] Clearly, if storage was costless, electricity would be

---

[1] For further (but mathematically fairly demanding) work on the Coase conjecture, see Gul *et al.* (1986), Karp (1996), or Driskill (1997).

[2] An individual is drawn to buy when she judges that the expected gain in consumer surplus from future price reductions is just balanced by the consumer surplus that would be gained for sure by purchasing now. With each price fall, the former gets smaller (as it gets increasingly likely that no garments will be available, the expected consumer surplus gain from waiting goes to zero), and the latter gets larger.

[3] To some extent, demand fluctuates in a systematic way by the minute, with pulses in demand during commercial breaks in TV soaps etc. Prices could in principle be made to vary on a continuous basis. However, there are issues beyond the question of to what extent demand is substitutable. There is also the question of the extent to which consumers can understand complex price messages. After all, they will only respond rationally to prices if they are actually aware of what they are. It can be argued that this means that too much complexity in the published tariff may be counter-productive (and may even put some customers off buying at all). Hence the prevalence of relatively simple schemes, such as, for electricity with day (peak) and night (off-peak) rates.

exclusively purchased in the 'off-peak' period (which would then cease to be off-peak). Thus storage by consumers must be difficult or expensive if peak-load pricing is to be sustainable. Such products are often termed **perishable goods**. Electricity is fairly perishable in this sense—but so too is a coach, train, or airline ticket if it specifies the date of departure, since it cannot be used thereafter.[4]

Difficulty of storage also affects the producer. If it is costly for the producer to store the product, then she will also favour just-in-time production. This means that the firm will have to meet the peak levels of demand directly, rather than by running down inventories. This also means that installed capacity needs to cope with this anticipated peak level of demand. In essence, it is the peak demand that determines how much capacity is needed. Opportunity cost reasoning suggests that peak demand is more costly to provide than off-peak. That is, the marginal cost of providing one more unit of output at the peak is the sum of the marginal running costs plus the marginal cost of providing the additional unit of capacity. By contrast, since the capacity is already there, the off-peak period marginal cost of production, it can be argued, is simply the running cost (fuel, materials, labour, etc.). An increase in demand at the off-peak period will not require additional investment in capacity, merely an expansion in output. These differences in cost will also translate into a desire by the firm to differentiate its pricing between peak and off-peak, and to charge a higher price during the peak.[5]

Peak-load pricing differs depending upon whether the objective of the firm is taken to be profit maximization or welfare maximization. Most texts dealing with the peak-load problem tend to discuss the welfare-maximizing case, usually on the grounds that the firm is a public utility. However, following extensive privatizations in many countries in Europe and North America etc., many of these utilities are now in the private sector. Hence it is of interest to explore both types of solution.[6]

23.3.1 The Profit-Maximizing Case

For simplicity, assume that there are just two periods, labelled 1 (**peak**) and 2 (**off-peak**), that capacity cost per unit[7] is β, and that marginal running cost, once capacity is installed, is constant at b per unit in both periods (it is straightforward to extend the analysis to the case where operating costs vary, but the added complexity adds little insight into the nature of the problem). Once installed, capacity is available for both periods. The problem is to determine the amount of capacity to install and the prices to charge for the product in the peak and off-peak periods.

Let p_1 and p_2 denote the prices charged in peak and off-peak periods respectively, with associated sales of q_1 and q_2, and let Q denote the capacity installed. The formal problem is

$$\text{Maximize } \pi = R_1 + R_2 - C = p_1 q_1 + p_2 q_2$$
$$- bq_1 - bq_2 - \beta Q \qquad (23.1)$$
$$\text{subject to } q_1 \leq Q \qquad (23.2)$$

and

$$q_2 \leq Q. \qquad (23.3)$$

This is an inequality-constrained problem of the type discussed in section 3.5. The solution is explored more formally in the Appendix to this chapter. However, it is reasonably straightforward to give an intuitive account of the nature of the solution(s), and this is the approach adopted below.

There are two types of solution to this peak-load pricing problem (when there are two periods, as here). Either capacity is chosen such that it is fully utilized in only the peak period, or it is chosen such that it is fully utilized in both periods.[8] These two solutions (termed the **firm peak** and **shifting peak** cases) are now examined in turn. The solutions are illustrated in Figures 23.2 and 23.3 respectively (these figures also give the solutions to the welfare-maximizing peak-load problem, discussed below).

---

[4] See Weatherford and Bodily (1992) for further discussion of this.

[5] Things are more complex when there is a network of electricity stations operating (since different stations have different capital and operating costs of production). A more detailed consideration is beyond the scope of the present chapter. See Crew and Kleindorfer (1979) for details of production planning problems when there are several plants to be operated.

[6] In so far as firms are private-sector regulated monopolies, it might also be of interest to explore the problem of peak-load pricing in the presence of regulatory constraints (but this is beyond the scope of this text).

[7] This is the capital cost converted into a cost per period (by an appropriate discounted cash flow calculation, which requires an assumption regarding the economic life of the plant etc.). The details of this type of calculation are omitted, given the object is merely to establish some basic principles.

[8] There is no purpose in having more capacity than is required in either period; this simply incurs unnecessary costs.

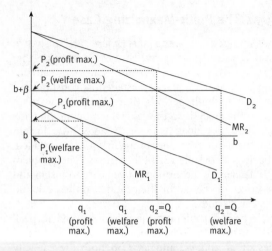

Fig. 23.2 Peak load, firm peak

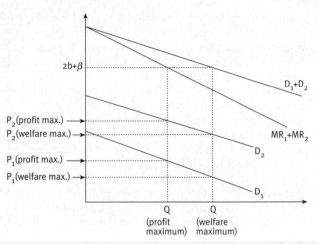

Fig. 23.3 Peak load, shifting peak

(a) Off-Peak Sales Less than Capacity (The Firm Peak Case)

In this case, the pricing rule is simply that

$$MR_1 = b + \beta \qquad (23.4)$$

and

$$MR_2 = b. \qquad (23.5)$$

The rationale for this solution is that profit maximization always requires equalization of marginal revenue with marginal cost. All that is required is a definition of marginal cost. As previously discussed, opportunity cost reasoning suggests the off-peak marginal cost is simply the marginal running cost b (expanding output by one unit in the off-peak merely incurs operating cost b; no extra capacity needs to be installed to supply this) whilst the peak marginal cost is the running cost plus the capacity cost (since expanding output by one unit at the peak requires not only the running cost to be incurred, but also that one more unit of capacity be provided, given that in this period, capacity is fully utilized). This type of solution is depicted in Figure 23.2.

(b) Peak and Off-Peak Sales Equal to Capacity (The Shifting Peak Case[9])

An alternative possible solution is that capacity is fully utilized in both periods. If we denote $MR_1(Q)$

as the peak period's level of marginal revenue at capacity output Q, with $MR_2(Q)$ for the off-peak period, the rise in revenue from adding one more unit of capacity is simply $MR_1(Q) + MR_2(Q)$. The total cost of supplying this is $2b + \beta$ (two units' worth of running costs, one for each period) plus the capacity cost associated with expanding capacity by one unit. Intuitively, this solution will involve setting marginal revenue equal to marginal cost; hence we should have

$$MR_1(Q) + MR_2(Q) = 2b + \beta. \qquad (23.6)$$

This type of solution is depicted in Figure 23.3. The marginal revenue curves are vertically summed (this gives the left side of (23.6)). The intersection with the horizontal marginal cost curve at $2b + \beta$ thus determines the level of capacity to install, and the prices can then be read off the appropriate demand curves. The level of price in each period depends in this case on the relative strength of peak and off-peak demand.

Which of the solutions described in Figures 23.2 and 23.3 in fact holds depends on the exact positions of the demand curves, in conjunction with the values for capacity and marginal operating cost. Broadly speaking, the bigger the vertical difference between the peak and off-peak demand curves, and the smaller the capacity unit cost, the more likely it is that there will be a firm peak, rather than a shifting peak, solution. Of course, in either case, the solution will involve a peak price that is higher than the off-peak price. For well-behaved demand curves, only one of these solutions will satisfy the

[9]   It is referred to as the 'shifting peak' case because, if the peak solution was invoked, the lower price in the off-peak would lead to sales which would exceed that of the peak; i.e. the off-peak would become the peak period at those prices, so the peak period would have 'shifted'.

necessary conditions of the formal optimization problem (given in the Appendix to this chapter). It is a simple matter to test which of the two solutions satisfies the necessary conditions in any given numerical application; this boils down to checking that the capacity constraints are satisfied and that the marginal revenues in both periods are at least covering marginal operating costs. The following numerical example illustrates this process.

EXAMPLE 23.2 (profit-maximizing peak-load pricing with linear demands). Consider the peak-load problem, as described in the text, when $b = £2$ per unit, $\beta = £6$ per unit, peak demand is given by the inverse demand function $p_1 = 20 - q_1$ (so $MR_1 = 20 - 2q_1$; marginal revenue has the same intercept and twice the gradient), and $p_2 = 12 - q_2$ (so $MR_2 = 12 - 2q_2$). Any potential solution must satisfy the constraints $q_1, q_2 \leq Q$, and, from the necessary conditions discussed in the appendix, it must also be that $MR_1, MR_2 \geq b$ (marginal revenue must not fall below marginal running cost in either period). Accordingly, the strategy is to solve for the firm peak and shifting peak cases, and then check these solutions to see which is valid.

(A) FIRM PEAK CASE
Here $q_1 = Q$ and $MR_1 = b + \beta \Rightarrow 20 - 2q_1 = 2 + 6$. Solving gives $q_1 = 6$, so $Q = 6$. The off-peak period output is given by $MR_2 = b \Rightarrow 12 - 2q_2 = 2$. Solving gives $q_2 = 5$. Prices are then given from the inverse demand curves as $p_1 = 20 - q_1 = 20 - 6 = 14$ and $p_2 = 12 - q_2 = 12 - 5 = 7$. This solution satisfies the marginal revenue conditions ($MR_1, MR_2 \geq b = 2$) and the capacity constraints ($q_1, q_2 \leq Q = 6$), and so constitutes the optimal solution. However, emphasize that this is so, I examine the alternative, shifting peak solution, and show that it does not satisfy all the necessary conditions.

(B) SHIFTING PEAK CASE
Here $q_1 = q_2 = Q$ and $MR_1(Q) + MR_2(Q) = 2b + \beta = (2 \times 2) + 6 = 10$. So $20 - 2Q + 12 - 2Q = 10$. Solving, this implies $q_1 = q_2 = Q = 5.5$. The prices are then read from the inverse demand curves as $p_1 = 20 - q_1 = 20 - 5.5 = 14.5$ and $p_2 = 12 - q_2 = 12 - 5.5 = 6.5$. This solution obviously satisfies the capacity constraint, but does not satisfy the marginal revenue conditions ($MR_1, MR_2 \geq b = 2$). Thus $MR_1 = 20 - 2q_1 =$

$20 - (2 \times 5.5) = 9 > b = 2$ but $MR_2 = 12 - 2q_2 = 12 - (2 \times 5.5) = 1 < b = 2$. Thus the shifting peak solution is not optimal (it violates the necessary conditions).

23.3.2 The Welfare-Maximizing Case

In this case, assume the problem is identical to that discussed in section 23.3.1, except that the objective is to maximize welfare W rather than profit. Recall that welfare is measured as willingness to pay minus costs (see Chapter 2 or 22), so the formal problem can be written as

$$\text{Maximize } W = WTP_1 + WTP_2 - C = WTP_1 + WTP_2 - bq_1 - bq_2 - \beta Q, \quad (23.7)$$

where WTP_i is the willingness to pay by consumers in period i (and is simply measured as the area under the appropriate demand function) and is subject to the capacity constraints (23.2) and (23.3). Again, this problem is one of inequality-constrained optimization and is analysed in the Appendix. However, the solution parallels that for the profit-maximizing case. Essentially, profit maximization requires that marginal revenue be equated with marginal cost, whilst welfare maximization requires price to be set equal to marginal cost. Thus, in the light of the discussion of the profit-maximizing case, we would again expect that there are two types of solution and that these solutions are identical to the profit-maximizing ones, except that prices replace marginal revenues in equations (23.4)–(23.6).

(a) Off-Peak Sales Less than Capacity (the Firm Peak Case)

Substituting price for marginal revenue in the profit maximizing solution gives the welfare-maximizing solution as

$$p_1 = b + \beta \quad (23.8)$$
$$p_2 = b. \quad (23.9)$$

Thus, price is set equal to marginal operating cost in the off-peak period, but marginal operating cost plus capacity cost in the peak. The solution is illustrated in Figure 23.2. Again, opportunity cost reasoning explains that the marginal cost in the peak period comprises both marginal running cost b and marginal capacity cost β, but only running cost b in the off-peak period.

(b) Peak and Off-Peak Sales Equal to Capacity (The Shifting Peak Case[10])

Replacing marginal revenues with prices in the profit-maximizing version of the shifting peak case, for welfare maximization we get

$$p_1 + p_2 = \beta + 2b, \qquad (23.10)$$

and of course, $q_1 = q_2 = Q$, so (23.10) implies

$$p_1(Q) + p_2(Q) = 2b + \beta. \qquad (23.11)$$

This solution is illustrated in Figure 23.3; the function $p_1(q) + p_2(q)$ is the vertical sum of the two demand curves (labelled $D_1 + D_2$). The intersection of this with the marginal cost line $2b + \beta$ gives the solution value for Q in this shifting peak case. The associated prices are then read off the individual demand curves associated with this level of output. The level of price here, as in the profit-maximizing case, depends on the relative strength of peak and off-peak demand.

As in the profit-maximizing case, which solution (firm peak or shifting peak) in fact holds depends on the exact positions of the demand curves, in conjunction with the values for capacity and marginal operating cost. Again, it is a simple matter to test which of the two solutions satisfies the necessary conditions in any given numerical application; as in the profit-maximizing case, this boils down to checking that the capacity constraints are satisfied and that, in this case, whether the calculated prices in both periods are at least covering marginal operating costs.

EXAMPLE 23.3 (welfare-maximizing peak-load pricing with linear demands). Consider the peak-load problem with data as in Example 23.2. As mentioned above, any potential solution must satisfy the constraints $q_1, q_2 \leq Q$, and, from the necessary conditions discussed in the Appendix, it must also be that $p_1, p_2 \geq b$ (price must not fall below marginal running cost in either period). As before, I solve for peak and shifting peak cases, and then check these solutions to see which is valid.

(A) FIRM PEAK CASE
Here $q_1 = Q$, $p_1 = b + \beta = 2 + 6 = 8$, and $p_2 = b = 2$. Solving for q_1 using the inverse demand curve gives $q_1 = 20 - p_1 = 20 - 8 = 12$, so $Q = 12$, and solving similarly for q_2 gives $q_2 = 12 - p_2 = 12 - 2 = 10$. This solution satisfies the price

conditions ($p_1, p_2 \geq b = 2$) and the capacity constraints ($q_1, q_2 \leq Q = 12$), and so constitutes the optimal solution. However, to check that this is so, I examine the alternative shifting peak solution, and show that it does not satisfy all the necessary conditions.

(B) SHIFTING PEAK CASE
Here $q_1 = q_2 = Q$ and $p_1(Q) + p_2(Q) = 2b + \beta = 2 \times 2 + 6 = 10$. The inverse demand curves imply $20 - Q + 12 - Q = 10$. Solving this gives $Q = 11$, so $q_1 = q_2 = Q = 11$. The prices are then read from the demand curves as $p_1 = 20 - q_1 = 20 - 11 = 9$ and $p_2 = 12 - q_2 = 12 - 11 = 1$. This solution obviously satisfies the capacity constraint, but does not satisfy the price condition ($p_1, p_2 \geq b = 2$), since $p_2 = 1 < b = 2$. Thus the shifting peak solution is not optimal (it violates the necessary conditions).

23.4 Pricing and Capacity Planning

This section considers the capacity planning problem and its relationship with optimal pricing. Most firms have to invest in capacity prior to production and selling of product. Thus the project appraisal question of how much capacity to install involves not only a consideration of the costs of installing capacity, but also of expected net operating profitability of the product in each year over the economic life of the plant.[11] Consideration of optimal capacity thus requires some assessment or forecast of expected future sales over the life of the product. This sort of information is notoriously difficult to pin down with any degree of confidence, and often all that can be done is to explore the sensitivity of the capacity decision to alternative growth forecasts (see Chapter 7 for a general discussion of sensitivity analysis).

The purpose of this section is not to attempt a realistic analysis, but rather to demonstrate the principles involved in conducting such an analysis. Hence, for simplicity, the case where there are just two periods is examined (since this suffices to introduce the time dimension into the pricing and investment decisions). At time 0, forecasts are made of the

---

[10] See n. 9 above.

[11] Economic life itself is theoretically endogenously determined. The problem of optimizing economic life was discussed in Chap. 7, and so will not be considered here.

demand curves the firm expects to face in time periods 1 and 2. Following this (still at time 0), the firm chooses to install some level of capacity, Q.

A major consideration is whether the product is storable, such that the firm can manufacture for inventory. In what follows, for simplicity, it is assumed that the product is effectively non-storable (either because the product is perishable, as with airline, coach, and train trips, or because storage is too costly, as, for the most part, with electricity).

It saves space if the core model is that used in section 23.3 above, with installed capacity Q, sales in periods 1 and 2 as q_1 and q_2, and the prices set being p_1 and p_2. As before, there is a constant operating cost of b per unit in both periods, and the capacity cost per unit is β. The problem is thus very similar to that in the peak-load pricing case, except that the period 1 demand curve can now lie either below or above that for period 2 (in the peak-load case, period 2 was the off-peak period, with lower demand). It follows that either period might be the firm peak demand.

Another feature, rather different from the peak-load pricing cases, is that capacity has to be chosen on the basis of expected future demands. Once the capacity is installed, the actual demands may turn out to be very different from what was initially expected; the problem here is that capacity cannot be varied in the short run, so the short-run pricing problem becomes one of doing the best one can, given the capacity there is. Capacity in the short run is a sunk cost, and the short-run marginal cost curve ($SRMC$) can be modelled as being flat at level b, finally turning vertical at the capacity output level Q (since output beyond Q is not possible). The pricing problem, once capacity has been installed, is then simply one of setting marginal revenue equal to marginal cost in each period as it arises. This is illustrated in Figure 23.4 below.

This short-run pricing solution applies to any period once capacity has been installed. It involves one of the following two principles:

(a) In a period where the demand curve is at a level such as D_A in Figure 23.4, such that the marginal revenue curve cuts the horizontal part of the short-run marginal cost curve, then, for profit maximization, price is set at p_A.

(b) If demand is sufficiently high for the marginal revenue curve to cut the vertical portion of the short-run marginal cost curve, as in the case of D_B, then the price is set so that demand is

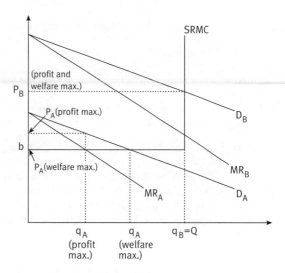

Fig. 23.4 Short-run pricing

restrained to be just equal to capacity (at p_B in Figure 23.4).

This kind of pricing policy applies no matter how many periods there are. If capacity is fixed, then one should set marginal revenue in the period equal to marginal short-run cost.

The same point applies if the aim is that of welfare maximization, except that this case requires price (rather than marginal revenue) to be set equal to marginal cost (as depicted in Figure 23.4). Thus, for maximum welfare, once capacity is installed, the optimal pricing policy involves:

(a) setting price equal to marginal running cost ($p = b$) if, at this price, there is spare capacity, and

(b) only if demand reaches capacity should the price start to rise above level b. In this case, price is chosen simply to restrict demand to available capacity (as with price p_B in Figure 23.4).

EXAMPLE 23.4 Consider the Humber Bridge in England, until recently the world's largest single-span bridge. This is hardly ever capacity-constrained: the carrying capacity at current prices substantially exceeds demand. If the bridge was publicly provided, then the above theory would suggest that the toll should be set at a very low level (merely to cover b, the wear and tear running cost per vehicle crossing). Indeed, taking collection costs into account, it would appear logical to make the bridge toll-free.[12] By contrast, an operator concerned with profit maximization should simply attempt to maximize revenue; this involves choosing a price at which marginal revenue is set equal to b, and hence is set close to zero (that is, the price is set at close to the revenue-maximizing level). Thus profit maximization is consistent with setting a significant toll.

To return to the ex ante problem of choosing capacity, this depends on the expected demand curves for the two periods (discounting will also play a role here). Let r denote the riskless rate of interest appropriate for discounting riskless cash flows;[13] the profit-maximizing problem may then be written as

$$\text{Maximize } \pi = \frac{R_1 - bq_1}{1 + r} + \frac{R_2 - bq_2}{(1 + r)^2} - \beta Q \tag{23.12}$$

$$\text{subject to } q_1 \le Q \tag{23.13}$$

and

$$q_2 \le Q. \tag{23.14}$$

In (23.12), the first two terms on the right represent the discounted operating profits earned in periods 1 and 2, whilst βQ represents the cost at time 0 of installing capacity Q. Once installed, this capacity cannot be exceeded, hence (23.13) and (23.14). Clearly, this assumes that the firm cannot produce something in one period and store it as inventory for demand in future periods. If this is possible, it is straightforward to extend the analysis to incorporate this possibility.[14] This problem is pretty much identical to the peak-load pricing

problem discussed above, except for the discount factors, and the fact that either period might turn out to be the peak period. That is, we have three possible regimes:

(a) $q_1 = Q$, $q_2 < Q$ (firm peak in period 1),

(b) $q_1 < Q$, $q_2 = Q$ (firm peak in period 2),

and

(c) $q_1 = q_2 = Q$ (shifting peak).

The analysis parallels that given in the appendix for the non-discounting peak-load problem, and the interested reader can easily establish the following pricing rules:

(a) $q_1 = Q$, $q_2 < Q$ (firm peak in period 1),

$$MR_1 = b + \beta(1 + r) \tag{23.15}$$

$$MR_2 = b \tag{23.16}$$

(b) $q_1 < Q$, $q_2 = Q$ (firm peak in period 2),

$$MR_1 = b \tag{23.17}$$

$$MR_1 = b + \beta(1 + r)^2 \tag{23.18}$$

(c) $q_1 = q_2 = Q$ (shifting peak).

$$\frac{MR_1(Q) - b}{(1 + r)} + \frac{MR_2(Q) - b}{(1 + r)^2} = \beta. \tag{23.19}$$

The economically relevant solution requires that the capacity constraint be respected in both periods, and that marginal revenues never fall below marginal operating cost b. The firm peak in period 1 can only occur if demand is declining over time, whilst a firm peak in period 2 occurs only if demand is expanding over time. The intuition is straightforward: given that capacity is fixed once installed, then if, for example, demand is expanding, it can pay to build more than is needed for the short run (and so on).

Naturally, the general problem of capacity choice is more complex than is indicated in this stylized two-period case. However, the two-period case suffices to illustrate some of the complexity involved in the decision (and formally, it is straightforward to extend the analysis to multiple periods). Furthermore, the above analysis indicates a general point: namely, that once capacity is installed, pricing becomes a (much simpler) short-run decision in which the price should be directly set equal to short-run marginal cost (for welfare maximization) or should be set such that marginal revenue is equal to short-run marginal cost (for profit maximization). Obviously, at some point, if demand keeps on rising, it becomes economic to install new capacity (and so on).

---

[12] However, second-best considerations would indicate that distortions elsewhere might motivate prices which deviate from marginal cost; for an extended discussion, see sect. 22.3.

[13] Note that uncertainty is ignored in this chapter; see sect 21.2 for some justification of such an assumption.

[14] The extension to the case where storage is possible is not very difficult, although it requires one to distinguish variables for production in each period and for sales in each period, since these are no longer necessarily equal. Letting q_t denote production, I_t the level of inventory at the start of the period, and s_t the sales through period t, then the capacity constraints apply to production, there is an adding-up condition for each period, namely that $I_{t+1} = I_t + q_t - s_t$ (inventory changes by the difference between production and sales), and there are additional holding costs associated with inventory. If these are h per period, there is an additional cost term hI_t in each period (there may also be limits on how much inventory can be stored). A committed reader might like to explore how such considerations affect the nature of the solution analysed in the text (for the two-period case, one might assume initial inventory is zero).

EXAMPLE 23.5 Suppose the demand curves for periods 1 and 2 are as in Example 23.2, that the rate of interest is $r = 0.1$, and that $b = 2$ as before, but $\beta = 6/1.1 = 5.4545$, so $\beta(1 + r) = 6$. Then the only solution which satisfies the necessary conditions is solution (a) above (the firm peak in period 1), which corresponds to prices and outputs as in Example 23.2.

Basically, if demand is increasing as time passes, then we can rule out period 1 as the firm peak in which capacity constrains output, whilst if demand is contracting, we can rule out period 2 as the firm peak.

A discussion of the welfare-maximizing case is omitted, as it parallels those already described in section 23.3; the solution merely involves replacing marginal revenue by price in equations (23.15)–(23.19).

23.5 Summary

This chapter examined some aspects of pricing and choice of capacity over time. Section 23.2 dealt with price-skimming, in which the firm gradually reduces price over time in order to extract more consumer surplus than can be got from applying a constant price. Section 23.3 examined the problem where the firm faces a systematically fluctuating demand, where consumers are unable to shift demand significantly between periods, and showed that peak-period prices will generally be set higher than off-peak prices, whether the objective is profits or welfare. Finally, section 23.4 examined the problem of capacity and pricing over time. The problem here is that initial choice of capacity depends on expectations regarding the level of future demand. Once installed, the capacity often takes the characteristic of a sunk cost (since it is difficult to vary capacity instantaneously) so the pricing rule becomes one of setting marginal revenue equal to short-run marginal cost. When this leads to demand which exceeds the available capacity, the firm then raises price to choke demand back to the available level of capacity. At time zero, the capacity installation decision may involve building excess capacity relative to initial demand, so as to provide better for future demand (when demand is expected to grow over time), or indeed, to install too little capacity initially, in the expectation that future demand is likely to fall away.

23.6 Review Questions

1. Consider the peak-load pricing problem (as in Example 23.2) for the case where $b = 2$, $\beta = 12$, $p_1 = 16 - q_1$, and $p_2 = 12 - 2q_2$.

   (a) Find the optimal profit-maximizing solution.

   (b) Find the optimal welfare-maximizing solution.

2. Under what conditions will a firm be able to (and wish to) practise peak-load pricing?

3. Many large-span bridges (the Humber, Severn, Firth of Forth, etc.) charge a toll for crossing (and the toll varies according to the type of vehicle). To what extent is the levying of tolls socially desirable; and to what extent is it socially desirable, if tolls are to be levied, that they vary by type of vehicle?

4. Consider a peak-load problem of the type described in section 23.3, where b and β, are constants and there are two periods; the peak period has demand $p_1 = \gamma_0 - \gamma_1 q_1$ and the off-peak $p_2 = \lambda_0 - \lambda_1 q_2$, where $\gamma_0, \gamma_1, \lambda_0$ and λ_1, are positive constants (such that the peak demand curve lies above the off-peak demand curve for positive prices and quantities). Show that if the optimal solution to the profit-maximizing peak-load problem is firm peak, then so is the solution to the welfare-maximizing problem, whilst if the profit-maximizing solution is shifting peak, then it is likewise for the welfare-maximizing case. Hint: examine and compare the conditions under which the firm peak solutions are optimal for the two problems (see Examples 23.2 and 23.3).

5. Consider a profit-maximizing two-period intertemporal problem of the type described in section 23.4. Suppose that $p_1 = 10 - q_1$ and $p_2 = 15 - q_2$, and that $r = 0.1$, $b = 2$ and $\beta = 6$. Determine the optimal solution. (Consider each of the possible solutions, and apply the checks, namely that $MR_i \geq b$, $q_i \leq Q$ for $i = 1, 2$; these tests rule out all non-optimal solutions.)

23.7 Further Reading

Coase (1972) is the seminal reference on the Coase conjecture regarding durable-goods monopolists; Gul *et al.* (1986) more formally establish necessary conditions for it to apply. Both Crew and Kleindorfer (1979) and Rees (1984) give good and clear accounts of the basic peak-load pricing problem. The former text goes on to give a variety of extensions (to multi-plant operations and stochastic models). The latter also discusses the intertemporal capacity planning problem discussed in section 23.4 in some detail, although only in the context of partial-equilibrium welfare maximization.

Appendix: Derivation of Peak-Load and Intertemporal Pricing Rules

(1) Profit-Maximizing Peak-Load Pricing

The formal problem is

$$\text{Maximize } \pi = R_1 + R_2 - C = p_1 q_1 + p_2 q_2 \\ - bq_1 - bq_2 - \beta Q \tag{A1}$$

$$\text{subject to } q_1 \leq Q \tag{A2}$$

and

$$q_2 \leq Q. \tag{A3}$$

If we set a Lagrangian for this problem, it takes the form

$$L = R_1 + R_2 - bq_1 - bq_2 - \beta Q \\ + \lambda_1(Q - q_1) + \lambda_2(Q - q_2), \tag{A4}$$

where the choice variables are Q, q_1, and q_2 and λ_1 and λ_2 denote the Lagrange multipliers for constraints (A2) and (A3) respectively. This problem involves inequality constraints, and the appropriate first-order conditions are termed the Kuhn–Tucker conditions (see section 3.5). These are now examined, although the solution is fairly intuitive, and the reader can pass over the following analysis on a first reading. The Kuhn–Tucker conditions are that

$$\partial L / \partial Q = -\beta + \lambda_1 + \lambda_2 = 0, \tag{A5}$$

$$\partial L / \partial q_1 = \partial R_1 / \partial q_1 - b - \lambda_1 = 0, \tag{A6}$$

and

$$\partial L / \partial q_2 = \partial R_2 / \partial q_2 - b - \lambda_2 = 0; \tag{A7}$$

the complementary slackness conditions, that

$$\lambda_1(Q - q_1) = 0, \tag{A8}$$

$$\lambda_2(Q - q_2) = 0, \tag{A9}$$

the constraints (A2) and (A3) hold, and the multipliers are non-negative, i.e. $\lambda_1 \geq 0$ and $\lambda_2 \geq 0$. Noting that $\partial R_i / \partial q_i = MR_i$ is simply the marginal revenue arising in period ($i = 1, 2$), we get from (A6) and (A7) that

$$MR_1 = b + \lambda_1 \tag{A10}$$

and

$$MR_2 = b + \lambda_2. \tag{A11}$$

This implies $MR_i \geq b$, $i = 1, 2$ (since the multipliers are non-negative). From (A5),

$$\lambda_1 + \lambda_2 = \beta. \tag{A12}$$

Basically, there are two types of solution possible here. Either capacity will be fully utilized in the peak period, whilst off-peak sales are lower, or capacity will be fully utilized in both periods.[15]

(1a) Off Peak Sales Less than Capacity (the Firm Peak Case)

In this case, from complementary slackness, (A9), if $q_2 < Q$ it must be that $\lambda_2 = 0$. Then, from (A12), $\lambda_1 = \beta$, so from (A8), $q_1 = Q$ and the pricing rule is that

$$MR_1 = b + \beta \tag{A13}$$

and

$$MR_2 = b. \tag{A14}$$

Thus, as usual, profit maximization requires equalization of marginal revenue with marginal cost, and opportunity cost reasoning can be invoked to show here that the marginal cost is operating and capacity cost in the peak period, but only operating cost in the off-peak period. This type of solution is depicted in Figure 23.2.

(1b) Peak and Off-Peak Sales Equal to Capacity (the Shifting Peak Case[16])

Adding (A6) to (A7) and rearranging slightly gives

$$MR_1 - b + MR_2 - b = \lambda_1 + \lambda_2, \tag{A15}$$

and of course, $q_1 = q_2 = Q$ and $\lambda_1 + \lambda_2 = \beta$, so (A15) implies

$$MR_1(Q) + MR_2(Q) = 2b + \beta. \tag{A16}$$

This determines the level of capacity to install,

---

[15] As mentioned above (n. 8), there is no point in having more capacity than is required in either period; this simply incurs unnecessary costs. Formally, a solution in which $q_1 < Q$ and $q_2 < Q$ will contradict the necessary conditions. To see this, note that from the complementary slackness conditions, these strict inequalities imply that both $\lambda_1 = 0$ and $\lambda_2 = 0$. However, by (A12), these must sum to $\beta > 0$, so there is a contradiction. Likewise it is easy to see that the other possibility, that off-peak demand equals capacity whilst peak demand is less, leads to a contradiction. (As the reader can verify, this solution would involve $MR_2 = b + \beta$ whilst $MR_1 = b$; for this to hold would require $q_2 < q_1$, which contradicts the assumption that it is off-peak demand which fully utilizes capacity—see Figure 23.2).

[16] See n. 9 above.

and the prices can then be read off the appropriate demand curves. The level of price in this case depends on the relative strength of peak and off-peak demand. This type of solution is depicted in Figure 23.3.

Which of the solutions described in Figures 23.2 and 23.3 in fact holds will depend on the exact positions of the demand curves, in conjunction with the values for capacity and marginal running cost. For given demand and cost parameter values, only one of these solutions will satisfy the necessary conditions (the key checks are that the capacity constraints are satisfied, and that marginal revenues in both periods are at least equal to marginal running cost, b). In either case, the solution will involve a peak price that is higher than the off-peak price. Example 23.2 gives a numerical instance of this type of problem.

(2) Welfare-Maximizing Peak-Load Pricing

In this case, assume the problem is identical to that discussed in section (1), except that the objective is to maximize welfare rather than profit. The formal problem is

$$\text{Maximize } W = WTP_1 + WTP_2 - C$$
$$= WTP_1 + WTP_2 - bq_1\, 2\, bq_2 - \beta Q,$$
$$\text{(A17)}$$

where WTP_i is the willingness to pay by consumers in period i (and is simply measured as the area under the appropriate demand function) and is subject to the capacity constraints (A2) and (A3). The associated Lagrangian is (cf. (A4)):

$$L = WTP_1 + WTP_2 - bq_1 - bq_2 - \beta Q$$
$$+ \lambda_1(Q - q_1) + \lambda_2(Q - q_1),$$
$$\text{(A18)}$$

where, again, the choice variables are Q, q_1, and q_2. It can be shown that the rate at which WTP increases as quantity increases is just equal to the price; that is, $\partial WTP_i/\partial q_i = p_i$ (see the appendix to Chapter 22, and especially Figure 22.5). The Kuhn–Tucker conditions are that

$$\partial L/\partial Q = -\beta + \lambda_1 + \lambda_2 = 0, \quad \text{(A19)}$$

$$\partial L/\partial q_1 = p_1 - b - \lambda_1 = 0, \quad \text{(A20)}$$

and

$$\partial L/\partial q_2 = p_2 - b - \lambda_2 = 0. \quad \text{(A21)}$$

Everything else is as for the profit-maximizing case. In effect, the solution is identical except that the solution here involves prices rather than marginal revenues. Since the multipliers are non-

negative, the solution must feature, $p_i \geq b$, $i = 1$, 2; that is, prices must always at least cover marginal running cost. Following through an identical analysis to that for the profit-maximizing case gives:

(2a) Off-Peak Sales Less than Capacity (the Firm Peak Case)

Substituting price for marginal revenue in (A13) and (A14) yields

$$p_1 = b + \beta \quad \text{(A22)}$$

and

$$p_2 = b. \quad \text{(A23)}$$

Thus, price is set equal to marginal running cost in the off-peak period, but marginal running plus capacity cost during the peak. This is a version of the standard result that to maximize welfare requires marginal cost prices.[17] Again, opportunity cost reasoning can be invoked to show here that the marginal cost in the peak period comprises both marginal running cost b and marginal capacity cost β, but only running cost b in the off-peak period. The solution is illustrated in Figure 23.2.

(2b) Peak and Off-Peak Sales Equal to Capacity (the Shifting Peak Case[18])

As above, replacing marginal revenue with price gives

$$p_1 - b + p_2 - b = \lambda_1 + \lambda_2 = \beta, \quad \text{(A24)}$$

and of course, $q_1 = q_2 = Q$, so (A24) implies

$$p_1(Q) + p_2(Q) = 2b + \beta. \quad \text{(A25)}$$

This determines the level of capacity to install, and the prices can then be read off the appropriate demand curves, as illustrated in Figure 23.3. The level of price in this case depends on the relative strength of peak and off-peak demand.

(3) Profit Maximizing Intertemporal Pricing

In this case, there are just two periods, with prices and expected sales quantities (viewed from the perspective of time 0) p_1, p_2 q_1, and q_2, and running costs and capacity costs are as above, b, and β. Capacity is chosen at time 0, and then remains fixed.

[17] Note that this is partial-equilibrium analysis, ignoring distortions elsewhere in the economy; for a discussion of how other distortions affect the marginal cost pricing rule, see sect. 22.3.
[18] See n. 9 above.

The optimization of capacity involves considering what prices are likely to hold in the future periods, and the profits these are likely to generate. The profit-maximizing problem may be written as

$$\text{Maximize } \pi = \frac{R_1 - bq_1}{1 + r} + \frac{R_2 - bq_2}{(1 + r)^2} - \beta Q \quad \text{(A26)}$$

$$\text{subject to } q_1 \leq Q \quad \text{(A27)}$$

and

$$q_2 \leq Q. \quad \text{(A28)}$$

In (A26), the first two terms on the right represent the discounted operating profits earned in periods 1 and 2, whilst βQ represents the time 0 cost of installing capacity Q. Once installed, this capacity cannot be exceeded, hence the constraints (A27) and (A28). This problem is pretty much identical to the peak-load pricing problem discussed above, except for the discount factors, and the fact that either period might turn out to be the peak period. The Lagrangian is

$$L = \frac{R_1 - bq_1}{1 + r} + \frac{R_2 - bq_2}{(1 + r)^2} - \beta Q + \lambda_1(Q - q_1)$$

$$+ \lambda_2(Q - q_2), \quad \text{(A29)}$$

where the choice variables are Q, q_1, and q_2. The Kuhn–Tucker conditions are that

$$\partial L / \partial Q = -\beta + \lambda_1 + \lambda_2 = 0, \quad \text{(A30)}$$

$$\partial L / \partial q_1 = \frac{\partial R_1 / \partial q_1 - b}{1 + r} - \lambda_1 = 0, \quad \text{(A31)}$$

and

$$\partial L / \partial q_2 = \frac{\partial R_2 / \partial q_2 - b}{(1 + r)^2} - \lambda_2 = 0, \quad \text{(A32)}$$

the complementary slackness conditions, that

$$\lambda_1 (Q - q_1) = 0, \quad \text{(A33)}$$

$$\lambda_2 (Q - q_2) = 0, \quad \text{(A34)}$$

the constraints (A27) and (A28) hold, and the multipliers are non-negative, i.e. $\lambda_1 \geq 0$ and $\lambda_2 \geq 0$. As $\partial R_i / \partial q_i = MR_i$, the results are those stated in the text (equations (22.15)–(22.19), as the reader can verify by following a parallel analysis to that given above for the peak-load problems).

A variety of extensions to this type of problem are possible, for example, where it is possible to hold inventory over time. Space precludes further analysis of such possibilities.

24 Cost-Plus and Mark-Up Pricing

Objectives This chapter examines different forms of cost-based pricing and discusses the apparent conflict between these and the economist's model, in which price is adjusted to equate marginal revenue with marginal cost.

Prerequisites None specific.

Keywords average cost pricing, cost-plus pricing, full cost pricing, marginalism, mark-up pricing.

24.1 Introduction

Several variants of the full cost pricing method are possible, but, in essence, the method simply involves adding a percentage or absolute mark-up to the cost of the item. The cost here is usually average cost or average variable cost, and is often based upon historic accounting data. For simplicity, it is assumed that there is a single product, so no problem of joint cost allocation arises (the more general and usual case of multiple products is considered in section 24.5). It is convenient to distinguish the following pricing concepts:

Definition 24.1 Cost-plus pricing is the general term used here for cost-based pricing, where price is determined by adding a mark-up to some measure of the cost of producing the product.

Definition 24.2 Mark-up pricing is the special case where the mark-up is applied to average variable cost.

Definition 24.3 Full cost (or **average cost**) **pricing** is the special case where the mark-up is applied to average total cost.

The subtle difference between mark-up and full cost pricing lies in the fact that full cost pricing requires overheads to be allocated across the products a firm produces and sells. In practice, for firms with many product lines (such as supermarkets), there is a tendency to prefer mark-up pricing. This is because average variable cost is generally much easier to estimate than full cost, so the mark-up pricing rule tends to be more straightforward to apply. The problem with the full cost pricing rule, from the perspective of the pricing decision, is that full cost requires overheads to be allocated to products. Overheads are often non-attributable (see Chapter 12) and the basis on which overheads are allocated is, from a pricing perspective, essentially arbitrary. It is not difficult to show that arbitrary overhead allocations can be detrimental to the firm's profitability, particularly when the firm is concerned with selling multiple products. It can also be argued that mark-up pricing is more likely to yield prices closer to those which maximize the firm's profitability (see in particular, section 24.4).

Let

C = total cost

F = fixed or overhead cost

VC = variable cost

AC = average cost

AVC = average variable cost

M = mark-up on AC

m = mark up on AVC.

Then the mark-up may be applied in the form of an absolute mark-up

$$P = AC + M \quad \text{or} \quad P = AVC + m \quad (24.1)$$

or as a proportionate (or percentage) mark-up

$$P = AC(1 + M) \quad \text{or} \quad P = AVC(1 + m) \quad (24.2)$$

In what follows, only the proportionate or percentage mark-up will be considered.[1] Clearly, given that,

---

[1] Mark-ups can be viewed as a mark-up on cost or on price. Thus equation (24.2) could have been written as $(P = AC)/AC = M$. A given mark-up on average cost implies a lower mark-up on price. Denote the mark-up on price as M'. Thus $(P - AC)/P =$

for any output level, $AC > AVC$, firms will tend to need to adopt higher mark-ups on AVC than on AC.[2]

The object of the pricing exercise is thus to choose a mark-up in order to achieve a satisfactory level of profitability (or return on capital or whatever); presumably it remains the case that more profit continues to be preferred to less, but this may not be the only goal of the firm. In particular, with the separation of ownership from control, managers of firms typically have some (often considerable) scope to pursue other objectives than simply short-run profit maximization (see Chapter 17). The key point to note about the cost-plus approach to pricing is that demand analysis appears to play no role in price setting. The idea is that price is determined through adding a standard mark-up to some estimate of unit cost. However, it is clear that, in the absence of knowledge of the sensitivity of demand to price, the choice of an inappropriate mark-up can lead to an unpleasant surprise for the firm; this point is discussed in section 24.6 and in a case study in section 24.8.2.

24.2 The Marginalist/ Cost-Plus Pricing Debate

The empirical evidence suggests that most firms, in determining selling prices, use cost-plus pricing rather than the economist's model, namely to choose price so that marginal revenue equals mar-

---

M'. Then $P - AC = M \times AC = M' \times P$. Since $P > AC$, $M' < M$. For example, a 10% mark-up on AC is equivalent to a 9.09% mark-up on price, as the reader may care to verify. Only the mark-up on cost is discussed in what follows, as this is the more usual form of the rule.

[2] For the single-product case, the mark-ups are easily related, since AC can be rewritten in terms of AVC. Thus, $AC = (VC + F)/q$ and $AVC = VC/q$, so it follows that

$$AC = AVC(1 + F/VC). \qquad (i)$$

Thus mark-ups m and M which give the same price can be related as follows;

$$P = (1 + M)AC = (1 + F/VC)(1 + M)AVC \qquad (ii)$$

and

$$P = (1 + m)AVC, \qquad (iii)$$

so

$$(1 + m) = (1 + F/VC)(1 + M) \qquad (iv)$$

Notice that overheads are allocated in proportion to total variable costs here (F/VC; see Chap. 10). Equation (iv) suggests that the equivalent mark-up on AVC to one on AC is of necessity larger. For example, if $F/VC = 0.5$, a mark-up of 20% on AC is equivalent to one of 80% on AVC.

ginal cost.[3] The questions that arises are 'Why?', and 'Does it matter?' The debate is presented in two parts. First, section 24.2.1 sets out and assess the marginalist critique of cost–plus pricing; following this, section 24.2.2 sets out and assesses the critique of marginalism. Finally, section 24.2.3 offers some concluding comments on the debate.

24.2.1 An Assessment of the Marginalist Critique of Cost-Plus Pricing

According to the (naive) marginalist critique of cost-plus pricing,

(i) Cost-plus pricing (in all its variations) does not explicitly focus on marginal revenue or marginal cost, and

(ii) the plus is usually added onto historic cost estimates of AC or AVC.

(iii) Setting marginal revenue equal to marginal cost is a necessary condition for profit maximization (see section 14.3). Therefore

(iv) cost-plus pricing will not, except as a fortuitous accident, maximize profits and so is inferior to the marginalist approach to pricing.

On the face of it, statements (i)–(iii) seem to be true and (iv) seems to follow logically from them. However, there is a certain vagueness in these statements and it is possible to construct a critique of marginalism and a defence of cost-plus pricing out of this. Anti-marginalists (as I shall dub the proponents of cost-plus pricing) do not claim that cost-plus pricing is the best of all possible policies, merely that it is not clearly inferior to marginalism in a real-world context.

Consider first points (i) and (ii). The cost basis for cost-plus pricing is typically that of standard costing; this methodology involves a per unit target cost estimated on the basis of a given planned/budgeted level of production (see e.g. Horngren and Foster 1987). Standard costs are usually based on historic (or at best current) cost data. However, as argued in

---

[3] Hall and Hitch (1939) is the seminal article claiming to establish the popularity of the full-cost rule of thumb. Many surveys since have noted that some form of cost-based pricing continues to be prevalent—see e.g. Hague (1949, 1971), and an excellent survey in Dorward (1987). The extent to which such surveys elucidate the truth is difficult to judge. What people say they do, and what they actually do, are often at variance. For example, managers may not be inclined to reveal how they actually behave, only how they would like to be seen to be behaving.

Chapter 12, cost analysis for decision-making should be forward-looking. That is, in choosing to set a price for a future period, the relevant costs are those which are expected to be incurred in that period. For example, if the firm is involved with importing inputs to production from abroad, this will in principle involve forecasting exchange rate movements; if wage rates are expected to change, these should also be forecast, and so on. Whilst this general critique of the use of historic costs is correct, it is also fair to point out that, in many applications, historic costs may provide reasonable estimates for future costs. This is likely to be true if inflation is low and the market environment is stable (no substantial shifts in demand, or the state of competition). In such cases, the accounting cost system provides a cheap source of relevant information for pricing decisions. Clearly this argument may be true in some situations and not in others. It would suggest that management should assess for each product what the best approach is for estimating the future costs of that product for the period over which the chosen price has to hold. Using historic costs will only be appropriate in some circumstances.

The lack of focus on demand (and hence marginal revenue) is also theoretically true; however, it should be noted that there is some evidence that decision-makers often adjust mark-ups in response to what the market will bear and it can be argued that this intuitive approach to the demand side can often yield prices which are close to optimal; this point is discussed further in section 24.4.

Turning to point (iii), that setting MR equal to MC is a necessary condition for profit maximization, this is clearly true for a monopolist faced with known and certain demand and cost functions in the case where price is set for a single period. In such circumstances, setting a price determines exactly how much product will be sold and how much profit will be made—and this is independent of what happens in future periods. In practice, of course, there is often uncertainty on both the cost and demand side, and intertemporal considerations are also important (for example, brand loyalty, but also the likely reactions of competitors etc.). It follows that the marginalist critique is not decisive.

24.2.2 The Anti-Marginalist Critique

Indeed, these observations suggest an anti-marginalist critique of (naive) marginalism which goes as follows:

(i) The marginalist model ignores the fact that the pricing problem is a dynamic one. The single-period model is inadequate. It ignores competitors' reactions and consumer brand loyalty and the fact that firms often sell a variety of different products. Therefore the naive marginalist model does not generally maximize the present value of future profits (and hence the value of the firm).

(ii) In practice, demand curves are rarely known in detail. Furthermore, there is uncertainty over the development of demand in the future. Likewise, marginal cost information may not be available and there may be uncertainty about marginal costs which lie in the future.

(iii) The full cost pricing rule should be viewed in the light of the above criticisms. It is often suggested that cost-plus pricing does not require detailed demand information, ensures a profit will be made, and promotes long-run profitability.

(iv) Although marginalism may be extended to take account of the above considerations, it becomes excessively complex: the risk of making mistakes is an important practical consideration.

Let's take these arguments in turn.

(i) The argument that marginalism ignores dynamics is a valid criticism only of the naive single-period marginalist model. As explained in Chapter 23, it is possible to extend marginalist reasoning to address decisions such as the frequency with which prices should be revised, depending upon assessments of the costs of revising prices (advertizing and other costs) and the impact upon customer loyalty and goodwill. Furthermore, although (i) is a criticism of the marginalist model, it is not an argument which unambiguously supports the cost-plus pricing approach. It is true that cost-based pricing tends to be less responsive to changes in demand conditions, and it can be argued that to an extent this promotes loyalty and a sense of fairness in pricing, but there are many products for which brand loyalty is largely unimportant (e.g. petrol). For such products, responsive pricing can increase short-term and hence long-term profitability. Furthermore, correctly applied, the marginalist model will recommend price stability in precisely those instances where such factors are important (as discussed in Chapter 23). Marginalism basically suggests that prices be adjusted over time in order to maximize the present value of profits. This motivates the deci-sion-maker to think about the knock-on effects of choosing price now for sales in the future (and so on). Likewise, the marginalist approach can be extended to deal with the problem of pricing mul-tiple products (Chapter 20), although the analysis does become significantly more complex. Complex-ity can be a significant drawback, as it increases the chances of making mistakes (the prune juice case study discussed in section 16.5 is illustrative of this point).

The idea that marginalism ignores competitors' reactions is again at best a critique of the most naive version of the theory. For example, the Cournot and kinked demand curve theories (Chapter 16) are essentially marginalist. The latter tells us, using mar-ginal reasoning, that it may be desirable in oligopoly (in the absence of collusion) to maintain price stability in the face of changing demand and cost conditions. By contrast, cost-based prices shift with changing cost conditions; in this case marginalist pricing may lead to greater stability. Thus, margin-alist reasoning can help to establish when price sta-bility is desirable and when it is not.

(ii) If the demand curve is not known, this clearly indicates that the marginalist model is not opera-tional. It should be noted that demand not known is not the same thing as demand being uncertain and fluctuating over time. Uncertainty can be incorpo-rated into marginal analysis (see Chapter 21); it turns out that it is often appropriate simply to take the best-guess demand and cost curves and to work with these, essentially treating the problem of pricing as though it is one under certainty. However, if the firm is completely ignorant of demand and how it varies with price, this is a rather worrying state of affairs. In particular, it may be worth spending some money on market research to explore the sensitivity of sales to price. Naturally this has to be judged; for some products, market research is likely to be important (e.g. the Jaguar case study in section 24.8) whilst for others it may not offer much reward. The criticism of marginalism not taking account of uncertainty is again only a criticism of the simplest textbook presentation of marginalism. The model can be extended to deal with pricing in the presence of uncertainty, and indeed, it can often be argued that uncertainty is not necessarily a problem for practical pricing policy (as explained in Chapter 21). On the cost side, this again suggests that it may be desirable to spend money on improving the cost information system (see Cato's Cleaners,

Section 12.4.2, page 207). It is also worth mention-ing that marginalism can be applied intuitively: all one needs in order to apply the principles is a rough idea of marginal costs and the demand elasticity (see section 24.4 below).

(iii) The arguments here are generally dubious. As already suggested, the argument that cost-plus pricing promotes long-run profitability is fallacious; there are situations where price stability may be beneficial, but equally there are situations where responsive pricing will increase profitability in both the short and long run. Without brand loy-alty, the long run is essentially a sequence of inde-pendent single periods; net present value (long-run profit) is maximized by maximizing the short-run profit for each individual period. Nor does cost-based pricing guarantee a profit; this is fairly obvious in the case of mark-up pricing (since the mark-ups must be such that there is a large enough contribution to cover the firm's overheads, but it can also be true for the full cost-plus approach. Losses can be incurred with full cost-plus pricing (1) if the cost-plus approach leads to prices such that sales are much lower than the expected/budgeted volumes, or (2) if prices are set on the basis of historic costs in an inflationary environment: cur-rent revenues obviously will cover historic costs, but may not cover current costs (this problem is most severe where stocks are held for appreciable periods, as is the case with booksellers).

(iv) None of the above discussion disarms the criticism that applying marginalism in the real world is not an easy task; it is clearly a fact that there is a significant increase in complexity if the marginalist model is to incorporate factors such as brand loyalty and competitive reactions, and the risk of getting things wrong in the analysis can be a clearly signifi-cant factor. Business decision-makers exposed to managerial economics courses (on MBA and Execu-tives programmes) are often wary of embracing marginalism precisely because they fear there are greater risks of getting it wrong. The prune juice case study reported in section 16.5 illustrates the possibilities for making such mistakes (in an oligo-polistic context). Cost-plus pricing at least has the merits of simplicity and transparency; everyone can at least see that such prices have been correctly calculated. Unfortunately, routine and uncritical application of simple pricing rules of thumb can *also* be disastrous. Marginalism, by contrast, expli-citly encourages consideration of the likely effects of price changes on sales.

24.2.3 Concluding Comments on the Debate

It is also often argued that cost-plus pricing is only ever used as a preliminary assessment of price. According to this view it is merely a way of finding out information about the demand curve at a price level that is not likely to be too damaging to the firm. Thereafter, observation of how sales progress relative to capacity, observation of any reactions by competitors in the market, and so on will be taken into account in deciding how to modify the level of the mark-up. These deliberations and adjustments may well result in cost-plus prices similar to these which would arise if a marginal or incremental approach was used. This point is taken up again in section 24.4 below.

Many economists are comfortable with the argument that, if observed behaviour survives in the market place, there must be good reasons supporting that form of behaviour. However, the argument that 'firms must be getting things right—for if they didn't, they would be driven out of the market' applies only in markets where there is significant competition *and* a stable environment where there are few innovations in product development or production technology. Even then, the argument that only the fittest survive is one which can take a long time to become manifest, even in a stable environment (see Dawkins 1976). In a world constantly in flux, efficient and inefficient firms can coexist for long periods of time, perhaps indefinitely. Only the grossly incompetent are likely to be weeded out; firms can generally survive so long as they are doing *something* right. That something does not have to be pricing policy. A firm which keeps ahead of the competition in terms of existing and new product development can, for example, turn in significant profits despite using the most defective costing and pricing systems.

To sum up, the marginalist perspective encourages explicit thinking about the key issues which should influence price policy, and best-practice cost-plus pricing (mark-up pricing with variable mark-ups) tends to approximate to this. Marginalism should not be rejected as too mathematically or conceptually complex. The basic ideas can be implemented without extended mathematical analysis; an intuitive grasp of how price sensitivity and marginal or unit cost assessments can be used to influence the choice of price is demonstrated in section 24.4.

24.3 Cost-Plus Pricing: Circularity and Stability

The argument that cost-plus pricing does not require knowledge of demand or demand elasticity can be both criticized and defended. The criticism is that the claim that cost-plus pricing does not require demand information involves circular reasoning. Thus, if average cost varies with output, you need to know how much you are likely to produce before you can say what average cost, AC, for that output will be—and you need to know AC in order to add a mark-up to arrive at the price. The problem is that the price determines the volume of sales, so we have a chicken-and-egg problem; you need to know the price in order to calculate the average cost, and you need to know the average cost in order to determine the cost-plus price. The same point applies to mark-up pricing if AVC varies with output, for precisely the same reasons.

Of course, in full-cost pricing, if average cost is constant with output over some relevant range, demand is irrelevant (and likewise in mark-up pricing, if AVC is constant). Figure 24.1 depicts this case (D_1 and D_2 represent different demand curves, to illustrate that the price is the same whatever the level of demand).

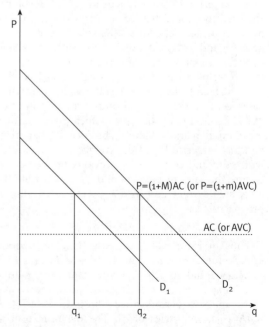

Fig. 24.1 Case where cost-plus price is independent of demand (constant *AC* or *AVC*)

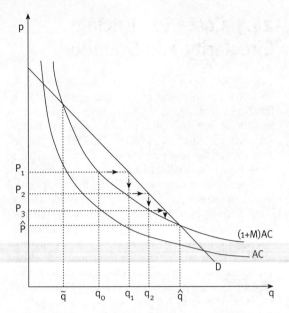

Fig.24.2 Case where cost-plus price depends on demand

Figure 24.2 illustrates the case where AC falls with output (a very common case in practice, although the diagram can easily be adapted to the more traditional U-shaped average cost curve). Clearly, in this case the price to be set depends on the volume expected to be sold (which in turn depends on the price set, which depends on the volume expected to be sold, and . . . so it goes). Apparently then, it is necessary to know the demand curve in order to set the cost-plus price. However, it can be argued that the usual cost-plus pricing rule, where prices are based on historic costs and output levels, will often quickly converge on the price which gives the firm the desired mark-up level. The idea is that firms typically set price based on average cost associated with sales and costs of the previous period. Let q_t denote the sales in period t and $AC(q_t)$ denote the associated average cost in that period. The full-cost pricing rule (24.2) becomes

$$P_t = (1 + M)AC(q_{t-1}). \qquad (24.3)$$

Thus in Figure 24.2, suppose that last period's sales volume was q_0. The firm sets $P_1 = (1 + M)AC(q_0)$ and so sells q_1. Note that the resulting mark-up, $(P_1 - AC(q_1))$, is greater than the desired mark-up. Next period, price adjusts to $P_2 = (1 + M)AC(q_1)$, with sales of q_2. The dynamic process clearly converges on $(\hat{P}, \hat{q})$, where the firm's realized mark-up is equal to its desired mark-up on average

cost. The same type of convergence process would have occurred if initially q_0 had been greater than $\hat{q}$ (but less than $\tilde{q}$). Thus for quite a wide range of starting values it would appear that convergence is achieved over time without the need for explicit knowledge of demand. Of course, if the market is misjudged such that q_0 starts to the left of $\tilde{q}$, a rigid application of a fixed mark-up pricing rule such as (24.3) would lead to the rule pricing the firm out of the market.[4]

Further complications are possible with more complex demand and average cost curves, since there may be more than two intersections, although it is reasonable to argue that these are likely to be little other than theoretical curiosities. (Further discussion of these types of adjustment processes can be found in Hanson 1992.) Finally, it is worth mentioning that the adjustment processes are much more complex in the (much more common) multi-product case.

All the above remarks apply equally to mark-up pricing. However, an important difference between the two cases lies in the empirical fact that AVC (unlike AC) is often reasonably constant over a wide range of output (as in Figure 24.1). When this is so, the desired mark-up is achieved immediately.[5] If, however, AVC does vary, then the above discussion of the adjustment process applies equally to this case.

Of course, this discussion is at best an indication that cost-plus pricers can achieve their desired mark-up in the absence of demand information using a simple fixed pricing rule. Observations of prices and traded quantities during such an adjustment process do, in the theoretical model at least, give information which can be used to modify the adjustment rule (24.3) in order to achieve more quickly the desired mark-up level. Once a few points on the demand curve are known, it should be possible to identify the fixed point $(\hat{P}, \hat{q})$ much more quickly than through the fixed adjustment process described here. Also, it remains true that the mark-up chosen arbitrarily by the firm is unlikely to correspond to the profit-maximizing mark-up; with information on the relationship between price and quantity afforded by observing such adjustment processes, a

---

[4] Notice that $\tilde{q}$ is also an equilibrium, although an unstable one. That is, if $q_0 \neq \tilde{q}$ the process diverges away, either to 0 or to $\hat{q}$.

[5] This is arguably another reason for preferring mark-up pricing to full cost pricing.

profit-maximizing mark-up is straightforward to establish.

24.4 Marginalist Advice for Cost-Plus Pricers

Clearly, there is some mark-up, whatever the particular mark-up model being used, which will maximize short-run profit. This section examines how this mark-up can be estimated. If there are long-run factors such as establishing market share, growth, and brand loyalty, short-run profit maximization may not be consistent with long-run profit maximization. However, suppose the following conditions hold:

(i) The pricing decision is time-separable; that is, it is effectively a one-period problem (so there are no intertemporal brand loyalty or competitor reaction effects, no inventories, etc.).

(ii) There is no demand or cost uncertainty—or, if there is, the conditions discussed in Chapter 21 which make uncertainty an irrelevance hold.

(iii) Over the relevant range of demand, average variable costs are constant.

(iv) The firm sells only a single product, or the products sold by the firm are not close substitutes or complements.

Then the following relationship between mark-up and demand elasticity holds: given the mark-up rule is

$$P = AVC(1 + m), \qquad (24.4)$$

where m denotes the mark-up, the profit-maximizing mark-up m^* is related to the elasticity of demand η by the formula

$$m^* = \frac{-1}{1 + \eta}, \qquad (24.5)$$

where the demand elasticity η is a negative number less than -1 (recall that in the single-period case, a profit-maximizing monopolist chooses a price in the elastic range of demand).[6]

The mark-up rule (24.5) can be derived as follows. Figure 24.3 illustrates a typical relationship between AVC and MC, in which these are constant over a fairly large output range. The key point to

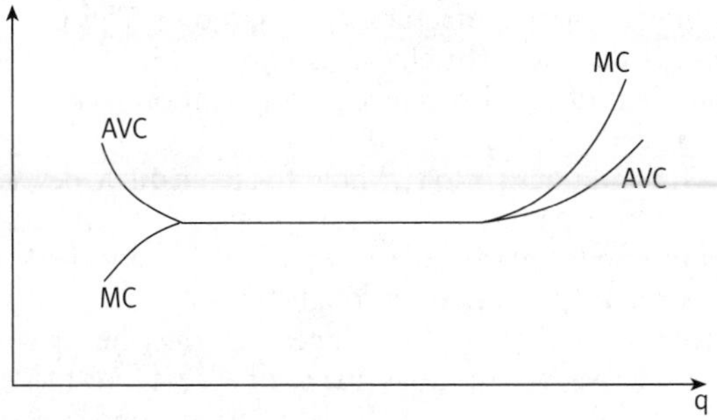

[6] See sect. 14.3.

Fig. 24.3 AVC may be approximately constant over quite a range of output

note about this figure is that, where AVC is flat, $MC = AVC$ (this is a mathematical fact[7]). The result is then obtained as follows. First note that profit maximization requires $MR = MC$ and that $MR = P(1 + /\eta)$. Given $MC = AVC$, the necessary condition is that

$$MR = P(1 + 1/\eta) = MC = AVC. \qquad (24.6)$$

When rearranged, this implies

$$p = \left(\frac{1}{1 + (1/\eta)}\right)AVC, \qquad (24.7)$$

thus identifying the mark-up as

$$1 + m = \left(\frac{1}{1 + (1/\eta)}\right), \qquad (24.8)$$

and rearranging this gives (24.5).

Equation (24.5) indicates that the profit-maximizing mark-up is related to demand elasticity. In practice, conditions (i) to (iv) may not hold exactly, but may hold to a reasonable approximation. That is, it may often be the case that uncertainty is not a critical factor and that the market is fairly stable, so significant intertemporal price changes are unlikely to be required. Also, the technology of production is often such that AVC is fairly constant over quite a range of output. The major difficulty is likely to rest with condition (iv), which is often violated in the multi-product firm context. Such firms typically manufacture a range of similar products, products which are relatively close substitutes for each other

---

[7] AVC constant with output implies $dAVC/dq = 0$. Recall that $AVC = VC/q$ and that marginal cost (MC) is the rate of change of variable cost ($MC = dVC/dq$). Applying the quotient rule for differentiation, we get $dAVC/dq = d(VC/q)/dq = (qdVC/dq - VC)/q^2 = 0$. Given $q > 0$, this implies $qdVC/dq - VC = 0$, so rearranging this establishes the equality of MC and AVC:

$$MC = dVC/dq = VC/q = AVC.$$

(think of car manufacturers for example). This problem is discussed (briefly) in section 24.5, whilst the problem of multi-product pricing is more generally considered in Chapter 20.

If conditions (i) to (iv) hold to an adequate degree of approximation, then (24.5) provides a useful rule of thumb for mark-up pricing. If the decision-maker has some (possibly only rough) idea of the responsiveness of demand to changes in price, he or she can derive an optimal mark-up. Thus if a 1% increase in price is expected to lose around 5% of sales, $\eta = -5$. From (24.5), the optimal mark-up is $m = 0.25$ or 25%. In general, the more elastic the demand, the lower the mark-up (as can be readily verified numerically).

Equation (24.5) can also be used as a check on the rationality of existing prices. Suppose the decision-maker currently has a mark-up of 20%, i.e. $m = 0.2$. Then from (24.5) this implies $\eta = -6$. The decision-maker can then be posed the question, 'Do you believe that a 1% increase in price would lead to a 6% fall in sales?' (that is, elasticity is -6). If the he or she replies 'No, much less,' then this suggests that if the mark-up is increased from its present level, profits will increase. So, in this case, some increase is bound to be beneficial. Of course there is always the danger of raising the mark-up too much too quickly. However, if the decision-maker is willing to put a figure on the likely percentage reduction in sales consequent on a 1% increase in price, equation (24.5) can be used to estimate the optimal mark-up, and hence the point beyond which prices should not be increased. Any increase up to this level will lead to an improvement in profitability. Naturally, one might choose to adjust prices in stages. This would allow some degree of monitoring of the impact on sales volume, which might in itself provide information regarding the sensitivity of sales to price.

It is worth emphasizing that this type of marginal reasoning can be applied in an intuitive way— the approach can be operational without formal demand analysis of the type discussed in Chapter 9. Thus, even in the absence of econometric estimates of demand elasticity, price sensitivity can still be subjectively guesstimated, and this suffices to implement the approach.

In principle, it would appear that the same procedure can be applied to each of the firm's products in turn. Unfortunately, the procedure is only formally correct if the products can be viewed as independent in terms of both costs and demand (cost and demand independence are defined in Chapter 20). The major problem is typically demand interdependence: multi-product firms typically manufacture products which are relatively close substitutes. In the next section, it is shown that the procedure will tend to underestimate the optimal mark-up in this case.

24.5 Multi-Product Cost-Plus Pricing

As discussed in Chapter 20, the multi-product firm is the norm rather than the exception. Many of the ideas and arguments discussed in sections 24.2–24.4 apply equally well to the multi-product case (the reader may find it useful to peruse the marginalist approach to multi-product pricing discussed in Chapter 20). Clearly the complexity of the marginalist problem increases—with demand and cost interdependencies likely, estimation of demand and cost structures can be quite complex and difficult statistical problems. Multi-product demand analysis is discussed in Chapters 8 and 9 whilst cost analysis and estimation are discussed in Chapters 10 and 11.

The key insight offered in Chapter 20 is that demand and cost interdependencies need to be recognized. In particular, formula-driven overhead allocations can lead to nonsense pricing. The 'what price progress?' peanuts case study set as question 3 in section 12.7, page 21, nicely illustrates this point. In that case study, Joe displays good incremental and opportunity cost reasoning in his analysis of peanut selling whilst the so-called 'efficiency expert' is obsessed with allocating overheads. The key marginalist idea is that prices should be chosen to maximize the contribution made by each and every product. In the case of the peanuts, Joe is right and the 'expert' wrong. If the 'expert' had his way, Joe would sell no peanuts at all. Once Joe has bought the rack, this is an historic and hence a sunk cost (and so should play no role in deciding the best price to charge). As Joe claims, if he sells nuts for 10 pence, he gets a contribution of 4 pence. Every bag sold will increase his profits by 4 pence. It may be that there is a better price to choose than 10 pence (there is no information here on whether this is a good price to charge), but clearly 60 pence a bag is nonsense. The issue raised here, that it is not necessary to cover full cost for all products, is discussed in some detail in the case study in section 12.2. In that example, routine overhead allocations (amongst other things) led to an incorrect branch closure decision. When teaching on MBA programmes, one always meets some managers who are reluctant to accept the marginalist principle that it may be desirable to go below full cost in pricing (for some products). They feel that if the firm prices on this basis, it could end up bankrupt. Clearly, if all prices were set below the accountant's measure of full cost, this would be (approximately) correct. However, marginalism does not recommend setting low prices per se. Marginalism recommends setting price such that the marginal revenue equals the marginal cost; only where demand is very elastic will this imply a price close to marginal cost. Indeed, price will be far above marginal cost on those products which are relatively inelastic in demand. However, marginalism is willing to push price down towards marginal cost if demand is highly elastic. The point is that setting low prices in this case at least gets some sales for the product, so the product makes some contribution (or incremental profit) towards covering overheads. By contrast, if price is set too high on such products, no contribution is made from them and the firm will inevitably earn lower profits as a consequence. In the case study, it is clear that the unattributable overheads continue whether Joe sells the peanuts or not; the peanuts, at 10 pence a bag, would make a contribution.

Equation (24.5), as a basis for setting mark-ups, is appropriate only if there are no strong interdependencies on the cost or demand side. In practice, the major interdependency problem arises on the demand side because firms often sell a set of closely related goods. If goods are close substitutes, changing price for one will affect not only the sales of that product, but also the sales of all the firm's other products. In this case, price setting should take into account the knock-on impacts of each price on the demand for the other products. These knock-on impacts are captured through estimates of cross-price demand elasticities. In practice, the elasticities may not be known in detail, but some consideration of the possible impacts should at least be considered in setting the prices of the various products. In what follows, an argument is presented for why equation (24.5) will tend to underestimate the profit-maximizing mark-up. An alternative practical procedure is then offered to cope with this.

Consider initially the two-product case. Products are labelled 1 and 2, and the demand functions are given as

$$q_1 = f_1(p_1, p_2), \qquad (24.9)$$

and

$$q_2 = f_2(p_1, p_2) \qquad (24.10)$$

where q_1 and q_2 denote the quantities demanded and p_1 and p_2 the prices for the two goods respectively. It is assumed that $\partial q_1/\partial p_1 < 0$, $\partial q_1/\partial p_2 > 0$, $\partial q_2/\partial p_1 > 0$ and $\partial q_2/\partial p_2 < 0$; ; that is, increases in a product's price decreases its own demand, but increases the sales of the other product. This is an example where the two products are (gross) substitutes. For simplicity, assume that $\partial q_1/\partial p_2 = \partial q_2/\partial p_1$ (see Chapter 20; if the demand functions were compensated demand functions, this would be true by virtue of the Slutsky condition). Then it can be shown that the profit-maximizing prices must satisfy the following equations:

$$\left(\frac{p_1 - MC_1}{p_1}\right)\eta_{11} + \left(\frac{p_1 - MC_1}{p_2}\right)\eta_{12} = -1 \quad (24.11)$$

and

$$\left(\frac{p_1 - MC_1}{p_1}\right)\eta_{21} + \left(\frac{p_1 - MC_1}{p_2}\right)\eta_{22} = -1, \quad (24.12)$$

where $\eta_{ij} = (\partial q_i/\partial p_j)(p_i/q_j)$ is the elasticity of demand for product j with respect to the ith price $(i, j = 1, 2)$. Thus η_{11} is the own-price elasticity of demand for product 1, η_{12} the cross-price elasticity of good 1 with respect to price of good 2, etc. If the elasticities are given specific values, equations (24.11) and (24.12) can be solved for the price–cost mark-ups, $(p_1 - MC_1)/p_1$ and $(p_2 - MC_2)/p_2$. Table 24.1 gives some results for fixed own-price elasticities and varying cross-price elasticities. The key point to note is the importance of cross-price elasticity. In the illustrative table, the cross-price elasticities are held equal ($\eta_{12} = \eta_{21}$), but varying their magnitude makes it clear that cross-price elasticities matter. In the example in Table 24.1, estimating own-price elasticity and ignoring cross-price elasticity would lead, using the rule of thumb, established in section 24.4, equation (24.5), to mark-ups on marginal cost (which, by the assumptions of that section, equals average variable cost) of 20% for good 1 and 50% for good 2 (this is the case in table 24.1 where $\eta_{12} = \eta_{21} = 0$). If the products are substitutes, the mark-ups should generally be higher than this. For example, with $\eta_{12} = \eta_{21} = 1$, the mark-ups on marginal cost become 56% for good 1 and 70% for good 2.

Clearly the impact of ignoring the cross-price effects can be substantial, and the tendency, given

Table 24.1 Multi-product case: Optimal markups and elasticities

Setting $\eta_{11} = -6$, $\eta_{22} = -3$, $\eta_{12} = \eta_{21}$ and solving (24.11) and (24.12).

$\eta_{12} = \eta_{21}$	$\left(\dfrac{p_1 - MC_1}{p_1}\right)$ (%)	$\left(\dfrac{p_2 - MC_2}{p_2}\right)$ (%)	Mark-up on AVC, good 1 (%)	Mark-up on AVC, good 2 (%)
−3	0	33	0	50
−2	7	29	8	40
−1	12	29	13	42
0	17	33	20	50
1	24	41	56	70
2	36	57	100	133

a firm's products are usually substitutes is for the effect to be one of underestimation of the profit-maximizing mark-up. This then is clearly an important caveat on the use of demand elasticities for setting price–cost mark-ups.[8] Many texts in managerial economics mention the use of the elasticity rule discussed in section 24.4. None of them (at the time of writing) note the fact that such an approach will tend to give significant underestimates for profit-maximizing mark-ups in the case where the firm sells several related products.

The argument in the single-product case (or where products are not interrelated on the demand or cost side) was that a rough estimate or guess at the elasticity of demand (the sensitivity of sales to price) could be useful in deciding what level of mark-up to set. Unfortunately, many firms (indeed most) produce several products, and these are often relatively close substitutes. The discussion in this section suggests that there is a need to estimate not only own-price elasticities, but also cross-price elasticities. Now, with two products, there are four elasticities to estimate; with three products, nine elasticities; and if there are n products, then n^2 elasticities need to be taken into account. Clearly the problem becomes more complex, and the hoped-for simple rule of thumb seems to break down.

In the light of these observations, is there then any (useful) alternative to full-blown statistical estimation of the demand systems, followed by the kind of mathematical analysis discussed in Chapter 20? The answer to this is a qualified yes. Suppose that the firm's products can be categorized into groups such that, within a group, the products are all fairly close substitutes, whilst between groups, it is reasonable to assume that the cross-price elasticities are small. Then it is reasonable to assume that a similar mark-up should apply within groups, whilst the mark-up between groups may vary. Assuming marginal costs can be treated as constant (empirically, often a reasonable approximation over the ranges of output typically under consideration), the problem simplifies to that of choosing a single mark-up for each product group. The decision-maker still has to make a judgement as to what the percentage effect on sales for a group would be from increasing all prices in that group by (say) 1%. But once this is done, the group elasticity implied by such a judgement can be used directly in the simple mark-up formula (24.5) to provide an estimate of the mark-up, which is then applied to all products in the group.

24.6 What People Do—and What They Say They Do

Although decision-makers often say they do not practise marginalism, it is common to observe that mark-ups do vary by product sold. Decision-makers often say they adjust mark-ups according to what the market will bear. From this, it might be inferred that they have an intuitive grasp of the concept of marginal revenue, of how revenue and sales vary with changes in price (even though they do not explicitly make use of marginal reasoning). Indeed

---

[8] It could be argued that there is a redeeming feature to this simplistic, equation (24.5) approach to determining the mark-up, namely that the analysis will tend to lead to prices being set too low rather than too high. This argument is correct if decision-makers are more comfortable with making the mistake of setting a price too low than setting with a price too high (which is probably the case).

it is often argued that this variable mark-up approach could approximate the profit-maximizing solution. However, note that focusing on average cost is not likely to improve the quality of the decision process. Indeed, if there is intuitive marginalism on the demand side but average rather than marginal costing, this will tend to lead to the firm setting prices too high. To see this note that, assuming that diminishing returns to scale have not set in too vigorously, AC will lie above MC at the kind of output levels under consideration. Setting MR equal to AC thus implies setting price above that associated with the profit-maximizing condition $MR = MC$. This is illustrated in Figure 24.4. (Recall that falling average cost was one of the stylized facts which motivated the early theory of monopolistic competition—see Chapter 15—so the assumption of $AC > MC$ is realistic.) It would thus seem to follow that if firms tend to allocate fixed cost to product lines and tend to focus on average costs whilst on the demand side taking into account what the market will bear, they may tend to overprice. However, mark-up pricing which takes into account what the market will bear would appear to be much more likely to get close to profit-maximizing prices (since, as discussed above, it is often the case that $MC \approx AVC$ over the relevant range of output).

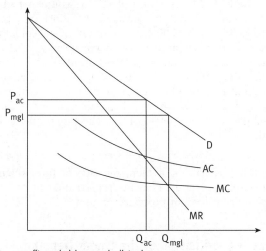

P_{mgl} = profit-maximizing marginalist price
P_{ac} = price a full cost pricer would set if she took into account price sensitivity and set MR=AC (this is an interpretation of setting price at 'what the market will bear'

Fig. 24.4 Cost-plus and 'what the market will bear'

24.7 The Psychology of Justifying a Price

Much of the emphasis in this text has been on incremental and opportunity cost reasoning, of marginal revenue and marginal cost as the basis for arriving at an optimal pricing decision. Sunk costs, historic costs, etc. are to be ignored. However, particularly when pricing one-off products, or in tendering for contracts, it is often extremely convenient to have a good story to explain how the price levied was derived. This story usually explains how price is derived from some cost basis plus a fair mark-up on it. The point of course is that to the customers, any given price looks a lot fairer if it is composed primarily of costs incurred, with only a small mark-up (to an extent, customers will judge quality by the apparent costs of production). Thus, from a promotional perspective it is often useful to explain that the price is largely due to costs of production. For this reason, even if the price is arrived at using marginal reasoning, for such contracts and tenders the firm may rationally choose to explain the price to a client in very different terms. Apart from imparting a feeling of fairness to the price, to the extent that clients judge quality by price only in so far as the latter reflects the costs of production these psychological ploys may in fact boost demand for the product. Thus there are several reasons why costs which economists regard as irrelevant can be highly relevant to the final selling of the product. Note that this discussion presupposes that consumers do not have full information about the product, or they would not be inclined to judge quality by price or the costs of production. With full information, customers can judge quality by direct observation.

24.8 A Case Study: The Jaguar XJ12

The following case study illustrates the problems that can arise when a firm does not adequately research the demand for its product and chooses an inappropriate mark-up.

24.8.1 The Facts Regarding The XJ12 Launch

Initial production capacity for Jaguar XJ12 was 6,000 cars per year. A cost-based approach to pricing suggested that a price of £3725 would yield a satisfactory profit margin, and this was in fact the price at launch in 1971. Demand outstripped supply and by the end of the year, a two-year waiting list had developed. Shortly afterwards, a second-hand XJ12 was auctioned for £1500 more than list price. The subsequent black market situation generated considerable embarrassment for the board of British Leyland. They argued that all would be well (and no one would have to wait) when they finally attained their long-term production target of 20,000 cars per anum. However, this would take time to realize, especially given the labour problems they were currently facing.

24.8.2 Linear Demand Curve Analysis of the XJ12 Pricing Problem

The Jaguar XJ12 pricing fiasco stimulated a modest academic debate—see for example Harrison and Wilkes (1973) and Barnard (1974). Clearly, the auction price suggests that Jaguar missed a significant profit opportunity. The question was, how much did they lose? One way to answer this question involves constructing a linear demand curve for the product, based on the above evidence. In what follows, it is assumed that the second-hand price represents the intercept on the vertical axis for the demand curve and also that the Jaguar board were right in stating that they would be able to sell 20,000 cars per annum at £3725. This demand curve is illustrated in Figure 24.5, where the vertical intercept is £5225 (£3725 + £1500). Given the intercept, and the fact that the gradient is −1500/20,000, it follows that the equation of the inverse demand function is

$$p = 5225 - \left(\frac{1500}{20,000}\right)q, \qquad (24.13)$$

whilst the marginal revenue function is given as

$$MR = 5225 - 2\left(\frac{1500}{20,000}\right)q, \qquad (24.14)$$

Marginal cost is presumably less than the price set by Jaguar (£3725). For £3725 to be the long-run profit-maximizing price, this would require that at the output of 20,000, $MR = LRMC$. Now,

$$MR = 5225 - 2\left(\frac{1500}{20,000}\right) \times 20,000$$

$$= 2225 \qquad (24.15)$$

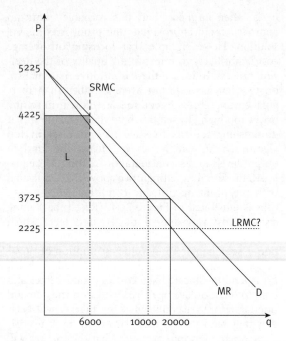

Fig. 24.5 Modelling the demand for the Jaguar XJ12 (not to scale)

Let's suppose then that $MC = 2225$. Figure 24.5 illustrates the situation.

Here, $LRMC$ is drawn at £2225, assumed to be constant with output. Now, in the short run, the capacity is only 6000 cars per annum. Conceptually, the short-run marginal cost curve turns vertical at this level of output, as indicated in the figure. Given this diagram, it is clear that $MR = SRMC$ at the output level of 6000 cars, as one would expect, and hence it follows, from (24.13), that the price that could have been set is £4225. The lost profit, L, is thus estimated as

$$L = (4225 - 3725) \times 6000 \approx £3,000,000. (24.16)$$

On the face of it then, the lack of forethought regarding potential demand has lost the company a significant level of profit per annum.

24.8.3 Criticisms of the Linear Demand Curve Analysis

Jaguar's error, however, is likely to be much less than indicated by the above naive analysis. Some of the points of concern are as follows (some might drive the estimate upwards; most would drive the estimated loss downward):

1. Considerable weight has been placed on the sale of one car at auction. A natural question to pose here is whether the auction was widely publicized—whether it did in fact attract the highest bidders. Perhaps there were many potential customers willing to pay even more who were simply not aware of the auction. This would push up the intercept and increase the estimate of lost revenue.

2. The estimate of 20,000 cars for the annual sales figure may be realistic for the first year. Is it realistic as a year-on-year figure? There are two points to note here. First, one should be aware that the car market is a market for durable goods, and so, as time goes by, a stock of second-hand vehicles also becomes established; this will tend to dissipate the demand for new vehicles to some extent. Secondly, new competition from other car manufacturers might erode the annual sales as time passes. Brand loyalty considerations might also influence the setting of the initial price (consider the effect of the firm having to reduce prices significantly at a later date were there to be significant increases in competition later on). These observations generally suggest that a lower price than indicated in linear demand analysis might be rational.

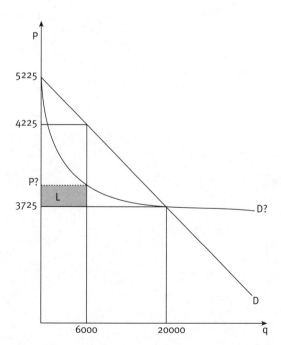

Fig. 24.6 An alternative view of the demand for the Jaguar XJ12

3. The demand curve need not be linear. This is the most important criticism to be levelled at the analysis of section 24.8.2 above. The skewed nature of the distribution of income and wealth, and the distribution of tastes in the population, tends to lead to demand curves which are often convex to the origin, as illustrated in Figure 24.6 by the demand curve "D?". Linear demand curves are at best good approximations only for small deviations around current sales levels. Clearly, with a non-linear demand function of the type illustrated, the price that would choke off demand at 6000 cars is still above £3725, but by much less than the linear demand function indicates.

24.9 Summary

Surveys of pricing practice indicate that cost-plus pricing in some form appears to be prevalent; when contrasted with marginalist theory, this seems to suggest that business pricing is likely to be suboptimal (non-profit-maximizing). This chapter has explored this apparent tension between business pricing practice and marginalism. In fact, the practice of cost-plus pricing tends to manifest variation in mark-ups of the type predicted by the marginalist model (that is, firms tend to set higher mark-ups on products that are perceived to be more inelastic), so it can be argued that cost-plus prices set in this way may not deviate significantly from profit-maximizing prices. There is a tendency to assume that, in the face of competitive pressure, business practice 'must be getting it right' on pricing. However, it is easy to exaggerate the extent to which competitive pressure has this effect. It would appear, for example, that the focus on historic average costs cannot be conducive to optimal pricing. Finally, the chapter focused on how marginalist reasoning can help improve the quality of extant pricing practice.

24.10 Review Questions

1. What reasons are given for the practice of cost-plus or mark-up pricing?

2. To what extent is the marginalist model practically operational?

3. A car manufacturer sells a particular model of car with a mark-up of 25% in the UK but only 12%

on the continent. If these were profit-maximizing mark-ups, what would this imply for the elasticity of demand for this product in the UK and the continent?

4. Daddy Toys plc manufactures and sells two products, Baby Joe and GI Jane, dolls to the under-sevens. They currently use a 40% mark-up on average variable cost for Baby Joe and 50% for GI Jane.

   (i) According to equation (24.5), what does this imply about the demand elasticities for these to be profit-maximizing prices?

   (ii) Name at least three reasons why this form of reasoning may be inappropriate in a particular practical application.

5. Here is a true case study involving a local car dealer. A man was considering purchasing a Rover 218SDT. The local garage had two second-hand cars available with very similar specification (PAS, full service history, etc.). They were both metallic red in colour, and in pristine condition. The man could hardly tell them apart—except for price! Further details:

   Car 1: 11,500 miles, 11 months old, price £8995;

   Car 2: 9900 miles, 9 months old, price £9800.

The man suggested to the dealer that £805 seemed too high a premium to pay for a car only two months and 1600 miles younger. The dealer shrugged his shoulders. He explained the price differential as follows. Car 2 was their ex-demonstrator. They had paid £14,000 for it new last year. ('It's a beautiful car, sir—and you would be saving over £4000 on the new price', he commented.) The other car, it turned out, had been acquired as a trade-in (purchased for much less, although he would not disclose the amount). He said he would get a satisfactory profit on the vehicle if he sold it at the advertised price.

Does this case study expose the irrationality of unthinking cost-plus pricing? Discuss.

24.11 Further Reading

Koutsoyiannis (1979) devotes a chapter to the marginalist debate. For a more extended discussion and also a guide to the literature on this topic, see Dorward (1987).

25 Buyer Market Power

Objective Much of this text is concerned with the case where there are many buyers of a firm's product, and no buyer has market power. This chapter, by contrast, considers the case where the buyer does have some power. The efficiency of alternative contracting arrangements is assessed.

Prerequisites Chapter 12 discusses incremental reasoning in detail; this is used in section 25.2.

Keywords bilateral monopoly, competitive bidding, controlability (in footnote), cost-plus contract, creative accounting, double marginalization, fixed-price contract, focal point, incentive contract, monopsony, oligopsony, price and quantity contract, profit-sharing contract, project, successive monopoly, tendering, threat point, winner's curse.

25.1 Introduction

In much of this text, it is assumed that firms set prices at which they are willing to supply output. Customers then choose how much to buy at the posted prices. However, a significant amount of arm's length economic activity takes place without such prices. This chapter discusses monopsony, competitive bidding, and bilateral monopoly.

In **monopsony**, there is a single buyer (the monopsonist) and a large number of sellers. The idea is that the sellers are price-takers, and that the buyer faces an upward-sloping supply curve. I deal briefly with this case in section 25.2. **Competitive bidding**, treated in section 25.3, is closely related to and numerically more prevalent than monopsony; in this case the buyer's requirements (a **project**) are satisfied by a single seller; there are many potential sellers, and they have to compete for the business by offering price quotes. This is referred to as a competitive bidding or **tendering** process. Such bids and tenders can be for multimillion- or indeed multibillion-pound contracts, as in the defence industry, or may be quite parochial, as for example when an individual householder invites builders to give a price quote for constructing a patio or length of trellis fencing. In the former case, there is a single buyer, whilst in the latter, there are many. However, in the latter, each buyer has individually distinct project requirements which need to be assessed by any potential seller. It follows that, in practice, each buyer is able to invite price quotes, and so is able to make the suppliers compete for her business.

Bilateral monopoly occurs when two economic agents (individuals, firms, etc.) trade with each other and neither has a satisfactory alternative to dealing with the other (alternatives either do not exist, or are significantly less financially attractive), as in negotiations between countries (over tariff barriers, smuggling, environmental pollution, etc.), or between union and management over wages and working conditions. However, bilateral monopoly is more widespread than one might think, simply because, even when there are many buyers and sellers, switching costs imply that, once a buyer and seller have agreed to trade, it becomes economically attractive for them to continue trading with each other in the future. This occurs, for example, when the supplying firm has to incur specific investment in tooling up to a particular design specification set by the buying firm. Such asset-specific investments are only likely to be incurred if the parties have contractually agreed to ongoing trade. There then ensues a bilateral monopoly relationship between the buyer and its supplier.

An important characteristic common to both competitive bidding and bilateral monopoly is that the individuals involved often have information private to themselves, information which is not observable, or not completely observable, by the other parties involved in the process. Obviously, the extent of the information asymmetry may vary; in particular, when two firms are involved in a long-term contracting relationship, one might expect familiarity to reduce the extent of the information asymmetry. However, the general point is that, where things are not completely observable, it can often seem advantageous to such parties not to reveal truthfully private information (used-car salesmen talk up the qualities of the cars they have for sale; they don't rubbish them).

The final difference between these two types of situation is that bilateral monopoly typically involves bargaining, and often there is more than one round to the bargaining process. By contrast, competitive bidding typically involves would-be suppliers having just one opportunity to make a bid, following which the firm is either awarded the contract or denied it.

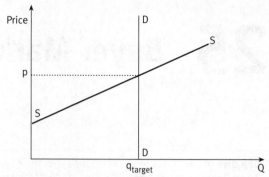

Fig. 25.1 Monopsony: fixed demand

25.2 Monopsony

Monopsony involves supply by price-taking agents (cf. monopoly, which features demand by price-taking agents). The idea is that different agents often have different reservation prices, so, as the offer price rises, more and more supply is called forth. The monopsonist sets a price so as to obtain the desired amount of the good (labour or whatever).

Definition 25.1 Monopsony occurs where a single buyer faces an upward-sloping supply curve (that is, there are a large number of suppliers, all price-takers). **Oligopsony** occurs when there are a small number of buyers.

EXAMPLE 25.1 The supply of nurses, teachers, etc. can be regarded as upward-sloping: that is, the higher the wage offered, the easier it is to recruit and retain such staff (at the time of writing, the UK government is under pressure to offer an above-inflation wage increase to nurses, as there is a shortfall of 6000 relative to the target employment number). The same point applies to many private sector firms which have the power to set the rate for a particular type of job.

The economic problem is thus to choose an optimal price. Clearly, if the monopsonist M requires a fixed number of units (of labour, say), then if she faces a rising supply curve, the solution is trivially to set the price (or wage rate) so as to secure the relevant number, as illustrated in Figure 25.1. More generally, the number of units M desires to buy may be influenced by the price she has to pay, as in Figure 25.2.

In Figure 25.2, M faces an upward-sloping supply

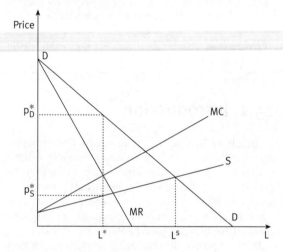

Fig. 25.2 Monopsony: downward-sloping demand

curve S for labour. For simplicity, the solution is illustrated for the special case where each unit of labour L produces exactly one unit of output q and there are no other costs of production. Suppose M also has some monopoly power in the final-product market, and so faces a downward-sloping demand curve DD there (the demand curve is horizontal in the special case where M is a price-taker in the final market). M offers a price p_s for labour, attracts a quantity of labour $L = q$, and sells the output q at a price p_D. After drawing straight-line demand and supply curves, we can see that the marginal revenue curve, MR, has the same vertical intercept and twice the gradient of the demand curve, whilst the marginal cost curve, MC, likewise has the same intercept and twice the gradient as the supply curve (as indicated in Figure 25.2). As usual, setting marginal revenue equal to marginal cost is a necessary condition for profit maximization. It follows that the optimal amount to purchase is $L^* = q^*$, with the price offered in the labour market being p_s^* and that in the final demand market as p_D^*. A general point to notice about the solution here (just as in the case of the monopolist in Chapter 14) is that the choice of employment and its price is part of a simultaneous solution, which includes the firm optimizing the price of the final product.

As in monopoly, the monopsonist restricts her purchase to below the socially optimal amount (given as L_s in Figure 25.2); note that this point applies whether or not the monopsonist has market power in the final market (to see this, reconstruct Figure 25.2 for the case where DD is horizontal).

25.3 Competitive Bidding

Competitive bidding can be thought of as a special case of monopsony in which the buyer wishes to purchase only one item, and there are many potential sellers:

Definition 25.2 Competitive bidding occurs when a single buyer is able to ask a multiplicity of potential sellers to tender for a contract (a project of some description). The buyer is then able to select the offer which represents the highest perceived value for money.

In many cases, there is scope for negotiation over what is to be delivered (quality and other characteristics). In such cases, would-be sellers must both design the product package and quote a price at which they are willing to make it available. The buyer then chooses the offer which appears to give the best value for money.

EXAMPLE 25.2 (Some examples of competitive bidding): Most countries put defence contracts up for tender. Firms such as Rolls-Royce are often involved in tendering for large private and public sector contracts to supply turbines, aircraft engines, etc. Waste disposal is often put out to tender by local authorities; likewise motorway construction. Catering and cleaning services are also often contracted out by many organizations. A house seller may get several quotes from estate agents before selecting one.

The above examples illustrate how widespread competitive bidding is, both in terms of numbers and types of project, and in particular the scale of these projects (from the parochial to those involving billions of pounds).

So long as the number of sellers is sufficiently large, it can be assumed that they will be unable to collude and so will compete against each other. Of course in many competitive bidding situations, the single buyer is not faced with such a large number of sellers. In such circumstances, it can be possible for the sellers to collude; this is discussed below in section 25.3.2.

25.3.1 Alternative Types of Contract

When a monopsonist invites firms to make bids, she may specify the basic structure that she expects the bid to take—or she may leave it up to the would-be seller to design and offer a contract. Different forms of contract have different characteristics, and create incentives for different types of behaviour. For simplicity, the focus is on two simple polar forms of contract often found in the competitive bidding process, namely the fixed-price contract and the cost-plus contract.

Definition 25.3 In a **fixed-price contract**, the firm offers to undertake the contract at a fixed price, whatever the costs it incurs.

Definition 25.4 In a **cost-plus contract**, the firm offers to undertake the contract at a price equal to the costs it incurs plus a fixed fee.

Naturally, it is possible to construct other forms of contract, including contracts which are intermediate between these two, often termed **incentive** or **profit-sharing contracts**. Furthermore, since different contracts perform with differing degrees of efficiency, the parties involved are likely to wish to negotiate over the detailed structure of the contract.

It will prove useful to set up a simple model. Suppose that V denotes the value of the project to the buyer. For simplicity, suppose this is a fixed value, known to the buyer. In practice, typically, the seller will not know the value of V, and can only form a subjective probability assessment as to its likely value. It is also the case that V could be a random variable (the value of the project to the buyer may turn out to be greater or less than its expected value). The cost of implementation, by contrast, is assumed to be uncertain; let $\tilde{C}$ denote the risky cost of implementing the project to the seller. The two parties may have asymmetric information concerning the possible cost of implementation; the seller usually has a better idea as to her costs of production, but the buyer may know more about hidden features contained in the project which may come as a (costly) surprise to the seller. After the project is implemented, there is a realized value for $\tilde{C}$, denoted C (known to the seller). Given this, I now consider alternative contracts, as follows.

(a) Fixed-Price Contracts

As its name suggests, the fixed-price contract involves the seller undertaking the project for a fixed price P, independent of realized value or cost. Clearly, unless there are quality differences across quotes, the lowest-priced quote is the one accepted by the buyer. Essentially, the fixed-price contract places all the risk associated with cost variability onto the seller and all the value risk onto the buyer. To see this, note that the profits to buyer (π_B) and seller (π_S) are given as

$$\pi_B = V - P \qquad (25.1)$$

and

$$\pi_S = P - \tilde{C}. \qquad (25.2)$$

Clearly π_B is constant (and riskless) whilst π_S is risky. If both parties are risk-averse, than ceteris paribus this is relatively good news for the buyer.[1]

Often a project's cost depends on the quality of the materials and workmanship that go into it, and this quality aspect may be only partially observable by the buyer.

EXAMPLE 25.3 If contractors skimp on foundation materials in motorway construction, this quality aspect is not observable once the asphalt has been laid. The consequences often become manifest only several years after the project is complete. For this reason, buyers try to monitor quality (usually by having their own resident engineer on site). Monitoring is clearly costly, and may not always be reliable (consider the incentives for bribery and corruption of the monitor).

Clearly, a fixed-price contract gives the supplier every incentive to minimize cost. This is good in so far as it encourages the supplier to operate cost-efficiently, but not so good when the costs are cut by reducing construction quality. Naturally, much depends upon how easily the buyer can observe these quality aspects. The problem of monitoring will be more severe in certain areas (motorway construction) than in others (trellis fencing). Notice that the incentive to cut corners on quality is at its greatest when observability is poor (where intrinsic

quality is hard to measure and is only revealed in the fulness of time). In these circumstances, a fixed-price contract will be attractive to the seller (because it can be exploited), and the buyer should take account of the costs associated with any monitoring that may be required.

EXAMPLE 25.4 (The Winner's Curse). When choosing a price at which to tender, the firm has to assess the likely costs it will incur if it wins the contract. Suppose the ith firm assesses the cost at C_i and then offers to undertake the contract for a price P_i. If all firms assess the cost at the same level, then the firm that wins is the one which sets the lowest profit margin. Now, suppose the true cost of the project is C, but that firms can only make an estimate of this; that is, let C_i now represent the ith firm's assessment of the true cost C. The firm that offers the lowest price gets the contract—and it offers the lowest price because it chooses a lower mark-up and/or because it has a low estimate of the cost. Now, it may have a lower estimate of the cost because it is more efficient than other firms. However, it is quite likely that the firm has simply underestimated what the true cost will eventually be. For example, if firms are all equally efficient and all choose the same mark-up rate, the winner is simply the firm with the lowest estimate of cost. If the average across firms of the implementation cost is unbiased, it follows that the firm who wins is the one which has most underestimated the project's true cost. This means that the resulting profit to the firm is likely to be much lower than it expected, and could well be negative. This is the winner's curse.

The winner's curse arises when there is imperfect observability by sellers of the likely costs that will be incurred—and because the contract is fixed-price.

(b) Cost-Plus Contracts

The cost-plus contract takes the form

$$\tilde{P} = M + \tilde{C}_R, \qquad (25.3)$$

where $\tilde{C}_R$ is the seller's reported cost and M denotes the agreed mark-up, a constant, on cost in the contract.[2] Once such a contract has been signed, it has the following characteristics. First, note that the

---

[1] Although risk averse sellers will tend to set higher price quotes so ceteris are not really paribus.

[2] The two parties will typically agree on an expected cost for the project, denoted $\overline{C}$, and a fair mark-up, m, such that the expected price is $\overline{p} = \overline{C}(1 + m)$. The actual price paid is thus $p = (1 + m)\overline{C} + (\tilde{C}_R - \overline{C}) = m\overline{C} + \tilde{C}_R$. Writing $M = m\overline{C}_R$, we get the simplified form above.

higher the actual incurred cost, the higher the reported cost is likely to be, so reported cost is, ex ante, a random variable, and hence so is the price the buyer is likely to have to pay ($\tilde{P}$). Secondly, note that the price paid by the buyer depends on what cost is reported by the seller. Profits for buyer and seller are

$$\pi_B = \tilde{V} - \tilde{P} = \tilde{V} - \tilde{M} - \tilde{C}_R \qquad (25.4)$$

and

$$\pi_S = \tilde{P} - \tilde{C} = M + \tilde{C}_R - C. \qquad (25.5)$$

Again, consider the simple case where there is no variation in value to the buyer, and only cost uncertainty. If the supplier tells the truth about cost, so $\tilde{C}_R = \tilde{C}$, then $\pi_B = V - M - \tilde{C}$, which is risky, whilst the seller receives $\pi_S = M + \tilde{C}_R - \tilde{C}_R = M$, which is constant and riskless. Thus the cost-plus contract with truth telling puts all the risk associated with cost variability onto the buyer. However, there is more to it than this. Suppose that the reported cost is greater than the true cost (because the supplier has managed, through **creative accounting**, to assign bogus costs to the project). If $\tilde{C}_R > \tilde{C}$, clearly this increases π_S and decreases π_B. Thus the cost-plus contract creates an incentive for the supplier to inflate reported costs (and to tell stories about how they arose). Furthermore, for this reason, there is also some incentive to economize on quality—if costs associated with 'full-quality' work can still be claimed.

Whilst the incentive for creative accounting is important, the main defect of the cost-plus contract is probably that it gives the seller no incentive to control actual costs at all. If the seller allows costs to rise, this does not damage the return that he makes (all that is required is a convincing story as to why costs have overrun, something which is hardly difficult in practice, given the information asymmetry). So, as with the fixed-price contract, there is a need for the buyer to undertake monitoring activity. With the fixed-price contract, this is concerned primarily with quality assurance; with a cost plus contract, monitoring quality is desirable—but it is also necessary to try to monitor project cost accounts (to try to control the incentive to allocate bogus costs to the project), so overall, monitoring costs are likely to be greater with the cost-plus in comparison to the fixed-price contract.

(c) Intermediate Forms of Contract

It is possible to design contracts where risks are shared between buyer and seller. These are often referred to as profit-sharing, risk-sharing, or incentive contracts. A typical contract agrees on the expected cost and a fair mark-up on this cost. Following this, any cost overrun or underrun is shared between the two parties. This amounts to a contract of the form

$$\tilde{P} = M + \theta \tilde{C}_R, \qquad (25.6)$$

where $0 < \theta < 1$. Notice that $\theta = 0$ corresponds to the fixed-price contract, whilst $\theta = 1$ corresponds to the cost-plus contract. The reader may find it instructive to write down the profits to buyer and seller arising from these two extreme forms of contract (cf. (25.4) and (25.5)). It follows that the incentive contract has characteristics associated with both the extreme forms; that is, it retains some incentive to be cost-efficient but skimp on quality etc., and also to overreport costs. Finally, it implies that risk is shared between the two parties. Given the different types of incentive created by cost-plus and fixed-price contracts, and given the possibility of different attitudes to risk by the two parties, contract design is clearly something which might potentially improve trading efficiency. Not only can contract design help to resolve (to an extent) the incentives for misreporting the truth, it can also prove beneficial when the two parties have different attitudes to risk. For example, if the seller is more risk-neutral than the buyer, then it makes sense, ceteris paribus, if the contract shares the risks such that the supplier bears more of the total risk. Contract design is beyond the scope of the present chapter; it is treated briefly in Chapter 29 (where the design of an incentive pay scheme is considered as part of a general discussion of the economics of principal and agent).[3]

(d) Discussion

Generally speaking one might expect fixed-price contracts where suppliers are involved in many similar contracts. One would expect such suppliers to be roughly risk-neutral, given the portfolio diversification effect (some projects might prove more costly than the average, but others will prove less costly). Buyers, by contrast, are often more risk-averse (individuals looking for household and auto repairs, etc.), simply because they are not involved in myriad similar transactions and so cannot fall back on this

---

[3] See Molho (1997) for accessible introduction, and Kreps (1983) for a somewhat more advanced (but reasonably user-friendly) discussion. Consult the index in each case for the fundamental concept involved, namely the 'revelation principle'.

effect. Hence it can pay the supplier to offer insurance in the form of a fixed-price contract.

In practice, cost-plus contracts appear to be more common where the level of uncertainty over the likely cost outcome is high, but also where monitoring is not very difficult (most repairs, e.g. to plant, machinery, housing, and automobiles). For example, most automobile repair work is on a cost-plus basis (where parts and labour are all billed separately, and the price for each incorporates a mark-up on cost).

The incentive for the supplier, once having obtained the contract, to cheat on it by either shirking on quality (in the case of fixed-price contracts) or massaging reported costs upward (in the case of cost-plus contracts) is mitigated to some extent when

(i) the supplier has hopes of being involved in repeat business, and/or

(ii) reputation (or the hope of building a reputation) matters. A tradesperson may not have extensive dealings with an individual client, but poor workmanship for one client can lead to a reputation effect, simply because such customers spread the word. Good-quality workmanship in such circumstances generates additional business through recommendation. In such circumstances, there is a clear rationale for not shirking on quality, even on a one-off job.

By contrast, where repeat business is unlikely, where customer networks are less important, say because contracts are geographically disparate, and when repeat contracts with an individual client are likely only in the distant future (so the consequences are more heavily discounted), the incentive to cheat on the contract is at its most severe.

Buyers who are able to offer large contracts (for example, the state, as in defence procurement) are often able to specify the type of contract. What type of contract is preferred depends upon a judgement as to which of the incentives described above is likely to be most counter-productive (from the buyer's perspective, of course). When the sellers have scope to offer different types of contract, sellers should weigh up their relative attractiveness (to themselves, and to potential buyers). It is also worth noting that choice of contract may induce a clientele effect (for example, ceteris paribus, the fixed-price contract will tend to attract the more risk-averse, whilst the cost-plus contract will attract the more risk-neutral

customer). It may even pay the seller to offer a menu of alternative contracts.

25.3.2 The Potential for Collusion

When the number of bidders is small, it may be possible for them to co-ordinate bidding activity. Cartel instability was discussed in some detail in Chapter 16, to which the reader is referred. The main insight there was that, given formal collusive agreements are illegal, there is no way the agreement can be legally enforced—and hence the players face the usual prisoners' dilemma; each will gain by cheating and offering a lower price quote than was previously agreed. Although it is possible to argue that, in multi-period games where there is no definitive last period, collusive outcomes may be sustainable, positive discounting of future benefits tends to induce chiselling, which undermines collusive agreements. Economic theory also suggests that collusive practices are easier to organize and sustain if the number of players is small (see Chapter 16, and also Selten 1983).

Interestingly, the empirical evidence suggests that large-number collusive agreements are by no means uncommon.

EXAMPLE 25.5 Large-number cartels are more difficult to sustain in theory; difficult perhaps, but in practice by no means impossible. In 1988, over 40 UK glass companies were implicated in a price-fixing agreement, whilst in 1991, 17 domestic fuel oil retailers colluded to fix prices in the north-east of England (see Moschandreas 1994 for other examples and further discussion).

It would appear that, in practice, firms are rather more successful at colluding than might be expected from a game-theoretic analysis, probably because the assumptions of the game-theoretic models are less than appropriate characterizations of individual behaviour (in particular, the assumption that agents are self-interested and rational expected-utility maximizers). Thus in practice, it often proves possible for firms to co-ordinate their bidding strategies so as to maintain artificially high bids, say with some form of bid rotation so that different firms win a 'fair' share of the overall tender business. (There is also some incentive for backhanders.) Of course, effective collusion effectively gives rise to a bilateral monopoly situation, as discussed below in section 25.4.

25.3.3 Bid Disclosure

Typically, private sector firms will not divulge the price outcomes of bidding and tendering processes. The point is that publication of such information helps the selling firms, since they are better able to calculate their bid price. Disclosure tends to reduce the variability of bids, and so tends to reduce the magnitude of the winning bid. A no-disclosure policy maximizes bid dispersion and so increases the winner's curse effect.

However, openness is often practised in government contracting to try to counter the scope for bureaucratic backhanders and corruption. Bids may be disclosed so as to show that the contest has been open and fair, and that the lowest bid was in fact the one that was taken—or, if a higher bid was taken, the reasons may have to be clearly specified (usually justified because of 'superior' quality or 'value for money'). Clearly, the trade-off is that the buyer is less likely to get a really good deal.

25.3.4 Optimizing the Bid Price

In practice many firms apply a standard mark-up to a measure of full cost when constructing a bid price. The example in section 12.4.1 illustrates how full cost pricing can lead to incorrect decisions. In that particular example, the firm wrongly rejected taking what would have been a profitable contract; the case study involved a reassessment using opportunity costing and incremental reasoning as a basis for deciding whether to accept the project or not. The same principles apply when considering the choice of bid to make; allocation of overheads and the use of the wrong cost categories (historic costs, depreciation, etc.) can lead the firm to choose a price which will not maximize expected value.

The focus is on expected profit in what follows; this is appropriate if the decision-maker is risk-neutral, or if the firm is involved in many projects, since the diversification effect suggests that, to good approximation, evaluating projects according to expected value is reasonable.[4] The argument that

using the wrong cost elements leads to wrong prices is illustrated in the following example.

EXAMPLE 25.6 (Bid Price Selection). The example in section 12.4.1 involved a project for which the firm had made a full cost estimate of £132,500 for completing the project. However, a reappraisal of the opportunity costs associated with the various items involved in the project indicated that the true overall (opportunity) cost was only £83,500. Given these cost figures, if this is a project for which the firm has to tender a price, what price should it choose? The team involved in the project have discussed the chances that their bid will succeed, and have settled on the subjective probability assessment as reported in Table 25.1.[5] The true expected profit, $E\pi$, is calculated as $E\pi = \text{prob(success)} \times (\text{price} - \text{true cost})$. Thus, for example, given a bid price of £120,000, the calculation is that $E\pi = 0.8 \times (£120,000 - £83,500) = £29,200$, as indicated in Table 25.1. The optimal bid price is thus £140,000. Notice that, if the wrong (full) cost figures are used, the firm is drawn into setting too high a price (£160,000). This increases the chance that it will not gain the contract, and the expected profit from setting this higher price is £10,950 lower (= £33,900 - £22,950).

The key idea behind the analysis in this example is the use of subjective probability. The optimal price reflects the trade-off that a higher price gives the firm more profit if it gets the contract, but reduces the probability of getting the contract. (For a review of an actual case which makes use of this type of analysis, see Bell 1984.)

Clearly, the decision can only be as good as the subjective probability assessments; changing the assessments can change the decision on the optimal price to charge. Thus the big questions here are how the team has managed to come up with its probability assessments, and then how confident it is in them. If the project is one of several, all of which are similar, the success rate (in winning

---

[4] This is likely to be true for projects that are small relative to size of the firm, both from the perspective of top management and from the perspective of owners, because of the effect of diversification. It may not hold, of course, for individual project managers; the success of an individual project to an individual project manager may be quite important (in so far as a project managed to a successful outcome is more likely to influence one's career path positively). Thus individual project managers may

incline to risk aversion when top management and owners would prefer them to be risk-neutral. In the case of large-scale projects, it is both the individual project managers and top management who are likely to take a risk-averse viewpoint, whilst diversified shareholders may be less concerned. Chap. 4 discusses how this treatment could be adjusted to take account of a decision-maker's degree of risk aversion.

[5] For more on subjective probability, see Chap. 4, particularly sect. 4.2.

Table 25.1 Optimizing the bid price

Tender price £	Probability of success	True expected profit	Expected profit over 'full cost'
100,000	1.0	16,500	−32,500
110,000	0.9	23,850	−20,250
120,000	0.8	29,200	−10,000
130,000	0.7	32,550	−1,750
140,000*	0.6	33,900	4,500
150,000	0.5	33,250	8750
160,000	0.3	22,950	8,250
170,000	0.1	8,650	3,750
180,000	0	0	0

* Optimal bid price.

contracts) may give some frequency basis for the probability assessments in Table 25.1. However, ceteris are rarely paribus; through the business cycle, the number of projects coming up for tender is likely to vary, as will the severity of competition for such projects.[6] So, in practice, probabilities can rarely be frequency-based, and must perforce be guesstimates.

Firms often apply standard mark-ups in deriving a tender price, particularly if they are involved in tendering for large numbers of similar projects. This reduces the cost of bid preparation. However, it still remains a useful exercise to monitor bid success rates. If the success rate is very low it may well pay to reduce (possibly substantially) the standard mark-up.[7]

Naturally, what the firm considers to be the opportunity cost will vary depending on circumstances. In particular, if the order book is short, if the firm is working at below capacity, if it wishes to maintain its skilled workforce, etc. then excess capacity and excess skilled labour have close to zero opportunity cost. Finally, although the price offered should normally be (significantly) above opportunity cost, there are cases where it might pay to set a price below it:[8]

[6] When times are hard, not only are there fewer contracts around, but competitors are likely to be discounting off their standard profit margins in order to maintain their order books — if the firm does not take this into account when assessing its probability of success, its assessments could well be wide of the mark.

[7] Mark-up and cost-plus pricing are discussed in some detail in Chap. 24.

[8] Conceptually, these spillover considerations can be included in the cost–benefit exercise, although, because it is often quite difficult to put a quantitative magnitude on such effects, they are often omitted. Clearly, some account of them is required, at least qualitatively, in coming to a decision.

1. If gaining the contract is likely to increase significantly the chances of gaining further contracts from the same purchaser. Familiarity with a satisfactory service can often induce purchasers to avoid the additional costs and uncertainties associated with searching out an alternative source of supply, once one has been satisfactorily established. This is particularly true of the Japanese way of conducting business (see e.g. Sako 1992). In such cases it is worth making some sacrifices to secure a contract in the first place.

2. If there is significant learning by doing; e.g. with a prototype military aircraft, the production of the first few units can lead to major reorganization and learning about the production process, such that future units cost significantly less to produce (the so-called learning or experience curve; see Chapters 9 and 11). It may also help the firm to stay ahead in the development of cutting edge technology, etc.

However, apart from spillovers of this type, the general rule is that the opportunity cost assessment (described in Chapter 12) gives a bottom line, a price below which the project is definitely not worth taking. Of course, the chosen bid price could be considerably in excess of this, although much depends on the probability assessment of likely success. In general, during slack times, a bid price based on full costing is likely to be set too high, whilst in boom times when capacity is already heavily utilized, bids based on full cost could well be too low.

25.4 Bilateral and Successive Monopoly

The term 'bilateral monopoly' is often taken to apply to a situation in which one firm exclusively sells its product to another firm, and the issue is taken to be how the two parties decide on how much to trade and at what price.

Definition 25.5 Bilateral monopoly occurs when one firm sells to another and it is costly for either firm to walk away from the relationship.

The difference between bilateral and successive monopoly lies in the fact that in the former, the seller and the buyer have some market power, whilst in the latter, only the seller does:

Definition 25.6 Successive monopoly occurs when a monopolist sells to several buyers, one or more of whom sells to several buyers. In this model, at each stage, only the sellers have monopoly power, and buyers have no monopsony power.

A further feature of successive monopoly lies in the fact that, because there are several buyers at each stage of production, the seller cannot practise price discrimination across buyers (since, if different firms were charged a different price, they would all buy in a secondary market from the firm offered the lowest price by the upstream seller).

Both bilateral monopoly and successive monopoly are most frequently found as a vertical relationship. Think of the river of production, with raw material extractors upstream, and, proceeding downstream, through the processors, refiners, and manufacturers of intermediate products which are essential inputs into the production of the final product, finally to the retail establishments which sell the product; there are many bilateral arm's length relationships crucial to completion of the manufacture and delivery processes.[9] The key to identifying a situation of bilateral monopoly lies in posing two questions:

(i) if the selling firm holds up production, can the buying firm quickly and easily obtain the product from alternative suppliers?

(ii) if the buying firm refuses to purchase, can the seller quickly and easily place the product elsewhere?

If the answer is no to both questions, then there is a situation of bilateral monopoly. In successive monopoly, only the first question is relevant, but it must apply at more than one stage in the chain of production (for monopoly to be successive).

As remarked in section 25.1, bilateral monopoly very commonly arises because of switching costs. That is, even when there are many buyers and sellers in the market place, once a buyer and seller pair off to undertake a trade, certain things change:

(i) Often, the seller needs to make buyer-specific investments in order to supply the appropriate design and quality etc. To get the seller to commit such investment, negotiations will typically

revolve around the need to guarantee a period of ongoing trade.

(ii) repeat trading reduces search and related trading costs, the firms get to know and trust each other, and so the efficiency of trade improves. To go outside the relationship then becomes costly because it involves search costs and new knowledge and trust etc. have to be built.

25.4.1 The Problem of Multiple Monopoly Mark-ups

When there is monopoly power at more than one stage in the production chain, it follows that, if uniform pricing is used at each stage, the successive monopoly mark-ups lead to a final price which is too high, a price which does not maximize total joint profit to the firms involved. This arises in successive monopoly, but can also arise in bilateral monopoly if the two firms trade using uniform pricing. To focus matters, consider the case of a manufacturer M who sells at a uniform price p_M to a distributor D, who then sells at a price p to final customers (an example which is revisited in Chapter 31, when we consider the related problem of transfer pricing within an organization).

(a) The Distributor's Problem

Given the selling costs, and given the purchase price p_M set by the manufacturer M, the problem for the distributor D is to find the optimal price p and quantity q to purchase in order to sell on to final customers. If we denote D's profits as π_D, the problem is to maximize

$$\pi_D = R_D(q) - C_D(q) - p_M q, \quad (25.7)$$

where $R_D(q)$ denotes the revenue gained by D from selling q, $p_M q$, denotes the payment to M (price times quantity purchased), and $C_D(q)$ represents D's other costs incurred in selling on output level q. Note that the price, p_M, is set by M, and is treated as a constant by D. Differentiating with respect to q_D gives the first-order condition as

$$\frac{d\pi_D}{dq} = \frac{dR_D(q)}{dq} - \frac{dC_D(q)}{dq} - \frac{d(p_M q)}{dq} = 0, \quad (25.8)$$

or, rearranging slightly, and using the usual notation,

$$MR_D = MC_D + p_M. \quad (25.9)$$

That is, the first-order condition states that marginal revenue MR_D should be set equal to marginal cost, which is the sum of D's own marginal cost

MC_D plus the price p_M that D has to pay to M. That is, the distributor purchases units up to the point where the marginal benefit from the last unit just balances the overall marginal cost of delivering it to the final customer. It follows that M faces a downward-sloping derived demand for her product. This is denoted $v(q)$ (see Figure 25.3), where

$$v(q) = MR_D(q) - MC_D(q). \qquad (25.10).$$

The point is that, if the distributor got the product for free, she would take the amount $\hat{q}$ (so setting her marginal revenue equal to her marginal cost). As p_M is increased, the amount taken decreases (thus, at a price $p_M^\star$, D takes $q^\star$, whilst at price p_M^s, D takes q^s, etc.). Note that the area below the curve MC_M represents the total costs incurred by M and the area below MC_D represents costs incurred by D, whilst the area below MR_D represents revenue taken by D in the final market. It follows that the area below $v(q)$ and above MC_M represents the total joint profit generated by the two firms.

(b) The Manufacturer's Problem

Suppose M knows the derived demand curve (how much D will buy as a function of the price the manufacturer sets).[10] It follows that M will compute a further marginal revenue curve to this derived demand curve (denoted $Mv(q)$ in Figure 25.3, lower panel). As usual, M will maximize profit by setting marginal revenue equal to marginal cost. That is, M chooses q^s so that

$$Mv(q^s) = MC_M(q^s) \qquad (25.11)$$

or, equivalently, in view of (25.10), such that

$$MMR_D(q^s) - MMC_D(q^s) = MC_M(q^s). \qquad (25.12)$$

(where MMR_D denotes a curve marginal to MR_D etc.). M thus sets a price p_m^s which sells the amount q^s. That is,

$$p_M^s = v(q^s). \qquad (25.13)$$

Total profit gained in this solution is equal to the shaded area A in the lower panel of Figure 25.3. This profit is shared between the two firms, with that part of A above the price line p_M^s being D's profit, and that part below the line being M's profit. It should be clear from the figure that a price $p_M^\star$ will increase total joint profit, by the amount equal to the shaded area B.

[10] In principle, this might be observed; in a stationary environment, changes in price lead to quantity adjustments, and the revelation of the demand function (so long as the parties do not play games, as they might in such a small-numbers case as this one).

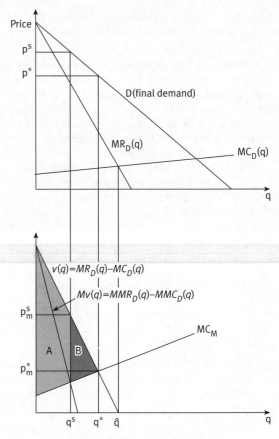

Fig. 25.3 The problem with uniform pricing

If the two firms merge and operate as one single entity, $M + D$, this simply sets marginal revenue equal to total marginal cost. That is, if these firms choose output level $q^\star$ and final price $p^\star$, then

$$MR_D(q^\star) = MC_D(q^\star) + MC_M(q^\star), \qquad (25.14)$$

or equivalently,

$$v(q^\star) = MC_M(q^\star). \qquad (25.15)$$

The fact that the two firms operate separately apparently leads them both to add a monopoly mark-up, and the overall impact is that the joint profit of the two firms is reduced relative to what is attainable. Furthermore, given that joint profit can be increased, it follows that each firm can be made better off by agreeing to trade $q^\star$ rather than q^s. This is illustrated in the following numerical example.

EXAMPLE 25.7 Let $p = 100 - q$ denote the final demand curve, so that $MR_D = 100 - 2q$ and

$MMR_D = 100 - 4q$ (recall that, with straight-line inverse demand curves, marginal curves have the same price intercept, and twice the gradient—see Chapter 9). Suppose D and M have constant marginal costs of 10 per unit; so $MC_D = MC_M = 10$. Hence $v(q) = MR_D - MC_D = 100 - 2q - 10 = 90 - 2q$. Since the marginal cost curve MC_D is flat, the curve MMC_D is also flat at 10.[11] Under uniform pricing, from (25.12) the amount traded is given by $MMR_D - MMC_D - MC_M = 100 - 4q - 10 - 10 = 0$, so $q^s = 20$.

M's price is then given by (25.13): $p_M^s = v(q^s) = 90 - 2 \times 20 = 50$ and $p^s = 100 - 20 = 80$. This implies that the two firms make profits of

$$\pi_M = (50 - 10)20 = 800$$

and

$$\pi_D = (80 - 50 - 10)20 = 400.$$

Total profit is thus $\pi = \pi_M + \pi_D = 800 + 400 = 1200$.

Now consider the joint-profit-maximizing solution. $\pi = (100 - q)q - 20q$; differentiating and solving gives $q^* = 40$, a final price of $p^* = £60$, and a total joint profit of $\pi^* = 60 \times 40 - 20 \times 40 = £1600$. Relative to the uniform pricing solution, both firms could be made better off if they agreed to trade 60 units. For example, a contract in which 60 units are traded in exchange for a payment by D to M of £1000 would leave D with profit of £600, and D and M both better off by £200, relative to the uniform pricing solution (although this is not a predicted bargaining outcome—see below).

25.4.2 Solutions to the Multiple Mark-up Problem

The problem with uniform pricing in section 25.4.1 is essentially that both the manufacturer and the distributor add a monopoly mark-up; this **double marginalization** (see equation (25.12)) gives a double dose of monopoly mark-up and this leads to the final price being too high to achieve joint-profit maximization.

On this argument, there is an incentive for vertical integration whenever there is a problem over successive monopoly power. The conventional wisdom on bilateral monopoly also follows from the above analysis; it states that simple uniform pricing will not realize maximum joint profits. However, whilst in successive monopoly there may be a rationale for the use of a single uniform price (to prevent the downstream buyers undertaking arbitrage or secondary trading), in the bilateral monopoly case there is no obvious reason to use it, simply because there is no one else to sell to.[12] In fact, if the outcome is suboptimal (as suggested above with uniform pricing), one or other of the firms would find it advantageous to talk and bargain with the other firm to come to some alternative contracting arrangement.

To replace uniform pricing, the outcome of bargaining could be a **price and quantity contract** in which the joint-profit-maximizing output is agreed on, and the bargaining is over the division of the total joint profit this generates. It was noted in Example 25.7 that such a bargain could increase both firms' profits, relative to a uniform pricing solution. However, the uniform pricing solution is not really the appropriate benchmark by which to gauge the likely outcome of such a bargaining process. In bargaining, each party has a **threat point**—if either walks away from the relationship, this entails zero profit to both parties. In such circumstances, a **focal point** outcome is that of equal or fair shares.[13] The following example illustrates this solution:

EXAMPLE 25.8 The joint maximum profit in Example 25.7 was £1600 if 40 units were traded (and zero to each if there is no trade). An equal shares bargaining solution would involve each party making a profit of £800. The price–quantity contract that does this involves D taking the optimal 40 units. The sum F to be paid over for this by D

---

[11] As demand is downward-sloping/flat/upward-sloping, so the marginal revenue curve lies below/on/above it. The same property applies to the curve which is marginal to the marginal cost curve (a conscientious student should be able to prove this). With linear demand curves, just as the marginal revenue curve has same vertical intercept and twice the gradient of the demand curve, so too the curve marginal to the marginal cost curve has the same intercept and twice the gradient.

[12] The only reselling that may be possible is to oneself over time (i.e. it may be possible to buy in bulk for future use, although there are storage costs plus the fact that you are tying up money over time, which has an opportunity cost—forgone interest).

[13] Equal shares is a commonly realized outcome in experimental bargaining games (see e.g. Kagel and Roth 1994). There are various arguments in favour of it; Waterson (1987) gives a brief review, in the context of bilateral monopoly. Bolton (1997) illustrates how it could be understood as a evolutionarily stable strategy; that is, it can be seen as something that has come to be (evolutionarily) hard-wired as a behavioural characteristic in *homo sapiens*.

can be calculated by noting that $\pi_D = 60 \times 40 - 10 \times 40 - F$, so if we set $\pi_D = 800$, we get $F = 2400 - 400 - \pi_D = 1200$. Thus the contract involves D paying M £1200. This leaves D with £800, whilst M incurs £400 in manufacturing costs, so making £1200 − £400 = £800 profit.

However, it is often a viable alternative to use non-uniform pricing. For example, a two-part tariff (or indeed a more complex tariff) could be used to realize the same optimal solution. This point can be understood by reconsidering Figure 25.3. Notice that if the manufacturer had set a uniform price p_M^* such that, at the output taken by D, price is equal to marginal cost, then D is induced to purchase the optimal quantity. The profit to the manufacturer in this case is the shaded area below the horizontal line at p_M^*. Notice that this is positive if the marginal cost curve has positive slope, as here, but that M's profit would be zero if it had constant marginal cost, and M would have negative profits if the marginal cost curve had negative slope (economies of scale etc.). Clearly, in the latter two cases, such profit consequences, associated with the uniform price which induces the efficient volume, would not be regarded as acceptable. However, a two-part tariff can resolve the problem. The uniform price in the two-part tariff is set equal to marginal cost, and the licence-fee part of the tariff can then be used to transfer profit from M to D to the point where both parties earn mutually acceptable levels of profit.

EXAMPLE 25.9 The two-part tariff that would underpin the equal-shares optimal solution described in Example 25.8 involves setting a marginal price of £10 per unit, with a fixed fee of $F = £800$. The profit made by this is $\pi_M = (F + 10Q) - 10Q = £800$. Thus in this case the marginal price brings in revenue which just covers the costs of production, and the fixed fee gives the firm a profit of £800. Faced with a marginal price of £10, D will naturally choose to buy 40 units, the optimal (joint-profit-maximizing) quantity.

There is thus no problem with the bilateral monopoly arrangement as set out above; one would expect joint profits to be maximized in a full-information environment. What one should not observe, however, is a uniform price being used to undertake the transaction. A uniform price is generally

unable to induce efficient trade and acceptable profit shares.[14]

Under asymmetric information, things are naturally more complex; much depends on what is assumed to be known and by whom. For example, it is still possible to achieve efficiency if we add only demand uncertainty,[15] so long as both parties are risk-neutral, and both parties know the structure and distribution of demand and also each firm's cost structures. In this case, the pricing solution involves setting a non-uniform pricing policy in which the buyer, D, faces marginal cost price on the range of possible demand. It then follows that the buyer will always choose to buy the joint-profit-maximizing quantity—and the seller does not need to know what the state of final demand is. This type of solution is illustrated in Figure 25.4. Notice that this solution involves the seller, M, making a certain profit (area A), whilst the buyer, D, makes a risky profit (area B, which varies with the position of the demand curve).

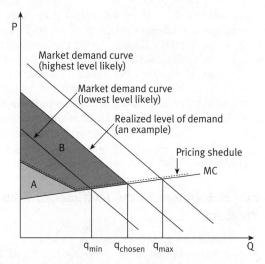

Fig. 25.4 Bilateral monopoly: demand uncertainty

When both parties are (possibly differentially) risk-averse and there is asymmetric information (about each other's cost structures, degrees of risk

---

[14] This is a general point about what is termed **controllability**. In general, you need as many control variables as there are targets; here there are two targets to hit (quantity and profit share) but only one control variable with the uniform price. The two-part tariff, or price–quantity contract, gives two control variables.

[15] Or cost uncertainty.

aversion, etc.) then an efficient outcome is difficult to achieve. It follows that there could well be gains from vertical integration in such cases (although there still remains the thorny problem of how to motivate the managers involved in such bilateral situations). An exploration of the problems that arise in such circumstances is beyond the scope of the present chapter.[16]

25.5 Summary

This chapter has explored situations in which the buyer has market power. Section 25.2 dealt with monopsony, where the buyer faces a competitive, upward-sloping supply curve. Section 25.3 examined the issues that arise in tendering (bidding) for contracts, whilst section 25.4 covered bilateral (and successive) monopoly. On competitive bidding, the contrasting properties of different forms of contract were considered (in particular, fixed-price and cost-plus contracts), and the issues that might determine the kind of contract likely to be seen in practice were discussed (issues such as incentives for cost efficiency, quality, etc. and the problems associated with monitoring contract outcomes). On bilateral and successive monopoly, the problem that can arise when firms utilize uniform prices in trading, was examined, along with ways in which such problems can be resolved through the use of price–quantity contracts, or non-linear pricing arrangements.

25.6 Review Questions

1. Suppose your firm is considering tendering for a contract. The team involved have assessed the opportunity cost of undertaking the project at £1 million and have also assessed the chances that their bid will succeed, as illustrated in Table 25.2 below:

[16] Dobbs and Hill (1993) gives a review of the bilateral monopoly problem and the problems associated with non-uniform pricing solutions when there is demand uncertainty. Rochet (1985) is a more general analysis of bilateral monopoly when there is uncertainty on both sides of the market (rather a difficult read). More generally, when there is asymmetric information, the analysis is much more complex. Molho (1997) provides an introductory discussion of how bargaining failure can occur in such circumstances; for a more thorough but still reasonably accessible treatment, see Kreps (1990).

Table 25.2 Tendering for a contract

Bid (£ million)	Probability of bid winning the contract
1.0	1.0
1.2	0.9
1.4	0.8
1.6	0.7
1.8	0.6
2.0	0.5
2.2	0.4
2.4	0.3

If the firm wishes to maximize the expected value associated with this contract, what price should it bid, and what is the resulting expected value? Given this price, what is the probability that the firm will not actually win the contract? (Note that this problem can be tackled by direct enumeration, as in Example 25.6, but note also that bid and probability vary linearly; try formulating the problem analytically and using calculus to determine the optimal solution.)

2. Mike's Minis is setting up its Oldcastle branch. Mike mainly undertakes servicing and repairs to old British Leyland cars. He is currently wondering whether to offer maintenance and servicing at a fixed or at a parts plus labour price. His clientele tend to run rather old and dilapidated vehicles. What are the pros and cons of the alternative methods of pricing for his services?

3. Does bilateral monopoly necessarily lead to inefficiency in the bilateral trading game? Examine the issues involved.

4. Suppose that in Example 25.7 the final inverse demand function is $p = 100 - q$ and the distributor has marginal costs of 10 per unit, but the manufacturer has marginal cost $MC_M(q) = 20/q$.

   (a) Find the outcome (prices, outputs, profits) if the manufacturer knows the derived demand curve and sets a uniform price, and contrast this with the joint-profit-maximizing solution.

   (b) Determine the price–quantity contract which yields equal profit shares.

   (c) Determine the two-part tariff that would

also support the joint-profit-maximizing solution.

25.7 Further Reading

Douglas (1992) gives an extended discussion of the issues raised by competitive tendering and bidding (but not the bilateral monopoly problem). Machlup and Taber (1960) gives a useful review of early literature on bilateral and successive monopoly, whilst Dobbs and Hill (1987) is a reasonably accessible discussion of how contracts and non-uniform pricing can be used under certainty and when there is demand uncertainty. For the more general problem where there is asymmetric and private information on both sides of the market, see Milgrom and Roberts (1992); Kreps (1990) covers similar material at a somewhat higher level.

26 Advertizing

Objective To examine the nature of advertizing, the choice of optimal level, and how the type of market structure influences the level and type of advertizing likely to be used in practice.

Prerequisites None.

Keywords advertizing elasticity, advertizing-to-sales-ratio, concentration, convenience goods, Dorfman–Steiner rule, endogenous sunk costs, exogenous sunk costs, experience characteristic, experience goods, inverse elasticity rule, prisoners' dilemma, search characteristic, search goods, shopping goods.

26.1 Introduction

What is the function of advertizing? Is it designed to inform or persuade? How much advertizing does a firm need? What types of advertizing are likely to prove most effective? How do these choices depend on market structure and how do they interact with pricing decisions? Is society better off with or without advertizing? Is there such a thing as the socially optimal level of advertizing? Unfortunately, as Nietzsche once observed, 'A fool can ask more questions than a wise man can answer.'

This chapter starts by first examining the nature and characteristics of advertizing (section 26.2). It then explores how market structure influences the level of advertizing undertaken by firms within an industry, and follows this by considering how advertizing acts as a strategic variable to increase entry barriers (section 26.3). Section 26.4 examines some simple models of what determines the firm's choice of advertizing level and section 26.5 discusses the extent to which, from the viewpoint of social welfare, advertizing is a waste of resources.

26.2 The Nature and Characteristics of Advertizing

Advertizing is simply a part of the overall selling or promotional effort.[1] It is a key element of a sales representative's job to inform potential customers about the firm's products, and to try to persuade them to make a purchase. Advertizing is concerned with exactly the same function, namely to inform and to persuade. However, the distinguishing feature of advertizing, in contrast to other selling activities, is that it involves getting a message across to a mass audience.

According to the simple model of consumer theory developed in section 8.2, advertizing has no purpose at all. Individuals have full knowledge as regards all existing and potentially existing products, and have preferences fully defined over all possible consumption bundles. Thus they do not need to be informed, and they cannot be persuaded. It follows that the very existence of advertizing testifies to the fact that something is amiss with this naive version of consumer theory. In practice, the consumer may lack knowledge of many commodities, never having previously experienced, or consumed, them. Furthermore, there are some products whose characteristics may be hidden and uncertain both at the point of purchase and even for some time thereafter; for example, second-hand cars and houses may only reveal their true quality only in the fulness of time. These observations suggest that advertizing does in practice perform the two types of function described above, namely to

(i) *inform*—to provide information about products and services (about the existence of the product, its price, where it can be bought, its characteristics, its quality, etc.)

---

[1] Sales promotions include: free samples; special offers; product bundling, including enclosing lottery tickets, coupons, etc. with the product; redesigning packaging; redesigning merchandising; setting up advertizing displays and exhibitions; and using direct mailshots.

(ii) *persuade*—to transform individuals' preferences about known goods.

Naturally, information can affect a consumer's preference ordering; for example, having a mechanic check over the second-hand car does not change its characteristics—but may well change your perception of those characteristics. However, there is no doubt that, as in fashion wear for example, advertizing can be persuasive; it can promote bandwagon/herd effects and can create 'characteristics' which hitherto were not there; for example, Levi jeans were just jeans until advertizing made them a fashion item.[2]

The following classifications can help to provide a useful way of thinking about the likely role of advertizing.

Definition 26.1 A **search characteristic** is one which can be understood without being experienced, whilst an **experience characteristic** is one that has to be tried before it is appreciated. Goods which comprise primarily search characteristics can then be categorized as **search goods** and those comprised of primarily **experience characteristics** as **experience goods** (see e.g. Martin 1994).

Definition 26.2: A **convenience good** is one with a relatively low unit price, frequently purchased by the consumer from outlets with easy access. A **non-convenience good** (or **shopping good**) is one with relatively high unit price, infrequently purchased (see e.g. Porter 1974, 1976).

Table 26.1 gives some examples. The categorization is fairly loose, since most goods are mixtures of these characteristics. The idea is that cosmetics, cars, foods, tobacco, drugs, etc. are probably better classified as experience goods (you have to try them to appreciate them fully) whilst clothes, furniture, computers, etc. are better classified as search goods. A search good is such that, given a good picture or description of the item, you know pretty much what you get, whilst with an experience good, you simply have to try it (try describing a perfume).

Fact 26.1 Advertizing on search goods is more likely to be informative, on experience goods, it is more likely to be persuasive.

Fact 26.2 Advertizing which imparts information is better done through newspapers, journals, and magazines. Advertizing concerned with persuasion is better done through television and related media (cinemas etc.).

Table 26.1 Examples of Different Types of Goods

	Convenience goods	**Shopping** goods
Search goods (mainly informative advertising).	Household consumables (soaps, polishes, disinfectants)	Consumer durables (washing machines). computers
Experience goods (mainly persuasive advertising)	Foods, beverages, cosmetics	Automobiles, HiFis, musical instruments

26.2.1 Advertizing on Search Goods

Take computers as an example of search goods. Advertizing typically sets out the full specification of what you get for your money (clock speed, RAM, drives, etc.). Such advertizing is enough for the consumer to make a judgement regarding whether or not to buy. There is little scope for persuading the consumer that the product is something that it isn't. This type of advertizing is also better placed in magazines and newspapers. Advertizements in these media are able to present a lot of factual information (think of computer hardware adverts). Advertizing on TV, on radio, or in the cinema is relatively poor at this form of advertizing.

26.2.2 Advertizing on Experience Goods

With experience goods, it is difficult to describe fully what you get (e.g. Camembert, Roquefort). Thus advertizing of this type is less likely to be concerned with imparting information about product details and more likely to be more concerned with persuasion. Simply by making the product more familiar, this type of advertizing makes the product more likely to be selected from a set of largely indistinguishable alternatives (as in the cola market). Hence we get the repetitive advertizing, for example, for perfume in women's magazines, or for cars in the colour supplements. Often these simply involve a picture of the product and the brand name. The pictures are primarily concerned with persuasion, with increasing familiarity with the product or trying to create a status niche for it.[3]

---

[2] It is often argued that advertizing does not affect the good, only people's perceptions of it. This is arguable. If status is regarded as a characteristic of a commodity, then advertizing can give the good more of it. Conceptually, this involves transforming the good.

[3] A typical strategy is to show the product as part of a desirable lifestyle, etc.

26.2.3 Advertizing on Convenience/Shopping Goods

Convenience goods are purchased on a regular basis, whilst shopping goods involve a relatively large expenditure. Porter (1974) argues that advertizing is more likely to concentrate on convenience goods, whilst for shopping goods, it is direct dealing with the sales force in the shop that is more likely to determine whether a customer makes a purchase. Hence convenience goods are likely to be more advertizing-intensive.

Advertizing is likely to be most cost-effective

1. where buyer awareness of the product is low; this is particularly the case for new products or services;

2. where the product has features or characteristics which are not immediately discernible to the potential customer. That is, the product is an experience good rather than a search good;

3. where there are good opportunities to differentiate the product from similar products.

Advertizing is also more likely to be important for final-consumption goods and services, rather than for intermediate goods being sold between firms, since in the latter case, the buying firms typically have purchasing departments who are responsible for finding out about the quality and the value of the goods they purchase. Thus there may be some informative advertizing for intermediate goods, but persuasive advertizing is unlikely to be significantly productive for such goods.

26.3 Advertizing and Market Structure

The empirical evidence suggests that there is a weak positive correlation between advertizing intensity and the level of concentration in an industry. This is consistent with the structure–conduct–performance (SCP) viewpoint,[4] which suggests that the nature of the market (structure) will naturally have an influence on the effectiveness of advertizing (conduct), and hence on the extent to which it is practised. However, as noted in Chapter 13, SCP also

[4] The structure–conduct–performance paradigm is introduced in Chap. 1 and discussed in more detail in Chap. 13.

envisages feed back influences. In particular, advertizing (conduct) is seen as a strategic variable controlled by the firm which has a feed back influence on market structure, in that it can be used not only to build monopoly power but also to create a barrier to new entry into the industry. Thus the direction of causation may be disputed, but the theoretical expectation, of positive correlation between advertizing intensity and concentration, does seem to be broadly consistent with the empirical facts. In what follows, the influence of market structure on the level of advertizing (26.3.1) is first examined, followed by a consideration the effect of advertizing on market structure (26.3.2) .

26.3.1 Advertizing in Different Market Structures

Advertizing is likely to vary across the four major types of market structure as follows.

(a) Perfect Competition

By definition, the product in this type of market is homogeneous; there is thus no role for advertizing, although advertizing may seek to differentiate what was previously thought of as a homogeneous product—coffee, for example, is increasingly differentiated and different brands and types can support different prices because of this.

(b) Monopoly

Advertizing can be used to increase the demand for the product at any given price. The general principle is to spend on advertizing and promotion until the extra profit generated by advertizing is just balanced by the extra cost of the advertizing (the familiar marginal principle). Models of this type are examined in sections 26.4.1 and 26.4.2. However, a major reason why a monopolist is likely to want to advertize is to deter entry and hence increase his ability to exploit his monopoly power without fear of entry. This idea is discussed in section 26.3.2.

(c) Monopolistic Competition

However one views monopolistic competition, advertizing is likely to play an important role. First, it can be used to increase the perceived product differentiation. This helps to increase the individual firm's monopoly power. In practice, as explained in Chapter 16, most monopolistically competitive markets are better characterized as a multiplicity of intersecting oligopolies. However, advertizing still remains important, since in this case each firm is in direct competition with a relatively small number of near neighbours; when faced with local competition, advertizing may be necessary simply to maintain market share.

(d) Oligopoly

This is the market structure where advertizing is likely to be most prevalent. Given the interdependence between firms, each firm faces a **prisoners' dilemma**,[5] not only in choosing output or price, but also in choosing the level of advertizing. The point is that every firm feels they will do better if they advertize more, so as to steal market share from competitors; the consequence is that all firms advertize heavily, the advertizing effects largely neutralize each other, and the firms are worse off, having incurred heavy advertizing expenditures. Clearly, such advertizing is also likely to represent a social waste of resources.

26.3.2 Advertizing, Concentration, and Entry Barriers

It is usually argued that there are often substantial economies of scale in advertizing and sales effort. This arises as follows (see e.g. Comanor and Wilson 1967):

(i) Through real economies of scale in advertizing. Often there are substantial indivisibilities, and hence substantial set-up costs, associated with advertizing. For example, think of the cost of making a thirty-second commercial vis-à-vis a five-minute commercial; many of the set-up costs will be the same. In general it is proportionately cheaper to have a larger or longer advertizing campaign.

(ii) Because of monopoly power in the market for advertizing. Media rate schedules are typically non-uniform; for example, the marginal price for air time typically falls with the amount purchased (the cost of supplying air time is probably approximately constant, but a monopoly seller of air time can practice second-degree price discrimination; see Chapter 19). It is also true that large-scale buyers can exert monopoly power of their own to extract lower rates (so-called 'pecuniary economies of scale').

The point is that a larger spend on advertizing buys proportionately more advertizing quantity. Economies of scale have already been mentioned in Chapter 14 as a barrier to entry, simply by making the minimum efficient scale large relative to the overall market size. One might suppose that economies of scale in advertizing may contribute to this kind of effect. However, it seems clear that the more important feature of advertizing which creates a barrier to entry is the extent to which it constitutes a sunk cost. Any entrant who wishes to set up in an industry must incur heavy advertizing expenditures simply to get it and its products known. Existing firms in the industry have already sunk this investment. The investment in advertizing builds up customer loyalty, goodwill, etc.; on exiting the industry, the value of this is likely to be substantially lost.[6] Thus advertizing constitutes what is termed an endogenous sunk cost:

Definition 26.3 Exogenous sunk costs are sunk costs which are outside the firm's control, whilst **endogenous sunk costs** are sunk costs which are induced or chosen by the firm.

For example, in building a plant of efficient scale, only a portion of its cost will be recoverable through reselling equipment in the second-hand markets. What is not recoverable is viewed as an exogenous sunk cost. By contrast, an endogenous sunk cost is incurred by the firm's choice. Advertizing and research and development (R&D) expenditures are usually viewed as the most significant endogenous sunk costs.

Given that sunk costs can be regarded as a source of barriers to entry, the expectation is that industry concentration might be positively related to the observed magnitude of such costs. Sutton (1991) presents an extended study of the role of endogenous and exogenous sunk costs in a variety of markets (primarily the food and beverage industries). The thesis is that the distinction between endogenous and exogenous sunk costs matters—and that entry amounts to a multi-stage game in which the entry decision is contingent on the outcome of the ensuing game of price/quantity/advertizing competition (or collusion). Sutton's analysis predicts that increases in market size lead, ceteris paribus, to increases in competition (concentration falling to zero) if the sunk costs are exogenous, but that

---

[5] Introduced in Chap. 5, and considered further in sect. 26.4.2 below.

[6] It may get something back, via selling brand names, so long as selling does not adversely affect the brand image.

increases in market size do not lead to concentration falling to zero (it remains bounded away from zero) if sunk costs are endogenous. With endogenous sunk costs, the toughness of competition matters; tough competition leads to higher levels of advertizing, higher endogenous sunk costs, and hence higher barriers to entry. By and large these insights into the role of advertizing seem to be borne out by the empirical evidence; there does seem to be some degree of positive correlation between advertizing intensity and concentration, and between the toughness of price competition, the level of advertizing, and barriers to entry (see e.g. Sutton 1991, Robinson and Chiang 1996).

26.4 Economic Models of Advertizing

This section outlines several alternative models in which the firm chooses the level of advertizing. Advertizing quantity is measured simply by the total expenditure on advertizing. The efficiency of advertizing, in terms of the sales response, is allowed to vary (the typical assumption is that, after perhaps some increasing returns, diminishing returns set in). However, it is worth noting that none of the models described below examine the relative efficiency of alternative forms of advertizing.[7]

26.4.1 Treating Advertizing in Isolation

The simplest model examines the problem of setting the level of advertizing in isolation from decisions regarding the rest of the firm's selling effort (pricing and other promotional activities). Figure 26.1 illustrates the basic idea. As a benchmark, suppose that, initially, the firm is gross-profit-maximizing (in the absence of advertizing), choosing price p and output q_1. Now introduce advertizing. An increase in advertizing shifts the demand curve to the right. Define gross profit, π_g, to mean profit before advertizing costs, and net profit, π_n, to mean the profit after advertizing costs.

Thus $\pi_n = \pi_g - A$. Note that the firm's gross profit is measured as the area below the price line and above the marginal cost curve in the upper panel in Figure 26.1 (since by assumption, price

[7] See Reekie (1986) for an examination of advertizing intensity and media selection.

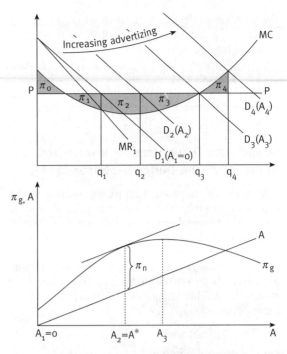

Fig. 26.1 Optimizing advertizing in isolation

remains unchanged as advertizing is increased). With zero advertizing, $A_1 = 0$, gross profit is $\pi_g = \pi_0 + \pi_1$ (where π_0 is negative). At level A_2, the gross profit is $\pi_g = \pi_0 + \pi_1 + \pi_2$, and so on. Clearly, any increment in advertizing above level A_3 will start to decrease the firm's gross profit. This point is indicated in the lower panel of Figure 26.1, which also incorporates advertizing costs. Maximum net profit is then given by the advertizing level A^*. This is the diagrammatic representation of the first-order condition for the problem of choosing A to maximize π_n; that is,

$$\frac{\partial \pi_n}{\partial A} = \frac{\partial \pi_g}{\partial A} - 1 = 0 \qquad (26.1)$$

must hold. As a consequence, the slope of the gross profit function must be equal to the slope of the advertizing cost function (unity) at the optimal level of advertizing.

This model is naive in the extreme. First, it should be clear that there is no consideration as to whether the price ought to remain constant as advertizing is varied. Clearly, shifts in the demand curve lead to shifts in the marginal revenue curve, and hence shifts in the profit-maximizing price, for a given level of advertizing. This observation suggests that the problem of determining the level of advertizing needs to be tackled simultaneously with that of determining the optimal selling price. This is the Dorfman–Steiner model, discussed in section 26.4.2. The other defects of the above model are identical to those of the Dorfman–Steiner model, and so are reviewed at the end of that section.

26.4.2 Joint Determination of price and Advertizing: The Dorfman–Steiner Model

The single-period profit-maximizing solution to the monopolist's problem suggests that price should be set so that marginal revenue equals marginal cost. If advertizing is also a variable under the control of the firm, the same principle applies: expand advertizing until the marginal benefit from it equals the marginal cost. At the optimum, both of these conditions should hold. This straightforward intuition can be formalized as follows.

(a) The Basic Model

Let the demand function be represented as

$$q = f(p, A). \qquad (26.2)$$

This suggests that quantity sold, q, is a function of price, p, and the expenditure on advertizing, denoted A. It is assumed that, for all p, $A > 0$, $\partial q/\partial p < 0$, and $\partial q/\partial A > 0$. That is, an increase in price leads to a fall in quantity sold, whilst an increase in advertizing expenditure increases quantity sold. The firm's cost of production for output q is denoted $C(q)$. Hence the firm's profits are given as

$$\pi = pq - C(q) - A. \qquad (26.3)$$

The first-order necessary conditions for a profit maximum are:

$$\frac{\partial \pi}{\partial p} = q + p\frac{\partial q}{\partial p} - \frac{\partial C(q)}{dq}\frac{\partial q}{\partial p} = 0 \qquad (26.4)$$

and

$$\frac{\partial \pi}{\partial A} = p\frac{\partial q}{\partial A} - \frac{\partial C(q)}{dq}\frac{\partial q}{\partial A} - 1 = 0. \qquad (26.5)$$

In performing these differentiations, recall that q is a function of p and A. The chain rule is used to differentiate $C(q)$.[8] The first of these conditions gives the standard inverse elasticity pricing formula (see section 14.2). To see this, first note that the own-price and the advertizing elasticity of demand are given as

$$\eta_P = \frac{\partial q}{\partial p}\frac{p}{q} \qquad (26.6)$$

and

$$\eta_A = \frac{\partial q}{\partial A}\frac{A}{q}. \qquad (26.7)$$

Now, from (26.4), writing $MC = dC(q)/dq$ as marginal cost, and rearranging, gives

$$(p - MC) = -\frac{q}{\partial q/\partial p}, \qquad (26.8)$$

so dividing both sides by p, and using (26.6), gives the inverse elasticity result,

$$\frac{p - MC}{p} = -\frac{1}{\eta_P}. \qquad (26.9)$$

This is the already familiar **inverse elasticity rule** (see Chapters 14, 18, and 24). It suggests that a higher mark-up is associated with a more inelastic demand. Now, firms tend to focus on what is termed the **advertizing-to-sales ratio** ($A/R = A/pq$) in deciding on how much to spend on advertizing. Equation (26.5) can be rearranged to show that the advertizing-to-sales ratio should be related to the ratio of advertizing elasticity to own-price elasticity of demand, as follows. First note that (26.5) simplifies to give

$$(p - MC)\frac{\partial q}{\partial A} = 1. \qquad (26.10)$$

Now, multiplying both sides by A/pq gives

$$\left(\frac{p - MC}{p}\right)\left(\frac{A}{q}\frac{\partial q}{\partial A}\right) = \frac{A}{pq}. \qquad (26.11)$$

From (26.9), the first term on the left is equal to $-1/\eta_P$, whilst the second term is the advertizing elasticity, hence

$$\frac{A}{pq} = \frac{A}{R} = -\frac{\eta_A}{\eta_P}. \qquad (26.12)$$

That is, the advertizing-to-sales ratio should be set equal to (minus) the ratio of the advertizing elasticity to the own-price elasticity of demand. To sum up in words, we have

The Dorfman–Steiner Rule The profit-maximizing policy, for the single-period single-product monopoly firm, involves setting the mark-up

$$\left(\frac{p - MC}{p}\right)$$

equal to the (absolute value of the) inverse of the demand elasticity, and the advertizing-to-sales ratio equal to the (absolute value of the) ratio of advertizing to demand elasticities.

---

[8] Since $dC(q)/dA = [dC(q)/dq][\partial q/\partial A]$.

(b) Characteristics of the Dorfman–Steiner Solution

Given equations (26.9) and (26.12), the following observations about the nature of this optimal pricing/advertizing solution are worth emphasizing:

(i) The more elastic demand is, the lower the optimal price (recall that the monopolist always operates at an elastic point on the demand curve).

(ii) The more elastic the advertizing elasticity, the higher the advertizing expenditure as a proportion of sales.

(iii) A rule of thumb commonly used in practice is to set a target level of advertizing expenditure as a percentage of sales revenue. Equation (26.12) suggests that this rule of thumb could be optimal if the target rate is set equal to the ratio of advertizing to demand elasticity (absolute value).

(iv) The optimal solutions for price and advertizing are interdependent. It is not, in general, possible to determine the optimal advertizing level independently of the optimal price—or vice versa. The simultaneous solution to equations (26.9) and (26.12) is only straightforward if it can be assumed that the estimated elasticities do not vary significantly with the choice of price and advertizing levels. This is often a reasonable assumption; indeed, demand functions are often estimated in constant elasticity form (see the presentation in Chapter 9 of the Cobb–Douglas type demand function of the form $q = KA^{\alpha}p^{-\beta}$, where K, α, and β are given constants; in this case, the advertizing-to-sales ratio should be set as $A/R = \alpha/\beta$ and the price–cost mark-up as $1/\beta$, as the reader may care to verify). By contrast, with a linear demand specification, the elasticities η_A and η_p both vary as A and p are varied.

Another general point regarding the Dorfman–Steiner solution is that the advertizing elasticity is not usually a constant but is likely to vary with the economic conditions and climate faced by the individual firm. Empirically, it has been shown to depend to an extent on:

(i) the past history of expenditure on advertizing: diminishing returns may set in;

(ii) the quantity currently being sold (the current level of market penetration, how saturated the market is);

(iii) the type of product: luxuries have higher advertizing elasticities than necessities;

(iv) advertizing reactions of competitors: these may reduce the impact of an individual firm's advertizing;

(v) the stage in the business cycle: for example, how much discretionary income is in people's pockets.

According to the Dorfman–Steiner model, if the advertizing elasticity varies, then so too should the proportion of sales revenue spent on advertizing.

Advertizing-to-sales ratios tend to be quite low, with many industries averaging around 0–3%. The major advertizers belong to pharmaceutical and related industries (drugs, cosmetics, soaps, etc.), as briefly illustrated in Example 26.1.

EXAMPLE 26.1 The advertizing-to-sales ratios vary significantly across industries (and across countries). Typical broad classifications for the UK give:

Drugs, cosmetics	15–30%
Soaps	5–15%
Cigarettes and beer	0–10%
Automobiles	0–5%

For more detailed reporting of advertizing-to-sales ratios, see e.g. Clarke (1985: chap. 9) and (for some specific examples in food and drinks industries) Sutton (1991).

It should be noted that A/R is subject to significant measurement problems (see Sutton 1991), and also only captures the percentage rate. The automobile industry has an unexceptionable advertizing-to-sales ratio, but its sales revenue is massive, so a low ratio is also consistent with automobile advertizing being a substantial part of the advertizing business.

(c) Marginalist Advice on Advertizing

Section 24.4 discussed the idea of using the marginalist model to investigate the rationality of existing price policy. To some extent the same idea can be applied to advertizing. The idea involves computing the firm's current advertizing-to-sales ratio, and its current price–cost margin. It is then possible to compute the advertizing elasticity that would validate these choices. If the advertizing elasticity seems out of line with reality, then this suggests the direction in which advertizing (and the price–cost margin) should be moved, as in the following example.

EXAMPLE 26.2 Suppose a product has A/R of 10% and the firm currently works with a mark-up of 30% on average variable cost. First we calculate the price–cost margin in equation (26.9): thus $p = 1.3 AVC = 1.3 MC$ (if, as in Chapter 25, it is assumed that AVC is constant and hence equal to marginal cost). Hence, (26.9) becomes

$$\frac{p - MC}{p} = \frac{1.3 MC - MC}{1.3 MC} = 0.231 = -\frac{1}{\eta_p}. \quad \text{(i)}$$

Thus, the elasticity of demand would need to be $\eta_p = -1/0.231 = -4.33$ for this price to be profit-maximizing. Then, applying equation (26.12), we have

$$\frac{A}{R} = 0.1 = -\frac{\eta_A}{\eta_p} = -\frac{\eta_A}{-4.333}, \quad \text{(ii)}$$

so that $\eta_A = 4.333 \times 0.1 = 0.4333$. Hence, for the advertising budget to be correctly set requires an advertising elasticity of 0.43 (that is, a 1% increase in advertising should increase sales by 0.43%).

Given the above analysis, it follows that, if the decision-maker believes advertising is more effective than the 0.43 advertising elasticity calculated here, then this is a signal for an increase in the level of advertising, whilst if it is believed that advertising is less effective, then the budget should be cut to some extent.

(d) Weaknesses of the Dorfman–Steiner model

Advertising expenditure positively affects sales in the model, but there is no detail regarding how it works, and whether different types of advertising might be more or less effective for a particular type of product (choice of media, length and frequency of messages, etc.). The model abstracts from these details, and, as a one-period model, also abstracts from the fact that the effects of advertising are not immediate; there is a time dimension to consider.

26.4.3 A Baumol-Type (Revenue-Maximizing) Advertising Model

Most managerial theories of the firm emphasize that profit is by no means the sole objective. Typically, firms concerned with growth or sales revenue maximization will tend to set lower prices and advertize more, ceteris paribus. This section briefly details how the Dorfman–Steiner model is affected if the firm operates in Baumol-fashion as a sales revenue maximizer (who also wishes to attain an acceptable level of profit). This model, without advertizing, was reviewed in section 17.3. As there, suppose that managers aim to maximize a managerial utility function of the form $U(\pi, R)$, where utility increases with both profits π and revenue R (the properties of this utility function are discussed in some detail in section 17.3).[9] As in the Dorfman–Steiner model outlined in section 26.4.2, demand is affected by price and by the level of advertizing. That is,

$$q = f(p, A), \quad (26.13)$$

where demand q is decreasing in price p and increasing in the level of advertizing expenditure A ($\partial f/\partial p$) $= f_p < 0$, $\partial f/\partial A = f_A > 0$. Profit is given as

$$\pi = pq - c(q) - A, \quad (26.14)$$

where $c(q)$ represents the cost function (total cost of producing and selling output q, aside from advertizing costs). Finally,

$$R = pq. \quad (26.15)$$

The problem is thus to maximize $U(\pi, R)$ subject to constraints (26.13)–(26.15) by choosing variables π, R, p, q, and A. Setting up the Lagrangian,

$$L = U(\pi, R) + \lambda_1(\pi - R + c(q) + A) + \lambda_2(R - pq) + \lambda_3(q - f(p, A)), \quad (26.16)$$

and writing out the first-order conditions associated with each of the choice variables π, R, p, q, and A, gives

$$L_\pi = U_\pi + \lambda_1 = 0, \quad (26.17)$$

$$L_R = U_R - \lambda_1 + \lambda_2 = 0, \quad (26.18)$$

$$L_q = \lambda_1 MC - \lambda_2 p + \lambda_3 = 0, \quad (26.19)$$

$$L_p = -\lambda_2 q - \lambda_3 f_p = 0, \quad (26.20)$$

and

$$L_A = \lambda_1 - \lambda_3 f_A = 0, \quad (26.21)$$

where $U_\pi = \partial U/\partial \pi$ is marginal utility of profit, $f_p = \partial f/\partial p$, etc. By using (26.17) to substitute for λ_1 in (27.18)–(26.21), and then (26.18) to eliminate λ_2, and so on, this system of equations can be reduced and manipulated in much the same way as described in section 26.4.2, which examined the Dorfman–Steiner model. Thus, using equations (26.6) and (26.7) to introduce the advertising and own-price

---

[9] It was argued in Chap. 17 that this is more realistic than the original version of the Baumol model, since the latter featured lexicographic preferences (in that the managers only, and suddenly, become concerned about profit once it falls below a fixed threshold level).

elasticities of demand into the formulae.[10] The outcome can be shown to entail

$$\frac{A}{R} = -\left(\frac{U_\pi + U_R}{U_\pi}\right)\frac{\eta_A}{\eta_p},\qquad(26.22)$$

which, since U_π and U_R are both positive quantities, implies that

$$\frac{A}{R} > -\frac{\eta_A}{\eta p}.\qquad(26.23)$$

That is, ceteris paribus, the advertizing-to-sales ratio is set to a value which is larger than the ratio of elasticities (in the Dorfman–Steiner model, (26.23) was an equality). The extent to which it is larger depends simply on the relative weights U_π and U_R placed on profit vis-à-vis sales revenue. If the management strongly emphasize the importance of sales revenue, this amounts to placing a higher value on U_R relative to U_π, and this can be seen to increase the level to which advertizing is seen to be desirable. By manipulating the first-order conditions (as in the Dorfman–Steiner model), it can also be shown that

$$\left(\frac{p - MC}{p}\right) < -\frac{1}{\eta_p}.\qquad(26.24)$$

That is, ceteris paribus, the firm sets a mark-up which is less than (the absolute value of) the inverse of the elasticity of demand (in the Dorfman–Steiner model, (26.24) was an equality). Again, the greater the emphasis placed by management on the importance of sales revenue relative to profit, the lower the price mark-up is.

To sum up, a firm interested in revenue as well as profit will set a lower price and advertize more (and hence sell more) than a pure profit-maximizing firm.

26.4.4 Advertizing in Oligopoly

Given the interdependence between firms, each firm faces the prisoners' dilemma, not only in choosing output or price, but also in choosing the level of advertising. It follows that firms may engage not only in price competition but also in advertising competition (and advertising wars). It is sometimes argued that firms focus on non-price competition because this is less destructive than price competition. The idea is that an advertizing war may adversely affect firms' profits, but at least it expands the total market size, whilst a price war merely involves the industry slipping down a fixed market demand curve. However, the logic of such an argument is dubious, since it is unclear which type of war will damage a firm's profitability the most.

Table 26.2 illustrates the idea that high advertizing is a dominant strategy in a prisoners' dilemma game. The payoffs indicate profit levels consequent on the different strategy choices of two firms in a duopoly (and the idea can be generalized to a multi-player game). A firm does well if it chooses high advertizing (HA) when the other firm chooses a low level of advertising (LA) with payoffs +20 and −5 to each respectively. This is because the HA-firm steals market share from the LA-firm. If both choose LA, they both do reasonably well because they share the market equally and have low advertizing costs (+10 each). If they both choose HA, they again share the market equally, but profit is poor because both incur heavy advertizing costs (+2 each); the bulk of the advertizing effect is simply to neutralize the advertizing effort of the other player.

Given the payoff matrix, it should be clear that, whatever the opponent's strategy, a firm is better off choosing HA. For example, if player B chooses low advertizing, LA, player A gets 20 from HA, and 10 from LA, whilst if B chooses HA, then A gets 2 from HA and −5 from LA. Thus whatever B does, A's best choice is to choose HA. HA is a dominant strategy. Of course, the same argument applies to B. It follows that the prediction is that both will choose HA and the outcome is a heavy advertizing equilibrium in which each firm's profit is low (2 each).

If both colluded, they would both be better off (LA by each gives 10 each). But in a one-shot game, both have an incentive to cheat on any agreement and to choose HA. In practice, the game is repeated (with an uncertain, possibly infinite number of future periods). In Chapter 5, it was argued that in such circumstances, there are possibilities for signalling and building co-operation (collusion). However, it has to be said that, once the number of players starts to increase, the incentives to cheat and go for higher levels of advertizing are likely to reappear.[11] Furthermore, in an industry in which all firms are advertizing heavily, as indicated in Table 26.2, no

---

[10] As in the above section, these are $\eta_p = (\partial q/\partial p)(p/q) = pf_p/q$ and $\eta_A = (\partial q/\partial A)(A/q) = pf_A/q$. Hence we can write $f_p = q\eta_p/p$ and $f_A = q\eta_A/A$ and use these expressions to replace f_p and f_A where they appear in the first-order conditions.

[11] See Chap. 5 for a more detailed consideration of the prisoners' dilemma, and Chap. 16 for a discussion of the problems of sustaining cartels and how this is affected by the number of players.

Table 26.2 Advertizing as a prisoners' dilemma game

		B's Strategies	
		Low advertizing expenditure, LA	High advertizing expenditure, HA
A's strategies	Low advertizing expenditure, LA	$\pi_A = 10$ $\pi_B = 10$	$\pi_A = -5$ $\pi_B = 20$
	high Advertizing expenditure, HA	$\pi_A = 20$ $\pi_B = -5$	$\pi_A = 2$ $\pi_B = 2$

firm can afford to stop doing it; each firm must continue advertizing in order to survive. Thus oligopolists are likely to advertize too much for their own good. They also advertize too much from the viewpoint of society as a whole (since the advertizing is primarily self-cancelling, it represents a social waste of resources).

The cola market is a classic example. The market leaders (Coca-Cola and Pepsi-Cola) maintain relatively high levels of advertizing expenditure despite the fact that this does not significantly expand the market for cola as a whole. Given the above discussion, this behaviour could be interpreted as that of players who are caught up in the prisoners' dilemma game. However, it is well to bear in mind the insight provided by section 26.3, namely that advertizing also creates a barrier to entry; heavy advertizing, an endogenous sunk cost, makes it harder for new firms to enter the market. In an industry dominated by a small number of players, one might expect some degree of tacit collusion and an ability to side-step the prisoners' dilemma. However, collusive dominant players might still choose heavy advertizing in order to keep entrants out.[12]

26.4.5 Dynamics

It has already been remarked that advertizing takes time to make an impact. Indeed, it is useful to think of the effect of advertizing as a stock. That is, advertizing requires substantial investment to build up the stock effect (reputation, brand loyalty, etc.). Once built, the stock depreciates unless a sufficiently positive level of advertizing is maintained. It follows that the major investment is in building the initial stock;

after this, it is relatively cheap to maintain the stock. However, the fact that advertizing requires investment (and time to make an impact) is not really in itself a barrier to entry.[13] Rather, it is the fact that the bulk of the advertizing investment represents a sunk cost; the value of the advertizing disappears if the product is no longer produced.[14]

26.4.6 Multi-Product Firms and Advertizing

Most firms manufacture a product line, typically of products that are fairly close substitutes. Chapter 20 discussed the problems of pricing a product line, and the need to take into account the interaction effects. The key idea raised there was that decisions made for products in isolation are likely to be suboptimal. The same argument applies to advertizing. Most advertizing for a single product will have an impact on sales of other products within the firm's product range. Often, advertizing increases generalized brand loyalty and customer familiarity with the firm as a whole. This 'visibility' effect suggests that other product sales will benefit from the advertizing of a single product. However, most of a firm's products are usually fairly close substitutes. Advertizing on a single product may thus make it seem better value relative to the rest of the product line. If so, there could easily be an adverse effect on the sales of these other products.

In principle, it is desirable to try to study the impact of a specific advertizing campaign on the sales of all the firm's products, either formally or informally. Formal analysis is often difficult, so it

---

[12] Clearly it is not easy to discriminate between these explanations of observed behaviour (however, see Sutton 1991 for a valiant attempt).

[13] Although the effects, lying in the future, are uncertain; to the extent that capital markets are short-termist and unduly risk-averse, it might be argued that this creates a barrier to entry. However, there is considerable dispute regarding the magnitude of such capital-market imperfections.

[14] Although see n. 6 above.

usually falls to gut reaction and qualitative judgements as to which of the two spillover effects is likely to be more important. The key idea is that, if advertizing on a single product is judged to benefit sales of all products, then more of it is justified than is revealed by an analysis of its impact on just the single product advertized. By contrast, if the advertizing has an adverse effect on the rest of the firm's products, then this suggests that less of it is desirable. Qualitatively, it will often be possible to make a judgement as to which direction the effect is likely to take. As discussed in Chapter 20, there is the danger that product managers may not be concerned with interaction effects of this type.

26.5 Advertizing and Economic Welfare

Judgements about economic welfare in this text have made use of consumer surplus as a measure of consumer gain. The measurement of a welfare gain for an individual is rooted in the idea that the individual's preference ordering is fixed (see Chapter 8). When preferences change, there is a problem of evaluation; should it be the pre-change or post-change preferences that are used in measuring the consumer's welfare gain? One possible strategy is to ask, in comparing two states of the world, whether one is preferred to the other under both pre- and post-advertizing preferences. The complexities involved in measuring welfare when tastes change is clearly of interest, but carries us beyond the scope of this text.[15] However, in the absence of formal analysis, it seems reasonable to conclude that

1. in so far as advertizing provides information that helps people make informed choices and fewer mistakes, it is likely to have social value, whilst

2. in so far as it is concerned to persuade, matters are fairly unclear, such that the advertizing could represent a waste of resources. In the extreme case where the advertizing is mutually self-cancelling, then it probably does represent a waste of resources.

Looking at more objective evidence, we can ask whether advertizing tends to lead to higher or lower

prices, higher or lower product quality, and less or more competition in the market place.

26.5.1 Effect on Prices and Competition

Advertizing will tend to increase prices in so far as it increases monopoly power, by increasing perceived product differentiation. However, to the extent that it is informative, advertizing could actually lead to lower prices, by increasing the amount of price information available to consumers (Koutsoyiannis 1982: 129 discusses some evidence for this). Overall, the empirical evidence appears to be that advertizing does tend to lead to higher prices (but identifying causality is complex).

26.5.2 Effect on Quality

Similar arguments apply to quality. If advertizing is informative, then it will increase customer awareness of the higher-quality products on offer, and increase competition amongst firms either to supply quality at a competitive price, or to reduce prices pro rata with the product quality on offer. Again, this is merely another way of saying that advertizing can promote market efficiency.

Hence, the concern over advertizing is usually over advertizing in oligopolies, where advertizing is most likely to be merely persuasive, and most likely to be largely a self-cancelling activity. Of course, concern is often expressed more widely about the nature and effects of advertizing—as part of a general concern regarding the influence of the media in moulding and manipulating tastes, preferences, and behaviour patterns.[16]

26.6 Summary

This chapter first sought to describe advertizing in terms of the nature of the goods it was concerned with: whether they were search or experience goods (section 26.2). It then noted the correlation between different types of market structure and the extent of advertizing observed (section 26.3.1). It was noted that advertizing has the characteristic of an endogenous sunk cost; such sunk costs create barriers to entry (section 26.3.2). The fact that these costs are endogenous indicates that the level of price competition in an industry can affect the

---

[15] See e.g. Dixit and Norman (1978). Clarke (1985) reviews some of this material.

[16] From an economic perspective, see e.g. Galbraith (1958).

level of advertizing and hence the barriers to entry into that industry. It was noted that as a consequence the conventional wisdom, that increasing the size of the market tends to reduce concentration, might no longer apply in the presence of endogenous sunk costs such as advertizing. Section 26.4 described a set of simple models concerned with the determination of the optimal level of advertizing. The three major points to observe there are that price and advertizing need to be jointly chosen, that sales revenue maximizers will tend to advertize more (and sell more at lower prices) than profit maximizers, and that oligopolists tend to get forced into what is often largely mutually self-cancelling advertizing. Thus, particularly in oligopolistic markets, a significant amount of advertizing probably is a waste of resources. Of course, this does not necessarily mean that state intervention is justified in the advertizing business (see Chapter 28; the usual economic argument is that it depends on weighing the likely costs of intervention against the anticipated benefits from it).

26.7 Review Questions

1. Contrast search and experience goods. Give three examples of each not mentioned in this chapter. What is the significance of this distinction for the type of advertizing likely to be observed?

2. Suppose that, in an econometric study involving a constant elasticity demand model, the price elasticity is estimated as -1.2 and the advertizing elasticity is 0.1. According to the Dorfman–Steiner model, what price–cost mark-up and advertizing-to-sales ratio should a profit-maximizing firm select?

3. Provide a full derivation of equations (26.22)–(26.24) for the Baumol sales-revenue-maximizing firm in section 26.4.3.

4. 'Changing price in oligopoly can trigger a price war. Price wars always make firms worse off. Hence the preference for non-price competition, through selective promotional efforts, or through advertizing.' Is advertizing a safer bet if one wants to get ahead of the competition? Discuss.

26.8 Further Reading

See Nelson (1975) or Martin (1994) for more discussion of search and experience goods. Most texts on industrial economics devote a chapter to advertizing (see e.g. Clarke 1985, Waterson 1984, or Martin 1994). Koutsoyiannis (1982) is a useful review of some earlier advertizing models. Sutton (1991) is a tour de force that confronts a class of theoretical models with extensive empirical evidence on the relationships between market size, concentration, and sunk costs such as advertizing. Finally, Becker and Murphy (1993) is an interesting recent attempt to model advertizing as just another good. Their idea is that advertizing can be viewed as a good in its own right, one which is linked to the product advertized by noting that the two goods are economic complements. Such an approach offers one way around the problem of welfare measurement.

Part VI

Regulatory Intervention

Part VI is concerned with the rationale for state intervention in the private sector economy, and the extent to which intervention is likely to improve economic welfare. The usual argument is that externalities, public goods, and imperfect competition give rise to welfare losses which might be reduced by state intervention either by state take-over or through state regulation of the private sector firms involved. State intervention tends to be imperfect and also costly, so the optimal arrangement can typically only be judged by weighing the expected costs of intervention against the expected benefits. Chapter 27 examines the problem of externalities and public goods, focusing in particular on the circumstances under which externalities are likely to be cured by those affected, and the circumstances where state intervention might prove beneficial. Chapter 28 then addresses the problem of market power. Market power, it has been argued (beginning in Chapter 2), leads to monopoly welfare loss; the issue is whether state intervention, through nationalization or through regulation, can improve on the unfettered market outcome. The pros and cons of public provision, and of alternative ways of regulating private sector firms, are then discussed.

27 Market Failure: Externalities and Public Goods

Objective To explain why markets do not deal with all goods and bads equally well, and why and under what circumstances (if any) problems such as noise, air and water pollution, and congestion require state intervention. Alternative mechanisms for dealing with these forms of market failure are then discussed.

Prerequisites None.

Keywords bargaining costs, Coase Theorem, contracting costs, externality, focal point, free riding, information acquisition costs, missing market, non-excludability, non-rejectability, non-rivalry in consumption, optimum externality, Pigovian tax, policing and enforcement costs, polluter-pays principle, private good, property right, public bad, public good, pure public good, regulation, search costs, second best, transaction cost.

27.1 Introduction

Roughly speaking, external effects or **externalities** occur when the activity of one agent or group of agents affects the utility levels of another agent or group of agents (whether consumers or firms) and the effect is unpriced in the market, whilst what is called a **public good** is a good or service which, when provided for consumption by one individual, is also an automatic spillover provided for others. In effect, consumption of the good by one individual does not deplete the amount available to others; for example radio broadcasts, or national defence. A public good can be thought of as a special kind of externality, since if I buy a unit of the good, such as the radio broadcast, other individuals get the good for free; that is, my activity affects the utility levels of others and the effects are not priced in a market.

To illustrate further the above ideas, consider the problem of noise pollution associated with airports. Typically, there will be many houses lying under the flight paths associated with this airport. The noise pollution, an unintended by-product of the airlines going about their normal business, adversely affects many individuals' welfare. Another feature of this noise is that there does not appear to be a market for it. We cannot buy or sell noise, or silence for that matter, on the open market.[1] Another feature of noise is that its impact on one person does not deplete the amount imposed on other individuals. Thus, this noise pollution has the characteristics both of an externality and of a public good (or **public bad**, since it generally makes recipients feel worse off).

Markets often cope badly with externalities, particularly those with public-good (or -bad) characteristics. Arguably, this provides an important intellectual rationale for the existence of the state—namely that there is a need for intervention in the market economy to resolve such problems. However, the need for intervention can be disputed, since intervention is never costless and state regulators cannot always be relied upon to act in the public interest. This issue is discussed further below. The major focus in this chapter is on the problem of externality, since state regulation of pollution, noise, etc. impinges on firms and how they should best behave. However, I start by giving a brief review of the special case of public goods, as this introduces some terminology useful in the more general discussion of externalities.

---

[1] Although the housing market prices locational attributes; thus one can always move, and so purchase peace and quiet. This observation is of considerable significance, and is discussed further in sect. 27.5 below.

27.2 Public Goods

Public goods are characterized by one or more of the following features:

1. **Non-rivalry in consumption.** A **private good** is one which, once consumed by one individual, is no longer available for consumption by another (e.g. pizza). A **pure public good** is one for which one individual's consumption in no way diminishes the amount available for consumption by others (noise pollution, television broadcasting, national defence, etc.). Some goods are intermediate between pure private and pure public goods, for example library books or football matches. If the stadium is half full, then my going to view the match does not preclude anyone else from doing so. However, as capacity is reached, my consumption does exclude another's.

2. **Non-excludability.** Once the good is provided for some individuals, it is impossible, or at least very expensive, to prevent others from consuming it. This is true for national defence, and to an extent for radio and TV broadcasting (although note that cable TV and the use of decoders provides the technology for excluding consumers).

3. **Non-rejectability.** This occurs when, once provided, the good has to be consumed by everyone. That is, you get it whether you want it or not (or, at least, it is expensive to avoid). This is the case with many types of pollution (radioactivity, noise, smog, acid rain, etc.).

Thus, non-rivalry in consumption is an essential characteristic of both public goods and public bads, whilst non-excludability is important for public goods, and non-rejectability for public bads.[2] To emphasize this point, focusing on goods, we have:

Fact 20.1: If a good features:
(i) non-rivalry in consumption + non-excludability ⇒ market provision is not possible.
(ii) non-rivalry in consumption + excludability ⇒ market provision is possible.

The point is that, when a public good has the characteristic of non-excludability, the problem of

free riding occurs. No rational consumer is willing to pay for a public good since they know that if someone else buys it, they will get it for free. As a consequence, the market tends to under-provide this type of good (or not provide it at all). By contrast, a good may feature non-rivalry in consumption but still be excludable. The football match falls into this category, since it is possible (at a cost) to exclude individuals from viewing; there is no problem with the market supply of such excludable public goods.

With public bads, it is non-rejectability that matters. A non-rejectable public bad impinges on everyone whether they like it or not. In bargaining with the perpetrator of the public bad, those affected by the pollution will likewise have an incentive to free ride. That is, they will understate their willingness to pay if asked to make a contribution to induce the polluter to reduce emissions. The end-product is that the market solution overprovides the public bad (there is too much pollution). In practice, therefore, public goods tend to be state-provided, and public bads tend to need state control.

Even if a public good is state-provided, there is still a difficult question associated with how much of the public good to provide. In theory, this involves summing each individual's marginal willingness to pay for the good, and then expanding output to the point where the marginal cost of provision equals the sum of these marginal valuations, as illustrated in Figure 27.1 for the case where the number of individuals affected is just two. The principle clearly generalizes to case where there are many individuals involved.

There is, of course, a problem in making such a solution operational. This is because, as previously

---

[2] It is worth noting that public goods and bads are rarely global (even carbon emissions do not evenly affect the whole globe); most are local to some community and/or geographical area. For example, river pollution affects only river users and those local to the river, urban congestion is local to a particular conurbation, and so on. However, some are relatively global.

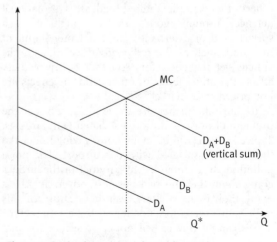

Fig. 27.1 Optimal provision of a public good

mentioned, individuals will understate their willingness to pay if they know they are going to be taxed in proportion to what they reveal. Equally, they will tend to overstate willingness to pay if the amount they have to pay is not directly related to the amount provided. The problem of discovering how much to provide thus requires the design of a mechanism which will reveal individuals' true valuations. Various schemes have been proposed which try to resolve the incentive problems of the type described above; the object of these schemes is to give individuals an incentive to tell the truth in reporting their valuation of the public good. However, space precludes our delving into such questions in more detail here.[3]

The above account suffices to give a flavour of the problem associated with public goods and bads. Section 27.3 examines the externality problem more generally. However, as we shall see, many of the most significant types of externality are those which constitute public bads (acid rain, CO_2 emissions, smog, congestion, etc.).

27.3 Externalities

Section 27.3.1 characterizes and provides a general definition of what constitutes an external effect. Following this, section 27.3.2 establishes the concept of optimum externality and discusses whether markets are likely to reach Pareto-efficient outcomes.

27.3.1 Defining Externality

There is some debate as to what constitutes an appropriate definition. The following is common and will serve:

Definition 27.1 An externality is said to exist when one agent's action directly affects the welfare of one or more other agents, where the effects are outside any form of exchange relationship. An externality is said to be a positive (negative) externality if the effect is beneficial (adverse).[4]

Consider the following example:

Example 27.1 Two firms located on the river bank both require clean water for their production processes. However, the upstream firm finds it cheaper to discharge polluted water rather than cleansing it prior to discharge. The pollution then affects the downstream firm's cost of production and the quantity and quality of the catch of downstream fishermen.

One of the key features of externality worth emphasizing is that it 'takes two to tango' (to quote Baumol 1976). That is, there are always two parties to any external effect, and when one of the parties is removed, the external effect disappears. Thus in Example 27.1, many readers might be inclined to blame the polluter—but notice that there is no damage if there are no firms or fishermen downstream. It could be argued, therefore, that those affected by the pollution are as much to blame for it as the polluter.[5]

The idea of exchange relationship in Definition 27.1 can be interpreted fairly widely. Thus, in Example 27.1, if the two firms negotiate a deal in which the upstream firm reduces its pollution levels in exchange for a cash payment, then we think of this as the establishment of a market for the external effect.

Definition 27.1 is sometimes referred to as a definition of what constitutes a technological externality, as distinct from a pecuniary externality. Clearly any agent's behaviour in the market place may affect other agents. For example, if George Soros purchases a large volume of a thinly traded equity stock, such that this trade moves the price upward, then if I also hold the stock, I benefit from his action. However, it can be shown that this kind of pecuniary effect, which flows through the market place, does not lead to under- or over-provision of goods. Only technological externalities can (potentially) lead to market failure.

If we classify agents as either consumers or producers (of course many are both at different points in time), then externalities may also be characterized according to Table 27.1. Externalities are usually

---

[3] One approach to attempting to elicit true valuations is through the use of the so-called Clarke–Groves tax. For an introductory discussion, see Atkinson and Stiglitz (1980) or Varian (1990); Tideman and Tullock (1976) examine the pros and cons of the Clark–Groves tax in more detail.

[4] Some writers include in the definition that externalities are unintended consequences of economic activity. However, intentionality is not a critical issue. Juveniles are often responsible for a significant level of litter (throwing away their sweet wrappers etc.); this is a negative external effect, whether it is intended or not.

[5] Some might take the 'common-sense' view that who is morally to blame depends on who was in place first. In a sense, this accords with the idea that 'possession is nine-tenths of the law'; that is, where property rights are not well defined, common law will usually ascribe the rights to those who have precedence. An alternative view is that anyone who harms the planet is morally culpable. Such questions are not explored further here.

Table 27.1 Externalities: classification and examples

		Affected party	
		Consumer	Producer
Affecting party	Consumer	Envy Altruism	Not so important (untreated sewage outfalls might affect downstream costs of production)
	Producer	Smoke Noise Airborne and waterborne pollution	Smoke Water abstraction (affecting availability downstream) Airborne and waterborne pollutants Fishing (and over-fishing)

unilateral (one-directional) effects, but occasionally they are bilateral. The classic example of a producer–producer bilateral, or reciprocal, externality, is that of beekeepers and orchards; in this example, bees in foraging and feeding pollinate apple trees. Thus the proximity of an orchard gives a positive external effect for beekeepers, and vice versa; without the bees, the orchard growers might need to expend resources on alternative methods of pollination.

Definition 27.1 emphasizes the idea that an externality exists when there is no exchange relationship. For this reason, the externality problem is often referred to as one of **missing markets**; for example, when firms produce airborne pollutants which impose costs on other economic agents, if there is no market for pollution, they have no incentive to take these costs into account. The same point applies to motorists who join in the congestion at rush hour; they take into account the costs they incur themselves, but ignore the additional costs their presence imposes on others; again, there is no market in congestion.

27.3.2 Optimum Externality and the Coase Theorem

(a) The Concept of Optimum Externality

Consider Figure 27.2. In this diagram, the level of an external effect is plotted on the horizontal axis. For concreteness, think of the external effect as smoke. Two classic examples from the literature which involve smoke are the following:

(*a*) A factory produces smoke as a by-product of its production process. Cutting back smoke emissions costs the firm (as it has to expend resources on abatement). The affected party is a laundry operating nearby. The higher the level

of smoke in the atmosphere, the higher its costs of production. (see e.g. Baumol 1972.)

(*b*) Two individuals, a smoker and a non-smoker (who dislikes smoke), are travelling by train, and are seated alone in a compartment (in the old carriages, a compartment would only seat about ten individuals). (See e.g. Mishan 1975.)

In both these examples, one agent generates smoke which harms the other. In (*a*), the factory earns profit and produces smoke. The area under the marginal benefit curve represents that total addition to profit obtained by producing the associated level of smoke (compared to producing no smoke), whilst the area under the marginal damage function represents the loss of profit to the laundry. In (*b*), the case of the smoker and the non-smoker, the marginal benefit and marginal cost curves represent each individual's marginal willingness to pay schedule. The area under the marginal benefit curve represents

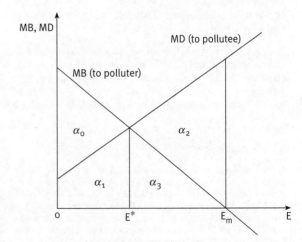

Fig. 27.2 Optimum externality (1)

the smoker's willingness-to-pay to be allowed to produce the associated level of smoke, whilst the area under the marginal damage curve represents the amount of money the non-smoker would be willing to pay to have the smoke eliminated.[6]

There are some complexities which, in the following discussion, are ignored. First, there is the obvious point that one or the other of the two parties might walk away from the relationship and so end it (the smoker or non-smoker can move to another more appropriate compartment; the factory or the laundry can relocate elsewhere). This is discussed further in section 27.5. Furthermore, the focus is purely on the benefits and harm to the two parties. In the case of the two firms, further complexities can arise if the firms are not operating in a price-taking environment (or may be driven into bankruptcy). This is because we would need to consider the knock-on welfare effects on consumers in the final-product markets, since what happens with regard to the externality question might have implications for the prices these firms set. The problem of market power in conjunction with externalities is an example of the general problem of second best (see Chapter 22).[7]

(b) The Role of Property Rights

Solutions to externality problems often turn on the issue of property rights, and who has them.

Definition 27.2 A **property right** is defined as a socially enforced right to be able (legally) to do something or use something.

A property right is said to be **alienable** if it is sellable; for example, you can sell your car to (almost) anyone else. Some rights (such as citizenship) are not (legally) alienable at all. It is also worth noting that there are often socially enforced limitations on usage. For example, there are legal restrictions on using your home as a place from which to conduct business activities (in the UK at least).

In what follows, I shall refer to the polluter as the 'smoker' and the affected party as the 'non-smoker'.

Property rights are of significance for externalities as follows. Suppose that, initially, the situation is that the polluter, the smoker, has the right to pollute. Thus, there is no law against the firm emitting smoke through its chimneys, or the individual smoking in the railway compartment (the compartment is not no-smoking). Then it would appear that the smoker would choose to pollute to the point where the pollution confers no further marginal benefit on him or her. This is the point E_m in Figure 27.2. The problem with this outcome is that the smoker is taking no account of the damage caused to the non-smoker. Taking 'society' as these two individuals, the benefit of a given level of externality E to the smoker is given as the area under the marginal benefit function MB, and the damage cost to the non-smoker is given as the area under the marginal damage function MD. It follows that economic welfare is equal to the difference in areas, and this is maximized by choosing the level E^*. Every unit of smoke produced beyond E^* damages the non-smoker more than it benefits the smoker. Every unit less than E^* deprives the smoker more than it harms the non-smoker. Hence total economic welfare rises up to the point E^*, but falls thereafter.

(c) The Coase Theorem

The market appears to fail in Figure 27.2 because, apparently, a high level of smoke E_m would result when the socially optimal level is really E^*. However, as Ronald Coase (1937) famously noted, in the absence of transactions costs, we would expect the optimal level of externality still to be achieved. Coase's argument is that, at the level E_m, there is a big incentive for the non-smoker to do a deal with the smoker. Thus the last unit of smoke at E_m hurts the non-smoker far more than it benefits the smoker. There are thus gains from trade to be had. It will pay the non-smoker to offer a bribe to the smoker if she will offer to cut back production by one unit. So long as the payment is less than the marginal damage to the non-smoker, and greater than the marginal benefit forgone by the smoker, this deal will make both parties better off. This argument applies to each and every unit of smoke[8] all the way back to E^* (if both parties recognize that E^* is optimal, the bargain can be struck immediately

---

[6] See Chap. 8 for some indication of the problems associated with measuring benefits for an individual consumer.

[7] Buchanan (1969b) gives an illustration of the type of second-best problem that arises. Basically, as we shall see, there is a tendency to produce too much pollution, relative to the socially optimal level. However, a monopolist restricts output and hence produces less pollution (assuming output is correlated with pollution). Hence there are offsetting effects.

[8] This abstracts from income effects, which can give rise to conceptual difficulties regarding the adequacy of the benefit measure (see e.g. Ng 1979).

for the smoker to pull back smoke production all the way to this level). The total gain in welfare in moving from E_m to E^* is equal to area α_2 in Figure 27.2. It can be argued that rational negotiators should end up realizing this maximum total gain—with bargaining skills determining the individual shares (50:50 is a common sharing rule or focal point in bargaining theory). Coase's insight is that, in the absence of transactions costs, there is an incentive to create a market in the external effect, and that this market will then resolve the problem.

However, there is more to it than this. Suppose, for example, the initial disposition of property rights had been different, such that there was no right to pollute: that is, in (a) there is a right to clean air or in (b) the railway carriage compartment is a no-smoking. In this case, it would appear that the outcome is for there to be no smoke, which is again suboptimal. However, in the absence of transactions costs, there is again an incentive for a market to spring up. In this case, the smoker gets a lot of benefit from producing even just one unit of smoke, and this benefit greatly outweighs the marginal damage of this smoke to the non-smoker. As before, a deal can be done in which the smoker pays the non-smoker in order to be allowed to create one unit of smoke (and again, so long as the payment is less than the marginal benefit, and exceeds the marginal damage, both parties are made better off). This process operates all the way up to E^*. It follows that the smoker should be able to offer a 'bribe' to the non-smoker in order to be allowed to generate smoke to the level E^*.

Thus Coase (1937) argued that, so long as property rights can be traded, there is an incentive to trade until the optimal level of externality is achieved (in the absence of transactions costs), and that this optimum level would be achieved independent of the initial disposition of property rights.

Theorem 27.1 (The Coase Theorem): Resource allocation is Pareto-efficient so long as there is a clear assignment of property rights (which are saleable) and so long as transactions costs are zero. Furthermore, in the absence of income effects, the optimum level of externality realized is independent of the initial disposition of property rights.

As Cooter (1989) points out, the validity of this theorem depends on the idea that bargaining will realize an efficient outcome when the costs of negotiating and enforcing agreements is zero. In practice, bargaining can fail, even a the small-numbers case (usually because of information asymmetries: underestimating the gains being made by the opponent, one may press too hard). However, the force of the argument is clear enough.

However, whilst a Pareto-efficient outcome may be achievable independent of the initial disposition of property rights, the individuals are not indifferent to that disposition of property rights, since it has wealth consequences for them. Property rights in favour of the smoker make her better off, and the non-smoker worse off, relative to an initial dispensation of property rights in favour of the non-smoker. Another point, in the case of the smokers in the carriage (two 'consumers'), is that the optimal level of externality may not be exactly the same, independent of the initial dispensation of property rights, because of income effects (in terms of Figure 23.2, one can argue that the willingness-to-pay curves are different depending on the initial dispensation of property rights). However, it remains true that negotiations will lead to a Pareto-efficient outcome. In the case of two firms, there are no income effects to consider, so the outcome will be independent of the initial dispensation of property rights in this case.

The Coase Theorem seems to indicate that the externality problem may be less of a problem than had previously been thought; all that is required is a clear initial assignment of property rights, one way or the other. Although negotiations can break down, and game playing can confuse the final outcome of such bargaining processes, the force of the argument is strong in the case where there are just two parties. In such small-numbers cases, we would expect a market to spring up to solve the externality problem.

As a corollary, it is precisely where property rights are unclear that externalities can go unresolved, and can be a major source of dispute. For example, I may feel that I have a right to peace and quiet, but my neighbour may wish to learn to play the piano (and believes she has a right to make the associated cacophony). Unless the law (implicitly or explicitly) underpins one of our preferences, it is hard to get the bargaining process going. Of course, in a dispute of this type, the law will typically rule in favour of one party or the other. This in effect determines who has the property rights (via case law). Thereafter, the bargaining process might then be expected to effect a solution.

Unfortunately, even where property rights are well defined, externality can still be a problem. Whenever transactions costs (associated with getting the parties together and also conducting the negotiations) are substantial, the theorem breaks down. This is most likely to occur when a large number of individuals are affected (as, for example, with airborne pollution).

EXAMPLE 27.2 Bees pollinate orchards (so conferring a positive externality on orchard owners) but also collect nectar from the orchards to manufacture honey (so conferring a positive externality on beekeepers). The Coase Theorem predicts that, since there are a small number of parties involved (maybe only two), transactions costs should be small, and so the externality should be resolved by negotiations and contracts. Cheung (1973) observed that this was in fact often the case, with beekeepers paying orchard owners in situations where there are high-nectar-bearing trees, whilst fruiters tended to pay beekeepers if their orchards provided little nectar.

27.3.3 Transactions Costs

The Coase Theorem focuses on zero transactions costs. However, this is only the starting point of Coase's (1937) contribution—which is really about how institutional or market arrangements arise to deal with externalities in ways which tend to maximize social welfare net of transactions costs. The types of transactions cost involved in the externality situation are as follows:

(i) **Search** and **information acquisition costs**: Those associated with finding out the nature of the circumstances, the extent of the damage, etc. and the way damages vary with the perpetrator's level of activity.

(ii) **Bargaining costs**: Those associated with getting the parties together plus the time and effort required to get agreement on the appropriate outcome.

(iii) **Contracting costs**: Those associated with drawing up of legal documents describing the agreement, legal fees, etc.

(iv) **Policing and enforcement costs**: For example, the polluter may have entered into an agreement in which the firm is required to curtail effluent. However, there is still an incentive to deposit effluent if the firm can get away with it (e.g. at night). Hence there is a need for some form of monitoring (which is costly). Any transgressions would then require some form

of action—further negotiations and/or legal actions (which again require legal fees).

The two-agent externality problem has relatively low transactions costs of the above type. In this case the affected parties should be willing to expend resources up to the point where these transactions costs just match the benefits that can be had from achieving an agreement. Naturally, if the transactions costs exceed the anticipated benefits, no attempt will be made to reach on agreement. The argument in the small-numbers case is that the transactions costs are sufficiently small for the process to actually happen. However, all the above costs increase significantly with the number of individuals concerned (in particular, because of the free rider problem). Thus, in larger-numbers cases, such costs are likely to preclude a market solution.

In the presence of significant transactions costs, no one can see a way of undertaking a trade which is a Pareto improvement. One might conclude that the extant state of affairs is in fact Pareto-optimal. However, this is an unduly Panglossian view of the situation. It is natural, in such circumstances, to ask whether some form of state intervention (such as taxes or direct regulation), or some alternative institutional arrangement (such as setting up an artificial market in tradeable pollution permits), might help in tackling the externality problem and increasing economic welfare. The idea is that the state can intervene, and it is possible that some alternative arrangement might be socially desirable even when the transactions costs associated with implementation are taken into account.[9] This is discussed below.

27.3.4 Alternative Solutions to the Externality Problem

Suppose an external effect has been identified, but no bargaining solution is forthcoming. The question then arises as to whether state intervention might be beneficial. This section considers the options of non-intervention, merger, taxes and direct regulation.

---

[9] There is considerable debate in the literature regarding the status of transactions costs, and any attempt to formalize them tends to make the analysis overly complex. For a recent discussion of such issues in relation to the Coase theorem, see DeSerpa (1994).

(a) Simply Leave the Situation Alone

This has the merit of avoiding all implementation costs, and can be the optimal solution if intervention costs outweigh the benefits of intervention.

(b) Allow Merger (Internalize the Externality)

Where transactions costs are significant, there are clearly benefits to internalizing the externality through merger. This is not always a meaningful option, of course. For example, it is hard to think of a merger between a river-polluting firm and downstream fishermen. However, in the case of producer–producer externalities, merger is an option. Thus, following a merger of the smoky factory and laundry, the merged firm would naturally take into account all the benefits and costs associated with the pollution.

Ceteris paribus, vertical and horizontal integration will be attractive to the extent that mergers internalize externalities and reduce the transactions costs associated with arm's length negations. It thus follows that there are long-run pressures within the economic system to minimize transactions costs and adverse external effects. As a consequence, regulatory agencies concerned with assessing the welfare consequences of mergers have to weigh the pros and cons; merger may increase monopoly power in the market place (increasing welfare loss) but may also reduce negative externalities and the associated transactions costs (so reducing welfare loss).[10]

(c) Pigovian Taxes (and/or Subsidies)

Suppose internalization of the externality, either through individual negotiation or through merger, is for some reason not feasible. Pigou (1920) noted that, in common law, any agent who causes a nuisance is typically required to pay damages. He argued that, so long as the level of damages set by the courts was appropriate, the externality would be internalized and a socially optimal outcome would occur. If the law failed to prosecute those who caused the nuisance, or if the law was unduly costly as a mechanism, then he suggested that it might be preferable for the state to levy a tax (now termed a **Pigovian tax**) in order to realize the Pareto-efficient outcome. In the smoke examples above, and at its simplest, this involves imposing a tax τ per unit of the externality, smoke, levied on the generator of the

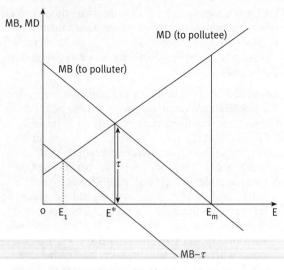

Fig. 27.3 Optimum externality (2)

smoke. The consequence of this is that the generator sees a net-of-tax marginal benefit curve $(MB-\tau)$ which falls to zero at the optimal level E^*, as in Figure 27.3. This Pigovian tax, τ, induces the polluter to restrict effluent to the optimal level E^*.

The idea that a tax would solve the externality problem seems quite appealing because it also accords with what some would consider to be environmental justice, namely the **Polluter-pays principle**.

(d) Regulation

A major problem with imposing such a tax is that it presumes the state has all the information necessary to determine what the level of the tax should be. That is, it needs to know the position of the marginal benefit and damage curves in order to know what tax level will induce the optimal level of externality. In such circumstances, a simple alternative to the Pigovian tax solution is to **regulate** the production of smoke. In the above situations, the smokers are given the right to produce smoke up to but not exceeding the level E^*.

27.3.5 Analysis of the Alternative Solutions

First consider the tax solution to realize the level E^* against the regulatory solution in which E^* is also attained. In the absence of transactions costs associated with implementing these interventionist strategies, the solutions are equally good. However, relative to doing nothing, there are clearly sub-

---

[10] For further discussion, see e.g. Jensen and Meckling (1995).

stantial costs involved in the implementation of either strategy. In order to regulate or to levy a tax per unit, it is first necessary to be able to measure the quantity of smoke produced, and to ensure that all emissions are in fact observed and measured (no clandestine dumping etc.). It further requires that transgressions (excessive discharges in the case of regulatory control, clandestine dumping in either case) be suitably punished. The policing and the legal processes usually required are far from costless. Thus it would appear that the choice between taxes and regulations turns on the relative transaction costs involved in their implementation. Interestingly, some types of regulation may be cheaper to monitor than others. For example, it is quite difficult to regulate such that some smoke is allowed. It is, however, relatively quite easy to police the regulation that no smoke is allowed. This observation probably accounts for the widespread existence of smokeless zones. The same point applies to parking; it is easier (less costly) to monitor and enforce a no-parking rule than one in which cars are allowed to park, but only for periods of one hour per day.

The optimal policy, according to this perspective, is the one that maximizes social benefits net of all the transaction costs involved in the implementation of policy. Consider Figure 27.2: the options discussed above are to do nothing, to impose the Pigovian tax to regulate to E^*, or to regulate to zero by imposing a total ban on emissions. In the simple setting described above, taxing to E^* is preferred to regulating to E^* if the costs of implementation are less (and vice versa). Suppose that the tax is more cost-efficient. There is still the question of whether the tax solution (result; E^*) is preferred to doing nothing (result: E_m), or an outright ban (result: $E = 0$). Denote the cost of implementing a total ban as C_{ban} and that of the implementing the Pigovian tax as C_{tax}. Which solution is preferable then depends on the relative magnitudes of the areas α_0 and α_2 in Figure 27.2 and the magnitudes of C_{ban} and C_{tax}. The options are shown in Table 27.2.

Figure 27.4 illustrates how the preferred solution depends on the relative magnitudes of α_0 and α_2 and C_{tax} and C_{ban}. For example, in the shaded region 'total ban', these costs are such that $W_{ban} > W_0$, W_{tax}, and so on. Depending on the relative magnitudes, any one of the solutions 0, E^*, or E_m can be optimal. Clearly, the higher the implementation costs are, the more likely it is that no intervention is worth while. Likewise, if intervention is worth

Table 27.2 Pigovian tax options

		Welfare level	Pollution level
1.	Do nothing	$W_m = \alpha_0 - \alpha_2$	E_m
2.	Impose outright ban	$W_{ban} = -C_{ban}$	0
3.	Impose Pigovan tax[11]	$W_{tax} = \alpha_0 - C_{tax}$	E^*

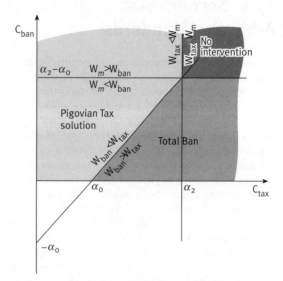

Fig. 27.4 Alternative solutions to the externality problem

while, the cheaper a particular form of intervention, the more likely it is to turn out to be optimal.

There has been much debate about Coase's contribution and also regarding the optimality of Pigovian taxes. For example, notice that, in Figure 27.3, after the Pigovian tax is imposed, there is still an incentive for the parties to get together to effect a bargaining solution. If they did, the outcome would not be E^*, but rather E_1, which is Pareto-inefficient. Usually, if there is no trade in the original position, then there is unlikely to be trade (to E_1) after the imposition of the tax. This is simply because the incentives to negotiate are now lower (as the reader can check by referring to Figure 27.3). However, it is also true that, in implementing a Pigovian tax, the

[11] The alternative, of regulating to E^*, gives net benefit $W_{reg} = \alpha_0 - C_{reg}$, where C_{reg} denotes the implementation cost of this form of regulation. Clearly this is preferred (in this naive analysis) to the tax solution if $C_{tax} > C_{reg}$. It is straightforward to replace the tax solution with this regulatory solution in what follows.

state interventionist needs to be fairly sure that the parties will not subsequently undertake any further bargaining (since this would tend to move the solution to the suboptimal point E_1). This amounts to being confident that transactions costs really do imply that no trade can take place.[12]

27.4 Second-Best and Arbitrary Standards

The focus in the above has been on optimum externality. Even in the absence of knowledge of what constitutes the optimum level, it may be clear that some reduction in the level of some type of pollution is socially desirable. This then raises the question of how a given level of pollution reduction might be best achieved. One option is to impose a per unit effluent tax. Firms then freely decide on how much pollution they want to produce and pay for. If there is then too much aggregate pollution, the tax can be increased—this will induce firms to cut their pollution outputs—and so in theory at least, it should be possible to adjust the tax iteratively to reach a situation where the target pollution level is reached.

Direct regulation of the quantity of pollution produced by individual firms is difficult to implement because of the difficulties of assessing what a fair level of abatement might be for each firm (clearly a contentious issue). One way of getting around this problem of setting individual firm abatement levels is through the issue and sale of tradeable pollution permits. For example, if a fixed number of permits is auctioned off, then those firms that derive most benefit from pollution will be able to outbid those which derive lower value. The fixed number of permits allocated then implies that the target quantity of pollution is realized

Tax and permit schemes have some attractive efficiency properties when there is a set of heterogeneous firms, since they offer the prospect of attaining a given target for the total level of pollution at minimum cost. However, space precludes further discussion of this kind of second-best control of pollution.[13]

27.5 The Role of the Property Market

It can be argued that the property market operates to minimize external effects, at least where they are local in character. Thus, consider the case of the smoky factory next to the laundry. If either firm relocates, the externality between them disappears. If laundries' production processes are adversely affected by a smoky environment, it makes sense for them to set up business in areas which are relatively smoke free. Indeed, ceteris paribus, they will be willing to pay a higher price for such premises (relative to the price paid next to smoky factories). As a consequence, laundries will tend to locate further away from smoky factories, and the externality is reduced and indeed may not be observed at all. Likewise (and again, ceteris paribus), a beekeeper will be willing to pay a higher price for a site close to an orchard—and the same holds true for orchard growers; they will be willing to pay more if they know that there are plenty of beekeepers in the neighbourhood.

Thus the property market will tend to maximize positive externalities and minimize negative ones. Agents with heterogeneous preferences are led by property prices to locate in particular geographic locations. A house located in a noisy environment will have a lower price because of that fact, but also, such a property will be relatively more attractive to someone who is less concerned about noise (a deaf person, for example). Thus we would expect smoky factories to tend to cluster in one place whilst laundries stay well clear.

Property prices will, of course, tend to reflect the value of the externalities that remain. The market tends to minimize negative external effects, but may not eliminate them. For example, the smoky factory and the laundry may need to locate close together if they have to serve the same community (and cannot make the sales without being in the proximity of that community). One interesting way of trying to value external effects involves looking at how property values vary as a function of the level of externality present. This form of analysis (hedonic pricing) is quite involved, as property prices reflect the whole bundle of characteristics on offer; in valuing one effect, there is a need to control for the impact of all the other determinants of site value.[14]

---

[12] See Buchanan and Stubblebine (1962) and Shibata (1972).

[13] See Baumol and Oates (1975) for the use of taxes in this context. For a more general review of instruments, implementation problems and the experience in using them (plus further bibliography), see Howe (1994) and Tietenberg (1994).

[14] A brief account of hedonic pricing is given in Pearce and Nash (1981).

27.6 Summary

Externalities (and public goods) are potential problems in which there is a Pareto-inefficient allocation of resources. Public goods tend to be under-provided. Externalities such as pollution (congestion, noise, etc.), in the absence of bargaining or merger solutions by the affected parties, tend to lead to overprovision, there being too much of these bads in the economy. This chapter explained the nature of the problem, and some of the possible approaches to solving it. It was noted that the property market tends to operate to minimize negative externalities (and to maximize positive ones), but that externalities were likely to remain. Of the ways of tackling persistent externality problems (such as smog and congestion), there is no single mechanism which is universally dominant. Alternative solutions may be appropriate, depending on the particular type of externality under consideration. This implies that a strategy for dealing with externalities (and public goods) needs to be conducted through cost–benefit analysis on a case-by-case basis.

27.7 Review Questions

1. List three producer–producer externalities and three producer–consumer externalities.

2. 'Consumer–consumer and consumer–producer externalities are of no great economic significance.' Is this correct? Discuss.

3. 'The externality problem is solved: all that is required is a clear initial assignment of property rights.' To what extent is this statement correct? Discuss.

4. 'The property market automatically deals with the problem of externality.' To what extent is this statement correct? Discuss.

27.8 Further Reading

Cornes and Sandler (1986) is an excellent text covering externalities, public goods, and club goods (goods you can enjoy when you join a club), whilst Ng (1979) remains one of the more interesting accounts at a fairly accessible level of the problems associated with externality and public goods. Cheung (1973) gives a beautiful account of (bilateral) externality in the context of a real-world example (bees and orchards) which emphasizes Coase's perspective (and the importance of transactions costs etc.). On the practical control of externalities, see e.g. Baumol and Oates (1975) or Fisher (1981).

28 State Intervention in Imperfectly Competitive Industries

Objective Monopoly power and anti-competitive practices are often cited as reasons for intervention. This chapter examines the case for intervention, and considers the pros and cons of the alternative policy instruments available.

Prerequisites Chapter 2 introduces the welfare criterion used here (see also Chapter 14 for more on monopoly welfare loss).

Keywords A–J effect, anti-competitive practice, concentration ratio, conduct, countervailing, power, dead-weight welfare loss, explicit collusion, free rider problem, Herfindahl index, implicit collusion, information asymmetry, Lerner index, monopoly welfare loss, nationalization, price cap, privatization, public provision, regulation, regulatory capture, regulatory uncertainty, RPI minus x, structure, tacit collusion, workable competition, X-inefficiency.

28.1 Introduction

Under certain restrictive assumptions, the market mechanism delivers a Pareto-optimal state of affairs (one in which no agent can be made better off without another being made worse off). However, the existence of externalities, public goods, and imperfect competition all indicate that there is some degree of Pareto suboptimality, and that there may be some merit in state intervention. Chapter 27 dealt with externalities and public goods, whilst this chapter deals with imperfect competition.[1] Dominant firms and oligopolies are far more prevalent than competitive markets, and equilibrium behaviour features prices above marginal costs, with an associated dead-weight welfare loss. The question then arises whether the state should (1) try to do something about mitigating this welfare loss associated with those firms who already have monopoly

power, and (2) try to prevent other firms getting such power (since it is the essence of corporate strategy to try to acquire such power).

The focus here is on the economic rationale for choices regarding the way big business is organized. Clearly, there are many other social and political considerations which may play a part. For example, state control may be justified on strategic grounds (for example, national defence; coal, steel, shipbuilding), or through concern for public safety (nuclear power). However, as this is a text in economic analysis, the focus here is on the specifically economic rationale behind the choice of alternative forms of industrial organization.

The relationship between structure, conduct, and performance (SCP, as introduced in Chapter 1, and discussed further in Chapter 13) is at the heart of the question of what is to be done about big business. The SCP paradigm suggests that the most appropriate way to organize the functioning of an industry is rooted in the technology of that industry. However, a crucial point to note about any industry which appears to be a natural monopoly is that such industries are rarely monolithic; they often have a variety of stages in the production process, and typically only some of these have natural monopoly charac-

---

[1] Individual consumers in theory have an incentive to bargain with the firm in order to realize the socially optimal outcome, a point which applies both to the problem of monopoly power and to externalities (see Chaps. 14 and 27). Unfortunately, bargaining, negotiating, and enforcing transaction costs typically rule out such solutions.

Table 28.1 Types of regulatory intervention

	Structure-focused intervention	Conduct-focused intervention
Policies dealing with existing monopoly power	Nationalization/privatization promotion of workable competition	Regulation of profit, rate of return or pricing. Restrictions on price discrimination, product bundling, tying etc.
Policies dealing with the prevention of the acquisition of monopoly power	Restrictions on mergers Restrictions on predatory pricing	Restrictions on advertizing, price discrimination, product bundling, tying etc.

teristics. Wherever elements feature approximately constant returns to scale, it is often possible to inject some degree of competition. By contrast, for those elements which feature economies of scale, competition is less likely to be an option. For such elements, the alternatives are either to publicly provide or to regulate (by placing controls or limits on pricing practices, and/or restrictions on allowable rates of return), although occasionally, a franchising scheme may prove workable (see section 28.3.2 below). Which of these options is preferable will often depend on the detailed structure of the industry. Intervention, either through direct operation of the industry or through regulation, is costly and involves agents who do not necessarily work selflessly for the good of society. For these reasons, non-intervention should also always be considered as a possible option.[2]

As illustrated in Table 28.1, intervention may be concerned with **structure** and/or with **conduct**. Structure concerns the number of players in the industry, whilst conduct concerns their behaviour (investment, marketing, pricing, advertizing, etc.). Thus, intervention on the structure side may take the form of direct alterations to the number of players involved. For example, the Bell telecommunications empire in the US was restructured as a set of independent 'baby Bells', and privatizations in the UK such as electricity, rail, etc. have also significantly increased the number of players involved. Merger policy is also concerned with market structure, in this case often with the object of preventing the industry becoming dominated by a small number of firms.

Intervention on the conduct side includes regula-

tion via prices and allowed rates of return. Firms may be restricted in the extent to which they are allowed to practise price discrimination, cross-subsidization, and predatory pricing. This can include fine-tuning restrictions, as when regulators get involved in the detailed structure of complex non-linear tariffs.[3] The aim, in restraining firms' conduct, is to reduce the monopoly welfare loss, although the focus on conduct can have a structural dimension (the prevention of predatory pricing, for example, may help protect a long-term competitive market structure).

Where monopoly power exists, the state has a variety of regulatory options available:

1. **Public provision.** The state runs the industry in the public interest, by setting prices, outputs, and investment so as to maximize economic welfare. In the absence of distortions elsewhere, this is often taken to mean setting prices equal to marginal costs.[4] The take-over by the state of previously private sector firms is termed **nationalization**. The opposite action, of returning public firms to the private sector, is termed **privatization**.[5]

2. **Regulation.** The firm is left in, or moved back into, the private sector, but its behaviour is restricted through state-imposed constraints on observable features of firm performance such as prices, profits, return on sales, and return on capital (possibly in addition to non-financial regulatory controls, such as controls on environmental pollution).

---

[2] The idea that regulation or intervention may not be desirable has already been discussed at some length in Chap. 27, and the arguments discussed there apply equally here. (If you have not read Chap. 27, it may be worth checking out the arguments for and against intervention discussed there.)

[3] See Chap. 19.

[4] See Chap. 22 for discussion of why marginal cost pricing may not be desirable in the presence of other distortions.

[5] Recent years have seen the extensive implementation of privatization programmes in many countries throughout the world. In some cases, these privatized industries have been allowed to operate without any form of external control or regulation, whilst in other cases, after privatization, the industry has been subject to some form of regulatory control.

3. Promotion of **workable competition**. The state alters the number of players in the game. Monopolies can sometimes be broken into smaller units which are then encouraged to compete against each other (either directly or through an artificial market[6]).

The benefits of intervention have to outweigh the likely costs if the intervention is to be worth while. If not, then no intervention is warranted, and the industry can be left to its own devices.

The above discussion has focused on the problem of existing monopoly power. Firms also try to acquire or create monopoly power by whatever means possible, and it is possible to limit this behaviour through policy pertaining to so-called **anti-competitive practices** (for example, through restricting the scope for mergers, predatory pricing and discriminatory pricing). Such policies are designed to reduce the ability of firms to acquire monopoly power in the first place.

Section 28.2 discusses the extent and measurement of monopoly power. Following this, section 28.3 deals with alternative policy options for dealing with monopoly power (including the policy of non-intervention) whilst section 28.4 looks at policy concerned with limiting firms' ability to acquire monopoly power.

28.2 Monopoly Power and Dead-Weight Welfare Loss

This section focuses on measures which may help to indicate whether or not monopoly power is likely to be a problem. Instinctively, a problem seems more likely if a small number of firms have a dominant market share. However, even a pure monopoly may not be so much of a problem if it is only just viable (as for example with UK railways) or if it is not abusing its dominant position. Hence, it is useful to consider first how it is possible to measure monopoly power (section 28.2.1). Section 28.2.2 then considers some qualifications regarding the likely magnitude of welfare loss due to monopoly power.

---

[6] Permits which allow a firm to produce a certain quantity of pollution can be issued or auctioned off. Thereafter, firms can trade such permits. Such permit markets can be shown to have various efficiency properties, if they can be made to function satisfactorily.

28.2.1 Simple Measures of Dead-Weight Welfare Loss

The static profit-maximizing model of the monopoly firm suggests there is a welfare loss which could be avoided if only the firm could be persuaded to set prices equal to marginal cost. For convenience, the standard diagram (presented in Chapter 2) is reproduced in Figure 28.1. With linear demand and marginal cost curves (and no fixed costs), the **dead-weight welfare loss**, *DWL*, is given as area *C*, and this is equal to 50% of the firm's profits (area *B*).

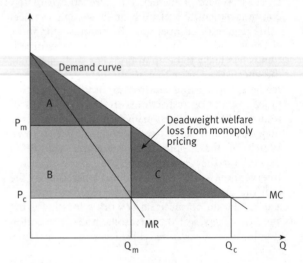

Fig. 28.1 Monopoly welfare loss

More generally, when the firm has economies of scale (including fixed costs), the relationship between observed profit and welfare loss is unreliable. However, it was shown in section 14.6 that, even in this case, if economies of scale occur outside the interval $[q_m, q_c]$ (so that marginal cost is constant on $[q_m, q_c]$), and if non-linearity in demand is also confined to output outside the region $[q_m, q_c]$, then the welfare loss is given by the formula

$$DWL = \tfrac{1}{2}R\left(\frac{p - MC}{p}\right) = -\tfrac{1}{2}\frac{R}{\eta}, \qquad (28.1)$$

where R denotes sales revenue and η is the elasticity of product demand. This result does depend on the assumption that the firm is setting a profit-maximizing price, in which circumstance the price–cost margin is given as

$$\left(\frac{p - MC}{p}\right) = -\left(\frac{1}{\eta}\right). \qquad (28.2)$$

Equation (28.1) suggests that DWL increases with the price–cost margin, $(p - MC)/p$, or with the degree of inelasticity of demand (note that $-1/\eta$ is larger the more inelastic the demand).

(a) Measuring Market Power via the Elasticity of Demand

Equation (28.1) suggests that the size of the monopoly welfare loss is positively related to the size of the price–cost margin, $(p - MC)/p$. This price–cost margin could be used directly as a measure of monopoly power, but the problem is that of measuring a firm's marginal cost. Typically, marginal cost information is not available outside the firm (and often not inside either). However, equations (28.1) and (28.2) also suggest using elasticity as an alternative measure of monopoly power and welfare loss. Indeed, this is the so called Lerner index of monopoly power:

Definition 28.1 The **Lerner index** of monopoly power is $-1/\eta$, where η is the elasticity of demand. The more inelastic the demand faced by the firm, the greater the monopoly power (Lerner 1934).

This makes intuitive sense; the more firms there are, the greater the competition they are likely to face and the more price-sensitive the individual firm's demand is likely to be. Thus in perfect competition, the firm's demand curve is infinitely elastic, so the Lerner index takes the value zero. At the other extreme, the elasticity can approach -1, so the Lerner index approaches 1 as a maximum value for a profit-maximizing firm.[7] It can go above unity, of course, if the firms in the industry are not pursuing profit-maximizing strategies. For example, the UK postal service is usually estimated to have an elasticity of somewhere between -0.1 and -0.3; its Lerner index is thus somewhere between 3 and 10.

Two important points to note regarding the Lerner index are

1. The relevant elasticity in the Lerner index is that facing the individual firm, not the market as a whole. The market elasticity can often be estimated, but the elasticity of demand at the firm level is more difficult to estimate and may tend to be less stable (it depends on other firms' behaviour, as well as that of the market as a whole).

2. There is no guarantee that the firm is exploiting its monopoly power; that is, a relatively inelastic demand could be associated with a relatively low price–cost margin. Equations (28.1) and (28.2) only hold if the firm is pursuing a profit-maximizing objective.

One case where it is reasonably straightforward to infer price–cost margins is where the firm practises price discrimination. So long as the cost of supply is the same to different market segments, the observed price in each segment can be used to infer the level of monopoly power. The point is that a profit-maximizing firm will never set price below marginal cost, so the price in the ith market segment will satisfy $p_i > MC$. Hence, once the lowest observed price has been identified (call it P_L), this can be used as a benchmark; if the price in some other segment is denoted p, the price–cost margin for that segment, $(p - MC)/p$, can then be assumed to be greater than $(p - P_L)/p$ (since $P_L > MC$). Table 28.2 gives some illustrative calculations for the automobile market.

Table 28.2 Examples of car price discrimination, 1991 (dealer price quotes)

Car model	Belgian pre-tax price (£)	UK pre-tax price (£)	Mark-up (%)	Implied elasticity
Audi 80E	10,017	11,273	11.14	−8.98
Citroen BX19GTi	8,305	10,133	18.04	−5.54
Rover 416GTi	9,153	12,004	23.75	−4.2105

Source: Locke *et al.* (1991).

The chief drawback to this type of calculation lies in the defence that costs are not the same across different market segments (see Lott and Roberts 1991 for examples).

(b) Measuring Market Power via Concentration

Section 16.3 showed that in an oligopoly in which firms have potentially different but constant marginal cost, the lower the average industry price–cost mark-up and aggregate profit, the lower the level of concentration in the industry. Concentration is typically measured either using concentration ratios or the Herfindahl index:

Definition 28.2 The m-firm **concentration ratio**, C_m, measures the share taken by the m firms with the largest shares in the industry (the share might be of sales revenue, profit, or employment). If s_i denotes the share of the ith

---

[7] Sect. 14.3 demonstrated that a monopolist always sets price such that demand is elastic.

firm, and there is a total of n firms in the industry, then $C_m = \sum_{i=1}^{m} s_i$.

C_4 is probably the most popular concentration ratio used in empirical work. Thus if, based on sales, $C_4 = 0.3$, this means that 30% of total industry sales are made by the top four companies. Table 28.3 gives some illustrative C_4 concentrations for different industries and countries.

Table 28.3 Some concentration ratios

Industry	C_4 concentration ratios (%)		
	UK	US	Japan
Salt	99.5	82	41.5
Flour	94	46	67
Sugar	38	27	48
Beer	59	81	99.9
Pet food	83	64	39

Source: Extracts from Sutton (1991: Table 4.3, p. 106).

Whilst concentration ratios do capture something of the dominance effect of big business, they are clearly rather crude; for example, if $C_5 = 0.5$, this could be because each of the top five has 10% of sales, or because the first has 46% and the other four 1%. The distribution within the top five may well make a difference to the effective degree of monopoly power within an industry, but it is not picked up by these types of measure. An alternative measure which takes account of *all* the firms in the industry is the Herfindahl index:

Definition 28.3 If s_i denotes the share (of sales, or some other measure of size, such as employment) of the ith firm, and there are n firms in the industry, then the **Herfindahl index** H of concentration is defined as $H = \sum_{i=1}^{n} s_i^2$.

The Herfindahl index takes a value between 0 and 1. Clearly with pure monopoly, $s_1 = 1$ and there are no other firms, and so $H = 1$. If all firms have an equal share and there are n of them, then

$$\sum_{i=1}^{n} (1/n)^2 = 1/n. \qquad (28.3)$$

Thus, the larger the number of similar sized firms, the smaller the index value; as $n \to \infty$, so $H \to 0$. Although the Herfindahl index takes account of all the firm shares, it is not a clearly superior measure; there are pros and cons with all measures of con-

centration (for an extended discussion of these, see Hannah and Kay 1977).

More firms usually means a more competitive industry. Cowling and Waterson (1976) show, in a simple Cournot oligopoly model, that industry profitability is positively related to industry concentration as measured by the Herfindahl index. The model is outlined in section 16.3. The basic assumption is that each firm has a constant marginal cost and no fixed cost (so average cost is equal to marginal cost), although each firm's marginal cost may be different. At the Cournot equilibrium,

$$\Pi = -(R/\eta)H, \qquad (28.4)$$

where Π, R, H, and η denote the aggregate industry profitability, aggregate industry revenues, market elasticity of demand, and Herfindahl index, respectively. What this Cournot equilibrium relationship tells us is that, ceteris paribus, industry profitability is positively correlated with industry concentration, as measured by H. Unfortunately such a simple mathematical relationship does not exist when firms have non-linear cost functions. The evidence is mixed in practice: although there is some evidence of a modest positive relationship between profitability and concentration in the US, in the UK the evidence is fairly mixed (see e.g. Clarke 1985).

It is important to note that increasing concentration may give rise to increased monopoly power, but also to increased efficiency (scale economies etc.); hence the welfare consequences of allowing mergers etc. are far from clear-cut (see section 28.5 below).

28.2.2 Other Factors Affecting Welfare Loss

Consider now the extent to which the one-period single-product analysis, which assumes profit-maximization, gives excessively high or low estimates of the likely welfare loss arising from monopoly power.

(a) Factors Reducing Welfare Loss

1. *Non-profit firm objectives* such as sales revenue or growth maximization suggest the firm will set prices below those of a profit maximizer. Lower prices imply less welfare loss.

2. *Market dynamics.* The higher prices earned by a monopolist can be ploughed back into improving production technology as well as new product research and development. Hence, relative to a competitive market, monopoly may in the long run foster better products with lower costs of produc-

tion. Both effects reduce the monopoly welfare loss when the benchmark is the competitive market.

3. *Economies of scale.* Under technological economies of scale, one single firm will have lower average costs than several smaller firms. This is a gain in welfare (a reduction in welfare loss) relative to a competitive market benchmark.

4. *The theory of contestable markets.* (see Chapter 14). Contestability theory suggests that, in an industry characterized by low sunk costs (so firms can enter or leave the industry at negligible cost—airlines are regarded as a good example[8]), the threat of potential entrants will keep prices close to average cost. For a critique of this argument, see section 14.4.3. Contestability is unlikely in practice to have a significant effect on an incumbent's choice of prices.

5. *Entry deterrence strategies.*

(*a*) *Excessive sunk costs.* Building excess capacity (a sunk cost) can be shown to help deter new entry; it also tends to lead to lower prices, which make better use of the capacity actually installed (see Dixit 1979).

(*b*) *Information asymmetries.* If there is uncertainty about the costs of production (and potential entrants have less knowledge than the incumbent) it can be shown that this may lead the incumbent to choose lower prices (see Milgrom and Roberts 1982*b*). The idea is that price can be used as a signal, and used in particular to signal that there is not much opportunity for profitable entry.

(b) Factors Increasing Welfare Loss

1. *X-inefficiency* (Leibenstein 1966). Monopoly, it is said, does not face the discipline of having to compete in the market place. The absence of competitive pressure reduces the drive toward production efficiency, and this may lead to higher costs and hence even higher prices. These types of behaviour pattern are discussed in some detail in Chapter 17.

2. *Countervailing power.* Galbraith (1952) suggested that there is a tendency, when there exists market power on one side of the market, for countervailing market power to develop on the other side. In particular, it can be argued that there are greater incentives to unionize within monopoly sectors of industry. Firms with monopoly power are thus likely

to face greater wage pressure, since there is generally less concern that the firm will incur financial distress or bankruptcy.

3. *Rent-seeking behaviour.* Posner (1975) suggested that, where there are supernormal profits, individuals have an incentive to expend resources trying first to find and then to protect such profit. According to the rent-seeking argument, it is worth spending resources on trying to acquire (or protect) monopoly power up to the point where the costs incurred are just equal to the expected increase in (present value of) profit obtained. In the extreme case, one could argue that the observed monopoly profit is merely an index of all the transaction and rent-seeking costs that have been incurred to acquire that monopoly position. The usual argument is illustrated in Figure 28.1: welfare under competition is equal to areas $A + B + C$, whilst under monopoly, it is just $A + B$ (consumer surplus plus firm profit). The welfare loss is thus simply area C. According to the rent-seeking argument, under monopoly, net social benefits are simply area A (consumer surplus); area B (profit) has an exactly offsetting (but unobserved) set of rent-seeking costs which have been previously incurred to acquire it. Thus, relative to the competitive paradigm, the welfare loss is really area $B + C$; that is, the sum of the usual welfare loss triangle plus the firm's profits. For the whole of the area B to count as a welfare loss, the 'industry' of rent-seeking needs to be fully competitive. Otherwise, firms or individuals involved in rent-seeking will get some value out of it (profit or consumer surplus), and this will in effect be simply a transfer.[9] However, whilst taking all of $B + C$ as the measure of welfare loss is perhaps an exaggeration, the idea behind rent-seeking contains an essential kernel of truth—and the consequence is that it increases the estimate of welfare loss relative to the competitive benchmark.

The above discussion suggests that the issue of welfare loss is far from clear-cut, although it is usually argued that, where there are substantial economies of scale (possibly including significant fixed costs), some form of regulatory action may be desirable.

---

[8] Because there is a reasonably efficient second-hand market for aeroplanes, the principal assets involved in setting up an airline.

[9] Recall (Chap. 2) that if I give you £1, economic welfare is unchanged; I am worse off and you are better off, but the sum over the whole of society is unaffected (£1 − £1 = £0). Distributional transfers do not affect the index of economic welfare used in this text.

28.3 Dealing with Existing Monopoly Power

This section gives a brief run-through of the pros and cons of different forms of intervention.

28.3.1 Non-Intervention

Non-intervention is the benchmark from which all the following policies are examined. The idea is that intervention is worth while if the benefits outweigh the implementation costs. Non-intervention is likely to be optimal if the unregulated private sector monopoly is unable to exploit its position significantly, either because of the threat of entry or the lack of product demand—or if, although the monopoly does have monopoly power, the profits are being ploughed back into R&D and new product innovation (so reducing future costs by more than would be possible if profitability was constrained).

28.3.2 Promoting Competition

(a) Competition for the Market

Demsetz (1968) suggested that, at least for some cases, franchise bidding might be used to circumvent the natural monopoly problem. The idea is that firms can be made to compete for the right to supply. The firm that offers the best deal (the lowest price with satisfactory quality) is offered the contract. Obviously the contract has to include a promise to set a particular price and deliver a satisfactory quality. In principle, if there is enough competition in the bidding process, the result will be a price close to average cost (which is better than the monopoly price, although still typically in excess of marginal cost). Naturally, there are many problems with getting the process working satisfactorily, and there may be problems with enforcement of the contract. However, where it is possible, it does seem to offer some benefits in keeping prices down. The approach has been used in TV franchising (US cable TV and UK independent TV franchises). However, it occurs at a more informal level for each and every household. Whenever you ask for quotes for some repair work (car, buildings, etc.), you are in effect getting around the problem of natural monopoly

(since it would rarely be optimal to have more than two suppliers of the service).[10]

(b) Creating a Competitive Market

It was suggested in section 28.1 that if an element of a monopoly business features approximately constant returns to scale, then it may be possible to create competition in that element. Privatization may be used, in some circumstances, to promote workable competition. For example, in electricity, it is possible to retain the national grid, but to have many generating companies competing with each other to supply electricity to the grid. This has proved a fairly effective form of competitive market. In general, the idea is that competition promotes more efficiency, lower costs, and, for given costs, lower prices (prices more in line with marginal costs). Unfortunately, there is often a trade-off in that, in order to create competition, it may be necessary to sacrifice some economies of scale. Furthermore, this solution is only applicable where economies of scale are largely absent.

28.3.3 Public Provision

This involves taking the industry into the public sector (nationalization), and then the operating of this industry in the public interest (taken here to mean maximizing the sum of consumer surplus plus profits).

(a) Advantages

Prices, investment in capacity, outputs, etc. can all be chosen in order to maximize social welfare. There are, of course, difficulties in implementation, primarily because of the problem of second-best (namely, there are distortions elsewhere in the economic system, and this means it is difficult to be sure what policy is for the best; see Chapter 22).

(b) Disadvantages

Public sector firms do not face the discipline of the market; since they can have their debts underwritten by the state, they will never go bankrupt. It can also be argued that there is a lower likelihood of management being disciplined for poor performance, at least in part because it is more difficult to judge what constitutes poor performance when a firm is not aiming to maximize profit. In the private sector,

---

[10] One of the problems associated with making bidding schemes work is that offering quotes is not a costless business.

monopolies are at risk of take-over if they are not run in a profit-maximizing and hence cost-efficient manner (although it is easy to exaggerate the extent to which this imposes a discipline on the behaviour of such firms). The general consequence is that such firms may be more likely to manifest **X-inefficiency** and be even less cost-efficient in the public than in the private sector. Similarly, **countervailing power** could easily be a greater problem here.

Many industries in the UK were brought into the public sector after the Second World War (including health, education, posts, telecoms, electricity, gas, coal, and railways). It was the continuing poor performance of many of these that stimulated the massive privatizations that occurred in the eighties and nineties. The jury is still out on how successful these have been.

28.3.4 Regulation

This involves leaving the firm in the private sector (or moving it there under a privatization programme) but monitoring and regulating its performance. Regulation necessarily focuses on observable statistics associated with the firm's performance (it is not possible to control what cannot be observed). Although the objective might be that of maximizing welfare, the regulator's job in practice seems to be that of trying to control profitability. Since it is difficult to judge whether the absolute level of profit is too large or too small, it is normal to focus on the firm's rate of return, its profitability expressed as a ratio to some measure of the firm's assets (usually what is termed 'book capital', an accounting valuation of the firm's assets). Whilst this may be the real target, there has been much debate amongst both academics and practitioners as to whether profitability is better restrained by a direct constraint on the rate of return, or by a restriction on prices (the so-called price cap). In what follows, I briefly discuss the characteristics of (1) a direct profit constraint, (2) a rate of return constraint, and (3) a price cap.

(a) Firm Behaviour Under a Profit Constraint

This takes the form

$$\pi \le \bar{\pi},$$

where $\bar{\pi}$ is some stated maximum allowable profit level. Such a constraint could have disastrous consequences for welfare if the firm is a profit maximizer. Essentially, with profit fixed, any way of achieving it is just as good as any other. This means that there is no incentive for the firm to be cost-efficient—and it gives a real incentive for managers to spend on managerial perquisites, secure in the knowledge that they can still set a price to attain the target profit level. For these reasons, direct profit constraints are never used.

(b) Firm Behaviour Under a Rate of Return Constraint

The common regulatory practice (particularly in the US) of setting a target rate of return on capital can be shown to give a firm concerned with maximizing profit an incentive to be cost-inefficient and to over-capitalize. The constraint takes the form

$$\pi/K \le s,$$

where K is some measure of capital employed, and s is the target rate of return which must not be exceeded. For any given value for K, reducing s would appear to be a method of restraining a firm's profitability. Unfortunately, once s is fixed, there is an incentive for the profit-maximizing firm to increase K in order to achieve a higher level of profit. It therefore has an incentive to over-capitalize, to 'pad the rate base' (the accounting value of K) and generally to operate with too high a level of capital intensity (and too little labour) relative to cost-efficient production. This is termed the **A–J effect** (after the seminal article by Averch and Johnson 1962). From a welfare perspective (and also an employment-creation perspective), the distortion is undesirable (although the overall effect of this type of regulation may be preferable to no regulation at all).

(c) Firm Behaviour Under a Price Cap

The **price cap** was really only first given serious attention following the work of Stephen Littlechild (see e.g. Beesley and Littlechild 1989 for a review). In the UK, it got started with the rule that the firm's price rise is limited to **RPI minus X**, where *RPI* denotes the percentage rate at which the retail price index is rising and *X* is a figure based on the regulator's view as to what technical progress was likely to offer in the way of a rate of cost reduction over time. In real terms, it meant that price was falling at the percentage rate *X*. With a single product, the constraint for a single point in time can be written simply as

$$p_t \le \bar{p}_t,$$

where $\overline{p}_t$ is the price that the firm must not exceed.[11]

The point about this form of constraint is that it appeared to avoid the inefficiencies associated with the rate of return constraint. That is, the firm still has an incentive to be cost-efficient, and to introduce cost-reducing innovation (since these all increase the difference between price and cost, they increase profitability).

The price cap is more complex to operate when there are multiple products; usually this involves defining a price index of the firm's products.[12] There is also the question of what is to be done about new products—how these are captured by the price cap (if at all). Finally, whilst the original plan was to set an *RPI* minus *X* and to leave it for several years, the experience in the UK has been that, if utilities then earn 'too high a rate of return', there is tremendous political pressure on regulators to tighten the regime. If increased profit (say from innovation) leads to a tightening price cap, this can adversely affect the firm's incentive to innovate. If the regulator really has a rate of return in mind as acceptable, such that he/she tightens the price cap to achieve this rate of return, then the rational firm will again have an incentive to over-capitalize (the A–J effect reappears), again with cost inefficiency. There is some evidence that firms are in fact refocusing on the rate of return, despite this not being the explicit regulatory constraint (see e.g. Neri and Bernard 1994).

(d) General Comments on Regulation

It can be seen that regulation may help to control profitability, but there are drawbacks. Here are a few others to consider.

1. Regulation involves standard-setting, monitoring, and enforcement, and all these activities are costly. It is also true that regulation is a bureaucratic activity; it confers power on regulators, and this sets up a variety of incentives for the individuals involved in the regulatory game. Effort is expended by the firms in trying to dupe the regulators and to sidestep the regulation. Given all the costs (along with often unintended outcomes of regulatory processes), it is only likely to be worth setting up a regulatory agency where the welfare gains are thought likely to be substantial.

2. The regulatory game involves **information asymmetry**; since the state does not run the firm, the state does not have full information on how well or badly the firm is performing. Only certain partial indicators of performance are available (accounting profitability, return on book capital, rates of change in prices, etc.). As can be seen above, regulatory constraints (targets) on any particular empirically observable aspect of a firm's performance with the aim of improving welfare will usually tend to distort the firm's behaviour, often with other undesirable effects. Furthermore, in debating how tight the constraints should be set, the asymmetry of information[13] means the firm has an incentive to understate what it can in fact achieve; it can get away with this to some extent because much of the information available to the regulator is available only from the firm itself.

3. **Regulatory uncertainty** may be induced by difficulties in predicting how tight the target will be. Such uncertainty can deter firms from undertaking cost-reducing investments (since it is uncertain how much of the cost savings they will be allowed to keep).

4. **Regulatory capture** is the idea that firms may be able to enter into implicit contracts (such that the regulator gets a job, or seat a on the board, etc. of the company when his/her time as regulator is up). The deal here is that the regulator, whilst in office, does not press down so hard on the firm. This potential for backhanders is an intrinsic problem in all forms of centralized control, planning, and bureaucracy.[14]

5. **Free rider problems** arise in trying to establish transstate or transnational regulatory agreements.

---

[11] In *RPI* − *X* form, the upper limit is then adjusted each year, such that

$$\overline{p}_t = \overline{p}_0 \left(1 + \frac{RPI}{100} - \frac{X}{100} \right).$$

[12] Capping individual products is too clumsy if the firm has a large number of products. The problem with a price index becomes one of choosing weights. The firm will also have scope to fiddle about with the pricing of individual items within the bundle, i.e. to practise price discrimination so the weights need to be chosen carefully.

[13] The regulator knows less about the potential for cost reduction, efficiency gain, product innovation, etc. than the firm itself.

[14] Thus economists no longer take it for granted that lawyers and regulators necessarily pursue the public interest. They are viewed as pursuing their own private objectives (which of course might include a moral and social dimension); there is no guarantee that such officials will automatically pursue the public interest—even if they comprehend what that is supposed to be. Martin (1989: chap. 18) provides a useful introductory discussion of the various issues involved.

One of the great difficulties facing governments who wish to regulate is the fact that the market is now much more international, and so is production. It is often inappropriate to focus on the local (or national) market when judging the state of competition in an industry. Furthermore, many of the firms which compete in local or national markets are world players. The problem for individual countries is that if they impose a tighter regulatory regime than exists elsewhere in the world, this simply encourages production to move to another country. This is true whether the regulation is financial (rate of return or price cap constraints) or environmental (emissions control etc.), and whether it applies to product markets (safety requirements etc.) or factor markets (minimum wage legislation). Following the Maastricht treaty, the UK 'benefited' from an opt-out from the European Community's social chapter (which imposes stricter controls on working hours and minimum pay, etc.) because such a country is viewed by multi-national companies as more attractive for inward investment. Lower wages may not be immediately attractive to workers, but they have the consequence of increasing the demand for labour (there are more jobs to be had). Similarly, if a country unilaterally imposes tighter environmental regulations on its companies (as has recently occurred for certain types of chemical product in the UK) this will in the longer run tend to induce such companies to move their production to countries where environmental controls are less tight. This of course is one reason (cheap labour being another) why countries such as China are so attractive for inward investment.[15]

28.4 Dealing with Anti-Competitive Practices

This section discusses primarily the economic problems associated with deciding whether an interventionist policy is beneficial, and the problems associated with identifying whether observed behaviour qualifies as an anti-competitive practice. It does not deal in any detail with the various laws, acts, and

bodies charged with implementing such policy. For details of the institutional background in Europe and America, see e.g. Martin (1994).[16]

28.4.1 Merger Policy

Chapter 31 discusses various types of integration (vertical, lateral, horizontal, etc.) and gives examples. Essentially merger often increases concentration, although conglomerate mergers may not do so. Merger will, however, usually increase monopoly power in some way or other; either through reducing the number of competitors in the market, or by increasing the scope for tying or bundling of products (see Chapter 20). Apparently then, merger seems likely to reduce economic welfare. However, this view forgets that merger also frequently reduces costs. First, competitive firms often have to engage in advertizing which is largely mutually self-cancelling; merger can reduce the need for this. Likewise, other marketing costs, the costs of reducing excess capacity, and especially, savings in R&D budgets (because of the avoidance of replication of research effort) can be substantial. Hence there is a trade-off (see e.g. Williamson 1968 for a formal model, and Cowling and Mueller 1978, 1981 and Littlechild 1981 for a debate regarding welfare measurement in such circumstances).

US policy has tended to be anti-merger on principle, whilst UK policy has always been one of judging a case by its merits. In the UK, mergers are typically assessed (after being referred to the Monopolies and Mergers Commission) to see whether or not they are likely to be in the public interest. The consideration is typically one of balancing the extent to which the merger leads to a significant increase in concentration[17] against the likely cost savings that such mergers might induce.

---

[15] Paradoxically, unilateral tightening of a regulatory regime on global emissions (such as sulphur, CO_2, etc.) can actually be counter-productive, as multi-nationals switch production to those countries which are more environmentally lax (where even dirtier technologies are permissible).

[16] For example, each of the newly privatized industries has a watchdog; thus the UK has OFFER (the office for the regulation of the electricity industry), OFWAT (the office for the regulation of the water industry), OFTEL (the office for the regulation of telecommunications), and so on. Further UK regulatory bodies include the Monopolies and Mergers Commission, the Restrictive Practices Court, and the Office of Fair Trading. Then there is possible intervention from DGIV (the directorate-general of the European Commission), and even the European Court of Justice.

[17] Merger proposals in the accounting sector, at the time of writing, would reduce the top 6 accounting firms to just 3 world players.

28.4.2 Policy/Detection of Collusion

Collusion may be explicit or implicit:

Definition 28.4 Explicit collusion involves a legally enforceable contract between the parties involved. **Implicit** or **tacit collusion** by contrast, involves an informal agreement; as there is no contract, tacit collusion cannot be legally enforced.

In both the US and Europe, both explicit and tacit collusion are deemed to be illegal.[18] Explicit collusion is in principle more straightforward to detect, since the agreements are underpinned by legal documents. By and large this form of collusion is never attempted, so the problem really concerns how best to detect tacit collusion.

First, there is the question of where to look. The modern view of collusion, or coalition formation, focuses on the benefits of joining vis-à-vis staying outside. Basically, it can be shown that the benefits of remaining outside the collusive coalition increase with the size of the coalition, so that large-number coalitions are less likely to be observed than small-number ones. In Selten's (1973) model, the probability of finding a coalition is 1 if there are four or fewer firms in the industry. With six or more firms in the industry, the probability of finding a cartel is less than 1%. Thus, in this model, four is few and six is many. The point to draw from this discussion is that it makes sense to focus attention on those industries which have a relatively small number of dominant players.

The problem then is what to look for. In a competitive market, firms have to charge pretty much the same price for their product in order to remain competitive. In such a market, it is observed that if one firm reduces price, other firms will tend to follow. If all firms face changes in the economic environment, their prices will tend to move together. Such a correlation in prices is also observed in markets where firms collude. Thus, in the price leadership model, when one firm changes price, pretty soon the others follow. It would thus appear that simply observing a correlation in prices, or price movements, tells us nothing; it neither predicts

collusion nor competition, as these theories are observationally equivalent.[19]

Thus the argument is that there is no simple test of tacit collusion, other than through studying the market outcomes: if an industry displays a supernormal profit rate, then this may be indicative of collusive practices.

Unfortunately, there is again an asymmetry of information between the regulators and the firms; the firms have a better idea of their costs and also the demand they face. Regulators can only get many of the numbers (particularly cost figures) from the firms they are trying to attack or control. Phlips and Harstad (1994), for example, argue that it is straightforward for firms to massage or report profit figures which will support their arguments in any attempt to test market outcomes for supernormal profits (i.e. profit levels above those which would arise out of a Cournot–Nash oligopolistic equilibrium).

28.4.3 Policy/Detection of Price Discrimination

Chapters 18 and 19 reviewed the practice and welfare consequences of price discrimination. The general insight there was that price discrimination does not necessarily decrease economic welfare, although it may often do so. In general, the principle enshrined in statutes is that prices are allowed to deviate only if the underlying costs of supply deviate. Of course, it can make a big difference whether 'cost of supply' is interpreted as short-run marginal cost, average variable cost, or full cost (especially since firms often have considerable discretion as to how the measure of full cost is arrived at). Even given a precise definition of cost here, it is still difficult for outsiders to test whether or not a firm is practising price discrimination.

Lott and Roberts (1991) suggest that attributing price differentials to monopoly power (and hence treating them as an abuse of a dominant or monopoly position) is too easy. They argue that in many cases it is possible to show that there are unrecognized cost (or opportunity cost) rationales for many

---

[18] US anti-trust legislation includes the Sherman Act 1890, the Clayton Act 1914, and the FTC (Federal Trade Commission) Act 1914; these are concerned with prevention of anti-competitive behaviour of various kinds. Likewise, the Treaty of Rome 1957 aimed at creating a level playing field in Europe (not that it achieved much).

[19] One might argue that the observation of cheating or chiselling is more a manifestation of collusive practices than of competitive markets, but even chiselling is a feature of competitive markets. And the non-existence of cheating is likewise consistent with all firms being equally efficient and market price being equal to marginal cost throughout the industry (see Phlips 1996).

observed price differentials.[20] They give a variety of examples, from petrol prices to the high prices for drinks, or lower prices for lunchtime meals, in restaurants. For instance, they argue that low prices for lunchtime meals makes sense because lunchers are under more time pressure and usually complete their meal quicker, so tying up the table for less time. The same applies to wine and coffee; people who partake of these tie up the table for longer, as they linger over their meal (and there are also inventory costs associated with wines etc.). Thus it is quite difficult to pin a price discrimination charge on a monopolist, given the asymmetry of cost information (that is, the firm knows better than the regulator what the true costs are).

28.4.4 Policy/Detection of Predatory Pricing

Predatory pricing can be viewed as the setting of low prices, so sustaining losses in the short run, in order to drive out competition. Once the competition has been expelled, higher prices can be set and higher profits earned.[21] Predatory pricing can be practised by a single-product monopolist in selective sub-markets (as in the case of Standard Oil; see below). However, predatory pricing is much more usually practised by a multi-product monopolist. In both cases, the idea is that profits elsewhere can be used to fund losses incurred in predatory pricing.

McGee (1958) claimed that predatory pricing is something that should be rare and unimportant (and hence not something that particularly needs to be regulated). He argued that, given the initial state of competition, the predator would be better off simply buying up the firms (whose values are depressed by the fact that there is competition in the market), and would then immediately enjoy the monopoly return from higher prices. With predatory pricing, the firm only gets the higher prices after a possibly significant period of time (and time is money), and must incur losses during this period. Hence take-overs are preferable to predatory pricing.

It would seem to follow that predatory pricing only becomes a possible problem if the state imposes restrictions on allowable take-overs. That is, anti-merger policy brings with it the need to be watchful

for predatory pricing. However, there are other reasons why firms may choose to undertake predatory pricing, for example because of asymmetric information or simply irrational behaviour (either might lead a privately owned firm not to sell at a reasonable price) or because of reputation-building by the predator in order to deter any future would-be entrants (see e.g. Kreps and Wilson 1982).

The standard test that has come to be used widely in the US courts (and in Europe) is that

(i) any price below average variable cost or short-run marginal cost is predatory;

(ii) any price above total cost is definitely not predatory;

(iii) a price between these levels may or may not be—and the court then uses other information to decide whether the intent was predatory or not.[22]

This test is probably popular[23] because it appears simple to apply. It probably is fairly simple in the case of a single-product firm. The test is much more difficult to apply in the case of a multi-product firm, simply because such a firm does not run deficits, and often there is a large gap between what the firm can claim is average variable cost, and what it can claim as average total cost. This is because there is usually considerable scope for manipulating the allocation of joint costs between products. Thus, in most practical cases, it is likely that (iii) applies—there is no clear-cut answer.

28.5 Summary

This chapter reviewed the economic arguments for and against alternative ways of dealing with the problem of natural monopoly and the attendant dead-weight monopoly welfare loss. No solution is universally dominant, and it would appear that the optimal organizational arrangement for a given industry can only be determined by a careful weighing of the various factors involved on a case-by-case basis. However, certain general principles were noted:

---

[20] This view is 'pure Chicago School'; if prices diverge, the Chicago view is that, assuming competition, it must be because there are real cost differentials which underpin them.

[21] The classic example is that of Standard Oil, which systematically drove out local competition by such aggressive pricing strategies. See *Standard Oil of New Jersey* v. *US*, 221 US 1 (1911).

[22] Such as entry conditions, or whether there is a reasonable explanation, for example a promotional campaign to introduce a new product etc.

[23] The paper by Areeda and Turner (1975) seems to have set the ball rolling.

(i) Monopolies can often be partitioned into aspects which do, and aspects which do not, feature significant economies of scale.

(ii) Where economies of scale are largely absent, it is often possible, and may be socially desirable, to set up a competitive structure (breaking up the organization into many competing units). In setting up a competitive market, it is desirable to have a reasonable number of players, with no player having a dominant share.

(iii) Where there are substantial economies of scale, the monopoly should probably be retained intact; if it is run in the private sector, then it may be desirable to regulate. The precise form which regulation takes then depends on individual circumstances.

28.6 Review Questions

1. 'In the absence of transactions costs, there is no monopoly problem.' Discuss. (See Chapter 27 for background material on the importance of transactions costs for bargaining solutions.)

2. One of the major problems associated with the return-on-capital constraint is the A–J effect. Explain the A–J effect and examine the extent to which price caps are a better method of regulating a private sector monopoly.

3. The privatization of the UK rail system has met with considerable difficulty. On the face of it, train operators probably operate under fairly constant returns to scale (a train is a train is a train), whilst it is the track which constitutes the natural monopoly element in the business. Hence, it seems logical to privatize so as to create a reasonably large number of competing operators. Is it possible to explain the problems experienced by the UK rail industry using the arguments presented in this chapter?

4. Examine the pros and cons of regulating the profitability of private sector firms.

28.7 Further Reading

Vickers and Yarrow (1988) gives a useful review of all the issues involved in the privatization versus nationalization debate. Martin (1993, 1994) gives a good account of the economics underpinning regulation—measurement of welfare loss, concentration etc.—and an account of the legislative frameworks underpinning regulatory practice in the UK and US. Waterson (1988) is a fairly short and readable text on economic theories of regulation. Phlips (1988: chap. 7, 1996) discusses policy against anti-competitive practices.

Part VII

Organizational Architecture

Part VII addresses the internal organization of the firm, something that, in Parts I–VI, has been taken pretty much as a 'black box'. In fact it remains the case that most managerial, business, and micro-economics texts do not discuss the firm's internal organizational structure. However, managerial economics is supposed to be concerned with decision problems of the firm, and fairly clearly the problem of how the firm should best organize itself, and indeed, what it should try to undertake itself as opposed to how much it should buy in, are questions which have a significant (and arguably, predominantly) economic dimension. Part VII thus addresses questions such as 'what organizational structure should a firm choose?', 'how should jobs be structured?', 'what sort of decision authority, incentives, and rewards, etc. should be attached to them?', and so on. Chapter 29 begins with a review of the key economic ideas that prove helpful in this context (transactions cost, information, and agency theory). Chapter 30 then addresses the issue of the design of organizational architecture, whilst Chapter 31 follows this with a further consideration of pros and cons of centralization/decentralization and of co-ordination through internal markets (through transfer prices), along with related issues such as what to make and what to outsource. Finally, Chapter 32 examines in more detail the economics of human resources, with a particular focus on employee recruitment, motivation, and retention.

29 Transactions, Information, and Agency

Objective To examine the key elements of economic theory which can be utilized in the analysis of organizations, namely transactions cost theory, the economics of information, and in particular agency theory, the economics of principal and agent.

Prerequisites Section 17.2 gives an overview of the idea that a firm's boundaries are determined by transactions and agency cost considerations (in conjunction with traditional ideas, such as the quest for monopoly rents and the resolution of externality problems).

Keywords adverse selection, agency costs, agency theory, asset specifity, exogeneity, game theory, hidden action, hidden information, implicit contract, incomplete contract, information economics, moral hazard, nexus of contracts, pre- and post-contract opportunism, relational contract, reputation effect, transaction, transactions cost, transactions cost theory.

29.1 Introduction

Organizational architecture comprises the structure of hierarchy, teams, and jobs, and the structure of decision authority, monitoring, and incentives. The term 'architecture' is apposite, because it suggests that the whole edifice can be designed and built from the foundations upwards, and that the result may be more or less functionally efficient as a result. This chapter looks at the principal economic ideas that can prove useful in the design process:

(i) **Transactions cost theory.** This focuses on the costs associated with undertaking transactions in different ways. Depending on the nature of the economic business at hand, this might entail trading on spot markets, long-term contracts with external suppliers, or the internalization of the transaction within the organization of the firm.

(ii) **Game theory.** Inter-firm and intra-firm transactions typically involve the strategic interaction of relatively small numbers of agents. It follows that game theory can provide a theoretical background, a general methodology, for the study of behaviour in organizations.

(iii) **Information economics.** This focuses on the existence of asymmetric and imperfect information and the scope this gives for agents within markets and firms to practise opportunistic behaviour ('lying and cheating' to get ahead), and on the consequences of such behaviour for the efficiency of markets and organizations.

(iv) **Agency theory.** This focuses on the information flows and incentives in vertical relationships where the individuals concerned do not necessarily manifest goal congruence (subordinates may pursue their own rather than their bosses' interests). The key feature of the agency problem is that the principal can only partially observe the agent's effort or behaviour. The 'agency problem' is seen as one of designing monitoring and incentive structures that encourage the agent to act more in line with the interests of the principal.[1]

---

[1] One might also add evolutionary economics: there has been a long tradition in economics that, in competitive markets, only the efficient will survive. On this view, only the best ideas will survive and come to be adopted throughout the industry. This suggests that the prevalent organizational architectures arise because they are more efficient than the available alternatives. The problem is then taken to be that of understanding why they are more efficient. The relevance of the evolutionary viewpoint clearly depends on the strength of the competitive process in weeding out the weak. For many markets, there is considerable doubt that such pressures are significant.

The above ideas overlap considerably. Game-theoretic ideas permeate the whole of agency theory and the economics of information generally, whilst transactions cost theory is often widened to include all the costs associated with agency, information imperfection and asymmetry, etc. However, not-withstanding the overlapping nature of the ideas, the rest of this chapter is concerned with identifying what is distinctive about each of strands (i), (iii), and (iv) (game theory has already been treated in some detail in Chapter 5).

The outcome of this analysis is a tool kit of ideas which can be utilized throughout the rest of Part VII; these ideas are used extensively in thinking about the design of organizational architecture (Chapter 30), the extent of integration, decentralization, and internal pricing (Chapter 31) and human resource management (Chapter 32).

29.2 Transactions Cost Theory

Section 17.2 introduced the basic elements of transactions cost theory. Coase's (1937) insight was that transactions, whether internal or arm's length (market transactions), involve contracting costs, and that the choice of

(1) trading on spot markets,

(2) long-term contracts, or

(3) internalizing the transaction within the firm

should be made depending on which of these was likely to minimize the transactions costs involved.

Definition 29.1 A **transaction** is simply an exchange of goods, services, or rights (to do certain things etc.).

In what follows, I first describe the key characteristics of a transaction (section 29.2.1), and follow this by identifying different types of transaction cost (29.2.2), and the idea of transaction cost minimization (29.2.3). Finally, section 29.2.4 discusses how transactions cost minimization has to be balanced against other factors (notably economies of scale) in considering whether or not to outsource (and if so, how).

29.2.1 Key Characteristics of a Transaction

1. *Frequency.* Some transactions occur only rarely (buying and selling houses, cars, etc.) whilst others are frequent transactions (food stores replenishing

their stocks, particularly of perishable items). If transactions are infrequent, they are usually provided for by spot markets, underpinned by community-wide common contract design (the customer having certain statutory rights). However, if transactions are frequent, then it can pay to set up special mechanisms and to trade with a single supplier (so that handling, billing, etc. can be streamlined and customized, and the associated transactions costs reduced). There is also less need for (costly) recourse to the law when things go wrong with a transaction if the transaction is conducted within a long-term supply relationship; informal arrangements can usually resolve such problems. The higher the frequency, therefore, the more likely it is that the transaction will be either a long-term contract with a particular supplier, or internalized within the firm.

2. *Timeliness/reliability.* The question here is of how precisely co-ordinated transactions have to be. If the transaction forms part of a JIT (just-in-time) system, timeliness and reliability may be crucial. By contrast, if supply is into inventory then timeliness may be less important.[2] The extent to which a transaction interconnects or needs to be co-ordinated with other transactions tends to influence the need for timeliness. If timeliness is important, there is a preference for long-term contracting rather than spot markets (because the ongoing relationship with a long-term supplier allows interaction and the building of trust between the partners to the transaction), although, when timeliness and reliability are crucial, it is commonly preferable to integrate and draw the transaction into the organization, where it is then under direct control. Internalizing the transaction in this way avoids the (costly) need to write or enforce complex contracts (which specify the punishments for a lack of timeliness/reliability).

3. *Complexity.* This occurs when the transaction involves a significant degree of private information (one party knows more than others about some aspects of the transaction). This often arises when there is a difficulty in measuring quantity or quality. If some characteristics of the transaction are difficult to measure, then the supplying party will have an incentive to indulge in post-contract **opportunism**,

---

[2] Holding inventory is costly, of course. In addition, buyers will, ceteris paribus, prefer a more reliable supply even if they do hold inventory, as reliability reduces the optimal inventory holding level, and hence associated inventory costs.

to 'economize' on these elements. This kind of problem often occurs in construction projects. Once a contract has been signed, there is an incentive to shirk on unobservable quality elements. For example, unless carefully monitored, a motorway contractor might skimp on the amount of hard-core foundation materials used in laying track; the consequence of such behaviour only becomes discernible many years later. If the transactions are complex but frequent, with a relatively short period of time before true quality is revealed, then long-term contracting may be satisfactory. If true quality takes some time to be revealed, and transactions are also relatively infrequent, then integration may be the preferred option.[3]

4. *Asset specificity*. Often an outside supplier is only able to supply inputs to an adequate quality specification if it makes buyer-specific investment. Theoretically, this is not a problem if the investment has zero sunk cost (if there are efficient second-hand markets for the equipment, and there are no significant transactions costs associated with reselling). However, in practice, most investment in plant and machinery involves a significant positive sunk cost, in that future resale involves the firm losing considerable value. With positive sunk cost, suppliers are only likely to be prepared to make the buyer-specific investment if the buyer offers a long-term contract which guarantees the supplier can get an adequate return on the investment. However, even long-term contracting may not solve the problem. The point is that, once the supplier has sunk the investment, this gives the buyer a stronger bargaining position, and an incentive to try to renegotiate more favourable terms. Thus, specific assets and private information suggest that external supply may be problematic and that, as a consequence, it may be more likely that the input will not be outsourced, but produced internally.

It is possible to categorize several types of asset specificity: (see Williamson [1975])

(a) *Site or locational specificity*: where the process etc. has to be located in proximity to other processes or has to be customized to the site (rolling mills next to blast furnaces; bridges, dams, tunnels, etc. in specific locations—clearly sunk costs once they are installed).

(b) *Type specificity*: plant and machinery that can only be used for producing an input for a particular firm, with no alternative use.

(c) *Human asset specificity*: individuals may have special skills or specific knowledge which is not easily transferable.

EXAMPLE 29.1 In the 1920s, General Motors and Fisher Body were separate firms; GM wanted Fisher Body to invest in a new and effectively dedicated plant adjacent to one of GM's assembly plants; (contiguity would significantly improve efficiency, by cutting transport time and cost and the need for inventory etc.). Fisher Body refused (naturally, as they were concerned about ex post opportunism once the investment had been sunk, for example by being asked to subsequently reduce prices). The 'solution' in due course was that GM bought Fisher Body to form a single company. See Brickley *et al.* (1995: 56).

29.2.2 Transactions Costs

Section 29.2.1 described the characteristics of a transaction and indicated that the choice of transaction format (spot market, long-term contract, or internal transaction) was likely to depend on transactions costs which arise because of these characteristics. The nature of these transactions costs is now discussed in more detail. Contracts involve a specification of the various conditions of exchange (prices, quantities, time and place, etc.) and the rights of the parties on either side of the transaction. Coase (1937), in the early development of transactions cost economics, focused in particular on the costs of developing an explicit contract.

(a) 'Coasian' Transactions Costs

1. *Search and information acquisition costs*. There are search and information acquisition costs in both markets and organizations:

(a) *In markets*, buyers need to search for best prices, check availability and quality, etc. Sellers have to decide on what prices to set (and so need to monitor competitors, do market research, invest in advertizing the product, etc.).

(b) *In organizations*, information has to be gathered at lower levels in the hierarchy and passed upward for the boss to make the decisions; this involves administrative effort. The boss then needs to take time to understand this

---

[3] The consequence of private information of the type discussed here is examined in more detail in sects. 29.3 and 29.4 below.

information and to formulate an overall plan based on this information. Following this, the plan has to be disseminated down through the hierarchy to those who are charged with implementation.

2. *Bargaining and negotiating costs*: the costs of getting the relevant parties together to negotiate, plus the time and effort required to get agreement. (Bargaining can often be long and protracted—consider the process of wage bargaining between management and union.)

3. *Contracting costs*: costs associated with the formal drawing-up of legal documents describing the agreement. These costs are incurred with the drawing-up of a new contract, but often there are also additional costs when a contract is terminated (for example, consider buying and selling a house; you have to pay the solicitor when you buy, and you pay again when you sell).

4. *Policing and enforcing costs*. For example, a polluting firm may have entered into an agreement to reduce its level of pollution. However, post-contract, the firm still has an incentive to dump effluent clandestinely. Hence there is a need for some form of monitoring (which is costly). Any verified transgression of the agreement then requires some form of action—further negotiations and/or legal action. All of these are costly.

(b) Agency-Based Transactions Costs

The concept of a transactions cost has more recently been widened from Coase's initial conception, to include many of what can be termed 'agency' or 'motivation' costs.

1. *Hidden information*. When parties to a transaction have private information, they can withhold the information, or misrepresent it (second-hand car sales, for example); this pre-contract opportunistic behaviour can lead to transaction inefficiency (mutually beneficial transactions may even fail to take place; this is discussed in more detail in section 29.3 below).

2. *Hidden action*. When the actions of one (or more) of the parties to a transaction are not fully observable, there is scope for post-contract opportunistic behaviour, again with the result that outcomes may be inefficient (see sections 29.3 and especially 29.4 below).

The overall consequence of such activity is transaction inefficiency. However, I shall generally refer to the above motivation costs as 'agency costs', and stick to the Coasian definition of the term 'transactions cost'; that is, costs directly associated with transactions.

29.2.3 Transaction Cost Minimization

The general idea behind transaction cost theory is that, taking the technology of production as given, the organization should be structured so as to minimize transactions costs. The argument is that market transactions (whether spot or long-term contract) may be attractive in some circumstances, but firms exist in order to reduce transactions costs by (1) reducing the number of transactions and (2) reducing the overall cost per transaction, as explained below.

(a) Cost Minimization by reducing the Number of Transactions Involved

All the Coasian transaction costs increase with the number of parties concerned. This provides a rationale for the existence of the firm; the point is that the firm is a **nexus of contracts**, a legal entity which enters into bilateral contracts with many different parties (suppliers, workers, customers, etc.). In the absence of the firm, there would either have to be complex multi-party contracts (in which case it might be difficult to get all the parties together to develop and negotiate the contract etc.) or a proliferation of bilateral contracts, as the following example illustrates.

EXAMPLE 29.2 Suppose a firm employs m differently skilled workers to produce and sell product to n customers. The firm would need to enter into $m+n$ bilateral contracts. In the absence of the firm, each customer would have to enter into m contracts (with the m workers) in order to get her product. The total number of contracts would then be mn. For example, with $m = 10$ and $n = 12$ the firm enters into 22 contracts; without the firm, the need is for 120 contracts.

(b) Cost Minimization by Allowing Implicit or Incomplete Contracting

The firm internalizes transactions, and as a consequence, can often reduce the associated costs involved in having to draw up, monitor, and enforce explicit contracts, as would be required if all production and distribution was done through markets. Although the firm enters into some explicit contracts such as employment contracts, it also enters into many which are either informal or incompletely specified. The point is that, for many transactions, it is difficult to write a complete contract which specifies the outcome under every eventuality, as illustrated in following example.

EXAMPLE 29.3 When a university offers a prospective student a place on a course, a complete contract would have to specify the cash flow or other consequences for all possible eventualities, such as: if all the best staff were suddenly head-hunted by another institution, so the status or quality of delivery of the course was adversely affected; if a member of staff left suddenly, and a course could not run; variations in the price of university campus accommodation, or meals; and any variations in sporting facilities.

Clearly, complete contracts are straightforward to write only in a very restricted set of circumstances. Thus most actual contracts are incomplete; not all consequences are spelled out. This makes them easier to write, but less easy to enforce. Most contracts within the firm are of this type; some things are set out formally, other things are not. (For example, employment contracts often spell out what kinds of behaviour are not acceptable—such as sexual or racial harassment, absence without leave, etc.—but can be quite vague on other elements, such as what constitutes grounds for promotion). Such contracts are often referred to as **relational contracts** (to emphasize the long-term collaborative nature of such contracts).

Explicit contracts are written contracts, whether complete or incomplete. For many of the transactions taking place within an organization, there is no written explicit contract; however, there is still an unwritten or implicit contract.[4] Explicit contracts are costly to write, monitor, and enforce; with implicit contracts, many of these costs are reduced (although there is still a need for monitoring and control—some transactions costs still exist).

EXAMPLE 29.4 (Implicit contracts.) There is an implicit contract between a superior and her subordinates in many organizations that 'good work'

[4] Of course, what is termed an implicit contract can often be thought of as part of what is omitted in some incomplete but explicit contract.

by a subordinate gives prospects of future promotion etc. There is no explicit contract, no clear definition of what counts as 'good enough', and no guarantee that promotion will result.

Implicit contracts are difficult to enforce, of course (try complaining about not getting that promotion). However, there are processes which help to enforce implicit contracts. In particular, **reputation effects** are important to underpinning and giving value to implicit contracts. A firm may honour an implicit contract for an individual as a motivating signal to others that it honours such implicit contracts. Implicit contracts are also likely to work even though there is some incentive for short-term opportunistic behaviour, so long as the short-term cheating does not give too high a return relative to the long-run returns available through sticking with the contract. If the short-term cheating incentive is high, then there is an incentive to increase the level of monitoring and control of the transaction.

It should be noted that incomplete contracting is not confined to intra-firm transactions. Long-term inter-firm contracts are also often incomplete (for exactly the same reasons as for intra-firm transactions). The point is that in a long-term relationship, an incomplete contract can still work because the parties involved have some leverage over each other. That is, having become used to working with each other, there are costs in terminating the relationship and beginning trade with a new partner, so the situation is one of bilateral monopoly. It follows that there is an incentive to resolve their bilateral difficulties by negotiation rather than through recourse to (usually more costly) external legal processes.

29.2.4 Caveats on Transactions Cost Theory

Coase (1937) argued that we observe exchange at arm's length on spot markets, or through long-term contracts, or within an organizational structure, depending on which method has lower transaction costs. This makes some sense, but Coasian transactions costs are only part of the story. There are other important factors to consider, as follows.

(a) Economies of Scale

The above discussion clearly assumes that the cost of transactions is something which is separable from the production technology and processes involved. This is a major weakness, because it ignores the fact that drawing a transaction inside the firm may throw away the economies of scale that may be had when the input is provided by an external supplier. The point is that the volume of an input required within the firm may be simply too small for the firm to produce the input internally in a cost-effective way.

EXAMPLE 29.5 Electricity, water, gas, etc. are inputs typically externally sourced by most firms. The point is that the minimum efficient scale in electricity generation, for example, is large relative to the amount typically required by most firms. The external supplier is able to gain these economies of scale by supplying many individual customers.

Thus transactions cost analysis is only one input into deciding on the best way to organize production. Consideration has to be given to the nature of the technology involved.

(b) Competitiveness of the External Market

The nature of the external markets in which the firm has to purchase the input will also influence the chance that internal production is economically attractive. If the external market is reasonably competitive, then the price at which the input can be got will be reasonably close to production cost. By contrast, if the market is imperfectly competitive, then price may be (significantly) above cost, and this increases the chance that internal production will be economic.

(c) Interdependencies between Transactions and Technology

Transactions and technology are often interdependent. Thus, the choice of a just-in-time technology may influence the type of contract used with suppliers (and indeed whether there is integration), but the efficiency of the latter form of contracting may influence whether it is worth moving to the new process technology in the first place. Given the technology, it is meaningful to ask how best to organize production. But then one has to step back and ask which arrangement is best overall.

29.2.5 Implications of Transaction Cost Theory

Basically, we would expect simple transactions, in the presence of competitive external markets, to be supplied via spot markets by external suppliers. As complexity, frequency, and asset specificity increase, ceteris paribus, there is a greater preference for long-term contracting or vertical integration. Integration will tend to be preferred if there are few economies of scale in the production of intermediate product or service, whilst if there are significant economies of scale, then one would expect long-term contracts with external suppliers to be preferred. Some of these influences are illustrated in Figure 29.1.[5]

The choice of transaction format theoretically requires a cost–benefit analysis in which the various types of transaction cost are quantified, along with an assessment of the level of internal production cost (if the input is taken in-house) and external price (if outsourced). However, it should be clear that quantification is often quite difficult for some types of transaction cost. Often the best that can be done is a fairly crude qualitative judgement about the relative magnitude of such costs (this is bigger than that). Indeed, transaction cost analysis may reveal no obviously dominant or superior organizational arrangement (in which case, the choice presumably becomes more a matter of taste, temperament, whim, or prejudice).

29.3 Information Economics

A useful way to start thinking about the nature of information is to consider the following variants on the game of poker, involving the dealing of five cards to each player.[6] For each game, after the deal, the players can bet on their holdings as in the usual game of poker.

1. *The Certainty Game.* The cards are all dealt face up, so everyone can see each player's holding.

2. *The Imperfect Information Game.* Three cards are dealt face up and two are dealt face down to each player.

3. *The Imperfect and Asymmetric Information Game.* Three cards are dealt face up and two face down. Each player is allowed to look at his own face-down cards.

---

[5] It is difficult to represent fully all the influences in a diagram of this type; for example, Fig. 29.1 ignores factors such as external market competitiveness, as well as other aspects of transactions, such as frequency.

[6] This pedagogical device is quite popular in the literature; see Milgrom and Roberts (1987), Phlips (1988), and Douma and Schreuder (1991).

Low economies of scale case		Asset specificity	
		Low	High
Transaction	Low	SPOT	VI (or perhaps LTC)
complexity	High	VI (or perhaps LTC)	VI

High economies of scale case		Asset specificity	
		Low	High
Transaction	Low	SPOT	LTC
complexity	High	LTC	LTC

LTC: Long term contract   SPOT: Spot market   VI: Vertical integration

Fig. 29.1 Transactional determinants

For the sake of clarity and simplicity, in each case, unlike poker, there is no opportunity to discard any of one's orginal cards and draw replacements.

In the first game, one would expect little betting to take place; the best hand should be obvious to all parties, so if there is a stake required prior to the deal, the player with the best hand simply wins these stakes. In the second game, each player is faced with imperfect but symmetric information; all players can see exactly the same cards. Some players may be better at weighing the odds of how the unseen cards might add value to those already revealed, and so there is a little more scope for skill (and thus betting becomes more likely). By contrast, the third game features imperfect and asymmetric information. Each player has private information in that she knows more about her own hand than she does about the others. Imperfect and asymmetric information creates much scope for strategic play; over the course of many hands, players can study the behaviour characteristics of the opponents in order to gain clues as to their current card holdings. In such a game, there is clearly much scope for bluffing and misleading signals through the use of both body language and betting behaviour. Real poker, which allows discards and replacements, is clearly an even more complex game.

Although some transactions in markets and organizations may feature full information, many more feature a degree of asymmetric and imperfect information, and this makes for potential inefficiency. In what follows, I discuss in turn the consequences of two forms of asymmetry, namely **hidden information** (where the party on one side of the transaction knows more about some aspect of the transaction) and **hidden action** (where the action of one party is not fully observable by the other party).

29.3.1 Hidden Information

Hidden information occurs when one party to a transaction has more information than the other parties about some **exogenous** facts relevant to the transaction. For example, I may try to take out life insurance, knowing I have a terminal illness, or I may try to sell you a second-hand car, knowing that it is a synthesis of two write-offs (where the car has the front end of one and the rear of another, welded together). At the point of entering into a contract, I know something the other party does not about some exogenous fact.[7] This gives an incentive for **pre-contract opportunism**, which induces what is termed **adverse selection**; such a problem can arise both in markets and in organizations, as follows.

(a) In Markets

The term 'adverse selection' originated as a problem manifest in insurance markets. The insurance industry offers insurance against a huge variety of risks. For any one of these, the insurer typically has limited information on the individuals being insured. For example, in medical insurance, individuals typically know more about their medical condition than the insurer. This means they have a better idea than the

---

[7] The idea is that I may have private information about some thing, but I cannot manipulate that thing; the hidden action case discussed below pertains to circumstances in which manipulation is possible. It is of course possible to have exogenously generated asymmetric information which arises after the contract is entered into. For example, in a contract for building some structure, the builder may discover after having signed the contract that there are foundation problems associated with the structure. At this point the builder has more information than the other party. Behaviour in such circumstances is likely to depend heavily on the details of the contract already signed (see Hart and Holmstrom 1987).

insurer as to whether the insurance represents a good deal or not. As a consequence insurers will tend to end up insuring only those who are a bad risk; this is termed adverse selection. In what follows I set up a (highly) stylized illustration of this type of effect.

Suppose the cost of some type of operation (heart by-pass, say) is a constant, c, and that an insurer has data on the size of the population, N, and the total number of operations per annum, n. If the whole population was insured, the average probability of an individual making a claim in a given year would thus be $\Pr_{ave} = n/N$. Now, suppose insurance is offered which pays for the cost of the operation. If everyone insured, the average pay-off would be $\Pr_{ave} \times c$, so an annual premium equal to $\Pr_{ave} \times c$ would allow the insurer to break even. However, this presumes that all individuals take up the insurance. What would happen if an insurer actually offered such insurance? For simplicity, suppose that all individuals are risk-neutral and that they have more information regarding their health than the insurer; let us suppose that the ith individual knows the probability, denoted $\Pr_i$, of needing the operation (by assumption, the insurer only knows the average risk in the population, $\Pr_{ave}$). Thus the individual's expected pay-off from buying insurance is $\Pr_i \times c$. It follows that individual i chooses to take out insurance only if the expected pay off exceeds the premium: that is, only if

$$\Pr_i \times c > \Pr_{ave} \times c \Rightarrow \Pr_i > \Pr_{ave}. \quad (29.1)$$

Thus only those with risk greater than the average in the population would choose to insure. Those with below-average risk would prefer to pay for the operation if and when it was required, without the benefit of insurance. From the perspective of the insurer, this is an adverse selection effect.

Unfortunately, if only those with above-average risk insure, the insurer makes a loss. To illustrate, suppose the risk distribution is that depicted in Figure 29.2. This assumes that the risk in the popu-

lation ranges from 0 through to a maximum of $2\Pr_{ave}$ and has a uniform distribution. For such a simple distribution, a premium equal to $\Pr_{ave} \times c$ leads to all those with risk less than $\Pr_{ave}$ remaining uninsured. Clearly, the average risk of those who do insure is higher, equal to $3\Pr_{ave}/2$. Thus for these individuals, the average cost of offering the insurance is $(3\Pr_{ave}/2) \times c$. However, yet again, if the insurer raises the premium to cover this, even more will choose not to insure. Thus an individual who has an expected pay-off of $\Pr_i \times c$ will only pay a premium of $(3\Pr_{ave}/2) \times c$ if there is a net benefit from doing so; that is, if

$$\Pr_i \times c > (3\Pr_{ave}/2) \times c \Rightarrow \Pr_i > (3\Pr_{ave}/2),$$
$$(29.2)$$

and so 75% of the population chooses not to insure. The average risk of those who do insure rises to $7\Pr_{ave}/4$. And so it goes. The end consequence, in this simple model, is that the insurer is forced to increase the premium to the point where no one wishes to insure.

In practice, individuals are (differentially) risk-averse, and may not precisely know their own level of risk (and the distribution of risk will not be uniform either). However, such complications do not alter the fact that there will still be some degree of adverse selection whenever the insurer is unable to distinguish the risk of different individuals; the insurer will always tend to end up with a clientele of higher-risk individuals (the ones who think they can exploit the insurance). The term 'adverse selection' is a description of the fact that the insurer gets an adversely unrepresentative selection of individuals choosing to buy insurance. However, the reason for the adverse selection is the fact that there is hidden information; the problem is that the insurer knows less than the individual about what that individual's risk level really is. This type of asymmetric and hidden information occurs in many types of markets, especially those where there

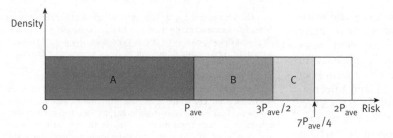

Fig. 29.2 Adverse selection

is some difficulty in discerning the true quality of the good—as with the market for second-hand cars, as discussed in a seminal article by Akerlof (1970).

(b) In Organizations

Information asymmetries can also lead to adverse selection problems within organizations. For example, consider the case of employees seeking jobs elsewhere within an organization; their bosses may know how good or bad they have been in their existing jobs, but they also have an incentive to hold back such information when writing a reference. That is, they have the incentive to extol poor-quality workers (to get rid of them) and to be grudging in their praise of genuinely good employees. This is not to argue that all references are dishonest; it merely points out that there are incentives for untruthful reporting which may influence outcomes. Notice that adverse selection here means that both parties lose out. The reference writer has an incentive to misreport the truth—but this means that the reference reader, recognizing this fact, will not trust the information contained in the reference. Signals simply cannot be trusted, and this reduces trading efficiency.

(c) Attempts to Reduce the Impact of Hidden Information

1. *By market segmentation.* Past evidence of claim behaviour in the population can be studied in order to discern whether there is a correlation with the characteristics of the individuals seeking insurance. For example, car insurance premiums vary not only with the value of the car, but the area in which it is used, the age and sex of the driver, and the number of years without a claim having been made. These observable individual characteristics allow the insurance company to discriminate price so as to align the premium being paid more closely with the risk level.[8]

2. *Through self-selection.* It is sometimes possible to offer individuals a menu of alternative insurance contracts. Individuals then self-select the contract they prefer, and in doing so, at least partially reveal their type. Thus, in car insurance, it is possible to select the level of cover: to opt for fully comprehensive or third-party only, and if comprehensive, to choose whether one pays nothing or the first £50, £100, £200, etc. of any future claim, and so on. The idea is that the seller can improve on setting a fixed fee by designing a non-uniform tariff (and the above range of options at different prices amounts to this). This is discussed in more detail in Chapter 19.

3. *By increasing monitoring.* Extending the level of knowledge the insurer has regarding each individual's characteristics can help to reduce the extent of private information. For example, in health insurance, a medical examination may be required, along with details regarding the state of health of other members of the family. Likewise, used-car dealers can offer refund guarantees to deal with the case where the car purchased turns out to be a lemon etc. Clearly, contract design of this type can help to reduce the asymmetry of information.

4. *By forced risk pooling.* For example, health care is state-provided in many countries; this means that everyone in the population has to 'pay the premium' whether they like it or not (through state taxes). Such a solution clearly avoids adverse selection because it forces everyone to 'insure'.[9]

5. *By internalizing transactions.* It can be argued that depending on the nature of the hidden information, the transaction will sometimes be better handled by the market and sometimes within the organization. For example, second-hand car sales cannot be meaningfully internalized (except within the family) but where internalization can be effected, there is a greater prospect that hidden information will be divulged. The inefficiencies associated with bilateral trading under asymmetric and imperfect information can often be reduced by integration and internal trading (although agency problems may still persist).

29.3.2 Hidden Action (Moral Hazard)

'Hidden action' refers to the idea that, having entered a contract, one party is unable fully to observe the behaviour of the other party; this in turn suggests that the party who cannot be fully observed may have an incentive for what is termed post-contract opportunism.[10] For example, in the good old days when lecturers were offered a post

---

[8] If there is imperfect competition in the insurance business, insurers will also be able to practice price discrimination by varying the mark-up over and above that 'justified' by the correlation of characteristics with observed risk (see Chap. 18).

[9] It also involves cross-subsidization; low-risk and high tax-rate individuals effectively cross-subsidize high-risk and low tax-rate individuals.

[10] Recall that hidden information usually gives an incentive for pre-contract opportunism.

'with tenure', having got such a job, some individuals might choose to put their feet up and simply enjoy the long vacations.

(a) In Markets

Consider the action of insuring your house or car against the theft of personal belongings. In the absence of insurance, there is an incentive to try to prevent burglaries or car thefts; this incentive typically translates into expenditure on detection systems, vigilance, neighbourhood watch schemes, etc. However, theory suggests that once insured, the individual is less concerned about theft, because the value can be recovered. Admittedly, the insurance does not usually cover the trauma and disruption during the time it takes to repurchase items, and of course some items are of sentimental value and in a sense irreplaceable. Nevertheless, the general point remains; insurance reduces the incentive to prevent crime. The insurer is unable to monitor whether or not you are maintaining your vigilance against crime at its pre-insurance level. This is where the term 'moral hazard' originates from: failing to prevent crime may not seem so immoral, but the incentive can extend to immoral behaviour—individuals have some incentive to claim for losses that have not been incurred, or indeed, having over-insured, actually to cause the damage themselves.[11]

EXAMPLE 29.6 Newcastle city centre has seen several fashion stores gutted by fire; a cynic would remark that this is a neat way of getting rid of old and outmoded stock. Boats famously sink in areas where it is sufficiently deep to make it difficult for insurers to check the veracity of the claim. Lord Brocket was jailed in 1998 for fraudulently hiding four of his classic cars and then making a claim against the insurers for £4.5 million.

(b) In Organizations

Hidden action is also pervasive within firms. In particular, the productivity of workers (consider coal miners, sales reps, managers, etc.) is often the product of a range of factors including efficiency and effort. Again there is a problem of hidden action; to what extent is the observed productivity a consequence of sloth or inefficiency, and to what extent is it due to factors beyond the control of the worker? The problem is that a manager cannot observe fully and completely the effort and efficiency of her subordinates. This gives subordinates the scope to pursue their own objectives rather than those of their superiors. With full information, there would be no such scope. It can be argued that the central problem within organizations is the problem of how to deal with hidden action.

(c) Attempts to Reduce the Impact of Hidden Action

1. Monitoring can be extended to try to directly enforce behaviour which is in the interests of the organization as a whole.

2. Monitoring and incentive pay may be used to align the individual's interests with those of the organization as a whole (see section 29.4).

3. Monitoring can be extended over time and across organizations. Such trans-organizational sharing of data can often reveal fraudulent individual behaviour (over-frequent claims, excessive claims, or indeed multiple claims for the same items; because claims can be made against a range of insurers, such behaviour can only be detected if insurers share information—which is, of course, why they do).

29.3.3 Comparing Hidden Information and Hidden Action

Hidden information and hidden action both turn on agents being able to conceal private information from others. Hidden information which gives rise to adverse selection is pre-contract; one party (at least) has pre-contractual information concerning some exogenous variable which is not available to the other parties to the transaction. It may pertain to past behaviour (e.g. past smoking habits, in the case of obtaining health insurance), but it is usually a characteristic of the agent prior to the transaction. Most importantly, it is exogenous; that is, it cannot be manipulated by the individual. All the individual can do is either report the truth about the exogenous variable, or tell a lie about it. By contrast, hidden action is post-contract; it pertains to unobservable behaviour of one of the agents or groups of agent, once the transaction is under way.

---

[11] Indeed, there is plenty of evidence that it actually induces a further type of crime; first, when theft occurs, there is an incentive to exaggerate the extent of the true loss. Secondly, there is an incentive to fabricate crimes; one merely claims to have lost a ring or piece of jewellery; many a yacht or sailing vessel has disappeared when it suited the owner; many a high street shop owner has 'suffered' an 'unexpected' fire which clears away all the clutter of unsold fashion lines.

29.4. Agency Theory

Agency theory, or the theory of principal and agent, takes individuals as creative, but selfish, utility maximizers. It recognizes that in hierarchical relationships, bosses ('principals') are only able to partially observe the behaviour and productivity of their subordinates ('agents'), and so face the moral hazard or hidden action problem. Agency theory focuses on the design of incentives which motivate such agents to act more in the interest of their bosses.

One of the most common types of agency problem arises when an individual's output depends not only on her own effort but also on other factors, some of which may be measurable, but some of which are not.

EXAMPLE 29.7 *Factors in principle measurable*: ambient temperature (may affect ice cream or beer sales), rainfall (may affect crop growth), machine down-time (unexpected breakdown), etc. *Factors often not easily measurable*: Often the most significant is that other agents' unobservable effort levels may affect the productivity of the agent in question. For example, the double glazing installer depends heavily on the accuracy of the individuals who make the initial measurements and then those who produce the units. If the windows don't fit, there is a lot more work to be done. There are also many inputs for which quality may be difficult to measure (for example, fuels such as coal or peat may have a variable calorific value); quality variations in inputs can make a job easier or harder to complete.

Often the boss is able to measure the output actually produced, but is unable to measure the effort the agent puts in, or many of the other factors which may influence the final output. The boss is thus unable to identify how much of the output is due to the agent's own effort and how much to other unmeasured factors.[12]

Consider what happens if the boss sets a flat salary for the agent. An effort-averse agent will then rationally exert no effort at all, with adverse consequences for the principal. Relating pay positively to output

will motivate the agent to exert more effort, but there are problems—such pay schemes can lead to windfall gains and losses arising out of fluctuations in non-effort-related output-influencing variables. In such circumstances, incentive pay means risky pay, and risk-averse agents, ceteris paribus, need to be paid more to compensate them for the risk. However, overall, there are usually gains to be had from offering agents an appropriate level of incentive pay, as illustrated in sections 29.4.1 and 29.4.2.

29.4.1 Honesty versus Greed

The following example is a typical textbook exposition of the value of incentive pay. Spiv Cars employs staff who are responsible for the preparation of used cars for sale and also for the sale of those cars. Staff are utility maximizers motivated by pay and by honesty. Staff can sell more cars by being dishonest (talking up the qualities of the cars, clocking the speedometer, undertaking cheap resprays to camouflage body rot, etc.) but, ceteris paribus, being dishonest lowers their utility level. Thus they are only prepared to be dishonest if there is a financial compensation. Honesty is indexed by the number of cars a salesperson can sell; if perfectly honest, she sells only 5 cars a week, and if perfectly dishonest, she is able to sell 10 cars.

Now, Mr Spiv currently offers a flat wage of w_0 and he gets 5 cars a week out of each member of staff. Staff are happy to work for him at this wage—but no lower. In Figure 29.3, this means that each employee has a reservation utility level $\bar{U}$. If their conditions of work offer them less than this utility level, they seek alternative employment. Spiv can introduce incentive pay; suppose he offers to pay sales staff a wage

$$W(N) = \alpha_0 + \alpha_1 N, \qquad (29.3)$$

where W is the total wage per week, N the number of cars sold, and α_0 and α_1 are positive constants; clearly, α_0 represents the individual's base wage and α_1 the incentive pay (per car sold). If $\alpha_0 < 0$, in effect the salesperson has to pay a 'franchise fee' for the privilege of selling cars. The wage received varies with the number of cars sold if $\alpha_1 > 0$.

Any wage schedule $W(N)$ which is tangential to the reservation-utility indifference curve will be acceptable to the salesperson. For example, if we set $\alpha_0 = 0$ and $\alpha_1 = w_1/7$, we get the wage schedule $W(N) = (w_1/7)N$, indicated as the 'Lower-commission incentive pay' schedule in Figure 29.3.

---

[12] There is a clear incentive to measure as many of these other factors as possible, so long as measurement is fairly low in cost, as this allows the boss better to identify the agent's contribution; this is the so-called informativeness principle, discussed in more detail in sect. 30.2.5. In practice, many variables that are in principle measurable are not.

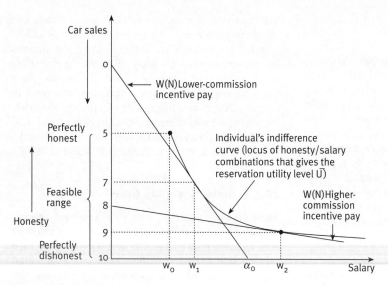

Fig. 29.3 Incentives and honesty

The salesperson chooses (by being sufficiently dishonest) to sell 7 cars. The 'Higher-commission incentive pay' schedule gives a wage of w_2 on sales of 9, but zero on sales of 8 or less. This corresponds to the wage schedule $W(N) = w_2(N - 8)$ for $N \geqslant 8$ (and zero for sales of less than 8). The incentive rate is clearly greater here; that is, in Figure 29.3, w_2 is much greater than $w_1/7$. A higher incentive per car sold induces more dishonesty, and hence more cars sold in total. Clearly, the overall pay to the salesperson is higher at the higher rate of commission. The increase in overall pay just compensates for the increased dishonesty, so as to maintain the salesperson at the reservation utility level. Offering the agent higher incentive pay may be attractive to the owner if it brings in a greater profit (net of payments to the salesperson).

The next question is that of optimally adjusting the magnitude of the base salary vis-à-vis the incentive pay element. Offering a lower base rate, but a higher incentive rate, induces greater output, but incurs greater cost. This suggests that the owner has to balance the extra profit contribution gained against the extra cost incurred; as usual, we would expect the usual marginal condition to apply; that is, α_0 and α_1 are adjusted to the point where the net return to the owner just flattens off. This is the fundamental idea behind the principal–agent problem; the owner recognizes that agents are motivated by incentives, and has to choose an incentive scheme which motivates them to work in such a way

that it maximizes his own profits. The computation of such a solution requires analytic form for the utility function etc. The type of analysis involved is discussed in more detail in section 29.4.2, where a slightly more realistic model is set up in analytic form.

EXAMPLE 29.8 In the UK in the 1990s, there has been a major issue with financial advisers selling life assurance policies and private pension plans in which they persuade individuals to take out policies that are not necessarily in those individual's best interests. The reason is that because the insurance advisers are on incentive commission, they have an incentive to sell policies, whether or not the individual needs them. The UK government has sought to reduce this form of exploitation by setting standards, and requiring these advisers to declare their interests.

The value of incentive pay in any type of selling in which the quality of the product may not be easily appreciated by the consumer is well recognized in business (hence we see such incentive pay in many types of selling activity) and is discussed further in section 30.2. However, an obvious problem for Spiv Cars is that its reputation may suffer (as customers realize they are not always getting what they pay for). The point is that word can get around and the short-term gains might be at the expense of the long-term future of the firm. If the firm decides it wishes to build a reputation for honesty and value for money, then one of the things it may have to do is to reduce the level of incentive pay—although clearly, some positive level of incentive pay is likely to prove desirable for motivational reasons.[13]

29.4.2 Effort Conflated with Other Unobservable (Random) Variables

Suppose an agent expends effort which, in conjunction with other, random factors determines the level of output. Thus observed output is only in part due to the agent's effort. The principal, who is assumed to be unable to observe the agent's effort, aims to maximize her expected profit (net of payments to the agent) by choosing an output-related incentive pay structure for the agent. Suppose also that the principal is risk-neutral and the agent risk-averse.[14] This means the principal faces a trade-off; adding a commission element or piece rate to the reward structure increases the agent's incentive to expend effort, which increases output, but also makes his pay risky. Assuming that the agent has a reservation utility level (below which he chooses to find employment elsewhere), risk aversion means that a higher average wage has to be paid if the agent is asked to face a riskier wage. The higher average pay is necessary to compensate for the extra risk associated with incentive pay.

To illustrate this argument, consider the following simple model. Suppose output is given by

$$Q = \alpha e + v, \qquad (29.4)$$

where Q denotes realized output, α is a positive constant, e is the effort exerted by the agent (I abstract from how effort is measured), and v is the random contribution to output. The random variable v has expected value zero, i.e. $E(v) = 0$, and

variance σ^2, i.e. $\text{var}(v) = \sigma^2$ (where σ^2 is simply a given constant).

By assumption, the principal, P, only observes output, and so can only reward the agent on the basis of this actual output. For simplicity, I shall restrict attention to linear pay schemes. Thus the agent, A, is offered a pay schedule in which pay Y varies with output Q:

$$Y = \beta_0 + \beta_1 Q. \qquad (29.5)$$

The problem for P is to select the constants β_0 and β_1 in order to maximize P's expected net profit. Clearly, β_0 represents basic pay to A, whilst $\beta_1 > 0$ gives incentive pay. (Setting $\beta_1 = 0$ would give a fixed salary). Now, suppose P is able to sell the output at a fixed price p (if the product market is competitive, p is simply the competitive price). P's net profit is

$$\pi = pQ - Y \qquad (29.6)$$

(revenue pQ minus the payment of wage Y to A). P's expected profit is

$$E(\pi) = pE(Q) - E(Y). \qquad (29.7)$$

From (29.4),

$$E(Q) = E(\alpha e + v) = \alpha e, \qquad (29.8)$$

since $E(v) = 0$, whilst $E(Y)$ is given by[15]

$$E(Y) = E(\beta_0 + \beta_1 Q) = \beta_0 + \beta_1 E(Q)$$
$$= \beta_0 + \beta_1 \alpha e. \qquad (29.9)$$

Hence expected profit is simply

$$E(\pi) = (p - \beta_1)\alpha e - \beta_0. \qquad (29.10)$$

In any principal–agent problem, the first step is to work out A's optimal response to a given reward structure offered by the principal P. Suppose that A has utility function

$$U = u_0 E(Y) - u_1 \text{var}(Y) - e^2, \qquad (29.11)$$

where u_0 and u_1 are fixed positive constants. This is a mean-variance utility function of a type often used in finance; it suggests that average income increases utility at the rate u_0 whereas variance of income decreases utility at the rate u_1, whilst in addition, utility is diminished (at an increasing rate) by the amount of effort e that has been exerted (the agent gets tired). First consider the term $\text{var}(Y)$:

$$\text{var}(Y) = \text{var}(\beta_0 + \beta_1 Q) = \beta_1^2 \text{var}(Q)$$
$$= \beta_1^2 \text{var}(\alpha e + v) = \beta_1^2 \text{var}(v)$$
$$= \beta_1^2 \sigma^2 \qquad (29.12)$$

---

[13] With incentive pay, individuals will tend to focus on the short-term gains to be had from being dishonest and selling more cars or insurance policies. The bad-reputation effect will have an impact primarily after these agents have moved on to other jobs. Notice there is also a free rider effect—even if all the other salesmen are honest, the incentive for the individual salesman is to be dishonest, since he can cash in on the reputation being maintained by others. This, of course, is another example of the prisoners' dilemma (Sect. 5.2.1). See also sect. 25.3 for an extended discussion of this type of issue.

[14] This is a typical simplifying assumption in the principal–agent literature. It certainly makes sense, for example, when it is shareholders who act as the principal; shareholders are relatively well diversified and so approximately risk-neutral, whilst most managers can be characterized as risk-averse precisely because they do not have a diversified portfolio (their major asset is often the job with the company).

[15] Recall that if x is a random variable, and a and b are constants, then $E(a + bx) = a + bE(x)$, where $E(x)$ denotes the expected value of x etc.

(since α, β_0, β_1, and e are constants).[16] A's utility can be written using (29.9) and (29.12), as

$$U = u_0(\beta_0 + \beta_1\alpha e) - u_1\beta_1^2\sigma^2 - e^2. \quad (29.13)$$

The parameters β_0 and β_1 are taken as given by A. A's problem is to decide whether to work for P, and if so, what level of effort to expend. As in the previous section, it is assumed that A has a reservation utility level $\overline{U}$ (below which A seeks a job elsewhere). Thus A will choose an effort level $e > 0$ only if this yields utility $U \geq \overline{U}$. If A does choose a positive level of effort, then the usual first-order condition must hold for effort:

$$\partial U / \partial e = u_0\beta_1\alpha - 2e = 0. \quad (29.14)$$

Hence the optimal level of effort by A, denoted e^*, is given as

$$e^* = u_0\beta_1\alpha/2, \quad (29.15)$$

so long as this satisfies

$$U^* = u_0(\beta_0 + \beta_1\alpha e^*) - u_1\beta_1^2\sigma^2 - e^{*2} \geq \overline{U}. \quad (29.16)$$

If A works, equation (29.15) tells us that A is induced to exert more effort the greater the piece rate (the larger β_1 is), the more important that income is to A (the larger u_0 is), and the more that effort increases output (the larger α is); all of which is intuitive.

Turning now to P's problem, the aim is to maximize expected profit subject to the constraint that the wage contract offered to A allows A, in choosing e^*, to attain the reservation level of utility. The object is thus to maximize (29.10) subject to (29.16). Fairly clearly, the optimal contract will keep A at the reservation level of utility; that is, the constraint will bind. Substituting for e^* from (29.15) into both the objective function and constraint, and forming the usual Lagrange function, gives

$$L = E(\pi) + \lambda[U^* - \overline{U}]$$
$$= (p - \beta_1)\alpha e^* - \beta_0 + \lambda[u_0(\beta_0 + \beta_1\alpha e^*) - u_1\beta_1^2\sigma^2 - e^{*2} - \overline{U}]$$
$$= (p - \beta_1)\alpha[u_0\beta_1\alpha/2] - \beta_0 + \lambda[u_0(\beta_0 + \beta_1\alpha[u_0\beta_1\alpha/2] - u_1\beta_1^2\sigma^2 - [u_0\beta_1\alpha/2]^2 - \overline{U}], \quad (29.17)$$

which looks messy but has a simple functional form. P has choice variables β_0 and β_1, so the first-order conditions for a maximum are that

$$\partial L / \partial\beta_0 = -1 + \lambda u_0 = 0, \quad (29.18)$$

so $\lambda = 1/u_0$ (nearly all terms are independent of β_0), and

$$\partial L / \partial\beta_1 = (u_0\alpha^2/2)(p - 2\beta_1) + \lambda[u_0^2\alpha^2\beta_1 - 2u_1\beta_1\sigma^2 - u_0^2\alpha^2\beta_1/2]. \quad (29.19)$$

Substituting for λ from (29.18), simplifying and solving for β_1, this gives

$$\beta_1^* = p/\left(1 + \frac{4u_1\sigma^2}{u_0^2\alpha^2}\right), \quad (29.20)$$

whilst the implied level of effort by A is given by substituting (29.20) into (29.15) to give

$$e^* = u_0\alpha p/2\left(1 + \frac{4u_1\sigma^2}{u_0^2\alpha^2}\right). \quad (29.21)$$

Given this, β_0^* can be calculated by substituting for β_1^* and e^* using (29.15) and (29.20), into the reservation utility constraint, (29.16), which clearly binds in the optimum solution. This calculation is rather tedious and not especially enlightening, and so is omitted. I focus instead on β_1^*, the rate of incentive pay; the larger this is, the more sensitive the agent's pay is to output. Inspecting (29.20), it is clear that the incentive rate in the pay structure is greater as

(i)   the risk aversion by the agent is lower (the higher the value of u_0, the lower the value of u_1);

(ii)   the random uncontrolled variation is lower (the lower σ^2 is);

(iii) the output is more responsive to effort (the larger α is).

All this makes sense. The more risk-averse the agent, the greater the preference for a stable wage (incentive pay in conjunction with random fluctuations in output creates an uncertain wage). Reducing the incentive rate β_1 helps with this. However, less random noise in the output increases accountability, and so tends to increase the attractiveness of incentive pay etc.

The optimal solution to the principal–agent model is very much second-best. If only effort could be observed, P could exercise her authority and simply require A to exert the efficient level of effort, subject only to giving A a wage which yields the reservation level of utility (otherwise A walks away from the job). That is, if effort is observable, a solution becomes possible which is a Pareto improvement on that characterized as $(\beta_0^*, \beta_1^*, e^*)$ above. If this solution is denoted $(\beta_0^{**}, \beta_1^{**}, e^{**})$, it can be shown that it involves[17]

$$\beta_1^{**} = 0 \quad (29.22)$$

---

[16] Note that, if a and b are constants, and x is a random variable, then $\text{var}(a + bx) = b^2\text{var}(x)$.

[17] See question 3 in sect. 29.6.

and

$$e^{\star\star} = \frac{u_0\alpha p}{2} \qquad (29.23)$$

That is, a flat salary is paid (this is attractive to A because A is risk-averse), and A is asked to work harder than in the agency solution (compare (29.23) with (29.21) and note that $1 + (4u_1\sigma^2/u_0^2\alpha^2) > 1$). A works harder, but still attains the reservation level of utility (through an appropriate choice of β_0) because A's pay is less risky. Thus the pincipal is better off in this solution and the agent no worse off; it is thus a Pareto improvement.

The point to understand is that the efficient solution described above is not attainable when the principal is only able to observe output, not effort. If a flat salary is set, then the agent will not choose to expend any effort at all (since utility decreases with effort). The principal cannot observe agent effort, and so is unable to command the agent to expend level of effort $e^{\star\star}$. The optimal solution to the agency problem, described in (29.20) and (29.21), is the best that can be done in the circumstances. Thus partial observability tends to put the solution into the realm of second-best.

29.4.3 Potential Difficulties with Incentive Pay

The above agency models suggest that by appropriate design, incentive pay can improve an organization's performance. However, there are often serious difficulties with implementing incentive schemes in practice. In a multi-task job, if only a subset of elements are explicitly rewarded through incentive pay, then the individual will tend to concentrate on these aspects of the job, so exerting too little effort on those aspects that are not monitored. This suggests that incentive pay is likely to work best for simple types of job (where most of the tasks involved can be monitored and rewarded in the pay structure)—and that it could be counter-productive in complex multi-task jobs where the outputs of important elements within the job are difficult to measure (these points are discussed in more detail in section 30.2).

Furthermore, one has to be clear that setting incentives is a matter of getting the balance right. In the Spiv Cars example in section 29.4.1, setting a flat salary would appear to be disastrous—but, as noted in that example, it is also possible that too much incentive pay could equally prove detrimental to the firm's reputation and long-term prospects, by inducing too much short-termism and dishonesty.

29.4.4 Agency Theory: Concluding Comments

The analytic models are helpful in that they clarify the trade-offs involved. In most applications, it is not possible to compute an optimal incentive scheme, and the alternative, of hill-climbing trial and error processes, is equally impractical.[18] In practice, the extent to which wages are based on flat fees, incentive elements, or career progression has to be judged qualitatively (although sometimes benchmarking may help—this involves looking at the levels of incentive pay used in other, and especially the most successful, organizations working in the same industry[19]).

29.5 Summary

This chapter gave a review of the key ideas on which the economic approach to organizational design is based; namely, transactions cost theory, information economics, and agency theory. These ideas are used as tools by which to examine the various elements that comprise a firm's organizational architecture (the organizational structure, the decision-making structures, and the monitoring and reward structures) in Chapters 30–32.

29.6 Review Questions

1. Many firms contract out catering, cleaning, and refuse collection, offering the suppliers a long-term contract (with duration in years rather than days). From a transactions cost perspective, does this make sense? Discuss.

2. Explain the difference between hidden information and hidden action, and give two examples of each type.

---

[18] It is difficult to play around with the wage structure, particularly at lower levels in the hierarchy, without adversely affecting pay relativities or worker morale (such processes typically require delicate negotiations).

[19] The practice of benchmarking is discussed further in Chap. 30.

3. In the principal–agent model developed in section 29.4.2, it was suggested that the solution deviated from what would be feasible under full observability. The solution under full observability is one in which the principal can choose not only the parameters of the pay schedule but also the agent's effort level, in order to maximize expected profit, subject only to the constraint that the agent must obtain the utility level $\overline{U}$. The problem is thus to choose e, β_0, and β_1 so as to maximize $E(\pi = (p - \beta_1)\alpha e - \beta_0$ subject to $u_0(\beta_0 + \beta_1\alpha e) - u_1\beta_1^2\sigma^2 - e^2 = \overline{U}$.

   Show that the solution to this problem involves, as stated in the equations (29.22) and (29.23), $\beta_1^{**} = 0$ and $e^{**} = u_0\alpha p/2$.

4. Suppose dentists are given an incentive pay contract in which they are paid a fixed price per tooth pulled, per filling, per crown, per routine inspection, etc. What are the pros and cons of setting up such a scheme?

29.7 Further Reading

Molho (1997) and Phlips (1988) give good and accessible accounts of the economics of information. Transactions cost and agency theory are presented fairly thoroughly at an accessible level in both Brickley *et al.* (1997) and Milgrom and Roberts (1992); both these texts give many applications and examples.

30 Organizational Architecture

Objective To show how the ideas discussed in Chapter 29 (information economics, transactions cost theory, agency theory, etc.) can help in the analysis and design of organizational architecture.

Prerequisites Chapter 30 is an essential preliminary; it discusses the background theoretical ideas utilized in this chapter.

Keywords agent-general, agent-specific, benchmarking, centralization, comparative advantage, decentralization, decision authority, decision-making rights, decision rights, hierarchical organization, hierarchy, influence costs, informativeness principle, inter-firm benchmarking, job rotation, matrix organization, motivation, multi-divisional form (M-form) organization, organizational architecture (OA), organizational structure, output manipulation, performance assessment, profit centre accounting, ratchet effect, reward structure, risk sharing, span of control, team production, unitary form (U-form) organization, within-firm benchmarking.

30.1 Introduction

Organizational architecture is concerned with the organization and co-ordination of economic activity within the firm, and of how to motivate the agents involved in the various stages of the overall process to advance the interests of the company as a whole. It can be thought of as comprising a set of inter-connecting elements as follows:

Definition 30.1 Organizational Architecture (OA) comprises:

1. **Organizational structures:** The choices of what is produced internally and what is outsourced; the choice of the hierarchies, teams, spans of control, layers of hierarchy, etc. which are used within the firm to co-ordinate all this economic activity; job design and the bundling of tasks into jobs.

2. **Decision-making structures:** At each level, the extent to which decision-making is by individual or team/committee, the extent of **decision authority** given to the individual or team, and the extent to which decision-making is centralized or decentralized.

3. **Performance assessment and reward structures:** The choices of performance monitoring, assessment, and reward structures for individuals and teams throughout the organization.

The design problem in organizational architecture is not usually 'greenfield', since, if the firm already exists, so too does an associated OA. Although root and branch redesign may be desirable in some cases, any major restructuring of OA is both risky and costly, so in practice design is more commonly concerned with incremental change in the search for improving the firm's overall operating efficiency. The idea is that the three key elements described above need to be in harmony if the overall structure is to work satisfactorily. The incremental approach is thus concerned with examining individual elements of architecture to see to what extent they are in harmony with the rest of the system.

The next three sections, 30.2–30.4, deal with the three elements of OA described in Definition 30.1. Section 30.2 starts with the pros and cons of alternative approaches to monitoring and reward systems. Following this, section 30.3 assesses the merits of alternative assignments of **decision authority** (the primary focus being on the extent to which it is centralized or decentralized). Section 30.4 then considers the pros and cons of bundling different tasks into jobs (the merits of specialization versus generalization), and then of bundling jobs into the overall organizational structure (the extent of hierarchy and span of control etc.). Section 30.5 then draws these strands together, emphasizing the idea that the three strands need to be in harmony if the overall organizational architecture is to be a success. This section finishes with an OA checklist which sets out the key questions one can ask about a given firm's architecture. Section 30.6 then shows how the checklist can prove useful in analysing elements of architecture, through various applications in the field of higher education.

30.2 Performance and Reward Structures

In this section we take the job as given, and consider the problem of monitoring performance and designing incentive structures. Agency theory suggests that, taking individuals on average as effort-averse, self-interested maximizers of their own utility, the firm needs to monitor and reward agent behaviour in so far as that behaviour contributes to corporate goals. Now, the idea of incentive pay often suggests a crude idea of piece rates. However, it is important to recognize that there are very many different forms of incentive pay, and that 'pay' should be interpreted widely, to include benefits in the utility dimension (such as status, power, congenial working conditions, etc.).

EXAMPLE 30.1 Types of incentive (carrots and sticks that may motivate) include: Piece rates; prospect of future promotion, demotion, or being fired (note also effects on pension rights); accelerated increments; bonuses and prizes for exceptional performance; perquisites (even if there is no official promotion, the range of tasks in a given job may be varied to make the job more attractive).

EXAMPLE 30.2 Academic Incentives. Apart from direct promotion, university academics can be rewarded for above-average research performance by getting lower teaching loads, better quality or more interesting teaching (post-graduate or MBA students rather than service courses to non-specialists, etc.), lower administrative loads, better offices, etc.

Thus a job may pay a fixed salary but there may still be significant incentives for the exertion of effort, as illustrated in the above examples. Agency theory suggests that the optimal level of incentive pay (of whatever form) involves a two-stage optimization process. First, the principal P needs to estimate how the agent A will react to different incentive schemes (this involves looking at the agent's optimization problem); then P needs to choose the scheme that gives the best overall return (net of payments to A). Sections 30.2.1–30.2.5 below examine some of the principal considerations involved in deciding whether to implement incentive pay, and if so, how.

30.2.1 Risk Sharing versus Motivation

The first issue to consider, in designing a reward system, is that it needs to balance the benefits of risk sharing against those of motivation.

(a) Risk-Sharing

It is conventional to argue that the firm, acting in the interests of diversified investors, is considerably less risk-averse than the individual worker. It follows that there are benefits to **risk sharing**. That is, if the firm offers the worker a flat salary, it is effectively offering the worker insurance against the risk that the business as a whole faces; the consequence is that other stakeholders (notably shareholders) have to take more risk. The idea is that the overall cost of risk-bearing is reduced by this process (since shareholders are more diversified than employees), so it can be used to make everyone better off (see Chapter 4).

(b) Motivation

The problem with offering a flat salary is that, whilst it helps through risk-sharing, it offers little incentive for the worker to exert any effort at all. This means that the firm will have to expend more resources on monitoring individual behaviour, in order to try to utilize the direct threat of firing, or demotion, as a motivator. By contrast, output-related incentive pay gives the agent A an incentive to exert effort, and if the output is easy to measure (and is simple—i.e. has a fixed combination of characteristics), this removes the need for extensive monitoring of effort. The trade-off is that, if there are random factors which also affect A's output, then the incentive pay scheme makes A bear risk over which A has no control (see section 29.4.2). There are also problems if output is complex and manipulable (see section 30.2.4 below).

30.2.2 Incentive Pay and Ratchet Effects

A major problem with implementing incentive pay is the so-called 'ratchet effect'. I first explain the nature of this effect, and then consider ways in which it can be mitigated.

(a) The Ratchet Effect

Incentives are often based on benchmarks or targets. Satisfactory performance means achieving certain output levels. Excellent performance is then gauged by the degree to which such targets are exceeded. Unfortunately it is only managerial human nature to shift the goalposts over time. If incentives work, output increases. There is then a tendency for managers to want to reset the output norm—one period's excellent performance can thus become the next period's expected output, and hence the new benchmark for performance evaluation. This is termed the **ratchet effect.**

If workers recognize that the ratchet effect is likely, this reduces their incentive to exceed the norm. Thus sales staff having a good year will often manipulate the figures so that some of one year's sales get reported in the following year. They do this output smoothing first to reduce the likelihood of inducing a shift in the benchmark, and secondly to give insurance against the possibility of poor sales in the following year (recall that staff are typically well modelled as risk-averse).

Apart from simply announcing there will be no ratchet effect—and then sticking to this promise (in the hope that a reputation effect may eventually give workers faith in the system), principals can also try **job rotation** or **benchmarking.**

(b) Job Rotation

One way of sidestepping the ratchet effect, and hence the agent's incentive to smooth performance over time, is to rotate jobs on the same time interval as the reward scheme operates. Thus, by being in a different job the next period, the individual has no concern regarding the possibility that her performance might affect the benchmark for that period. Unfortunately, job rotation often incurs significant training costs, along with loss of learning-by-doing efficiency, and so is only likely to be attractive in jobs where these effects are likely to be small.

(c) Benchmarking

A more often useful way of overcoming the disincentive effect associated with the ratchet effect lies in benchmarking. The idea behind benchmarking is that the output of individuals who undertake a very similar job can be compared, with rewards then being based on relative performance. For example, additional pay could be based on the amount by which the individual's output exceeds that of the group average, or simply through a ranking procedure (an extra fixed percentage for being the top, the second, etc. salesperson). Jobs can be benchmarked within the firm, (**within-firm benchmark-**

ing), but it is also possible to compare output for a similar job across firms (**inter-firm benchmarking**).

WITHIN-FIRM BENCHMARKING
Within-firm benchmarking is clearly more straightforward to implement than inter-firm benchmarking—since in principle all the data are ready to hand. The major difficulties are likely to be as follows:

(i) It is often difficult to apply because too few people have a sufficiently similar job. Sales staff, for example, often deal with different geographic areas or product markets (which may be going through different economic cycles etc.).

(ii) Benchmarking gives some incentive to both sabotage and coercion. If the average or norm is based on a relatively small number of individuals, sabotaging the output of other members of the group can improve an individual's pay. Small group numbers can also lead to the group coercing deviant individuals. The Hawthorn experiments (Parsons 1974) famously illustrated this coercion effect. The group of workers, aware that general increases in output would lead to ratchet effects, attempted to discipline individuals who sought to exceed the normal, acceptable level of output. Both sabotage and coercion are small-numbers problems which tend to disappear as numbers increase.

INTER-FIRM BENCHMARKING (IFB)
Inter-firm benchmarking helps to increase the numbers of individuals being compared; this reduces the likelihood of coercion or sabotage being a problem. IFB can be operationalized if firms exchange information, for example, through trade associations, or through the use of an external consulting body. The trade association or consultant can offer the participating firms individual anonymity, and the consequence is that the firms are able to share an industry-wide database of performance on some given job or task. The main difficulties lie in the fact that, again, jobs may not be similar enough to compare performance directly (different firms are not necessarily subject to the same environmental conditions).

Inter-firm benchmarking is also used in a wider sense; this involves looking to other successful companies to identify best praxis in organizational design. For this type of benchmarking to be effective, it is necessary that the firms operate in a similar environment and culture, since if these are different, the best practice may not be transferable (so one needs to think carefully about the implications of differences in such environmental factors). Abstracting ideas out of context can prove dangerous and counter-productive.[1] However, looking across firms to get an overview of industry practice can prove helpful, as it can generate ideas about how best to change current practices (for more details on the practice of benchmarking, see e.g. Atkinson *et al.* 1997).

EXAMPLE 30.3 Recently Newcastle University commissioned a consultant to report on the organization of its estate management function. The consultant was able to get co-operation from several other universities, and this gave a picture of practice and performance levels across the industry. Each was given anonymity as a case within the study, and each university received a copy of the final report.

30.2.3 Incentives for Teams

The key feature of **team production** is that it is difficult to measure separately the individual performance of team members. Because it is difficult to measure individual productivity, it is also difficult to design a scheme that rewards the individuals in the team differentially.[2] As a consequence, there is always the incentive to free ride, and, except at the extremes, team members are often reluctant to 'blow the whistle' (to report on other team members slacking). However, in smaller teams, individual team members are more likely to monitor each other and to apply moral suasion if there is serious slacking. By contrast, the larger the team, the lower the emotional bonding, and the less likely there will be intra-team monitoring; for this reason, it is generally advisable to keep teams as small as practicable for the business in hand.

Whilst it may be difficult to offer team members

individually differentiated incentive pay, there *is* merit in offering the team as a whole incentive pay (with each member receiving a fixed share, which might be an equal share or a fixed percentage based on age, seniority, etc.). If the team is given incentive pay,

(i) this helps to emphasize teamwork and co-operation amongst team members (since this increases the total output, and hence total pay, to the team, with each individual's share also increasing pro rata);

(ii) it gives the members an additional incentive to monitor each other for effort. Teams often discipline slackers in various non-pecuniary ways (not discussed here!).

The following example provides an interesting illustration of how a team can be induced to exercise internal control.

EXAMPLE 30.4 A scheme designed to tackle absenteeism involved employees accumulating points for attendance; these were translated into prizes (such as holidays). The amusing twist was that the prize was not given to the employee but to the employee's spouse. The idea, apparently effective, was that this motivated spouses to monitor their partner's attendance (to get them out of bed and off to work). For more details, see Ehrenberg and Smith (1988) (or Brickley *et al.* 1997).

The interesting additional question regarding team organization concerns the possibility of teams hiring and recruiting their own members. Competition for places might then provide a powerful further incentive against slacking. Naturally, this can only be implemented in large organizations, where there is a relatively large pool of workers who are potential team candidates.

30.2.4 Jobs, Tasks, Task Characteristics, and Incentive Pay

The type of job can influence the effectiveness of incentive pay as a motivating device. The four key job characteristics of importance here are as follows:

(a) Team Member or Independent Agent

The problem with individuals who are team members is that individual output is often not possible to measure, merely that of the team as a whole. This tends to mean that incentive pay can only be based

---

[1] The point is that it is not generally desirable to extract one component of design from a company with the idea that it is this and this alone which makes that company successful. The case study of Cato's Cleaners, discussed in sect. 12.4.2, gave an illustration of how a rule of thumb (a target labour-to-sales ratio) applied to a particular firm could prove counter-productive.

[2] It is possible to give the responsibility for determining individual team members' pay to the team leader (who must then subjectively judge the productivity of individual members). However, this usually puts undue peer pressure on such an individual.

on the output of the team as a whole, with individual team members being rewarded a share of the team's total pay. This gives some incentive to free ride (see section 30.2.3 above).

(b) Involves Single Task or Multiple Tasks

Multi-task jobs give more scope for the individual to allocate his or her time amongst the various tasks. Whilst multi-tasking has benefits (individuals prefer more varied jobs, which also means employers can pay lower wages, ceteris paribus), multi-tasking creates the danger that the individual will spend too much time on certain tasks to the detriment of others. In the absence of incentive pay, individuals will tend to concentrate on those tasks they enjoy the most. If there is incentive pay for only some tasks, then these tasks will get greater attention, again at the expense of others.

(c) Task Output Simple or Complex

If we think of products or services as having characteristics, as in Lancaster's theory (see Chapter 8), then output can characterized as simple if every unit of output contains the same combination and quantity of each product characteristic.

EXAMPLE 30.5 An example of a simple product is a litre of distilled water. Contrast this with a ton of coal; coal can vary in its calorific value, its sulphur content, and so on, and these variations are not easy to discern ex ante (before it is burnt). Not every ton of coal offers the same quantity of heat-generating or effluent-producing potential.

Now, the quality that comes with a ton of coal, for example, may not be easy to control by the individuals who produce it. However, when characteristics of the product which are difficult to measure or observe are under the control of the individual who produces it, this can give rise to **output manipulation**. With incentive pay based purely on physical output, elements of the product which are not measured (quality dimensions) will be economized on heavily.

EXAMPLE 30.6 The author recently employed a builder to re-slate the roof of a house; a fixed price quote was agreed for re-slating using the original tiles where these were of adequate condition, with the builder supplying other second-hand slates where they are not. This is a classic case where one can expect output manipulation. The builder has the incentive to use the existing slates even when they have significant wear and tear (as he then has to provide fewer himself). All that is required is that the slates last a few years before problems become manifest. Clearly it is fairly difficult for the buyer to verify the quality of the work done (which will be manifest only several years later if slates start to fall off).

(d) Output Controllability

Agency theory tells us it matters to what extent output depends on variables under the agent's control, and to what extent on variables outside the agent's control. What these variables are (and how costly they are to monitor) are clearly characteristics of the task itself. Incentive pay works best when it is based solely on agent-controllable variables, and clearly the extent to which task output depends solely on agent input will vary across tasks. Note that in assessing the agent's contribution to output, there is an incentive for the principal to try to measure the impact of variables outside the agent's control. However, there is always a trade-off, since monitoring any variable can be costly, and this has to be weighed against the fact that it may allow the principal to sharpen the incentives faced by the agent (and to reduce exogenous sources of risk affecting agent pay).

30.2.5 The Informativeness Principle

As explained in section 30.2.4, in a multi-task job, if the incentive structure omits to monitor and reward a given task, the individual is likely to put too little effort into that task. The **informativeness principle** states that, so long as measurement costs are sufficiently low, it benefits the principal, P, to measure as many as possible of the variables which enter into the determination of agent A's output, and to design an incentive structure which incorporates all these variables (see Holmstrom 1982 and Holmstrom and Milgrom 1991 for further discussion). This includes both those elements A controls and those that A does not. The idea is that measuring the factors which A does not control allows P to take account of their effect on output, and hence to be better able to identify the contribution made by the agent.

If monitoring is costly, of course, then it would seem sensible to include additional variables in the pay-off function only if they are likely to generate expected gains which outweigh the costs of monitoring such variables. If there are many such variables, the informativeness principle would also appear to suggest a fairly complex reward structure. In practice, individuals may have difficulty in understanding complex reward structures, so additional complexity can prove counter-productive (see e.g. Simon 1982, Kagel and Roth 1995).

The informativeness principle also applies when task output is complex, in that the composition of its characteristics can be varied (even if the job involves just one task). In this case, the argument is that each characteristic of the task output should be measured, with the overall reward being a function of these characteristics. The following is a good example of output manipulation when output is complex in the above sense.

EXAMPLE 30.7 One of a professor's duties, specified in a teaching document, is to deliver a course of, say, 20 hours of lectures. But what is a lecture? It could involve watching a video, or playing a team business game, or it could be on the teacher's latest research topic. The teacher could have spent many hours preparing it, or taken the overhead slides from someone else and delivered the material without any prior preparation. The characteristics of a lecture and the level of inputs required to produce it are clearly manipulable by the teacher.

In the above example, it is difficult to measure all the characteristics of task output. The problems of assessing teaching quality are discussed further in section 30.6 below.

30.2.6 Hard Versus Soft Evaluation

Hard evaluation occurs when objective elements of output are measured, and performance is judged on these data. By contrast, soft evaluation occurs when a boss makes a subjective judgement of the level of performance of a subordinate. This is typically based on a checklist of elements of performance (such as forecasts or targets achieved, punctuality, instances of adverse client feedback, contribution to teamwork, and timely completion of assignments). Naturally, the appropriate list of elements varies from job to job.

(a) Pros and Cons of Hard and Soft Evaluation

1. Hard evaluation means there are usually greater direct monitoring costs (physical equipment to measure output, computing hardware and software, accounting systems, etc., plus the manpower to operate all these monitoring systems).

2. Hard evaluation removes the need for bosses to spend so much time on appraisal; it also removes the subjectivity of the reward system, and hence probably reduces what are termed **influence costs**. Influence costs occur when individuals expend resources trying to influence outcomes. If evaluation is subjective, subordinates will expend resources trying to impress or pressure their bosses into reporting a good evaluation.

EXAMPLE 30.8 For assessments where there are objectively right or wrong answers, student complaints are infrequent, and easily resolved. By contrast, where performance is more complex, such that evaluation is necessarily more subjective, students rationally exert more effort seeking to influence rewards (grades received). Teachers then have to exert more effort in defending their assessments. These are all termed influence costs. (See e.g. Milgrom 1988 or Brickley *et al.* 1996: 210).

3. Hard evaluation is typically best for simple, single-task jobs with easily measurable outputs. For complex multi-task jobs, hard evaluation is more likely to be manipulable, and some form of subjective evaluation is likely to be preferable (as in Example 30.7 above).

(b) Subjective Evaluation, Implicit Contracts, and Reputation

The above discussion suggests that we would expect to see more subjective evaluation when task output is more complex. Subjective evaluation also tends to be more informal, based on implicit rather than explicit contracts between principal and agent; such implicit contracts are not easily enforceable, but do motivate agents and help to economize on transactions costs (see section 29.2.3 for further discussion).

30.2.7 Performance and Reward Structures: Concluding Comments

It has been argued by many organization theorists that incentives (carrots and sticks) do not motivate people. Often this is on the basis of spurious evidence. For example, if a firm offers its workforce profit-related pay, this may look like incentive pay, but agency theory tells us it will not motivate individuals to work harder—because additional effort by an individual does not lead to any significant additional reward for that individual. Incentive pay has to operate on variables over which the individual has control. The evidence on schemes in which incentive pay *is* designed in this way is that incentives can work extremely powerfully.

In fact, the problem is not so much that individuals do not respond to incentives, but that they often respond to incentives in creative ways which can be quite unexpected by those who set up the incentive schemes (see Baker 1993). The point is that, where jobs involve multiple tasks, and tasks often embody multiple characteristics, there is much scope for individuals to manipulate the output so as to maximize their return. However, the possibility of output manipulability does not mean that there should be no incentives at all. It merely shows that they work best when the output is simple and is easily measurable.

When incentives are manipulable, it may be worth expending resources on measuring more of the elements of individual task output, and perhaps also considering more subjective forms of incentive pay. It may also pay to restructure jobs (by making them more specialized with fewer tasks) and to centralize decision authority (so giving individuals rather less scope for output manipulation). The pros and cons of centralization versus decentralization are discussed below.

30.3 Decision-Making Structures

This section addresses the pros and cons of, first, committee versus individual decision-making, and secondly, of centralized versus decentralized decision-making. Decision-making can be viewed as consisting of basically four elements:

(i) Defining the range of alternatives (projects, courses of action, etc.) to be considered.

(ii) Assessing and ranking the alternatives.

(iii) Implementing the alternative which has been chosen.

(iv) Monitoring and control after implementation.

Often (i) and (ii) are undertaken by the same agent, whilst (iii), implementation, may sometimes be delegated. However, the crucial point is that (iv) should be undertaken by someone different from those responsible for (i)–(iii). The point is that if

an individual is responsible for all four elements, this gives plenty of scope for cooking the books. For this reason, there is usually a separation of decision-making from control in most organizations, with higher-level managers typically exerting the control function.

Definition 30.2 An individual is said to have **decision authority** or **decision rights** when she has the right to make a choice and the authority either to directly implement that choice or to instruct someone else to implement it.

The importance of separating (i)–(iii) from (iv) has long been recognized and emphasized (see Fama and Jensen 1983, Watts and Zimmerman 1983). The following example illustrates the importance of having independent monitoring and control.

EXAMPLE 30.9 The collapse of Barings Bank, 1995. The remuneration structure for traders working for Barings Bank emphasized rewards for good profit performance but did not significantly penalize bad performance. There was thus an incentive for staff to engage in risk-taking behaviour. This kind of incentive scheme can be logical; staff may tend to be too risk-averse, so incentive pay can help to overcome this. In the celebrated case of Nick Leeson, 'rogue trader', the demise of the bank essentially arose because he was motivated to get good performance by inappropriate dealing (taking huge bets on future currency swings, as opposed to what he was supposed to be doing, namely making essentially riskless profits by arbitrage actions associated with small-price mismatches across different stock markets). However, the key problem was not so much the trader's behaviour as the fact that he was able to cover up this behaviour when it started to go systematically wrong, because he also did the book-keeping. There was no independent monitoring of or control over his actions.

I now focus on the issue of whether decision authority should be given to teams or individuals, and the extent to which it should be devolved through the hierarchy, taking the hierarchy and the jobs within it as given.

30.3.1 Individual versus Team/Committee Decision-Making

It is usually argued that team decision-making is slower and more costly (more person-hours input for any given choice problem). This is because there is more bilateral communication in horizontal compared to hierarchical organizational structures, as illustrated in Figure 30.1. This figure illustrates the idea that hierarchy economizes on the amount of bilateral communication necessary to undertake a given task. The idea is that the number of bilateral communications (C) needed to inform fully all members in a team is given by $C = n(n - 1)/2$, whilst it is $C = (n - 1)$ in a simple hierarchical structure. As the number of individuals n increases, the hierarchy clearly and significantly economizes on the number of bilateral communications needed to keep all members informed, as illustrated in Figure 30.2. Of course, this idea of counting the number of communications is extremely naive, as it abstracts from the quantity of information that needs to be interchanged, and from who needs to know what with respect to a given decision problem (there are also agency costs to consider). However, Figures 30.1 and 30.2 do illustrate the idea that there can be too much unproductive communication in teams and committees. Anyone who has been a member of a committee (and university teachers are typically on many such committees) will confirm that a significant quantity of material dealt with in committee could often be dealt with more efficiently by a single individual or a small working party. Hierarchy allows the organization to economize on the necessary information flows.

There are a number of reasons to prefer teams to individuals in decision-making:

1. Teams draw together a range of skills, experience

n=4: C=n(n-1)/2=6   n=4: C=n-1=3

Fig. 30.1 Bilateral communications

Number of individuals	n	3	4	5	10	20
Team bilateral communications	$C=\frac{n(n-1)}{2}$	3	6	10	45	190
Simple hierarchy, bilateral communication	$C=(n-1)$	2	3	4	9	19

Fig. 30.2 Communication efficiency

and perspectives; as a consequence, team decision-making may be less prone to fundamental error, and so may be more secure, less risky.

2. Teams encourage communication and creativity (as in brainstorming sessions); new ideas may be generated through the cross-fertilization arising out of different perspectives.

3. Teams are social processes, and so can increase the level of commitment of those involved, especially if the team is also given the authority to manage the whole process (Volvo was one of the first automobile manufacturers to develop the small-team approach in production).

On the other hand, decision-making by individuals has certain advantages over decision-making by teams:

1. Teams are often slower at reaching decisions.

2. Depending on the form of team decision-making process (unanimity, consensus or majority vote, etc.), outcomes may tend towards excessive risk-taking (because individuals are not individually accountable or responsible for the team decision) or excessive conservatism (if the decision rule is one of unanimity, the status quo rules).

3. Team decision-making becomes significantly more costly; there are more individuals involved in making the decision, and they typically take longer to decide.

4. As with team production, there are potential free rider problems.

5. Some individuals also enjoy meetings for their own sake, and indulge in the sport of debate; such individuals can significantly and unproductively prolong the length of meetings.

Therefore, team decision-making is likely to be best:

(i) When the specific knowledge which is important to the decision is dispersed across a group of individuals.

(ii) Where free riding is relatively easy to observe, monitor, and control.

(iii) Where it is important not to make mistakes. The risk that one individual can go badly wrong is possibly greater than with a team.

Thus whether team decision-making or individual decision-making is preferable may well depend upon the circumstances. Big decisions are more likely to be team decisions—or at least decisions which have a significant team input. Thus the overall direction of the firm, its corporate strategy, is likely to be developed as a consequence of teamwork and deliberations at top management and board level.

30.3.2 Centralization Versus Decentralization

An individual's job description will normally specify to some degree the tasks and associated decision authority associated with those tasks. In principle, a manager can choose to exert her decision authority over subordinates in a centralized way (giving subordinates no leeway or scope for decision-making within their jobs), or can decentralize decision authority to those subordinates. The relative benefits and costs associated with decentralizing authority depend on the nature of the tasks involved. The main trade-off is clearly that centralizing, and restricting an agent's decision-making authority, helps to reduce incentive problems. Unfortunately, centralizing decision authority restricts an agent's freedom to do an even better job. Thus any degree of decentralization has to go hand in hand with a careful consideration of what types of monitoring and reward structure should also be put in place. Once an agent has been given greater freedom, the need is to provide that agent with an incentive to utilize his local knowledge and creativity in ways which, while furthering his own interest, also contribute to the goals of the principal, as illustrated in the following example.

EXAMPLE 30.10 Car distributors usually find it advantageous to give their salesmen some discretion over the price at which a car can be sold. In this way, local knowledge about the type of customer faced, the level of local competition, and the level of local demand can be utilized to improve the firm's overall profitability. However, it should be clear that the seller needs to be motivated via a reward structure to do this, hence the prevalence of a commission basis for pay.

(a) Advantages of Decentralization

1. *Better utilization of local and specific knowledge.* Centralized decision-making can slow the process down, such that beneficial deals at the sharp end can be missed.

2. *Better alignment of decision-making with seniority.* Decentralization devolves workload from senior staff, who no longer need to get bogged down in the operational details (so releasing their time to attend to more strategic issues). This is important, since in most organizations, most managers at most levels appear to spend most of their time 'fire-fighting' (answering the phone and dealing with administrative minutiae) rather than thinking about more fundamental reform and strategic issues.

3. *Aids career development.* Having decision authority and responsibility is an important part of the value of a job, valued for its own sake and for the CV (as an indicator of success, of promotion potential, etc.). A manager who has decision authority also has more scope to indicate his or her quality. Devolving it to lower levels takes away this potential signal of quality and ability (through making good decisions, getting good results, being generally more pro-active). However, devolving decision authority allows the specific and local knowledge to be activated by those closer to the cutting edge.

(b) Disadvantages of Decentralization

1. *Agency costs.* Decentralization of authority creates more of a control problem. Devolved decision authority gives managers at lower levels greater scope to pursue their own objectives. Hence, decentralization needs to go hand in hand with setting up appropriate performance monitoring and incentive schemes. Managers at lower levels may have more of the relevant information at hand with which to make decisions, but they do have to be motivated to make decisions which contribute toward the goals of the organization as a whole.

2. *Greater co-ordination problems.* The problem with decentralization is that local managers tend to have only local knowledge. Central management may have a better view of more general trends, and of the overall position of the firm. It is costly to make managers lower down the hierarchy aware of the overall corporate strategy, and of how their contribution fits into it.

(c) Horses for Courses?

The pros and cons of decentralization vary depending upon the specific application at hand—hence the optimal level of decentralization is likely to vary too. Decentralization works best, generally, when there is complexity, since complexity tends to mean that central management will lack the specific knowledge to do all the tasks satisfactorily. That is, decentralization works best

(i) If the firm sells in a diverse set of markets or produces a diverse set of products, or operates in dynamic and rapidly changing markets. In such cases, it is harder for central staff to be responsive to the needs of these markets. The firm can often benefit from decentralized decision-making, which makes better use of the more local and product-specific knowledge available at the sharp end.

(ii) In larger, more complex organizations. The larger the organization, the more difficult it is for the CEO to be able to get and process all the local knowledge necessary for the implementation of the central planning solution.

30.4 Organizational Structures

This section looks at the considerations involved in deciding (1) how best to bundle tasks into jobs and (2) how best to bundle jobs into larger-scale organizational structures. These are dealt with in turn.

30.4.1 Bundling Tasks into Jobs

Jobs can be described as comprising a range of tasks, and, for each task, an assignment of decision authority. The general issue, in drawing up a job description, is to consider the pros and cons of specializing versus generalizing the job.

(a) In Favour of Generalization

1. Multi-tasking can be more efficient, since there is less need for interpersonal communication.

2. It is also true that variety makes for a more interesting job, and this, ceteris paribus, means that, if the theory of compensating wage differentials holds, the job can be adequately recruited at a lower wage level.

3. Job specificity may lead to an inability to adapt to changing technology and market forces. Job specificity (with endless job demarcation disputes) was notoriously counter-productive for British firms and workforces in the 1960s, notably in car and motorcycle manufacturing.

4. Job specificity increases agency costs. Unless there is close monitoring of the quality of work done, the specialist may have an incentive to shirk on quality. In many types of production, a bad job

done on one element of the overall product can make other jobs harder. The merit of making one person undertake all the tasks (along with rewarding her for the overall product) is that she then has the incentive to maintain quality in the production of all the individual components.

5. Specialization also increases co-ordination costs as well as the control costs referred to above. In particular, specialists tend to suffer from what might be described as functional myopia. Specialization can be counter-productive if it leads to a narrow perspective on the job, and rigid rather than flexible thinking.

6. Specialization may also be more risky. If only one member of the department knows how to undertake a task (e.g. how to get the local network server back on line), it can be somewhat annoying if that person is on holiday or ill when the need arises. Flexibility, and the ability to be able to do a variety of tasks, reduces this kind of indivisibility problem; indivisibilities create a risk of bottlenecks in production processes.

(b) In favour of Specialization

1. Specialization allows individuals to be matched to jobs which maximize their **comparative advantage**.[3]

2. An individual's efficiency in the given task may be higher than when the task is one of several in a multi-tasking job (but note that efficiency also depends on motivation, and so also on monitoring and incentives).

3. Specialization can also reduce overall training costs (because the training for each individual is for just one skill area).

4. There are also problems with the appropriate design of monitoring and incentive schemes for multi-task jobs, particularly when the tasks are also complex, as discussed in section 30.2. There, it was suggested that, if an individual or team is given the job of producing the complete product (for example, an automobile), then there is an incentive to maintain quality through all the elements of the process. However, if the tasks are not all concerned with a single end-product, as is often the case, then there is the problem that the individual may not allocate an appropriate amount of time to each individual task. This is especially a problem for those

---

[3] For a discussion of comparative advantage, see any basic text on economics.

elements of the job where task outputs are not easily measured (see Holmstrom and Milgrom 1991).

EXAMPLE 30.11 It is generally easy to measure the volume of sales, but it is less easy to measure the quantity and quality of after-sales service. If the sales force is responsible for both elements, and they are given incentive pay (sales commissions), this means they may tend to put too much emphasis on selling, and too little on after-sales care. After-sales care gives the firm a longer period return (repeat custom, because good after-sales increases customer satisfaction), and this is likely to go to different salespersons (since individuals move on, up, or away, and are likely to take a more short-termist view than may be good for the firm).

The solution, for some multi-task jobs, may be to split the tasks into separate jobs. In the above example, one possibility is to have separate personnel responsible for selling and after-sales care (with the salesperson rewarded by commission and the after-sales person with a flat salary). An alternative is to try to devise an incentive structure which yields a balance of effort amongst the tasks (for example, there might be incentive pay both for sales and for after-sales care based on subjective performance assessments of the latter). Recall that individuals prefer variety in jobs, as in life, so the trade-off is not straightforward (as previously remarked, ceteris paribus, a more interesting job can be filled at a lower wage rate).

30.4.2 Bundling Jobs into Larger Organizational Structures

Technology may determine the optimal scale of plant to install, and it may also favour certain levels of teamwork in the running of that plant. However, manufacturing technology is only one aspect of any business; given there are also the aspects of marketing, finance, personnel, research and development, etc., there arises the question as to how the overall firm is to be organized. The key feature of the firm is that it is a **hierarchical organization** in which information flows up through the levels, whilst decisions taken at higher levels are implemented at lower levels on the basis of authority. Figure 30.3 illustrates the idea of levels of hierarchy and also **span of control**. It is assumed that, at the top of the hierarchy, there is the chief executive officer (CEO) or managing director (MD) who runs the overall

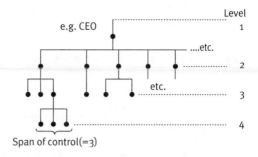

Fig. 30.3 Hierarchical levels and the span of control

show.[4] Below this person, the hierarchy fans out; individuals at each level in the hierarchy report to the individual at the next level above, as indicated in the hierarchical tree, and have authority (as defined in job descriptions etc.) over those within their span of control in the level below.

The larger the span of control (the greater the number of subordinates a manager has), the more difficult it becomes to monitor each subordinate effectively; agency costs are thus likely to increase with the span of control. However, ceteris paribus, agency costs also decrease with the number of layers in the hierarchy, and greater spans of control clearly imply fewer bosses and possibly fewer levels to the hierarchy. This is illustrated in Figure 30.4; 13 individuals could be organized with 2 levels of hierarchy and a span of 12, or in, say, 3 levels, each with a span of 3. The design of the hierarchical structure involves balancing the benefit of smaller spans of control against the increase in the number of levels of hierarchy (since there are agency costs at every interface between levels). Naturally, the trade-off is likely to depend on the nature of the jobs involved. For simple single-task jobs, it may be possible for a single foreman to monitor adequately quite a large number of agents. With complex multi-task jobs, the span will usually need to be smaller.

(a) The U-form Organization

The technological view of the firm focuses on economies of scale associated with grouping functions

---

[4] In practice, stockholders elect a board of directors, who may in turn appoint a president and/or a managing director or chief executive officer. I shall simply assume that there is one person in overall charge (the CEO), with that person ultimately accountable to the board as a whole.

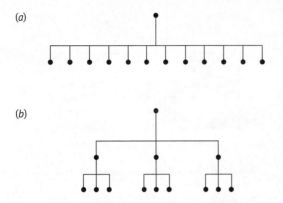

Fig. 30.4 Levels versus spans

together. This is the rationale for the so-called **unitary form** or **U-form organization**, in which activities are gathered together at the functional level, as illustrated in Figure 30.5. This kind of organizational chart depicts not only the work units (boxed) but also the levels of management, and the reporting relationships (lines linking boxes) between superiors and subordinates (the levels of hierarchy within each functional category are suppressed in this diagram, for clarity). The idea of having, say, a marketing department, is that by grouping all people concerned with selling and advertizing products together, there may be organizational economies of scale in that functional area (and so on).

It can be said in favour of U-form structures that they provide good promotion paths (since there are relatively large functional groups, with hierarchy within a given specialism). They also help with training, as there are greater numbers of older, more experienced people within the functional unit available to train incomers. Co-ordination within functional areas is also relatively good (people speak the same language).

On the other hand, U-form structures tend to lead to relatively poor co-ordination across functional areas (marketing and production do not speak the same language, do not understand each other's perspective on operational problems, etc.). This costs time and effort as top management has to resolve the co-ordination problems. Now, the U-form organization seems logical from a technological perspective, but it faces the problem of how to get the functional divisions to run efficiently (since divisions do need to communicate and trade with each other). Essentially, this is a problem of **centralization** versus **decentraliza-**

tion. That is, the firm can make its decisions in one of two ways:

1. *Centralized decision-making*. Here, the chief executive officer (CEO) functions effectively as a central planner who dictates to everyone what they must do. For this to work effectively, the local and specific knowledge at the sharp end has to filter up through the organization to the CEO, who must be up to the task of processing it. Decisions are then taken and implemented, by authority, down through the hierarchy. For small to medium-size firms, this organizational structure can work quite well. However, the larger the firm, the less effective the structure becomes. The problem is that the CEO tends neither to get the relevant information, nor to be able to cope with the volume of information, as the organization grows beyond a certain size.

2. *Decentralized decision-making*. Here, the CEO decentralizes decision-making down through the organization (this requires that performance be monitored and rewarded, in order to motivate managers at lower levels to act more in the interests of the firm as a whole). Decentralization is increasingly preferable the larger the organization, since decentralization gives power to individuals to tap their own local creativity and specific knowledge. However, with the U-form arrangement described in Figure 30.5, the output and productivity of individuals within many functional divisions may be hard to measure or control (for example, within the finance division, or the research and development division). It follows that motivation and efficiency may become problematic.

The above observations suggest that, for small and medium-sized firms with stable and small numbers of products, the U-form structure with centralized planning and control can work effectively. With larger organizations, the benefits of decentralization increase, and this has led to alternative organizational arrangements of the type discussed in the rest of this section.

(b) M-form Organizations

In what is known as the **multi-divisional** or **M-form organization**, the overall organization is split into divisions which are effectively mini-firms, as illustrated in Figure 30.5. M-form (1) illustrates the idea of the firm being split geographically into smaller operational units (which may each manufacture and produce all the firm's products). These smaller units are then organized functionally, in

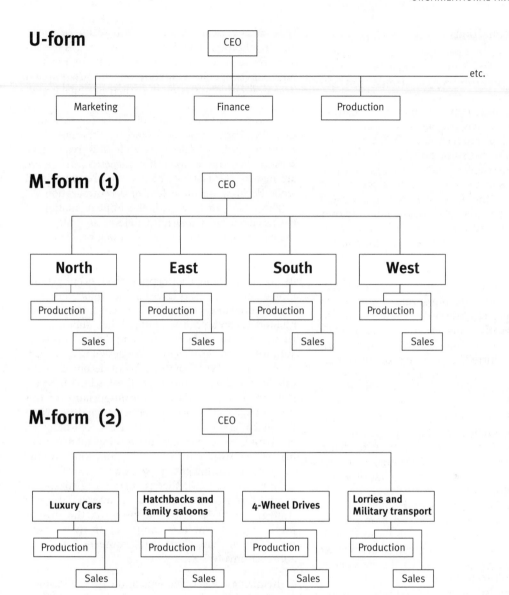

Fig. 30.5 Organizational structures

U-form. An alternative arrangement is depicted in M-form (2), in which the divisions or mini-firms are separated out into product groupings, again with each division being organized on a U-form basis.

The benefit of a well-designed M-form organizational structure is that it reduces the size of the resulting divisions to the point where they can function efficiently as U-form organizations. Finally,

each division can be made a profit centre, and the manager in charge of each division can then be monitored and rewarded on the basis of financial performance. As usual, there are some agency costs associated with decentralizing authority to divisions, but with appropriate incentive structures, these costs can be minimized. Chapter 31 addresses in some detail the organizational problems associated with M-form structures.

(c) Matrix Organizations

Before moving on, it is perhaps worth mentioning the hybrid form referred to as the **matrix organization**, a type common in project-oriented firms (in defence, construction, management consulting, etc.). This involves an overlapping U- and M-form structure in which there may be functional departments (finance, marketing, production, etc.) but members are also assigned to cross-functional product or project teams. Team members then report not only to their functional superiors but also to a product or project manager (the functional manager would typically be the one given the decision authority over setting incentives, and the responsibility for monitoring and rewarding an individual's performance).

Matrix organizations have various pros and cons. On the plus side, decision-making is decentralized, skills are allocated to where they are most needed, communication across the organization is increased (through multiple reporting), individuals learn to be more collaborative, and there are greater alternative career pathways upwards. On the debit side, accountability is blurred because subordinates report to more than one superior. Efficiency may also be reduced by influence costs, as managers expend time and effort competing for control over subordinates. Furthermore, there is an inevitable increase in the volume of information passing up, down, and across the organization, along with a tendency toward greater democracy in decision-making (more team or committee decision-making), all of which can adversely affect overall firm efficiency.

In practice, it would appear that the matrix organizational form can be made to work reasonably effectively, although its success is likely to depend on the quality of the managers involved at all levels throughout the organization. Agency theory suggests that there are still benefits from keeping the teams involved relatively small, and in setting up appropriate monitoring and reward schemes for such project teams. That is, the matrix organizational structure needs the appropriate support systems described in sections 30.2 and 30.3 above in order for it to function effectively.

30.5 A Design Checklist

Ultimately, organizational architecture is the responsibility of the CEO (although to some extent, the power may be delegated to lower levels). However, this makes it clear why the CEO is so important to any organization. The CEO can move the OA toward a more, or a less, centralized system. In practice, most CEOs operate a mixture of centralization and decentralization, depending on their personal knowledge. For things they feel they know, they are inclined to want direct control, whilst for areas outside their own personal expertise, they are more likely to wish to delegate. While this may make some sense, this chapter has suggested that there are many other factors which should be considered when deciding on the extent of decentralization.

The CEO can help with the implementation of OA by educating managers at all levels to understand the nature of the organizational design problem they face (since each manager at each level has a similar design problem). The idea is that, if decision authority is devolved down with appropriate incentives, the individuals at the next layer have a similar choice—either to operate a centralized system in which they retain decision authority (and tell their subordinates what to do) or to decentralize and delegate decision authority to the level below. The design issue at each level is one of whether the gains of decentralization can be expected to outweigh the losses. Managers need to be made aware of the importance of this design issue—and of how performance depends on the incentives individuals face. In a well-designed enterprise, each manager, in working to maximize his or her own return, should contribute to the performance of the enterprise as a whole.

One can test whether a firm's organizational architecture is well adjusted to its overall corporate strategy, taking as fixed the products the firm is producing, the way it is competing in the markets in which it has chosen to compete, etc. The approach involves the following:

1. Itemizing the key elements of the overall business strategy (the long-term strategic goals of the firm).

2. Itemizing the key features of organizational architecture:

   (a) The organizational structure (developing and extending in more detail the firm's organizational chart: hierarchies, teams, spans of control, etc.).

   (b) For each job at each node in the hierarchy:

      (i) A job description, itemizing the tasks involved, and for each task, some assessment of its complexity.

(ii) The extent to which decision authority is decentralized.

(iii) The monitoring and control systems.

(iv) The reward systems.

Naturally, in a large organization, different parts of the organization are likely to have different arrangements. Consistency of elements (i)–(iii) across the whole organization may well not make sense, given the possibly very different nature of the functions of different jobs within the organization.

3. Examining the extent to which the organizational architecture described in 2 above (*a*) is internally consistent (the extent to which elements (i)–(iii) support each other) and (*b*) fits with the firm's strategic goals in 1 above.

(*a*) (Internal consistency) For each job one can ask:

(i) Are decision rights appropriately specified: is an appropriate level of decentralisztion chosen such that specific and local knowledge is used effectively in the interests of the organization as a whole?

(ii) Are the monitoring systems adequate? In particular, are they adequate as a basis for the incentive schemes that are in place?

(iii) Do the incentive schemes encourage the best use of decision rights? Are the incentive schemes in place well designed (hard versus soft incentive schemes, etc.)?

(iv) Are there control systems in place? Is there adequate monitoring of ex post performance? Is there an appropriate separation of those who have decision authority from those who monitor them?

(*b*) (Fit with corporate strategy) I have suggested that different types of architecture are more suited to different types of firm (see the discussion in section 30.4.2 of U-form, M-form, and matrix organizations, and of the pros and cons of centralization versus decentralization). Given a market strategy (choice of products, markets, modes of competition, etc.) and given the current size and organization of the firm, it is possible to ask whether an alternative structure might improve organizational performance.

4. If there is a mismatch, the question arises as to what to do about it. The need here is to try to assess the likely costs and benefits of change—are the benefits likely to outweigh the costs?

One of the great difficulties with making organizational change is that change, any change, is both risky and costly. Reorganization may improve the efficiency with which the firm operates, but there are short-term adjustment costs to be borne, as individuals have to relearn working habits and need to adjust to the new demands that are put upon them. Furthermore, the gains to be had from reorganization lie in the future and are therefore necessarily uncertain. Expected longer-term benefits could turn out to be simply further costs if the organizational re-engineering turns out to be inappropriate. Thus any change has to be carefully thought out. For change to be beneficial, the expected benefits of reorganization need to outweigh significantly these short-term adjustment costs. Often there are ways of piloting organizational change within a sub-division of the overall firm. This is usually a good idea when possible, as it not only limits the potential damage to the overall organization of making mistakes, but also allows the firm to move faster up the learning curve—often there is a need for further fine-tuning etc.; if this is explored on a pilot scale, considerable adjustment costs can be avoided when change is finally implemented globally throughout the organization.

30.6 Applications in Higher Education

I give below some examples to illustrate the application of the economics of organizational architecture to universities as organizations. (The motivation for choosing higher education to illustrate these principles is quite natural; it is the one area pretty much all readers of this text will have had direct experience of.)

30.6.1 Decentralization in Universities

Many universities have or are considering some degree of decentralization, with profit centres at the faculty level, the school level, or indeed the level of the individual department. Berry (1994) provides a useful set of case studies reporting on the experience of a range of such institutions. The decentralization attempted at Bath (reported in Tomkins and Mawditt 1994) gives a good account of a restructuring toward making schools into profit centres. Broadly speaking, this was done by giving each school the revenue it generated (student fee income, UFC funding, research and contract income) minus a percentage deduction (of around 40%) to cover central services such as administration (registrars, bursars, etc.), computing services, stationery, library, etc.

Typically, university objectives can be described (somewhat tritely) as

(a) to be financially viable;

(b) to promote excellence in teaching;

(c) to promote excellence in research.

At the University of Bath, school heads were expected to develop a rolling three-year plan regarding income and expenditure, the objective being to pursue goals (b) and (c) whilst attaining (a) (to a reasonable approximation).

Clearly, there are a range of transitional difficulties associated with such a system (in particular, that some schools were in sizeable deficit so there was a need to transfer funds between schools on an interim basis). However, putting these to one side, consider some of the issues that arise when introducing such a scheme:

1. The flat rate levied for central services gives no incentive for cost control on those services. Nor does it recognize that different schools place different burdens on central services (indeed, there is a free rider problem; schools pay an average percentage, and so have an incentive to demand more than this level of service).

2. The system focuses directly only on profit and loss. The real goals of the university, at least as perceived by academic staff, are (b) and (c), but there is no clear guidance as to how these are to be pursued within the new framework.

3. Transfer pricing becomes a major issue. Service teaching, if it is not properly priced, can be given short shrift; indeed, departments have an incentive to withdraw from service teaching unless they get 'an appropriate reward'.

4. Effective decentralization requires that profit centre managers understand the system and the incentives that exist within the system. Furthermore, the incentives should be such as to promote the goals of the institution as a whole. Academic heads of department (and indeed many pro-vice- and vice-chancellors) often have only limited understanding of the issues involved (and indeed of management accounting concepts such as a budget). In practice some heads are simply not interested in running their schools or departments as businesses. They are also placed in a situation where they are merely exhorted to do their best; there are no direct incentives in place (no incentive pay).

Thus it would appear that the Bath experiment looks very much like a case where the organizational structure is left alone whilst decision rights are changed (at the level of the vice-chancellor, and at school level). However, these decision rights seem to have been changed without due care being taken with regard to the third element of OA, namely that of monitoring, control, and incentives.

Interestingly, the initial attempt at decentralizing authority at the University of Bath ended up as what Tomkins and Mawditt (1994) describe as **profit centre accounting**. That is, the university reverted back to a centralized decision-making structure, but one in which the quality of information being transmitted to central management regarding the performance of the various schools was much improved. The merit of setting up profit centre accounting is that it makes it very clear who is subsidizing who, and this gives the centre the information it needs to consider where serious strategic intervention or investment may be desirable. Of course, crude allocations (such as the percentage rate for central services) and inappropriate transfer prices can lead to spurious measures of profit or contribution at the divisional level, and hence to poorly informed decisions, but these are matters of detail which can in principle be addressed (see Chapter 31).

It has been argued in this chapter that organizational change should endeavour to improve the harmony between the three key elements (organization structure, decision authority, and monitoring/ incentive systems). In the absence of proper monitoring and incentive structures, it can be preferable to operate with a relatively centralized system. Whether it is possible or desirable to move to a decentralized system in universities probably turns on the extent to which it is possible to devise adequate performance monitoring and reward structures. Although not impossible, this is not an easy task.

30.6.2 Measuring and Rewarding Research Output

The attempt in the 1990s to shake up academic research in the UK has met with decidedly mixed success. Universities are funded in part by income they generate themselves (through contract research, revenues from non-centrally funded teaching etc.) and in substantial part through state funding, both through a block grant based on the number of undergraduate students taught and through funding for research (administered by research councils). Originally, the amount of funding for research was not tied to the quality or quantity of the research that universities undertook. However, in the 1980s and 90s, there has been a concerted attempt to create research incentives by tying funding to some measure of research output, the idea being that if university funding depends on university research performance, there will be a trickle-down effect, since universities will then have an incentive to try to motivate and reward high-performance research.

The problem with the idea of performance-related funding is that of how to measure research output. The problem is that research is a complex output; as such it is manipulable. If only some elements of what constitutes research are rewarded, then it follows that academics will have an incentive to manipulate output toward those measured elements.

For example, suppose research is measured and rewarded by the number of articles, or indeed the number of published pages, in refereed academic journals. In so far as quality is not included in the measure, we would predict that the response by academics will be to publish more in low-quality journals (where articles are more easily and quickly accepted), and to publish the same material (with different titles) in multiple outlets. The increased demand to publish will also be catered for by the launch of a greater number of lower-grade academic journals. None of these responses increase the quantity of real academic research. Indeed, such responses could actually reduce the quantity and quality of real academic research output, given the opportunity cost (more time spent repackaging and publishing essentially the same material in multiple outlets means less time spent on new research).

The initial attempts at research assessment thus suffered from being manipulable[5] and led to much counter-productive activity.[5] However, the research assessment exercise (RAE) is in a continuous state of development, and the output measures continue to be refined in order to reduce the scope for such output manipulation. A revised system involves academic journals being rated on a quality scale (such as from 1, worst, to 5, best); an article published in a 4–rated journal then gains a 4 rating and so on. Following this, an individual academic's research contribution is based only on that individual's best m articles published in an n-year research window (initially m and $n = 4$). The idea of focusing on quality and limiting the number of admissible publications restricts academics' ability to manipulate the system; indeed, it gives them some incentive to try to improve the quality of their research. There is less of an incentive to try to get something written, no matter what its value, merely to hit the RAE target date. Naturally, this type of measure remains to an extent manipulable (for example, some journals may be underrated, others overrated, relative to the ease of getting material published—leading to academics expending resources trying to maximize the perceived rather than real 'value' of their research). However, the above discussion does indicate that, with care, it is often possible to design incentive systems which can improve performance.

A predictable consequence of the new system is that academic pay for 'high flyers' (as measured by RAE assessments) has been invigorated, in much the same way as the market for footballers; such academics have gained considerably as institutions chase their research potential. As yet it is unclear whether introducing market forces into the academic sector has increased the total real output from that sector. In reality, the analogy with football is probably fairly close. The increased pay levels for higher performance do not actually improve the ability levels of those currently in the game, but they do give an encouraging signal to potential entrants into the game. Thus competition for key players may seem a prisoners' dilemma as far as clubs and universities are concerned, but it could yield a longer-term pay-off to the game as a whole. Possibly only time will tell.

---

[5] Given the large numbers of articles being claimed as published, it became a costly and difficult job to verify the research output claims (and some bogus returns did eventually come to light).

30.6.3 Measuring and Rewarding Teaching Quality

The ability of a university academic to teach was, historically, never a concern. Indeed, it was often a matter of pride that academics could choose to put little effort into developing teaching programmes, and then little effort into delivering those programmes. Teaching was a necessary evil, something which intruded on the 'real' job of doing research. These days, students are 'customers' who are increasingly being asked to pay for their education. Both they and the government thus expect value for money—so there is increasing pressure on universities to put teaching quality onto the agenda. As with research, it is possible to give incentive funding for teaching quality, based on some form of quality assessment of a university's departments. Teaching quality assessment is now monitored centrally; in England, by HEFCE, the Higher Education Funding Council for England. Essentially, HEFCE teams visit individual university departments and examine the documentation and delivery of programmes.

The impact of the threat of evaluation (and the potential carrots and sticks that might ensue) on the quality of teaching over the last few years has been quite significant, and many universities have set up their own quality assurance departments, in order to monitor and improve teaching in time for the external assessments by HEFCE. For example, at the University of Newcastle, in the areas of business, economics, and accountancy studies, the level and quality of documentation used in course delivery has vastly improved (with ongoing development of multi-media delivery, including TV, video, overheads, PC lab sessions, etc., and different modes of learning, including workshops, game-playing, and teamwork as well as the traditional lectures, tutorials, and seminars). Buddy systems have been introduced in which colleagues (after suitable training) monitor the quality of teaching delivery, and questionnaire feedback from students on lecture, seminar, and workshop content and delivery is now implemented on a regular cycle. Some of these developments are a consequence of the onrush of new technology, but there is no doubt that the major impetus has been the expectation that there is, or is going to be, external monitoring, with rewards or punishments as a consequence.

The substantial effort that has gone into monitoring teaching quality suggests there must be an opportunity cost, an adverse impact on the level of research output. However, it would appear that the carrots (and potential sticks) have thus far generally induced greater effort from academics on all fronts, presumably with some diminution in on-the-job leisure.[6]

I argued that setting up monitoring and reward systems tied to research output was not straightforward, simply because the output is complex. I have also noted that teaching is a complex output. Again, we would predict some output manipulation, at least outside of the lessons directly monitored by HEFCE officials. In fact, there are many ways in which the systems described above could be improved. For example:

1. The buddy system is manipulable. In fact individuals are expected to write a report on the teaching quality of their buddy, which is then filed with the head of department as a potential input into that individuals annual review of performance. It can pay individual's to do deals in such circumstances. This is the 'Leeson problem': inadequate separation of implementation from monitoring and control systems.

2. Teachers give out questionnaires to students, collect and collate their own results, and file these with the head of department. Again, this is manipulable, since, first, the teacher can choose at what point in the programme to hand out the material, and secondly, it is open to binning adverse questionnaires, and even fabricating good results.

Since teaching quality measures could well form part of the overall assessment of the contribution of an academic, and so, potentially, could translate into financial rewards (promotions, accelerated increments in pay, etc.), it may be desirable to set up systems which are less manipulable; for example, the independent quality assessment unit could be charged with the task of evaluating all staff, and of administering the student questionnaires.

---

[6] Casual empirical observation suggests that stress levels and sick leave may be increasing as a consequence. In considering the benefits and costs of organizational change, it is important to track all the benefits and costs to the organization.

30.7 Validity of the Economic Approach to Organizations

The exposition in this chapter, and indeed, the rest of Part VII takes the view that individuals may be other things, but they are at least in part self-interested and hence responsive to the explicit and implicit reward structures contained within an organizational framework. By contrast, many management gurus stress that individuals do not behave like *homo economicus* and that Taylor's (1923) 'scientific management' simply does not work (see e.g. Kohn 1993). However, the empirical evidence really suggests otherwise; people do respond to reward systems (see Baker 1993), and this is why every organization has one. The point to understand is that incentives do not have to be hard-nosed piece rates. A whole panoply of both monetary and non-monetary rewards can be mobilized as incentives: the prospect of rewards such as a more satisfying/interesting set of tasks, a larger office, more job flexibility, more travel, more status, more job security, more managerial perquisites generally (tickets to the opera or football match, etc.) can all be utilized as carrots to induce individuals, in pursuing their own interests, to identify these more with those of the organization as a whole.

Thus it can be argued that, whilst individuals are clearly not purely selfish utility maximizers, this does not invalidate the economic approach to organizations. The economic approach can be stoutly defended by noting that the key element that organizational architecture should manifest is that it be robust to individual variation. Not all individuals are the same; what the economic model proposes is that there is an element of selfishness in all of us, and this means there is an element of responsiveness to carrots and sticks (all appropriately designed, of course—the wrong kind of carrots can induce mayhem). The following example illustrates this argument.

EXAMPLE 30.12 In the UK, the motorway speed limit is 70mph. However, it is common knowledge that there is a sliding scale of penalties for speeding offences; the punishment increases with the speed, with a tendency for significantly increased levels of punishment for speeds in excess of 100mph. Now it may be that some individuals will obey a rule (such as this speed limit) even in the absence of a fine. However, clearly some do not; in the UK

probably the majority, if they get the chance, break the speed limit. However, very few exceed 100mph. As far as alterations in the probability of detection, and in the magnitude of the fine, go, it would seem that motorists give every indication of, on the average, responding pretty much like *homo economicus*. That is, higher fines, or increased probability of detection, on average lead to greater compliance with the regulation.

The same point applies to the organization; some individuals will work hard even in the absence of any incentive pay or career prospects. The problem is that only some do; incentives can prove helpful in motivating the others.

The economic approach thus looks toward organizational structures which are fairly robust to abuse. This means the aim, particularly at lower levels of the hierarchy, is for organizational architecture to be agent-general rather than agent-specific. That is, the organization should not be overly dependent on particular agents with particular skills (as Barings was with Leeson). As can be seen in this chapter, economic analysis can be very helpful in thinking about the design of agent-general organizational architecture.

30.8 Summary

This chapter uses the tools developed in Chapter 29 (transactions cost, information, and agency theory) to examine the various elements that comprise a firm's organizational architecture (in section 30.2, the monitoring and reward structures, in 30.3 the decision-making structures, and in 30.4 the overall organizational structure). Section 30.5 then set out a diagnostic checklist by which an organization can check its architecture to see whether changes may be desirable, with section 30.6 giving various applications. Organization theorists tend to be rather dismissive of the economic approach to organizations, basically arguing, albeit in different ways, that *homo sapiens* is not *homo economicus*; section 30.7 gave something of a defence against such critiques.

30.9 Review Questions

1. It has been proposed that university teachers should be rewarded in part on the basis of

their performance ratings, as measured by a standard questionnaire sent to their students. The questionnaire asks students to rank the teacher on a scale of 1 to 5 for each of a range of teaching quality elements, such as 'was well prepared and organized', 'communicated clearly', 'conveyed enthusiasm', 'made appropriate use of visual aids', 'encouraged class participation', etc. Examine the pros and cons of such a scheme.

2. The registrar's examinations section routinely allocates invigilation duties to academics, but not to administrative staff. Furthermore, it typically allocates senior invigilation duties to senior academic staff. The 'benefit' of being a senior invigilator is that one has to collect examination papers, and to ensure that everything is tied up administratively at the end of the exam. For a 3-hour exam, invigilation costs about 3.5 hours, whilst senior invigilation costs more like 4.25 hours. Is this allocation of duties rational? Examine the incentives faced by the registrar's department in your university. Do they face any pressures to be efficient? Does the above appear to be an efficient use of an academic's time? Would it pay to contract out this type of activity? Discuss.

3. The new ethos in universities is that they are expected to compete for students. This puts them in a prisoner's dilemma. Each department (and university) can make itself more attractive by lowering standards and granting a higher number of firsts and upper seconds, and this is easy enough to achieve since output is manipulable and standards are not required to be uniform across institutions. Is this a problem? Should there be uniform standards?

4. In the UK, there has recently been a major drive towards improving school education in reading, writing, and arithmetic, etc., with the introduction of a range of country-wide standard tests, starting as early as age 7. The results are being used to assess both individual teachers and their schools. Examine the incentives this creates for teachers and schools, and then consider and assess the likely consequences.

30.10 Further Reading

Milgrom and Roberts (1992) is perhaps the seminal text on the economics of organizations; it is lucid and gives an extensive range of examples and applications. The text by Brickley *et al.* (1997) provides an excellent coverage of similar material; although entitled *Managerial Economics and Organizational Architecture*, it concentrates principally on organizational architecture, and deals in much less detail with many of the other topics more usually covered in the managerial economics syllabus.

31 Integration, Decentralization, Transfer Pricing, and Related Decisions

Objective This Chapter focuses on the decision whether to integrate or outsource (through spot markets or long-term contracts), and whether and how to use internal markets and transfer pricing. The factors involved in setting the transfer price are then examined.

Prerequisites Chapters 29 and 30 give essential background material. Chapter 25 deals with the problem of bilateral monopoly, which is also essential background to the discussion in this chapter on transfer pricing (since bilateral monopoly is the arm's length trading equivalent to the internal trading problem associated with transfer pricing).

Keywords asset specifity, backward vertical integration, derived demand curve, firm-specific assets, forward vertical integration, horizontal integration, incentive compatability, incomplete contract, internal market, lateral integration, long-term contract, non-uniform transfer price, outsource, post-contract opportunism, spot market, transfer price.

31.1 Introduction

The primary focus in this chapter is on the vertical chain of production from upstream raw materials through the conversion processes and on downstream to the distribution of finished goods and services. It examines the incentives to integrate (to produce within the firm) and to **outsource** (to buy in components from external suppliers). Finally, it examines the incentive within such integrated organizations to **decentralize** and to use **internal markets**. The traditional reasons for integration of upstream and downstream operations relate to technology (economies of scale and scope), monopoly rent-seeking, the internalization of externalities, and the reduction of transactions costs (see Chapters 14, 17, 25, and 29). It was noted in Chapter 29 that as the size of the firm increases, organizational diseconomies of scale are likely to set in, and the unitary-form, or U-form, organizational structure suffers increasingly from agency problems. One way of tackling the information/communication and motivation problems associated with the U-form organization is to restructure it in multi-divisional or M-form. This effectively divides the overall organization into a set of smaller (usually U-form) operating units, each of which has a degree of autonomy.

In the M-form organization, the divisions are usually set up as profit centres, with the managers of these divisions exhorted to maximize their divisional profit (or given incentive pay structures which motivate them to do this). To be a meaningful profit centre, all flows across the boundaries between divisions (and between divisions and the outside world) must be priced. Prices for internal interdivisional trading are referred to as **transfer prices**.

Making divisions into profit centres is attractive as a device for motivating efficiency within divisions. The idea is that if each sub-unit is motivated to operate efficiently and to maximize its own profit, then the overall firm profits will also be maximized. This idea works if each division is unaffected by other divisions' behaviour—but in practice, interdependence is the norm. Profitability of one division typically depends on the behaviour of other divisions; for example, divisions selling related products can adversely affect each other's sales performance through their pricing and advertizing tactics (see chapter 20). Likewise, in the vertical chain of production, monopoly pricing practices upstream can adversely affect downstream profitability. In theory, these interdependencies must somehow be taken into account, if the firm's overall profitability is to be maximized.

Price is the co-ordinating and motivating device in markets. When the price is wrong in a market (say because of external effects or monopoly power), there is market inefficiency.[1] The same point applies in the case of the transfer price used internally. If the transfer price is set incorrectly, the wrong quantities will be traded, inappropriate decisions will be made as to whether to outsource, to make or buy, etc., and overall firm profits will not be maximized. However, transfer prices not only influence the volume of trade between divisions (and hence the overall profit earned by the firm as a whole), they also allocate that overall profit between the divisions who trade. The central tension in the transfer pricing problem is that the transfer price is trying to do two jobs (efficient allocation and reward/motivation) in a situation where there is typically imperfect and asymmetric information (each division having private information about its own operations). As we shall see, with private information, first-best efficiency is difficult to achieve.

31.2 Integration and Outsourcing

After presenting some basic definitions and illustrative examples of integration and outsourcing, this section reviews the pros and cons of vertical integration and outsourcing.

Definition 31.1 Outsourcing occurs when an intermediate product previously produced within the firm is purchased on external spot markets or contracted out to external suppliers.

EXAMPLE 31.1 Many elements of what firms term 'non-core' business are contracted out. Catering, cleaning, and rubbish collection are typical examples. Inputs such as electricity, gas, and water are also usually provided by external suppliers.

Definition 31.2 Types of integration:
 (i) **Lateral** or **conglomerate integration** occurs when firms which have little in common are brought under the umbrella of a holding company.
 (ii) **Horizontal integration** occurs when firms which produce different products are taken over, but those products are related to existing products.
 (iii) **Backward vertical integration** occurs when the firm begins to manufacture inputs it previously bought in from external suppliers.
 (iv) **Forward vertical integration** occurs when the firm takes over downstream activities, activities previously done by its customers.

EXAMPLE 31.2 (examples of the above types of integration)
 (i) Lonrho, Mitsubishi, and Virgin are all examples of conglomerate integration. For example, Virgin has interests in the music business, in drinks (Virgin Cola), in finance, and in rail transport (Virgin Trains).
 (ii) Horizontal integration is perhaps the most prevalent type of merger, particularly in recent years. Many firms diversify into related product markets, for example, BMW's recent take-over of Rover and Rolls-Royce.
 (iii) and (iv) The oil industry provides classic examples of both backward and forward integration. Most major oil companies now own their own oil fields, refineries, oil pipelines, and final distribution networks (forecourt filling stations). The automobile industry is also highly integrated, with many of the components originally outsourced now produced within the firm.

Section 31.2.1 reviews the circumstances under which vertical integration may prove attractive; section 31.2.2 follows this by discussing those which favour outsourcing, either through spot markets or long-term contracts.

---

[1] That is, the outcome is Pareto-inefficient. For monopoly welfare loss, see Chaps. 2, 14, and 28, and for inefficiencies arising out of externality, see Chap. 27.

31.2.1 Reasons for Vertical Integration[2]

The reasons for vertical integration are various, although the factors discussed below broadly contribute to improving market power, improving organizational economies (reducing transactions costs), or improving operational economies.

(a) Security of Supply

For inputs which are critical for continuity of production, integration can reduce the risks of incompetence or hold-ups on the part of suppliers. It can also bring the problem of quality assurance in-house, and hence under direct control. Naturally, security can be improved to an extent without integration if the supply contracts specify appropriate penalties should problems of supply arise. However, the transactions costs of writing, and more especially enforcing, such contracts can often be reduced through integration.[3]

(b) Asset Specificity

Many of the problems described above are associated with asset specificity (discussed in detail in Chapter 29). When external suppliers need to invest in assets specific to the buying firm, once such investment is sunk the supplier is at risk of post-contractual opportunism. Complex contractual arrangements may be needed to try to protect against exploitation of the bilateral monopoly situation that then ensues. Often the transactions costs associated with writing and enforcing contracts are reduced by taking the activity in-house.

(c) Increased Productive Efficiency

Often physical contiguity of processes can lead to increased efficiency through the design of integrated production processes. For example, in steel production, physical contiguity of blast furnaces, converters, and primary reduction mills reduces the need for reheating between processes.[4]

(d) Reduced Stockholding Costs

Integrated production, or physical contiguity and internal control, often allow the firm to reduce the levels of inventory which buffer each stage in the production process—simply because of the greater level of assurance that there will be no hold-up or bottlenecks. Integrated production may even do away with stockholding of some elements altogether (JIT: the 'just in time' philosophy).

(e) Reduced Marketing Costs

Integration reduces the need on the part of the supplier to advertize and market her supplies, and reduces search costs for the buyer.

(f) Reduced Co-ordination and Administration Costs

Co-ordination and bargaining problems associated with arm's length bilateral monopoly (see Chapter 25) give a reason for firms to integrate vertically. The point is that independent firms incur significant transactions costs in negotiating, contracting, and enforcing contracts. These transaction costs can often be reduced if everyone operates within the structure of the same organization. Integration does not get rid of the problem that the parties to any transactions may not have the same goals; a buying and selling division can still pursue selfish interests rather than those of the organization. However, there is a greater chance of goal alignment when individuals are drawn into the same organization, given that the firm can also institute procedures designed to improve goal alignment.

(g) Internalization of Externalities

Chapter 27 dealt in detail with externalities. It was suggested there that, where efficient bargaining

---

[2] Given the focus in this chapter on vertical relationships, I do not discuss reasons for horizontal or lateral integration. However, the reasons for horizontal integration are broadly the same as in (b) to (f) in sect. 31.2.1 below. The benefits of lateral integration lie in diversification (this may reduce risk for managers within the company, even if this is of little concern to investors, who hold relatively diversified portfolios in any case). The conglomerate can also homogenize and improve management practices and use its financial muscle to improve managerial access to cash for new investment (managers in practice prefer internal to external sources of finance—see sect. 31.7 for further discussion of this point). It may also reduce the cost of capital associated with external finance.

[3] Contractual rights may be on your side, but the legal process can often prove to be expensive, slow, and fraught with uncertainty. Often the compensation comes too late, as was the experience of many UK haulage firms, who in March 1997 won their case for compensation in the European Court of Justice for the French lorry drivers' embargo on cross-Channel freight. Many UK contractors were forced into bankruptcy as a consequence; for them, the compensation arrived too late.

[4] It could be argued that, so long as there are clear-cut interfaces between the various elements of the overall process, it is possible for such elements to be retained under separate ownership. But then the other factors discussed here usually weigh in (security of supply etc.), so that in practice single ownership is usually preferable.

solutions prove difficult to achieve, the parties may be able to internalize the externality through merger. The externality then typically becomes one between individuals or groups within the firm; if these individuals have the firm's interests at heart, they will then take into account the knock-on effects of their actions on other parts of the business (although, as above, agency problems arise to some extent within the firm too).

(h) To Increase Monopoly Power

Vertical integration (along with horizontal integration) can also increase the ability to exploit monopoly power. It is sometimes argued that it helps to increase barriers to entry, and may improve the ability to cross-subsidize products, so creating barriers to entry or facilitating predatory competition. For example, the old CEGB (Central Electricity Generating Board) in the UK was regularly criticized for deterring entry by setting an 'unfairly low' price for electricity inputs from external suppliers (see e.g. Peters 1976, Muller 1980).

Vertical integration can also facilitate price discrimination. A classic example of this is discussed in some detail by McGee (1988: 275):

EXAMPLE 31.2 (Forward integration): Alcoa, who sold aluminium for cabling and piston manufacture (amongst other things), wished to charge a higher mark-up on the aluminium supplied to piston manufacturers, but faced the arbitrage problem that piston manufacturers would then be able to buy from the lower-priced cabling sector. By integrating forward into cabling, and so eliminating this as an external market, Alcoa was then free to charge the higher price to piston manufacturers

(i) Evasion of Price Regulation

Increasingly, regulators are taking an interest not only in final-goods prices but also in the prices offered for intermediate products. For example, electricity generators are now allowed to supply electricity, gas, etc. to central grids at a given (often time-varying) access price. If such suppliers are taken over, then the access price disappears within the organization, and so is no longer subject to intervention or control.

31.2.2 Reasons for Outsourcing

Integrated production means that all elements in the process are carried out within the firm. However, for many elements, there is the alternative of outsourcing to external suppliers, either through

(*a*) **spot markets**, or

(*b*) **long-term contracts**.

The reasons for choosing spot or long-term contract outsourcing are as follows.

(a) Reasons for Using Spot Markets

Many inputs are bought on spot markets (e.g. fleet cars, trucks, stationery and administrative consumables, fuel and power). This can be rational; it all depends on the relative costs of outsourcing versus insourcing. Some reasons for buying on spot markets are as follows.

1. If the spot market is reasonably competitive, supply will be efficient and priced at close to the marginal cost of production.

2. If there is low **asset specificity**—that is, the supplier does not need to lay down much buyer-specific investment in order to supply the product—then this implies that there is no bilateral monopoly problem, no risk of bottlenecks or strategic hold-up of supply to extract monopoly rents (if one supply fails, there are good alternative suppliers available).

3. If there are economies of scale associated with the outsourced product, it is often the case that these cannot be realized by internal production, simply because the level of demand within the firm is too small. For example, electricity is normally outsourced by nearly all companies. This makes sense; the total demand by industry (and consumers) enables the electricity supply industry to attain plant economies of scale (and also reliability from multi-plant generation etc.).

4. Spot contracts can be advantageous if there are internal motivational or operational problems. In-house production does carry with it the responsibility for realizing internal organizational and productive efficiency. Outsourcing can often help as an engine for change in the quest for improved organizational and productive inefficiency. For example, outsourcing has often been used to break a union stranglehold on production (as occurred in the UK newspaper industry in the 1980s)—and the threat of outsourcing has also been used to force through more flexible working practices, to break down the traditional demarcation lines between jobs.

5. Spot contracts are also more likely if the transaction is simple in nature (clear quality and quantity measures, etc.) such that a complete contract (which covers all possible contingencies) is easy to write.

(b) Reasons for Using Long-term Contracts

1. If there are economies of scale in supply of the intermediate good such that these cannot be realized within the firm (as for spot markets).

2. If transactions are repetitive, so there are benefits from working with a single supplier to reduce the complexity of billing etc., and to streamline delivery, product handling, etc. through firm-specific investment by both buyer and seller.

3. If **firm-specific assets** are required, i.e. if firm-specific investment is required by the supplier in order to effect supply. The security of a long-term contract is that it makes it economic for both parties to make firm-specific investments.

4. It is difficult to write a complete contract, because it is difficult to envisage all the possible contingencies that might arise. In such cases, short-term **incomplete contracts** can give rise to post-contract opportunism. For example, if quality or reliability aspects of supply are relatively difficult to monitor, then in one-off contracts there is an incentive to cheat on quality. Setting up an (incomplete) long-term contract (often with many aspects of the supply relationship implicitly remaining for future negotiation) gets around this to some extent because the supplier has less of an incentive to exploit the buyer if the two parties are committed to working with each other in the future. This is particularly true with respect to quality and reliability standards. In long-term relationships, it is common for the firms involved to work together to achieve adequate quality assurance (see Sako 1992 for a discussion of long-term contracting in the UK and Japan).

(c) Summary

The choice of internal or external provision involves weighing the relative pros and cons of the alternative forms of provision (vertical integration, spot markets, long-term contracts). Economies of scale tend to make external provision more likely, and if outsourcing is preferred, it is more likely to be by long-term contract rather than spot market if the trade is repetitive, if the transaction is complex in nature, and if it requires firm-specific investment.

In recent years there has been a general trend for organizations to increase the level of outsourcing of intermediate products and services. Much of this outsourcing has involved long-term contracting rather than spot markets. Indeed, there has generally been something of a move away from firms acquiring inputs on spot markets. The reasons for this are probably several:

1. New technology, new methods of production are continually being developed. Suppliers have a big incentive to keep abreast of the latest developments, whilst it is more difficult for an integrated firm to keep up with the pace of change in areas of non-core activity. Outsourcing avoids the problem.

2. Supplier reliability also tends to increase with the adoption of new techniques (JIT—just in time, TQM—total quality management, etc. all improve the quality in supply chain performance, etc.). As a consequence, there is less risk associated with external supply (of delays or inadequate quality).

3. With the globalization of markets, more competitive pressure, means that firms have a greater range of alternative external suppliers to choose from. Competition amongst suppliers not only reduces prices but also improves supply quality and reliability.

4. Technology, in becoming more flexible, tends to make assets less firm-specific and also reduces the level of investment required in firm-specific assets. For example, the supplier of parts for a new car can now tool up much more quickly and cheaply than in the past.

5. Information technology reduces many of the transactions costs associated with arm's length contracting (inventory control, billing and the managing of creditors/debtors, etc.).

31.3 Decentralization and Transfer Pricing

When integrated production is desirable, there is still the question of how to internally organize and co-ordinate the various elements of the production process. Chapter 29 suggested that, to reduce agency costs, large organizations usually operate with an M-form structure, with individual divisions operating as profit centres.[5] Profit centres have a clear performance measure (profit) and so managers of such centres can be monitored and motivated toward operating their units efficiently and hence in the interest of the firm as a whole. However, as remarked in section 31.1, for a meaningful measure of profit, there is a need for all flows across the boundary of a division to be priced. When the flow involves trading between divisions of the same firm, the price used is referred to as a transfer price. Transfer pricing is in fact widespread across most large organizations—and it does not require that the whole organization be set up in the form of profit centres:

EXAMPLE 31.3 Most universities practise transfer pricing. Not only are consumables such as stationery and computer supplies either purchased by academic departments from central stores or sourced externally, but they often trade in students; when a department delivers a course to a student from another department, it typically gains a proportion of the unit of resource which that student represents. The prices offered then affect behaviour. For example, if the price per student on offer for a service course is inadequate, a department will seek to withdraw that course.

The curiosity of transfer pricing is that it seems to undo the benefits that are supposed to be obtained by vertical integration. That is, if vertical integration reduces transactions costs, it would appear that introducing divisions and forcing them to trade as if at arm's length merely reintroduces the bilateral monopoly problem, and the transactions costs and inefficiency associated with it (see Chapter 25). However, there is a subtle difference between the cases of transfer pricing and genuinely arm's length bilateral monopoly, in that central management potentially has direct control over the divisions, and can thus impose the rules by which transfer prices are set. This can make a significant difference to the efficiency of the internal market (see section 31.5 below).

The problem of transfer pricing (TP) is that of trying to attain several goals simultaneously. The TP system should ideally

(i) lead to efficient levels of trade between divisions,

(ii) facilitate performance evaluation for divisions and their managers, and

(iii) form the basis for setting up incentives and reward structures for managers.

Section 31.4 begins by examining the marginalist approach to transfer pricing and continues in section 31.5 with how this can be implemented. The marginalist approach focuses on setting prices so as to attain internal trading efficiency. However, it presupposes that private information held by individual divisions is reported honestly to the centre (when it is asked for). Section 31.6 then examines the question whether such a system is likely to encourage truthful reporting.

31.4 The Marginalist Approach to Transfer Pricing

The example discussed in section 25.4 is used as a vehicle for discussing the marginalist approach to transfer pricing.[6] In that example, there was a manufacturer M and a distributor D who were separate companies; in this section, M and D are divisions within the same M-form firm. The key assumptions under which the standard marginalist analysis is conducted are as follows:

(i) There is a single period and there is no uncertainty in demand or costs.

(ii) The goal of the M-form firm is that of maximizing overall profit. Divisions are profit centres; each of their managers aim to maximize their division's profitability.

(iii) There are no cost or demand interdependencies for intermediate or final products. That is, a division's cost of supplying a given quantity depends only on that quantity; the price at which a division sells externally and the

---

[5] It is also possible to set up cost or revenue centres. However, these are much less common. For some discussion of their use, and the pros and cons, see Horngren and Foster (1987: chap. 25).

[6] Although perhaps not the earliest writings on transfer pricing, Hirshleifer (1956) and Gould (1964) are the seminal early references for this type of marginal analysis.

quantity sold do not affect the demand for the other divisions' products.[7]

(iv) Truth-telling is assumed. If the centre asks for information known privately to one division, that division truthfully reports that information. The impact of not telling the truth is examined in section 31.6.

(v) There are no taxes, or taxes are such as to have a neutral effect. The impact of taxes, of particular significance for multinational corporations, is discussed in section 31.7.

The basic transfer pricing model is presented for the following cases:

1. where no intermediate-good external trade is possible;

2. where there is an external market for the intermediate good. This case subdivides into

2a. the perfectly competitive external market, with or without selling costs;

2b. the imperfectly competitive external market, with or without selling costs.

31.4.1 With No Intermediate-Good External Market

The manufacturing division has, by assumption, a cost function $C_M(q)$ and associated marginal cost function $MC_M(q)$ associated with producing output q. The distributor takes this output q and sells it on to the final-product market, gaining revenue $R_D(q)$ and incurring distribution costs $C_D(q)$ from doing so. The firm's overall profit from the two divisions is thus given as

$$\pi = (R_D(q) - C_D(q)) - C_M(q). \qquad (31.1)$$

This is maximized if the two divisions trade the output level which satisfies the first-order condition

[7] In practice, some degree of interdependence is quite common, and it is not difficult to take this into account (in theory at least). In the example involving a manufacturer and distributor, it might be expected that sales by the manufacturing division to outside distributors would adversely affect the demand curve faced by the distribution division. It can be shown that this sort of demand interdependence does not alter the marginal cost pricing rule for internal transfers, as derived in sect. 31.4.2(b) below, but it does affect the price the manufacturer should charge for external sales (and naturally complicates the computation of the transfer price).

$$\partial \pi / \partial q = [MR_D(q) - MC_D(q)] - MC_M(q)$$
$$= 0 \qquad (31.2)$$

(using the standard notation in which the prefix M stands for 'marginal'; thus $MR_D(q)$ stands for $\partial R_D(q)/\partial q$ etc.). The marginal benefit function for the distributor can be defined as

$$v(q) = MR_D(q) - MC_D(q). \qquad (31.3)$$

Essentially, $v(q)$ represents the distributor D's **derived demand function** for output from the manufacturer M. The functions $v(q)$ and $MC_M(q)$ are illustrated in Figure 31.1.[8] The point at which they intersect is denoted $(\hat{q}, \hat{p})$. Equation (31.2) requires that joint profits are maximized if output is determined by the intersection of $v(q)$ and $MC_M(q)$ in Figure 31.1. At this point,

$$v(\hat{q}) = MC_M(\hat{q}). \qquad (31.4)$$

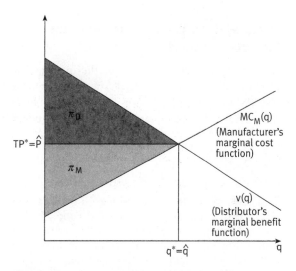

Fig. 31.1 Transfer pricing with no external market

Clearly the optimal quantity to trade, denoted q^*, is given as $q^* = \hat{q}$; this maximizes total firm profit (the area below $v(q)$ but above the MC_M curve; the

[8] Which is identical in form to the lower panel in Fig. 25.3, which describes the bilateral monopoly problem. In Figure 31.1, it is assumed that $v(q)$ is downward-sloping (which is reasonable, given that final demand has negative slope). M's marginal cost curve is drawn as upward-sloping. This is the traditional way that textbooks present the model. Naturally, it can be argued that it may be more realistic to draw MC_M as an (also traditional) U-shape curve, or, if there are economies of scale in manufacturing, as falling continuously with output. I stick for the moment with the case depicted in Figure 31.1, and then later comment on the impact of changing this assumption.

area below the MC_M curve is manufacturing cost). The optimal transfer price is $TP^* = \hat{P}$ (the price level at which the net marginal value curve $v(q)$ of the distributor D intersects the marginal cost curve MC_M of the manufacturer M). At this price, M wants to sell q^* and D equally wants to buy this quantity.[9] Thus, if the transfer price is set at TP^*, the two divisions can then be left to their own devices; both parties, in trying to maximize their own profits, will wish to trade q^*, and this will also maximize the profits of the firm as a whole. Notice that the transfer price is equal to the marginal cost of the last unit traded. For this reason the pricing principle is:

Fact 31.1 In the absence of an external market for the intermediate good, joint-profit maximization is achieved by setting a uniform transfer price equal to marginal cost (of the last unit traded).

31.4.2 With an External Market in the Intermediate Good

If there is an external market for the intermediate product, it becomes possible for M to sell to outside distributors as well as to D, whilst D can outsource and buy in product to distribute, rather than using M's output. Now it is possible to consider the external market as either competitive or imperfectly competitive. These are dealt with in turn.

(a) With a Competitive External Market

Two cases are worth distinguishing. In the first, it is assumed that the costs to M are the same whether she sells internally or externally. In the second, it is assumed that there is a fixed per-unit cost associated with selling externally (due to marketing costs, billing, handling of debtors and creditors, etc.).[10] These two cases are referred to as the 'zero selling costs case' and the 'positive selling costs case'.

1. *The zero selling costs case.* In the case where there is a competitive intermediate market, it is essentially a matter of indifference whether the two divisions trade with each other, or merely trade with the external market. Basically the rule is that

---

[9] To spell this out, M wants to sell q^* because, for all units to the left of q^*, $MC_M < TP^*$ (each unit adds profit), whilst for all units to the right, $MC_M > TP^*$ (cost outweighs revenue, and so reduces profit). A similar analysis applies for D.

[10] One could model selling costs as varying in a more complex way with total output sold externally, but the assumption of a fixed per-unit selling cost keeps things simple without losing any insight.

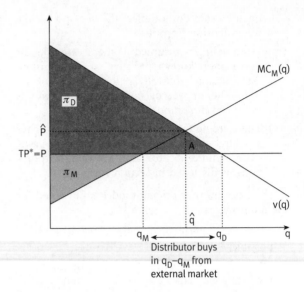

Fig. 31.2 Transfer pricing with external market (Transfer price=External price)

Fact 31.2 If there exists a competitive market for the intermediate product, then in the absence of selling costs, the transfer price should be set at the external market price.

This solution is illustrated in Figure 31.2. This figure has been arbitrarily drawn so that the external market price P is below the transfer price that would have been set if there had been no external market $\hat{P}$. In this case it is optimal for D to take the output q_M produced by M and then buy in additional units $q_D - q_M$ from the external market. Profits to D and M are marked π_D and π_M respectively. Notice that the overall profits to the firm are greater by setting the transfer price $TP^* = P$ (and allowing external sales by M) to that which would have been achieved if the CEO had forced the two divisions to deal exclusively with each other. The additional profit generated for the firm is the area labelled A in Figure 31.2. The reader can explore the profit consequences of the case where the external price is above the transfer price that would have been charged in the absence of an external market (by appropriately redrawing Figure 31.2). In this case, M will supply D's demand and then sell additional output on the external market.

2. *The positive selling costs case.* In practice, of course, the firm will typically save on certain selling costs (marketing costs, transport costs, management of debt/credit, etc.) by internalizing the transaction

as opposed to using the external market. Assuming these selling costs amount to S per unit, then D incurs the external market price P if she buys externally, whilst M receives the price net of selling costs, $P - S$, if she sells externally. $\hat{P}$ continues to represent the transfer price that would be optimal if there was no external market. The optimal price TP^* depends on the values of P and $P - S$ and how they relate to $\hat{P}$. Three cases arise:

Fact 31.3 With a competitive external market and positive selling costs, the joint-profit-maximizing transfer price is given as

(i) $P > P - S > \hat{P} \Rightarrow TP^* = P - S$
   M sells to external market;

(ii) $P > \hat{P} > P - S \Rightarrow TP^* = \hat{P}$
   No external trade;

(iii) $\hat{P} > P > P - S \Rightarrow TP^* = P$
   D buys in from external market.

The logic behind these results is straightforward. Thus consider case (i), illustrated in Figure 31.3. Recall that the stand-alone firm (which makes no use of the external market) can only realize total profit equal to the area between the curves $v(q)$ and MC_M to the left of $\hat{q}$. In case (i), where $P > P - S > \hat{P}$, the high external price means that it is clearly profitable for M to sell additional output to the external market. Since she gets a net price $P - S$ for doing this, she is willing to expand output up to q_M. Since she can get a price $P - S$ externally, this is the opportunity cost of selling units internally to D. Hence the internal transfer price should be $P - S$. At this transfer price, D only buys the amount q_D. However, it should be clear that total firm profit has been increased by the area A relative to operating as a stand-alone unit. A similar situation arises in case (iii) (Figure 31.4). Here there is a low external price, making it attractive for D to buy additional units from the external market. Since D can get units externally at the price P, it is never worth buying internally at a price higher than this. Hence P is the transfer price in this case. The intermediate case, (ii), as the reader might guess, is the case where it is best for the firm to operate in stand-alone mode, with the two divisions trading solely with each other. This case is illustrated in Figure 31.5. Here, the dark-shaded areas indicate the profits each division would make if they used the external market only, and the light-shaded area represents the gain in profit to the firm as a whole from using the marginal-cost transfer pricing rule (at this price, neither division uses the external market).

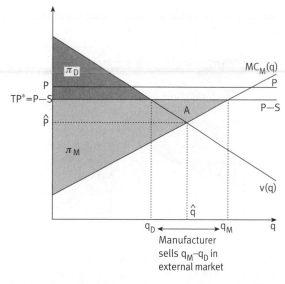

Fig. 31.3 Transfer pricing with external market and selling costs: case (i) $P > P - S > \hat{P}$

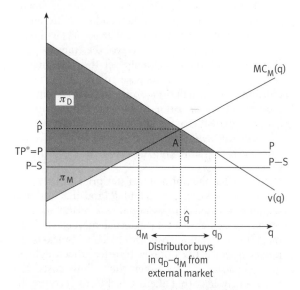

Fig. 31.4 Transfer pricing with external market and selling costs: case (iii) $\hat{P} > P > P - S$

It is worth mentioning that in case (i) (Figure 31.3), the manufacturer is indifferent, given the transfer price, as to whether she sells to D or entirely to the external market. However, it matters to D that she is able to buy from M. The point is that D can get the product from M at the price $P - S$, whilst she would have to pay P to get product on the open market. In case (iii) (Figure 31.4), by contrast,

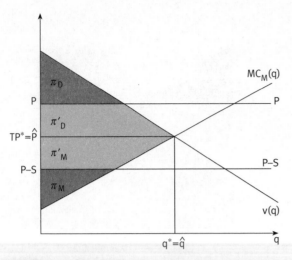

Fig. 31.5 Transfer pricing with external market and selling costs: case (ii) $P > \hat{P} > P - S$

the boot is on the other foot; in this case it is D who is buying from the open market, and is indifferent as to whether she takes the output from M (whilst M cares, since in this case M receives the transfer price P from D, whilst M can only get the price net of selling cost $P - S$ on the open market). However, divisions are usually required to satisfy internal requirements first, prior to having recourse to the external market, so the potential difficulty (of the division who is indifferent choosing solely to trade externally) is unlikely to prove a problem in practice.

Notice that the optimal transfer price in Fact 31.3 always lies between $P - S$ and P (and that the zero selling cost case is just a special case of this model). Thus the existence of an external market, and the magnitude of selling costs, immediately brackets the range in which the optimal transfer price ought to lie. Furthermore, the larger the selling costs, the more likely it is that there will be no recourse by either party to the external market. Selling costs make internal transfers relatively more attractive.

(b) With an Imperfectly Competitive External Market

In practice, many external markets are imperfectly competitive. Suppose that M faces a downward-sloping demand curve for external sales—that is, the lower the price M sets for external sales, the greater the volume she can sell. For simplicity, only the case where there is a per-unit selling cost

S is considered (setting this to zero obviously gives the special case of zero selling costs).

The optimal internal and external trading levels are first established, and then the transfer price and external selling price which support these trading volumes. Suppose the internal trade between M and D is the quantity q, whilst the external sales by M are the additional quantity q_x (x for 'external'). External sales raise revenue $R_x(q_x)$ but incur selling costs $S \times q_x$. Sales by D in her final market generate revenue $R_D(q_D)$ but incur distribution costs $C_D(q_D)$. Finally, the manufacturing division incurs costs $C_M(q + q_x)$, since it produces for both internal and external markets. The firm's overall profit is thus

$$\pi = [R_x(q_x) - Sq_x] + [R_D(q) - C_D(q)] - C_M(q + q_x). \quad (31.5)$$

So the first-order conditions are that

$$\partial\pi/\partial q_x = MR_x(q_x) - S - MC_M(q + q_x) = 0 \quad (31.6)$$

and

$$\partial\pi/\partial q = MR_D(q) - MC_D(q) - MC_M(q + q_x) = v(q) - MC_M(q + q_x) = 0 \quad (31.7)$$

(where $MR_D(q)$ stands for $\partial R_D(q)/\partial q$ etc. in the standard economist's notation). The function $v(q) = MR_D(q) - MC_D(q)$ is the net marginal benefit function of the distributor (as before, the graph of $v(q)$ depicts D's derived demand curve). Equations (31.6) and (31.7) give a familiar marginal condition, namely that

$$v(q) = MR_x(q_x) - S = MC_M(q + q_x). \quad (31.8)$$

This simply says that the marginal benefit from selling internally should be equal to the (net of selling cost) marginal benefit of selling externally, and that both should be equal to the marginal cost of manufacture. This solution is illustrated graphically in Figure 31.6.[11]

A perusal of Figure 31.6 should make it clear that the optimal transfer price is defined by:

Fact 31.4 When the manufacturing division M faces a downward-sloping demand for external sales of its product, the internal transfer price should be set equal to the marginal cost of production.

With downward-sloping demand in the external market, the internal transfer price lies necessarily (and potentially significantly) below the price set for external sales.

[11] Compare this diagram with that for price discrimination (Fig. 18.2, page 282).

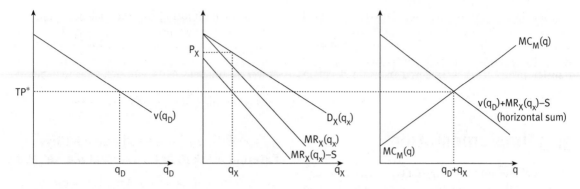

Fig. 31.6 Transfer pricing: Imperfect competition and selling costs in external market

Notice that an increase in selling costs shifts the curve $v + MR_x - S$ to the left and down in the right panel in Figure 31.6. The impact of an increase in selling cost is thus to reduce the internal transfer price (and to also increase the optimal price at which M sells externally[12]). In the case where the external market is competitive, a £1 increase in selling costs will reduce the internal transfer price by fully £1. With an imperfectly competitive market, the effect is still in the same direction, but the impact is less pronounced.

31.4.3 Criticisms of the Marginalist Approach to Transfer Pricing

Notice that in Figure 31.1 a uniform price divides the total joint profit of the two divisions in a particular way. For example, if the figure is redrawn such that the manufacturer has a flat marginal cost curve, she would clearly make no profit at all. Worse still, if M had economies of scale, such that MC_M was downward-sloping, then M would necessarily make a loss, although it remains true that, under certainty at least, the marginal-cost transfer pricing solution continues to give maximum joint profits to the firm as a whole. However, in many cases, there is no need to restrict the transfer price to being uniform. The adverse division of profits can be adjusted by the use of a **non-uniform transfer price** schedule (such as a two-part tariff). All that is required is that the marginal price schedule passes through the intersection point of the curves $v(q)$ and MC_M, as illustrated in

[12] This can be established by a formal comparative statics exercise. Naturally the result is contingent on the assumptions regarding the slopes of the various curves in Fig. 31.6.

Figure 31.7, for the case where the manufacturer has a continuously falling marginal cost curve, of the type that would arise if there were global economies of scale. Naturally, there may be considerable negotiation between the parties regarding the choice of schedule (equal profit shares is a focal point for such bargaining; this would involve the parties agreeing on a schedule such that $\pi_D = \pi_M$ in Figure 31.7).

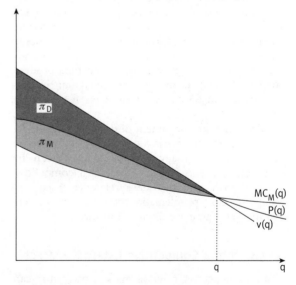

Fig. 31.7 Non-uniform transfer pricing

Unfortunately, fixing the profit shares does not necessarily resolve motivational problems. The key difficulty lies in the fact that the divisions typically have private information, and cannot be relied upon to divulge this truthfully. For example, in the case where M has constant marginal cost, it would appear that she has an incentive to exaggerate true marginal cost, in order to get a higher ex post profit share. This is the idea that the marginal approach to transfer pricing does not yield incentive-compatible transfer prices. This is explored in more detail in section 31.6 below.

31.5 Implementation

The chief executive officer (CEO) needs to assign decision authority over transfer price setting—and the way this is done matters. In principle this authority could be given to the buyer or the seller, or the price could be imposed centrally by the CEO. There is also scope for the CEO to restrict the form the transfer price is allowed to take (uniform price, two-part tariff, price–quantity negotiated contract, etc.). For example, a bad choice would be to assign the buying division the right to set the level of a uniform transfer price, a price at which it must then supply as much as is requested by the selling division. Such a set-up would not be in the interests of the firm, because (as shown in section 25.4, on bilateral monopoly), uniform pricing leads to the problem of successive monopoly, in which everyone in the vertical chain of production levies a monopoly mark-up, with the consequence that the firm ends up charging too high a price in the final-product market. Individual maximizing behaviour in this case proves to be counter-productive for the firm as a whole (overall firm profits are not maximized).

Given that the assignment of decision rights matters, what transfer pricing system is likely to prove satisfactory? Essentially, a good solution can be achieved in the case where there is a competitive external market to provide a reference price, but things are more problematic when there is no external market. These are discussed in turn.

31.5.1 With a Competitive External Market

With a competitive external market, the centre can monitor and impose the transfer price since this is directly observable. If there are selling costs involved, then the transfer price must lie somewhere between external market price, and this price minus selling costs. When there is external trade, the transfer price is set by reference to the observed external price, and so is not manipulable by internal divisions. In this case it makes little difference to whom the CEO gives

the job of monitoring the external price and then setting the transfer price. It can be given to either division, or left as a central task. Decision authority can be devolved to either division, because the power is unlikely to be abused, precisely because transfer price setting can also be monitored and verified by the other parties concerned.

31.5.2 With an Imperfectly Competitive External Market, or no External Market at all

By contrast, with no external market in use, there is a need for the truthful revelation of private information. Typically, M knows more about its cost structure than either the centre or D—and D knows more about the state of final demand, and its distribution and selling costs, than either M or the centre. Thus to calculate the optimal transfer price in such a case requires one of the following:

(a) The centre requests the relevant information (the structures of the functions $v(q)$ and $MC_M(q)$) from the two divisions. Assuming these are truthfully reported, it then calculates the optimal transfer price and sets this as the transfer price at which the divisions are allowed to trade.

(b) The centre gives the decision authority to D to set the transfer price, and requires M to pass the estimate of its marginal cost curve to D, with D being instructed to treat this as a supply curve when determining the transfer price.

(c) The centre gives the decision authority to M, with D required to pass the estimate of its demand curve to M, and M instructed to treat this as a marginal revenue curve in deciding on the transfer price to set.

The idea is that, once the transfer price has been determined, the divisions can be left to undertake what trades they wish at the set price.

It should be clear that, in a single-period context, there is not much decentralization going on in any of these schemes (a)–(c). Indeed, one could argue that the centre might just as well forget about pricing and simply impose the optimal transfer quantity. The problem here lies with the assumption in the model of single-period certainty. Extending the model to a multi-period setting (with uncertain demand) naturally makes the idea of transfer pricing more meaningful. Thus, suppose that there are in fact multiple periods, and that once the transfer price is set, the divisions trade in a decentralized way on the basis of the fixed transfer price. It should be clear that, so long as marginal cost does not vary much over the normal range of output, a fixed transfer price will perform fairly efficiently in decentralized internal trading (having a fixed transfer price and decentralized decision-making based on it is clearly less cumbersome than requiring divisions to report information to the centre, with the centre calculating the optimal trading quantity period by period).[13]

However, the major drawback with trying to implement the marginal-cost transfer pricing rule (as is required in the above theory when there is no external trading) is that it only really works if divisions initially report private information truthfully. In practice, if they know that the above form of transfer pricing scheme is to be implemented on the basis of the private information they divulge to other parties, they are likely to bias their reports; this idea is discussed in more detail in section 31.6.

31.6 Incentive Compatability and Transfer Pricing

If there is an external market, as remarked above, setting price using external market price as a reference means that both M and D have an incentive to operate efficiently and to trade the optimal amounts both internally and externally. The key point is that, because the transfer price is determined by external reference, it is not manipulable by the divisions involved. By contrast, in the case where there is no external market for the intermediate good, the transfer price depends on the point at which $v(q)$ intersects MC_M. This is endogenously determined, and so can be manipulated by both divisions, since each has to report one of the two functions involved ($v(q)$ or MC_M).

Typically, the manufacturing division M has much better knowledge regarding what its true fixed and variable costs are, and likewise the distributor D has a clearer idea of what its costs are—and also the state of demand it faces (and the centre has less information than either division). The agency problem arises because misreporting of benefit and cost structures may be attractive to each division—in

that misreporting may increase that division's profitability. The problem is that telling lies is a dominant strategy in a prisoners' dilemma game. It is individually rational to tell lies, but the overall consequence for the firm is that total profit is lower as a result.[14]

The following highly simplified model illustrates the idea that there is an incentive to tell lies when the firm is trying to implement a marginalist transfer pricing solution. Assume that everyone knows the distributor D's true net marginal benefit function, $v(q)$, but that only the manufacturer M knows her cost structure (and hence marginal cost structure MC_M). The transfer pricing regime involves both M reporting her cost structure and D reporting her demand structure to the centre, with the centre then calculating the marginal-cost transfer price at which the two divisions trade. Now, M's revenues and costs will be observable by everyone once the trade takes place. Naturally M, in order to increase her profit, may choose to report a possibly untruthful cost structure. Clearly, it makes sense for M to report a cost structure which has the property that it will give a reported cost equal to the actual cost at the volume of trade that actually occurs. In this way, the centre, or D, will not know that M has been lying.

Suppose that the true net marginal benefit function is

$$v(q) = \alpha_0 - \alpha_1 q, \qquad (31.9)$$

where α_0 and α_1 are positive constants. Suppose that M's true cost function (privately known only to M) is

$$C_M(q) = F + \tfrac{1}{2}cq^2, \qquad (31.10)$$

where the parameters F and $c > 0$. The true marginal cost function is thus

$$MC_M(q) = \partial C_M(q)/\partial q = cq. \qquad (31.11)$$

Again to keep things simple, also let everyone know the general shape of M's cost function (i.e. that it is a quadratic of a simple type), but not the actual values of the parameters. It follows that M has the option of reporting different values for these parameters F and c. Suppose then that M reports the cost function

---

[13] See for example Ronen and Balachandrian (1988) for an analysis of transfer pricing under uncertainty.

[14] It follows that if only everyone told the truth, a bargain could be had that would yield a gain to all parties. The problem is that it is individually tempting to cheat on any truth-telling agreement—and there is no way to punish cheating because the lies are not detectable.

$$\hat{C}_M(q) = \hat{F} + \tfrac{1}{2}\hat{c}q^2 \qquad (31.12)$$

and hence also the associated marginal cost function

$$\widehat{MC}_M(q) = \hat{c}q, \qquad (31.13)$$

where the reported values $\hat{F}$ and $\hat{c}q$ may differ from the true values F and c, as illustrated in Figure 31.8.

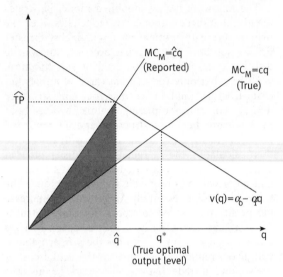

Fig. 31.8 The problem of incentive compatibility

Clearly the actual traded quantity will depend on the announced marginal cost function parameter $\hat{c}$. Thus the output that will be traded, denoted $\hat{q}$, is given by the intersection of the functions $v(q)$ and MC_M. That is,

$$v(\hat{q}) = \widehat{MC}_M(\hat{q}) \Rightarrow \alpha_0 - \alpha_1\hat{q} = \hat{c}\hat{q}, \quad (31.14)$$

so, by rearranging,

$$\hat{q} = \frac{\alpha_0}{\hat{c} + \alpha_1}. \qquad (31.15)$$

This suggests that the choice of $\hat{c}$ allows M to manipulate the quantity D will choose to buy, $\hat{q}$. The reported value of $\hat{c}$ given to the centre means the centre calculates the transfer price, $\widehat{TP}$, as in Figure 31.8, as

$$\widehat{TP} = \hat{c}\hat{q} = \alpha_0 - \alpha_1\hat{q}. \qquad (31.16)$$

M's actual profit can then be written as

$$\begin{aligned}\pi_M &= \hat{q} \times \widehat{TP} - C_M(q) \\ &= \hat{q}(\alpha_0 - \alpha_1\hat{q}) - F - \tfrac{1}{2}c\hat{q}^2\end{aligned} \qquad (31.17)$$

(note the use of the true cost function). Now by the chain rule,

$$\frac{d\pi_M}{d\hat{c}} = \frac{d\pi_M}{d\hat{q}}\frac{d\hat{q}}{d\hat{c}} = 0 \qquad (31.18)$$

is a necessary condition for the reported marginal cost $\hat{c}$ to maximize M's profit. Notice from (31.15) that $d\hat{q}/d\hat{c} = -\alpha_0/(\hat{c} + \alpha_1)^2 < 0$, so for (31.18) to hold, it must be that $d\pi_M/d\hat{q} = 0$. Basically, $\hat{c}$ is chosen to induce the output which maximizes M's profit (note, from Figure 31.8, the higher the marginal cost reported, the steeper the reported curve $\widehat{MC}_M$ and so the smaller $\hat{q}$ will be). Thus from (31.17),

$$\frac{d\pi_M}{d\hat{q}} = \alpha_0 - 2\alpha_1\hat{q} - c\hat{q} = 0. \qquad (31.19)$$

Rearranging this implies that π_M is maximized if D chooses

$$\hat{q} = \frac{\alpha_0}{2\alpha_1 + c}. \qquad (31.20)$$

The idea is that M can choose $\hat{c}$ to induce D to choose this output level because of (31.15). That is, M can set (31.20) equal to (31.15), so finding the value of $\hat{c}$ that induces the optimal level of output. That is,

$$\hat{q} = \frac{\alpha_0}{2\alpha_1 + c} = \frac{\alpha_0}{\hat{c} + \alpha_1}. \qquad (31.21)$$

This simplifies to give

$$\hat{c} = c + \alpha_1. \qquad (31.22)$$

Thus the reported marginal cost is greater than the true marginal cost (since $\alpha_1 > 0$). Now given that actual costs are observable, M needs to choose her reported fixed costs so that

$$\hat{F} + \tfrac{1}{2}\hat{c}\hat{q}^2 = F + \tfrac{1}{2}c\hat{q}^2. \qquad (31.23)$$

If this holds, there will be no evidence that M lied in reporting her cost structure (since the cost calculated under the reported cost function at $\hat{q}$ is precisely equal to that actually incurred, and observed). Rearranging (31.23), and substituting in for $\hat{q}$ from (31.20), gives the reported fixed cost as

$$\hat{F} = F - \tfrac{1}{2}\alpha_1\hat{q}^2. \qquad (31.24)$$

That is, whilst marginal cost is over-reported, this is compensated for by an under-reporting of fixed costs.

The basic story is that, by reporting a figure higher than true marginal cost, M induces a higher transfer price and so makes a greater profit. Although I have chosen a very special case, to keep the analysis as simple as possible, it should be clear that there is a general tendency for a division to cheat if a marginal-cost transfer pricing solution is implemented in a situation where true divisional benefit and cost functions are not fully observable. Because the end result is not the optimal volume of trade ($\hat{q} < q^*$ in Figure 31.8), the firm's overall profitability is less than its potential. In the particular case discussed, M increases her profit at the expense of D, with the aggregate overall profit being adversely affected.

Naturally, the same type of incentive incompatibility problem also applies to the distributor as well as the manufacturer. That is, there is an incentive both for M to exaggerate its marginal cost, and for D to misreport its marginal benefit function $v(q)$. The general consequence is that too little gets traded internally, so the firm sets too high a final price and fails to realize its maximum profit level. Thus, incentive incompatibility could prove to be a major source of inefficiency within the firm in the case where there is no competitive external market for the intermediate product (the availability of an external market gives an independent, non-manipulable basis for setting the transfer price).

To reduce the level of inefficiency that could arise out of the incentive compatibility problem, it is possible to:

(i) Try to improve the monitoring of divisional cost and benefit structures. The individuals involved in such monitoring and assessment must be independent of the divisions involved, of course.[15]

(ii) Try to devise transfer pricing rules which are less manipulable. It is possible to abandon the quest for efficiency, and in so doing reduce the incentive for untruthful reporting. Some pricing practices which may help in this regard are discussed in section 31.8. The formal theory of incentive-compatible transfer pricing (beyond the scope of this text[16]) has yet to find much application, although it can be argued that some actual practices do move in this direction.

31.7 Multinational Transfer Pricing

Multinational companies practising transfer pricing can use such prices to manipulate reported profits in the operating divisions in different countries. This can be advantageous to firms for the following reasons.

31.7.1 For Inward Investment

Managers tend to prefer internally generated finance to the alternative of using external financial markets (new equity issues, corporate bond issues, or bank borrowing), simply because it reduces various transactions costs (share issue costs etc.) and avoids the use of external finance, which leads to greater external scrutiny of the firm's operations (see e.g. Ross *et al.* 1993; there is a pecking order of preference in terms of sources of finance). If a company wishes to expand in a given country, it can facilitate this without recourse to external financial markets by setting low transfer prices for those items that the subsidiary purchases from elsewhere within the multinational, and also through high prices for the products it sells to other subsidiaries within the group. Such a pricing strategy will boost the subsidiary's profit performance, and hence increase its ability to fund investment from retained earnings.

31.7.2 For Minimizing Tax Liabilities

The tax system, and in particular the taxation of corporate enterprise, can vary across countries. It follows that multinational corporations (MNCs) will have an incentive to manipulate transfer prices so as to realize more profit where taxes are lower.[17] This type of behaviour is quite common in practice

---

[15] No easy task; auditors external to the division will usually have to rely to some extent on information provided internally, so there typically remains some scope for internal manipulation and bias in the estimation of cost structures.

[16] Incentive compatibility in bilateral relationships is studied in Rochet (1985). See also Besanko and Sibley (1991), Ronen (1992), and in the context of MNCs, Prusa (1990).

[17] Note that, with simple uniform transfer pricing rules, it appears that this would be at the expense of efficiency—however, it is typically the case that when this type of profit shifting is desired, the transfers are not based on arm's length quantities which the divisions are free to choose. That is, it is typically the case that divisions are required by the centre to take a certain quantity at a certain price. Thus the price—quantity contract is in operation (even though the quantity part of the contract may not be clear to any tax authorities).

(see e.g. Brook and Remmers 1972, Rahman and Scapens 1986).[18]

EXAMPLE 31.4 A Monopolies and Mergers Commission report (1973) into pharmaceutical transfer pricing revealed that a certain Swiss pharmaceutical company admitted to setting transfer prices for tax purposes; in particular, it set prices for two products at £370 and £922 per kilo at a time when these same products were available on the open market at £9 and £20 per kilo respectively (see Stewart 1973 for other examples).

Of course, countries (and their tax authorities) pay a great deal of attention to the strategies of multinationals, and are continually trying to limit the extent to which MNCs can get away with such tax avoidance strategies.

31.7.3 Exchange-rate Risk Management

Although typically, price itself is not actively used (albeit fluctuations in exchange rates affect real transfer prices, depending on the currency in which transfer price is fixed), MNCs undoubtedly do manipulate the volume of trade depending upon their expectations about future exchange rate movements (trade can be accelerated if adverse movements are expected, or held back to take advantage of expected favourable movements).

31.8 Transfer Pricing in Practice

Transfer price in practice is typically the external market price if available, and if not, is usually some form of full-cost plus or negotiated transfer price. Surveys suggest that marginal cost pricing is sometimes used, but certainly not extensively.[19]

38.8.1 External Market Price

Market price is probably the most widely used transfer price (see e.g. Dorward 1987 for some surveys), often less selling costs when the firm sells to an external market in addition to engaging in internal transfers.[20]

31.8.2 Full Cost

In the absence of external markets, many firms use a full cost-plus transfer pricing rule (see Emmanuel and Mehafdi 1994). In part, this can be seen as a response to the incentive compatibility problem. However, Kaplan and Atkinson (1989) have suggested that full cost transfer pricing may give reasonable results on average. The point is that the opportunity cost of using capacity rises as maximum output is approached and can indeed rise above full cost. This suggests that the opportunity cost of capacity varies with the state of demand. If there is a desire to maintain stable long-run transfer prices so as to give clear price signals, then a price equal to full cost may perform adequately. This argument does not, of course, support the practice of adding a significant mark-up to full cost in setting transfer prices.

Full cost-plus pricing has the usual merit that it is simple to understand and reasonably straightforward to implement, and it has additionally been suggested that it also stops the classification of fixed and variable costs being a bone of contention (there is less scope for misreporting costs). However, this is a reasonable argument only in the case of a single-product division. In practice, most divisions have multiple products, and the concept of full cost then suffers the usual problem of arbitrariness in joint-cost allocation (of the type discussed in detail in Section 11.3). In such situations, there is great scope for creative accountancy and the manipulation of transfer prices via the allocation of overhead across different product cost headings.

According to marginalist theory, full cost or worse, full cost-plus, transfer prices overstate the cost of transferring resources between divisions. Furthermore, full cost transfer pricing gives little incentive for the manufacturing division to be cost-efficient, simply because it can pass on its inefficiency in a higher transfer price.

---

[18] The usual test by such authorities turns on their determining the price that an unrelated third party would pay for the item under consideration (the so-called arm's length trading test). In practice this test is often inapplicable (because there are no such external dealings).

[19] Although see Chap. 24 for some discussion of how what people do and what they say they do matches up.

[20] MNCs may deviate from this on occasion because of tax considerations.

31.8.3 Negotiated Price

Some companies leave it to divisions to negotiate transfer prices. It can be argued that this could lead to reasonably efficient outcomes—but only in the case where there is no asymmetry of information. When the parties have private information, there is no guarantee that an efficient outcome can be realized—and the process can be time-consuming and costly (the outcome will depend on the respective parties' negotiating skills), particularly if it requires continual re-negotiation as circumstances change.

31.9 Summary

Section 31.2 summarized the pros and cons of integration and outsourcing and 31.3 those of decentralization. Integration creates a larger unit, and this brings with it certain motivational difficulties along with difficulties regarding the upward transmission of local and specific information; hence the M-form organization and the move toward some degree of decentralization. This induces the problem of transfer pricing. If divisions are to be profit centres, then inter-divisional trade must be priced. The problem with divisionalization and transfer pricing is that it almost returns the situation to one of arm's length trading. Whilst this is between divisions of the same company, if the managers are rewarded on their divisional performance there is potential for inefficiency if the decision rights are inappropriately specified. However, the subtle difference in the transfer pricing problem as compared to the bilateral monopoly problem is that the centre can instruct the divisions as to what transfer pricing rule has to be used. It was seen that, when there is a competitive external market, the transfer price should be set simply at the level of the market price, or the external price minus selling costs if there are external sales as well. In this case there is no problem with incentive compatibility; the transfer price is set with respect to an external reference and so cannot be manipulated. By contrast, if there is no external market for the product being transferred, then marginal reasoning suggests that the transfer price should be set at marginal cost. Unfortunately, the marginal cost pricing rule is manipulable. When divisions have private information, it was shown that there can be incentives to misreport the truth in ways that in practice are hard to uncover. The end-product is that a naive marginal cost pricing rule may perform quite poorly in terms of the objective of maximizing overall firm profit. The problem then becomes one of either trying to improve independent monitoring (to assess more accurately the true marginal cost) or to design a transfer pricing scheme which gives the divisions a greater incentive to report the truth. In practice, firms use external prices wherever possible (minus selling costs where appropriate), and tend to use full cost where this is not possible. Of course, if it is not possible to get the transfer pricing system working reasonably efficiently, then it may well pay the firm to re-centralize the divisions, to run them as a single unit with a single manager in charge.

31.10 Review Questions

1. Compare and contrast the considerations which are likely to be of importance in setting transfer prices for (*a*) an M-form organization operating in a single country; (*b*) an M-form multinational organization.

2. Suppose there are two divisions, a manufacturer M and distributor D as in section 31.4, with the inverse derived demand curve for the intermediate product by D given as

$$v(q) = 100 - q,$$

whilst M has marginal cost function

$$MC_M = 10 + 5q.$$

(*a*) If there is no external market for the product, calculate the marginal-cost transfer price.

(*b*) If there is an external market for the product, with external market price £90, calculate the optimal transfer price and the optimal choice by M of how much to produce and sell to D and to the external market, and the optimal choice by D of how much to take from M and how much to buy in from the external market. Calculate each division's profit, and the firm's total profit in each case.

(*c*) Recalculate the answers to (*b*) with an external price of £80.

(*d*) How would your answers to (*b*) and (*c*) be affected if (i) there were selling costs of £3 per unit for sales to the external market, and (ii) there were selling costs of £6 per unit?

(*e*) Explain why it is that firm joint profits

generally increase when an external market is introduced (relative to the case where there is no external market). Under what circumstances, at least within the context of the above model, would the introduction of an outside market have no effect on the firm at all?

3. Explain why, in the absence of an external market for an intermediate product, the marginal-cost transfer pricing rule has, in practice, proved to be the least popular of the approaches used by firms.

4. What drawbacks would you envisage in the use of full cost as the basis for a transfer price (in the absence of an external market)?

5. Explain the marginalist approach to transfer pricing when there is an imperfectly competitive external market.

31.11 Further Reading

Useful reviews of transfer pricing theory and practice are given in Abdel-Khalik and Lusk (1974), Grabski (1985), and Emmanuel and Mehafdi (1994); the last is accessible and gives a reasonably comprehensive bibliography on transfer pricing. It also discusses, at an informal level, the problem of transfer pricing in the presence of private information and uncertainty.

32 Economic Aspects of Human Resource Management

Objectives To examine the economics of recruitment and retention of staff, along with related issues such as whether to invest in employee training.

Prerequisites Chapters 29 and 30 provide background material. Chapter 29 deals with transaction costs and agency theory, whilst Chapter 30 examines the economics of job and organizational design, the allocation

of decision rights, and issues concerning monitoring and incentives.

Keywords compensating wage differentials, efficiency wages, firm-specific skills, fringe benefits, general skills, human capital, influence costs, job matching, job-specific skills, non-transferable skills, seniority pay, transferable skills.

32.1 Introduction

Chapters 29 and 30 developed the economics-based approach to organizational architecture, focusing on the three key elements: (1) how tasks are best bundled into jobs, and jobs into larger hierarchical structures, (2) how decision rights are best assigned, and (3) whether performance should be measured and rewarded. In a sense, therefore, I have already addressed some of the key issues involved in the economics of human resource management, namely those associated with job design and motivation. This chapter reviews some background theory regarding labour markets and then focuses on some of the elements not already covered, in particular the recruitment and retention of staff and the incentives for the firm to invest in the training of employees.

32.2 Characteristics of Labour Markets and Pay Structures

This section briefly outlines some simple models of labour employment, including the theory of compensating wage differentials, and then discusses how these relate to pay and employment conditions in practice.

32.2.1 Labour Demand in the Competitive Firm

In a competitive labour market, individuals get paid the value of their marginal product. That is, in trying to maximize profits, firms are naturally led to expand their labour input to the point where the marginal cost (the wage) of employing an additional worker just matches the value that worker contributes to the firm. Example 32.1 gives a more formal derivation of this result.

EXAMPLE 32.1 Suppose that p represents the competitive price for a profit-maximizing firm's output, and q its output level. Suppose L denotes labour employed at a competitive wage rate w, whilst K denotes capital input at a price r. Suppose the production function is $q = f(K, L)$; that is, output depends on the capital and labour inputs. Assume, as usual, that the production function is smooth and concave, with positive but diminishing marginal products. The problem for the firm is to choose K, L, and q so as to maximize π subject to the production function constraint: that is, to

$$\text{maximize } \pi = pq - rK - wL \qquad (32.1)$$

$$\text{subject to } q = f(K, L). \qquad (32.2)$$

Setting up the usual Lagrangian, denoted as $\mathcal{L}$ we have

$$\mathcal{L} = pq - rK - wL + \lambda(f(K, L) - q). \quad (32.3)$$

The first-order conditions are that

$$\partial\mathcal{L}/\partial q = p - \lambda = 0, \quad (32.4)$$

$$\partial\mathcal{L}/\partial K = -r + \lambda f_K(K, L) = 0, \quad (32.5)$$

and

$$\partial\mathcal{L}/\partial L = -w + \lambda f_L(K, L) = 0 \quad (32.6)$$

(note that p is a constant as far as the individual pricetaking firm is concerned). Making λ the subject of each of equations (32.4)–(32.6), and putting them together, gives the usual efficiency result that

$$r/f_K(K, L) = w/f_L(K, L) = p \,[= \lambda]. \quad (32.7)$$

Here, $f_L(K, L)$ is the marginal product of labour;[1] rearranging slightly, we get

$$w = pf_L(K, L). \quad (32.8)$$

The term $pf_L(K, L)$ represents the value of the marginal product of labour; this equation thus suggests that the firm chooses to employ workers up to the point where the value of the marginal product of labour is just equal to the wage. It is this result which lies behind the common but rather loose saying that in competitive markets, workers get paid a wage equal to their marginal products (what is meant is 'their marginal value products').

It can also be shown that, in the model in Example 32.1, the higher the wage, the lower the firm's demand for labour. Aggregating over all firms in the industry, we get a downward-sloping aggregate demand curve for labour, denoted D_L in Figure 32.1. Assuming an upward-sloping supply curve for labour S_L (a higher wage attracts more labour supply to the industry), we get an equilibrium wage and employment level (w_c, L_c) given by the intersection of the supply and demand curves.

32.2.2 Labour Demand with a Monopoly Supplier of Labour

Suppose firms operate in a competitive product market, but are faced by a monopoly supplier of labour. I shall refer to these monopoly suppliers as unions, although many professional associations also fall into this category (for example, the British Medical Association, the Law Society, and the various

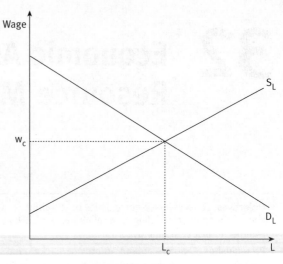

Fig. 32.1 Competitive labour market

professional accountancy bodies such as ACAEW, the Association of Chartered Accountants of England and Wales). The central purpose of such bodies is to promote the welfare and wages of their members. If we focus purely on the ability of the union to raise the wage rate above the competitive level, the union must clearly have the ability to prevent firms employing labour from outside the union. That is, it must be able to enforce a closed shop. This is easier to do if there are only a small number of firms involved. As firm numbers become large, it becomes more difficult for the union to prevent firms, especially new entrants, from hiring outside the union. However, many of the professions have been quite successful, essentially by getting state legal backing for their closed shops.

Figure 32.2 illustrates a model in which the union chooses a wage, and the firms then decide how many individuals to employ. In effect, the union can pick any point on the aggregate demand for labour schedule, D_L, and so faces a trade-off: setting a high wage restricts its membership size, assuming all union members are to be fully employed. The union could, for example, choose to maximize employment by setting the competitive wage w_c, or to maximize the total wage payment to its members by setting wage w_R, or to maximize the sum of economic rents

---

[1] The marginal product of labour, (MP_L) is defined as $MP_L = f_L(K, L) = \partial f(K, L)/\partial L \,(> 0)$; the assumption of a diminishing marginal product is that $\partial MP_L/\partial L = f_{LL}(K, L) = \partial f^2(K, L)/\partial L^2 < 0$ (see Chap. 10).

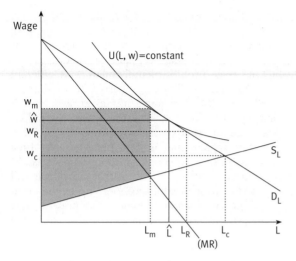

Fig. 32.2 Monopoly supplier of labour

accruing to its members by setting wage w_m.[2] However, if we model the union as being concerned about *both* the numbers of union members in employment *and* the wage, then this suggests that the union aims to maximize a utility function of the form $U(w, L)$. This utility function $U(w, L)$ gives rise to indifference curves in (w, L) space, and the solution features a tangency between the indifference curve and the outer boundary of the feasible set, which in this case is the demand for labour schedule (so long as the tangency occurs to the left of L_c); the solution is illustrated as the point $(\hat{w}, \hat{L})$, although note that such a point of tangency could occur at any point on D_L, depending on the union's relative preference for high wage versus membership size.

It is possible to model the behaviour of the leadership of such a union in a more sophisticated way through an agency treatment (in which union leaders may not necessarily have their members' interests at heart)—but the general consequence of any such modelling is that the resulting wage is higher than would be the case if there were no such monopoly power on the labour supply side

(see e.g. Gravelle and Rees 1987 for some simple examples).

Given that theory suggests unions tend to raise wages above competitive levels, then, *ceteris paribus* one might expect this to entail a welfare loss (see Chapter 28). However, as usual, ceteris are not paribus. The presence of unions can help to reduce transactions costs associated with employment. The avoidance of such transactions costs can make some firms quite sanguine about having to deal with unions. Furthermore, the impact of unionization on wage levels also depends on how competitive the industry is. Karier (1985), for example, working with US data, noted that there was some positive wage effect in concentrated industries, but no discernible effect in relatively competitive industries, as one would expect.

It is also possible to examine the spillover impacts of union monopoly power. The general idea is that if unions are successful at raising wages and restricting employment in the unionized sector, this suggests that those who do not find work in the unionized sector will move across to swell supply to the non-unionized sector. The ensuing rightward shift in the supply curve in such a competitive market will in theory depress the equilibrium wage in that market.[3]

32.2.3 Labour and Bilateral Monopoly

It was mentioned in section 32.2.2 that unions tend to find it harder to exert an impact in industries where firms are essentially competitive, the major reason being that it is difficult to control entry by firms employing cheaper, non-unionized labour. It follows that we would expect to see unions playing more of a role in industries in which there are relatively small numbers of firms (with significant barriers to entry etc.), as is in fact the case.

The relationship in such cases is one of bilateral monopoly; that is, the union is involved in bilateral bargaining with the management of each firm. Bilateral monopoly is a market structure that was analysed in section 25.4 (to which the reader is referred). Under full information, theory predicts that bilateral monopoly leads to efficient trades

---

[2] Compare these solutions with that of a monopoly firm setting a marginal cost price, a revenue-maximizing price, or a monopoly price. It may also help, in thinking about this type of figure, to recall that economic rent is the sum of money paid to factors of production over and above that needed to keep them in employment. Thus the supply curve depicts the wage at which the marginal individual is just willing to supply labour, with the area below the wage line and above the labour supply curve representing economic rent accruing to union members. It is maximized if the union sets the wage w_m.

[3] This is a similar argument to that sometimes presented regarding the minimum wage legislation. That is, introducing a minimum wage reduces employment in the markets subject to a minimum wage, so pushing labour supply to the right in those not subject to it (the unregulated black markets), so depressing the often already low wages in those sectors even further.

(here, an efficient level of employment),[4] with the wage at which this amount is employed being subject to negotiation. However, it was also noted that, if there is asymmetric information regarding the size of the pie over which negotiations take place, there is the possibility of bargaining failure, or of an efficient outcome failing to be realized. In practice, given the long-term nature of the bargaining situation in which they find themselves, unions and management are usually able to resolve this type of bargaining game to some degree of satisfaction for the parties involved.[5]

32.2.4 The Theory of Compensating Wage Differentials

In a competitive labour market, the theory of **compensating wage differentials** is supposed to apply. The idea is that every job has particular characteristics and that wages reflect both supply-side and demand-side characteristics; for example,

· individual abilities, skills, and education;

· job location (ease of commuting, attractiveness of local housing, etc.);

· job risk (accident rates may be known to be high—as in, say, deep mining);

· other job characteristics (quality of the work environment; monotony, unsocial hours, dirt, noise, etc.).

This suggests that, *ceteris paribus*, a less congenial job will command a higher wage; likewise, one which requires investment by the individual in skills that are costly and difficult to acquire will also yield a higher wage rate.

In a competitive labour market, the investment in skills might be thought to be a broadly zero net present value exercise: that is, if it costs £X to acquire a skill, then the ensuing wage differential (net of taxes etc.), present-valued at a suitably risky

discount rate over the working life, ought to just balance the initial outlay. In fact it is possible to estimate the discount rate, usually referred to as the 'return to **human capital**', by looking at the lifetime wage profiles of individuals with different education and skills. It is referred to as 'human capital' because it requires an investment, and it yields a return to that investment over the individual's lifetime (and it has the properties of other forms of capital: that is, it depreciates over time but can be supplemented, or topped up, by additional training etc.). The idea is that individuals will choose to invest in education only up to the point where the incremental cost equals the present value of the expected increment in income that will ensue from such training.

The other important aspect of the theory of compensating wage differentials is that it induces a process of **job matching**, in which the most relevant people are attracted to particular jobs. To take some extreme examples, deaf people might be attracted to the high wages offered in noisy environments.[6] Likewise, risk lovers will be attracted to riskier jobs, while the more risk-averse will be attracted to more secure employment (people do differ in their attitude to risk and their attitude to risk can change over their lifetimes—as their commitments etc. change).

EXAMPLE 32.2 In 1994, US labour secretary Robert Reich charged a Bridgestone Tyre subsidiary with 107 safety code violations and Bridgestone had to pay a fine of $7.5 million. This did not meet with approval from the employees. With Bridgestone having to implement safety codes, the jobs became much safer, and the compensating wage differential (danger money) disappeared. The point of course is that the risk-takers who went for the danger money were quite happy with the level of risk they faced in their original job situation—and they did not appreciate being forced to take more safety for less pay. (For more details, see Brickley *et al.* 1997: 248.)

Economic liberals argue that, so long as individuals are aware of the risks they face, and so long as markets are reasonably competitive, there is no need

---

[4] Efficient, that is, for the parties concerned (management and union); this does not entail global efficiency, because a firm with monopoly power will set prices above marginal costs; see Chaps. 14 and 28.

[5] The fact that it is a long-term relationship means that union and management both have a reasonable understanding of the nature of the business and the pressures that it faces (although management may have superior information). Thus information is more complete regarding the size of the pie to be divided, so the transactions costs associated with such negotiations are rather less than they would otherwise be—and an efficient outcome is more likely.

[6] Hence some care needs to be taken when analysing cause and effect; if one were to look simply at correlations between hearing impairment and noisy jobs, this type of job selection might well induce a positive correlation. One would need to get evidence of damage actually caused whilst in a job.

to legislate such 'protection'; they argue that the market will efficiently solve the problem. Furthermore, they argue that well-meaning intervention can often make matters worse. The above example illustrates the kernel of truth in this view. However, there would appear to be a role for state intervention when markets are imperfectly competitive or when individuals have a poor understanding of the risks they face.

In practice, the competitiveness of labour markets varies considerably across different types of job and across countries. For example, job markets in the US tend to be far more competitive than those in Europe, where monopoly power on both sides of the market is still quite common. The theory of compensating wage differentials will apply only to an approximation if markets are imperfectly competitive, and it is possible in such markets for significant wage differentials to persist (by age, by sex, by ethnicity, etc.) even where individuals do similar work. However, the theory clearly does hold to an extent; wages for unsocial hours (night shifts and weekend shifts) are routinely higher, risky occupations command higher wages, and so on.[7]

32.2.5 Pay in Practice

In practice, the structure of pay is only partly captured by the above economic models, primarily because, except for simple, relatively unskilled jobs, most employment takes place in the context of long-term contracts. The general characteristics of pay in such circumstances may be summarized as follows:

1. Pay is geared to the level in the hierarchy; the higher the level in the organization, the higher the pay.

2. Pay structures are set for jobs, and do not vary much across individuals in the same type of job within the firm.

3. Most promotion is internal, with recruitment from the level below in the hierarchy.

4. Wages tend to increase with seniority.

The first observation, that pay goes with level, may suggest a correspondence with marginal productivity theory (high level = high productivity),

although there is some evidence that individuals higher up the hierarchy get paid less than their marginal products whilst those further down get paid more. Frank (1984), for example, suggests this is because of a compensating wage differential effect; job characteristics at a higher level include status, decision authority, etc., and these are characteristics which are valued by individuals for their own sake, so such individuals can end up with relatively lower financial rewards.

The second observation fits in with what transaction cost theory would predict. Standardization of jobs and the pay structures associated with them clearly reduces transactions costs which would otherwise be required if an employer had to negotiate terms with each and every employee. It should be noted that what is typically standardized is the pay *structure*. If this includes incentive pay elements, then differential productivity is differentially rewarded. However, the main point is that all employees at a given level have equal earning opportunities. This helps reduce transactions costs, and also tends to reduce envy within peer groups.

The third observation also makes considerable sense from the perspective of transactions cost theory. There is often significant firm-specific human capital which individuals within the organization build up over time (knowledge of the firm's idiosyncratic modes of operation, including its technological systems, information systems, and organizational systems); furthermore, the firm builds up knowledge of the attributes of its employees, and so can seek to place them where they are most productive. Both parties lose firm-specific asset value when an individual leaves and has to be replaced.

The fourth observation can also be justified as a way of creating incentives for individuals to stay with an organization (so reducing turnover costs), and of motivating such individuals; this point is discussed in more detail in section 32.3.4 below.

32.3 Recruitment and Retention of Employees

Outsourcing was discussed in Chapters 30 and 31. Naturally, in deciding to recruit to a given job, one has to ask first whether the job is best placed inside the firm or outsourced (such as when a firm hires an external contractor or consultant). If the firm recruits rather than outsources, the issues that arise

---

[7] The focus in this chapter is purely on the problem faced by the firm in human resource management. The important wider social concerns associated with discrimination in labour markets may, through legislation, have an impact on the firm, but these issues are not considered in any further detail here.

concern employment contracts (incentives and prospects for internal promotion etc.), the age–wage structure, the opportunities for employees to acquire human capital (and whether or not this is at the expense of the firm), and whether the firm should try to hold on to workers through matching outside offers. These are discussed below.

32.3.1 Transactions Cost Minimization

The theory of transactions cost minimization described in Chapter 29 suggested that the type of transaction which was most likely to minimize transactions costs depended on the characteristics of that transaction. These characteristics were (1) frequency, (2) timeliness/reliability, (3) complexity, and (4) asset specificity; they are now reviewed in the context of the labour transaction.

Frequency. For jobs that occur only infrequently, indivisibilities can be a problem internally (not fully utilizing the resource), and so outsourcing can prove attractive. As frequency increases, indivisibility becomes less of a problem; the larger the number of transactions the more fully they are likely to fill a job or jobs, so making internal provision more attractive.

Timeliness/reliability. Jobs critical for core production are usually internalized. Long-term contracting might be possible, but is only usually attractive if there are significant economies of scale (see Chapter 30). Economies of scale tend to be less important in the human resource field than for plant and machinery,[8] so internalization is usually preferable.

Complexity. For simple jobs, where the output is relatively easy to measure, it can pay to contract out. However, for complex outputs, where output quality is manipulable and there may also be private information about quality etc., then internal provision is usually preferable. However, note that when there is complexity, and hence the potential for output manipulability (Chapter 30), considerable care needs to be taken regarding the design of the labour contract.

Human asset specificity. This concerns the extent to which the job requires job-specific and firm-specific skills. The higher the level of firm-specific skills, the more likely it is that provision will be internal.

---

[8] For example, electricity is usually outsourced because internal use is generally small relative to plant-efficient scale.

EXAMPLE 32.3 Infrequent or complex tasks, such as installing a new information system, are often contracted out to specialists or consultants. Bottleneck jobs are usually internally sourced, although some may be on long-term contracts (such as photocopier and computer repairs). Simple jobs with low asset specificity are often hired on short-term contracts (as casual labour).

If transactions are taken into the firm, the objective becomes one of minimizing total costs, including the transaction costs associated with recruitment and staff turnover. Sections 32.3.2–32.3.4 review strategies widely used in practice by firms to this end.

32.3.2 Efficiency Wages

In a competitive labour market, theory suggests that individuals get paid their marginal products. There is no purpose in a firm offering a higher wage than the going rate for the job. However, in practice, there is some evidence that setting an above-average rate, so-called **efficiency wages**, can be beneficial for a firm:

1. High pay may act as a motivational device: higher pay, even if not in the form of direct incentive pay, can be motivating if it is backed by the possibility of being fired for less than satisfactory work. The point is that, if the firm pays only the going rate, sacking a worker only imposes on that worker the cost of going and finding another job (at the same wage). If the firm offers above-average pay, then the worker also loses the wage differential if he or she gets the sack. In practice, behaviour often has to be significantly worse than satisfactory before firing becomes a realistic threat (given that such action may induce a variety of transaction costs, including union action and litigation for unfair dismissal, in addition to the usual transaction costs involved); as a consequence, the motivational argument probably does not often carry much weight.

2. Above-average pay reduces employee turnover (equally, paying below the going rate increases turnover). There are transactions costs associated with advertizing, interviewing, and selecting, followed by on-the-job training costs and learning-by-doing efficiency losses. Also, for some types of job, there is the potential leakage of confidential information (if an employee who has specialist knowledge specific to the firm takes up a job with a competitor). For jobs

in which these costs are high, it can pay the firm to raise its wage because the additional wage bill is more than offset by the reduced turnover costs. Indeed, theory suggests raising the wage until the marginal cost in terms of the wage bill just balances the marginal benefit in terms of reduced transactions costs.

3. It can be argued that a higher wage induces a beneficial screening or selection bias effect. Imagine that individuals looking for jobs have different reservation wage rates, and that reservation wage rates correlate with ability. If a firm offers a low wage rate, only those with reservation wages below the offered rate will apply. Some of these will get such jobs and drop out of the pool of job seekers. Firms offering higher wages will attract more job seekers in total, but will also get, on average, a better quality of applicant than those firms who offer lower wages.

4. A higher wage not only improves the average quality of applicants, due to the screening effect, but also increases the total number of applicants. This cuts two ways: it increases the difficulty of selection, but, if the selection process can be made to work, it suggests that it may be possible to recruit an even better employee.

5. A higher wage also makes it more worth while for applicants to expend resources in trying to signal their quality (by investing in education, training qualifications, etc.).

6. A higher wage may also create more team spirit and identification with the company if that company is a good employer and pays above-average wages. Although agency theory suggests that higher wages per se will not motivate employees (putting to one side the threat-of-redundancy effect), individuals are not simply selfish utility maximizers, so there may be some additional beneficial productivity arising out of efficiency wages.

EXAMPLE 32.4 Perhaps one of the most famous examples of efficiency pay in action occurred when Henry Ford, circa 1914, more than doubled the wage rate for his automobile workers (to $5 per hour). All of the above consequences ensued: applications for posts increased dramatically, turnover fell, productivity rose, and most important of all, firm profitability was significantly increased by the strategy.

Thus pay above the average can be beneficial for the firm. However, much depends on the transaction costs associated with turnover. For jobs where there are significant firm-specific skills to be acquired, it may well benefit the firm to offer pay above the going rate.[9] By contrast, if a job involves a relatively low skill level, with little firm-specific knowledge, then turnover costs will be relatively low, and a wage near the going rate is more appropriate. Note also that appointment procedures can be streamlined for unskilled posts since, if it does not matter very much who does the job, there is little point in expending many resources on the selection process, whilst for jobs involving significant firm-specific skill etc., it is worth expending more time and effort on the selection process (since getting the right candidate is more important in such a case).

At a practical level, the two obvious indicators of whether the wage rate advertized is appropriate for a given job are:

1. the number of job applicants (or more precisely, the number of job applicants who are deemed appointable);

2. the resignation rate (in particular, with regard to employees leaving to go to outside and similar jobs).

If there is a low resignation rate and a large number of adequately qualified applicants, then the wage rate is probably set too high (although more generally, the level of transactions costs etc. described above needs to be taken into account in judging the appropriate wage level to set).

EXAMPLE 32.5 Lectureships in UK universities all offer the same pay scale (with the exception of medical staff, who have a separate and significantly higher scale). At the author's university (and this is fairly typical across the country), history lectureships attract many applicants, all highly qualified (with many publications etc.). By contrast, lectureships in accounting attract few appointable applicants, and even those that are deemed appointable typically have a limited publication track record. The main problem is that there is plenty of competition from the private sector job market for accountants. As a consequence, academic research in the area of

---

[9] Although efficiency wages are a rational strategy for an individual firm, there are elements of the prisoner's dilemma here. That is, each firm has the incentive to raise wage above the going rate, but if all do so, then firms get no benefit (with all the other firms paying high wages, one firm's high wage is no longer a motivating device since workers can get the same pay elsewhere).

accountancy is relatively weak in the UK. Likewise, academics in other vocational areas (engineering, medicine, law, even economics) are more likely to quit academia in order to take up employment in the more lucrative private sector.

To sum up, if the firm offers a higher rate for a given job, the number of applications for such posts will rise, the quality of the resulting recruitment should also improve, and the incentive for employees to move on will be diminished. The firm needs to balance these benefits against the additional wage bill that will be incurred. For jobs where there is significant learning by doing and training in order to become productive within the firm, it will usually pay to incur a higher wage because the non-wage benefits can be significant.

32.3.3 Attitudes to Outside Offers

Should the firm match an outside offer? Matching outside offers tends to reduce turnover costs but incurs a higher wage bill. The argument against it is that if the firm always does so, and this becomes known within the organization, then there is an incentive for staff to expend resources and effort actively seeking outside offers in order to crank up their wages; these are so-called **influence costs**. Furthermore, the impact is not only on wages, as there is also an opportunity cost in that more effort expended on such activities implies less effort exerted productively within the firm.

In theory, the decision on whether or not to match an outside offer should be influenced by the level of firm-specific human capital in a given job. If this is significant, the firm will usually find it economic to match or more than match any outside offer, quite simply because the latter is based on the value of the individual without the firm-specific capital. It follows that a mutually beneficial bargaining outcome should be reachable, in which the employee stays with the firm and the added value of firm-specific human capital, which would be wasted if the worker moved on, is beneficially shared between the employer and the worker.

32.3.4 Seniority Pay Structures

Pay structures in which individuals receive low pay in the early years, and increasing levels of **seniority pay** (even though still doing the same job), are widespread, particularly in managerial and professional employment. This may seem to fit with marginal productivity theory since, if individuals have to acquire significant firm-specific human capital, and there is also firm-specific learning by doing, then productivity may well increase with seniority. However, such efficiency improvements typically occur only for a relatively small number of years, and age can also lead to some fall-off in productivity (particularly for those in physically demanding jobs). Thus, the general consequence of a rising pay structure over time is that it under-rewards early productivity, and over-rewards the later years, as illustrated in Figure 32.3 (and there is some empirical evidence to bear this out—see Kotlikoff and Gokhale 1992, for example).

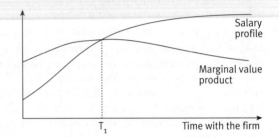

Fig. 32.3 Age-for-wage pay structures

Seniority pay may be rational even if it is not backed by productivity. One argument is that it helps to increase motivation, and to reduce shirking and staff turnover. In the early years, individuals become increasingly motivated by each additional year of employment, because if they exit the firm (either voluntarily or compulsorily), they lose the investment they have built toward the later years of high pay (and high pension). Thus, seniority pay, in conjunction with some degree of monitoring of performance and a credible threat of job loss if the individual is found shirking, can prove a useful motivational device. One might think that it is in the interests of the firm to offer a seniority pay contract, and then sack the employee at the point where the wage starts to rise above the marginal revenue product curve (time T_1 in Figure 32.3). However, this is not in fact the case. If the firm were to do this, it would give a signal to would-be employees that the contract would not be honoured, and individuals taking a job look at the overall package on offer: if they observe that the firm disposes of staff early, this will have a disincentive effect. Overall, the present value of the income stream on offer must be satisfactory. From the firm's perspective, whilst seniority pay has motivational plus points, it is clearly desirable to impose a compulsory retirement age, to avoid the post-contract opportunism of workers staying too long aboard the gravy train.

32.4 Training of Employees

The firm can improve the human capital of its workers by either in-firm, on-the-job training, or by funding outside training bodies to do the training for them (as for example when firms fund university provision of MBA or specialist masters' programmes). The traditional theory regarding whether a firm will choose to provide or fund training for its employees suggests that the decision depends on whether or not the training can be classified as the acquisition of transferable or non-transferable skills (see e.g. Mincer 1962, Becker 1984).

Definition 32.1 General skills are those which are not job-specific but which are transferable both across jobs and across firms. General skills are **transferable skills**. By contrast, job-specific skills are those which have no value outside a given job. Job-specific skills are, of course, transferable across firms. Finally, **firm-specific skills** are those which have no value outside a particular firm. Thus firm-specific skills are **non-transferable skills**.

EXAMPLE 32.6 At the extreme of general skills we have numeracy, literacy, etc. Somewhat less general, but still counting as transferable skills, are typing, word processing, and a familiarity with dominant software such as Microsoft Windows and Office. Job-specific skills are widespread; most apprenticeship-trained skilled workers (lathe operators, fitters, electricians, etc.) fall into this category. Firm-specific skills arise when the firm makes a unique product, or operates idiosyncratic systems; computing and production control systems often fall into this category, but generally, detailed knowledge of how a firm works, its administrative and control systems (and of how to take short-cuts through such systems), etc. all count as firm-specific knowledge; that is, such knowledge has little value outside the particular firm.

32.4.1 Transferable Skills (General or Job-Specific Skills)

The key distinction in early theory was whether the skill was transferable or non-transferable. For transferable skills, the employee can take these with her to any new job, and so can obtain elsewhere a wage which reflects these skills. It then follows that a firm which trains such an individual in such skills will have to match the new skilled wage level after educating the worker. That is, the training cost cannot be recouped; the firm therefore does better simply to hire such skilled workers from outside. If individuals wish to acquire such skills, they must pay the price themselves.

32.4.2 Non-Transferable Skills (Firm-Specific Skills)

By contrast, conventional theory suggested that firms are more likely to invest in non-transferable (firm-specific) skills. The idea here is that the worker who acquires firm-specific skills effectively enters into a bilateral monopoly relationship with the employer. Both sides have some monopoly power because first, the firm can threaten to sack the worker (which would extinguish the worker's firm-specific human capital), whilst the worker can threaten to withdraw her labour (so imposing on the firm the cost of having to train another worker in the firm-specific skills required for the job). The usual argument is that there are gains from the employment bargain, and the two parties should be able to negotiate a wage somewhere between the marginal value product to the firm of such a worker, and the wage she could get if she had to go elsewhere and lose the firm-specific human capital. In this case, therefore, the firm is able to capture some of the increased productivity that training gives, and so is more likely to be prepared to supply such training.

32.4.3 Why Firms Offer Transferable Skill Training

The early theory described above does not appear to square too well with the evidence, as many firms do seem to provide transferable skill training (of all types, from general administration and office training to support for MBA and related programmes). On the face of it, this does not make sense, because training is a benefit in kind and, so the argument goes, individuals prefer to take the cash equivalent and the freedom that goes with cash as to how to spend it. However, if we enquire more deeply into the problem, it turns out that there are many reasons why firms are likely to wish to offer general, non-firm-specific training.

One obvious reason why firms provide fringe benefits (such as training and health insurance) is that, relative to salary income, this form of income faces a lower effective tax rate. If the total tax taken by government can be reduced by giving pay in one form rather than another, then it is in the mutual interest of both firm and employee to agree on a reward structure which does this.

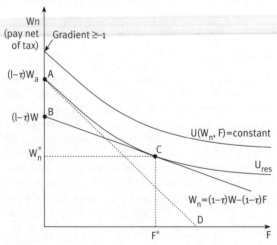

F= Fringe benefits (health insurance, general training, etc.)

Fig. 32.4 Salary versus fringe benefits

Figure 32.4 illustrates the general argument that, in the absence of a differential tax treatment, an employee prefers cash to kind; that is, to be given cash rather than specific commodities which are not easily or costlessly resellable (medical health insurance and individual training come into this category). The idea is that the individual can always choose to purchase the commodities herself—but cash gives her the option of buying other things instead. To explain Figure 32.4, let W be the amount of money handed over by the firm to the employee, split between F, the amount given as fringe benefits, and $W - F$, the gross salary. Suppose fringe benefits are not taxed as income at all, whilst salary is taxed at the rate τ. Thus the individual receives F in fringe benefits and net salary W_n, given as

$$W_n = (W - F)(1 - \tau) = (1 - \tau)W - (1 - \tau)F.$$
$$(32.9)$$

Clearly, for a fixed gross payment W by the firm, increasing F decreases W_n; that is, for a given W, the firm can choose to offer a net-of-tax package (W_n, F), where W_n is defined by (32.9). In other words, for a given gross payment of W, the firm is able to offer a net pay/fringe benefit package at any point on the straight line passing from point B through point C (all points on the line from B through C have the same total cost W to the firm). The individual is viewed as having a utility function of the form $U(W_n, F)$ which gives rise to the usual indifference curves. These indifference curves are drawn so as to always have gradient greater than -1 (i.e. flatter than a negative 45° slope), since £1 of cash is always as least as good as £1 of income in the form of a particular fringe benefit. As in the agency models (Chapter 29), it is assumed that an individual will have a reservation utility level denoted U_{res}; the reward package must offer this level of utility, or the individual will seek employment elsewhere.

(a) Case 1: No Income Taxes

First, consider the case where there are no taxes. In the absence of taxes ($\tau = 0$), equation (32.9) simplifies to give $W_n = W - F$, and the wage/fringe benefit line has gradient -1: that is, it is a straight line such as AD. Notice that reducing W causes a parallel shift in the line downwards and to the left. The firm aims to choose a package that gets the individual to the level U_{res}, and this is most cheaply done by offering a gross wage W_a and no fringe benefits (point A on the line AD). Thus, in the absence of taxes, there is no point in the firm offering fringe benefits (this is also true if salary and fringe benefits are taxed at the same rate).

(b) Case 2: Positive Income Tax, Fringe Benefits not Taxed

Now consider the case where there is a positive tax τ on income whilst fringe benefits are completely untaxed. In this case, from equation (32.9), the net wage/fringe benefit trade-off line has a slope of $-(1 - \tau)$ (which is flatter than that of the no-tax case), as in the case of the line from B through C. Again, a reduction in W causes a parallel shift in this line down and to the left. The firm once more wishes to minimize W, but must choose a reward package which offers the reservation utility level U_{res} needed to keep the employee in the post; hence W is reduced until the line just gives a tangency with the U_{res} indifference curve (at the point C). The solution involves the firm offering total pay W, split up into a fringe benefit payment F^* and a gross salary of $W-F^*$, which after tax leaves the individual with net pay W_n^*. This reward package minimizes the gross amount of money the firm needs to pay out to retain the employee. Clearly, in the presence of taxes, it is cheaper to offer the package at point C, which gives the individual (W_n^*, F^*), rather than the one at point A, which gives $((1 - \tau)W_a, 0)$, since the gross cost to the firm is less: $W < W_a$.

In practice some fringe benefits get counted as taxable income, at least in part, but the general idea holds; offering a package in which part of the pay is in tax-sheltered fringe benefits can be to the advantage of both the firm and the employee. In the above model, all the benefits go to the firm (employees remain on their reservation utility levels). With firm-specific skills or imperfectly competitive labour markets, both employees and the firm will share some of the benefits of the tax shelter (at the expense of government tax receipts).

A reward package which includes fringe benefits can also be tailored to select employees with characteristics which are desirable, from the firm's perspective. Thus offering health insurance will tend to attract those with families, whilst jobs with low or no fringe benefits, *ceteris paribus*, will tend to attract those without family commitments. Offering general training *which leads to a graded qualification* (which may also be failed) will be more attractive to an abler individual (if you think you would fail, then you would rather just have the extra salary, even if it is taxed more heavily). Thus offering a reward package in which part of the reward is general training which is then assessed (and might be failed) can be a useful way not only of improving tax efficiency but also of tending to screen out the less able; *ceteris paribus*, they are simply less likely to apply for such jobs.[10]

---

[10] See Acemoglu and Pischke (1998) for a slightly different perspective on this issue of why offering general training may be attractive to firms. They focus on the information asymmetry—and the idea that training can help to reveal which employees are the most able. They claim that not only do abler employees add more value from such training, but other employers are unable to detect such employees' ability: since it is revealed through in-house training, it is difficult to signal this externally. As a consequence, employees cannot go elsewhere to claim the added value. Hence the firm gains some value out of such general training.

32.5 Summary

This chapter has reviewed some of the issues concerning the economics of human resource management not covered in Chapters 29 and 30 (where issues of job design, of assigning decision authority, and of monitoring and reward systems were addressed); it began by examining the traditional theory of employment (marginal productivity theory, compensating wage differentials, etc.), and then looked at some of the key features observed in the workplace, notably efficiency wages, seniority pay, fringe benefits, and firm-sponsored or in-house training.

32.6 Review Questions

1. In Figure 32.2, suppose the tangency point betweeen the indifference curve and the demand for labour, D_L, occurs to the left of L_m or to the right of L_c. Explain the nature of the optimal solution in each case.

2. For what reasons might wages deviate from the marginal revenue product of labour? Discuss.

3. Examine the pros and cons of state intervention in labour markets to impose a maximum number of working hours per week, as is intended by the European Union.

4. British universities offer few perks and relatively low pay. By contrast, many private sector organizations offer significant fringe benefits (company cars, medical insurance, etc.). Why do the pay structures differ, and what are the likely consequences for recruitment in each case?

5. A recent proposal has suggested that sick pay should no longer be borne by the firm, but rather by the individual. That is, if you do not turn up for work, for whatever reason, you do not get any pay. Analyse and assess the consequences of such a proposal.

6. 'In a free market economy, in which there was no state intervention, it would be a matter of individual choice how long one worked.' Would it? Discuss.

7. (a) Show that, in the model illustrated in Figure 32.4, if salary and fringe benefits are taxed at the same rate, then it is never optimal for the firm to offer a reward package which includes fringe benefits.

(*b*) The model assumed in (*a*) suggests that if fringe benefits are fully taxed as income, then firms will not offer such fringe benefits. Can you think of any reasons why a firm might provide such benefits even if they are fully classified as income?

32.7 Further Reading

A recent general text which covers the economics of human resource management is Ehrenberg and Smith (1988). Brickley *et al.* (1997) and Milgrom and Roberts (1992) also cover this area in some detail. Becker (1983) gives an account of early theory and evidence on human capital, whilst Acemoglu and Pischke (1998) is a good example of recent thinking on labour market theory (emphasizing the importance of asymmetric information on the design of labour contracts).

References

Abdel-Khalik, A., and Lusk, E. J. (1974), 'Transfer Pricing: A Synthesis', *Accounting Review*, 49: 8–23

Acemoglu, D., and Pischke, J.-S. (1998), 'Why Do Firms Train? Theory and Evidence', *Quarterly Journal of Economics*, 113: 79–119

Akerlof, G. (1970), 'The Market for "Lemons": Qualitative Uncertainty and the Market Mechanism', *Quarterly Journal of Economics*, 84: 488–500.

Alchian, A. (1950), 'Uncertainty, Evolution and Economic Theory', *Journal of Political Economy*, 58: 211–22.

—— and Demsetz, H. (1972), 'Production, Information Costs and Economic Organisation', *American Economic Review*, 62: 777–95.

Allais, M. (1954), 'Le Comportement de l'homme rationnel devant le risque: critique de postulats et axiomes de l'école americaine', *Econometrica*, 21: 503–46.

Anderson, D. R., Sweeney, D., and Williams, T. A. (1982), *An Introduction to Management Science*, St Paul, Minn.: West Publishing Co.

Annual Abstract of Statistics, London: HMSO.

Ansoff, H. I. (1970), *Corporate Strategy*, London: Penguin Books.

Apostol, T. M. (1974), *Mathematical Analysis*, 2nd edn. Reading, Mass.: Addison Wesley.

Areeda, P., and Turner, D. (1975), 'Predatory Pricing and Related Practices under Section 2 of the Sherman Act', *Harvard Law Review*, 88: 697–733.

Armstrong, M., and Vickers, J. (1993), 'Price Discrimination, Competition and Regulation', *Journal of Industrial Economics*, 41: 335–59.

Arnold, J. (1973), *Pricing and Output Decisions*, Accountancy Age Books, London: Haymarket Publishing Ltd.

Arrow, K. J. (1962), 'The Economic Implications of Learning by Doing', *Review of Economic Studies*, 29: 155–73.

—— (1963), 'Uncertainty and Medical Care', *American Economic Review*, 53: 941–73.

—— (1971), *Essays in the Theory of Risk Bearing*, Chicago: Markham.

Atkinson, A. A., Banker, R. D., Kaplan, R. S., and Young, S. M. (1997), *Management Accounting*, 2nd edn. Englewood Cliffs, NJ: Prentice Hall.

Atkinson, A. B., and Stiglitz, J. E. (1980), *Lectures on Public Economics*, New York: McGraw-Hill.

Averch, H., and Johnson, L. L. (1962), 'Behaviour of the Firm under Regulatory Constraint', *American Economic Review*, 52: 1053–69.

Bain, J. (1956), *The Barriers to New Competition*, Cambridge, Mass.: Harvard University Press.

Baker, G. (1993), 'Rethinking Rewards', *Harvard Business Review*, Nov–Dec.: 44–5.

Barnard, N. R., *et al.* (1974), 'A Comment on "A Note on Jaguar's Pricing Policy"', *European Journal of Marketing*, 8: 182–3.

Battalio, R. C., and Ekelund, R. B., Jr. (1972), 'Output Change under Third-Degree Price Discrimination', *Southern Economic Journal*, 39: 285–90.

Baumol W. J. (1959), *Business Behaviour, Value and Growth*, London: Macmillan.

—— (1972*a*), *Economic Theory and Operations Analysis*, Englewood Cliff, NJ: Prentice Hall.

—— (1972*b*), 'On Taxation and the Control of Externalities', *American Economic Review*, 62: 307–22.

—— (1976), 'It Takes Two to Tango, or Sind "separable externalities" überhaupt möglich?', *Journal of Political Economy*, 84: 381–7.

—— (1982), 'Contestable Markets: An Uprising in the Theory of Market Structure', *American Economic Review*, 72: 1–15.

—— and Oates, W. (1975), *The Theory of Environmental Policy*, Englewood Cliffs, NJ: Prentice Hall.

—— and Quandt, R. E. (1964), 'Rules of Thumb and Optimally Imperfect Decisions', *American Economic Review*, 54: 23–46.

Baumol W. J. Panzer, J. C., and Willig, R. D. (1982), *Contestable Markets and the Theory of Market Structure*, New York: Harcourt Brace Jovanovich.

Beavis, B., and Dobbs, I. M. (1990), *Optimisation and Stability Theory for Economic Analysis*, London: Cambridge University Press.

Becker, G. (1983), *Human Capital*, Chicago: Chicago University Press.

—— and **Murphy, K. M.** (1993), 'A Simple Theory of Advertising as a Good or Bad', *Quarterly Journal of Economics*, 108: 941–63.

Beesley, M., and Littlechild, S. C. (1989), 'The Regulation of Privatised Monopolies in the United Kingdom', *Rand Journal of Economics*, 20: 454–72.

Begg, D. K. (1982), *The Rational Expectations Revolution in Macroeconomics*, Oxford: Philip Allan.

Belkaoui, A. (1986), *The Learning Curve: A Management Accounting Tool*, Westport, Conn.: Quorum Books.

Bell, D. (1984), 'Bidding for the *SS Kuniang*', *Interfaces*, Mar.–Apr.: 17–23.

Bernoulli, D. (1738), 'Exposition of a New Theory of the Measurement of Risk', English trans. in *Econometrica*, 22 (1954): 23–36.

Berry, R. H. (1994), *Management Accounting in Universities*, London: CIMA.

Bertrand, J. (1883), 'Théorie mathématique de la richesse sociale', *Journal des savants*, 67: 499–508.

Besanko, D., and Sibley, D. (1991), 'Compensation and Transfer Pricing in a Principal Agent Model', *International Economics Review*, 32: 55–68.

—— **Dranove, D., and Shanley, M.** (1995), *The Economics of Strategy*, New York: Wiley.

Binmore, K. (1992), *Fun and Games: A Text on Game Theory*, Lexington, Mass.: D. C. Heath and Co.

Blair, R. D., and Esquibel, A. K. (1995), 'Some Remarks on Monopoly Leveraging', *The Antitrust Bulletin*, 40: 371–96.

Blaug, M. (1968), *Economic Theory in Retrospect*, 2nd Edn. London: Heinemann.

Boadway, R. B. and Bruce, N. (1984), *Welfard Economics*, Oxford: Blackwell.

Bolton, G. (1997), 'The Rationality of Splitting Equally', *Journal of Economic Behaviour and Organisation*, 32: 365–81.

Bonini, C. P., Jaedicke, R. K., and Wagner, H. M. (eds.) (1964), *Managerial Controls: New Directions in Basic Research*, New York: McGraw-Hill.

Box, G. E. P., and Cox, D. R. (1964), 'An Analysis of Transformations', *Journal of the Royal Statistical Society*, Series B, 26: 211–34.

Braithwaite, R. B. (1968), *Scientific Explanation: A Study of the Function of Theory, Probability and Law in Science*, Cambridge: Cambridge University Press.

Brealey, R. A., and Myers, S. C. (1996), *Principles of Corporate Finance*, 5th edn., New York: McGraw-Hill.

Brickley, J. A., Smith, C. W., and Zimmerman, J. L. (1997), *Managerial Economics and Organisational Architecture*, Chicago: Irwin.

Brook, M. Z., and Remmers, L. (1972), *The Strategy of Multinational Enterprise*, London: Longman.

Brown, S. J., and Sibley, D. S. (1986), *The Theory of Public Utility Pricing*, Cambridge: Cambridge University Press.

Buchanan, J. M. (1969*a*), *Cost and Choice: An Enquiry into Economic Theory*, Chicago: Markham.

—— (1969*b*), 'External Diseconomies, Corrective Taxes and Market Structure', *American Economic Review*, 59: 174–7.

—— and **Stubblebine, W. M. C.** (1962), 'Externality', *Economica*, 29: 371–84.

—— and **Thirlby, G. F. (eds.)** (1973), *L.S.E. Essays on Cost*, London: Weidenfeld and Nicolson.

Bultez, A. V., and Naert, P. A. (1979), 'Does Lag Structure Really Matter in Optimising Advertising Expenditures', *Management Science*, 25: 454–65.

Chamberlin, E. (1929), 'Duopoly: Value where Sellers are Few', *Quarterly Journal of Economics*, 43: 63–100.

—— (1933), *The Theory of Monopolistic Competition*, Cambridge, Mass.: Harvard University Press.

—— (1937), 'Monopolistic Imperfect Competition?', *Quarterly Journal of Economics*, 51: 557–80.

Chambers, R. G. (1988), *Applied Production Analysis: A Dual Approach*, London: Cambridge University Press.

Cheung, S. (1973), 'The Fable of the Bees: An Economic Investigation', *Journal of Law and Economics*, 16: 11–34.

Clarke, D. G. (1976), 'Econometric Estimation of the Duration of Advertising Effect on Sales', *Journal of Marketing Research*, 13: 354–7.

Clarke, R. (1985), *Industrial Economics*, Oxford: Blackwell.

—— and Low, A. (1993), 'Risk Analysis in Project Planning: A Simple Spreadsheet Application using Monte-Carlo Techniques', *Project Appraisal*, 8: 141–6.

—— and McGuinness, T. (eds.) (1987), *The Economics of the Firm*, Oxford: Blackwell.

Coase, R. (1937), 'The Nature of the Firm', *Economica*, 4: 386–405.

—— (1960), 'The Problem of Social Cost', *Journal of Law and Economics*, 3: 1–44.

—— (1972), 'Durability and Monopoly', *Journal of Law and Economics*, 15: 143–9.

Comanor, W. S., and Wilson, T. A. (1967), 'Advertising, Market Structure and Performance', *Review of Economics and Statistics*, 49: 423–40.

Cooter, R. D. (1989), 'The Coase Theorem', in Eatwell *et al.* (1989), 456–60.

Cornes, R., and Sandler, T. (1986), *The Theory of Externalities, Public Goods, and Club Goods*, Cambridge: Cambridge University Press.

Cosh, A. D., and Hughes, A. (1987), 'The Anatomy of Corporate Control: Directors, Shareholders and Executive Remuneration in Giant US and UK Corporations', *Cambridge Journal of Economics*, 11: 285–313.

Cournot, A. (1838), *Recherches sur les principes mathématicques de la théories des richesses*, English trans. in N. Bacon (ed.) (1897), *Researches into the Mathematical Principles of the Theory of Wealth*, New York: Macmillan.

Cowling, K., and Cubbin, J. (1971), 'Price, Quality and Advertising Competition: An Econometric Investigation of the United Kingdom Car Market', *Economica*, 38: 378–94.

—— and Mueller, D. (1978), 'The Social Costs of Monopoly Power', *Economic Journal*, 88: 727–48.

—— —— (1981), 'The Social Costs of Monopoly Power Revisited', *Economic Journal*, 91: 721–5.

—— and Waterson, M. (1976), 'Price Cost Margins and Market Structure', *Economic Journal*, 43: 267–74.

Crew, M. A. (1975), *Theory of the Firm*, London: Longman.

—— and Kleindorfer, P. (1979), *Public Utility Economics*, London: Macmillan.

Cuthbertson, K., and Dobbs, I. M. (1996), 'A Robust Methodology for Ramsey Pricing with an Application to UK Postal Services', *Journal of Industrial Economics*, 44: 229–49.

—— and Richards, P. (1990), 'An Econometric Study of the Demand for Inland Letters', *Review of Economics and Statistics*, 72: 640–8.

Cyert, R. M., and March, J. G. (1963), *A Behavioural Theory of the Firm*, Englewood Cliffs, NJ: Prentice Hall.

Darnell, A. C., and Evans, J. L. (1990), *The Limits of Econometrics*, Aldershot: Gower.

David, P. A. (1985), 'Clio and the Economics of QWERTY', *American Economic Review*, 75: 332–45.

Davidson, R., and MacKinnon, J. G. (1993), *Estimations and Inference in Econometrics*, Oxford: Oxford University Press.

Davis, D. D., and Holt, C. A. (1993), *Experimental Economics*, Princeton, NJ: Princeton University Press.

Davis, O. A., and Whinston, A. (1965), 'Welfare Economics and the Theory of the Second Best', *Review of Economic Studies*, 32: 1–14.

Dawkins, R. (1976), *The Selfish Gene*, London: Oxford University Press.

—— (1986), *The Blind Watchmaker*, London: Longman.

Deaton, A. (1975), *Models and Projections of Demand in Post-war Britain*, London: Chapman and Hall.

—— and Muellbauer, J. (1980), *Economics and Consumer Behaviour*, Cambridge: Cambridge University Press.

Debreu, G. (1959), *Theory of Value: An Axiomatic Analysis of General Equilibrium*, New York: Wiley.

Demsetz, H. (1964), 'The Exchange and Enforcement of Property Rights', *Journal of Law and Economics*, 7: 11–13.

—— (1968), 'Why Regulate Utilities?', *Journal of Law and Economics*, 11: 55–65.

DeSerpa, A. C. (1992), 'The Pure Economics of the Coase Theorem', *Eastern Economic Journal*, 18: 287–304.

—— (1994), 'Pigou and Coase: A Mathematical Reconciliation', *Journal of Public Economics*, 54: 267–86.

Dixit, A. K. (1979), 'A Model of Oligopoly Suggesting a Theory of Entry Barriers', *Bell Journal of Economics*, 10: 20–32.

—— (1980), 'The Role of Investment in Entry Deterrence', *Economic Journal*, 90: 95–106.

—— (1982), 'Recent Developments in Oligopoly Theory', *American Economic Review*, 72: 12–17.

—— and **Nalebuff, B.** (1991), *Thinking Strategically: The Competitive Edge in Business, Politics and Everyday Life*, New York: Norton.

—— and **Norman, V.** (1978), 'Advertising and Welfare', *Bell Journal of Economics*, 9: 1–17.

—— and **Pindyck, R. S.** (1994), *Investment under Uncertainty*, Princeton, NJ: Princeton University Press.

Dixon, H. (1986), 'The Cournot and Bertrand Outcomes as Equilibria in a Strategic Meta-game', *Economic Journal*, 96 (supp.): 59–70.

Dobbs, I. M. (1980), 'Externality, Efficiency and the Pareto Principle', *International Review of Law and Economics*, 1: 167–81.

—— (1988), 'Risk Aversion, Gambling and the Labour–Leisure Choice', *Scottish Journal of Political Economy*, 35: 171–5.

—— (1991), 'A Bayesian Approach to Decision-Making under Ambiguity', *Economica*, 58: 417–40.

—— (1992), 'UK Car Prices: Taken for a Ride? An Alternative View', *Consumer Policy Review*, 2: 100–3.

—— (1995), 'Hiring and Leasing with Nonuniform Prices', *Management Science*, 41: 1793–1807.

—— (1996), 'On the Use of Payback Thresholds in Devolved Budgeting', *Project Appraisal*, 11: 51–9.

—— and **Beavis, B.** (1994), 'On the Relative Performance of Alternative Regulatory Instruments for Constraining a Firm's Profitability', *Zeitschrift für Nationalokonomie*, 60: 125–40.

—— and **Hill, M.** (1993), 'Pricing Solutions to the Bilateral Monopoly Problem under Uncertainty', *Southern Economic Journal*, 60: 479–89.

—— and **Richards, P.** (1994), 'Entry and Component Pricing in Regulated Markets', *International Journal of the Economics of Business*, 1: 355–76.

Dorfman, R., and **Steiner, P. O.** (1954), 'Optimal Advertising and Optimal Quality', *American Economic Review*, 44: 826–36.

Dorward, N. (1987), *The Pricing Decision*, London: Harper Row.

Douglas, E. J. (1992), *Managerial Economics: Analysis and Strategy*, 4th edn. Englewood Cliffs, NJ: Prentice Hall.

Douma, S., and **Schreuder, H.** (1991), *Economic Approaches to Organizations*, Hemel Hempstead: Hall International (UK).

Driskill, R. (1997), 'Durable Goods Monopoly, Increasing Marginal Cost and Depreciation', *Economica*, 64: 137–54.

Drury, C. (1992), *Standard Costing*, London: Academic Press.

Dunne, T., Roberts, M., and **Samuelson, L.** (1988), 'Patterns of Firm Entry and Exit in US Manufacturing Industries', *Rand Journal of Economics*, 19: 495–515.

Earl, P. (1995), *Microeconomics for Business and Marketing*, Aldershot: Edward Elgar.

Eaton, B. C., and **Lipsey, R. G.** (1981), 'Capital, Commitment, and Entry', *Bell Journal of Economics*, 12: 593–604.

Eatwell, J., Milgate, M., and **Newman, P.** (eds.) (1989), *The New Palgrave: A Dictionary of Economics*, London: Macmillan.

Edgeworth, F. J. (1897), 'La teoria pura del monopoly', *Geornale degli Economisti*, 40: 13–31; trans. into English as 'The Pure Theory of Monopoly', in F. J. Edgeworth (1925), *Papers Relating to Political Economy*, London: Macmillan.

Efroymson, C. W. (1955), 'The Kinked Demand Curve Reconsidered', *Quarterly Journal of Economics*, 69: 119–36.

Ehrenberg, R., and Smith, R. (1988), *Modern Labour Economics*, 3rd edn. Glenview, Ill.: Foresman.

Ellsberg, D. (1961), 'Risk, Ambiguity, and the Savage Axioms', *Quarterly Journal of Economics*, 75: 643–69.

Emanuel, C., and Mehafdi, M. (1994), *Transfer Pricing*, CIMA Advanced Management Accounting Series, London: Academic Press.

Encaoua, D., Geroski, P., and Jacquemin, A. (1986), 'Strategic Competition and the Persistence of Dominant Firms: A Survey', in Stiglitz and Mathewson (1986), 55–87.

Fama, E., and Jensen, M. (1983), 'Separation of Ownership and Control', *Journal of Law and Economics*, 26: 301–26.

Ferguson, C. E. (1969), *The Neoclassical Theory of Production and Distribution*, Cambridge: Cambridge University Press.

Fisher, A. C. (1981), *Resource and Environmental Economics*, Cambridge: Cambridge University Press.

Frank, R. H. (1984), 'Are Workers Paid their Marginal Products?', *American Economic Review*, 74: 549–71.

Friedman, M. (1953), 'The Methodology of Positive Economics', in M. Friedman, *Essays on Positive Economics*, Chicago: University of Chicago Press, 3–43.

Fudenberg, D., and Tirole, J. (1991), *Game Theory*, Cambridge, Mass: MIT Press.

Galbraith, J. K. (1952), *American Capitalism: The Concept of Countervailing Power*, New York: Houghton Mifflin.

—— (1958), *The Affluent Society*, Boston: Houghton Mifflin.

Geroski, P. (1995), 'What do we Know about Entry?', *International Journal of Industrial Organisation*, 13: 421–40.

Gibbons, R. (1992), *A Primer in Game Theory*, London: Harvester-Wheatsheaf.

Goldman, M. B., Leland, H. E., and Sibley, D. S. (1984), 'Optimal Nonuniform Prices', *Review of Economic Studies*, 51: 305–19.

Gould, J. R. (1964), 'Internal Pricing in Firms when there are Costs of Using an Outside Market', *Journal of Business*, 37: 61–7.

Grabski, S. V. (1985), 'Transfer Pricing in Complex Organisations: A Review and Integration of Recent Empirical and Analytical Research', *Journal of Accounting Literature*, 4: 33–75.

Gravelle, H. S. E., and Katz, E. (1976), 'Financial Targets and X-efficiency in Public Enterprises', *Public Finance*, 31: 218–34.

—— and Rees, R. (1992), *Microeconomics*, 2nd edn., London: Longman.

Green, H. A. J. (1976), *Consumer Theory*, London: Macmillan.

Griffiths, W. E., Hill, R. C., and Judge, G. G. (1993), *Learning and Practicing Econometrics*, New York: Wiley.

Grossman, S., and Hart, O. (1983), 'An Analysis of the Principal–Agent Problem', *Econometrica*, 51: 7–45.

Gul, F., Sonnenschein, H., and Wilson, R. (1986), 'Foundations of Dynamic Monopoly and the Coase Conjecture', *Journal of Economic Theory*, 39: 155–90.

Hague, D. C. (1949), 'Economic Theory and Business Behaviour', *Review of Economic Studies*, 16: 144–57.

—— (1971), *Pricing in Business*, London: George Allen and Unwin.

Hall, R., and Hitch, C. J. (1939), 'Price Theory and Business Behaviour', *Oxford Economic Papers*, 2: 12–45.

Hamburger, W. (1967), 'Conscious Parallelism and the Kinked Oligopoly Demand Curve', *American Economic Review*, 57: 266–8.

Hannah, L., and Kay, J. A. (1977), *Concentration in Modern Industry: Theory and Measurement*, London: Macmillan.

Hanson, W. (1992), 'The Dynamics of Cost-Plus Pricing', *Managerial and Decision Economics*, 13: 149–61.

Hansson, I., and Stuart, C. (1990), 'Malthusian Selection of Preferences', *American Economic Review*, 80: 529–44.

Harberger, A. C. (1971), 'Three Basic Postulates for Applied Welfare Economics: An Interpretative Essay', *Journal of Economic Literature*, 9: 785–97.

—— (1978), 'On the Use of Distributional Weights in Social Cost Benefit Analysis', *Journal of Political Economy*, 86 (suppl.): 87–120.

Hare R. M. (1952), *The Language of Morals*, Oxford: Oxford University Press.

—— (1963), *Freedom and Reason*, Oxford: Oxford University Press.

Harrison, R., and Wilkes, F. M. (1973), 'A Note on Jaguar's Pricing Policy', *European Journal of Marketing*, 3: 242–6.

Harsanyi, J. (1973), 'Games with Randomly Disturbed Pay-offs: A New Rationale for Mixed Strategy Equilibrium Points', *International Journal of Game Theory*, 2: 21–3.

Harstad, R. M., and Phlips, L. (1995), 'Information Requirement of Collusion Detection: Simple Seasonal Markets', mimeo; extracts in L. Phlips (ed.), *Competition Policy: A Game-Theoretic Perspective*, Cambridge: Cambridge University Press, 124–48.

Hart, O., and Holmstrom, B. (1987), 'The Theory of Contracts', in T. Bewley (ed.), *Advances in Economic Theory*, 5th World Congress, Cambridge: Cambridge University Press.

Hartman, R. S. (1989), 'Hedonic Methods for Evaluating Product Design and Pricing Strategies', *Journal of Economics and Business*, 41: 197–212.

Hayek, F. A. (1945), 'The Use of Knowledge in Society', *American Economic Review*, 35: 519–30.

Haynes, W. W. (1969), *Managerial Economics*, 2nd edn., New York: Business Publications Inc.

Hertz, D. B. (1964), 'Risk Analysis in Investment Appraisal', *Harvard Business Review*, 42: 95–106.

—— (1968), 'Investment Policies that Pay Off', *Harvard Business Review*, 46: 96–108.

Hey, J. D. (1979), *Uncertainty in Microeconomics*, Oxford: Martin Robertson.

—— (1991), *Experiments in Economics*, Oxford: Basil Blackwell.

Hicks, J. R. (1935), 'Annual Survey of Economic Theory—Monopoly', *Econometrica*, 3: 1–20.

—— (1940), 'The Valuation of Social Income', *Economica*, n.s., 7: 105–24.

Hirshleifer, J. (1956), 'On the Economics of Transfer Pricing', *Journal of Business*, 29: 172–84.

—— (1957), 'Economics of the Divisionalised Firm', *Journal of Business*, 30: 96–108.

—— (1964), 'Internal Pricing and Decentralised Decisions', in Bonini *et al.* (1964), 27–37.

—— (1977), 'Economics from the Biological Viewpoint', *Journal of Law and Economics*, 20: 1–52.

Hofbauer, Josef, and Sigmund, Karl (1988), *The Theory of Evolution and Dynamical Systems*, Cambridge: Cambridge University Press.

Holmstrom, B. (1982), 'Moral Hazard in Teams', *Bell Journal of Economics*, 13: 324–40.

—— and Milgrom, P. (1991), 'Multi-task Principal Agent Analyses: Incentive Contract, Asset Ownership and Job Design', *Journal of Law, Economics and Organisation*, 7: 24–52.

Horngren, C. T., and Foster, G. (1987), *Cost Accounting: A Managerial Emphasis*, 6th edn., Englewood Cliffs, NJ: Prentice Hall.

Hospers, J. (1967), *An Introduction to Philosophical Analysis*, London: Routledge Kegan Paul.

Howe, C. W. (1994), 'Taxes versus Tradable Discharge Permits: A Review in Light of the US and European Experience', *Environmental and Resource Economics*, 4: 127–50.

Huang, C. F., and Litzenberger R. C. (1988), *Foundations of Financial Economics*, Amsterdam: North Holland.

Hume, D. (1739/1960), *A Treatise on Human Nature*, ed. L. A. Selby-Bigge, Oxford: Clarendon Press.

—— (1751/1975), *Enquiries Concerning Human Understanding and Concerning the Principles of Morals*, ed. L. A. Selby-Bigge, Oxford: Clarendon Press.

Ingersoll, J., and Ross, S. A. (1992), 'Waiting to Invest: Investment and Uncertainty', *Journal of Business*, 65: 1–29.

Jarque, C. M., and Bera, A. K. (1980), 'Efficient Tests for Normality, Homoscedasticity, and Serial Independence of Regression Residuals', *Economics Letters*, 6: 255–9.

Jarrow, R. A. (1988), *Finance Theory*, Englewood Cliffs, NJ: Prentice Hall.

Jensen, M. (1983), 'Organisation Theory and Methodology', *Accounting Review*, 58: 319–39.

—— (1986), 'Agency Costs of Free Cash Flow, Corporate Finance and Take-overs', *American Economic Review*, 76: 323–9.

—— and Meckling, W. J. (1976), 'Theory of the Firm: Managerial Behaviour, Agency Costs and Ownership Structures', *Journal of Financial Economics*, 3: 305–60.

—— —— (1994), 'The Nature of Man', *Journal of Applied Corporate Finance*, 7: 4–19.

—— —— (1995), 'Specific and General Knowledge, and Organisational Structure', *Journal of Applied Corporate Finance*, 8: 4–18.

Jevons, W. S. (1871), *The Theory of Political Economy*, London: Macmillan.

Johnston, J. (1960), *Statistical Cost Analysis*, New York: McGraw-Hill.

—— (1972), *Econometric Methods*, 2nd edn., New York: McGraw-Hill.

Jones, S. (1994), 'Modeling and Muddling: Resource Allocation in British Universities', in Berry (1994), 37–54.

Kagel, J., and Roth A. (1995), *The Handbook of Experimental Economics*, Princeton, NJ: Princeton University Press.

Kahneman, D., and Tversky, A. (1979), 'Prospect Theory: An Analysis of Decision under Risk', *Econometrica*, 47: 263–91.

Kaldor, N. (1939), 'Welfare Propositions and Interpersonal Comparisons of Utility', *Economic Journal*, 44: 549–52.

Kanodia, C. (1979), 'Risk Sharing and Transfer Pricing Systems under Uncertainty', *Journal of Accounting Research*, 5: 367–79.

Kaplan, R. (1982), *Advanced Management Accounting*, Englewood Cliffs, NJ: Prentice Hall.

—— and Atkinson, A. A. (1989), *Advanced Management Accounting*, 2nd edn., Englewood Cliffs, NJ: Prentice Hall.

—— and Norton, D. P. (1992), 'The Balanced Scorecard—Measures that Drive Performance', *Harvard Business Review*, Jan.–Feb.: 71–9.

Karier, T. (1985), 'Unions and Monopoly Profits', *Review of Economics and Statistics*, 67: 34–42.

Karp, L. (1996), 'Depreciation Erodes the Coase Conjecture', *European Economic Review*, 40: 473–90.

Kay, J. A. (1993), *Foundations of Corporate Success: How Businesses Add Value*, London: Oxford University Press.

Knight, F. (1921), *Risk, Uncertainty and Profit*, Boston: Houghton Mifflin.

Koening, R. (1990), 'Du Pont Plan Linking Pay to Fibres Proft Unravels', *Wall Street Journal*, 25 Oct., B-1.

Kohn, A. (1993), 'Why Incentive Plans Cannot Work', *Harvard Business Review*, Sept.–Oct., 54–63. (For further discussion and his responses, see also 'Rethinking Rewards: What Role—If any—should Incentives Play in the Workplace?', *Harvard Business Review*, Nov.–Dec. 1993, 37–45.)

Kotlikoff, L. J., and Gokhale, J. (1992), 'Estimating a firm's Age-Productivity Profile Using the Present Value of Workers' Earnings', *Quarterly Journal of Economics*, 107: 1215–42.

Koutsoyiannis, A. (1979), *Modern Microeconomics*, 2nd edn., London: Macmillan.

—— (1982), *Non-price Decisions*, London: Macmillan.

Kreps, D. M. (1990), *A Course in Microeconomic Theory*, London: Harvester-Wheatsheaf.

—— and Scheinkman, J. (1983), 'Quantity Pre-commitment and Bertrand Competition Yield Cournot Outcomes', *Bell Journal of Economics*, 14: 326–37.

—— and Wilson, R. (1982), 'Reputation and Imperfect Information', *Econometrica*, 27: 253–79.

Lambert, P. J. (1985), *Advanced Mathematics for Economists: Static and Dynamic Optimisation*, Oxford: Blackwell.

Lancaster, K. (1966a), 'A New Approach to Consumer Theory', *Journal of Political Economy*, 74: 132–57.

—— (1966b), 'Change and Innovation in the Technology of Consumption', *American Economic Review*, 56: 14–23.

—— (1971), *Consumer Demand: A New Approach*, New York: Columbia University Press.

Lazear, E. P. (1981), 'Agency Earning Profiles, Productivity and Hours Restrictions', *American Economic Review*, 71: 606–20.

Lazear, E. P., and Rosen, S. (1981), 'Rank Order Tournaments as Optimal Labour Contracts', *Journal of Political Economy*, 89: 841–64.

Leamer, E. E. (1978), *Specification Searches*, New York: Wiley.

Leamer, E. E. (1983), 'Let's Take the Con out of Econometrics', *American Economic Review*, 73: 31–44.

Leech, D., and Leahy, J. (1991), 'Ownership Structure, Control-Type Classifications and the Performance of Large British Companies', *Economic Journal*, 101: 1418–37.

LeGrand, J. (1984), 'Optimal Taxation, the Compensation Principle and the Measurement of Changes in Economic Welfare', *Journal of Public Economics*, 24: 241–47.

Leibenstein, H. (1950), 'Bandwagon, Snob and Veblen Effects in the Theory of Consumers' Demand', *Quarterly Journal of Economics*, 64: 183–201.

—— (1966), 'Allocative Efficiency versus X-inefficiency', *American Economic Review*, 56: 392–415.

Leland, H. (1972), 'The Theory of the Firm facing Uncertain Demand', *American Economic Review*, 62: 278–91.

Lerner, A. P. (1934), 'The Concept of Monopoly and the Measurement of Monopoly Power', *Review of Economic Studies*, 1: 157–75.

Levy, H., and Sarnat, M. (1990), *Capital Investment and Financial Decisions*, 4th edn., New York: Prentice Hall.

Lewellen, W. G., and Long, M. S. (1972), 'Simulation vs. Single-Valued Estimates in Capital Expenditure Analysis', *Decision Sciences*, 3: 19–34.

Lieberman, M. (1984), 'The Learning Curve and Pricing in the Chemical Processing Industry', *Rand Journal of Economics*, 15: 213–88.

Lipsey, R. G., and Lancaster, K. (1958–9), 'The General Theory of the Second Best', *Review of Economic Studies*, 26: 225–6.

Liston, C. (1993), 'Price Cap versus Rate of Return Regulation', *Journal of Regulatory Economics*, 5: 25–48.

Littlechild, S. C. (1981), 'Misleading Calculations of the Social Costs of Monopoly Power', *Economic Journal*, 91: 348–63.

Loasby, B. J. (1976), *Choice, Complexity and Ignorance*, Cambridge: Cambridge University Press.

Locke, S., Scribbins, K., and Greensmith, J. (1991), 'Taken for a Ride? The Price of Cars and the Future of the Selective Distribution System', *Consumer Policy Review*, 1: 159–66.

Lockwood, B. (1985), 'Nonlinear Pricing and the Exclusion of Consumers', *Economic Letters*, 18: 313–16.

Loomes, G., and Sugden, R. (1982), 'Regret Theory: An Alternative Theory of Choice under Uncertainty', *Economic Journal*, 92: 805–24.

Lopatka, J. E., and Page, W. H. (1995), 'Microsoft, Monopolisation and Network Externalities: Some Uses and Abuses of Economic Theory in Antitrust Decision-Making', *Antitrust Bulletin*, 40: 317–70.

Lott, J. R., and Roberts, R. D. (1991), 'A Guide to the Pitfalls of Identifying Price Discrimination', *Economic Enquiry*, 29: 14–23.

Luce, H., and Raiffa, H. (1964), *Games and Decisions*, New York: Wiley.

Lumby, S. (1994), *Investment Appraisal and Financial Decisions*, 5th edn., London: Chapman and Hall.

Machina, M. (1979), 'Expected Utility without the Independence Axiom', *Econometrica*, 50: 277–321.

Machlup, F. (1978), *Methodology of Economics and Other Social Sciences*, New York: Academic Press.

—— and Taber, M. (1960), 'Bilateral Monopoly, Successive Monopoly, and Vertical Integration', *Economica*, 27: 101–19.

Malcomson, J. M. (1984), 'Work Incentives, Hierarchy and Internal Labour Markets', *Journal of Political Economy*, 92: 486–507.

Mansfield, E. (1996), *Managerial Economics*, 3rd edn. New York: Norton.

Markham, J. W. (1951), 'The Nature and Significance of Price Leadership', *American Economic Review*, 41: 891–905.

Marris, R. (1963), 'A Model of the Managerial Enterprise', *Quarterly Journal of Economics*, 7: 185–97.

—— (1964), 'The Economic Behaviour of Managerial Capitalism', London: Macmillan.

Marschak, J., and Radner, R. (1972), 'The Economic Theory of Teams', New Haven: Yale University Press.

Marshall, A. (1890), *Principles of Economics*, London: MacMillan.

Martin, S. A. (1993), *Advanced Industrial Economics*, Oxford: Blackwell.

—— (1994), *Industrial Economics: Economic Analysis and Public Policy*, 2nd edn., Englewood Cliffs, NJ: Prentice Hall.

McGee, J. S. (1958), 'Predatory Price Cutting: The Standard Oil (N.J.) Case', *Journal of Law and Economics*, 1: 137–69.

—— (1988), *Industrial Organisation*, Englewood Cliffs, NJ: Prentice Hall.

McGuigan, J. R., and Moyer, R. C. (1993), *Managerial Economics*, 6th edn., St Paul: West Publishing Co.

Mead, R. (1988), *The Design of Experiments: Statistical Principles for Practical Applications*, London: Cambridge University Press.

Milgrom, P. (1988), 'Employment Contracts, Influence Activities and Efficient Organisational Design', *Journal of Political Economy*, 96: 42–60.

—— and Roberts, J. (1982a), 'Limit Pricing and Entry under Incomplete Information', *Econometrica*, 50: 443–60.

—— —— (1982b), 'Predation, Reputation and Entry', *Journal of Economic Theory*, 27: 280–312.

—— —— (1987), 'Information Asymmetry, Strategic Behaviour, and Industrial Organisation', *American Economic Review*, 77: 184–93.

—— —— (1992), *Economics, Organisation and Management*, Englewood Cliffs, NJ: Prentice Hall.

Miller, G. (1993), *Managerial Dilemmas: The Political Economy of Hierarchy*, Cambridge: Cambridge University Press.

Miller, M. H. (1955), 'Declining Average Cost and Theory of Railway Rates', *Southern Economic Journal*, 21: 390–404.

Mills, E. S. (1961), 'Uncertainty and Price Theory', *Quarterly Journal of Economics*, 73: 116–30.

Mincer, J. (1962), 'On-the-Job Training: Costs, Returns and some Implications', *Journal of Political Economy*, 70: 16–36.

Mishan, E. J. (1975), *Cost–Benefit Analysis*, London: George Allen and Unwin.

Molho, I. (1997), *The Economics of Information*, Oxford: Blackwell.

Monopolies and Mergers Commission (1973), *Chlordiazepoxide and Diazepam*, London: HMSO.

Morey, E. R. (1981), 'The Demand for Site-Specific Recreational Facilities: A Characteristics Approach', *Journal of Environmental Economics and Management*, 8: 345–71.

—— (1985), 'Characteristics, Consumer Surplus and New Activities: A Proposed Ski Area', *Journal of Public Economics*, 26: 221–36.

Moschandreas, M. (1994), *Business Economics*, London: Routledge.

Muller, J. (1980), 'Industrial Self-generation of Electricity in a Public System', in P. Mitchell and P. R. Kleindorfer (eds.), *Regulated Industries and Public Enterprise: European and United States Perspectives*, Lexington, Mass.: Lexington Books, 229–46.

Musgrave, R. A. (1959), *The Theory of Public Finance*, New York: McGraw-Hill

Myers, S. C. (1976), 'Postscript: Using Simulation for Risk Analysis', in S. C. Myers (ed.), *Modern Developments in Financial Management*, New York: Dryden, 457–63.

Myerson, R., and Satterthwaite, M. (1983), 'Efficient Mechanisms for Bilateral Trading', *Journal of Economic Theory*, 28: 265–81.

Nagel, T. (1984), 'Economic Foundations for Pricing', *Journal of Business*, 57: 3–26.

Nash, J. (1950a), 'The Bargaining Problem', *Econometrica*, 21: 155–62.

—— (1950b), 'Equilibrium Points in *n*-Person Games', *Proceedings of the National Academy of Sciences*, 36: 48–9.

Nelson, P. (1974), 'Advertising as Information', *Journal of Political Economy*, 82: 729–54.

Neri, J. A., and Bernard, K. E. (1994), 'Price Caps and Rate of Return', *Public Utilities Fortnightly*, 15 Sept.: 34–6.

Ng Y. K. (1979), *Welfare Economics: Introduction and Development of Basic Concepts*, London: Macmillan.

Oren, S. S., Smith, S. A., and Wilson, R. B. (1984), 'Pricing a Product Line', *Journal of Business*, 57 (suppl.): 73–99.

—— —— —— (1987), 'Multi-product Pricing for Electric Power', *Energy Economics*, 9: 104–14.

Page, A. N. (1980), 'Marshall's Graphs and Walras' Equations: A Textbook Anomaly', *Economic Inquiry*, 18: 138–43.

Panzar, J. C., and Willig, R. D. (1981), 'Economies of Scope', *American Economic Review*, 71: 268–72.

Pappas, J. L., Hirschey, M., and Whigham, D. (1995), *Managerial Economics*, European edn., London: Dryden.

Pareto, V. (1909), *Manuel d'économie publique*, Paris: Girard and Briere.

Parfit, D. (1984), *Reasons and Persons*, Oxford: Oxford University Press.

Parsons, H. (1974), 'What Happened at Hawthorne', *Science*, 183: 927.

Pascoa, M. R. (1997), 'Monopolistic Competition and Non-neighbouring Goods', *Economic Theory*, 9: 129–42.

Pearce, D. W., and Nash, C. A. (1981), *The Social Appraisal of Projects*, London: Macmillan.

Penrose, E. T. (1959), *The Theory of Growth of the Firm*, Oxford: Blackwell.

Peters, C. M. D. (1976), 'The Electricity Supply Industry and Private Generation: An Alternative View', mimeo.

Phillips, A. W. (1958), 'The Relation between Money Wages and Unemployment in the United Kingdom 1861–1957', *Economica*, 25: 283–94.

Phlips, L. (1983), *The Economics of Price Discrimination*, Cambridge: Cambridge University Press.

—— (1988a), *The Economics of Imperfect Information*, Cambridge: Cambridge University Press.

—— (1988b), 'Price Discrimination: A Survey of the Theory', *Journal of Economic Surveys*, 2: 135–67.

—— (ed.) (1995), 'Competition Policy: A Game-Theoretic Perspective', Cambridge: Cambridge University Press.

—— (1996), 'On the Detection of Collusion and Predation', *European Economic Review*, 40: 495–510.

Pigou, A. C. (1920), *The Economics of Welfare*, London: Macmillan.

Polinsky, A. M. (1972), 'Probabilistic Compensation Criteria', *Quarterly Journal of Economics*, 86: 407–25.

Pollitt, R. G. (1995), *Ownership and Performance in Electric Utilities*, Oxford University Press.

Popper, K. R. (1963), *Conjectures and Refutations: The Growth of Scientific Knowledge*, London: Routledge Kegan Paul.

Porter, M. (1974), 'Consumer Behaviour, Retailer Power and Market Performance in Consumer Goods Industries', *Review of Economics and Statistics*, 56: 419–36.

—— (1976), *Inter-brand Choice, Strategy and Bilateral Market Power*, Cambridge, Mass.: Harvard University Press.

—— (1980), *Competitive advantage: Techniques for Analysing Industries and Competitors*, New York: Free Press.

—— (1985), *Competitive Advantage: Creating and Sustaining Superior Performance*, Englewood Cliffs, NJ: Prentice Hall.

Posner, R. A. (1975), 'The Social Costs of Monopoly and Regulation', *Journal of Political Economy*, 83: 807–27.

Prusa, T. J. (1990), 'An Incentive-Compatible Approach to the Transfer Pricing Problem', *Journal of International Economics*, 28: 155–72.

Rahman, M. Z., and Scapens, R. (1986), 'Transfer Pricing in Multinationals: Some Evidence from Bangladesh', *Journal of Business Finance and Accounting*, 13: 383–91.

Ramsey, F. P. (1927), 'A Contribution to the Theory of Taxation', *Economic Journal*, 37: 47–61.

Rao, V. R. (1984), 'Pricing Research in Marketing: State of the Art', *Journal of Business*, 57 (suppl.): 39–60.

Reder, M. W. (1982), 'Chicago Economics: Permanence and Change', *Journal of Economic Literature*, 20: 1–38.

Reekie, W. D. (1986), 'Advertising Intensity and Media Selection', *Applied Economics*, 18: 557–64.

—— and Crook, N. (1987), *Managerial Economics*, 3rd edn., London: Philip Allan.

Rees, R. (1984), *Public Enterprise Economics*, London: Weidenfeld and Nicolson.

Roberts, K. W. S. (1979), 'Welfare Considerations of Nonlinear Pricing', *Economic Journal*, 89: 66–83.

Robinson, J. (1934), 'What is Perfect Competition?', *Quarterly Journal of Economics*, 49: 104–20.

Robinson, W. T., and Chiang, J. (1996), 'Are Sutton's Predictions Robust? Empirical Insights into Advertising, R&D and Concentration', *Journal of Industrial Economics*, 44: 389–408.

Rochet, J-C. (1985), 'Bilateral Monopoly with Imperfect Information', *Journal of Economic Theory*, 36: 214–36.

Ronen, J. (1992), 'Transfer Pricing Reconsidered', *Journal of Public Economics*, 47: 125–36.

—— and Balachandrian, K. R. (1988), 'An Approach to Transfer Pricing under Uncertainty', *Journal of Accounting Research*, 26: 300–14.

—— and McKinney, G. (1970), 'Transfer Pricing for Divisional Autonomy', *Journal of Accounting Research*, 8: 99–112.

Rosen, S. (1985), 'Implicit Contracts', *Journal of Economic Literature*, 23: 1144–75.

Ross, S. A. (1995), 'Uses, Abuses, and Alternatives to the Net Present Value Rule', *Financial Management*, 24: 96–102.

—— Westerfield, R., and Jaffe, J. F. (1996), *Corporate Finance*, 4th edn. Chicago: Irwin.

Sako, M. (1992), *Prices, Quality and Trust*, Cambridge: Cambridge University Press.

Samuelson, P. A. (1977), 'St Petersburg Paradoxes: Defanged, Dissected and Historically Described', *Journal of Economic Literature*, 15: 24–55.

Savage, L. (1974), *The Foundations of Statistics*, 2nd edn., New York: Dover.

Scherer, F. M. (1980), *Industrial Market Structure and Economic Performance*, 2nd edn., New York: Rand McNally.

Schmalensee, R. (1981), 'Output and Welfare Implications of Monopolistic Third-Degree Price Discrimination', *American Economic Review*, 71: 243–7.

—— and Willig, R. D. (eds.), (1989), *Handbook of Industrial Organisation*, 2 vols., Amsterdam: Elsevier North-Holland.

Schoemaker, P. (1982), 'The Expected Utility Model: Its Variants, Purposes, Evidence and Limitations', *Journal of Economic Literature*, 20: 529–63.

Scholes, M., and Wolfson, M. (1992), *Taxes and Business Strategy: A Planning Approach*, Englewood Cliffs, NJ: Prentice Hall.

Seiler, E. (1984), 'Piece Rate versus Time Rate: The Effect of Incentives on Earnings', *Review of Economic Studies*, 66: 363–76.

Selten, R. (1973), 'A Simple Model of Imperfect Competition in which Four are Few and Six are Many', *International Journal of Game Theory*, 2: 141–201.

—— (1978), 'The Chain Store Paradox', *Theory and Decision*, 9: 127–59.

Shapiro, C. (1986), 'Theories of Oligopolistic Behaviour', in Schmalensee and Willig (1989), ii. 329–41.

Sharkey, W. W. (1982), *The Theory of Natural Monopoly*, Cambridge: Cambridge University Press.

Sharpe, W. F. (1964), 'Capital Asset Prices: A Theory of Market Equilibrium under Conditions of Risk', *Journal of Finance*, 19: 425–42.

Shavell, S. (1979), 'Risk Sharing and Incentives in the Principal and Agent Relationship', *Bell Journal of Economics*, 10: 55–73.

Shibata, H. (1972), 'Pareto Optimality, Trade and the Pigovian Tax', *Economica*, 39: 190–202.

Shleifer, A. (1985), 'A Theory of Yardstick Competition', *Rand Journal of Economics*, 16: 319–27.

Shubik, M. (1984), *Game Theory in the Social Sciences*, Cambridge, Mass.: MIT Press.

Silberburg, E. (1978), *The Structure of Economics: A Mathematical Analysis*, New York: McGraw-Hill.

Simon, H. A. (1955), 'A Behavioural Model of Rational Choice', *Quarterly Journal of Economics*, 69: 99–118.

—— (1982), *Models of Bounded Rationality*, 2 vols., Cambridge, Mass.: MIT Press.

Skinner, R. C. (1970), 'The Determination of Selling Prices', *Journal of Industrial Economics*, 19: 201–17.

Smith, Adam (1776), *The Wealth of Nations*, London: Strahan and Cadell, repr. (Bks. I–III), New York: Penguin, 1986.

Spanos, A. (1986), *Statistical Foundations of Econometric Modelling*, Cambridge: Cambridge University Press.

Spence, A. M. (1977), 'Entry, Capacity and Oligopolistic Pricing', *Bell Journal of Economics*, 8: 534–44.

Sraffa, P. (1926), 'The Laws of Returns under Competitive Conditions', *Economic Journal*, 36: 535–50.

Stackelberg, H. von. (1934), *Marktform und Gleichgewicht*, Vienna: Julius Springer, trans. into English as *The Theory of the Market Economy*, London: William Hodge, 1952.

Starrett, D. (1972), 'Fundamental Non-convexities in the Theory of Externalities', *Journal of Economic Theory*, 4: 542–52.

—— (1988), *Foundations of Public Economics*, Cambridge: Cambridge University Press.

Stewart, J. C. (1977), 'Multinational Companies and Transfer Pricing', *Journal of Business Finance and Accounting*, 4: 353–71.

Stigler, G. (1947), 'The Kinked Oligopoly Demand Curve and Rigid Prices', *Journal of Political Economy*, 55: 442–4.

—— (1958), 'The Economies of Scale', *Journal of Law and Economics*, 1: 54–71.

—— (1963), '*United States* versus *Loew's Inc.*: A Note on Block Booking' *Supreme Court Review*, 152–7.

Stiglitz, J., and Mathewson, F. (eds.) (1986), *New Developments in the Analysis of Market Structure*, Cambridge, Mass.: MIT Press.

Strong, N., and Waterson, M. (1987), 'Principals, Agents and Information', in Clarke and McGuinness (1987), 18–41.

Sugden, R. (1981), *The Political Economy of Public Choice*, Oxford: Martin Robertson.

Sutton, J. (1991), *Sunk Costs and Market Structure*, Cambridge, Mass.: MIT Press.

Sweezy, P. M. (1939), 'Demand under Conditions of Oligopoly', *Journal of Political Economy*, 47: 568–73.

Sylos-Labini, P. (1962), *Oligopoly and Technical Progress*, Cambridge, Mass.: Harvard University Press.

Taha, H. A. (1992), *Operations Research: An Introduction*, 5th edn., New York: Macmillan.

Takayama, A. (1985), *Mathematical Economics*, 2nd edn., London: Cambridge University Press.

Taylor, F. (1923), *The Principles of Scientific Management*, New York: Harper and Row.

Teece, D. J. (1982), 'Towards an Economic Theory of the Multi-product Firm', *Journal of Economic Behaviour and Organization*, 3: 39–63.

Thomas, A. L. (1980), *A Behavioural Analysis of Joint Cost Allocation and Transfer Pricing*, Arthur Andersen and Co. Lecture Series, Champaign, Ill.: Stipes Publishing Co.

Thomas, R. L. (1993), *Introductory Econometrics: Theory and Applications*, 2nd edn., London: Longman.

—— (1997), *Modern Econometrics: An Introduction*, Harlow: Addison Wesley Longman.

Tideman, N., and Tullock, G. (1976), 'A New and Superior Way for Making Social Choices', *Journal of Political Economy*, 84: 1145–59.

Tietenberg, T. H. (1994), 'Economic Instruments for Environmental Regulation', *Oxford Review of Economic Policy*, 6: 17–33.

Tirole, J. (1986), 'Hierarchies and Bureaucracies', *Journal of Economics and Organisation*, 2: 181–214.

—— (1993), *The Theory of Industrial Organisation*, Cambridge, Mass.: MIT Press.

Tomkins, C., and Mawditt, R. (1994), 'An Attempt to Introduce Profit Centre Management within the University of Bath: A Case Study', in Berry (1994), 25–36.

Trivol, G. W., and McDaniel, W. R. (1987), 'Uncertainty, Capital Immobility and Capital Rationing in Investment Decisions', *Journal of Business Finance and Accounting*, 14: 215–28.

Utton, M. A. (1970), *Industrial Concentration*, Harmondsworth: Penguin.

Varian, H. (1985), 'Price Discrimination and Economic Welfare', *American Economic Review*, 75: 870–5.

—— (1989), 'Price Discrimination', in Schmalensee and Willig (1989), i. 597–654.

—— (1990), *Intermediate Microeconomics: A Modern Approach*, 2nd edn., New York: Norton.

Vickers, J., and Yarrow, G. (1988), *Privatisation: An Economic Analysis*, Cambridge, Mass.: MIT Press.

von Neumann, J., and Morgenstern, O. (1944), *Theory of Games and Economic Behaviour*, Princeton, NJ: Princeton University Press.

Ward, R. W. (1976), 'Measuring Advertising Decay', *Journal of Advertising Research*, 16: 37–41.

Waterson, M. (1984), *The Economic Theory of the Industry*, Cambridge: Cambridge University Press.

—— (1988), *The Regulation of the Firm and Natural Monopoly*, Oxford: Blackwell.

Watts, R., and Zimmerman, J. (1983), 'Agency Problems and the Theory of the Firm: Some Evidence', *Journal of Law and Economics*, 26: 613–33.

Weatherford, L. R., and Bodily, S. E. (1992), 'A Taxonomy and Research Overview of Perishable Asset Management: Yield Management, Overbooking and Pricing', *Operations Research*, 40: 831–44.

Weingartner, H. M. (1977), 'Capital Rationing: N Authors in Search of a Plot', *Journal of Finance*, 32: 1403–31.

White, H. (1980), 'Using Least Squares to Approximate Unknown Regression Functions', *International Economic Review*, 21: 149–70.

Williamson, O. E. (1964), *The Economics of Discretionary Behaviour: Managerial Objectives in the Theory of the Firm*, Englewood Cliffs, NJ: Prentice Hall.

—— (1966), 'Peak Load Pricing and Optimal Capacity under Indivisibility Constraints', *American Economic Review*, 56: 810–27.

—— (1968), 'Economies of Scale as an Anti-trust Defence: The Welfare Trade-offs', *American Economic Review*, 58: 18–36.

—— (1975), *Markets and Hierarchies: Analysis and Antitrust Implications*, New York: Free Press.

—— (1985), *The Economic Institutions of Capitalism: Firms, Markets, Relational Contracting*, New York: Free Press.

Willig, R. D. (1976), 'Consumer's Surplus without Apology', *American Economic Review* 66: 589–97.

Wilson, R. B. (1993), *Nonlinear Pricing*, Oxford: Oxford University Press.

Wonnacott, R. J., and Wonnacott, T. H. (1991), *Introductory Statistics for Business and Economics*, 4th edn., New York: Wiley.

Yarrow, G. K. (1976), 'On the Predictions of the Managerial Theory of the Firm', *Journal of Political Economy*, 24: 267–79.

Zeithaml, V., et al. (1970), 'Problems and Strategies in Services Marketing', *Journal of Marketing*, 49: 33–46.

Index